Consumer Behavior in Theory and in Action

The Wiley Marketing Series

WILLIAM LAZER, Advisory Editor *Michigan State Univesity*

MARTIN ZOBER, *Marketing Management*

ROBERT J. HOLLOWAY AND
ROBERT S. HANCOCK
*The Environment of Marketing
Behavior—Selections from the
Literature*

GEORGE SCHWARTZ, Editor
Science in Marketing

EDGAR CRANE
*Marketing Communications—A
Behavioral Approach to Men,
Messages, and Media*

JOSEPH W. NEWMAN, Editor
On Knowing the Consumer

STEUART HENDERSON BRITT, Editor
*Consumer Behavior and the
Behavioral Sciences—Theories and
Applications*

DONALD F. MULVIHILL AND
STEPHEN PARANKA
Price Policies and Practices

DAVID CARSON
*International Marketing: A
Comparative Systems Approach*

BRUCE E. MALLEN
*The Marketing Channel: A
Conceptual Viewpoint*

RONALD R. GIST
*Management Perspectives in
Retailing*

JOHN K. RYANS AND JAMES C. BAKER
*World Marketing: A Multinational
Approach*

JOHN M. BRION
Corporate Marketing Planning

NORTON E. MARKS AND
ROBERT M. TAYLOR
*Marketing Logistics: Perspectives
and Viewpoints*

JAMES BEARDEN
*Personal Selling: Behavioral Science
Readings and Cases*

FRANK M. BASS, CHARLES W. KING, AND
EDGAR A. PESSEMIER, Editors
*Applications of the Sciences in
Marketing Management*

ROBERT J. HOLLOWAY AND
ROBERT S. HANCOCK
Marketing in a Changing Environment

RONALD E. GIST
Retailing: Concepts and Decisions

KENNETH P. UHL AND BERTRAM SCHONER
*Marketing Research: Information
Systems and Decision Making*

JOHN M. RATHMELL
*Managing The Marketing Function
in Industry*

GEORGE DOWNING
Sales Management

W. J. E. CRISSY AND ROBERT M. KAPLAN
*Salesmanship: The Personal Force
in Marketing*

HARRY A. LIPSON AND JOHN R. DARLING
*Introduction to Marketing
Administration*

HARRY A. LIPSON
Cases in Marketing Administration

WILLIAM LAZER
Marketing Management

STEPHEN H. GAMBLE AND
JOHN R. WISH, Editors
Social Issues in Marketing

STEUART HENDERSON BRITT: Editor
JAMES L. LUBAWSKI
*Consumer Behavior in Theory and in
Action*

STEUART HENDERSON BRITT
*Psychological Experiments in
Consumer Behavior*

RONALD R. GIST, Editor
*Management Perspectives in Retailing
2nd edition*

Consumer Behavior in Theory and in Action

Edited By

STEUART HENDERSON BRITT

Ph.D in Psychology
Professor of Marketing, Graduate School of Management
and Professor of Advertising, Medill School of Journalism
Northwestern University

With the Editorial Collaboration of
JAMES L. LUBAWSKI

M.B.A. in Marketing
Department of Business
Instructor in Marketing
Business and Business Education
University of Northern Iowa

JOHN WILEY & SONS, INC.

New York · London · Sydney · Toronto

Library of Congress Catalogue Card Number: 71-126225

ISBN 0-471-10482-5

Printed in the United States of America

10 9 8 7 6 5 4 3 2 1

Dedicated to P.Y.E.

Preface

This book—*Consumer Behavior in Theory and in Action*—deals with the social psychology of consumer motivation and behavior.

Parts One through Five show how anthropological, sociological, psychological, and economics materials can help us to understand the behavior of consumers. This is a necessary background for Parts Six through Nine, which demonstrate how behavioral-science materials can be utilized to help us to understand the behavior of business firms with respect to products, promotion, and consumer decision making.

An earlier book of mine, *Consumer Behavior and the Behavioral Sciences* (Wiley, 1966), also dealt with consumer behavior. But the present volume is *not* a replacement of that book and is *not* a revision of it. Instead, the present book of readings is a *logical extension* of the previous one.

1. The fairly short abridged readings in the first book are supplemented in the present volume with longer edited readings.

2. The 348 selections in the first book, mostly from the 1950s and early 1960s, have been added to in the present volume with 144 selections—129 from the 1960s, with 84 of these published after 1964.

3. In order that the two books can be used together, the plan of organization is identical:

      I.   Foundations of Consumer Behavior
     II.   Cultural Influences
   III.   Individual Influences
   IV.   Group Influences
    V.   Economic Influences
   VI.   The Business Firm and the Consumer
  VII.   Product Attributes and the Consumer
 VIII.   Promotion and the Consumer
   IX.   Decision Making by Consumers

4. The chapter headings in the two books are essentially the same.

To round out the important theories and applications in these two volumes, a third book, *Psychological Experiments in Consumer Behavior*

(Wiley), is being published as a companion volume. It consists of 32 articles reproduced in their entirety as significant examples of practical experiments on consumer behavior.

Thus the three books together complement one another, and provide an overall view of the best materials on consumer motivation and behavior.

* * *

The significance of the editorial collaboration of my former student, James L. Lubawski, now Instructor in Marketing at the University of Northern Iowa, is indicated by including his name on the title page of the present book. I also acknowledge the aid of my superb secretary, Mrs. Irene E. Peach.

STEUART HENDERSON BRITT, PH.D.

Northwestern University
Evanston, Illinois
October, 1970

Contents

PART III

INDIVIDUAL INFLUENCES

Consumer Behavior in Theory and in Action

FOUNDATIONS OF CONSUMER BEHAVIOR

1 / The Consumer in Society

A. BACKGROUND AND THEORY

The first article (Sommers and Kernan) indicates why consumer behavior is a study of *human* behavior. This is followed by an article (Kassarjian) about a field theoretical approach to consumer behavior.

1-A CONSUMER BEHAVIOR AS HUMAN BEHAVIOR

Montrose S. Sommers (Marketing Educator)
and Jerome B. Kernan (Marketing Educator)

Applications of rat psychology notwithstanding, consumers are humans and their behavior is obviously a reflection of their human qualities. Whether it follows that consumer behavior is not therefore a distinct discipline but only an approach to the study of human behavior, or that consumer behavior is as much a discipline as political science, law, or medicine seems to be a matter of perspective. How macroscopic should one's view be?

Regardless of one's perspective, the inescapable fact is that much about humans can be understood by studying them in their roles as consumers. Indeed, two distinct areas are rendered more pregnable. First, because consuming is such a complex phenomenon, to understand it is to enrich one's *concepts* of human behavior. Learning, for example, can be seen in a very rich dimension as one contemplates all that a buyer must "learn." Second, because consuming is such a ubiquitous

SOURCE: Montrose S. Sommers and Jerome B. Kernan, "Consumer Behavior in Retrospect and in Prospect," in Montrose S. Sommers and Jerome B. Kernan, Editors, *Explanations in Consumer Behavior* (Austin, Texas: The Bureau of Business Research, The University of Texas, 1968), pp. 5 and 7.

and continuing phenomenon, its data bank is virtually bottomless. There will always be consumers whose behavior can be measured. Methodological refinement depends on practice. Thus with repeated attempts the research community's *ability to measure* the behavior of humans develops.

If the consumer is a problem solver, then he chooses among alternatives on the strength of what he knows, or thinks he knows, about them. In this sense information becomes a critical factor in the consumer's choice process. It determines which alternatives he perceives and how he perceives them.

The key issues relative to information concern its nature, its acquisition, and its function. Perhaps the most elusive of these is the *nature* of information. In other words, what does the consumer regard as information? Is this concept uniform among consumers and/or in decision situations?

Acquisition concerns the sources of information and the processes by which it is acquired. In addition to the many external sources, one must account for internal retrieval of information—that is, remembering. Whatever the source, however, processes clearly affect phenomena like selective acquisition and distortion.

Function asks: "How does the consumer use information?" Obviously, he possesses some sort of processing facility (he thinks), but its precise nature is not understood. Why do things like repression exist? What about so-called impulse buying? What is the meaning of a consumer's assertion that he really doesn't know why he bought Brand X?

1-B CONSUMER BEHAVIOR: A FIELD THEORETICAL APPROACH

Harold H. Kassarjian (Psychologist)

A common characteristic of many of these approaches to consumer behavior is their reliance to a greater or lesser extent upon Aristotelian logic and modes of thought rather than the Galileian and post-Galileian scientific logic that has served so well in the physical sciences.

Aristotelian Concepts[1]

Aristotelian logic is distinguishable by several characteristics. The first of these is its heavy dependence upon valuative and normative concepts. There exist ethical and unethical influences on behavior, rational and irrational consumers, good and bad decisions. Much of the justification and criticism of marketing and advertising relies on this form of anthropomorphism.

Secondly, when Galileian and post-Galileian physics extended the field of natural law, it was due not only to the exclusion of value concepts but also to a changed interpretation of classification.

For Aristotelian physics the membership of an object in a given class was of critical importance, because for Aristotle the class defined the essence or essential nature of the object and thus determined its behavior in both positive and negative respects.

The basic logic of market segmentation, the classification of goods and the attempts to derive distinct "laws of behavior" for the separate classifications, approach the Aristotelian conceptualizations of nature.

Aristotle's classification schema in turn determined lawfulness and chance. Those things are lawful which occur without exception. And, also, those things are lawful which occur frequently.

Excluded from the class of the conceptually intelligible as mere chance are those things which occur only once, individual events as such. Actually the behavior of a thing is determined by its essential nature, and this essential nature is exactly the abstractly defined class (*i.e.*, the sum total of the common characteristics of a whole group of objects), it follows that each event, as a particular event, is chance, undetermined.

Finally, in premedieval Aristotelian logic, regularity is to be understood entirely in historical terms. Behavior is determined by past events, not the immediate present. The purchase of a product, the decision process, is to be understood in terms of childhood frustrations and fixations for the motivation researcher, the personality development for the Neo-Freudians, and the number of trials for stimulus-response and mathematical theorists. Present behavior is either predetermined by past events or is to be explained by chance and not by law.

Galileian Concepts

Turning to the Galileian and post-Galileian concepts in physics and to their counterpart in psychology—Gestalt and Field Theory—one finds a new set of conceptualizations about nature, reality and lawfulness. First, there are no valuative or classificatory schema. The same laws govern the course of the stars, the falling of stones, and the flight of supersonic jets. The behavior of the ghetto Negro can be explained in the same terms as that of a rural

SOURCE: Harold H. Kassarjian, "Consumer Behavior: A Field Theoretical Approach," in Robert L. King, Editor, *Marketing and the New Science of Planning* (Chicago: American Marketing Association, 1968), pp. 285–289.

[1] Portions of this and the following section have been taken from, "The Conflict Between Aristotelian and Galileian Modes of Thought in Contemporary Psychology," in Kurt Lewin, *A Dynamic Theory of Personality* (New York: McGraw-Hill, 1935), pp. 1–42.

Peruvian peasant or a pretender to the throne on the Riviera. Such assumptions as rational and irrational behavior, logical or illogical decisions, or even normal or psychotic actions become meaningless. Classification can be made only according to the underlying genotypic laws rather than the observable phenotypic properties. Behavior cannot be explained or understood by resorting to a statistical or historical analysis. For example, the law of falling bodies, $s = \frac{1}{2}gt^2$, applies to stars, baseballs, and dead butterflies, irrespective of their observable phenotypic differences. The law does not state that the relationship holds regularly or frequently, 60% of the time, or even at the .05 level of statistical confidence. And in fact, outside of theory, the relationship can never be observed and can only be approximated under the most carefully constructed and artificially controlled conditions. The law is not determined historically, by historical actuary, or by counting and empirically measuring falling apples to see what percentage behave according to hypothesis and what percentage do not. In short, the falling of all bodies is determined by genotypic relationships—the fortuitousness of the individual case is not undetermined, random, chance or an exception to the data to be ignored.

Although some evidence exists that previous purchases of coffee, orange juice, or bread will allow for predictions of future behavior, the relationship does not hold for any given individual or even for an aggregate in the purchase of a new home, a fruit tree to be planted in the back yard, or the color and design of a new tie. To create a separate behavioral law for the purchase of an orange tree, and for the purchase of orange juice appears most Aristotelian in logic.

Theory of consumer behavior must be able to explain in similar terms the purchase of furniture by the Rigby family, the purchase of a swimming pool, a new shirt for Juan, or the acquisition of the peach-faced parrot. One must not ask, is the behavior of the Rigby family common to all families, or 60% of the families, or what proportion of the previous purchases of children's bedroom furniture consisted of early American maple from a particular retail outlet? One must not claim that these are random events, single instances that need not concern the consumer behavior theorist, any more than one may claim that the rate of fall of a fortuitous meteor is not related to the laws of astronomy.

A Field Theoretical Approach

THE CONSTRUCTIVE METHOD. The classificatory approach, rampant in marketing and consumer behavior, has as a basic assumption that concepts can be derived from data that somehow capture the essential characteristics of that data, and that somehow by collecting data on the aggregate, we will understand the consumer and his actions. Hence generalizations from individual consumers lead to concepts about housewives in a given socioeconomic class and to female consumers in general. However, using such a phenotypic approach, there is no logical way back from the concept "lower-class female consumer" to the individual. Hence, one resorts to statistics and probability. Perhaps it was fortunate for the development of the physical sciences that modern statistics, representative samples and factor analysis were not available to Galileo and Newton. Seldom do the physical sciences resort to statistics, since it is not the purpose of laws to summarize the distribution of observed events. Once a law of consumer behavior is proposed, it must be tested against all conditions included under the law whether these occur frequently or not. Laws, then, cannot be developed by generalizing from molecular data. In other words, in studying some event or act, say purchase behavior, one cannot study the isolated parts such as price, personality, reference groups, frequency of purchase, or political conditions, separately in the expectation that it will eventually be possible to reconstruct the whole by adding together the parts. This is the familiar Gestalt dictum: the whole is different from, if not greater than, the sum of the isolated parts. To understand the entire event one must study the whole problem, then by continuous experimentation and logical manipulation the parts of the whole can be differentiated and placed in correct relationship with each other.

If one studies the effect of price of, say, early American style furniture, the influence of the retail outlet, pressures exerted by children in a family decision, and the personal influence of neighbors, and hence develops abstractions and generalizations, these individual parts cannot be put together to describe or predict why any individual, Professor Rigby, made the purchase he did. What is lost is the interrelationship of the parts, the interactions and confounding of one influence with the other. Hence, a field theoretical approach, a level of analysis that attempts to transform the phenotypic language of data into a language of constructs or genotypes; a mode of analysis that starts with the entire behavior pattern and attempts to extract the relevant relationships rather than first studying the individual parts and from them futilely attempting to reconstruct the purchase act.

AHISTORICAL APPROACH. A second basic foundation of a field theoretical approach to consumer behavior is its emphasis on an ahistorical approach. Only facts that exist in the present can directly affect present events. Since consumer behavior depends upon the forces and influences acting upon the individual at a given moment in time, the moment the behavior itself occurs, past events and future events which do not exist now cannot effect his behavior. The relationship of the past to the present is so indirect that its explanatory value is slight. This is not to deny completely the effect of previous experiences in the behavior of the consumer, but rather to keep it in perspective. Only the directly relevant facts from previous behavior which exert an influence on the present are to be considered, rather than childhood experiences in general as used by the motivation researcher or number of previous trials for the learning theorist or Markov analyst. Further, future events, aspirations and expectations, as they are relevant and represented in the present, are accounted for by field theory, concepts difficult to deal with in many of the theoretical approaches to consumer behavior. Consumer behavior, however, must be explained in terms of the properties which exist at the time the event occurs.

THE LIFE SPACE. The most fundamental of the Lewinian concepts is that of the life space or psychological field. All behavior—consuming, purchasing, thinking, crying—is a function of the life space, which in turn consists of the total manifold of "facts" which psychologically exist, all of the influences, for an individual at a given moment in time. The life space is the totality of the individual's world as he himself

perceives it; it is the individual's perception of "reality," the totality of possible events.

The life space, thus, includes the person and the environment. The person is represented by a differentiated region within the life space in a dynamic interrelationship with the environment. The environment, in turn, does not refer to the objective world of physical stimuli, but rather is the psychological world as it exists for the individual under study. It contains only those facts which exist for him at a given point in time, somewhat analogous to a phenomenological field, although unconscious determinants of behavior are not excluded. The term behavior has been employed by Lewin to refer to any change within the life space. For behavior to occur, some perceived change within the life space must exist. A change in the geographic world or "objective" environment, such as a change in package design, color of label, price or physical characteristics of a consumer product which is not represented by a change in the psychological field of the consumer, cannot lead to a behavior change.

The life space of the newborn child may be described as a field which has relatively few and only vaguely distinguishable areas, perhaps only greater or less comfort. No definite representations of objects or persons exist, future events or aspirations do not exist, nor is there even an area that can be called "my own body." The child is ruled by the situation immediately at hand; he has no conception of past experiences. As he grows there is an increased differentiation within this life space. Areas such as his own body, his mother, edible food, non-edible objects can be distinguished. Included also is a differentiation of the time dimension as plans extend further into the future, and activities of increasingly longer duration are cognitively organized as one unit. A mature adult can differentiate between brands of products, two models of an automobile, or two candidates within the same political party.

The various differentiated regions, however, are not equally accessible to the person. The boundaries of the region may from time to time become more or less permeable, and in fact may act as a barrier to locomotion into the region. To the child the region representing his mother may be easily accessible at all times. Roller skating with much older children may be a less permeable region, while consuming a bottle of Scotch may represent an impermeable area. Movement or locomotion from one region to another is usually carried out in a definite sequence of steps or a path that is perceived by the person as necessary to move from where he is to his goal.

Thus, the behavior of the consumer, either in a supermarket selecting among products or in the living room semi-consciously planning the purchase of a dishwasher or a new home, can be represented as a function of the psychological field or cognitive structure of the individual—a dynamic relationship in which change in any one region will lead to changes in the entire field.

MATHEMATIZATION. A final foundation to consumer behavior from a field theory approach is an emphasis on the need to mathematize the theoretical structure. One of the most significant features of the work of Lewin and his followers has been the use of mathematics to quantify the theory.

DYNAMIC CONCEPTS. The life space, then, is a topological representation of the cognitive organization of the individual. However the topological or nonmetric concepts in and of themselves are not enough to account for behavior—why one purchases Standard Oil products rather than a private brand. To explain consumer behavior fully several dynamic concepts are needed.

Tension. The first of these concepts is that of tension, a state of the person within the life space. Just as the environment is differentiated into regions, so too the person can be considered a system of dynamically inter-dependent regions. These in turn consist of two sub-systems, the more central inner-personal or need-value system and the peripheral perceptual-motor system. A tension is a state of an inner-personal region relative to other inner-personal regions. The concept of tension can probably replace such undefinable and vague generalizations as needs, wants, motives, drive or urge. Physiological conditions such as hunger or sex, and social demands such as high fashion clothing, a new hat, a Corvette or a candy bar, are best conceptualized as tension or pressure against the boundaries of some

region within the inner-personal system. A need or drive can be defined as a term trying to explain a syndrome of behavior which takes into account the tension within a person to achieve some goal. As soon as the goal is reached the region is no longer in tension; that is, the system achieves equilibrium.

A state of tension in a particular region will tend to equalize itself with the amount of tension in the surrounding regions. Hence a need for sexual gratification may lead to a need for sports cars, cosmetics, group membership, high fashion, clothing and an expensive apartment, or *vice versa*. The tension can be equalized by any process such as thinking, remembering, purchasing, consuming or even daydreaming to achieve equilibrium.

Energy. Further, the person can be seen as a complex energy system. This psychical energy is released as the person attempts to return to equilibrium, after it has been thrown into a state of disequilibrium by the arousal of a tension or need in one part of the system.

Valence. The third dynamic property of a field theoretical approach is that of valence, a conceptual property of a region of the psychological environment representing its attractiveness or unattractiveness. A valence is obviously coordinated with a need; that is, whether a particular region of the environment has a positive or negative value depends directly upon a system in a state of tension. To a hungry person food will have a positive valence; to a satiated individual even the odor of food can be quite repelling or negative. Although food in general may well have a positive valence, a particular product that is sold by a disliked retailer, or manufactured by a producer that supports lunatic political causes, is responsible for obnoxious advertising or engages in disagreeable labor practices, may well take on a negative valence. Hence, even to a hungry person a particular food may be repelling. The strength of the "need" in combination with other prevailing factors determines the strength of the valence.

Force of Vector. A valence plus energy creates a force—a property of the environment rather than of the person. The strength and direction of the force can be represented as a vector acting upon the person, causing locomotion, or in our terminology, behavior. Of course, more than one vector at any given moment is likely to exist—the decision between two brands of gasoline, both of which have a positive valence, the choice between being drafted or branded a coward, both with negative valence, or the purchase of a dishwasher with a positive valence related to its function and a negative vector created by its cost. In such cases the direction of locomotion will be the resultant of the various vectors. The net valence, if above threshold, will determine whether or not the dishwasher is purchased. Similarly, the selection of a service station will depend upon the relative strength of the valences. Presuming both brands are perceived to be exactly identical within the life space of the individual—vacillation, indecision, greater tension and a high non-pecuniary cost of consumption should result. Perhaps it is the need to reduce the non-pecuniary cost of consumption that leads to very fine discriminations among brands and manufacturers and to brand loyalty, when in fact the physical products are "known" to be identical.[1]

With the topological structure of the life space and the dynamic properties of tension, need, valence, and vectors let us consider an example. On a midweek afternoon a housewife considers going downtown to see a motion picture. The need to "do something" and the desirability or positive valence of the goal—the motion picture—create a vector or force in the direction of the goal within her life space. Her life space is structured to contain two paths to the goal: one, walk to the corner, take the bus, buy a ticket and enter the goal region; and two, get the car keys, walk to garage, drive car, park car, buy ticket and enter goal region. Suddenly remembering that the garage is locked and her husband walked off with the key, the region of the life space en-

compassing "drive car" is inaccessible, the boundaries of her life space are impermeable. To overcome the barrier to her psychological movement requires a circuitous route. She decides to walk, and in preparation for the trip, passes by the refrigerator. A new stimulus has now entered her life space as she remembers she has no vegetables for dinner that evening and that she must go to the supermarket.

Suddenly, plans for the theater are discarded, her life space is restructured around her grocery shopping. The new regions of her life space consist of walking to the market, selecting the produce, paying for it and entering the positive goal region to reduce the tension. Other possible paths or methods of obtaining vegetables such as planting seeds and raising carrots do not occur to her, are not part of her life space. Having selected the carrots at the market, her life space again is restructured as she contemplates a new path for entering the goal region. Rather than pay for the vegetables she can shoplift; however, the negative consequences of this behavior and the concomitant negative vector induce her to pass through the check-out stand to reach the goal, reduce the tension and restore equilibrium.

Summary

In conclusion, consumer behavior can be and should be conceptualized from a field theoretical perspective. Causality is the resultant of co-existing forces and is not probabilistic. Analysis of the consumer's actions must begin with the entire situation as a whole, from which the relevant parts can be differentiated, rather than study of the isolated parts leading to reconstruction of the behavioral act. The behavior of the consumer is a function of the psychological field which exists at the time the behavior occurs. This field of life space consists of the person and environment interacting in a mutually interdependent relationship. And finally, the field can be represented mathematically by the use of non-Euclidian geometry and vector theory.

[1] For a discussion of factors influencing brand choice, see William F. Brown, "The Determination of Factors Influencing Brand Choice," *Journal of Marketing*, Apr. 1950, pp. 699–706.

B. RESEARCH AND APPLICATIONS

The two selections in this section deal with an interpersonal orientation to the study of consumer behavior (Cohen) and simulation of consumer preference (Day).

1-C   AN INTERPERSONAL ORIENTATION TO THE STUDY OF CONSUMER BEHAVIOR

Joel B. Cohen (Marketing Educator)

Consumer decision making and market behavior seem in part to be a response to significant others, who are either physically or referentially present at the time. To the extent that consumers use other people as a frame of reference, a sufficiently inclusive interpersonal framework may well be an essential part of a broader theoretical paradigm in which to study consumer behavior.

This study attempts to provide such a framework. To determine the potential usefulness of the approach, a two-step research program was conducted. The first step involved the development of an instrument to make the key theoretical constructs operational. The second step focused on testing hypotheses that related these constructs to selected product choice and media preference decisions.

A Theory of Interpersonal Response Traits

Much of previous work with interpersonal variables focused on relatively specific personality needs and dispositions. Detailed lists of interpersonal response traits have been suggested.[1] Yet marketing's diverse and complex behavioral applications seem to demand more than an exhaustive listing of traits. It may be far more useful to organize traits into meaningful categories that are descriptive, not only of a single interpersonal act, but of a person's

SOURCE: Joel B. Cohen, "An Interpersonal Orientation to the Study of Consumer Behavior," *Journal of Marketing Research*, Vol. 4 (August, 1967), pp. 270–278.
[1] For example, Krech, Crutchfield, and Ballachey [8] list 12 "primary" interpersonal response traits. French [2], after factor analyzing a number of personality tests, was able to "reduce" the number of apparently unrelated factors to 49.

relatively consistent means of relating to and coping with others.

Karen Horney [4, 5, 6, 7] has constructed a tripartite interpersonal model that fits the stated goals. Rather than merely listing a group of needs or traits, Horney attempted to provide a rationale for thinking in terms of three basic interpersonal configurations. These configurations help to explain a person's perception of his social environment and his action tendencies toward the objects in his life space.

According to Horney [6], people can be placed into three groups, which reflect their predominant mode of response to others: (1) those who move toward people (compliant), (2) those who move against people (aggressive), and (3) those who move away from people (detached). Each mode of response involves a different strategic method of coping with other people.

COMPLIANT ORIENTATION. Compliant-oriented people want to be part of the activities of others. They wish to be loved, wanted, appreciated, and needed. They see in other people a solution for many problems of life and wish to be protected, helped, and guided. Because of the importance given to the companionship and love of others, compliant people become oversensitive to others' needs, overgenerous, overgrateful, and overconsiderate. Such people tend to avoid conflict and subordinate themselves to the wishes of others. They are inhibited in criticism, and apologetic and willing to blame themselves rather than others if things go wrong. Among the most important attributes associated with a compliant tendency are: goodness, sympathy, love, unselfishness, and humility. The compliant person dislikes egotism, aggression, assertiveness, and power-seeking. The compliant type seeks to manipulate others by being weak and dependent and relying on others to help him achieve his goals. Since many of his goals are tied to finding an accepted place in society, he will go out of his way to conform to what he believes are accepted forms of behavior.

AGGRESSIVE ORIENTATION. Aggressive-oriented people want to excel, to achieve success, prestige, and admiration. Other people are seen as competitors. Aggressive people strive to be superior strategists, to control their emotions, and to bring their fears under control. Strength, power, and unemotional realism are seen as necessary qualities. People are valued if useful to one's goals. Everyone is thought to be motivated by self-interest, with feelings simply a cover for hidden objectives. The aggressive person seeks to manipulate others by achieving power over them. Yet he needs people to confirm his self-image, to bolster what may well be uncertain confidence in his competitive talents. He will go out of his way to be noticed, if such notice brings admiration.

DETACHED ORIENTATION. Detached-oriented people want to put emotional "distance" between themselves and others. Freedom from obligations, independence, and self-sufficiency are highly valued. Such people do not want to be influenced or to share experiences. Conformity is repellent; intelligence and reasoning are valued instead of feelings. Detached people consider themselves more or less unique, possessing certain gifts and abilities that should be recognized without having any need to go out of their way to show them to others. The detached type is distrustful of others, but does not wish to "stay and fight." Horney suggested that people frustrated in their compliant or aggressive tendencies, or both, may well adopt this response trait. If one is uncertain as to how to deal effectively with people, and receives negative reinforcement from early social interaction, this latter mode may be a solution. Goals and values that support this individualistic orientation will acquire positive reinforcement character.

DEVELOPMENT OF A PRIMARY ORIENTATION. The child seeks to obtain satisfaction and safety in dealing with his parents and others. The strategy that proves most successful becomes part of his value system, and will continue to dominate the other two until it no longer leads

to optimum rewards in interpersonal relationships. The selection of a particular strategy or predisposition toward others leads the person to adopt an appropriate set of values and attitudes consistent with his view of others (compliance becomes unselfishness, friendliness; aggressiveness becomes leadership, strength, etc.). These values achieve significance in their own right as they become a model toward which the person strives and have a powerful role in supporting the chosen interpersonal strategy. The other two strategies are inconsistent with these values and attitudes; they reflect different feelings toward life and require a different set of skills to achieve optimum results. The increasing ability with which one uses a predominant strategy provides a certain amount of security and self-confidence for the person [3].

The probability of a predominantly compliant, aggressive, or detached response should be a function of (1) previous reinforcement and accompanying attitudinal development for each orientation and (2) the perceived relevance of compliant, aggressive, or detached behavior in a situation. A detailed analysis of a person's previous reinforcement would be most difficult to obtain. Measurement of present attitudes will have to serve as an operational approximation of the strength of each predisposition.

The relevance of compliant, aggressive, and detached responses in different situations remains to be empirically determined even though we may have some feel for the interpersonal significance of certain aspects of consumer behavior. For example, there are some consumer acts and decisions that one might expect to be strongly motivated by interpersonal response traits, such as the purchase of a new car or clothing style. Not only do these purchases communicate the desired interpersonal orientation to other people, but they reinforce and are consistent with the values associated with the person's self-image. Other product choices, such as which brand of hairpins to buy or which vegetable to serve, may have little interpersonal orientation.

Measurement of Complaint, Aggressive, and Detached Traits

The Horney classification system, which may deal with the interpersonal dimension of personality in an especially meaningful way, has lacked an adequate means of measurement.

A 35-item, Likert-type instrument was designed to measure compliant, aggressive, and detached interpersonal orientations, as shown in the appendix. The instrument was shown to have adequate test-retest reliability and internal consistency reliability. Several studies were then undertaken to determine the instrument's validity.

The first of these served to ensure that CAD adequately represented the theory on which it was based and would thus be definitive in testing hypotheses based on that theory. High interjudge agreement among qualified people familiar with Horney's typology indicated that each of the items did measure the desired trait. On a 10-item compliant scale, all seven judges agreed on the compliant designation for nine items; the other item received six out of seven compliant responses. On a 15-item aggressive scale, two items received six out of seven aggressive responses, and the other 13 received perfect scores. A 10-item detached scale received perfect agreement on seven items and six out of seven agreement on three items.

Another frequently used technique for determining validity is a comparison with other psychological tests that have been demonstrated to measure, at least partly, many of the same underlying qualities as the test being validated. If the test under study converges on the same underlying qualities as the criterion measures, support is given to the instrument's ability to measure these qualities. Of course, perfect correspondence between two tests would eliminate the need for one of them.

Schutz [10] developed an instrument, FIRO-B (Fundamental Interpersonal Relations Orientation, 2nd ed.) designed to measure three interpersonal needs: inclusion, control, and affection, each dichotomized into expressed behavior and wanted behavior. This instrument received considerable use and validation in studies of group interaction. Consistent predicted similarities were found between CAD and FIRO-B when the scores of 50 students on both measures were correlated.

A somewhat different dimension of validity relates to how well test scores correspond to measures of concurrent criterion performance or evaluation. Following Rosenberg's work [9] with the Horney classification scheme in gaug-

ing occupational preference, it was felt that a similar approach might yield an adequate concurrent criterion measure. Two studies were undertaken using different measures of occupational preference. The first used the preference-report technique, and the second was a study of vocational preparation.

The preference-report study used three specially constructed scales of occupations validated by high interjudge agreement. The occupations were chosen by reference to Rosenberg's short list of compliant, aggressive, and detached occupational values and occupational choices, and by attempting to add similar-appearing occupations to each category. Students responded to these scales by indicating how desirable each occupation was to them. They were told to assume that all the occupations had the same salary and prestige, and required skills which the students possessed.

Table 1 shows that the intercorrelations among the compliant and detached CAD scores and corresponding occupational scales are significant at the .01 level. The correlation between the CAD aggressive scale and the scale of aggressive occupations is significant at the .05 level. Deficiencies in the reliability of the occupational scales, as indicated by internal consistency analysis, have in all probability led to an understatement of the correlations between the two sets of variables.

The magnitude and signs of the other correlations are interesting. The compliant orientation toward life may partly be described as acquiescent. Although a strong preference exists for compliant occupations, the others may be tolerated. Both aggressive and detached people may adopt a more negative

TABLE 1

Correlations of CAD Scales with Occupational Scales

CAD Scale	Occupational Scale		
	Compliant	Agressive	Detached
Compliant (n = 78)	.48[b]	.10	.21
Aggressive (n = 78)	—.20	.24[a]	—.29[b]
Detached (n = 78)	—.28[a]	—.40[b]	.34[b]

[a] Significant at .05 level.
[b] Significant at .01 level.

attitude toward situations and values not in harmony with their own views.

Vocational preparation was adopted as a particularly meaningful criterion measure in a second study of occupational preference. Using Rosenberg's evidence that the occupational choice of social work carried with it compliant values; business administration, aggressive values; and natural science, detached values, the following groups were selected for comparative purposes: students studying in the graduate school of social welfare, students working on their M.B.A., and students taking an advanced undergraduate course in geology.

Each group was given CAD, and the hypotheses were:

1. Social welfare students will score higher on the compliant scale than either business administration or geology students.
2. Business administration students will score higher on the aggressive scale than either social welfare or geology students.
3. Geology students will score higher on the detached scale than either social welfare students or business administration students.

Mean CAD scores for each group are in Table 2. Both compliant and detached scales contain 10 items; the aggressive scale contains 15 items. "T-tests" confirmed each hypothesis. Five of the six comparisons involved in the hypotheses may be accepted beyond the .001 level of confidence. The remaining comparison (social welfare compliant scores exceed geology compliant scores) may be accepted at the .01 level. Of all other possible comparisons for a given scale, only one was statistically significant at the .05 level: geology students score higher on the aggressive scale than social welfare students.

As a final measure of validity the criterion

variable "susceptibility to personal influence" was studied experimentally.

In his study of the relative effectiveness of alternative group communication processes in the estimation of economic indices, Campbell [1] selected CAD to measure interpersonal response traits. The following predictions were made regarding the extent of a person's change of estimates when compared with the group average after each person had participated in a face-to-face conference group.

1. High changers[2] would score lower on the CAD aggressive scale than low changers.
2. High changers would score higher on the CAD compliant scale than low changers.
3. High changers would score lower on the CAD detached scale than low changers.

Results of this study (Table 3) confirm the first two hypotheses but fail to confirm the third. The "high change" profile consists of a high compliant, low aggressive combination of traits.

Hypotheses and Method

It was felt that general interpersonal dispositions might be reflected in a wide range of consumer decisions, to the extent that other people are taken into account by the decision maker. A study was designed to explore several possible relationships between CAD scores and consumer market behavior. This discussion will focus on the two main areas of investigation: product and brand usage, and media preferences. The objective of the study was to indicate whether and in what more specific areas the schema might be useful. For this reason, emphasis was given to the scope of possible relationships, rather than to a few particular relationships. Results to be presented, therefore, cannot resolve the important question, "How important are these variables in a more general theory of consumer behavior?"

An in-class questionnaire was given to a convenience sample of 157 undergraduate students in business administration at UCLA and San Fernando Valley State College. This

TABLE 2
CAD Scores for Three Fields of Study

CAD Scale	Social Welfare	Business Administration	Geology
Compliant	39.41	35.70	36.67
Aggressive	41.88	50.87	44.96
Detached	23.88	25.03	28.60
Sample size	32	30	25

[2] High changers were operationally defined as those people whose shifts in indicator estimates toward the group mean comprised the highest third of the scores. Low changers comprised the lowest third of the change scores.

TABLE 3

CAD Scores and Group-Induced Opinion Change

Degree of Change	Compliant Mean Score	Aggressive Mean Score	Detached Mean Score
High (n = 15)	39.33[b]	45.53[a]	26.07
Low (n = 15)	34.80	50.20	26.40

[a] Significant at the .05 level.
[b] Significant at the .01 level.

questionnaire included instruments designed to measure product and brand usage and media preferences as well as the CAD scale. A wide range of products were selected with the limitation that students would be expected to purchase all products for their own use. Many consumer durables were excluded because students typically are not responsible for such purchases. The products were cigarettes, men's dress shirts, men's deodorant, mouthwash, toothpaste, razors, headache remedies, gasoline, men's hair dressing, toilet soap, and beer. In addition, the questionnaire included four products—tea, wine, Metrecal and similar diet products, and cologne and after-shave lotion— for which frequency of use was felt to be more important than brand preferences. Most of the popular brands for each product were included in the questionnaire. Not all students responded to each product category.

The 157 subjects were divided into high and low groupings for each of the three interpersonal response traits. High groupings on each trait were composed of people scoring above the median on that trait.[3]

[3] Other means of classifying people were also considered. Most rule-of-thumb criteria for placement offer competing solutions. One might use the person's highest score, which would often be lower than another person's second highest score, or a normative level, which may not be reached by one or more of his scores. Probably the best approach would have been to use each set of three scores to assign each individual to his appropriate grouping. However, the exact interpretation of a CAD profile is not yet clear. The procedure adopted for this study treated a person's three scores as though each came from different and unrelated instruments, following the logic that a high score on a trait should be associated with behavior consistent with that trait.

Results and Discussion

Differences in patterns of brand preference (or frequency of use) within each of the three high-low comparisons are reported in Table 4 for each product. In addition, specific brand or frequency responses are reported when differences among interpersonal groupings were most pronounced and cell sizes were thought reasonable for this purpose. It should be emphasized that such a "picking and choosing" process has severe limitations. Its strength lies in focusing on more initiatory findings and trying to discover unifying threads that may exist.

CIGARETTES. When high and low groupings on each of the three response traits are compared (high compliant subjects compared with low compliant subjects, etc.) no significant differences are observed in each comparison. However, an interesting result is that 60 per cent of the compliant and aggressive people were nonsmokers, as compared with 68 per cent of the detached people.

MEN'S DRESS SHIRTS. When high-aggressive men are compared with low-aggressive men, the pattern of their shirt preferences approaches statistical significance ($p < .10$). Based on recent advertising for "Van Heusen" shirts, it was expected that more aggressive men would be attracted to the brand. Prior predictions were not made for other brands. High-aggressive men did prefer "Van Heusen" to other shirts to a significantly greater extent than low-aggressive men ($p < .01$). Interesting also is that a slightly greater percentage of high-detached individuals than high-compliant or high-aggressive individuals did not know what brand they used most frequently. It is expected in general that detached individuals are less concerned with brand names as indicators of "social status" than aggressive or compliant individuals.

MOUTHWASH. It was felt that high-compliant people would be more likely to use a mouthwash than low-compliant people and, thereby, reduce the risk of offending others. This expectation is confirmed. The direction of the percentage differences supports the theoretical interpersonal dispositions of the Horney paradigm. Aggressive individuals must, of necessity, facilitate their ability to interact with others. Detached individuals are less concerned with others' opinions of them.

TABLE 4

Summary of Product and Brand Study

Product	Within-trait Comparison[a]	Brand or Category	N	C(n= 66)	A(n= 67)	D(n= 75)
				Percent of High Grouping in Each Brand or Product Category		
Cigarettes	NS	Smoker	47	40	40	32
		Nonsmoker	83	60	60	68
Men's dress shirts	NS	Arrow	26	20	15	22
		Van Heusen	21	16	25	20
		Brand not known	15	8	5	12
		Other	67	56	55	46
Mouthwash	Compliant	Used	91	74	64	56
		Not used	54	26	36	44
Men's deodorant	Aggressive	Old Spice	33	34	41	24
		Right Guard	53	45	38	52
		Other	33	21	21	24
Men's cologne and after shave lotion	Aggressive	At least several times a week	119	88	91	82
		Several times a month or less	25	12	9	18
Toilet or bath soap	Compliant	Dial	50	47	36	31
		No preference	39	19	23	38
		Other	46	34	41	31
Men's hair dressing	NS	Not used	46	41	43	39
		Other	65	59	57	61
Toothpaste	NS	Crest	77	61	60	60
		Colgate	28	16	24	20
		Other	29	23	16	20
Razors	Aggressive	Electric	48	38	25	38
		Manual	92	62	75	62
Beer	NS	Coors	54	41	49	35
		Not consumed	29	19	19	24
		Other	60	40	32	41
Tea	Detached	At least several times a week	41	26	22	33
		Several times a month or less	116	74	78	67
Wine	Compliant	At least several times a month	38	35	33	23
		Several times a year or less	119	65	67	77
Metrecal and similar diet products	NS	At least a few times a year	18	15	12	11
		Never	139	85	88	89
Gasoline	NS	Standard	32	17	23	19
		Shell	32	28	18	23
		Other	83	55	59	58
Headache remedies	NS	Bayer aspirin	44	32	38	30
		Other aspirin	33	13	23	21
		Bufferin	23	18	11	15
		Other remedy	47	37	28	34

[a] High and low groupings on each trait were compared using the chi-square test. Differences significant at the .05 level are reported by trait designation.

MEN'S DEODORANT. A statistically significant pattern of deodorant brand purchase was found for high-aggressive people when compared with low-aggressive people, but not for the other two comparisons. The most interesting finding in the significant aggressive pattern of responses is the preference for "Old Spice" over other brands. "Right Guard" is preferred by compliant and detached people. It is possible that "Old Spice" is thought of as a particularly masculine deodorant.

COLOGNE AND AFTER SHAVE LOTION. High-aggressive people—who desire notice—used cologne significantly more often than low-aggressive people. No other significant relationship was observed.

TOILET OR BATH SOAP. High- and low-compliant people differed significantly in brand purchasing habits. In the compliant grouping, high-compliant subjects were less likely to have no brand preference than low-compliant subjects (p < .05). The opposite relationship holds for high-detached people when compared with low-detached people. High detached subjects had no brand preference to a significantly greater extent than low-detached subjects (p < .05).

High-compliant people showed a preference for "Dial" soap when compared with low-compliant people (p < .05). "Dial" had been advertised using a strong interpersonal appeal similar to that of many deodorants. High-compliant people should be the best targets for such advertising, because of their greater concern for possibly offending others.

MEN'S HAIR DRESSING. No significant patterns of brand differences emerged between high and low groupings in any of the three classifications.

TOOTHPASTE. No significant patterns of toothpaste brand usage emerged between the highs and lows for each classification. This is not unexpected, since the competition among brands seems to have shifted in recent years to dental health.

RAZORS. A statistically significant relationship was observed between the type of razor customarily used by high and low aggressive people. Seventy-five percent of the aggressive people prefer a manual razor rather than an electric razor as compared with 62 percent of the compliant and detached groups. Use of a manual razor may be seen as more masculine by aggressive males.

DISCUSSION OF PERSONAL GROOMING PRODUCTS. Many personal grooming products may be purchased, in part, to help the person attain basic interpersonal goals and to reflect appropriate interpersonal values. The compliant person should want reassurance that he is *capable* of being liked by others. To this end, he obtains the extra security afforded by a mouthwash, deodorant, or anti-bacteria soap. Interpersonal qualities are seemingly inherent in such products, providing that a degree of anxiety is present or induced in the person. Brands of such products may themselves acquire a certain interpersonal aura, yet this seems to be secondary.

The aggressive person should desire more distinctive brands of personal grooming products. Acceptance by others is not enough. He wants to establish his separate identity and style of behavior at first contact with others. Thus he should select brands conveying such a tone by virtue of their advertising or other characteristics. He may, for example, choose an especially manly deodorant. To reinforce his feelings toward himself, he may select more masculine shaving products.

The detached person should not be overly concerned with products or brands that help ensure his interpersonal attractiveness. He might be expected to show the least brand preference for products with interpersonal appeals in their advertising.

Certain personal grooming products, such as toothpaste and men's hair dressing, carry less significant interpersonal overtones. Toothpaste might represent a category of products, which through general usage, becomes an accepted standard. It is only when certain brands of such generally accepted products acquire specific interpersonal character that we should expect differences in purchasing behavior of compliant, aggressive, and detached people.

Men's hair dressing may represent a category of products that are purchased, in large part, in response to specific grooming needs of the person. Differences in product attributes are of more overriding importance than differences in interpersonal brand imagery. This is especially true when a multiplicity of brands use rather similar advertising appeals, and therefore minimize differences in consumer predispositions toward the product.

In summary, personal grooming products appear to differ initially among themselves in relevance to interpersonal goals and values. In addition, the ability of a specific brand to attract either compliant, aggressive, or detached people may reflect the application of a consistent and enduring program of marketing and advertising emphasizing one or another set of interpersonal values. To be most relevant to a particular interpersonal classification, a product should possess clearly perceived aids to goal attainment.

BEER. No significant patterns of brand usage emerged for beer. Age may have been a factor, because most of the students were under 21 and may have had little choice in such consumption habits.

Twenty-four percent of the detached people did not drink beer as compared with 19 percent of the compliant and aggressive groups. Though this difference is slight, once again it fits the model. The social influence and possible group pressure to drink and smoke decreases for detached people. Thus, to speculate, the adoption rate of a product may be faster among aggressive or compliant individuals, who may be more receptive to social influence.

Another interesting finding is the significant difference (p < .05) between high and low aggressive people in their preference for "Coors" beer. Forty-nine percent of the agressive people listed "Coors" as their usual brand compared with 41 percent of the compliant and 35 percent of the detached. The result seems reasonable because "Coors" may have attracted more aggressive students as it is a popular tap beer at local beer joints, which cater to an outspokenly masculine group of students.

TEA. High-detached people were significantly greater consumers of tea than were low-detached ones: 33 percent of the detached subjects drank tea at least as often as several times a week compared with 26 percent of the compliant and 22 percent of the aggressive subjects.

WINE. The number of people who drank wine several times a month (5) was too small to examine this relationship over a range of frequency categories, though high-compliant people drank wine more frequently than low-compliant people. Yet demographic differences between the present sample and a more appropriate sample for this product suggest that

a satisfactory test of this relationship remains to be undertaken.

METRECAL AND SIMILAR DIET PRODUCTS. It was felt that dieting might be related to interpersonal values since probably not all dieting is undertaken merely to please the dieter. The interpersonal nature of much of the advertising for Metrecal strengthened this belief. Unfortunately, the number of people who reported using such products even a few times a year was very small, and the data revealed no significant interpersonal differences.

GASOLINE. The pattern of gasoline brands used most frequently by high-detached people was somewhat different from that used by low-detached people (p < .10). Cell sizes were too small to examine brand differences in detail.

HEADACHE REMEDIES. High-compliant people were found to use "Bayer" aspirin more than other aspirin compared with low-compliant people (p < .10). Only 13 percent of the compliant subjects used some other brand of aspirin as compared with 23 percent of the aggressive and 21 percent of the detached subjects. Compliant people might prefer the security of name brands more than aggressive or detached people in cases where the brands themselves do not carry significant interpersonal overtones. This result is consistent with similar findings for toilet or bath soap.

TELEVISION AND MAGAZINE PREFERENCES. Interpersonal differences in television and magazine preferences were investigated by examining students' reported interest in 23 television programs and 15 magazines. As an example of the contingency tables developed, the following is the absolute number cross-classification of the "Ben Casey" television program.

Interest	High C	Low C	High A	Low A	High D	Low D
High	21	26	25	22	17	30
Low	44	62	41	65	55	51

The overall pattern of television viewing preferences between high- and low-aggressive students and between high- and low-detached students was significantly different well beyond the .05 level of significance. The pattern of differences between high and low compliant groupings was not. High- and low-aggressive students have significantly different patterns of magazine preferences, while overall differences between the two compliant groupings approach significance. Significant differences were not found between high- and low-detached groupings.

That detached people are often high in both interest and disinterest for television programs and magazines leads to an interesting hypothesis: detached people may exhibit at least two different kinds of behavior in similar situations, apathy-avoidance or detached-interest behavior. The second is simply the detached behavioral counterpart of compliant or aggressive interests. Apathy-avoidance behavior may reflect a low level of interest in many subjects regardless of content or tone— a desire not to be involved. For example, many of the news, current events, and discussion programs and magazines were felt to offer an intellectual involvement rather than an emotional involvement and, therefore, to be generally attractive to detached people. Though results indicated a predictably high level of interest in such programs, detached people also had the *least* interest in such programs. Apathy-avoidance may be partly topic-bound and closely associated with issues seemingly beyond the control of the person (the world situation, the state of the economy, etc.). The detached person may wish either to retreat in the face of them or to reduce their potential danger by learning more about problems and alternative logical solutions.

In general, the results are in agreement with the expectation that programs and magazines having a compatible format (stories, characters, etc.) will be preferred by each interpersonal group. Aggressive people prefer such programs as "The Untouchables," "Voyage to the Bottom of the Sea," "Combat," and "The Fugitive." They also prefer such magazines as *Playboy* and *Field and Stream*. Compliant people prefer such programs as "Dr. Kildare," "Peyton Place," and "Bonanza" and have a much greater preference for the *Reader's Digest*.

Detached people, as discussed previously, have mixed patterns of interest. Results indicate that the detached have little interest in such programs as "Dr. Kildare," "Peyton Place," "The Fugitive," and "The Man From U.N.C.L.E." and have ambivalent attitudes toward news content.

Assessing the significance of these results is difficult. The directions of interest for most programs tend to support the compatibility hypothesis, but the magnitude of the differences is generally not large. Of course, there are reasons why interpersonal differences are not more pronounced. On the one hand there are built-in levelers in each program's content and characterizations. Programs are not pure types seeking to cater only to compliant, or aggressive, or detached people. A program generally attracts more than one type.

In addition, students are constrained far in excess of normal adult television viewers and magazine readers. Most students, living at home with their parents or in dormitories, fraternities, or other such facilities, are not completely free to choose their television programs and magazines. It seems reasonable to assume that the results of this study are affected by these factors, and, in fact, the rather consistent support given the theory in this section may well be impressive.

Conclusion

The Horney classification of interpersonal response traits seems to bring a high degree of integration to bear on otherwise diverse individual needs, values, and attitudes. These elements are brought together in an interpersonal dimension. Since much of human action, and probably an even greater segment of consumer behavior, is interpersonal, Horney's model may have special relevance for marketing.

Some products and brands appear to express either compliant, aggressive, or detached responses to life. Products reflecting differences in the goals and values of the respective interpersonal types may be important both in terms of the presentation they make to others and for the consistency and enhancement they offer the person's self-concept. Television programs and magazines are capable also of offering formats compatible with each interpersonal disposition. Most current offerings are not differentially selected by compliant, aggressive, and detached people, though patterns of program and magazine selection vary.

REFERENCES

1. Robert Campbell, *The Utilization of Expert Information in Business Forecasting,* Unpublished doctoral dissertation, Graduate School of Business Administration, University of California, Los Angeles, 1966.

2. Thomas French, *Summary of Factor Analytic Studies of Personality,* Princeton, N.J.: Educational Testing Service, 1956.

3. Erving Goffman, *The Presentation of Self in Everyday Life,* Garden City, N.Y.: Doubleday Anchor Books, 1959.

4. Karen Horney, *The Neurotic Personality of Our Time,* New York: W. W. Norton & Co., Inc., 1937.

5. Karen Horney, *New Ways in Psychoanalysis,* New York: W. W. Norton & Co., Inc., 1939.

6. Karen Horney, *Our Inner Conflicts,* New York: W. W. Norton & Co., Inc., 1945.

7. Karen Horney, *Neurosis and Human Growth,* New York: W. W. Norton & Co., Inc., 1950.

8. David Krech, Richard Crutchfield, and Egerton Ballachey, *Individual in Society,* New York: McGraw-Hill Book Co., 1962.

9. Morris Rosenberg, *Occupations and Values,* Glencoe, Ill.: The Free Press, 1957.

10. William Schutz, *FIRO: A Three-dimensional Theory of Interpersonal Behavior,* New York: Rinehart and Company, 1958.

1-D SIMULATION OF CONSUMER PREFERENCE

Ralph L. Day (Marketing Educator)

Manufacturers of consumer goods gauge consumer preferences for product attributes in many ways. They study sales records, both of their own brands and competitors', and conduct field surveys on how products are used and which features are preferred. Further, they may conduct motivation research studies to probe basic attitudes and beliefs underlying purchase behavior. While such methods provide useful information, each has shortcomings. Sales records reveal little about preferences for product features because so many other factors influence sales. Survey findings are susceptible to biases from many sources, and motivational data are often quite difficult to relate to consumer actions. Consequently, product tests in which consumers use alternative versions of the product and express their preferences by overt choices may provide important information. Though it too has shortcomings, the product-use test is becoming more important because it attempts to measure preferences directly under controlled conditions.

PAIRED COMPARISONS. Product-use tests can

SOURCE: Ralph L. Day, "Simulation of Consumer Preference," *Journal of Advertising Research,* Vol. 5 (September, 1965), pp. 6–11; © 1965 by the Advertising Research Foundation, Inc.

be conducted in several ways, but this paper focuses on the blind forced-choice paired-comparison test which reduces the choice situation to its simplest terms and requires the subject to demonstrate his preference through an overt choice. In the typical paired-comparison test, two product versions are prepared such that all influences external to the test items are minimized. Every precaution is taken so that the subject's choice reflects his reaction to the test items per se, rather than to advertising or experiences associated with brand names, or other merchandising factors such as colorful packaging. Participants in paired-product tests typically are asked to use both items in the same way they would use the corresponding products they normally purchase, and then are asked to indicate the item which they like best overall.

The paired-comparison test lends itself well to the study of preference for product attributes considered one at a time. By holding constant all other product features while one is varied, the influence of the experimental attribute can be analyzed. For example, tests might be conducted to determine whether most consumers preferred a hot chili sauce to a mild sauce, or a high-sudsing dishwashing detergent to a low sudser.

A FIELD PREFERENCE STUDY. The balance

of this paper briefly reports on a field preference study and the development via simulation of an estimate of the underlying preference distribution. Pennsylvania State University students made systematic paired comparisons on their preferences for chocolate ice cream samples, which varied as to the quantity of chocolate flavoring materials. Ice cream specialists at Penn State estimated that few students would like chocolate ice cream with more than 5.0 pounds of cocoa solids per hundred pounds of mix, or less than 2.2 pounds. Since ice cream manufacturers usually use about 3.6 pounds per hundred, this represented a range from 60 to 140 per cent of the customary amount.

On economic grounds we decided to test five levels of "chocolatiness," representing five equal steps over the 2.2 to 5.0 pound range. Test batches were carefully prepared, with other attributes such as solids, fats, and sweeteners carefully controlled across all batches. Paired-comparison tests were conducted systematically, with servings from every batch being tested against servings from every other batch. A different sample of students tested each of the ten resulting pairs. In all, 928 students, selected by cluster sampling techniques, participated. Each subject was given, in random order, two cups containing two-ounce servings, and asked to indicate an overall preference. Table 1 summarizes the results by preferred batch across all pairs.

The results of the ice cream study suggest a unimodal preference distribution. Table 1 also suggests that the distribution is skewed toward the 5.0 pound end and is heavy in the tails. However, the apparent skewness could result from a failure of the test levels to span the entire range of consumer preferences for the attributes toward the 2.2 pound end. This would force those preferring a lower level than any available into the lowest available level. The apparent heaviness in the tails could be an illusion. The assumption that consumers cannot recognize with a perfect 1.00 probability the item they prefer in a paired comparison test implies that the peak of a unimodal distribution of preferences will be understated and the tails overstated. The degree of flattening would depend on the basic ability of consumers to discriminate between levels of the attribute.

FIRST SIMULATION STUDY. In order to test the hypothesis that the ice cream study findings were consistent with a normal distribution of preferences over the five segments (five test levels) used in the field test, a model was developed and programed to generate simulated tests for comparison with the actual results. Since the field study was designed on the assumption that the distribution of preferences was centered on the third level (commercial norm) with only small percentages of the population preferring as little or less chocolate than level one and as much or more than level five, the area of the standard normal distribution ($\mu = 0$ and $\sigma = 1.0$) was assigned to the five segments as shown in Figure 1. The area between $-.5$ and $.5$ was assigned to segment three, the area from $-.5$ to -1.5 to segment two, from $.5$ to 1.5 to segment four, and the remaining area in the tail five each were assigned 6.68 per cent of the area, segments two and four each received 24.17 per cent, and segment three 34.30 per cent.

The expected value of the number choosing each item in each of the ten simulated paired

TABLE 1
Total Choices of Each Test Level (Adjusted for Variations in Sample Size)

Test Batch	Choices	Per Cent
1 (2.2 lbs.)	184.6	19.9
2	220.6	23.8
3 (commercial norm)	202.8	21.8
4	183.5	19.8
5 (5.0 lbs.)	136.5	14.7
	928.0	100.0

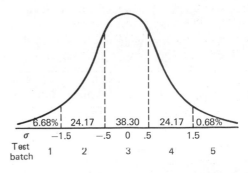

Figure 1. Standard normal distribution allocated to five segments.

comparison tests was computed using the following equations:

$$C_j = \sum_{i=1}^{n} p^i_{jk} \cdot A_i \cdot N_{jk} \qquad (1)$$

$$C_k = \sum_{i=1}^{n} (1 - p^i_{jk}) A_i \cdot N_{jk} \qquad (2)$$

where n is the number of segments, A_i is the area assigned to the ith segment, and N_{jk} is the size of the sample testing level j against level k. Exploratory runs iterating on d with large increments suggested that the value of d which would provide simulated results closely matching the actual results would be around .65 to .80. The final run was begun with d = .60 and tests with samples of 1,000 (100 for each of the ten paired tests) were simulated, iterating 25 times on d in steps of +.01. The simulated results were summarized in the same way as the actual results and were compared with the results of the field study after they were adjusted to the same overall sample size (1,000). Using the chi-square test of goodness of fit, the best fit was found when the value of d was .71. The simulated results are compared with the adjusted actual results in Table 2. Using a chi-square test of goodness of fit and the .05 critical level, the hypothesis that the results obtained in the ice cream study were generated by a population with the parameters of the simulated population would be rejected.

SECOND SIMULATION STUDY. To investigate the possibility that the apparent weakness in the ice cream study resulted from the resistance of a small but significant group preferring even less chocolate than the amount contained in level one, with more than the assumed small number preferring level two, it was decided to simulate a preference distribution with an additional segment at the lower end of the scale. This segment would represent those who would like the level of chocolatiness produced by 1.5 pounds of flavoring materials per hundred pounds of mix, maintaining the spacing of .7 pounds used in the actual test. The standard normal distribution was allocated to the six steps with each of the inner segments one standard deviation wide as in the first simulation study. Thus segments one and six were each assigned 2.27 per cent, segments two and five 13.60 per cent, and segments three and four 34.13.

The field study was then simulated with the test batches corresponding to the same levels as before, now numbered two through six. Twenty tests each involving 1,000 simulated consumers were performed, iterating on d in steps of .01 from a start with a d of .55. The simulated results best fitted the results of the ice cream study at a d of .65. The fit was quite good. In the goodness of fit test, a chi-square value as large as that obtained ($\chi^2 =$ 1.123, four df) could occur by chance more than 80 per cent of the time if the observed values were from the theoretical distribution. The simulated results are shown along with the field results in Table 3.

SOME MONTE CARLO RUNS. Both simulation studies were conducted without statistical variation so that the results represent the expected value with a random sample from the infinite simulated population. In order to simulate field product tests subject to sampling error, a Monte Carlo model was developed with areas under the normal curve assigned to six segments as in the second simulation study. Each simulated consumer's innate preference was determined by a draw from a gen-

TABLE 2

Five Segment Simulation and Actual Results

Test Batch	Simulation Results	Field Study Results[a]
1	176	199
2	211	238
3	228	218
4	211	198
5	176	147

[a] Adjusted to a sample size of 1,000.

TABLE 3

Six Segment Simulation Results

Test Batch	Simulation Results	Field Study Results[a]
1	195	199
2	230	238
3	231	218
4	196	198
5	149	147

[a] Adjusted to a sample size of 1,000.

erator of pseudo-random deviates from a normal population with mean 0.0 and standard deviation 1.0. Each simulated consumer was assigned to one of the six segments (assigned a value of i) according to the value drawn. Thus the expected distribution of simulated consumers would be as shown in Figure 2. The probability that the simulated consumer would choose the lower-numbered item in a particular pair was developed by assigning the appropriate values of i, j, and k as well as a value of d in equation 1. The choice between items with levels j and k was simulated by a draw from a uniform distribution on the segment 0.0 to 1.0. The simulated consumer was assigned to segment j if the random number was equal to or less than p^i_{jk}, and to segment k if it was greater.

The first run with the Monte Carlo model was made with a d of .65, the level of best fit to the field results. Twenty preference studies involving 1,000 respondents in ten subsamples of 100 were simulated. The simulated results in each test were compared with the results of simulation model two, with a d of .65 as the theoretical frequencies for chi-square, the same comparison made with the actual field study results. In 13 of the twenty simulated tests, the fit of the simulated results (reflecting only sampling variation) to the theoretical results was poorer than the fit of the actual field results.

As yet no extensive sensitivity analysis has been done to study the effect of variations in the estimated value of the parameter d. However, two additional runs of the Monte Carlo

model with different values of d were made. In the first case, the d was reduced by .10 to .55 and again twenty tests involving 1,000 respondents were simulated. When tested against the theoretical results obtained with d of .65, the fit of the simulated results was worse than the fit of the actual field results in 19 of the twenty replications. When d was raised by .10 to .75, the fit of the simulated results was worse in all twenty cases.

Applications

The results obtained so far strongly suggest that systematic paired comparison tests, the concept of a preference distribution, and a probabilistic model of choice in the paired comparison situation can, in combination, provide a useful basis for studying consumers' preferences for many product attributes. While these techniques are likely to be applicable to relatively few products, they provide a starting point for developing more complex models having wider applicability. Experience to date in studying preferences for levels of chocolatiness in ice cream has demonstrated the practical feasibility of scientific research on consumers' preferences for significant product attributes.

Experience suggests that computer simulation also has potential utility in research on consumer preferences. In the research reported here, simulation was very helpful in checking out the assumption that the apparent skewness in the ice cream study results was due to an inadequate preference scale rather than an actual skewed distribution of preferences. The ability of a simulation model based on a normal distribution over six segments to produce simulated results very much like the results of the field test supported the assumption. As a consequence, a new study of preferences for the chocolatiness of ice cream is now being conducted. An extra-mild chocolate ice cream containing one level less chocolate is being tested against the same five levels used in the initial study. If the results appear to provide an adequate delineation of the distribution of preferences for chocolate ice cream, we planned to perform simulation experiments to investigate the possibility of estimating the preference distribution with fewer tests than $n!/(n-2)!2!$ paired comparison tests required by the procedure now being utilized.

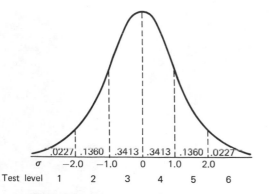

Figure 2. Six-segment distribution.

REFERENCES

Boyd, Harper W., and Ralph Westfall. *Marketing Research: Text and Cases.* Homewood, Ill.: Irwin, 1964.

David, H. A. *The Method of Paired Comparisons.* London: Griffin, 1963.

Metropolis, N., and S. Ulam. The Monte Carlo Method. *Journal of the American Statistical Association,* Vol. 4, 1949, pp. 335–341.

Saaty, Thomas. *Mathematical Methods of Operations Research.* New York: McGraw-Hill, 1959, pp. 292–295.

2 / Behavioral Sciences and the Consumer

A. BACKGROUND AND THEORY

The first two selections provide specific information as to how materials from anthropology, psychology, and sociology can contribute to an understanding of consumer behavior: an explanation (Katona) of consumer psychology, and the role of the consumer psychologist (Twedt). The third selection (Kotler) describes five different behavioral models for interpreting the transformation of buying influences into purchasing responses.

2-A WHAT IS CONSUMER PSYCHOLOGY?

George Katona (Psychologist)

Some social scientists, not well informed about consumer psychology, maintain views which I wish to contradict in this paper. According to one of these notions consumer psychologists merely apply findings of experimental or social psychology to practical problems of marketing goods and services to consumers. According to a related notion, the work of consumer psychologists consists of collecting a variety of raw facts. It is conceded that finding out how consumers think and feel at a given time, either about spending or saving in general or about buying the one or the other brand, has practical value, but it is not thought that such studies would contribute much to the progress of science.

It will be argued in this paper that:

1. The purpose of consumer psychology is acquisition of knowledge for the sake of understanding and predicting important aspects of real-life behavior.

2. Consumer psychology contributes to the development of a theory of social action. Programmatic research is undertaken, starting with hypotheses derived from economic, sociological, or psychological findings and the-

ories, and consisting of the never-ending process of testing hypotheses, formulating more comprehensive hypotheses on the basis of the tests, testing the new hypotheses, etc.

3. At the same time, consumer psychology is policy-oriented and practical, in the sense that nothing is more practical than good theory (as Kurt Lewin said). Major changes in the economy of the country (for instance, the tax cut of 1964) or in the situation of a business firm (e.g., the introduction of new products) offer the opportunity for many studies in consumer psychology which are basic and practical at the same time.

Consumer psychology, to define it in one sentence, is the study of the dynamics of the behavior of masses of consumers. The term "dynamic" means that the studies are directed toward the understanding and prediction of factors that make for changes over time. The term "masses" implies that unique features in the behavior of a few people are of no interest to consumer psychology, nor is it concerned with idiosyncratic behavior or with random movements in all directions (resulting perhaps from temporary moods) which cancel out in the aggregate. Consumer psychology studies changes in the behavior of groups of consumers and attempts to identify the factors responsible

SOURCE: George Katona, "What Is Consumer Psychology?" *American Psychologist*, Vol. 22 (March, 1967), pp. 219-226, pp. 219-220.

for those changes. Differences among consumers are studied by comparing the behavior of groups which differ with respect to economic variables (e.g., the "rich" versus the "poor"), demographic variables (young versus old), as well as psychological variables (optimists versus pessimists, achievement-minded versus security-minded people, etc.). From understanding changes in one form of behavior in one country at one time (for instance, an increase in installment buying in the United States in the 1960s) as well as changes in other forms of behavior at different times, broad generalizations and theories are derived.

The topic of research carried out by consumer psychologists is real-life behavior. Certain limitations to which many experimental studies are subject are thereby overcome. For instance, traditional problem-solving experiments usually begin with the subjects being strongly and extraneously motivated to tackle a task presented to them. In consumer psychology, however, the questions of whether or not consumers perceive a problem, and whether they are motivated to take steps toward its solution, are studied in addition to their methods of solving a problem. Furthermore, the final variable of consumer psychology is action rather than verbal behavior. The entire process, stimuli-intervening variables-expressed opinions-action, is studied because one outstanding feature of consumer behavior is that easily identifiable forms of action occur frequently in this field (such as buying specific consumer goods, putting money in a bank or in stocks, etc.).

Consumer psychology is concerned with a variety of psychological problems. The following tentative list is presented so as to indicate some principal areas for the study of which consumer behavior offers great opportunities.

1. DECISION MAKING. Choosing between two possible forms of action is constantly studied by consumer psychologists. The two alternatives may be doing something or doing nothing (e.g., buying common stock or deciding not to touch the money in the bank account) or proceeding in one way or the other (e.g., buying a car on the installment plan or by paying cash). Among the explanatory variables for the choice process, we may list enabling conditions (e.g., cash in the possession of people), demographic variables (age, education, etc.), new stimuli (change in the enabling conditions such as an increase in income as well as information received, for instance, about new products or about the change in the price of a product), past experience (including long-established attitudes and motives), and personality traits that prevail among large groups of people.

2. CHANGE IN ATTITUDES AND BEHAVIOR. Social learning, that is, the acquisition of new opinions, attitudes, and expectations, as well as of new forms of behavior by masses of people, represents a central topic of consumer psychology. Two settings of social learning may be distinguished. In one setting we study response (or its absence) to intentional attempts to change the response, such as marketing and advertising campaigns. Second, learning may occur without being closely related to the process of persuasion or of inducing change. Whether or not, and if so how, information transmitted by the news media or by word of mouth makes for a change in attitudes and behavior is studied.[1] News about price increases, international tensions, increase or decrease in unemployment, etc., has been shown to change behavior.

3. INFLUENCE OF TIME PERSPECTIVE AND OF UNCERTAINTY. People's time perspective extends both backward and forward. How distant past events may influence behavior and how far into the future influential expectations extend are questions raised in consumer psychology. Topics of research include planning or its absence, and carefully weighed decisions influenced by confidently held expectations as against continuation of habitual behavior. Uncertainty is practically always attached to expectations, and its impact may differ greatly according to a variety of factors.

4. STUDIES OF GROUP BELONGING, SOCIAL FACILITATION, AND LEADERSHIP MAY PROFIT FROM RESEARCH ON CONSUMER BEHAVIOR. Such research extends not only to face-to-face

[1] Important differences are neglected when both kinds of settings are subsumed under the concept of "effects of communication on attitudes." The differences between the two settings are related to but are not the same as the differences between experiments and survey studies discussed by C. I. Hovland (1959).

groups (family, neighbors, etc.) and reference groups (e.g., "keeping up with the Joneses") but also to the influence of such broad demographic and socioeconomic groups as age and income groups, or "businessmen" and trade union members. The salience of news heard has been found to be strongly group influenced.

2-B THE CONSUMER PSYCHOLOGIST

Dik Warren Twedt (Psychologist)

The outstanding consumer psychologist of the first quarter of this century was Walter Dill Scott. In 1900, he established a psychological laboratory at Northwestern University.

In *The Psychology of Advertising*, Scott showed how the experimental method could be applied to problems in consumer psychology. He reported experiments he had conducted in magazine reading habits (by random observation of readers in the Chicago Public Library), and investigations on the attention value of magazine advertisements of different size. He also developed questionnaire and sampling techniques that were widely used in early marketing surveys. Many of the questions first raised by Scott were later studied by Starch, Strong, and Hollingworth.

In 1931, Daniel Starch inaugurated the first continuing measurement of advertising readership. By 1933, the Psychological Corporation had begun its Psychological Brand Barometer service—continuing national polls of public opinion and buying habits. In the 1936 presidential election, public opinion polling was popularized independently by Gallup, Crossley, and Roper. But it was not until the postwar period that the consumer psychologist came into his own. At the end of World War II, there were only about a dozen qualified individuals in the U.S. who were working full-time as consumer psychologists.

Current Activities of Consumer Psychologists

What kinds of activities occupy today's consumer psychologist? His primary function is to serve as the missing *communications link* between producer and consumer. There are

SOURCE: Dik Warren Twedt, "The Consumer Psychologist," in Martin M. Grossack, Editor, *Understanding Consumer Behavior* (Boston: The Christopher Publishing House, 1964), pp. 53-63.

now more than 300,000 brand names actively competing for shelf space, and almost 7,000 different products available in a typical large supermarket. Thus it becomes increasingly important to the manufacturer to establish a clear image of his product in the consumer's mind.

The manufacturer must set up a two-way channel of communication, so that he is aware of changes in product demand and preference *as these changes occur*—so that he can immediately respond to them.

Since the beginning of this century, there have been three great stages of our economy. First was the *production-oriented* economy, in which the emphasis was on the efficiency of production of large quantities of goods at the lowest unit cost. The early years of the Ford Motor Company, with its highly efficient production of a very limited number of models, is an example of such production orientation.

The second stage was the *sales-oriented* economy. Such mottos as "Nothing happens until a sale is made" reflected management's growing awareness of the distributive function in modern business. An extreme example of sales-oriented thinking is the praise given the legendary salesman who was so persuasive that he could "sell ice boxes to Eskimos."

The third stage is the orientation of *consumer needs*. Management is learning the implications of the First Law of Marketing: "Make what people want to buy—don't try to sell what you happen to make."

The problem, of course, is finding out what people want to buy. Rarely is it feasible to make a census of the consumer population, and so we resort to the tools of statistical sampling, with estimated errors of measurement. The ways in which we frame our questions, to ensure that the answers are valid, reflect the collective experience of social scientists, statisticians, and marketing management.

The consumer psychologist contributes to

the study of consumer needs in three major ways: through his knowledge of scientific method, experimental design, and psychological theory and its applications.

1. *Scientific Method.* The psychologist, as a behavioral scientist, starts an investigation with an attitude of objectivity. He also starts with an optimism that the problem can be solved, agreeing with the dictum of Dr. E. L. Thorndike, who once observed that "if a thing exists at all, it exists in some amount—and can be measured." The psychologist also recognizes that sometimes the cost of measurement is greater than the price of being wrong—in which case he may recommend that no research be undertaken, unless it is likely to shed light on some future problems. Often, too, the psychologist makes a major contribution simply by his insistence upon a clear statement of what the problem is, and what kinds of answers may be useful, before *any* research is undertaken.

2. *Experimental Design.* The psychologist knows appropriate statistical tools, and how to design experiments that yield a maximum amount of truth at minimum cost. He may also be a specialist in, or is at least likely to be familiar with, instrumentation and special techniques of the psychophysical methods of measuring human perception.

3. *Psychological Theory.* Because of his broad knowledge of motivation and learning theory, the psychologist can interpret and relate the results of a particular experiment within a psychological framework that permits generalization to other similar problems of predicting consumer behavior.

There are problems, of course, in the measurement of human motivation. There *is* error in measurement, just as there is in the supposedly more precise physical sciences. Consider the problem of measurement in nuclear physics. In the measurement of the location of sub-atomic particles in a Wilson cloud chamber, a beam of light is focused on the particles to determine their relative positions. But unfortunately, the light itself has enough free energy to shove the particles aside so that the reflective angle changes at the very moment of measurement.

In physics, this has been called the "Uncertainty Principle"—and the consumer psychologist also is likely to find that the very act of measuring consumer opinion introduces change which we call "bias." This is one of the principal reasons advanced for the indirect measurement of motivation through the projective techniques.

We should remember, however, that not only is psychology one of the newer sciences (more than three-quarters of all the psychologists who have ever lived, are alive right now!)—it is certainly concerned with, by all odds, the most complex subject matter of any science—the understanding and prediction of human behavior, both singly and in group interaction. Without complaint, but as a simple fact, it is fair to say that psychologists share the greatest problems, and the greatest opportunities, of any branch of scientific inquiry.

2-C　BEHAVIORAL MODELS FOR ANALYZING BUYERS

Philip Kotler (Marketing Educator)

What are the most useful behavioral models for interpreting the transformation of buying influences into purchasing responses? Five different models of the buyer's "black box" are presented in the present article, along with their respective marketing applications: (1) the Marshallian model, stressing economic motivations; (2) the Pavlovian model, learn-

SOURCE: Philip Kotler, "Behavioral Models for Analyzing Buyers," *Journal of Marketing*, Vol. 29 (October, 1965), pp. 37-45.

ing; (3) the Freudian model, psychoanalytic motivations; (4) the Veblenian model, social-psychological factors; and (5) the Hobbesian model, organizational factors. These models represent radically different conceptions of the mainsprings of human behavior.

The Marshallian Economic Model

Economists were the first professional group to construct a specific theory of buyer behavior. The theory holds that purchasing decisions are the result of largely "rational" and conscious economic calculations. The individual buyer seeks to spend his income on those goods that will deliver the most utility (satisfaction) according to his tastes and relative prices.

Alfred Marshall was the great consolidator of the classical and neoclassical tradition in economics; and his synthesis in the form of demand-supply analysis constitutes the main source of modern micro-economic thought in the English-speaking world. His theoretical work aimed at realism, but his method was to start with simplifying assumptions and to examine the effect of a change in a single variable (say, price) when all other variables were held constant.

He would "reason out" the consequences of the provisional assumptions and in subsequent steps modify his assumptions in the direction of more realism. He employed the "measuring rod of money" as an indicator of the intensity of human psychological desires. Over the years his methods and assumptions have been refined into what is now known as *modern utility theory*: economic man is bent on maximizing his utility, and does this by carefully calculating the "felicific" consequences of any purchase.

MARKETING APPLICATIONS OF MARSHALLIAN MODEL. Marketers usually have dismissed the Marshallian model as an absurd figment of ivory-tower imagination.

From one point of view the Marshallian model is tautological and therefore neither true nor false. The model holds that the buyer acts in the light of his best "interest." But this is not very informative.

A second view is that this is a *normative* rather than a *descriptive* model of behavior. The model provides logical norms for buyers who want to be "rational." Although the consumer is not likely to employ economic analysis to decide between a box of Kleenex and Scotties, he may apply economic analysis in deciding whether to buy a new car. Industrial buyers even more clearly would want an economic calculus for making good decisions.

A third view is that economic factors operate to a greater or lesser extent in all markets and, therefore, must be included in any comprehensive description of buyer behavior.

Furthermore, the model suggests useful behavioral hypotheses such as: (a) The lower the price of the product, the higher the sales. (b) The lower the price of substitute products, the lower the sales of this product; and the lower the price of complementary products, the higher the sales of this product. (c) The higher the real income, the higher the sales of this product, provided that it is not an "inferior" good. (d) The higher the promotional expenditures, the higher the sales.

The validity of these hypotheses does not rest on whether *all* individuals act as economic calculating machines in making their purchasing decisions. For example, some individuals may buy *less* of a product when its price is reduced. They may think that the quality has gone down, or that ownership has less status value. If a majority of buyers view price reductions negatively, then sales may fall, contrary to the first hypothesis.

But for most goods a price reduction increases the relative value of the goods in many buyers' minds and leads to increased sales. This and the other hypotheses are intended to describe average effects.

Economic factors alone cannot explain all the variations in sales. The Marshallian model ignores the fundamental question of how product and brand preferences are formed. It represents a useful frame of reference for analyzing only one small corner of the "black box."

The Pavlovian Learning Model

The designation of a Pavlovian learning model has its origin in the experiments of the Russian psychologist Pavlov, who rang a bell each time before feeding a dog. Soon he was able to induce the dog to salivate by ringing the bell whether or not food was supplied. Pavlov concluded that learning was largely an associative process and that a large component of behavior was conditioned in this way.

Experimental psychologists have continued this mode of research with rats and other animals, including people. Laboratory experiments have been designed to explore such phenomena as learning, forgetting, and the ability to discriminate. The results have been integrated into a stimulus-response model of human behavior, or as someone has "wise-cracked," the substitution of a rat psychology for a rational psychology.

The model has been refined over the years,

and today is based on four central concepts—those of *drive, cue, response,* and *reinforcement.*[1]

Drive. Also called needs or motives, drive refers to strong stimuli internal to the individual which impels action. Psychologists draw a distinction between primary physiological drives—such as hunger, thirst, cold, pain, and sex—and learned drives which are derived socially—such as cooperation, fear, and acquisitiveness.

Cue. A drive is very general and impels a particular response only in relation to a particular configuration of cues. Cues are weaker stimuli in the environment and/or in the individual which determine when, where, and how the subject responds. Thus, a coffee advertisement can serve as a cue which stimulates the thirst drive in a housewife. Her response will depend upon this cue and other cues, such as the time of day, the availability of other thirst-quenchers, and the cue's intensity. Often a relative change in a cue's intensity can be more impelling than its absolute level. The housewife may be more motivated by a 2-cents-off sale on a brand of coffee than the fact that this brand's price was low in the first place.

Response. The response is the organism's reaction to the configuration of cues. Yet the same configuration of cues will not necessarily produce the same response in the individual. This depends on the degree to which the experience was rewarding, that is, drive-reducing.

Reinforcement. If the experience is rewarding, a particular response is reinforced; that is, it is strengthened and there is a tendency for it to be repeated when the same configuration of cues appears again. The housewife, for example, will tend to purchase the same brand of coffee each time she goes to her supermarket so long as it is rewarding and the cue configuration does not change. But if a learned response or habit is not reinforced, the strength of the habit diminishes and may be extinguished eventually. Thus, a housewife's preference for a certain coffee may become

extinct if she finds the brand out of stock for a number of weeks.

Forgetting, in contrast to extinction, is the tendency for learned associations to weaken, not because of the lack of reinforcement but because of nonuse.

Cue configurations are constantly changing. The housewife sees a new brand of coffee next to her habitual brand, or notes a special price deal on a rival brand. Experimental psychologists have found that the same learned response will be elicited by similar patterns of cues; that is, learned responses are *generalized.* The housewife shifts to a similar brand when her favorite brand is out of stock. This tendency toward generalization over less similar cue configurations is increased in proportion to the strength of the drive. A housewife may buy an inferior coffee if it is the only brand left and if her drive is sufficiently strong.

A counter-tendency to generalization is *discrimination.* When a housewife tries two similar brands and finds one more rewarding, her ability to discriminate between similar cue configurations improves. Discrimination increases the specificity of the cue-response connection, while generalization decreases the specificity.

MARKETING APPLICATIONS OF PAVLOVIAN MODEL. The modern version of the Pavlovian model makes no claim to provide a complete theory of behavior—indeed, such important phenomena as perception, the subconscious, and interpersonal influence are inadequately treated. Yet the model does offer a substantial number of insights about some aspects of behavior of considerable interest to marketers.[2]

An example would be in the problem of introducing a new brand into a highly competitive market. The company's goal is to extinguish existing brand habits and form new habits among consumers for its brand. But the company must first get customers to try its brand; and it has to decide between using weak and strong cues.

Light introductory advertising is a weak cue

---

[1] See John Dollard and Neal E. Miller, *Personality and Psychotherapy* (New York: McGraw-Hill Book Company, Inc., 1950), Chapter III.

[2] The most consistent application of learning-theory concepts to marketing situations is found in John A. Howard, *Marketing Management: Analysis and Planning* (Homewood, Illinois: Richard D. Irwin, Inc., revised edition, 1963).

compared with distributing free samples. Strong cues, although costing more, may be necessary in markets characterized by strong brand loyalties. For example, Folger went into the coffee market by distributing over a million pounds of free coffee.

To build a brand habit, it helps to provide for an extended period of introductory dealing. Furthermore, sufficient quality must be built into the brand so that the experience is reinforcing. Since buyers are more likely to transfer allegiance to similar brands than dissimilar brands (generalization), the company should also investigate what cues in the leading brands have been most effective. Although outright imitation would not necessarily effect the most transference, the question of providing enough similarity should be considered.

The Pavlovian model also provides guide lines in the area of advertising strategy. The American behaviorist, John B. Watson, was a great exponent of repetitive stimuli; in his writings man is viewed as a creature who can be conditioned through repetition and reinforcement to respond in particular ways.[3] The Pavlovian model emphasizes the desirability of repetition in advertising. A single exposure is likely to be a very weak cue, hardly able to penetrate the individual's consciousness sufficiently to excite his drives above the threshold level.

Repetition in advertising has two desirable effects. It "fights" forgetting, the tendency for learned responses to weaken in the absence of practice. It provides reinforcement, because after the purchase the consumer becomes selectively exposed to advertisements of the product.

The model also provides guide lines for copy strategy. To be effective as a cue, an advertisement must arouse strong drives in the person. The strongest product-related drives must be identified. For candy bars, it may be hunger; for safety belts, fear; for hair tonics, sex; for automobiles, status. The advertising practitioner must dip into his cue box—words, colors, pictures—and select that configuration of cues that provides the strongest stimulus to these drives.

[3] John B. Watson, *Behaviorism* (New York: The People's Institute Publishing Company, 1925).

The Freudian Psychoanalytic Model

The Freudian model of man is well known, so profound has been its impact on 20th century thought. It is the latest of a series of philosophical "blows" to which man has been exposed in the last 500 years. Copernicus destroyed the idea that man stood at the center of the universe; Darwin tried to refute the idea that man was a special creation; and Freud attacked the idea that man even reigned over his own psyche.

According to Freud, the child enters the world driven by instinctual needs which he cannot gratify by himself. Very quickly and painfully he realizes his separateness from the rest of the world and yet his dependence on it.

He tries to get others to gratify his needs through a variety of blatant means, including intimidation and supplication. Continual frustration leads him to perfect more subtle mechanisms for gratifying his instincts.

As he grows, his psyche becomes increasingly complex. A part of his psyche—the id—remains the reservoir of his strong drives and urges. Another part—the ego—becomes his conscious planning center for finding outlets for his drives. And a third part—his superego—channels his instinctive drives into socially approved outlets to avoid the pain of guilt or shame.

The guilt or shame which man feels toward some of his urges—especially his sexual urges—causes him to repress them from his consciousness. Through such defense mechanisms as rationalization and sublimation, these urges are denied or become transmuted into socially approved expressions. Yet these urges are never eliminated or under perfect control; and they emerge, sometimes with a vengeance, in dreams, in slips-of-the tongue, in neurotic and obsessional behavior, or ultimately in mental breakdown where the ego can no longer maintain the delicate balance between the impulsive power of the id and the oppressive power of the superego.

The individual's behavior, therefore, is never simple. His motivational wellsprings are not obvious to a casual observer nor deeply understood by the individual himself. If he is asked why he purchased an expensive foreign sportscar, he may reply that he likes its maneuverability and its looks. At a deeper level he may have purchased the car to impress others, or to feel young again. At a still deeper level, he may be purchasing the sports-car to achieve substitute gratification for unsatisfied sexual strivings.

Many refinements and changes in emphasis have occurred in this model since the time of Freud. The instinct concept has been replaced by a more careful delineation of basic drives; the three parts of the psyche are regarded now as theoretical concepts rather than actual entities; and the behavioral perspective has been extended to include cultural as well as biological mechanisms.

Instead of the role of the sexual urge in psychic development—Freud's discussion of oral, anal, and genital stages and possible fixations and traumas—Adler[4] emphasized the urge for power and how its thwarting manifests itself in superiority and inferiority complexes; Horney[5] emphasized cultural mechanisms; and Fromm[6] and Erickson[7] emphasized the role of existential crises in personality development. These philosophical divergencies, rather than debilitating the model, have enriched and extended its interpretative value to a wider range of behavioral phenomena.

MARKETING APPLICATIONS OF FREUDIAN MODEL. Perhaps the most important marketing implication of this model is that buyers are motivated by *symbolic* as well as *economic-functional* product concerns. The change of a bar of soap from a square to a round shape may be more important in its sexual than its functional connotations. A cake mix that is advertised as involving practically no labor may alienate housewives because the easy life may evoke a sense of guilt.

Motivational research has produced some interesting and occasionally some bizarre hypotheses about what may be in the buyer's mind regarding certain purchases. Thus, it has been suggested at one time or another that

- Many a businessman doesn't fly because of a fear of posthumous guilt—if he crashed, his wife would think of him as stupid for not taking a train.
- Men want their cigars to be odoriferous, in order to prove that they (the men) are masculine.
- A woman is very serious when she bakes a cake because unconsciously she is going through the symbolic act of giving birth.
- A man buys a convertible as a substitute "mistress."
- Consumers prefer vegetable shortening because animal fats stimulate a sense of sin.
- Men who wear suspenders are reacting to an unresolved castration complex.

There are admitted difficulties of proving these assertions. Two prominent motivational researchers, Ernest Dichter and James Vicary, were employed independently by two separate groups in the prune industry to determine why so many people dislike prunes. Dichter found, among other things, that the prune aroused feelings of old age and insecurity in people, whereas Vicary's main finding was that Americans had an emotional block about prunes' laxative qualities.[8] Which is the more valid interpretation? Or if they are both operative, which motive is found with greater statistical frequency in the population?

The Veblenian Social-psychological Model

While most economists have been content to interpret buyer behavior in Marshallian terms, Thorstein Veblen struck out in different directions.

Veblen was trained as an orthodox economist, but evolved into a social thinker greatly influenced by the new science of social anthropology. He saw man as primarily a *social animal*—conforming to the general forms and norms of his larger culture and to the more specific standards of the subcultures and face-to-face groupings to which his life is bound. His wants and behavior are largely molded

---

[4] Alfred Adler, *The Science of Living* (New York: Greenberg, 1929).

[5] Karen Horney, *The Neurotic Personality of Our Time* (New York: W. W. Norton & Co., 1937).

[6] Erich Fromm, *Man For Himself* (New York: Holt, Rinehart & Winston, Inc., 1947).

[7] Erik Erikson, *Childhood and Society* (New York: W. W. Norton & Co., 1949).

[8] L. Edward Scriven, "Rationality and Irrationality in Motivation Research," in Robert Ferber and Hugh G. Wales, editors, *Motivation and Marketing Behavior* (Homewood, Illinois: Richard D. Irwin, Inc., 1958), pp. 69-70.

by his present group-memberships and his aspired group-memberships.

Veblen's best-known example of this is in his description of the leisure class.[9] His hypothesis is that much of economic consumption is motivated not by intrinsic needs or satisfaction so much as by prestige-seeking. He emphasized the strong emulative factors operating in the choice of conspicuous goods like clothes, cars, and houses.

Some of his points, however, seem overstated by today's perspective. The leisure class does not serve as everyone's reference group; many persons aspire to the social patterns of the class immediately above it. And important segments of the affluent class practice conspicuous underconsumption rather than overconsumption. There are many people in all classes who are more anxious to "fit in" than to "stand out." As an example, William H. Whyte found that many families avoided buying air conditioners and other appliances before their neighbors did.[10]

MARKETING APPLICATIONS OF VEBLENIAN MODEL. The various streams of thought crystallized into the modern social sciences of sociology, cultural anthropology, and social psychology. Basic to them is the view that man's attitudes and behavior are influenced by several levels of society—culture, subcultures, social classes, reference groups, and face-to-face groups. The challenge to the marketer is to determine which of these social levels are the most important in influencing the demand for his product.

CULTURE. The most enduring influences are from culture. Man tends to assimilate his culture's mores and folkways, and to believe in their absolute rightness until deviants appear within his culture or until he confronts members of another culture.

SUBCULTURES. A culture tends to lose its homogeneity as its population increases. When people no longer are able to maintain face-to-face relationships with more than a small proportion of other members of a culture, smaller units or subcultures develop, which help to satisfy the individual's needs for more specific identity.

The subcultures are often regional entities, because the people of a region, as a result of more frequent interactions, tend to think and act alike. But subcultures also take the form of religions, nationalities, fraternal orders, and other institutional complexes which provide a broad identification for people who may otherwise be strangers. The subcultures of a person play a large role in his attitude formation and become another important predictor of certain values he is likely to hold.

SOCIAL CLASS. People become differentiated not only horizontally but also vertically through a division of labor. The society becames stratified socially on the basis of wealth, skill, and power. Sometimes castes develop in which the members are reared for certain roles, or social classes develop in which the members feel empathy with others sharing similar values and economic circumstances.

Because social class involves different attitudinal configurations, it becomes a useful independent variable for segmenting markets and predicting reactions. Significant differences have been found among different social classes with respect to magazine readership, leisure activities, food imagery, fashion interests, and acceptance of innovations. A sampling of attitudinal differences in class is the following:

Members of the *upper-middle* class place an emphasis on professional competence; indulge in expensive status symbols; and more often than not show a taste, real or otherwise, for theater and the arts. They want their children to show high achievement and precocity and develop into physicists, vice-presidents, and judges. This class likes to deal in ideas and symbols.

Members of the *lower-middle* class cherish respectability, savings, a college education, and good housekeeping. They want their children to show self-control and prepare for careers as accountants, lawyers, and engineers.

Members of the *upper-lower* class try to keep up with the times, if not with the Joneses. They stay in older neighborhoods but buy new kitchen appliances. They spend proportionately less than the middle class on major clothing articles, buying a new suit mainly for an important ceremonial occa-

[9] Thorstein Veblen, *The Theory of the Leisure Class* (New York: The Macmillan Company, 1899).

[10] William H. Whyte, Jr., "The Web of Word of Mouth," *Fortune*, Vol. 50 (November, 1954), pp. 140 ff.

sion. They also spend proportionately less on services, preferring to do their own plumbing and other work around the house. They tend to raise large families and their children generally enter manual occupations. This class also supplies many local business-men, politicians, sports stars, and labor-union leaders.

REFERENCE GROUPS. There are groups in which the individual has no membership but with which he identifies and may aspire to—references groups. Many young boys identify with big-league baseball players or astronauts, and many young girls identify with Hollywood stars. The activities of these popular heroes are carefully watched and frequently imitated. These reference figures become important transmitters of influence, although more along lines of taste and hobby than basic attitudes.

FACE-TO-FACE GROUPS. Groups that have the most immediate influence on a person's tastes and opinions are face-to-face groups. This includes all the small "societies" with which he comes into frequent contact: his family, close friends, neighbors, fellow workers, fraternal associates, and so forth. His informal group memberships are influenced largely by his occupation, residence, and stage in the life cycle.

The powerful influence of small groups on individual attitudes has been demonstrated in a number of social psychological experiments.[11] There is also evidence that this influence may be growing. David Riesman and his co-authors have pointed to signs which indicate a growing amount of *other-direction*, that is, a tendency for individuals to be increasingly influenced by their peers in the definition of their values rather than by their parents and elders.[12]

For the marketer, this means that brand choice may increasingly be influenced by one's peers. For such products as cigarettes and automobiles, the influence of peers is unmistakable.

The role of face-to-face groups has been recognized in recent industry campaigns attempting to change basic product attitudes. For years the milk industry has been trying to overcome the image of milk as a "sissified" drink by portraying its use in social and active situations. The men's-wear industry is trying to increase male interest in clothes by advertisements indicating that business associates judge a man by how well he dresses.

Of all face-to-face groups, the person's family undoubtedly plays the largest and most enduring role in basic attitude formation. From them he acquires a mental set not only toward religion and politics, but also toward thrift, chastity, food, human relations, and so forth. Although he often rebels against parental values in his teens, he often accepts these values eventually. Their formative influence on his eventual attitudes is undeniably great.

Family members differ in the types of product messages they carry to other family members. Most of what parents know about cereals, candy, and toys comes from their children. The wife stimulates family consideration of household appliances, furniture, and vacations. The husband tends to stimulate the fewest purchase ideas, with the exception of the automobile and perhaps the home.

The marketer must be alert to what attitudinal configurations dominate in different types of families, and also to how these change over time. For example, the parent's conception of the child's rights and privileges has undergone a radical shift in the last 30 years. The child has become the center of attention and orientation in a great number of households, leading some writers to label the modern family a "filiarchy." This has important implications not only for how to market to today's family, but also on how to market to tomorrow's family when the indulged child of today becomes the parent.

THE PERSON. Social influences determine much but not all of the behavioral variations in people. Two individuals subject to the same influences are not likely to have identical attitudes, although these attitudes will probably converge at more points than those of two strangers selected at random. Attitudes are

[11] See, for example, Solomon E. Asch, "Effects of Group Pressure Upon the Modification & Distortion of Judgments," in Dorwin Cartwright and Alvin Zander, *Group Dynamics* (Evanston, Illinois: Row, Peterson & Co., 1953), pp. 151-162; and Kurt Lewin, "Group Decision and Social Change," in Theodore M. Newcomb and Eugene L. Hartley, editors, *Readings in Social Psychology* (New York: Henry Holt Co., 1952).

[12] David Riesman, Reuel Denney, and Nathan Glazer, *The Lonely Crowd* (New Haven, Connecticut: Yale University Press, 1950).

really the product of social forces interacting with the individual's unique temperament and abilities.

Furthermore, attitudes do not automatically guarantee certain types of behavior. Attitudes are predispositions felt by buyers before they enter the buying process. The buying process itself is a learning experience and can lead to a change in attitudes.

Alfred Politz noted at one time that women stated a clear preference for G.E. refrigerators over Frigidaire, but that Frigidaire continued to outsell G.E.[13] The answer to this paradox was that preference was only one factor entering into behavior. When the consumer preferring G.E. actually undertook to purchase a new refrigerator, her curiosity led her to examine the other brands. Her perception was sensitized to refrigerator advertisements, sales arguments, and different product features. This led to learning and a change in attitudes.

The Hobbesian Organizational-factors Model

The foregoing models throw light mainly on the behavior of family buyers.

But what of the large number of people who are organizational buyers? They are engaged in the purchase of goods not for the sake of consumption, but for further production or distribution. Their common denominator is the fact that they (1) are paid to make purchases for others and (2) operate within an organizational environment.

How do organizational buyers make their decisions? There seem to be two competing views. Many marketing writers have emphasized the predominance of rational motives in organizational buying.[14] Organizational buyers are represented as being most impressed by cost, quality, dependability, and service factors. They are portrayed as dedicated servants of the organization, seeking to secure the best terms. This view has led to an emphasis on performance and use characteristics in much industrial advertising.

Other writers have emphasized personal motives in organizational buyer behavior. The purchasing agent's interest to do the best for his company is tempered by his interest to do the best for himself. He may be tempted to choose among salesmen according to the extent they entertain or offer gifts. He may choose a particular vendor because this will ingratiate him with certain company officers. He may shortcut his study of alternative suppliers to make his work day easier.

In truth, the buyer is guided by both personal and group goals, and this is the essential point. The political model of Thomas Hobbes comes closest of any model to suggesting the relationship between the two goals.[15] Hobbes held that man is "instinctively" oriented toward preserving and enhancing his own well-being. But this would produce a "war of every man against every man." This fear leads men to unite with others in a corporate body. The corporate man tries to steer a careful course between satisfying his own needs and those of the organization.

MARKETING APPLICATIONS OF HOBBESIAN MODEL. The import of the Hobbesian model is that organizational buyers can be appealed to on both personal and organizational grounds. The buyer has his private aims, and yet he tries to do a satisfactory job for his corporation. He will respond to persuasive salesmen and he will respond to rational product arguments. However, the best "mix" of the two is not a fixed quantity; it varies with the nature of the product, the type of organization, and the relative strength of the two drives in the particular buyer.

Where there is substantial similarity in what suppliers offer in the way of products, price, and service, the purchasing agent has less basis for rational choice. Since he can satisfy his organizational obligations with any one of a number of suppliers, he can be swayed by personal motives. On the other hand, where there are pronounced differences among the competing vendors' products, the purchasing agent is held more accountable for his choice and probably pays more attention to rational factors. Short-run personal gain becomes less motivating than the long-run gain which

[13] Alfred Politz, "Motivation Research—Opportunity or Dilemma?" in Ferber and Wales, op. cit., pp. 57-58.

[14] See Melvin T. Copeland, *Principles of Merchandising* (New York: McGraw-Hill Book Co., Inc., 1924).

[15] Thomas Hobbes, *Leviathan*, 1651 (London: G. Routledge and Sons, 1887).

comes from serving the organization with distinction.

Summary

Think back over the five different behavioral models of how the buyer translates buying influences into purchasing responses.

1. Marshallian man is concerned chiefly with economic cues—prices and income—and makes a fresh utility calculation before each purchase.
2. Pavlovian man behaves in a largely habitual rather than thoughtful way; certain configurations of cues will set off the same behavior because of rewarded learning in the past.

3. Freudian man's choices are influenced strongly by motives and fantasies which take place deep within his private world.
4. Veblenian man acts in a way which is shaped largely by past and present social groups.
5. And finally, Hobbesian man seeks to reconcile individual gain with organizational gain.

Thus, it turns out that the "black box" of the buyer is not so black after all. Light is thrown in various corners by these models. Yet no one has succeeded in putting all these pieces of truth together into one coherent instrument for behavioral analysis. This, of course, is the goal of behavioral science.

B. RESEARCH AND APPLICATIONS

This section consists of an article (Markin) dealing with consumer choice as dependent on concepts from economics, psychology, and sociology.

2-D ALTERNATE THEORIES OF CONSUMER CHOICE

Ron J. Markin (Marketing Educator)

Any comprehensive theory of consumer choice must rely upon the concepts developed in the various fields of the social sciences—economics, psychology and sociology—and for this reason an attempt is made here to relate an example of the type of thinking and the aproach to problems which has been undertaken by some of these various disciplines.

ECONOMICS. The economists have provided us with a rather widely adopted theory of consumer behavior based upon the concept of indifference curves which represent different combinations of two goods, to which the consumer is indifferent. The consumer attempts to move to the highest indifference curve, limited by qualifying factors such as income and the product price. The consumer is visualized as substituting one good for another until the highest level of equilibrium is achieved. Having reached this equilibrium point, he is spending his income in such a way

that the last dollar spent on each kind of good results in the same additional satisfaction or marginal utility.[1] Most of us are well aware of the shortcomings of this approach. It rules out the impact of motivations and social status on the consumers in question. Furthermore, it assumes that tastes are autonomous and that changes in taste do not occur, except of an autonomous nature.

The main fact which emerges from a survey of the economic literature is the contrast between the detailed theory of the influence on demand of income and prices in a static situation and the almost complete lack of concern with the way in which tastes and habits, as dictated by social status, affect consumers' behavior.

PSYCHOLOGY. The psychologists have approached the problem of consumer choice and consumer behavior on the basis of observations and data usually subsumed under the catego-

[1] For a more detailed description and analysis, see Ruby T. Norris, *The Theory of Consumer's Demand* (New Haven, Conn.: Yale University Press, 1952), pp. 11-58.

ries of needs, desires, and motives. Such terms refer to something which apparently lies behind the observed behavior of people.

A noteworthy application of this type of approach is the Shepherd-Bayton study for the U.S. Department of Agriculture.[2] The study began by using six values which were culled from the literature: comfort, orderliness, economy, pleasure, social approval, and recognition. From interviews, the investigators found that these values were closely associated with four attributes of men's suits which served as means of attaining these goals: color, style, material, and fit. When possible, value-means relationships were coded as a unit. The number of value statements were converted into a score. This score was a percentage based on the total number of each type, that is, the value or means made by a person. For example, if a person made forty value statements and ten of these indicated a desire for social approval, his score for social approval would be twenty-five. Median scores were then computed for both values and means. An attempt was made to find the relationship between income groups, i.e., lower, middle, and upper, and median scores for value and means. This process was repeated. The relation between income and means for obtaining comfort was established, and the same procedure was followed for occupation and age as well as for other values and means.

The study of values or motives has a rather long and, in many instances fruitful history, but there remain many shortcomings to this approach as a sole predictor of consumer behavior. It would appear to have the following limitations: (1) Semantics, the meaning and interpretation of words—this becomes largely a personal matter for the individual who is responsible for interpretation. (2) The data have not been quantified nor do they seem to be quantifiable, given the present state of psychological measurement devices. (3) Finally, this means that there is a positive validation of conclusions about the number of values and their individual tendencies.

While both the economic and psychological approaches make important contributions, the major limitation in each case has been the tendency to treat each as a separate, independent explanation and to ignore other factors which affect consumer behavior. Most certainly, any theory of consumer behavior must recognize the importance of social forces as they shape consumer behavior.

SOCIOLOGY. The sociologists have made many noteworthy contributions in terms of insights into consumer behavior and product choice. Many of these studies have been in connection with social stratification and reference groups as they influence buying and product decisions. The importance of reference groups in buying behavior has been reviewed by a whole symposium of marketing students.[3]

Special attention should be called to one study which takes into account varying kinds of personal attitude: the popularity of a beverage among one's friends can override a person's desire to stay slim and his moral objections to the beverage; but if he dislikes its taste, he is not likely to drink it, even if his friends do.[4]

Buying habits can also be used to characterize social position and conceptions of role. Thus, Stone has shown that isolated city dwellers prefer to buy in small stores because this provides them with personal contacts.[5]

A number of activities are considered the sign of a good housewife by some women and old-fashioned by others: home sewing,[6] doing one's own laundering,[7] and shunning instant coffee.[8]

[2] Jane A. Shepherd and James A. Bayton, *Men's Preferences Among Wool Suits, Coats and Jackets,* Agricultural Information Bulletin No. 64 (Washington, D.C. U.S. Department of Agriculture, 1951).

[3] Francis S. Bourne, "Group Influences in Marketing and Public Relations," in Rensis Likert and Samuel P. Hayes, Jr., eds., *Some Applications of Behavioural Research* (Paris, France: UNESCO, 1961), pp. 205-207.

[4] *Ibid.,* p. 223.

[5] Gregory Stone, "City Shoppers and Urban Identification," *American Journal of Sociology,* Vol. LX (July, 1954), pp. 36-45.

[6] Joseph Newman, *Motivation Research and Marketing Management* (Boston: Harvard Graduate School of Business Administration, Division of Research, 1957), p. 313.

[7] American Marketing Association, *The Technique of Market Research* (New York: McGraw-Hill Book Company, 1936), p. 275.

[8] Mason Haire, "Projective Techniques in Market Research," *Journal of Marketing,* Vol. XIV (April, 1960), pp. 649-656.

The difficulty of predicting human behavior is often lamented. But it is almost as hard to evaluate the effect of past efforts. Amid all today's turmoil of propaganda and advertising, one can rarely tell whether a specific "campaign" has reached its goal. One of the devices which has been tried is to interview people who have performed a desired act. Is is possible to trace in retrospect the influence we are interested in? Lazarsfeld has attempted to assess the comparative role of personal advice and of advertising.[9] He concludes that the former is stronger and suggests that his statistical results could be developed in many directions. In what situations and with what kinds of people is personal influence especially strong or weak? Who are the influential ones?

A final illustration of the sociological approach, one which emphasizes the importance of social class or social status, is that of Barber and Lobel.[10] This study attempted to correlate women's fashion magazine advertising copy with Warner's social class concept. Social class

differences in the meanings of the word "fashion" were found to exist, by virtue of the various copy approaches examined. Social status is based largely on occupational position. This holds true for all classes except those at the top, among whom family lineage is an additional factor. This is Warner's Upper-Upper category. According to this study, women in this class do not need to compete for status through consumption; thus their quality clothes may remain roughly the same for several years. It is in the Lower-Upper class that most of the "high fashion" is found. Clothes, as symbols,´ are related to wealth rather than to family connection. Fashion has a different meaning for the upper middle class. These women have a distaste for high style, or that which is daring or unusual. Their clothes must be conservative and respectable.

While this approach makes an important contribution to the study of consumer behavior in terms of class orientation, it has, along with many of the sociological studies, several important shortcomings. In many instances, the methodology has inherent deficiencies. Terminology is often "forced" and without standards and little if any mention is made of the importance of the learning process as conditioned by personality and income over a period of time.

[9] Elihu Katz and P. F. Lazarsfeld, *Personal Influence* (Glencoe, Ill.: Free Press, 1955).
[10] Bernard Barber and Lyle S. Lobel, "Fashion in Women's Clothes and the American Social System," *Social Forces*, No. 31 (December, 1952), pp. 124-131.

3 / Fact Finding About Consumers

A. BACKGROUND AND THEORY

The four readings selected for this section provide special insights into fact-finding methodology. A search of the relevant literature is a sensible way to begin any scientific research, as well as to have some understanding of the techniques of observing and experimenting (Wilson). The logic and method of science (Cohen and Nagel) also needs to be understood; and this includes an understanding and appreciation of why nonscientific observations are not acceptable (Hyman) in analyzing human behavior. The next discussion (Boyd and Britt) points up the need for the use of the administrative process in order to make fact-finding (that is, research) more effective than otherwise.

3-A READING, OBSERVING AND EXPERIMENTING

E. Bright Wilson, Jr. (Physical Chemist)

Six hours in the library may save six months in the laboratory. In undertaking to acquire a background in a given subject, it is best to read the most general treatment first, as for example in an encyclopedia. This can be followed by a more detailed but still quite broad discussion in a handbook. At this point it is desirable to search the library or book catalogues for books on the subject. If there is a quite recent specialized book, the search may end right there, because such books often contain bibliographies sufficient for most purposes.

Usually, however, no book exists which is complete or entirely up to date. The next stage will normally be to look for a survey or review article in one of the journals which specializes in such or in one of the annual survey publications. These can be most helpful in providing orientation and key references.

Eventually it becomes necessary to consult the appropriate abstract journals, working

SOURCE: E. Bright Wilson, Jr., *An Introduction to Scientific Research*, Copyright 1952. Used with permission of the McGraw-Hill Book Company, pp. 10, 17–18, 22–23, 36–37.

backward in time until the desired coverage has been obtained or until a year is reached which has been adequately dealt with in a book.

The final stage is the reading of current original articles. The latest of these will not yet have been abstracted and can therefore be found only by searching through the current issues of appropriate journals. By the time this step is reached, the reader will know the small list of journals most likely to contain papers on the subject. He will also know the names of the principal workers in the field.

Each paper will contain references to earlier work, and in this way the search can be carried backward with the object of picking up references missed in going through the abstract journals. There will be such missed items because of the deficiencies of all systems of indexing.

Finally, the easiest way to find out about anything is to ask someone who knows, provided such a person is available. It is not safe to assume, however, that the most expert specialist knows all the literature of his subject. He may well have the most surprising gaps in his knowledge. It is also a good idea to acquire a pretty good general background before seeking personal assistance.

Wise selection rather than all-inclusive coverage is the key to library work. On the other hand, this does not mean specializing too narrowly. It is most important to keep a steady stream of new ideas flowing into a research project. These often come from browsing in apparently unrelated fields. It is consequently hard to give any useful rules for this kind of reading.

Searching the literature to find a particular piece of information or to determine whether a proposed project has already been carried out is a somewhat different task. It is obviously much easier for the specialist in the field than for an outsider. The principal reliance must be placed on books, abstract journals, and specialized, classified bibliographies. Every possible clue should be used, including the probable range of dates, the general field of knowledge, the most likely country, the journals specializing in the topic, and any authors who have worked in the subject. The advice of an expert is particularly useful here, but again negative statements should be used with caution. In going through indices, all synonyms for the topic must be examined because all papers on a given subject will almost never be listed in one place.

The second point involves the question of bias. It is probably impossible for anyone to free himself completely from preconceived prejudices, and in a certain sense this is not desirable. It is important to have some hypothesis in mind before making an observation; if this were not so, how would one know what to observe? On the other hand, it is equally important to arrange the conditions of observation so that the observer's bias will not distort the observations. This is far less easy than it sounds and often elaborate stratagems must be devised to enable the observer to outwit his own bias and get the true facts recorded in his notebook.

A scientific observer is never afraid to allow others to view the phenomena in which he is interested. He should welcome checks and repetitions of his work as adding to their certainty. Some events, such as eclipses, cannot be reproduced at will and occur naturally rather rarely. These especially need multiple independent observers and in addition instrumental methods of recording portions of the phenomena for later study, as, for example, by photography.

A feature of scientific observation is a tendency to be quantitative. Numbers are used as part of the description where possible. Even rather untractable qualities like hardness are given numerical scales, even if of a somewhat arbitrary nature. Thus the mineralogist rates hardness according to a scale with diamond 10, topaz 8, quartz 7, orthoclase 6, etc. If B scratches C but A scratches B, then B lies between A and C. The use of numerical measures permits a more precise description and ultimately may make possible the application of mathematics.

Of course not all science is numerical, qualitative statements play a very large role which should not be belittled. It all depends upon the object of the investigation; if "green" is sufficient for the purpose in mind, it is foolish and wasteful to give a table of wavelengths.

Another distinguishing characteristic is the use of instruments as aids to the senses. Much of nature can be observed with the naked eye, but far more becomes accessible when microscopes, telescopes, measuring instruments, and all the vast and formidable array of scientific paraphernalia can be used. Even very simple instruments such as a meter stick, stethoscope, or test tube help considerably. In spite of the arrival of the age of the superbillion-volt synchro-cyclotron, there still must be a good deal left worth observing with simple instruments.

Observation and Description

Observation implies selection. A forest can be observed as a forest, but not easily as ten thousand trees. A tree can also be observed as a whole, but not easily as thousands of leaves, twigs, platelets of bark, etc. The powers of man are limited, and it is necessary to limit what is to be observed to a portion of the universe small enough to be encompassed. An unwise choice yields items so remotely connected that no amount of study would ever determine their interrelations.

Observation leads to description. Precise definitions are adopted so that a specific word carries the same meaning to all scientists.

Many nonscientists are excellent observers, but there are certain points emphasized more in scientific observation. One of the most important of these is the immediate recording of the data in a notebook. An experimental scientist without his notebook is off duty. Human memory is entirely too fallible to be trusted in such matters. There is a well-known law professor who annually stages a mock trial and calls witnesses to testify concerning some event previously enacted before all his students. The disagreements of the different witnesses are always vivid evidence of the fallibility of human memory.

Design of Experiments

Before planning actual experiments, the investigator should obviously have a good basic understanding of the nature of the problem and of any relevant theory associated with it. Even a very imperfect theory will often provide existence theorems, limiting values, etc., of considerable utility in guiding experiments. Furthermore, it is almost essential that an experiment be designed on the basis of one or more preliminary hypotheses. These can be constructed more intelligently if a full knowledge of the theory and background of the situation is available.

The experimenter will next be wise if he analyzes his problem and is thereby enabled to cast it into the simplest form. It is possible to break most problems into parts which are much more easily answered separately than together. Furthermore, it is almost always desirable or even necessary to approach the answers in stages, starting with the most idealized and simplified version possible. When this has been unraveled, more general cases can be attacked.

For example, in studying the problem of detonation in explosives, it would have been hopeless to start with a high-explosive shell, whose shape, composition, and mode of initiation are too complicated to permit the basic principle to be discovered. Instead, essentially one-dimensional detonations in pipes were studied. The length was made great enough so that the conditions of initiation were unimportant, and the simplest possible chemical mixtures, particularly gases, were used. In this way a very successful theory of detonation processes has been reached.

Practical people often balk at this approach since the idealized situations may be so far removed from those of use as to appear highly academic. It is true that many practical problems can and often must be answered by direct empirical experiment, but there are few fields where a simultaneous attack by the method of analysis and simplification would not in the long run pay dividends. The experimental designs to be discussed are applicable to both methods.

CRUCIAL EXPERIMENTS. In some cases it is possible to set up a single experiment whose outcome largely determines the fate of a given hypothesis or theory. The Michelson-Morley experiment, which showed the absence of any measurable motion of the earth through the "ether," disposed of the ether hypothesis and is therefore a good example of such a *crucial* experiment. However, it is rather rare that a single experiment is decisive. Usually evidence either for or against a theory is built up from several directions at once, and the final acceptance of a state of affairs by the scientific community is the result of a large mass of observations, some of which may be contradictory. Nevertheless it is important to design experiments that are as far as possible crucial with respect to the hypothesis under consideration. This is not as easy as it sounds because there are alternative interpretations for the results of most experiments.

AIM OF EXPERIMENT. It is rather poor policy to carry out an experiment without a clear-cut idea in advance of just what is being tested. Purely exploratory experiments are necessary in a new field, and such preliminary searches are of great importance. Very often, however, a certain objective is the reason for undertaking a research, and yet when the experiments are over, it becomes apparent that the questions asked were not the ones whose answers were really needed. It is safest here to go right back to the origin of the inquiry and ask at every stage: "Why am I doing this particular thing? Will it really tell me what I want to know?"

3-B LOGIC AND METHOD OF SCIENCE

Morris R. Cohen (Philosopher) and Ernest Nagel (Philosopher)

If we look at all the sciences not only as they differ among each other but also as each changes and grows in the course of time, we find that the constant and universal feature of science is its general method, which consists in the persistent search for truth, constantly asking: Is it so? To what extent is it so? Why is it so?—that is, What general conditions or considerations determine it to be so? And this can be seen on reflection to be the demand for the best available evidence, the determination of which we call logic. Scientific method is thus the persistent application of logic as the common feature of all reasoned knowledge. From this point of view scientific method is simply the way in which we test impressions, opinions, or surmises by examining the best available evidence for and against them. The various features of scientific method can naturally be seen more clearly in the more developed sciences; but in essence scientific method is simply the pursuit of truth as determined by logical considerations. Before determining this in detail, it is well to distinguish between scientific method and other ways of banishing doubt and arriving at stable beliefs.

Most of our beliefs rest on the tacit acceptance of current attitudes or on our own unreflective assumptions. Thus we come to believe that the sun revolves around the earth daily because we see it rise in the east and sink in the west; or we send a testimonial to the makers of a certain toothpaste to the effect that it is an excellent preserver of teeth because we have had no dental trouble since we have used that preparation; or we offer alms to some beggar because we perceive his poverty by his rags and emaciated appearance. But too often and sometimes, alas! too late, we learn that not all "seeing" is "believing." Beliefs so formed do not stand up against a more varied experience. There is too little

SOURCE: Abridged from Morris R. Cohen and Ernest Nagel, *An Introduction to Logic and Scientific Method* (New York: Harcourt, Brace & World, Inc., 1934); copyright renewed, 1962, by Ernest Nagel and Leonard Cohen Rosenfield. Reprinted by permission of the publishers, pp. 191–96.

agreement in opinions so formed and too little security in acting upon them. Most of us then find ourselves challenged to support or change our opinions. And we do by diverse methods.

The Method of Tenacity

Habit or inertia makes it easier for us to continue to believe a proposition simply because we have always believed it. Hence, we may avoid doubting it by closing our minds to all contradictory evidence. That frequent verbal reiteration may strengthen beliefs which have been challenged is a truth acted upon by all organized sects or parties. If anyone questions the superior virtues of ourselves, our dear ones, our country, race, language, or religion, our first impulse and the one generally followed is to repeat our belief as an act of loyalty and to regard the questioning attitude as ignorant, disloyal, and unworthy of attention. We thus insulate ourselves from opinions or beliefs contrary to those which we have always held. As a defense of this attitude the believer often alleges that he would be unhappy if he were to believe otherwise than he in fact does. But while a change in opinion may require painful effort, the new beliefs may become habitual, and perhaps more satisfying than the old ones.

This method of tenacity cannot always secure the stability of one's beliefs. Not all men believe alike, in part because the climate of opinion varies with historical antecedents, and in part because the personal and social interests which men wish to guard are unlike. The pressure of opinions other than one's own cannot always be so disregarded. The man who tenaciously holds on to his own way occasionally admits that not all those who differ from him are fools. When once the incidence of other views is felt, the method of tenacity is incapable of deciding among conflicting opinions. And since a lack of uniformity in beliefs is itself a powerful source of doubt concerning them, some method other than the method of tenacity is required for achieving stable views.

The Method of Authority

Such a method is sometimes found in the appeal to authority. Instead of simply holding on doggedly to one's beliefs, appeal is made to some highly respected source to substantiate the views held. Most propositions of religion and conduct claim support from some sacred text, tradition, or tribunal whose decision on such questions is vested with finality. Political, economic, and social questions are frequently determined in similar fashion. What one should wear at a funeral, what rule of syntax one should follow in writing, what rights one has in the product of his labor, how one should behave in some social crisis like war—these are problems repeatedly resolved by the authoritative method.

We may distinguish two forms of the appeal to authority. One form is inevitable and reasonable. It is employed whenever we are unable, for lack of time or training, to settle some problem, such as, What diet or exercise will relieve certain distressing symptoms? or, What was the system of weights which the Egyptians used? We then leave the resolution of the problem to experts, whose authority is acknowledged. But their authority is only relatively final, and we reserve the right to others (also competent to judge), or to ourselves (finding the time to acquire competence), to modify the findings of our expert. The second form of the appeal to authority invests some sources with infallibility and finality and invokes some external force to give sanction to their decisions. On questions of politics, economics, and social conduct, as well as on religious opinions, the method of authority has been used to root out, as heretical or disloyal, divergent opinions. Men have been frightened and punished into conformity in order to prevent alternative views from unsettling our habitual beliefs.

The Method of Intuition

A method repeatedly tried in order to guarantee stable beliefs is the appeal to "self-evident" propositions—propositions so "obviously true" that the understanding of their *meaning* will carry with it an indubitable conviction of their *truth*. Very few men in the history of philosophy and that of the sciences have been able to resist at all times the lure of intuitively revealed truths. Thus, all the great astronomers, including Copernicus, believed it to be self-evident that the orbits of the planets must be circular, and no mathematician or physicist before Gauss seriously doubted the proposition that two straight lines cannot en-

close an area. Other examples of propositions which have been, or still are, believed by some to be self-evident are: That the whole is greater than any one of its parts; that the right to private property is inalienable; that bigamy is a sin; that nothing can happen without an adequate cause.

Unfortunately, it is difficult to find a proposition for which at some time or other "self-evidence" has not been claimed. Propositions regarded as indubitable by many, for example, that the earth is flat, have been shown to be false. It is well known that "self-evidence" is often a function of current fashions and of early training. The fact, therefore, that we feel absolutely certain, or that a given proposition has not before been questioned, is no guarantee against its being proved false. Our intuitions must, then, be tested.

The Method of Science or Reflective Inquiry

None of the methods for settling doubts we have examined so far is free from human caprice and willfulness. As a consequence, the propositions which are held on the basis of those methods are uncertain in the range of their application and in their accuracy. If we wish clarity and accuracy, order and consistency, security and cogency, in our actions and intellectual allegiances, we shall have to resort to some method of fixing beliefs whose efficacy in resolving problems is independent of our desires and wills. Such a method, which takes advantage of the objective connections in the world around us, should be found reasonable, not because of its appeal to the idiosyncrasies of a selected few individuals, but because it can be tested repeatedly and by all men.

The other methods discussed are all inflexible, that is, none of them can admit that it will lead us into error. Hence none of them can make provision for correcting its own results. What is called *scientific method* differs radically from these by encouraging and developing the utmost possible doubt, so that what is left after such doubt is always supported by the best available evidence. As new evidence or new doubts arise, it is the essence of scientific method to incorporate them—to make them an integral part of the body of knowledge so far attained. Its method, then, makes science progressive because it is never too certain about its results.

It is well to distinguish between scientific method and general skepticism. The mere resolution to doubt all things is not necessarily effective. For the propositions most in need of questioning may seem to us unquestionable. We need a technique that will enable us to discover possible alternatives to propositions which we may regard as truisms or necessarily

true. In this process formal logic aids us in divising ways of formulating our propositions explicitly and accurately, so that their possible alternatives become clear. When thus faced with alternative hypotheses, logic develops their consequences, so that when these consequences are compared with observable phenomena, we have a means of testing which hypothesis is to be eliminated and which is most in harmony with the facts of observation.

3-C   WHY NONSCIENTIFIC OBSERVATIONS ARE NOT ACCEPTABLE

Ray Hyman (Psychologist)

Here we shall consider more systematically factors that lead to distortion of observations. In doing so, we shall borrow examples both from nonscientific and from scientific situations. Such illustrations will make the point that even a scientist, in scientific activities, is fallible as a perceiver. And this should not surprise us. The scientist is, after all, a human being with the same afflictions of pride, emotion, prejudice, enthusiasm, and sensory limitation that beset us all. The illustrations will also serve to remind us that the goal of objective observation is an ideal rather than a reality. Scientific observation does not differ from everyday observation by being infallible, although it is quantitatively less fallible than ordinary observation. Rather, it differs from everyday observation in that the scientist gradually uncovers his previous errors and corrects them; and he uses the example of these errors to improve his observational procedures and to build in new safe-guards against future repetition of distortion. Indeed, the history of psychology as a science has been the development of procedural and instrumental aids that gradually eliminate or correct for biases and distortions in making observations.

The Limits of Sensory Discrimination

One of the chief values of instrumentation in science is the increase in range it gives to the scientist's observational powers. Another advantage comes from the substitution of a more reliable and objective judgment for an incon-

SOURCE: Ray Hyman, *The Nature of Psychological Inquiry,* © 1964. Reprinted by permission of Prentice-Hall, Inc., Englewood Cliffs, New Jersey, pp. 37–40.

sistent and subjective one. It is much easier to obtain agreement on pointer readings than it is to get different observers to agree whether a subject shows "anxiety" or not. Where observation involves poor viewing conditions or fine discriminations on the part of the observer, distortions of judgment are especially likely to occur. A particularly tragic example is the case of the so-called *n-rays.*

The n-ray was discovered in 1902 by the eminent French physicist, M. Blondlot. The discovery was confirmed and extended by other French scientists. In the year 1904 alone, there appeared 77 different scientific publications devoted to the n-ray. Controversy over the n-ray quickly arose when it was realized that German, Italian, and American physicists could not duplicate Blondlot's findings. The n-ray, it seemed, could be observed only on French soil. Eventually, the American physicist R. W. Wood, who had unsuccessfully attempted to duplicate n-rays in his own laboratory at Johns Hopkins, visited Blondlot in Nancy. Wood's own encounter with Blondlot is best described in his own words.

He first showed me a card on which some circles had been painted in luminous paint. He turned down the gas light and called my attention to their increased luminosity when the n-ray was turned on. I said I saw no change. He said that was because my eyes were not sensitive enough, so that proved nothing. I asked him if I could move an opaque lead screen in and out of the path of the rays while he called out the fluctuations on the screen. He was almost 100% wrong and called out fluctuations when I made no movement at all, and that proved a lot, but I held my tongue.

Wood conducted other tests which clearly demonstrated that the n-rays existed only in Blondlot's imagination. By 1909 there were no more publications involving the n-ray. Blondlot himself never recovered from this incident and died in disgrace.[1]

Frameworks Within Which "Observations" Are Interpreted

As we have shown, the same events can be "seen" as different "facts" when two observers bring different frames of reference to the situation. The case of the n-rays illustrates their difficulty in addition to the difficulties of observation near the sensory threshold. Listen to what the physiologist W. B. Carpenter had to say in 1877:[2]

> The two different modes in which Spiritualists and their opponents view the same facts, according to their respective predispositions, is well brought out in cases of the so-called "materialization"—a party being assembled in a front drawingroom, the "medium" retires into a backroom separated from it by curtains, and professes there to go into a trance. After a short interval, during which the lights are turned down so as to make "darkness visible," a figure dressed in some strange guise enters between the curtains, and displays itself to the spectators as an "embodied spirit." Precluded from any direct interference with the performance, a sceptic among the audience slyly puts some ink on his fingers, and whilst this is still wet, grasps the "spirit-hand," which he finds very like a mortal one. The "spirit" withdraws behind the curtains, after a short interval the lights are raised, and the "medium" returns to the company *in propria persona*. The sceptic then points out inkstains on one of the "medium's" hands, and tells what he has done.
>
> These are the *facts* of the case. Now, the "common-sense" interpretation of these facts is, that the "medium" is a cheat, and the "embodied spirit" a vulgar ghost personated by him; and until adequate proof shall have been given to the contrary, I maintain that we are perfectly justified in holding to this interpretation, confirmed as it is by the ex-posure of the trick in every instance in which adequate means have been taken for its detection. But the explanation of his inked fingers given by the "medium" is, that the impress made on the hand of the "embodied spirit" has been transferred "according to a well-known law of Spritualism" to his own; and this assumption is regarded as more probable, by such as have accepted the system, than that their pet "medium" is a cheat, and their belief in him a delusion.

The Aspects Attended To

In the area of selective attention, psychologists have demonstrated over and over again the limitations of the human being as an eyewitness. F. K. Berrien describes a demonstration of a type that has been done before many audiences under a variety of circumstances with the same outcome:[3]

> A great many informal classroom experiments have demonstrated the influence of attention and expectation on subsequent recall. For example, the author arranged to have a student walk into the class late and interrupt the lecture by a declaration of having lost some white rats. He walked slowly across the room in front of the class, turned around, and went out, all the while carrying on a previously rehearsed conversation with the instructor concerning the loss of, and search for, the rats. In spite of the fact that the student-actor was well known to the class, estimates of his weight ranged from 145 to 210 (actual weight 190); eight of the forty-three students declared he wore a maroon-colored sweater (actually he wore a gray-tan, double-breasted coat); and a majority declared vehemently he searched in the corners looking for his rats (he made one furtive glance toward the corner of the room contrary to instructions to keep his eyes on the instructor). The reports on the sweater and his searching were at least partly due to expectation, the prevailing color of sweaters on this particular campus being maroon, while the searching was expected in view of the conversation.

Self-deception

Other studies on memory, rumor transmission, and personality have demonstrated the

[1] See also E. Z. Vogt and R. Hyman. *Water Witching U.S.A.* Chicago: University of Chicago Press, 1959.

[2] W. B. Carpenter. *Mesmerism, Spiritualism, &c.* New York: Appleton, 1877, pp. vii–viii.

[3] F. K. Berrien. *Practical Psychology.* Rev. ed. New York: Macmillan, 1952, pp. 482–483.

variety of ways in which our perceptions and reports can be influenced and distorted by such personal factors as values, motivation, prior expectations, social norms, and the like. In the area of self-deception comes a variety of phenomena that occur because an individual has poor feedback from his muscles. Tables can seemingly move of their own accord, divining rods dip, the ouija board spells out a message—all such things can occur because, without adequate feedback from our muscles, we can unwittingly respond to our subconscious expectations and move objects in such a way that we are convinced that the objects are self-propelled.[4]

The psychologist as a scientist, then, rejects many sources of observations—of his own as well as of others. He knows that man is a highly fallible observer. Despite the best intentions the human onlooker is limited by the sensitivity of his perceptual apparatus, by the

[4] For a detailed discussion of self-deception, see Vogt and Hyman, *ibid.*

frameworks and categories he has for ordering his perceptual experience, by the limited span of things he can attend to at any one time, and by motivational and physiological aspects that lead to self-deception. The growth of psychology as a science goes hand in hand with the gradual discovery and elimination of these human defects in the gathering of data.

Even under conditions where the observers know that they will be immediately tested for the accuracy of what they are going to witness, such distortions inevitably take place. No wonder, then, that the scientist has learned to be skeptical about data from casual observation. The psychologist, in particular, knows quite well how his own and others' observations can be misleading. He has learned to trust neither his own reports nor those of others—unless these reports are accompanied by clear specification of how anyone else might check the same facts if he so desires. This clear specification must include a statement of the relevant conditions, what is to be looked for, what is to be done, and how it is to be recorded.

3-D MAKING MARKETING RESEARCH MORE EFFECTIVE BY USING THE ADMINISTRATIVE PROCESS

Harper W. Boyd, Jr. (Marketing Educator) and Steuart Henderson Britt (Psychologist)

Too often marketing research deals only with fragments of a problem; but this may be due to a tendency by both management executives and research executives to view the decision-making process too narrowly.

Decision-making in business is a continuing process, and only well-designed and executed research can help decision-makers in solving problems. While the marketing researcher can and should be creative in designing studies, usually it is not his function also to be creative in the formulation of the goals and strategies of the enterprise.

It is, however, his function to be well versed in new and important concepts pertaining to decision theory, which are coming from the be-

SOURCE: Harper W. Boyd, Jr., and Steuart Henderson Britt, "Making Marketing Research More Effective by Using the Administrative Process," *Journal of Marketing Research*, Vol. 2 (February, 1965), pp. 13–19, at pp. 13–14.

havioral sciences, as well as from higher mathematics.

Since the primary role of the researcher is one of providing valid information which management can and should use in its decision-making activities, how can the research function be performed most effectively? It is too easy to say that improvement will come only when management specifies what kinds of information are needed. This is not the answer.

Instead, the answer is that researchers *and* decision-makers must strive to interact in such a way as to make explicit the use to which research information will be put. This interacting can best be accomplished through the use of the *administrative process* which consists of (1) *setting objectives;* (2) *developing the plans to achieve these objectives;* (3) *organizing to put these plans into action;* and (4) *controlling and reappraising the program that has been carried out,* in order to determine whether or not the objectives, the plans, and the organization are functioning properly.

Decision-Making and the Administrative Process

The researcher must participate in the formulation of problems, as well as contribute to effective action.

ANATOMY OF A DECISION. Decisions are made *only* because decision-makers want to achieve something and have certain goals or objectives. Without understanding these goals, both the researcher and the decision-maker cannot proceed. The problem, however formulated, is not solvable.

Most problems of any consequence tend to cut across functional lines; any attempt to solve them on a piece-meal basis will often prove unsuccessful or even disastrous. In fact, the solution of a problem in one area may cause a new but related problem to spring up elsewhere. For example: A large manufacturer of consumer goods recently altered its distribution system. The change to franchise dealers and direct selling was accompanied by the decision that the company would absorb more of the stock-carrying function. This decision was made only after considerable marketing research was done on the subject. Six months later this old, well-financed company suffered a severe cash-flow problem. A detailed investigation of this situation indicated that the change in distribution was responsible. Furthermore, and more important, the conclusion was reached that this shift was ill-advised and destined to fail because it was incompatible with the long-run objectives of the company, which were ultimately to produce a variety of related items appealing to different market segments.

In the above illustration, there were two difficulties: First, the decision to effect a change in the functional area was made without considering its impact on another area; second, and equally important, the decision was made with reference to a higher-order prior decision, which was designed to guide the activities of *all* parts of the firm. The decision was made out of context.

Had the research director probed deeply enough and long enough with the various decision-makers involved, he might have been successful in understanding the totality of the problem and thereby helped the other executives to avoid the costly mistake which was made.

THE ADMINISTRATIVE PROCESS. One possible way to ensure that a problem is properly dissected is to focus on the *administrative process* in some detail. In this process, which consists of a series of interlocking steps, no one step can be considered independently.

The process is not only useful in visualizing and understanding the activities of management but also in diagnosing problems through the establishment of a basic framework. This framework, which might at first appear to be relatively simple, is complicated by the division of each of the four major steps into a number of parts.

Moreover, the framework typically features several layers, namely, processes within processes. Top management, for example, will set major policies having to do with each step; in turn, each department will operate within these policies by establishing its own *objectives, plans, organizations,* and *control-and-reappraisal systems.*

Research conducted on problems having to do with "the plan" runs the risk of being ineffective unless both the researcher and the decision-maker agree that the problem is not one having to do with the objectives of the firm. If the objectives present difficulties, research in the plan's area usually will not be very helpful. Likewise, it will do little good to focus attention on the organization if the plan is in error.

B. RESEARCH AND APPLICATIONS

To illustrate the importance of fact-finding, excerpts are included from an analysis (Britt) of "proofs of success" for 135 campaigns by 140 advertising agencies.

3-E ARE SO-CALLED SUCCESSFUL ADVERTISING CAMPAIGNS REALLY SUCCESSFUL?[1]

Steuart Henderson Britt (Psychologist)

To what extent do advertising agencies know whether their advertising campaigns are successful? Even more to the point, to what extent do agencies really set specific objectives for their campaigns? And in attempting to judge the success of a campaign, are the "proofs of success" relevant to the objectives stated?

For the first time, public statements by advertising agencies of campaign objectives and "proofs of success" of various campaigns have been set forth publicly in a form that permits systematic investigation of this question. The United States Trade Center for Scandinavia held an exhibition in Stockholm, Sweden, during May 1967, that featured advertisements from successful American advertising campaigns. One Swedish advertising agency, Annonsbyrå, prepared and distributed a special booklet that contained descriptions of 135 "successful advertising campaigns" created by 40 American advertising agencies.

The statements of campaign success in this booklet are presented in a consistent form. For each of the 135 campaigns, the agency states its "campaign objectives" and also the "proofs of success." A knowledge of what is said about both of these variables is essential in order to evaluate objectively the criteria by which each agency determines the success of its campaigns.

Each of the 40 agencies had submitted materials to be printed in the booklet, describing

SOURCE: Steuart Henderson Britt, "Are So-called Successful Advertising Campaign Really Successful?" *Journal of Advertising Research*, Vol. 9 (June, 1969), pp. 3–9; © 1969 by the Advertising Research Foundation, Inc.
[1] This article was written with the help of Miss Sabra E. Brock, who analyzed the data.

what they considered to be representative of their most successful campaigns. Although some agencies listed all major clients, most did not.

The format for each campaign described was:

Agency
Client
Length of service
Market situation
CAMPAIGN OBJECTIVES (of special importance in the present investigation)
Individuals responsible
Media plan
PROOF OF SUCCESS (of special importance in the present investigation)

As an example, here is the description by Papert Koenig Lois for Wesson Oil:

Client:
Hunt-Wesson Foods
Wesson Oil Campaign

Length of service: two years

Market situation:
Wesson Oil, the cooking oil leader, has been steadily losing share of market to Procter & Gamble's Crisco oil. Wesson's share has declined from a high of 36 per cent to below 32 per cent when the campaign started.

Campaign objectives:
To first arrest, then reverse the trend. In terms of creative objectives, the advertising was to say that Wesson's high heat tolerance made it desirable for frying (the largest cooking oil in use), specifically, that it was better than the competition for making fried foods crisp.

Individuals responsible:
This was a group effort, no individuals can be cited.

Media plan:

The magazine ads ran in McCall's, Reader's Digest, Good Housekeeping; the television commercials were largely in eight week waves in the prime time shows "My Three Sons," and spot daytime locations, throughout 1966.

Proof of success:

Although details are confidential, three months after the campaign started, Wesson showed its first month-to-month share increase. Procter & Gamble's Crisco oil showed a sharp decline, and that trend seems to have been maintained.

Three Questions

The following is a summary of an analysis of each of the 135 different campaigns, based on answers to the following three questions:

A. Did the agency set *specific objectives* for the campaign, that is, objectives specific enough to be measured?

B. Did the agency attempt to measure the effectiveness of the campaign by clearly stating *how the campaign fulfilled the previously-set objectives?*

C. Were there any differences in the results . . . in either specificity of the objectives or in fulfillment of objectives in terms of (a) *size of agency* or (b) *product classification?*

SPECIFIC OBJECTIVES. A. *Did the agency set specific objectives for the campaign, that is, objectives specific enough to be measured?*

As a basis for analysis, an *operational definition* for a specific objective was established. An operational definition entails defining a term by stating the procedures (or operations) employed in distinguishing the item referred to from others.

Four points were established as the criteria of a specific objective. All four of these had to be given in the stated objective for it to be considered a specific type of objective. Thus, the statement of the advertising objective had to make it clear:

1. *What basic message* was to be delivered . . .
2. *to what audience* . . .
3. *with what intended effect(s)* . . .
4. and as to *what specific criteria* were

going to be used later on to measure the success of the campaign.

Analysis of the stated campaign objectives in the present instance showed a majority—87 of the 135, or 64 per cent—fulfilled the first three of the four criteria of the operational definition of a specific objective. *But in only two campaigns—less than two per cent of the 135 campaigns—were all four criteria met as to having specific objectives.*

DEFICIENCIES IN STATEMENTS OF OBJECTIVES. The major deficiencies of the stated campaign objectives are of four kinds:

1. Failure to state the objective(s) in quantifiable terms
2. Apparent failure to realize that the results of the advertising could not be measured in sales
3. Failure to identify the advertising audience
4. Use of superlatives (which are unmeasurable).

FULFILLMENT OF OBJECTIVES. B. *Did the agency attempt to measure the effectiveness of the campaign by clearly stating how the campaign fulfilled the previously-set objectives?*

In 93 instances of the 135—69 per cent of the cases—proofs of success were not directly related to the previously-stated campaign objectives. Only in 42, or 31 per cent, of the cases were proofs of success related directly to the objectives the agency set.

DEFICIENCIES IN FULFILLMENT OF OBJECTIVES. Careful analysis showed that deficiencies of the agencies in relating proofs of success to stated campaign objectives were of three principal kinds:

a. With the objective of *awareness*, success stated in sales.

b. With the objective of a *new image*, success stated in terms of readership or inquiries.

c. With *more than one objective* set forth, success stated only in relation to one of these, with the others ignored.

SIZE OF AGENCY AND PRODUCT CLASSIFICATION. C. *Were there any differences in the results in either specificity of the objectives or in fulfillment of objectives in terms of (a) size of agency or (b) product classification?*

Of the 135 campaigns, 62 represented campaigns of agencies billing over $20 million. There is a trend toward the larger agencies stating specific objectives, and a fairly significant trend toward the larger agencies using the terms of the objective to state proofs of success.

Implications

Advertising of a product or service must prove its success as advertising by *setting specific objectives.* Such general statements of objectives as "introduce the product to the market," "raise sales," and "maintain brand share" are not objectives for advertising. Intead, they are the objectives of the entire marketing program. And even when considered as marketing goals, such statements still are too general and broad to be used to determine the extent of a plan's success or failure.

ADVERTISING GOALS. Advertising goals should indicate (1) what basic message is to be delivered, (2) to what audience, (3) with what intended effect, and (4) what specific criteria are going to be used to measure the success of the campaign.

When the advertising campaign is over, the advertiser can best judge the results by comparing them with the intended results, as expressed in the campaign objective. Only when he knows what he is intending to do can he know when and if he has accomplished it.

The present analysis shows the need for emphasis on the setting of specific objectives in advertising campaigns, and an even greater need for agencies to use their campaign objectives as means of measuring campaign success or failure.

Why does a business firm or organization spend money on advertising without knowing exactly what is supposed to be achieved by the advertising?

When a business firm purchases a new line of production equipment, management is quite sure of the advantages to be gained for the price paid. But why has management not consistently established the same types of objectives and results with respect to advertising expenditures?

When asked for a statement as to company advertising goals and objectives, many companies can supply such a statement only after the advertising has run (see Wolfe, *et al.,* 1962). Actually management ought to decide exactly what advertising is expected to achieve, and then at that time develop the necessary plans to test, so as to find out how successful the advertising was in terms of the expected results.

Precise, specified goals and objectives ought to be set and measured for advertising as advertising. Perhaps the agencies represented in the Annonsbyrå AB book actually are doing so; but their publicly-stated objectives for successful campaigns indicate that the majority are *not* doing this, at least in the campaigns discussed.

SUCCESSFUL CAMPAIGN? What is the answer to the central question posed at the outset: "To what extent do advertising agencies know whether or not their campaigns are successful?"

The answer is that most of the advertising agencies do *not* know whether their campaigns are successful or not. In the majority of the 135 campaigns analyzed here, the agencies did *not* prove or demonstrate the success of the campaigns which they themselves had publicly stated were successes.

There is even a further implication. That is that most of the advertising agencies did *not* state (and possibly did not know) what the objectives for determining success were for a particular campaign, and consequently they could not possibly demonstrate whether a "successful" campaign was actually a success.

Advertising may consist of doing something right or of doing something wrong. But do most advertisers and advertising agencies actually know just what that "something" is?

REFERENCES

Lucas, Darrell B. and Steuart Henderson Britt. *Measuring Advertising Effectiveness.* New York: McGraw-Hill Book Company, 1963, pp. 180–187.

Wolfe, Harry Deane, James K. Brown, and G. Clark Thompson. *Measuring Advertising Results.* New York: National Industrial Conference Board, 1962.

CULTURAL INFLUENCES

4 / Cultural Antecedents of Behavior

A. BACKGROUND AND THEORY

This section of Chapter 4 contains three readings. The first selection (Kuhn) is a brief discussion of the topic of this chapter. The second one (Bonner) gives a definition of culture. The third reading (Barnhill) points up the importance of cultural anthropology and its concepts in marketing.

4-A CULTURAL ANTECEDENTS OF BEHAVIOR

Alfred Kuhn (Economist)

It is relatively easy to define the boundaries of a society for a people who have been isolated for centuries, as in the culture of an island small enough so that all its inhabitants interact among each other, but far enough from others to make communication difficult. Only a relatively primitive culture can retain this condition, since transportation brings advanced societies into contact. Many islands of the South Seas show this situation. So do the Eskimos and Laplanders, whose contacts remain limited by virtue of climatic isolation. Even within the same continent, however, it is possible to have little enough interaction for cultures to remain distinct. The culture of the Hopi Indians is quite distinct from that of the Iroquois, and the Aztecs and Incas showed very little interconnection.

Within a large cosmopolitan area, such as Europe or the United States, cultural lines can be drawn on varied bases. We can, for example, refer to Western society, as distinct from Eastern. The culture of each includes certain broad attitudes toward the origins and purpose of life, toward work, toward animals, and toward other human beings. Within the West there are distinguishing features which mark off the attitudes and beliefs of the French, the

Source: Alfred Kuhn, *The Study of Society* (Homewood, Illinois: Richard D. Irwin, Inc., 1963), pp. 212–213.

German, the British, and the American cultures—among others. Each of these can be considered a society, with its own subculture within the general heading of Western culture. But American society is not a unitary thing. The Southern mountain white, the sharecropper, the plantation owner, the semiskilled Northern factory worker, the New York business tycoon, the New England fisherman, and the Iowa corn and hog farmer all belong to societies whose habits, beliefs, language, and life patterns differ widely from one another. Each has its own subculture within the American culture. Each can be divided and subdivided in turn, almost without end. The mountain whites on one ridge differ from those on the adjoining ridge, and the skilled culturologist might tell them apart by certain attitudes or pronunciations. Even in the relatively homogeneous small town, the inhabitants of the east end differ in some ways from those of the west end, and the precise set of attitudes in one family differs from that of its next door neighbors. It seems possible that the unit recently much analyzed under the heading of the "small group" can meaningfully be viewed as a small subsociety with its own miniature and partial subculture. We cannot subdivide culture further, for to do so would bring us to differences among individuals, and these are matters of personality, not culture.

On the basis of whatever traits we choose to distinguish cultures, a given society and its culture are, by definition, coextensive. The society is the group of people who have a common culture, and a culture is the set of external manifestations of the common motives and concepts of a society. If two widely separated and noncommunicating groups of people were to show identical *bodies* of culture, we would, nevertheless, not consider them as parts of the same society, since they are not part of the same cultural *system*. Interaction within the group is thus an indispensable attribute of a society.

4-B ENCULTURATION

Hubert Bonner (Psychologist)

The study of the effect of culture on personality is to a great extent a continuation of the investigation of socialization begun in the preceding chapter. We defined the group as a collection of people in various degrees of interaction. However, people in groups are invariably carriers of culture. When people interact with others in a group they not only relate themselves to these others in required ways, but they act in accordance with rules and customs that are in various degrees shared by all. In the preceding chapter we indicated, without elaboration, that the mode of child training is dictated by the culture, although there are wide latitudes in which the personalities and emotional tone of the family can operate freely. The school as an educational group is not only a form of teacher-pupil interaction but a complex of norms and values inherited from the past, as well as those determined by present needs. The anchorage groups are not only associations of people which gratify certain needs, but social forms whose being and behavior are partly regulated by custom and tradition.

These brief observations underline the inseparability of group processes and cultural values. There are no functional groups without a culture, and no culture exists outside a group. This inseparability is not a mere interrelatedness, but an overlapping of functions and a deep structural-functional interpenetration. The chief purpose in separating them is the recognition that the elementary fact regarding group structure is interpersonal *contacts*, whereas the essence of culture is a complex of *values*.

DEFINITION OF CULTURE. A definition of culture which adheres to anthropological usage and at the same time is relevant to the study of personality, has been given by a distinguished anthropologist as "the configuration of learned behavior and results of behavior whose component elements are shared and transmitted by the members of a particulaı society.[1]

This definition is useful for several reasons. First, it shows that culture is not a static structure, but a dynamic process. It denotes that culture is not only the sum of accumulated traditions, but even more the transmission of ideas, values, artifacts, and ways of doing things. Further, it implies the organic nature of culture, its togetherness, by stressing its distributive character: culture is mutually shared. Next, culture is a form of learned behavior, thus making it compatible with modern social psychology which denies the instinctive origin of universal social patterns. Again, the term *results of behavior* allows room for innovation and individual creativeness. While in themselves the results of behavior, by virtue of their individuality and idiosyncrasy, are noncultural, their sharing by others makes for their eventual cultural integration. Finally, the definition has a special relevance for the psychology of personality by conceiving culture as a *behavioral* configuration, and not wholly a determinate social structure. Culture, in short, is a way of *behaving*, a way of doing things, rather than a static social structure.[2]

CONTENT OF CULTURE. Although culture is a dynamic process, it is nevertheless, a structure composed of institutions and practices

SOURCE: Hubert Bonner, *Psychology of Personality*. The Ronald Press Company, Copyright © 1961, New York, pp. 191–193.

[1] R. Linton, *The Cultural Background of Personality* (New York: Appleton-Century Crofts, Inc., 1945), p. 32.

[2] For a similar analysis, see *ibid.*, pp. 32–38.

that tend to remain relatively stable. These relatively stable cultural forms serve as marks of its identification. A culture is recognized over a period of time—in other words, by the institutionalized ways of life of a people in a group. These institutionalized ways of life, while differing among various cultural groups seem to be universal.

4-C MARKETING AND CULTURAL ANTHROPOLOGY: A CONCEPTUAL RELATIONSHIP

J. Allison Barnhill (Economist)

In the past, cultural anthropology generally has been excluded from marketing theory and practice. Little systematic conceptualizing or research has been undertaken which logically relates cultural anthropology to marketing. This absence of *explicit* cultural anthropological theory as well as research methods having functional applicability to marketing comprises the fundamental problems of a recent exploratory investigation.[1]

The paucity of cultural anthropological concepts and research has not gone unnoticed in the past. Winick has stated,

Marketers have been relatively slow in using anthropological insights and approaches, even though anthropology is also concerned with man and society.[2]

Two tendencies have hindered the relating of cultural anthropology to marketing. First, cultural anthropologists have concentrated on studying "exotic" groups of people. Unfortunately for marketers, most of these "exotic" peoples do not constitute major markets. Second, marketing practitioners and educators have tended to ignore cultural anthropology as a discipline and seek bases other than cultural anthropological theory or facts upon which to develop meaningful marketing relationships.

However, marketing managers and theorists, faced with the perpetual problem of changing market situations, must endeavor to encompass as many parameters and variables in their infinite relationships as exist in the modern, complex market. The failure by marketers to develop meaningful anthropological concepts and research methods hinders the understanding of markets (domestic and foreign) that is so essential to efficient marketing. For example,

As recently as a few years ago, United States food processors attempting to sell canned vegetables to Europeans met with little success. Canned corn in particular had little sales appeal in Europe because it was considered food for animals.[3]

During the past two decades, behavioral science concepts have been utilized increasingly in marketing. However, the behavioral science theories and research used in marketing have been limited to the disciplines of psychology and sociology. Unfortunately, little effort has been made to expand the scope of behavioral science research and theory by marketers to encompass cultural anthropology.[4]

Numerous contributions to marketing appear to be forthcoming from cultural anthropology. Winick, in his pioneering article, identifies three things which cultural anthropology can contribute to marketing:

1. specific knowledge,
2. awareness of themes of a culture, and
3. sensitivity to taboos.

Alderson has argued that to understand marketing behavior the marketing man must come to grips with the organized behavior system.[5]

SOURCE: J. Allison Barnhill, "Marketing and Cultural Anthropology: A Conceptual Relationship." *University of Washington Business Review*, Vol. 27 (August, 1967), pp. 73–84, at pp. 73–74.

[1] J. Allison Barnhill, *Cultural Anthropology and Marketing: Concepts and an Empirical Investigation*, unpublished doctoral dissertation, University of Washington, Seattle, 1966.

[2] Charles Winick, "Anthropology's Contributions to Marketing," *Journal of Marketing* (July, 1961), p. 53.

[3] "Will United States Methods Apply Abroad?" *Printers' Ink*, October, 1962, p. 59.

[4] One major exception is the recent book by Gerald Zaltman, entitled *Marketing: Contributions from the Behavioral Sciences*, in which one section emphasizes subcultures and market communication.

[5] Wroe Alderson as quoted by Lawrence Tarpey,

Consequently, marketing men should endeavor to develop the capacity to understand organized cultural systems which are fundamental components of a holistic behavioral approach to marketing. Credence to this mandate is given by Duesenberry who postulates that

"Marketing Research and Behavioral Science," *Business Topics*, Vol. 13 (Winter, 1965), p. 65.

. . . in every case the kinds of activities in which people engage are culturally determined and constitute only a small subset of the possible actions in which people might participate.[6]

[6] James S. Duesenberry, *Income, Saving and the Theory of Consumer Behavior* (Cambridge: Harvard University Press, 1949), p. 19.

B. RESEARCH AND APPLICATION

The reading in this section (Sommers and Kernan) points out six value orientations that underlie market behavior; and different cultures are compared with respect to these attributes.

4-D WHY PRODUCTS FLOURISH HERE, FIZZLE THERE

Montrose Sommers (Marketing Educator)
Jerome Kernan (Marketing Educator)

Of the many forces that bear on buying decisions culture is perhaps the one most often taken for granted. Cultural values typically come in dead last in the parade of exhortations about economic variables, social class, buyers' psyches, and so on. This attitude probably stems from a common misconception regarding the relevance of culture to marketing, the consequence of which is almost always lost sales opportunities.

New products succeed; old products maintain entrenched market positions; promotional campaigns for diet foods, soft drinks, or kitchen appliances stand or fall in direct relation to how well marketers create products and product information which are meaningful and persuasive in the eyes of those who comprise markets. While it can always be said that consumers are individuals with different needs, motivations, or desires, it is also axiomatic that individuals within a culture generally rely on basic hard-core values for all types of decisions—those dealing with consumption as well as others.

This common core of values is reflected in

this country in "the American way of life." Part of this way of life results in a characteristic approach to the evaluation of goods and services as well as the product information that supports them. For the marketing manager, a knowledge of this approach and its role in the consumer's evaluation of products and product claims is essential. It helps him to decipher the seemingly random success experience of both new and established products in this country. Further, the ability to compare the characteristics of a number of national markets results in guidelines for adapting domestic marketing strategies to other countries. It is such adaptations that facilitate successful overseas market expansion.

What are the value orientations that underlie characteristic market behavior? Talcott Parsons and Seymour Martin Lipset isolated six categories to help identify the relevant values. To these authors cultural patterns can be distinguished by the degree to which people: (1) are either egalitarian or elitist; (2) are prone to lay stress on accomplishment or inherited attributes; (3) expect material or nonmaterial rewards; (4) evaluate individuals or products in terms of objective norms or subjective standards; (5) focus on the distinctiveness of the parts (intensiveness) rather than the general characteristics of the whole (extensiveness); and (6) are oriented toward personal rather than group gain.

If the Pair Fits

Where do different cultures find themselves with respect to these paired attributes? Citizens of the U.S. for the most part share the attributes described by the first term of the paired groups discussed above and listed in Table 1. In the United States people are encouraged to improve their social position. They can expect: (1) to receive, within limits, recognition for their activities; (2) to be rewarded with material perquisites; (3) to be viewed objectively—what you can do—rather than subjectively—who you are; (4) to be judged in terms of those specific activities pertinent to the situation; and (5) to make evaluations in terms of personal gain. This does not mean that there are no elitist, qualitative, nonmaterial, subjective, extensive or collective values in American society. There very obviously are, but such traits cannot be called dominant in the sense that they are in the British system.

Although in Great Britain values are obviously in flux, the dominant ones are still elitist, qualitative, nonmaterial, subjective, extensive and collective. The British system does not encourage the individual to improve his social position; class structure is an acknowledged fact of life. Recognition is very much bound up with the question of class or category relationship—the right people or objects do the right things. The rewards the system offers for appropriate activity, while they include material perquisites, are to a very important degree positional or status rewards which confer power or prestige rather than tangible gain. The evaluation of an individual or an object is made not so much by an impersonal standard applied to specific activities or functions, but rather by more personal or subjective standards which again vary with group, category or class. Whereas Americans are more liable to apply an objective standard to a narrow range of activities or functions, the British apply a more subjective standard across a broader range of activities. Finally, the British tend to look at persons or objects less in terms of their uniqueness and distinctiveness (less intensively) than do Americans.

Australia and Canada stand between these two extremes for most of the paired variables. One exception is the Australian orientation toward equality. Australians are even more concerned with questions of equality and general worth than are Americans. It can be maintained that Australians, because of their overriding concern for equality, have value orientations that are more closely allied with those of Americans and that the orientations of Canadians generally parallel those of the British.

TABLE 1

Estimates of Rankings of Countries According to Strength of the Six Pattern Variables (Ranked According to First Term in Each Pair)

Pattern Variable	United States	Australia	Canada	Britain
Equal—Elite	2	1	3	4
Performance—Quality	1	2.5	2.5	4
Material—Nonmaterial	1	3	2	4
Objective—Subjective	1	3	2	4
Intensive—Extensive	1	2.5	2.5	4
Individual—Collective	1	3	2	4

5 / Norms of Behavior

A. BACKGROUND AND THEORY

The first of the two articles in this section (Homans) contains a delineation of the determinants of conformity. The second selection (Morris) supplies a functional definition of a norm, and delineates a classification method to aid in establishing and predicting the salience of norms.

5-A DETERMINANTS OF CONFORMITY

George Caspar Homans (Sociologist)

When we say that some people conform to a norm "for its own sake," we mean that they are rewarded by the result that the norm itself, if obeyed, will bring. In our example, some workingmen conform to an output norm because it brings them some kind of protection from management. So long as management does nothing, regardless of its reasons for doing so, their behavior is rewarded. We make no assumption that all members of a group find conformity to a norm valuable for its own sake, but only that some of them do. Suppose that Person is a man who finds it valuable that his own behavior conform to a norm, and that Other's behavior do so too. If Other holds the same values as Person, so that the conformity of each is valuable to the other, then Person rewards Other and Other rewards Person in much the same degree. The exchange between the two is balanced, and we have argued that when the condition of distributive justice is realized, each party is apt to emit, over and above the immediate exchange itself, sentiments of liking or social approval rewarding to the other.

Even if Other does not hold quite the same values as Person, even if, to return to our example, he is not much worried about what management may do, he may still conform. For as we saw in the last chapter, people often reward conformity with social approval, as they reward other activities they find it valuable to receive; and Other, though himself indifferent to the norm, may still conform for the sake of the approval it gets him from people that are not indifferent. He conforms for the approval's sake and not for the norm's sake. Several experiments suggested that he is the more apt to conform, the warmer the approval he may expect to get for it.

Mind you, once Other has conformed, he is not likely to admit that he did so because he was bought by social approval. He will say that he really believes that conformity to the norm is valuable for its own sake. Indeed he may come to talk just like Person, a true believer from the beginning. So far we have talked as if men brought to their current groups the values precipitated by their past experience; but what is happening now will be past experience in just a moment, and besides bringing old values to new groups, men acquire new values within them. What they have once done for the sake of something else, they come to do, for all we can tell, for its own sake.

Mind you, too, Other in conforming may not get a particularly high grade of social approval from Person. If many members of

SOURCE: George Caspar Homans, *Social Behavior: Its Elementary Forms* (New York: Harcourt, Brace and World, Inc., 1961), pp. 116–119; © 1961 by Harcourt, Brace, and World, Inc., and reprinted with their permission.

the group are conforming so that conformity is not a scarce good or one at all hard to come by, Person may not give Other more than perfunctory approval. The highest approval goes to activities that are both valued and rare. But Person will certainly not dislike Other or ostracize him.

Only if Other values an activity incompatible with conformity strongly enough to forgo the approval that conformity would have brought him will he fail to conform. Whether or not he holds such values depends on his past history, on how he has behaved and how that behavior has been rewarded. In the case of output norms in American industry, we have reason to believe that people who have had a certain kind of past history, a rural, white-collar, or Protestant background or some combination of these—people, that is, who have picked up the values Max Weber called the Protestant Ethic—are more likely to be non-conformists and produce more than the output norm than are people with urban, blue-collar, or Catholic backgrounds.[1]

If Other fails to conform, then, as everyday experience suggests, Person will direct much communication to him in an effort to get him to change his behavior. When the attempt fails, and his behavior remains unrewarding to Person, the latter will not simply disapprove of him but positively dislike him. For if many people have conformed, so that conformity appears to be something a member could provide with little cost to himself, Person will expect Other to conform; his failure to do so becomes not just a failure to reward Person but an active withdrawal of reward from him, and the withdrawal of reward is met with hostility. Other has not lived up to the standards of fair exchange. At the extreme, Person will strike back at him or try to get the other members of the group to ostracize him, to send him to Coventry, so that he will have no chance whatever of getting any social reward.

Whether or not Other conforms does not depend simply on whether he finds sufficiently rewarding some activity—like hard work as a

moral value—that is incompatible with his conforming to a norm—like the norm of pegged production. It also depends on whether he can find companions in his nonconformity. Should he fail to conform, he forgoes social approval from at least some of the members of his group, and this cost will be the greater the less open to him are alternative sources of social approval. If, for instance, there is no other group he can escape to, he is more apt to give in. Savages, who seldom have another tribe than their own that they can join, are great conformers. He is also more apt to give in if no other members of his own group share his values: the lot of the isolate is often hard. But if there are such persons—not just nonconformists but nonconformists of his own stripe—then he may not have to give up social approval altogether. Even a single such man seems to be a great comfort, and robs the group at one stroke of the greater part of its power. In this man the nonconformist has a source of support and social approval alternative to the approval offered by the rest of the group and now forgone by him. This is what the investigators meant in one of the experiments in the last chapter when they said that a member was less likely to conform if he saw the formation of subgroups was possible. If, indeed, there are enough members who share values opposed to those of other members, the group may split up into mutually hostile subgroups. We are far from knowing just what conditions are necessary in order that a norm should become accepted as a norm for a whole group, to which all members give lip service even if they do not all conform fully. We suspect that what is needed is a certain number of members that value conformity to the norm for its own sake, a certain number that are indifferent to the norm but value the social approval that conformity gets them, and an opposition that is divided against itself: its members fail to conform, but in different ways and for different reasons.

It should be clear that in this discussion the author and readers of this selection are not Organization Men: we are not assigning a high moral value to conformity, to the man who goes along with the gang. We are only making the obvious point that nonconformity often has a price; and if we take any moral stand it is that the good nonconformist pays the price

[1] M. Weber, *The Protestant Ethic and the Spirit of Capitalism*, translated by T. Parsons (London, 1930); W. F. Whyte, *Money and Motivation* (New York, 1955), pp. 39–49.

without feeling sorry for himself. Too many people complain when they can't have their nonconformity and eat it too. They want the best of both worlds, and if they got it they would be unfair to the rest of us.

Most studies of groups in practical equilibrium are not geared to testing all we have said about the relations between conformity and social approval. But they are geared to testing and have tested one corollary that seems to follow from our argument. Suppose a piece of research is pretty coarse-meshed: of a number of groups it tells us only that so many members of each conformed to a norm or failed to do so, and only that so many members of each expressed liking for other members or failed to do so. The research may lump together as conformists people who conformed for different reasons, some for the norm's sake and some for the approval's. It may lump together liking of different degrees, or confuse a low degree of approval with a high degree of positive disapproval. But so long as our argument is right in finding any link between conformity and social approval, we should expect such a study to show that the larger the number of members that conform to a group norm, the larger is the number that express social approval for other members. We cannot say that one variable in this corollary is the cause and the other the effect, for the liking may have produced the conformity as well as conformity the liking. But grossly and statistically we should expect the relationship to hold good.

5-B   A TYPOLOGY OF NORMS

Richard T. Morris (Sociologist)

The typology of norms presented here, while based in part upon these prior efforts, attempts a classification employing additional dimensions (or criteria), directed toward the establishment of the *salience* of particular norms in any given hierarchical, normative system.

It should be pointed out at once that the rather considerable literature[1] on the classification of values is relevant to the problem of typing norms; nevertheless, there is a difference between values and norms, which precludes the direct application of value classifications to the study of norms. To make a very brief distinction between values and norms it may be said, following Kluckhohn,[2] that values are individual or commonly shared conceptions of the desirable, i.e. what I and/or others feel we justifiably want—what it is felt proper to want. On the other hand, norms are generally accepted, sanctioned prescriptions for, or prohibitions against others' behavior, belief, or feeling, i.e. what others *ought* to do,

believe, feel—*or else*. Values can be held by a single individual; norms cannot. Norms must be shared prescriptions and apply to others, by definition. Values have only a subject—the believer—while norms have both subjects and objects—those who set the prescription, and those to whom it applies. Norms always include sanctions; values never do. Although it is true that commonly held values often result in the formation of norms that insure the maintenance of the values, this is not always the case. Nor does it follow that every norm, at the point of its application, involves a presently held value, even though most norms are based upon established values.

As Turner has pointed out,[3] there may be a widely-held value placed upon baseball skills in a society, but no norm which states that baseball *ought* to be played by the individuals in that society, or they will suffer the consequences. On the other hand, there may be a norm that recommends stopping at a red light even when there is no traffic, without a value attached to the instance. A demonstration of the difference between norms and values may be found in attempting to answer the question of when and how children begin to develop values in distinction to norms, i.e. ideas of what is desirable as distinct from

SOURCE: Richard T. Morris "A Typology of Norms," *American Sociological Review*, Vol. 21 (October, 1965), pp. 610–613.
[1] Cf. the bibliographic footnotes in Clyde Kluckhohn and others, "Values and Value-Orientations in the Theory of Action" in Talcott Parsons and Edward A. Shils (editors), *Toward a General Theory of Action*, Cambridge: Harvard University Press, 1951, pp. 388–433.
[2] *Ibid.*, pp. 395–396.

[3] Ralph H. Turner, "Value Conflict in Social Disorganization," *Sociology and Social Research*, 38 (May-June, 1954), pp. 301–303.

shared ideas of what others ought to do, with sanctions attached.[4]

It follows that norms and values must be classified and operationalized in different fashions, using different criteria. Whereas Kluckhohn[5] has suggested a classification of values on the bases of modality, content, intent, generality, intensity, explicitness, extent, and organization, and although this scheme provides valuable insights for the classification of norms, it does not mean that norms can be classified in the same manner, since other criteria are involved, such as degree and kind of sanction, extent and kind of deviation, and the like.

The development of the typology presented here arose partially from the realization that other schemes of classification dealt only with certain aspects of norms. Sumner's classification is based largely upon the degree of conformity required and the kinds of sanction applied. Linton's classification is based upon the mixed criteria of extent of acceptance (universals and alternatives) and extent of application (specialties). Sorokin's classification utilizes the mixed criteria of content, i.e. what areas of behavior or belief the norms regulate, in his distinction between the technical norms and norms of etiquette and fashion, and the criterion of degree of conformity required (obligatory vs. free norms), in his distinction between law norms and moral norms. He also uses the criterion of reciprocity or "two-sidedness" in the latter distinction. Williams uses content criteria, i.e. what areas of behavior are regulated, in his classification of technical, conventional, aesthetic, etc., norms, and suggests the use of such characteristics as extent of agreement, modes of enforcement, explicitness, and specificity as criteria, although he never proceeds to a systematic classification on these bases. He does suggest a single type, institutional norm, which has several of the characteristics.

[4] Piaget's distinction between "the morality of constraint" and "the morality of cooperation" may be viewed in present terms as the distinction between the obeying of norms and the establishing of values. Although he discusses it (pp. 180–182), Piaget does not fully develop the third theme, that of setting norms for others. Cf. Jean Piaget, *The Moral Judgment of the Child*, Glencoe: The Free Press, n.d., Ch. 2, 3.

[5] Kluckhohn, *op. cit.*, pp. 412–421.

The various classifications based upon these selected criteria, or characteristics of norms, are useful for the particular problems which these writers had in mind, e.g., the developmental problems of Sumner, the cultural homogeneity problems of Linton, and so on. The present classification is based upon the somewhat different problem of establishing and predicting the salience of norms. It is but a first step, prior to the development of empirical measures of the variables outlined below.

The characteristics of norms selected for the classification are presented as grouped continua. These are arranged so that types or profiles can be constructed by a vertical reading of the characteristics of a given norm on all continua.

I. Distribution of Norm

Extent of knowledge of norm

1. By subjects (those who set the norm)
   very few . . . . almost everyone
2. By objects (those to whom the norm applies)
   very few . . . . almost everyone

Extent of acceptance, agreement with norm

3. By subjects
   very few . . . . almost everyone
4. By objects
   very few . . . . almost everyone

Extent of application of norm to objects

5. To groups or categories
   very few . . . . almost everyone
6. To conditions
   in specified few . . . . in almost all

II. Mode of Enforcement of Norm

7. Reward—punishment
   more reward   more punishment
   than punishment . . . . than reward
8. Severity of sanction
   light, unimportant . . heavy, important
9. Enforcing agency
   specialized,   general,
   designated   universal
   responsibility . . . . responsibility
10. Extent of enforcement
    lax, intermittent . . . . rigorous, uniform
11. Source of authority
    rational,   divine, inherent,
    expedient,   absolute,
    instrumental . . . . autonomous

12. Degree of internalization by objects
    little,   great,
    external enforcement   self-enforcement
    required . . . . sufficient

III. Transmission of the Norm
13. Socialization process
    late learning,   early learning,
    from secondary   from primary
    relations . . . . relations
14. Degree of reinforcement by subjects
    very little . . . . high, persistent

IV. Conformity to the Norm
15. Amount of conformity attempted by
    objects
    attempted by   attempted by
    very few . . . . almost everyone
16. Amount of deviance by objects
    very great . . . . very little
17. Kind of deviance
    formation of   patterned   idiosyncratic
    sub-norms . . evasion[6] . . deviation

It should be noted at once that the above selection of characteristics of norms *is* a selection: it does not intend to represent all of the features of norms which may be useful in analysis. For example, the following characteristics were considered as candidates for inclusion in the typology: specificity and explicitness in the statement of the norms, formal vs. informal sanctions, repressive vs. restitutive sanctions, degree and kind of conflict with other norms, locus of conflict (intragroup vs. inter-group), perceived consequences of deviance by subjects and objects. These characteristics were excluded from the typology, either because they seemed not to vary consistently in possible polar types with the other criteria used, or because they were subsumed under the criteria listed in the typology. Probably the most striking omission is the content of the norms.[7]

[6] Robin M. Williams, *American Society* (New York: Knoff, 1951), pp. 347–371.
[7] "Content" is used here in two senses: classification of norms according to the area of behavior regulated, e.g. technical and aesthetic, as in Sorokin or Williams; or classification of norms according to the nature of action called for by the norms, e.g. norms regulating behavior, belief, or feeling, as in Parsons. Cf. Talcott Parsons, "The Superego and the Theory of Social Systems," in Talcott Parsons, *et al., Working Papers in the Theory of*

The classification here is not based upon content criteria, e.g. between technical and aesthetic norms, norms referring to behavior vs. norms referring to beliefs, feelings, or cognition. The position taken here is that these various norms, classified according to content, may all have the characteristics selected for the typology just outlined. In other words, constructed types based upon the characteristics listed above apply equally well to norms in any of the content areas. A further step in the application of the type is to investigate the relations between the types of norms and the content areas to which they apply.

The two types which appear most obviously are the polar ones. Reading down the extreme right-hand end of each of the continua, one may construct a polar type of norm which may be called an *absolute norm:* a norm which is known and supported by everyone, which applies to everybody under all conditions, which is rigorously enforced by heavy sanctions. Reading down the left-hand end of each continua, the opposite polar type may be constructed which may be designated a *conditional norm,* suggesting its limited application and sporadic enforcement.

The arrangement of the continua above points up at once the similarity between the present typology of norms and the familiar folk-urban, sacred-secular typology of Tönnies, Redfield, Becker, and others. This is not surprising since it has long been hypothesized, sometimes in other terms, that a folk society has a high ratio of absolute norms, and an urban society a high ratio of conditional norms. There is also some resemblance between the absolute norm and Williams' concept of institutional norm.[8]

The placement of existing norms, group, organizational or societal, along the various continua in the typology should result in the formulation of additional mixed types which will be useful in the analysis and prediction of changes in single norms or in the normative structure.

Action, Glencoe: The Free Press, 1953. Chapter 1.
    It may be argued that it is stretching the meaning of the term "content" to make it apply to two such basically different classification schemes. Both, however, point toward what is included in the prescription, rather than focusing on implementation as does the present classification.
[8] Williams, *op. cit.,* pp. 28–29.

B. RESEARCH AND APPLICATIONS

The research in the article (Andreason and Durkson) selected for this section was carried out to determine the learning of brand alternatives in a new market, and to discover the patterns of change in brand knowledge and brand behavior over time in a new community.

5-C MARKET LEARNING OF NEW RESIDENTS

Alan R. Andreason (Marketing Educator)
and Peter G. Durkson (Marketing Educator)

The present study focuses on one small phase of the complex adjustment process, learning of brand alternatives in a new market, and stresses patterns of change in brand knowledge and behavior over time in the new community. The authors' major hypotheses compare new movers to the community's settled residents with similar basic needs and wants and with access to about the same market availabilities. These hypotheses are:

1. The new group's knowledge of available brands and their purchase preferences at the time they enter the community will be different from those of old residents,
2. As length of time in the community increases, brand knowledge and behavior will become like those of old residents,
3. Differences across brands in initial knowledge, behavior, and rate at which these differences disappear over time will be explained by differences in brand distribution nationally and brand promotion locally. Specifically, (a) For brands with national distribution and presumably national promotion, no differences in brand knowledge will be found between new and settled residents; in some cases, differences in brand purchase behavior will be found between new and settled residents because of local differences in competitive promotion and brand penetration; and differences in purchase behavior will tend to disappear over time under the impact of new market influences. (b) For brands with regional or

local distribution, differences in both awareness and behavior will exist initially because of new resident ignorance or lack of experience, but these differences will tend to disappear over time under the impact of new market influences. (c) Exceptions to the above hypotheses and differences in rates of adoption of community norms can be explained by promotional variables within or among product categories.

Methodology

A cross-sectional research design was developed in which data on brand knowledge and behavior were gathered at one time for three sample groups: persons who had very recently moved into the Philadelphia metropolitan area, persons who had been there about 18 months and had partially or entirely completed the market learning process, and persons who had lived in the community long enough to be considered settled residents. To control for different needs, wants, and local availabilities, matching of the three samples was considered necessary.

The study design was based on a subsample of 75 female heads of households randomly selected for the Marketing Science Institute's 1964 Philadelphia study. At the time of the present study, the housewives had resided in the Philadelphia area 16 to 20 months and were assumed to be representative of new residents part way through the market learning process. This basic sample was then matched to a sample of 75 new residents who had been in the community about three months at the time of interviewing. Each of the two samples was then matched to a sample of 75 residents who had lived at their present ad-

SOURCE: Alan R. Andreason and Peter G. Durkson, "Market Learning of New Residents." *Journal of Marketing Research*, Vol. 5 (May, 1968), pp. 166–176.

dresses for not less than three years.[1] Since household needs and wants were assumed to vary with place of residence, (matching was based on broad income groupings, age of youngest child, and geographic proximity) To control one major source of difference in transferable past experience, both new resident groups were restricted to housewives who had moved from outside the Philadelphia metropolitan area and who had not lived within the area more than six months.

Data collection was based on telephone interviews over the four-week period from November 2 to 30, 1965, under the supervision of the Opinion Research Corporation and the Marketing Science Institute. The matching procedures resulted in close correspondence between movers and settled residents on most demographic characteristics. The most noticeable difference was in educational attainment. More movers than settled residents had been to college. Movers were also somewhat younger than the settled residents and had fewer children. In general, the differences between movers and settled families followed known patterns.

The following sections are intended to describe and explain the process by which new residents learn about and use old and new brands in a new market. It is assumed that the only difference among the three groups is length of residence, which permits sample measures of knowledge and behavior of the three groups to be considered as three stages in long-term adjustment processes of new residents. Specifically, the assumption permits interpretation of the pooled responses of the 150 old residents as indicators of completed adjustment stages for new residents.

It should be noted that adjustment as treated here is not adjustment in the usual sense of describing changes in one person over time.

[1] Average length of residence for the 150 old residents was approximately ten years. Although it is clearly inappropriate to describe this group as non-movers since many of them had moved sometime, the assumption made here is that their new-market learning is essentially complete. The fact that they, too, have moved further supports the assumption that the mover groups are not fundamentally different from the matched settled residents except for their length of time in the community.

TABLE 1

Average Number of Brands Named

Product	New Movers	1964 Movers	Matched Families
Coffee	4.3	4.5	4.9
Gasoline	4.3	4.5	4.5
Soft drinks	4.0	4.5	4.8
Facial tissue	2.4	2.5	2.6
Bread	2.7	3.1	3.9
Milk	2.1	2.9	3.5
Total	3.3	3.7	4.0

The data represent summaries of dichotomous responses (aware-not aware; purchase-not purchase) of groups of persons. Adjustments are therefore defined as changes in the total number of respondents who are aware of or have purchased a particular brand or group of brands between two points in time.

The Findings

MARKET KNOWLEDGE. The acquisition of market knowledge was investigated by studying differences in brand awareness among the three sample groups—new, somewhat new, and settled residents. Respondents were asked to name on an unaided basis as many different brands as they could in six categories of frequently purchased nondurable convenience goods—milk, bread, coffee, gasoline, facial tissue, and soft drinks. The results appear to support the first two of our major hypotheses (Table 1)[2] in all six product categories, 1965 movers (the very new residents) named fewer brands than settled residents. Second, in all categories, residents who moved in 1964 (18-month residents) were aware of more brands than the very new movers and the same or fewer brands than old residents.

Sections a and b of Hypothesis 3 imply, however, that these differences in awareness will be attributable only to the local and regional brands. In general, Table 2 tends to support the hypothesis.[3] Relatively small dif-

[2] Planned interdependencies among the sample groups preclude statistical test of this finding.
[3] Characterizations of the extent of each brand's distribution coverage are based on a variety of sources including personal experience, telephone calls, personal conversations, and correspondence

TABLE 2

Total Brand Awareness

Product	Distribution	Total Mentions		
		New Movers	1964 Movers	Settled Residents[a]
Coffee	National[b]	234	229	227
	Local-regional[b]	44	81	110
	Other	43	31	26
Gasoline	National	220	222	159
	Local-regional	69	86	119
	Other	37	27	23
Soft drinks	National	216	250	255
	Local-regional	24	41	70
	Other	62	47	36
Facial tissue	National	113	111	108
	Local-regional	27	48	58
	Other	42	23	27
Bread	National	79	104	107
	Local-regional	29	58	111
	Other	91	68	76
Milk	National	35	38	44
	Local-regional	69	103	128
	Other	57	76	92
Total	National	897	900	940
	Local-regional	262	417	596
	Other	332	272	280
		1491	1589	1816

[a] One-half the total for the two settled resident groups.
[b] Includes brands mentioned by at least five percent of settled residents.

ferences are found in total mentions of national brands across the three sample groups, and large differences are found in the expected direction for the major[4] regional-local brands in the Philadelphia market.

with persons in the various industries. Nationally distributed brands are defined as those available in most or all of the 50 states and the District of Columbia. Local brands are those essentially available only in the Philadelphia metropolitan area. Regional brands comprise the rather broad middle ground. To illustrate, gasoline brands were divided as follows by the American Petroleum Institute data:

National brands—represented in 45 or more states (including D.C.)
Regional brands—represented in 3 to 44 states (including D.C.)
Local brands—represented in 1 or 2 states (including D.C.)

[4] "Major" defines brands mentioned by at least five percent of settled residents.

The relatively higher mention of other brands by new movers in Table 2 undoubtedly reflects a tendency to mention (presumably regional-local) brands from the previous community. This finding along with the previous one emphasizes that the gross figures in Table 1 substantially obscure the underlying process by combining disparate types of brands with different change patterns, by understating the extent of change in awareness of those brands (i.e., the local and regional brands) that do change, and by ignoring the fact that adjustment of brand cognition over time involves both acquiring new information and forgetting old.

It should also be noted in Table 2 that the patterns are not identical across all six product categories. For example; some differences in national brand mentions across the three groups appear to exist for bread, for milk, and somewhat for soft drinks. Also, the extent of difference, i.e., the relative ignorance of new

TABLE 3

Percent Reporting Individual Brand Awareness

Brand	Product	Distribution	Settled Residents Matched To					Significance Level		
			New Movers	1964 Movers	New movers	1964 movers	Total	1	2	3
A & P	Coffee	National	36	40	35	35	35	—	—	—
Chase & Sanborn	Coffee	National	57	55	53	61	57	—	—	—
Maxwell House	Coffee	National	89	92	83	84	83	—	—	—
Sanka	Coffee	National	29	31	29	35	32	—	—	.20
Yuban	Coffee	National	43	33	40	44	42	—	—	—
American (AMOCO)	Gasoline	National	31	28	28	31	29	—	—	—
Citgo (Cities Service)	Gasoline	National	24	40	21	20	21	—	.025	.20
Esso (Humble)	Gasoline	National	67	67	63	64	63	—	—	—
Gulf	Gasoline	National	63	60	55	51	53	—	—	—
Sinclair	Gasoline	National	16	21	31	28	29	.05	—	—
Texaco	Gasoline	National	44	40	40	40	40	—	—	—
Mobil	Gasoline	National	19	21	23	25	24	—	—	—
Canada Dry	Soft Drinks	National	41	51	55	53	54	.20	—	.10
Coca-Cola	Soft Drinks	National	76	84	84	76	80	—	—	—
Hires	Soft Drinks	National	17	16	25	24	25	—	—	—
Pepsi-Cola	Soft Drinks	National	75	76	75	69	72	—	—	—
Seven Up	Soft Drinks	National	43	53	43	56	49	—	—	—
Kleenex	Facial tissue	National	93	79	77	77	77	.025	—	.05
Scott	Facial tissue	National	57	69	64	69	67	—	—	—
Bond	Bread	National	41	68	93	83	88	.001	.10	.001
Pepperidge Farm	Bread	National	29	28	33	31	32	—	.10	—
Wonder	Bread	National	35	43	19	28	23	.05	.10	—
Sealtest	Milk	National	47	51	57	60	59	—	—	—
Chock Full O'Nuts	Coffee	Regional	11	25	20	23	21	.20	—	.20
Horn & Hardart	Coffee	Regional	5	17	35	31	33	.001	.20	.05
Savarin	Coffee	Regional	16	28	19	33	26	—	—	—

Brand	Product	Distribution	New Movers	1964 Movers	Settled Residents Matched To			Significance Level		
					New movers	1964 movers	Total	1	2	3
Atlantic	Gasoline	Regional	32	49	63	67	65	.001	.05	—
Sunoco	Gasoline	Regional	52	51	65	81	73	.20	.001	—
Booth's	Soft Drinks	Regional	4	7	24	21	23	.01	.025	—
Frank's	Soft Drinks	Regional	7	17	35	32	33	.001	.05	.025
Hudson	Facial tissue	Regional	17	32	43	32	37	.01	—	.10
Marcal	Facial tissue	Regional	15	31	31	29	30	.05	—	.20
Freihofer	Bread	Regional	11	28	68	67	67	.001	.001	.10
Stroehmann	Bread	Regional	11	31	48	55	51	.001	.01	.20
Abbot's	Milk	Local	17	28	56	55	55	.001	.01	.20
Harbison's	Milk	Local	4	12	27	20	23	.20	.20	.20
Martin-Century	Milk	Regional	32	44	44	45	45	—	—	—
Sylvan Seal	Milk	Regional	35	49	37	40	39	—	—	—

movers compared with that of settled residents for regional and local brands ranges from very substantial for bread to much less substantial for gasoline.

To explore some of these variations, individual brands are reported in Table 3. Although as in the previous section, summary brand data could be used to describe differences in awareness of individual brands across residence groups, it is possible through the use of matched-pair analysis to analyze these patterns statistically.

Matched-pair analysis is used to make three statistical tests of the data.[5] These tests in their null form are:

Test 1. There is no significant difference in brands named between the 1965 movers and the sample of settled residents to which they were matched.

Test 2. There is no significant difference in brands named between the 1964 movers and the sample of settled residents to which they were matched.

Test 3. There is no significant difference in the degree of similarity of brands named between the 1965 movers and their matched sample of settled residents and the 1964 movers and their matched sample of settled residents.

In effect, Test 1 examined the study's first hypothesis that new residents are unlike old residents in their brand awareness, and Test 3 examined the second hypothesis that new residents become like settled residents over time. Test 2 indicated whether, among brands where change exists, 18-month residents are as aware of the brands as old residents; that is, whether change had effectively been completed after 18 months in the new community.

Table 3 presents matched-pair analyses for 38 brands for which statistically significant results were found. In 19 cases, no significant differences were found across the three residence groups.[6] Hypothesis 3a predicts that

all these cases will be national brands and, reciprocally, that all national brands will exhibit this pattern. It turned out that 17 of the 19 brands are national brands, but these 17 constitute only a portion of the 23 national brands for which statistically significant results were obtained. It is, however, reasonably strong support for our hypothesis.

A second basic pattern suggested by Hypothesis 3b is that for the remaining 19 cases where differences across groups were found, changes over time will exhibit more or less gradual increases in awareness. New movers will be less aware of given brands than old residents with 18-month residents somewhere between the two degrees of awareness. Conceivably, in some cases 18-month residents could be at a level equal to either of the other groups, i.e., not having had any change or having completed all change. The hypothesis further suggests that this pattern will apply only to regional and local brands and conversely that all regional and local brands will follow this pattern.

In Table 3, the pattern described can be assumed to exist where significant differences on the three tests are indicated in any of the following three combinations:

1. *Significance on Tests 1 and 3.* Here, new residents will appear to have become as aware as settled residents after 18 months in the new community. This pattern describes six brands including Sinclair and Canada Dry[7] but excluding Kleenex, discussed later.

2. *Significance on Tests 1, 2, and 3.* In this pattern, 18-month residents will appear to have moved toward, but not to, the awareness levels of settled residents. This pattern describes six brands.

3. *Significance on Tests 1 and 2.* In this pattern, 18-month residents will appear not to have increased awareness from that indicated for very new movers. This pattern describes four brands not

---

[5] A description of matched-pair analysis is included in the appendix. A probability of .20 or less as computed from the chi-square statistic was considered significant for purposes of the analysis.
[6] Strictly, the null hypothesis was not accepted statistically for two of these brands. Sanka and Coca-Cola were found statistically significant on Test 3 at the .20 and .10 levels respectively. The

findings, however, are assumed to be sampling errors associated with the high variation between old resident groups that obscure a lack of real differences among all resident groups.
[7] Significance on both tests was not strictly found for Sinclair and Canada Dry, requiring a judgment that this was the "true" pattern for these cases.

including Wonder Bread, discussed later. (Strictly speaking, brands in the third combination do not support the study's second major hypothesis that new residents become over time like old residents.)

Of the 16 brands in these three combinations, all but three are regional or local brands as the hypothesis predicted. These 13 represent a substantial proportion of the 15 significant regional-local brand cases. Again this would seem to be strong support for the hypothesis.

Sections a and b of Hypothesis 3 account for all but three of the brands in the analysis. Among the 34 brands accounted for, the hypotheses misplaced three national brands—Canada Dry, Sinclair gasoline, and Bond bread—and two regional-local brands—Sylvan Seal Milk and Savarin Coffee. Hypothesis 3c suggests that these exceptions can be attributed to promotional variables. Thus the authors were encouraged to hypothesize that the three national brands for which awareness increases over time acquire stronger promotional support and market shares in the market *locally* than they do nationally. This would lead to higher-than-average awareness levels locally and a consequent pattern of new resident increases in awareness after arrival in the new community. Of the two local-regional brands where no change in awareness appears to take place, it may be hypothesized that all learning for these brands has been completed before our first interview.

Alternatively, the pattern may result from more active or more effective promotional impact of these brands in the local community in general or specifically among new residents in the periods when market learning was taking place. Unfortunately, our understanding of the promotional variables operating in the Philadelphia market, particularly as they might affect new movers, is still too imperfect to permit more than offering these hypotheses as speculations at the present time.

The three cases unexplained by the above hypotheses are all national brands—Kleenex, Wonder Bread, and Citgo. Wonder Bread is unclear although it may be categorized as an aberrant national brand showing decreased awareness over time. Kleenex, however, appears to be a clear case of a brand new residents

become less aware of over time in the new community. A promotional variable may be also operative here since the Philadelphia market is known to be strong Scott territory, and the decline of Kleenex awareness may be a reflection of Scott's more effective local promotion. If so, the pattern would fit the general conception of market learning as adaptation to community norms.

Though Citgo may also be a result of sampling variation, a historical accident suggests an alternative, if highly speculative, explanation. In May, 1965, about six months before interviewing for this study and about 12 months after the 1964 movers had arrived in Philadelphia, Cities Service Company changed its corporation trademark, renamed itself, its retail outlets, and its products "Citgo." The introduction was accompanied by substantial brand promotion, suggesting that the heightened awareness of the 1964 movers is the consequence of above-average information seeking activity for these movers, taking place just when Cities Service was getting above-average brand dissemination. This accidental conjunction would not be true of the very new movers who would not have begun presumed information-seeking by May, 1965, or for the settled residents whose interest in brand information is assumed to be average. This reasoning leads us to ask whether new movers when they are actively seeking brand information might not be more sensitive than others to brand learning programs.

MARKET BEHAVIOR. The establishment of market behavior patterns was investigated by observing last-reported purchases in four of the six product categories discussed earlier in the brand awareness section: coffee, gasoline, facial tissues, and soft drinks. Table 4 gives an overall view of purchasing behavior within these categories. Most data follow the patterns described in Table 2. There are initial overall differences between new movers and settled residents in purchase behavior, but these differences tend to disappear over time. The principal changes take place mostly in the purchase of local-regional brands. There is, however, somewhat less variation among product categories in the strength of these patterns than with the awareness data although this is, in part, a function of the small sample sizes. Mention of other purchases again tends

TABLE 4

Total Brand Purchases

		Total Mentions		
Product	Distribution	New Movers	1964 Movers	Settled Residents[a]
Coffee	National[b]	54	51	57
	Local-regional[b]	9	12	13
	Other	10	11	5
Gasoline	National	47	51	36
	Local-regional	14	21	21
	Other	1	2	2
Soft drinks	National	53	63	56
	Local-regional	4	6	11
	Other	18	5	7
Facial tissue	National	50	54	42
	Local-regional	8	13	18
	Other	12	6	12
Total	National	204	219	191
	Local-regional	35	52	63
	Other	41	24	26
		280	295	280

[a] One-half the total for the two settled resident groups.
[b] Includes brands mentioned by at least five percent of settled residents.

to decline as one moves from new to settled resident data.

It should be noted that the finding of little change over time among national brands does not support that part of Hypothesis 3a that predicted some adjustments in national brand use over time as a response to local promotional pressures.

Purchase behavior for individual products was investigated by looking at reported purchases by each of the sample groups in the four product categories. The same matched-pair testing procedure was applied to the data for the more prominent brands. Because of small sample sizes, only five brand patterns— four national and one regional—were statistically supportable.

Two of the four national brands showed no difference among the three groups, and the one regional brand followed the pattern predicted by Hypothesis 3b. The first of the two exceptions is Maxwell House Coffee that can be attributed to sampling variability. The second exception is Kleenex.

For Kleenex, new residents seemed more likely to purchase the brand than settled

residents. This was the same pattern found in the Kleenex awareness data described earlier. Here, however, unlike the awareness data, Kleenex purchases do not seem to tend toward the community norm over time. Again, our market understanding does not offer a ready explanation for this finding. One is tempted to speculate that new community promotional influences may affect brand cognitions much more rapidly than the perhaps more deeply rooted past purchase preferences for strong national brands such as Kleenex.

The following seem to be the principal conclusions from the study:

1. The assumption that active brand learning is done by new residents is well supported by the data,

2. The overall pattern of brand learning is one of movement toward community norms,

3. Brand learning involves acquiring knowledge about new brands in the new community and forgetting brands from the old community,

4. Although adjustments in brand aware-

ness and purchasing behavior take place primarily for regional-local brands, some adjustment in national brand awareness apparently does take place,

5. There is substantial variation in the rate and kind of change in knowledge and behavior among and within product types,

6. Differences in adjustment patterns among brands are probably only partially explainable by promotional variables in the local market.

6 / Socialization

A. BACKGROUND AND THEORY

This section begins with a definition (Secord and Backman) of the socialization process. The second selection (Krech, Crutchfield, and Ballachey) discusses the various determinants of conformity. The final reading (McDavid and Harari) explains how the socialization process is instrumental in governing particular behavioral traits.

6-A THE SOCIALIZATION PROCESS

Paul F. Secord (Psychologist) and Carl W. Backman (Psychologist)

One of the most significant and remarkable processes occurring in human beings is the transformation of the helpless infant into the mature adult. No other species goes through as long and as intensive a process of development, and in no other species is the contrast between infant and adult so great. As he develops, the child learns one or more languages, a wealth of empirical facts about his physical and social environment, and a variety of special skills and bodies of knowledge. He also acquires attitudes and values, some of them pertaining to moral standards and others that are ways of relating to people, such as loving or hating and helping or hurting other persons. This transformation takes place largely as a result of what have been termed *socialization processes*.

The principal agents in socialization are other persons, most notably the child's parents, teachers, siblings, playmates, and others who are significant to him. Much of what the child learns in the process of growing up is not systematically and consciously taught. Parents do not generally define themselves as teachers,

yet they serve this role. Most of what they teach is not conveyed with deliberate intent; nevertheless, the child learns effectively.

Formerly, the term *socialization* had not been applied to adult learning experiences, but had been restricted to children. This traditional usage of the term was almost synonymous with the everyday phrase "bringing up the child." More recently the concept of socialization has been broadened to include aspects of adult behavior as well. Currently, socialization is thought of as an interactional process whereby a person's behavior is modified to conform with expectations held by members of the groups to which he belongs. This more inclusive definition recognizes that socialization does not stop at a certain age, but instead continues throughout life. Socialization processes are especially active each time a person occupies a new position, as when he joins a fraternity or sorority, gets promoted in a business organization, becomes a parent, or is inducted into military service.

Two aspects of socialization distinguish it from other processes of change. First, only the attitudinal and behavioral changes occurring through *learning* are relevant. Other changes, such as those resulting from growth, are not a part of the socialization process. Second, only the changes in behavior and attitude having

SOURCE: Paul F. Secord and Carl W. Backman, *Social Psychology.* Copyright 1964 McGraw-Hill Book Company, New York. Used with permission of the McGraw-Hill Book Company, pp. 525–527.

their origins in *interaction with other persons* are considered products of socialization. The term *interaction* is here defined broadly to include communication through the mass media, as when a student nurse reads a biography of Florence Nightingale.

Several illustrations may clarify these distinctions. Learning motor skills without tutelage by other persons, such as learning to run or jump, is not a socialization process. Learning to speak in the vernacular of one's own locality, on the other hand, is clearly a product of socialization because such learning is heavily dependent on interaction with other local inhabitants. Other illustrations of socialization include learning the folkways and customs of one's society or regional group and the religious beliefs and moral values of one's society and family.

Socialization should not be thought of as molding a person to a standard social pattern, however. Individuals are subjected to different combinations of socialization pressures, and they react differently to them. Consequently socialization processes can produce distinctive differences among persons as well as similarities.

Socialization processes receive considerable attention in such fields as developmental psychology, sociology of the child, portions of clinical psychology, certain aspects of group psychology, and culture and personality. Over the years, however, a certain division of labor has developed, reducing the overlap between these areas. In particular, social psychologists have usually limited their interest in socialization to four aspects:

1. Social learning processes such as imitation, identification, and role learning.

2. The establishment by means of social learning of internal controls or conscience, the self concept, and social roles.

3. The development of various behavior systems such as dependency, aggression, and affiliation and the formation of various strategies of goal achievement and defense.

4. The relation of the social structure to these processes and to their effects.

A number of questions have been posed concerning socialization processes and their effects. What is the nature of the learning processes underlying socialization? How are these processes linked to their effects? What role is played by social structural and cultural factors in shaping these processes? The last two questions may be illustrated by reference to concrete behaviors. For example, what behaviors of parents will lead children to be strongly dependent upon their parents? How are these parental behaviors related to certain features of the family system, such as its size and the relation between the parents? How are they related to the cultural system, especially to the prevailing ideology of child rearing found in a particular group?

Socialization has been defined in terms of learning processes associated with interaction between persons. How does the behavior of one person affect the behavior of another? Anyone familar with the psychology of learning will answer that one individual may influence another when he rewards or punishes him for certain responses. A parent, for example, praises his child for an action just performed or punishes him in order to eliminate its recurrence.

6-B CONFORMITY

David Krech (Psychologist), Richard S. Crutchfield (Psychologist), and Egerton L. Ballachey (Psychologist)

Why are some people high in conformity-proneness and others low? By this time a large

SOURCE: David Krech, Richard S. Crutchfield, and Egerton L. Ballachey, *Individual in Society*, Copyright 1962 by the McGraw-Hill Book Company Inc., New York. Used with permission of the McGraw-Hill Book Company, pp. 523–525.

body of individual and personality test data has been accumulated, which, together with a great deal of theoretical speculation about the psychology of conformity, gives a fairly clear picture of some of the basic determinants of conformity-proneness. Some of these determinants have to do with the effect of the individual's specific past experiences. Others have to do with his social roles. Others have to do with his basic personality make-up. These three classes of determinants are intimately and intricately interwoven.

PAST EXPERIENCE AND CONFORMITY. Every individual growing up in his society necessarily goes through a great many group-pressure situations, varying from the trivial to the deadly serious. The concrete nature of these events and the particular manner in which the individual has behaved in them play a major role in the shaping of his generalized "habits" of conforming or of resisting. The interpersonal response dispositions of the individual are the end products of his characteristic experiences in satisfying his wants.

The nature of the particular culture in which the individual grows up significantly shapes his conformity experiences. As many anthropologists have shown, primitive societies vary widely in the degree of conformity to social norms that they demand of their members. There is some evidence that modern national cultures, too, differ in the extent to which they inculcate conformity-proneness in their members. Cultures also differ in the salient wants engendered in their members, and this may differentially affect the way the individual learns to conform in satisfying these wants.

As part of this learning process the individual also comes to develop particular beliefs, values, attitudes with respect to the abstract concepts of "conformity" and "independence." And these values help govern in a powerful way just how ready he is to conform or to resist when he is faced with group pressure. He may, for instance, come to accept the idea that conforming is appropriate to a given social role and inappropriate to another.

SEX ROLE AND CONFORMITY. In our culture, and in many others, there would appear to be a pronounced difference in the definition of *sex roles* in regard to the matter of conformity. The typical feminine role tends to be defined as involving promulgation of the conventional values of the culture, dependence upon the group, submissiveness to the male, avoidance of disagreement with others in the interests of group harmony. The typical masculine role tends to lay more stress on the ideals of self-sufficiency, self-assertion, independence of thought, "standing on one's two feet and casting a shadow."

Thus the socially dictated *meaning* of the group-pressure situation might be expected to differ in significant aspects for males and for females, and females might be predicted to conform more readily in it. In Crutchfield's studies females consistently earned higher conformity scores than did males. Moreover, this difference tended to get larger as the testing session continued; on the average the conformity scores for males tended to decline over the duration of the session, whereas the average score for females tended to rise. Finally, there was evidence that high-conforming females tended to be generally characterized by easier acceptance of the conventional feminine role. On the contrary, many of the females who independently resisted the group pressure tended to be characterized by marked signs of conflict in their feelings about the conventional feminine role, by rejection of a dependent relationship with parents and with others, and by hostile attitudes toward family. On a personality scale intended to measure "socialization"[1] the independent females scored significantly lower than did the conforming females. Among males, it is interesting to note, there was little difference in socialization scores between the independents and the conformers.

It should be emphasized that, though females and males do differ on the average in conformity-proneness, there are still very large individual differences in conformity in both groups. In the many samples of persons tested, females, like males, ranged all the way from complete independence to complete conformity in their test performance. Obviously, there is much more to individual differences in conformity than is accounted for by "habits" or social roles. There still remain the basic personality variables.

[1] Gough, H. G., Theory and measurement of socialization, *J. Consult. Psychol.*, 1960, 24, 23–30.

6-C SOCIALIZATION AND BIOGENICALLY MOTIVATED BEHAVIOR

John W. McDavid (Psychologist) and Herbert Harari (Psychologist)

The physiological origins of biogenic motives are, of course, independent of social learning. Nevertheless, the socialization process is instrumental in governing the particular behavioral habits an individual uses to satisfy these motives. For several kinds of biologically based motivation, the mechanisms for their satisfaction are rather specific and automatic: breathing satisfies the need for oxygen and carbon dioxide elimination, and the behavior involved in breathing is subject to limited voluntary individual control. For others, such as the elimination of waste materials from the body, the specific mechanisms are at first automatic, but social learning may induce the individual to inhibit these mechanisms temporarily, allowing them to operate only under specific socially defined circumstances, in acceptable places at acceptable times. Several of the motivational systems in man for which the criteria of biogenic origin have been fairly well demonstrated are discussed below to give some general indication of the importance of the role of socialization in steering the individual's behavior, even when it is directed toward biologically defined objectives.

Hunger, Thirst, and Nourishment

Biologically based motivation directs behavior toward the maintenance of the living organism through ingestion of food and water. There is some evidence that under conditions of very extreme deprivation of specific nutritive substances, animals and men may unconsciously and automatically begin to show preferences for the deprived substance. But in the normal flow of behavior in the adequately nourished individual, his food preferences and food habits are largely products of socialization. Although human flesh may be adequately nutritive, most cultures forbid cannibalism under normal circumstances. Anthropological evidence suggests that even in the most primitive societies, the eating of human

SOURCE: John W. McDavid and Herbert Harari, *Social Psychology: Individuals, Groups, Societies* (New York: Harper & Row, Publishers, 1968), pp. 49–51.

flesh is sanctioned only in connection with isolated magical ceremonial rites. Members of our own society are normally horrified by even the thought of consuming human flesh. Most people acquire a preference for cooked meat and a keen distaste for raw flesh of any kind. Although among gourmets, highly seasoned raw beef may constitute a delicacy known as steak tartare, the uninitiated individual (that is, one not yet socialized into the elite society of gourmets) may be nauseated by this dish. Fried ants, rattlesnake steaks, and snails may be regarded as delectable by one individual, but as repulsive by another. What Americans know as corn was once regarded by the English (who know it as maize) as more suitable for stock feed than for human consumption. The thoroughly assimilated member of a vegetarian cult may keep himself adequately nourished on foods of vegetable origin and experience genuine distaste for meats of all kinds. The completely identified orthodox Jew systematically eliminates pork from his diet, and the devout Roman Catholic may rigidly shun certain foods during the Lenten season.

Human beings do not eat continuously, like grazing animals. The capacity of the stomach sets an upper limit on the amount that can be eaten at one time, and the time required for the digestive processes to be carried out places limits on the interval before the motive will again become sufficiently intense to dominate the direction of behavior. But within these limits, considerable variation occurs. Most Americans families concentrate their eating behavior into three fairly brief intervals during each 24-hour cycle. Some families habitually take a larger meal in the middle of the day and a smaller one at nightfall, but the majority make a larger meal of dinner than of lunch. The old English custom of tea in the midafternoon, the continental Latin American custom of a late supper shortly before retiring, and the Jamaican custom of "elevenses" in midmorning, all represent formalized subcultural consistencies in introducing an additional small meal into the 24-hour cycle. While the determination of these intervals is related to socialization, one should not assume that the hunger experienced by the Englishman in midafternoon, the Jamaican in midmorning, or the Latin American at midnight, is merely fantasied: his subjective experience of the desire for food at those times, a consequence of his learned adaptation to the prescriptions of his culture, is very real, at least to him.

The handling of utensils in the mechanics of eating behavior is also a product of socialization. The complexity of cultural prescriptions about the "manners" (i.e., socially acceptable patterns of behavior) of eating behavior, as well as the rapidity with which they are imposed upon the child during the course of the socialization in our culture are remarkable. While the nipple provides an entirely practical means of handling liquid foods, infants in our culture are at a very early age induced to utilize a cup or glass such as that used by adults. Furthermore, they are induced almost as soon as possible to supplement the milk diet with solid foods, and to use a spoon for handling them. But the spoon is not a socially acceptable utensil for solid foods for the adults, so the child is coerced into the use of a fork. He is further trained to hold it between certain fingers at a certain angle, and in a certain hand. Eventually, he is taught to recognize certain foods as requiring the use of a fork, rather than a spoon. By the time he is halfway to the social maturity of adulthood, he is expected to have learned an exceedingly complex catalog of proper and acceptable ways of handling the simple task of getting food into his mouth to supply his bodily needs. Many of these complexities are very practical (ice cream might melt and run through the tines of a fork, but meat is conveniently speared by the same tines), but others are not (round peas roll off a fork more readily than they would from a spoon and even though the best part of a stew might be its gravy, the spoon must not be used). Europeans learn to use the fork with the left hand, Americans with the right. Some foods may even be more practically and conveniently handled with the fingers than with utensils, but many subcultures are unrelentingly rigid about even this. In the southern United States, where fried chicken is prepared with a relatively ungreasy crust, it is permissible to use one's fingers for this food, but in Boston, where it is prepared in an oven and is therefore greasier, the use of one's fingers to eat fried chicken is considered gauche and unacceptable. But the Bostonian who has dry chicken and the Alabaman who has greasy chicken each will be considered socially proper only if he adheres to the conventions with which he has been socialized.

The complexity of our culture's social pronouncements about behavior that is basically motivated by biologically based hunger is fantastic, but not without reason. Eating behavior in our culture is highly interrelated with social interactions. Mealtime is a social time in our culture: a time of convocation of a family or friends. Since it serves also to satisfy a number of affiliative social needs, it is at least partially understandable that cultural conventions should be very elaborate in this area of behavior. The banquet, the ceremonial dinner, and the businessman's luncheon have all been used to serve more social than nutritional purposes.

B. RESEARCH AND APPLICATIONS

The first selection in this section (Krech, Crutchfield, and Ballachey) reviews research done on the effect of nationality and conformity. It is followed by a study (Stevenson and Odom) of the effectiveness of social reinforcement after social deprivation.

6-D NATIONALITY AND CONFORMITY

David Krech (Psychologist), Richard S. Crutchfield (Psychologist), and Egerton L. Ballachey (Psychologist)

Stanley Milgram, a social psychologist at Yale University, compared conformity-proneness of Norwegians and Frenchmen through the use of a modified form of the group-pressure technique. The subject judged which of two tones, delivered through headphones, was the longer. On prerecorded tape recordings, he would hear five taped judgments before he was asked to give his own. In 16 of the 30 trials (the "critical trials"), the prerecorded judgments were unanimously wrong. Milgram reports that the "synthetic groups" thus created were accepted as real groups by his subjects.

In the first experiment, the conformity-proneness of 20 Norwegian students at the University of Oslo was compared with a matched sample of French university students. The Norwegian students conformed to the group on 62 per cent of the critical trials; the French students, on 50 per cent.

In a second experiment the subjects were told that the results of the study would be used in the design of aircraft safety signals, thus linking their performance to a life-and-death matter. (This same instruction was used in all subsequent experiments.) As expected, the over-all amount of yielding was lower than in the first experiment. But, once again, the level of conformity was higher among the Norwegians (56 per cent) than among the French (48 per cent).

In the first two studies, the subjects made

SOURCE: David Krech, Richard S. Crutchfield and Egerton L. Ballachey, *Individual in Society*. Copyright 1962 by the McGraw-Hill Book Company, Inc., Used with permission of the McGraw-Hill Book Company, pp. 524–525.

their judgments aloud for all (or so they thought) to hear. In a third study, the subjects recorded their judgments on a secret ballot. As anticipated, the over-all amount of yielding dropped considerably, but once again the Norwegian students yielded more often (50 per cent) than the French students (34 per cent).

A fourth experiment tested the sensitivity of Norwegian and French subjects to various kinds of criticism from the group when they opposed majority opinion. Thus, for example, the Norwegian subject who opposed a majority opinion would hear *"Skal du stikke deg ut?"* ("Are you trying to show off?"); the French subject, *"Voulez-vous vous faire remarquer?"* ("Trying to be conspicuous?"). Criticism of nonconformity significantly increased conformity, but still again, the Norwegian subjects were less independent (yielding on 75 per cent of the trials) than the French (who yielded on 59 per cent). The Norwegian subjects accepted the criticism impassively. In dramatic contrast, more than half of the French subjects retaliated to the criticism of the group. Two of the French students became so enraged that they "directed a stream of abusive language at their taunters."

Many of the Norwegian subjects rationalized their yielding by saying that they doubted their own judgment and that, if they had been given an opportunity to dispel their doubts, they would have been more independent. In a fifth experiment, they were provided with this opportunity. The subjects were told if they wished to hear a pair of tones again they were to sound a bell. As in the fourth experiment, the subjects were censured for failure to conform, but not for asking to have a pair of tones repeated. Only 5 of the 20 Norwegian subjects asked for a repetition of a tone on any trial, whereas 14 of the French subjects were "bold" enough to do so. And, once again, the French students were more independent.

Milgram's impressions of the Norwegian and French societies throws some light upon his experimental findings.[1]

I found Norwegian society highly cohesive. Norwegians have a deep feeling of group identification, and they are strongly attuned to the needs and interests of those around them. Their sense of social responsibility finds expression in formidable institutions for the care and protection of Norwegian citizens. The heavy taxation required to support broad programs of social welfare is borne willingly. It would not be surprising to find that social cohesiveness of this sort goes hand in hand with a high degree of conformity.

Compared with the Norwegians, the French show far less consensus in both social and political life. The Norwegians have made do with a single constitution, drafted in 1814, while the French have not been able to achieve political stability within the framework of four republics. Though I hardly propose this as a general rule of social psychology, it seems true that the extreme diversity of opinion found in French national life asserts itself also on a more intimate scale. There is a tradition of dissent and critical argument that seeps down to the local *bistro*.

[1] Milgram, S. "Nationality and Conformity." *Sci. Amer.*, 1961, **205**, 45–51.

6-E THE EFFECTIVENESS OF SOCIAL REINFORCEMENT FOLLOWING TWO CONDITIONS OF SOCIAL DEPRIVATION

Harold W. Stevenson (Psychologist) and Richard D. Odom (Psychologist)

Gewirtz and Baer (1958a, 1958b) have demonstrated that the effectiveness of social reinforcement in modifying children's performance is increased by a brief period of social isolation preceding the experimental task. The results are interpreted as indicating that the effectiveness of a social reinforcer is increased by its own deprivation.

Another interpretation of these findings is possible. Isolation resulted in the deprivation of not only social but also of other types of stimuli. The children, therefore, may have been subjected to general stimulus deprivation rather than merely to deprivation of social stimuli. As a consequence, the effectiveness of social stimuli as reinforcers may be reduced when other types of stimuli are available during the deprivation period. One approach to determining the degree to which the increased effectiveness of social reinforcement is due specifically to the deprivation of social stimuli would be to isolate subjects in a setting providing a wide variety of other types of stimuli and to compare their performance with that occurring in a condition where other subjects were isolated without such stimuli.

This study investigates the effect of social reinforcement on children's performance in a simple operant task following three conditions: a control condition with no isolation; a "toy" condition in which the subject is left alone in a room filled with unusual and interesting toys with which he can play freely for a 15-minute period; an isolation condition in which the subject is left alone in the room with no toys for 15 minutes.

Method

SUBJECTS. The subjects were 30 boys and 30 girls attending kindergarten, first, and second grades of the Laboratory School of the University of Minnesota. The subjects were above average in intelligence and socioeconomic status.

APPARATUS. EXPERIMENTAL TASK. The apparatus was a red rectangular box, 22 inches long, 16 inches wide, and 12 inches deep. Two 8-inch square sunken bins were located on the top of the box. The right bin was covered

SOURCE: Harold W. Stevenson and Richard D. Odom, "The Effectiveness of Social Reinforcement Following Two Conditions of Social Deprivation"; *Journal of Abnormal and Social Psychology*, Vol. 65 (—, 1962), pp. 429–431.

by a Masonite plate with six ⅝-inch holes randomly placed on its surface. The floor of the right bin was covered with foam rubber and sloped toward a small aperture. As a marble passed through the aperture it activated a microswitch which in turn activated an electric counter. The left bin was filled with approximately 600 marbles of different colors.

The apparatus was placed on a child-sized table in an 8 foot × 7 foot room. The only other furnishing in the room was a chair for the experimenter behind the apparatus.

Pretraining Task. The pretraining room was 10.5 feet long and 10 feet wide and was located two rooms away from the experimental room. It contained two tables, two chairs, a sink, windows with drapes drawn and a one-way vision mirror.

For subjects in the Toy condition the tables and chairs were filled with toys. The toys included a drumming clown, a drinking rabbit, a rocking-telephoning bear, a ballon-blowing bear, a typewriting doll, a bouncing bird, a butterfly-chasing duck, a spiral shooting gun, a large stuffed bear, a stuffed rabbit, a beach ball, and a xylophone. All except the last seven toys were powered by batteries and were equipped with 2-foot extension cords with switches which could be easily operated by the children.

PROCEDURE. The subjects were randomly divided into three groups with an equal number of boys and girls in each group. For the two pretraining groups a 15-minute period in the pretraining room preceded the experimental task. In the Toy group the pretraining room contained the toys described above. In the Isolation group no toys were present. The preliminary 15-minute period was eliminated for the control group.

The subjects were obtained individually by the experimenter from their classroom. While the experimenter escorted the subject to the laboratory room, the experimenter attempted to gain rapport with the subject by talking about school and related matters. The experimenter was a female elementary teacher trained for the experiment.

Pretraining Task. For subjects in the Toy and Isolation groups the experimenter approached the experimental room and told the subject:

Now the game is in that room right there, but I have to get it ready. You wait in here and I will come and get you when the game is ready.

The experimenter walked with the subject into the pretraining room.

For the Isolation group the experimenter told the subject:

As soon as I get the game ready I will come back and get you. You wait in here until I get the game ready.

The experimenter went out of the room leaving the door partly open.

For the Toy group the experimenter told the subject:

I have a lot of toys in here and you can play with them while you are waiting. Play with any of the toys you want to and have fun.

The experimenter demonstrated how one of the mechanical toys worked. Again, the experimenter left the door partly open.

As the experimenter left the pretraining room she started a stopwatch and went to a hallway from which she could observe the subject's behavior through the one-way mirror of the pretraining room. At the conclusion of the 15-minute period the experimenter returned to the pretraining room and told the subject:

The game is ready. You can come with me now.

Experimental Task. The experimenter took the subject to the experimental room and said:

This is a game called Marble-in-the-Hole. I'll tell you how to play it. See these marbles. Well, they go in these holes like this. (The experimenter demonstrated.) You pick up the marbles one at a time and put them in these holes. I'll tell you when to stop. Remember, pick them up one at a time, and I'll tell you when to stop.

The task was concluded after 7 minutes.

After an average of every 15 responses the experimenter made a supportive comment about the subject's performance. The comments were delivered after every tenth, fifteenth, or twentieth response according to a prearranged random schedule. Six statements were used in a random order: Fine, Very good, That's fine, You're really good, Good, and Swell.

The experimenter counted the subject's responses in order to follow the reinforcement schedule, but the responses were also recorded electrically for each successive minute.

Results

The score used in the analysis of the results was a difference score obtained by subtracting the number of responses made during the first minute of the task from that for each successive minute. This procedure was adopted to reduce the effect of individual differences in response rate.

The average number of responses during the first minute of the game was 25.8. A 2 × 3 analysis of variance with entries for sex of subject and condition resulted in no significant main effects and in a nonsignificant interaction ($Fs < 1.00$). Performance during the first minute of the game may be assumed to be approximately the same in all conditions.

The major results of the study are summarized in Figure 1, which presents the average difference score obtained by each group for 2-minute intervals after the first minute of the task. The highest scores occurred in the Isolation group and the lowest in the Control group. The scores of subjects in the Toy group were slightly below those of the Isolation subjects. A facilitating effect, which persisted throughout the task, was evident in the Isolation and

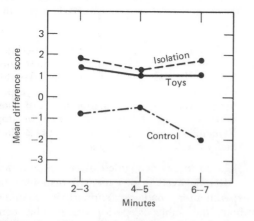

Figure 1. The average difference score for each group for 2-minute intervals following the first minute.

Toy groups. The subjects in the Control group showed a decrement in performance after the first minute of the task which increased during the last 2 minutes.

These data were subjected to a 2 × 3 analysis of variance. The F associated with condition was significant at the .05 level ($F = 3.76$, $df = 2/54$). The F associated with sex of subject was not significant ($F < 1.00$), nor was the interaction term ($F = 2.64$, $df = 2/54$, $p > .05$).

Discussion

The toys appeared to be very attractive to the subjects and they played with them with enthusiasm. When no toys were present the subjects sat quietly, sighed, peered around the room, and showed other indications of impatience and boredom. Although some subjects in the Toy group showed some of these types of behavior towards the end of the 15-minute period, the behavior of the two groups was in general quite dissimilar.

The greater effectiveness of social reinforcement in modifying performance in the Isolation group compared to the Control group corroborates the results of Gewirtz and Baer (1958a, 1958b). The greater effectiveness of a female experimenter with boys than with girls found by Gewirtz and Baer was not obtained; however, older subjects were used in the present study.

The presence of other stimuli during the Isolation period did not result in a significant decrease in the effectiveness of social reinforcement over that obtained when no toys were present. Although the difference scores for the subjects in the Toy group are consistently below those in the Isolation group, the difference is not significant ($t < 1.00$). Perhaps with a larger number of subjects or with a more sensitive measure of performance a significant difference would emerge. For the present, however, it may be tentatively concluded that the greater effectiveness of social reinforcement following isolation is primarily dependent upon deprivation of social stimuli, rather than on more general stimulus deprivation.

Summary

Three groups of elementary school children were presented with a simple operant task in which the insertion of marbles into a series of holes was verbally reinforced. The first group of subjects played alone for 15 minutes in a room containing a variety of interesting toys. The second group was left alone for 15 minutes with no toys. A control group received no pre-experimental treatment. Analysis of variance indicated a significant difference among conditions. The Isolation group showed the greatest increase in response rate after the first minute of the task and the Control group the lowest. The performance of the Toy group did not differ significantly from that of the Isolation group. The results are interpreted as tentatively supporting the hypothesis that the increased effectiveness of social reinforcement following isolation is primarily dependent upon the deprivation of social stimuli rather than upon more general stimulus deprivation.

REFERENCES

Gewirtz, J. L., & Baer, D. M. Deprivation and satiation of social reinforcers as drive conditions. *J. Abnorm. Soc. Psychol.*, 1958, **57**, 165–172. (a)

Gewirtz, J. L., & Baer, D. M. The effect of brief social deprivation on behaviors for a social reinforcer. *J. Abnorm. Soc. Psychol.*, 1958, **56**, 49–56. (b)

INDIVIDUAL INFLUENCES

7 / Motivation

A. BACKGROUND AND THEORY

This section begins with a statement (Brink and Kelley) on human motivation. This is followed by a description (Edwards) of a personality scale for assessment of motives.

7-A HUMAN MOTIVATION

Edward L. Brink (Marketing Educator) and
William G. Kelley (Marketing Educator)

When physiological cell activity burns up energy and exhausts food compounds, the organism's homeostasis is upset, and food-seeking activities are set in motion to replace the material in question. The pressure of waste products arouses activities which eliminate both the waste products and the pressure. Accumulation of fatigue products inhibits activity and gives the organism a chance to dispel them. In abnormally high temperatures normal body temperature is maintained by withdrawal or other suitable adjustment by simple organisms and sweating by more complex creatures.

In very simple terms, the disturbance of homeostatic equilibrium results in a deprivation; the deprivation *drives* the organism to take action to restore homeostasis. Thus, we speak of a hunger drive, thirst drive, and sex drive. The altered physiological state creates a deprivation or need. As soon as a higher organism is aware of the need, it becomes a want. The appropriate action which the creature takes to fulfill or satisfy that need is called motivated behavior. The organism has a drive (hunger); it has an incentive (objects in the external environment suitable for food); it has

a motive (incentive-directed behavior). The motive leads it to explore its surroundings and capture a suitable supply of food objects. Drives provide the "push from within"; motives afford a "push in some relevant direction." However, it is more useful to speak of "motivation" or "motive" than of "drives," since a motive is purposeful. The organism has a drive or felt need for something and knows what kind of substance or object from its environment is required to lessen the tension created by the deprivation; its resulting activities are goal-directed toward the incentive.

Writers on motivation often differentiate between needs and wants. A need arises from a deprivation drive; when the human senses this need, when it breaks through the threshold of his consciousness and he becomes aware of it, then a want is created. We are all busy satisfying our various wants, but we must not lose sight of the fact that more primitive motivation lies behind them.

By now it should be obvious that a study of human motivation is vital to an understanding of the selling and advertising processes. Nothing happens so long as the organism's homeostasis is maintained in a constant state. Only when disturbed by a biological drive or some external event does action occur. The job of the sales or advertising man is to induce an alteration of behavior through suitable conditioning. He must call attention to the need,

SOURCE: Edward L. Brink and William G. Kelley, *The Management of Promotion: Consumer Behavior and Demand Similation.* © 1962 Reprinted by permission of Prentice-Hall Inc., Englewood, New Jersey, pp. 86-101.

changing it to a want. Then he must demonstrate how his product or service provides the best solution to the want. Sometimes he actually creates a want for the kind of product he is promoting, although it is doubtful that he can ever create a need for it.

7-B THE ASSESSMENT OF HUMAN MOTIVES BY MEANS OF PERSONALITY SCALES

Allen L. Edwards (Psychologist)

The process of socialization, as I view it, is concerned with teaching a child to do those things that are considered desirable and not to do those things that are considered undesirable by society. The child may not learn to behave in accordance with society's norms of desirability, but it seems reasonable to believe that he will learn what these norms are. I would think that by the time an individual has reached adolescence, if not earlier, he has a very good understanding of what is considered socially desirable and socially undesirable by others, that is, by society.

In the discussion that follows, I shall describe one way in which we might quantify norms of social desirability. I shall then consider the role that these norms may play in our attempts to study and describe human motives by means of self-reports of the kind ordinarily obtained with personality scales.

If one wishes to study or to describe the motives of an individual one must make appropriate observations of his behavior. We may have observed how an individual has behaved in the past or we may design experimental situations and observe how an individual behaves under the specific conditions of the experimental setting. Our observations may be made in the course of a clinical or nonclinical interview. We may observe responses to cards in the Thematic Apperception Test (TAT) or to Rorschach ink blots or to statements of the kind found in personality inventories and scales. On the basis of the observations made, we may then attempt to infer something about a given motive or group of motives. Thus, a motive may be regarded as a construct or as a response-inferred organismic variable. As a construct, a motive has the same status as any other psychological construct. The validity

of any proposed index or measure of a motive can then be investigated by the same methods and procedures that are ordinarily used in studies of construct validity.[1]

Although, as I have indicated, one might observe various kinds of responses in attempting to devise an index of a motive, I propose to confine my remarks to one particular kind of response: a True or a False response to an item or statement in a scale. Presumably, if we want to develop a scale to measure a particular motive, we would include in the scale those items or statements that we believe to be relevant to the particular motive under consideration. For example, if we want to develop a scale to measure a student's motivation to achieve good grades in college, we would include in the scale those items we believe to be relevant to this motive. One candidate for inclusion in the scale might be the statement "I study very hard." Another might be "I think there are many things more important in college than getting good grades." The statements included in the scale may refer to behavior, to feelings, or to beliefs.

If we have developed a scale consisting of *n* statements which we believe may provide an index of a given motive, we could give the scale to an individual and ask him to respond True or False to each item or statement in the scale. The responses that he makes to each of the items can, in turn, be described as keyed or non-keyed. A keyed response is one which we believe indicates the presence of the motive and a non-keyed response is one which we believe indicates the absence of the motive. For example, the keyed response to the item "I study very hard" would be True and the keyed response to the item "I think there are many things more important in college than getting good grades" would be False. The individual's score on the scale would be the

SOURCE: Allen L. Edwards, "The Assessment of Human Motives by Means of Personality Scales," *Nebraska Symposium in Motivation* (Lincoln, Nebraska: University of Nebraska Press, 1964), pp. 135–139.

[1] Cronbach, L. J., & Meehl, P. E. "Construct Validity in Psychological tests," *Psychol. Bull.*, 1955, **52**, 281–302.

number of keyed responses he has given to the set of *n* items or statements.

Since I am concerned with general principles and no specific motives, I want to cite a few other selected examples of the kinds of statements we might have in various scales without specifying the particular motives which the statements might possibly measure. Here are some of the kinds of statements I have in mind:

I don't like to make things with my hands.
I have been known to throw or break things when I am angry.
I have difficulty in admitting I am wrong about something.
I can be counted upon to see that a job gets done.
I often get so involved in my work that I lose track of what time it is.
I never received a grade lower than a C in any of my courses in high school.

I stated earlier that I believe that the process of socialization involves the association of a value with every act of behavior, every belief, every feeling. To take this position is not to deny the possibility of acts which may be neutral, that is, acts which are considered neither desirable nor undesirable. I would argue, therefore, that there exists a continuum, ranging from highly socially undesirable, through neutral, to highly socially desirable and that every descriptive statement such as we might have in a scale can be located on this continuum. I call this continuum the *social desirability continuum.*

Suppose, for example, that we have a large population of *N* statements. This population may include many subsets of *n* statements with each of these subsets representing the set of statements which we might include in a scale to measure a particular motive. We can present the complete population of *N* statements, one at a time, to a group of judges and ask them to rate each statement on a 9-point scale ranging from highly undesirable, through neutral, to highly desirable. We would find that some statements are judged, on the average, as being highly desirable, others as highly undesirable, and still others would fall between these two extremes. I refer to this average rating of a statement as the *social desirability scale value* of the statement.

B. RESEARCH AND APPLICATIONS

Motivational theory is valuable if applied and tested. Two aspects of consumer motivation are developed in the selections in the present section: the reclassification of product buying motives (Udell), and a method of discovering people's aspirations (Cantril).

7-C A NEW APPROACH TO CONSUMER MOTIVATION

Jon G. Udell (Marketing Educator)

The importance of customer buying motives in the marketing success of a product was emphasized forty years ago in the pioneering work of Melvin T. Copeland.[1] In an attempt to present a classification of motives useful to business management, Copeland proposed separating them into two categories, rational and emotional:

SOURCE: Jon G. Udell, "A New Approach to Consumer Motivation," *Journal of Retailing*, Vol. 40 (Winter, 1964–65), pp. 6–10.
[1] Melvin T. Copeland, *Principles of Merchandising* (New York: A. W. Shaw Company, 1924), pp. 155–167.

Rational buying motives are those which are aroused by appeals to reason. The group includes such motives as dependability in use, durability, and economy in purchase.[2]

Emotional buying motives include emulation, satisfaction of the appetite, pride of personal appearance, cleanliness, pleasure of recreation, securing home comfort, and analogous motives. These motives have their origin in human instincts and emotions and represent impulse or unreasoning promptings to action.[3]

[2] *Op. cit.,* p. 162.
[3] *Ibid.*

Copeland's approach is still widely used in the literature of marketing and advertising. Each year thousands of college men and women, preparing to take their place in the world of business, learn that buying motives fall into these two categories, and that the type of motive should determine the nature of the appeal to be used in merchandising the product.

Despite the appeal and continued use of Copeland's rational-emotional distinction, the classification is not adequate to meet today's needs. It is, at best, confusing and may be damaging in the implications it conveys to marketing management.

Many objections can be raised to its continued use, three of which are covered by the following remarks:

1. The choice of expressions to describe the two types of motives is very unfortunate. By labeling one set of motives rational, the other group is assumed to be not rational or irrational. However, it is not irrational to seek emotional satisfaction. Vast numbers of American consumers are far beyond satisfying their basic physical needs for survival, and consequently are also striving to satisfy their emotional and psychological desires. Such satisfaction often constitutes very real utility for both individuals and society as a whole. In short, *emotionally based purchases are often very rational purchases.*

2. The definitions used to differentiate between emotional and rational motives are meaningless and contradictory. Emotional buying motives, according to Copeland, have their origins in human instincts and emotions and, as such, represent impulse buying and unreasoned purchasing. However, many goods are purchased for emotional and psychological reasons after considerable deliberation and thought. Surely this is the application of the process of reasoning to the purchasing decision (which contradicts the original definition). A similar criticism can be leveled at Copeland's assertion that rational buying motives are those which are aroused by appeals to reason. Most buying motives can be aroused by appeals to reason. Many advertising campaigns have hit pay dirt by using reason to help the customer rationalize his emotional desire for a product. In addition, it is often effective to appeal directly to the customer's judgment by emphasizing the emotional satisfaction to be gained from a particular product or service. In brief, there may be a continuous interplay of emotion and reason in all types of consumer buying motives.

3. In light of the above comments, it follows that the rational-emotional classification is of little value to management in designing a marketing program. Should the vendors of sailboats use a rational or an emotional appeal? If an emotional appeal is used, should it appeal directly to the desires for recreation and prestige, or should it appeal indirectly by attempting to rationalize these desires for the consumer? The classification gives little guidance in answering these and other important questions.

A Reclassification of Product Buying Motives

The objective of this reclassification is to identify buying motives in a way that will guide managerial decision-making toward the development of effective marketing programs. The buyer's needs and desires must be appealed to and satisfied, and this satisfaction can be derived from the following sources:

1. The product's physical performance, or
2. The consumer's social and psychological interpretation of the product and its performance, or
3. A combination of the product's physical performance and the consumer's social and psychological interpretation of the product.

Given the two basic sources of satisfaction, physical performance and sociopsychological interpretation, product buying motives may be classified according to two extremes, those which are *operational* and those which are *sociopsychological.*

Operational buying motives include those reasons for the purchase that are directly related to the anticipated performance of the product. In other words, their satisfaction is derived from the product's physical performance. The majority of product buying motives for industrial goods falls within this class. For example, a road construction company purchases a new dump truck because it will serve the firm by hauling construction materials. A consumer's operational buying motive may be illustrated by a Michigan homeowner's desire to have an efficient oil burner to heat his home.

Sociopsychological buying motives comprise those reasons for the purchase that are indirectly related to the anticipated performance of the product and directly related to the consumer's social and psychological interpretation of the product. The utility that the consumer receives is only indirectly derived from the product's physical performance. The direct source of utility is the psychological satisfaction that the consumer receives through the ownership, use, and social prestige of the product. This psychological satisfaction may be received at the buyer's conscious or subconscious level of thought. If a young lady receives psychological satisfaction from a bottle of expensive French perfume because she associates it with an advertisement picturing a heavy romance, she is probably receiving psychological satisfaction at a subconscious level. However, if the satisfaction is primarily derived from her belief in the social prestige of the perfume, the psychological satisfaction is received at a more conscious level.

THE BUYING MOTIVE CONTINUUM

Operational Buying Motives	Psychological Buying Motives
Satisfaction to be derived from physical performance of product	Satisfaction to be derived from consumer's social and psychological interpretation of the product and its performance

The potential source of satisfaction is the controlling factor in distinguishing between the two types of buying motives. However, it is important to recognize that a product is rarely purchased on the basis of one motive, and that the motives inducing a purchase can seldom be classified as entirely sociopsychological or entirely operational. Therefore, the motives inducing the purchase of a product should be visualized as existing on the continuum between the two extreme types of buying motives.

The suggested classification takes on a fuller meaning when it is applied to the marketing strategy of the business firm. Although all aspects of the marketing program may relate to both the sociopsychological and operational buying motives, advertising and sales efforts are most closely related to the sociopsychological buying motives, whereas the quality of the product and product service are most closely related to the operational buying motives.

It is suggested that this set of relationships can be used in allocating marketing efforts between product and sales efforts. Suppose a cosmetics manufacturer were to analyze the buying motives and purchasing behavior involved in the purchase of cosmetics. The manufacturer finds that some minimum quality level is important, but that many major factors in the consumer's purchase relate to the individual's psychological interpretation of the product and the social prestige of the product. Assuming that the minimum quality level is met, the manufacturer will find it most profitable to invest his marketing efforts in advertising and sales promotion. These efforts should be designed to create a favorable product image, an image which would appeal to the consumer's sociopsychological buying motives.

7-D DISCOVERING PEOPLE'S ASPIRATIONS: THE METHOD USED

Hadley Cantril (Psychologist)

The methodological problem faced in this study was essentially that of devising some means to get an overall picture of the reality worlds in which people lived, a picture expressed by individuals *in their own terms*; and to do this in such a way that without sacrificing authenticity or prescribing any boundaries or fixed categories it would still be possible to make meaningful comparisons between different individuals, groups of individuals, and societies. The aim was to uncover the limits and boundaries to aspirations set by internalized social norms, by all the group identifications that people learn in their particular social milieu and that serve as subjective standards for satisfaction or frustration.

The problem is a very basic one for the social scientist. For everyone—whether of high or low status, a Communist or a democrat, a sophisticated Westerner or a caveman—has subjective standards which guide behavior and define satisfactions. These standards can change radically within an individual's lifetime so that what was once regarded as a goal may disappear or be taken for granted as new sights come into play. Furthermore, the quality of any person's relationship to his group or his society is determined by the assumptions he has built up which define for him the degree and nature of his satisfactions or dissatisfactions with that group or society. The problem is to learn what these standards are in a person's own terms and not judge them by our own standards.

Thus, what is needed, of course, is a method that will not obscure the close interdependence between an individual's purposes and his perceptions and one that will differentiate frustrations due to an uncertainty of what goals to strive for from frustrations due to the means of achieving goals that were clearly in mind. Clearly, an accurate appraisal of an individual's reality world can never be obtained if he is forced to make choices or selections between categories, alternatives, symbols, or situations as these are posed in the usual type of ques-

tionnaire. Yet, without some such preconceived classifications, how can a final research instrument be obtained that allows for quantitative comparisons?

The Self-Anchoring Striving Scale

The solution was to invent what I call the Self-Anchoring Striving Scale, a direct outgrowth of the transactional point of view. This scale seems to provide a simple, widely applicable, and adaptable technique for tapping the unique reality world of an individual and learning what it has in common with that of others.

A person is asked to define on the basis of *his own* assumptions, perceptions, goals, and values the two extremes or anchoring points of the spectrum on which some scale measurement is desired—for example, he may be asked to define the "top" and "bottom," the "good" and "bad," the "best" and the "worst." This self-defined continuum is then used as our measuring device.

While the Self-Anchoring Striving Scale technique can be used on a wide variety of problems, it was utilized in this study as a means of discovering the spectrum of values a person is preoccupied or concerned with and by means of which he evaluates his own life. He describes as the top anchoring point his wishes and hopes as he personally conceives them and the realization of which would constitute for him the best possible life. At the other extreme, he describes the worries and fears, the preoccupations and frustrations, embodied in his conception of the worst possible life he could imagine. Then, utilizing a nonverbal ladder device (see Figure 1), symbolic of "the ladder of life," he is asked where he thinks he stands on the ladder today, with the top being the best life *as he has defined it*, the bottom the worst life *as he has defined it*. He is also asked where he thinks he stood in the past and where he thinks he will stand in the future. He is then asked similar questions about the best and worst possible situations he can imagine for his country so his aspirations and fears on the national level can be learned.

SOURCE: Hadley Cantril, *The Pattern of Human Concerns* (New Brunswick, New Jersey: Rutgers University Press, 1965), pp. 21–24.

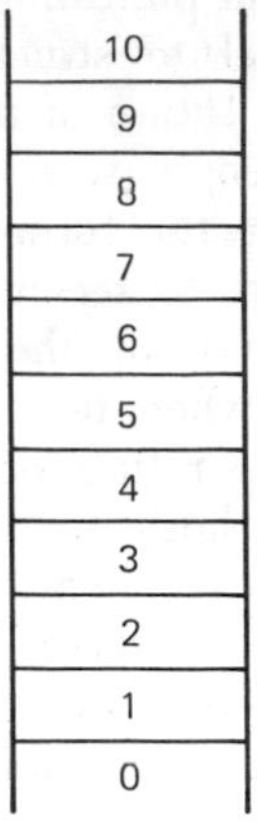

```
10
 9
 8
 7
 6
 5
 4
 3
 2
 1
 0
```

Figure 1. Ladder device.

Again, the ladder is used to find out where he thinks his country stands today, where it stood in the past, and where it will stand in the future.

The actual questions, together with the parenthetical instructions to interviewers, are given below:

1. (A) All of us want certain things out of life. When you think about what really matters in your own life, what are your wishes and hopes for the future? In other words, if you imagine your future in the *best* possible light, what would your life look like then, if you are to be happy? Take your time in answering: such things aren't easy to put into words.

   Permissible Probes: What are your hopes for the future? What would your life have to be like for you to be completely happy? What is missing for you to be happy? (Use also, if necessary, the words "dreams" and "desires.")

   Obligatory Probe: Anything else?

   (B) Now, taking the other side of the picture, what are your fears and worries about the future? In other words, if you imagine your future in the *worst* possible light, what would your life look like then? Again, take your time in answering.

   Permissible Probe: What would make you unhappy? (Stress the words "fears" and "worries.")

   Obligatory Probe: Anything else?
   Here is a picture of a ladder. Suppose we say that the top of the ladder (*pointing*) represents the best possible life for you and the bottom (*pointing*) represents the worst possible life for you.

   (C) Where on the ladder (*moving finger rapidly up and down ladder*) do you feel you personally stand at the *present* time? Step number _____.

   (D) Where on the ladder would you say you stood *five years ago?* Step number _____.

   (E) And where do you think you will be on the ladder *five years from now?* Step number _____.

2. (A) Now, what are your wishes and hopes for the future of our country? If you picture the future of (name of country) in the *best* possible light, how would things look, let us say, ten years from now?

   Obligatory Probe: Anything else?

   (B) And what about your fears and worries for the future of our country? If you picture the future of (name of country) in the *worst* possible light, how would things look about ten years from now?

   Obligatory Probe: Anything else?

   (C) Now, looking at the ladder again, suppose your greatest hopes for (name of country) are at the top (*pointing*); your worst fears at the bottom (*pointing*). Where would you put (name of country) on the ladder (*moving finger rapidly up and down ladder*) *at the present time?* Step number _____.

   (D) Where did (name of country) stand *five years ago?* Step number _____.

   (E) Just as your best guess, where do you think (name of country) will be on the ladder *five years from now?* Step number _____.

A number of questions were then asked to give details about the individual's background: age, occupation, religion, education, whether or not he owned his own land or was an agricultural worker, marital status, political preference, economic status, and the like. These items, of course, had to be varied in different cultures according to what was and was not relevant, what was and was not pos- sible to obtain, such as political preference in certain countries.

It will be noticed that on the questions deal- ing with personal aspirations and fears, when a person was asked to imagine his future in the best and worst possible lights, the ques- tion was left open without any specification of what was meant by the future; whereas when asked about the future with respect to the nation, the question included the phrase "How would things look, let us say, ten years from now?" But in both the personal and national questions when the ladder ratings were ob- tained, people estimated where they felt they, or the nation, stood five years before or would stand five years from then. The reason for this was that in careful pretesting it was found un- wise and artificial to structure the personal future, but if the future of the nation was left indeterminate, people were bewildered. Peo- ple could imagine the future of their country as they might like to see it or as they might fear it a decade from the time they were questioned. But when it came to the actual task of making a rating on the ladder, the ten-year interval both for personal and na- tional seemed too far away to be predictable, and so the five-year interval was used.

Interviewers were instructed to take verba- tim reports as much as possible. All interviewers were, of course, natives of the country, or, where it was important, of the region of the country in which they interviewed.

8 / Emotions

A. BACKGROUND AND THEORY

The first section consists of two brief statements by psychologists: the first one (Baughman and Welsh) about anxiety, and the other (Brehm and Cohen) about commitment and cognitive dissonance.

8-A REDUCTION OF ANXIETY

E. Earl Baughman (Psychologist) and George Schlager Welsh (Psychologist)

We investigate anxiety because it does affect performance, but beyond that, since it is a painful experience, we also attempt to discover its origin and development so that we can learn how to reduce it. Before scientists began to attack the problem of anxiety, however, people, through trial and error, had worked out a number of methods to cope with it. Ordinarily, of course, we all make use of defense mechanisms to ward off anxiety. But when these are not adequate to the task, we seek relief through (1) increasing our mastery of, or competence in, the anxiety-provoking situation, (2) securing reassurance or support from others [and certain other means].

Increasing Competence

Many people feel anxious when they have to undertake some new and unfamiliar task. Complaints of tension and nervousness are common under novel circumstances, such as learning to drive a car or going away to school for the first time. But with experience in driving, a person acquires confidence in his ability—sometimes too much—and speeding down a highway becomes a pleasure rather than an anxiety-ridden affair. And although the first day on campus—amidst strange surroundings,

SOURCE: E. Earl Baughman and George Schlager Welsh, *Personality: A Behavioral Science.* © 1962. Reprinted by permission of Prentice-Hall, Inc., Englewood Cliffs, New Jersey, pp. 446–448.

with complicated forms to be filled out in registration and time schedules to meet in unfamiliar and ill-marked buildings—tends to make a student anxious, when the second semester begins, he is used to the routine and less anxious—even though the routine may arouse other feelings, such as annoyance. In general, then, when a person has attained competence in some skill and is familiar with the demands that will be made on his abilities, his level of anxiety tends to be reduced. This, indeed, is why we noted earlier that the constructive effects of anxiety must not be neglected—for to reduce our anxieties, we are often spurred on to learn new skills or to increase our competence in old ones.

Support from Others

Competence does not always guarantee freedom from anxiety, however. For example, if you ask a friend who is a highly competent football player how he feels just before a game, he is likely to admit that he is anxious. Or take a student who has learned his lessons letter-perfectly; even he may fail to respond accurately to a teacher's question because of anxiety. In situations like these, we commonly turn to other persons for support. We might say that anxiety stimulates affiliative behavior because, somehow, association with others is reassuring.

Developmentally speaking, seeking reassurance through contacts with others seems to go back to the early mother-child relationship. Disturbed children, for example, regain their poise by being cuddled in their mothers' arms, just as Harlow's monkeys sought contact with cloth-covered inanimate mothers when they were frightened. As we grow older, we learn to be less directly dependent on our mothers, but we still find that some type of psycholog-

ical contact with others is helpful during our anxious periods. Our football player, for example, would probably be even more anxious before the game if he had to wait alone rather than in the company of his coaches and fellow players. And our anxious student, if he is supported and assisted by an understanding teacher rather than threatened, may be able to proceed more effectively and less anxiously.

8-B   THE THEORY AND THE ROLE OF COMMITMENT

Jack W. Brehm (Psychologist) and Arthur R. Cohen (Psychologist)

Cognitive dissonance, according to Festinger, is a psychological tension having motivational characteristics. The theory of cognitive dissonance concerns itself with the conditions that arouse dissonance in an individual and with the ways in which dissonance can be reduced.

The units of the theory are cognitive elements and the relationships between them. Cognitive elements or cognitions are "knowledges" or items of information, and they may pertain to oneself or to one's environment. Knowledge of one's feelings, behavior, and opinions as well as knowledge about the location of goal objects, how to get to them, what other people believe, and so forth, are examples of cognitive elements.

The relation that exists between two elements is *consonant* if one implies the other in some psychological sense. Psychological implication may arise from cultural mores, pressure to be logical, behavioral commitment, past experience, and so on. What is meant by implication is that having a given cognition, A, leads to having another given cognition, B. The detection of psychological implication is frequently possible by measurement of what else a person expects when he holds a given cognition.

A *dissonant* relationship exists between two cognitive elements when a person possesses one which follows from the obverse of another that he possesses. Thus, if A implies B, then holding A and the obverse of B is dissonant. A person experiences dissonance, that is, a motivational tension, when he has cognitions

among which there are one or more dissonant relationships. Cognitive elements that are neither dissonant nor consonant with each other are said to be irrelevant.

The amount of dissonance associated with a given cognition is a function of the importance of that cognition and the one with which it is dissonant. The magnitude of dissonance is also a function of the ratio of dissonant to consonant cognitions, where each cognitive element is weighted for its importance to the person. As the number and/or importance of dissonant cognitions increases, relative to the number and/or importance of consonant cognitions, the magnitude of dissonance increases.

In general, a person may reduce dissonance by decreasing the number and/or importance of dissonant elements compared to consonant, or he may reduce the importance of all relevant elements together.

In order to be perfectly clear about how the theory works, we will give a hypothetical example, to illustrate how dissonance may be aroused and reduced when a person chooses between two attractive alternatives. Suppose that a person is going to buy a new car and is considering both sedans and station wagons. Since he cannot afford to buy both, and since he ordinarily buys a car once every 3 or 4 years, he must choose carefully. Prior to making his final decision, he will carefully weigh the pros and cons of each kind of car. Let us suppose, then, that the person in our example has gone through this process and has finally decided to buy the station wagon. What can we say about him in terms of dissonance theory?

It should be clear that all of the good or positive aspects of the station wagon that the

SOURCE: Jack W. Brehm and Arthur R. Cohen, *Explorations in Cognitive Dissonance* (New York: John Wiley & Sons, Inc., 1962), pp. 3–6.

buyer knows about constitute cognitive elements that "lead to," or are consonant with, his knowledge that he has bought the station wagon and will be using it for the next 3 or 4 years. Other cognitions that are consonant are those knowledges of bad or unpleasant aspects of the sedan that he rejected. Still other cognitions, however, will almost inevitably be dissonant with—that is, follow from the obverse of—knowledge of this choice. These are the knowledges of bad or unpleasant aspects of the station wagon and good or favorable aspects of the sedan. Any of these latter cognitive elements would have led the person to buy the sedan rather than the station wagon. If the person holds any cognitions that would have led him to buy the sedan rather than the station wagon, he will experience dissonance consequent to choosing the station wagon.

The amount of dissonance experienced by the person depends on the ratio of dissonant to consonant elements, where each element is weighted according to its importance to him. Thus, if the only dissonant element is that the sedan has a softer ride than the station wagon, and if the individual really doesn't consider a soft ride to be an important quality of his car, then little dissonance will be created. It could also happen that a soft ride is considered very important, but the advantages of having a station wagon outweigh this factor so much that, again, little dissonance would be experienced. In sum, the magnitude of dissonance experienced depends directly on the number and/or importance of dissonant cognitions *relative* to the number and/or importance of consonant cognitions.

Many derivations follow from the above formulation. For example, with the attractiveness of the chosen alternative held constant, the greater the attractiveness of the rejected alternative, the greater the magnitude of dissonance. With the relative attractiveness of two alternatives held constant, the more attractive they both are, the greater is the magnitude of dissonance. And with the attractiveness of two alternatives held constant, the greater the amount of cognitive overlap (qualities in common) between them, the less the magnitude of dissonance. The extreme case of this latter derivation is that there will be no dissonance aroused by a choice between two identical alternatives, for there are no cognitions that lead to choosing one rather than the other.

Returning to our buyer who has just chosen a station wagon, let us see how he may try to reduce his dissonance. In general, of course, he may try to reduce the number and/or importance of dissonant, relative to consonant, cognitive elements, or he may try to reduce the general importance of all of these relevant elements. What this means specifically is that he may try to eliminate or reduce the importance of dissonant elements, such as the good or favorable aspects of the sedan or the unfavorable aspects of the station wagon. At the same time he may try to increase the number and/or importance of cognitions that are consonant with buying the station wagon, such as favorable aspects of the station wagon and the unfavorable aspects of the sedan. He might also try to eliminate dissonant cognitions and add consonant cognitions by trying to convince other people that station wagons are better than sedans and thereby gain social support for his selection. Similarly, he might seek out information, such as advertisements, that is expected to point out the benefits of owning a station wagon. These, then, are some of the consequences that we might expect from dissonance aroused by a choice.

B. RESEARCH AND APPLICATIONS

A number of psychologists have developed theories as to the individual's analysis of various situations as influenced by emotional factors. One of the best known of these theories is Leon Festinger's theory of cognitive dissonance. The first reading (Holloway) describes a test of the theory that involved four dissonant-producing factors simultaneously. The second selection (Oshikawa) raises questions about the theory's applicability to many areas of consumer behavior.

8-C AN EXPERIMENT ON CONSUMER DISSONANCE

Robert J. Holloway (Marketing Educator)

How can the theory of cognitive dissonance be applied or used by marketing practitioners? The theory itself is fairly well known—that there may exist dissonant or "nonfitting" relations among cognitive elements.[1]

But how is this idea relevant to the field of marketing? Three articles dealing with cognitive dissonance have appeared in the *Journal of Marketing*;[2] but even so, substantial research remains to be carried out before marketers can be sure of the value of the theory to marketing.

Consumers continually are receiving various kinds of information about products from friends, advertisements, and salesmen. These pieces of information are *cognitions* which, according to the theory of cognitive dissonance, consumers like to have consistent with one another. The theory is that if cognitions are inconsistent, consumers try to reduce the inconsistency, that is, to reduce dissonance, and that consumers try to reduce dissonance *after* making a buying decision.

Thus, a buyer who selects Brand A over other brands might experience dissonance because he is aware of attractive features of the rejected brand and unattractive features of chosen Brand A. One way for him to reduce dissonance would be to read advertisements of Brand A that would reinforce his buying decision.

However, an analysis of consumer behavior involves many interacting forces, and the post-decision emphasis of dissonance theory represents only one facet of the multi-facet problem. Even so, the theory may be useful.

Consider such questions as the following. Does dissonance relate to brand loyalty? Can marketers improve their position by helping consumers reduce any dissonance they might have developed? How does a salesman handle anticipated dissonance on the part of a potential customer? What can a salesman do in the pre-decision conflict period? How similar should alternatives be for the buyer? How many alternatives should be presented? Are impulse purchases apt to be dissonance-producing? Does planning on the part of the buyer aid the process of dissonance reduction?

Post-decision dissonance is caused by a number of factors identified by psychologists in experiments, and most of these factors relate to buying decisions. Table 1 represents an attempt to place these dissonance-arousing factors in a buying context.

As indicated in Table 1, dissonance may operate in one buying situation and not in another. Further, several factors may operate simultaneously: one may be dissonance-producing and two others may not be. Subsequently, the aroused dissonance may be reduced in a variety of ways. The buyer may

SOURCE: Robert J. Holloway, "An Experiment on Consumer Dissonance," *Journal of Marketing*, Vol. 31 (January, 1967) pp. 39–43.

[1] Leon Festinger, *A Theory of Cognitive Dissonance* (Evanston, Illinois: Row, Peterson and Company, 1957).

[2] James F. Engel, "Are Automobile Purchasers Dissonant Consumers?" *Journal of Marketing*, Vol. 27 (April, 1963), pp. 55–58; Bruce C. Straits, "The Pursuit of the Dissonant Consumer," *Journal of Marketing*, Vol. 28 (July, 1964), pp. 62–66; James F. Engel, "Further Pursuit of the Dissonant Consumer: A Comment," *Journal of Marketing*, Vol. 29 (April, 1965), p. 34.

TABLE 1

Dissonance and Buying Situations

Factors Affecting Dissonance	Buying Situation	Conditions with High Dissonance Expectation	Conditions with Low Dissonance Expectation
1. Attractiveness of rejected alternative	A high-school graduate decides which of several pictures to order.	Three of the proofs have both attractive and desirable features.	One of the proofs clearly is superior to the rest.
2. Negative factors in chosen alternative	A man chooses between two suits of clothing.	The chosen suit has the color the man wanted but not the style.	The chosen suit has both the color and style the man wanted.
3. Number of alternatives	A teacher shops for a tape-recorder.	There are eight recorders from which to choose.	There are only two recorders from which to choose.
4. Cognitive overlap	A housewife shops for a vacuum sweeper.	A salesman offers two similarly priced tank types.	A salesman offers a tank type and an upright cleaner.
5. Importance of cognitions involved	A child buys a present for her sister.	The sister has definite preferences for certain kinds of music.	The sister has no strong tastes for certain records.
6. Positive inducement	Parents decide to buy a photo-enlarger for their son.	The son already has hobby equipment and does not need the enlarger.	The son never has had a true hobby and needs something to keep him occupied.
7. Discrepant or negative action	A man purchases an expensive watch.	The man had never before paid more than $35 for a watch.	Fairly expensive watches had been important gift items in the man's family.
8. Information available	Housewife buys a detergent.	The housewife has no experience with the brand purchased—it is a new variety.	The housewife has read and heard a good deal about the product, and has confidence in the manufacturer.
9. Anticipated dissonance	A small boy buys a model airplane.	The boy anticipates trouble at home because of the cost of the model.	The boy expects no trouble at home relative to the purchase.
10. Familiarity and knowledge	A family buys a floor polisher.	The item was purchased without much thought.	The item was purchased after a careful selection process.

change his evaluations, select supporting information, ignore conflicting information, distort his perceptions, or even return the item to the seller.

Description of the Dissonance Experiment

It was decided to carry out an experiment in which several dissonance-producing factors

Inducement	High								Low							
Anticipated dissonance	High				Low				High				Low			
Additional information	Yes		None		Yes		None		Yes		None		Yes		None	
Cognitive overlap	High (1)	Low (2)	High (3)	Low (4)	High (5)	Low (6)	High (7)	Low (8)	High (9)	Low (10)	High (11)	Low (12)	High (13)	Low (14)	High (15)	Low (16)

Figure 1. The experimental design. An example of 1 of the 16 conditions is: high inducement, low anticipated dissonance, no additional information, high cognitive overlap.

could be manipulated: (1) inducement to buy, (2) anticipated dissonance, (3) information, and (4) cognitive overlap.

Each of these four conditions had two levels—one with high-producing dissonance features and one with low. A factorial design was used, and 80 persons were randomly assigned to the 16 experimental conditions—as shown in Figure 1.

HYPOTHESES. The following hypotheses were developed relative to the four main conditions.

1. *Individuals with low inducement to buy will have more dissonance than those who have high inducement to buy.* As an example, a person who needs a new pair of shoes (high inducement) should experience less dissonance than one who buys an extra pair (low inducement).

2. *Individuals exposed to a condition of high anticipated dissonance will reflect greater dissonance than those in the low anticipated dissonance condition.* For instance, a buyer of a sports car, who wonders what comments his colleagues will make, should experience more dissonance than when he buys a traditional type of car which would likely not draw criticism (anticipated dissonance).

3. *Individuals to whom additional positive information is provided to aid their decision-making will experience less dissonance than those to whom no additional positive information is provided.* In other words, additional positive information concerning a purchased item should make a buyer more confident and less dissonant than when he was not given that additional information.

4. *The high cognitive overlap condition will create more dissonance than the low cognitive overlap condition.*

Hypotheses based on interactions among the four factors were not developed because we did not know what to anticipate. However, the following procedure was carried out.

PROCEDURE. Male college students of the University of Minnesota were asked to play the role of buyers of automobile batteries. They were given class credit for participating, plus a chance of receiving a new automobile battery in the several drawings that were held. The four graduate students who conducted the experiments were systematically rotated over all 16 conditions.

Twelve brands of batteries were used in the experiment:

Allstate	Goodrich	Penneys
Atlas	Goodyear	Pure
Delco	Gould	Riverside
Fisk Ambassador	National	Wizard

Each participant in the experiment was asked to complete a rating form, indicating how favorable he considered each of the 12 brands. This rating form was actually the pre-rating score, later to be compared with an identical post-rating score, so that the difference in the two rating scores would be a measure of the amount of dissonance reduction experienced.

After completing the form, each person was taken to another room for three minutes. On the walls of the room were diagrams of the electrical system of the automobile, annual sales figures for the battery industry, and a list of battery brands sold in Minneapolis and St. Paul. These materials were expected to help the person become involved in the study without biasing him in any way.

The person was next greeted with the purchase-decision situation which contained (1a) a *high-inducement factor* or (1b) a *low-inducement* factor, and (2a) a *high-anticipated dissonance* condition or (2b) a *low-anticipated dissonance* condition.

1. *Inducement*
   a. *High Inducement*

   You have been in northern Minnesota for the weekend and are driving back to the Twin Cities. After a stop for coffee, you find that you cannot start the engine of your car. You return to the cafe and locate the phone number of a nearby garage. The attendant arrives in a few minutes, checks your car, and reports that your battery probably has a leaky cell which is shorting out.

   The attendant tows your car into his garage and determines that your battery is dead and cannot be recharged. The long winter has apparently taken its toll.

   b. *Low Inducement*

   You were planning on running several errands today. After the first stop,

however, your car will not start. After
several attempts to start it, you give
up and call the nearest garage. The
attendant arrives in a few minutes and
starts your car with the aid of his
booster battery.

You follow him to his garage where
he checks over your engine and battery. He believes that you may have a
leaky cell in the battery and that, with
a little luck, it may be possible for you
to get along for a few weeks.

2. *Anticipated Dissonance*
   a. *High-anticipated Dissonance*

As the attendant checks your car,
you notice the brand of the battery
and you reflect that it has done a
pretty good job. You also recall that
your regular service station dealer is
quite proud of his brands of batteries,
and the thought runs through your
mind that he will notice a new battery
in your car the first time he checks
under the hood.

   b. *Low-anticipated Dissonance*

As the attendant checks your car,
you notice that the battery is so en-
cased and hidden that you cannot
even see what brand of battery you
now have. Since you normally trade
at several statons and purchase several
brands of automobile products, you
cannot even guess what brand of battery it is.

Each person was then told orally:

"At this point the garage attendant
where you are now suggests that you
look at several of the new batteries he
has in stock."

The experimenter then stepped out of the
room and wheeled in a battery-display cart
on which were three batteries—the batteries

available in the hypothetical situation. The
three brands shown the person were selected
according to a decision rule in which brands
rated very high or very low in the pretest were
excluded.

3. The manipulation of the positive *information* factor occurred at this time; that is, half
the subjects received no additional information, and the other half were given a card on
which appeared the following:

The batteries displayed here are conventional 12-volt batteries. They are heavy
duty with plenty of reserve power. Specifications range around the 75-Ampere Hour
Rating, which means the amount of power
stored for normal driving needs. Their Zero
Start Ratings range around 6.6 minutes—
the number of minutes a battery will crank
in zero cold without dying out.

4. The condition of *cognitive overlap* was
handled by placing cards beside each of the
batteries on the display rack. See Table 2.

The experimenter then said:

"Now look at these three batteries. We
would like you to decide which one of these
batteries you would buy under the conditions you are in, that is, in the garage talking to the attendant. Think about it carefully now and then tell me which one you
would select. Take your time and make
what you think would be your real decsion."

As soon as the person decided, the experimenter thanked him and reminded him that he
had chosen Brand A, for example. The person
was then asked for a "little more information,"
which meant that he filled out the post-rating
form.

Following this the experimenter discussed
the study with the individual, in an effort to
determine his reactions, battery knowledge,
and buying experience.

TABLE 2

Cards on Display Rack

| Battery | High Overlap | | Low Overlap | |
	Price	Warranty	Price	Warranty
A	$22.88	30 months	$36.88	48 months
B	22.29	30 months	27.77	36 months
C	22.49	30 months	23.49	39 months

Results

Reduction of dissonance was measured by comparing the prerating and postrating scores. A higher postrating score for the chosen battery or a lower postrating score for the rejected batteries, or both, indicated dissonance reduction.

The overall mean change was 2.51, a statistically significant change, which indicated that dissonance had been experienced by the participants. The mean changes for each of the 16 conditions shown in Figure 1 ranged from a low of 0.8 to a high of 4.8.

MAIN EFFECTS. Dissonance reduction was measured for each of the four independent variables. Three of the four results were in the direction predicted, although none of them was statistically significant.

However, the results concerning *anticipated dissonance* were *contrary to expectations*, and contrary to preliminary results.

INTERACTION. As to the results on interaction, two of the interactions were significantly different from the mean change and support two of the hypotheses.

In the first significant interaction, when *high inducement* interacted with the two levels of information, a significantly different amount of dissonance was measured. Thus, hypothesis 3 was in part confirmed, as the amount of positive informaton did affect dissonance somewhat.

When there was *low inducement*, the information effect was not apparent. The explanation probably is that because low inducement by itself produced substantial dissonance, a manipulation of information had no further effect.

In the second case, with *low anticipated dissonance combined with cognitive overlap*, a significant effect was measured. Thus, hypothesis 4 was in part confirmed, as the interaction showed the effect of high versus low cognitive overlap.

With *high anticipated dissonance*, however, the overlap manipulation produced no additional dissonance.

Several other results were in the anticipated direction but not statistically significant. As an example, the condition expected to produce the least amount of dissonance (high inducement—low anticipated dissonance—additional information—low cognitive overlap), yielded a change score of only 0.8, the lowest of all conditions and considerably below the 2.5 overall mean.

Generalizing from the experiment, there appears to be more possibility of dissonance when buyers purchase without need and without sufficient information, and when alternatives are similar to the point of making the decision difficult.

Implications

Although the results of the experiment were not as positive as anticipated, they did provide a number of *tentative findings* about dissonance and buying behavior:

1. Consumers who buy when they have *strong inducement* should experience *less dissonance* than those who buy without inducement.

2. Consumers who obtain *adequate information* probably will have *less dissonance* than those who buy without sufficient information.

3. Product alternatives with very *similar attributes* may cause *greater consumer dissonance* than dissimilar alternatives.

4. *Interaction effects* occur when *various dissonance-arousing factors* are combined in one buying situation.

8-D   CAN COGNITIVE DISSONANCE THEORY EXPLAIN CONSUMER BEHAVIOR?

Sadaomi Oshikawa (Marketing Educator)

More than a decade has passed since the publication of Festinger's original book on the theory of cognitive dissonance.[1] Marketing researchers and psychologists have conducted numerous experiments to test the theory.

SOURCE: Sadaomi Oshikawa "Can Cognitive Dissonance Theory Explain Consumer Behavior?" *Journal of Marketing*, Vol. 33 (October, 1969), pp. 44–49.

[1] Leon Festinger, *A Theory of Cognitive Dissonance* (Stanford, California: Stanford University Press, 1957).

Whether dissonance theory can be applied to marketing is a question which has raised considerable interest among marketing writers.[2] The theory asserts that a person has certain cognitive elements which are "knowledges" about himself, his environment, his attitudes, his opinions, and his past behavior. If one cognitive element follows logically from another, they are said to be consonant to each other. They are dissonant to each other if one does not follow logically from the other.

Dissonance can be aroused in three ways and can motivate the person to reduce this tension in a variety of ways. Dissonance may be aroused (1) after making an important and difficult decision, (2) after being coerced to say or do something which is contrary to private attitudes, opinions, or beliefs, and (3) after being exposed to discrepant information.

The theory does not specify the mode of dissonance reduction but indicates that there are many possible ways to reduce dissonance. Attitude change, opinion change, seeking and recall of consonant information, avoidance of dissonant information, perceptual distortion, and behavioral change are some of the common modes of dissonance reduction.[3]

Since the theory does not designate the expected mode of reducing dissonance, most researchers have adopted the experimental method in which subjects could reduce dissonance in only one predetermined way. When the subjects responded to the experimental manipulation in the manner predicted by dissonance theory, the dissonance researcher took the results as evidence for the support of the theory. However, some psychologists have suggested that many of the findings are the results of built-in artifacts (or biases) or can be explained by other competing theories, and that the affirmative result is not necessarily unequivocal evidence for the theory.[4] This article will attempt to assess this possibility.

This article will also attempt to examine theoretical issues and experimental findings for each of the three dissonance arousal conditions mentioned above to determine the relevance of the theory to the study of consumer behavior. In general, it appears that the findings are contradictory and are not always supportive of the theory; however, an attempt will be made to sort out and evaluate the evidence.

Post-decision Dissonance

A review of literature on the psychological study of decision making led Festinger to hypothesize that decision making almost always provokes dissonance because, after a decision is made to choose one alternative, a person has to cope with the cognitive elements

[2] James F. Engel, "Are Automobile Purchasers Dissonant Consumers?" *Journal of Marketing*, Vol. 27 (April, 1963), pp. 55–58; James F. Engel, "Further Pursuit of the Dissonant Consumer: A Comment," *Journal of Marketing*, Vol. 29 (April, 1965), pp. 33–34; Robert J. Holloway, "An Experiment on Consumer Dissonance," *Journal of Marketing*, Vol. 31 (January, 1967), pp. 39–43; Harold H. Kassarjian and Joel B. Cohen, "Cognitive Dissonance and Consumer Behavior," *California Management Review*, Vol. 8 (Fall, 1965), pp. 55–64; Gerald D. Bell, "The Automobile Buyer After the Purchase," *Journal of Marketing*, Vol. 31 (July, 1967), pp. 12–16; Donald Auster, "Attitude Change and Cognitive Dissonance," *Journal of Marketing Research*, Vol. 2 (November, 1965), pp. 401–405; Gerald D. Bell, "Self-Confidence and Persuasion in Car Buying," *Journal of Marketing Research*, Vol. 4 (February, 1967), pp. 46–52; and James F. Engel and M. Lawrence Light, "The Role of Psychological Commitment in Consumer Behavior: An Evaluation of the Theory of Cognitive Dissonance," in *Applications of the Sciences in Marketing Management*, Frank M. Bass, Charles W. King, and Edgar A. Pessemier (eds.), (New York: John Wiley and Sons, Inc., 1968), pp. 179–206.
[3] Jack W. Brehm and Arthur R. Cohen, *Explorations in Cognitive Dissonance* (New York: John Wiley & Sons, Inc., 1962), pp. 306–308.
[4] S. E. Asch, "Review of L. Festinger, A Theory of Cognitive Dissonance," *Contemporary Psychology*, Vol. 3 (July, 1958), pp. 194–195; Milton J. Rosenberg, "When Dissonance Fails: On Eliminating Evaluation Apprehension from Attitude Measurement," *Journal of Personality and Social Psychology*, Vol. 1 (January, 1965), pp. 28–42; Alan C. Elms, "Role Playing, Incentive, and Dissonance," *Psychological Bulletin*, Vol. 68 (August, 1967), pp. 132–148; Karl E. Weick, "When Prophecy Pales: The Fate of Dissonance Theory," *Psychological Reports*, Vol. 16 (June, 1965), pp. 1261–1275; Howard L. Fromkin, "Reinforcement and Effort Expenditure: Predictions of 'Reinforcement Theory' Versus Predictions of Dissonance Theory," *Journal of Personality and Social Psychology*, Vol. 9 (August, 1968), pp. 347–352.

concerning the attractive attributes of the rejected alternatives.[5]

Since decision making entails the rejection of alternative(s), the theory asserts that post-decision dissonance is an inevitable consequence of decision making. The magnitude of dissonance depends upon the importance of the decision and the relative attractiveness of the rejected alternative(s). Therefore, the more important the decision and/or the more attractive the rejected alternative(s), the greater the dissonance.

One derivation of the theory is that the greater the number of alternatives a consumer considers before his purchase decision and/or the more equal the positive and negative attributes of the alternatives, the greater the post-purchase dissonance.

EQUIVOCAL EVIDENCE FOR POST-PURCHASE DISSONANCE. The experimental evidence frequently quoted to support the existence of post-purchase dissonance was reported by Ehrlich *et al.* They found that the larger number of alternative automobiles the consumer considered before his purchase, the greater the frequency of reading the automobile advertisements of the make he bought. This finding supported dissonance theory. They also found, however, that both recent and not-recent purchasers noticed and read more advertisements of considered-but-rejected makes of automobiles than those of not-considered makes. This evidence cast doubt on the hypothesis that purchasers experienced dissonance. According to dissonance theory they should have avoided the advertisements of the rejected makes.[6]

It may be that, soon after the purchase of a new automobile, Ehrlich *et al*'s consumers read automomobile advertisements not because they experienced dissonance but because automobile buying was an infrequent undertaking and the topic of automobiles was relevant and useful to them. An experiment by Berkowitz and Cottingham supports the view that people tend to be interested in the topics

which are relevant to themselves.[7] They found that safety-belt users were more interested in communication on safety-belts than were non-users because the topic was relevant to them, their interest having been aroused previously.

Canon, Freedman, and Lowe and Steiner found that when information is dissonant but also useful, utility outweighs dissonance and the information will not be avoided.[8] However, Berkowitz and Cottingham's relevance hypothesis and Canon's utility hypothesis explain the finding equally well and the evidence is not unequivocally supportive of dissonance theory.

In an attempt to reconcile the Ehrlich *et al* finding with dissonance theory, Mills hypothesized that automobile purchasers liked considered-but-rejected makes better than not-considered makes. He reasoned further that, if they preferred to read ads of a chosen (and liked) product to those of a considered-but-rejected (less liked) product, then the Ehrlich *et al* finding that considered-but-rejected makes were noticed more frequently than not-considered makes could be explained by their liking for the former makes.[9]

In an experiment Mills proceeded to show that consumers preferred to read advertisements of the chosen product to those of the unchosen product. However, in this experiment the consumers had been promised that they would receive the chosen product as a free gift, but had not received it when they expressed their ad preferences. Consequently,

[5] Same reference as footnote 1.

[6] Danuta Ehrlich, Isaiah Guttman, Peter Schonbach, and Judson Mills, "Post-Decision Exposure To Relevant Informaton," *Journal of Abnormal and Social Psychology*, Vol. 54 (January, 1957), pp. 98–102; Table I.

[7] L. Berkowitz and D. Cottingham, "The Interest Value and Relevance of Fear Arousing Communications," *Journal of Abnormal and Social Psychology*, Vol. 60 (January, 1960), pp. 37–43.

[8] L. K. Canon, "Self-Confidence and Selective Exposure to Information," in L. Festinger (ed.), *Conflict, Decision, and Dissonance* (Stanford: Stanford University Press, 1964), pp. 83–95; Jonathan L. Freedman, "Confidence, Utility, and Selective Exposure: A Partial Replication," *Journal of Personality and Social Psychology*, Vol. 2 (November, 1965), pp. 778–780; Rosemary H. Lowe and Ivan D. Steiner, "Some Effects of the Reversibility and Consequences of Decisions on Postdecision Information Preferences," *Journal of Personality and Social Psychology*, Vol. 8 (February, 1968), pp. 172–179.

[9] Judson Mills, "Avoidance of Dissonant Information," *Journal of Personality and Social Psychology*, Vol. 2 (October, 1965), pp. 589–593.

their preference may have been influenced by their curiosity about the free gift. His findings would have been less ambiguous if the consumers had, in fact, received the gift. Even granting that Mills proved his hypothesis, the Ehrlich *et al* experiment showed that their consumer subjects did not experience strong enough dissonance to overcome the interest-in-the-liked product tendency.

Ehrlich and others ascribed their unexpected finding to the possibility that some recent purchasers sought the advertisements of unchosen makes in order to find faults and reduce dissonance. This, however, is not a satisfactory explanation regarding the behavior of the purchasers in their attempts to reduce dissonance. If the experimenter is allowed to do this, the findings will always support predictions and there is no room for the rejection of the theory. A better research approach would have been to clearly specify the predicted mode of dissonance reduction and to block other possible modes before the execution of the experiment.

PROBLEMS IN EXPERIMENTAL DESIGN. One of the criticisms raised by Chapanis and Chapanis and Janis and Gilmore was that some of the experimental findings in support of the theory were the results of built-in bias. They argued that some experiments were designed and manipulated in such a way as to produce supporting results. Consequently, the findings could not be accepted as evidence for dissonance theory.[10]

An experiment reported by LoSciuto and Perloff illustrates this problem. Dissonance theory postulates that if a person, given a choice between two equally desirable products, chooses one and rejects the other, he will experience dissonance. Such dissonance will lead the person to evaluate the chosen product more favorably and the rejected product less favorably. In their experiment, LoSciuto and Perloff had their subjects rank nine phonograph records according to desirability. To

arouse strong dissonance, one group of subjects was given a choice between the third- and fourth-ranked albums; the other group was given a choice between the third- and eighth-ranked albums.[11]

The experimenters found that the first group of high-dissonance subjects tended to rerank the chosen albums as more desirable and the rejected albums as less desirable. The low-dissonance group did not show this tendency as strongly. According to dissonance theory, a greater proportion of high-dissonance subjects would show divergent changes in ranking (that is, reranking of the chosen albums as more desirable and the rejected ones as less desirable), while a greater proportion of low-dissonance subjects would show convergent changes. A chi-square test supported this prediction at the .001 level of significance.

Analysis of the design showed that the experiment was set up in such a way as to make it easier for high-dissonance subjects to show divergent changes and for low-dissonance subjects to show convergent changes. Since high-dissonance subjects chose between the third-ranked and fourth-ranked albums, the third-ranked albums had two places to move up, and the fourth-ranked albums had five places to move down, totaling seven places to move divergently. Seven (44%) of the total 16 movements would be considered divergent and the remaining nine movements (56%) would be convergent. For the low-dissonance subjects, 13 of the possible 16 movements (81%) contributed to convergent changes and only three (19%) to divergent changes.

If all subjects reranked the albums randomly, a greater proportion of low-dissonance subjects would show convergent changes and a greater proportion of high-dissonance subjects divergent changes. Although dissonance theory indicates that cognitive dissonance produces the above pattern of changes, an alternative explanation is that the observed pattern of changes is the result of the experimental design.

A REPLICATION OF THE EXPERIMENT. This

[10] Natalia P. Chapanis and Alphonse Chapanis, "Cognitive Dissonance: Five Years Later," *Psychological Bulletin,* Vol. 61 (January, 1964), pp. 1–22; I. L. Janis and J. B. Gilmore, "The Influence of Incentive Conditions on the Success of Role Playing in Modifying Attitudes," *Journal of Personality and Social Psychology,* Vol. 1 (January, 1965), pp. 17–27.

[11] Leonard LoSciuto and Robert Perloff, "Influence of Product Preference on Dissonance Reduction," *Journal of Marketing Research,* Vol. 4 (August, 1967), pp. 286–290.

writer conducted an experiment to test this possibility.[12] One hundred fifty-four undergraduate students were told that he was conducting a survey among college students on the popularity of nine record albums. The students were asked to rank each of the nine albums. One week later they were given the impression that the first preference questionnaires had been misplaced and were asked to rank the same albums again. Because the subjects were not asked to choose between any two albums, dissonance was not provoked.

The pattern of changes of the third-, fourth-, and eighth-ranked albums from the first to the second survey was studied. The chi-square test rejected the null hypothesis of independence between the pattern of changes and the initial location of albums at the .0005 level of significance ($\chi^2 = 25.58$). This finding showed that the experimental design ensured the statistically significant outcome even when subjects did not experience cognitive dissonance. Sheth's experimental findings in support of dissonance theory can be largely explained as the result of the same built-in bias of using changes in rank positions as the dependent variable.[13]

SUMMARY: POST-DECISION DISSONANCE. The Ehrlich *et al* study did show that new car owners sought out dissonance-reducing information, and supported dissonance theory. The difficulty, however, is that alternative explanations (or theories) predict the same results. Consequently, the findings were not unequivocal in support of dissonance theory. Furthermore, dissonance theory also postulates avoidance of dissonance-increasing information. Although some experiments supported this postulate, many others failed to do so. Thus, the theory has not fared too well in the area of information seeking and avoidance. In addition, problems associated with the experimental design may have produced a "built-in" bias for many post-decision dissonance studies.

Forced Compliance

Another way to create dissonance is to have a person verbalize or behave in a manner which is contrary to his original attitude, belief, opinion or conviction. In most experiments, subjects were forced to comply with the request of the experimenter to create dissonance. Hence, this process is called "forced compliance."[14] The theory has some support in forced compliance experiments.

As applied to automobile-purchasing behavior, forced compliance resulted in dissonance when a consumer clearly knew that a particular make was superior to other makes in relevant attributes but was induced, *on his own volition*, to buy an inferior make. The knowledge of superior attributes of rejected makes is dissonant with the knowledge that he bought an inferior make. The less the amount of inducement to buy the inferior make and the greater the freedom he had in rejecting superior makes, the greater his post-purchase dissonance.

The importance of volition cannot be overemphasized. Without it, the person will not experience strong enough dissonance to motivate a dissonance-reducing behavior. Its importance was well illustrated in the Festinger and Carlsmith experiment.[15]

FORCED COMPLIANCE IN CONSUMER BEHAVIOR. When the forced compliance paradigm is applied to consumer behavior, the consumer has to be induced to buy the make he knows is inferior if his dissonance is to be aroused. If he believes that one alternative is not a good one but is forced to choose that alternative, he will not experience dissonance because he can explain the poor choice as forced upon him. If, on the other hand, he has complete freedom in making the decision and chooses the wrong alternative, then he will experience dissonance as he cannot ascribe his poor choice to the force imposed upon him. The problem, however, is that in a realistic market situation it is impossible to force a customer to buy a product which he knows is inferior.

One methodological problem of the forced

---

[12] Sadaomi Oshikawa, "The Theory of Cognitive Dissonance and Experimental Research," *Journal of Marketing Research*, Vol. 5 (November, 1968), pp. 429–430.

[13] Jagdish N. Sheth, "Cognitive Dissonance, Brand Preference and Product Familiarity," in Johan Arndt (ed.), *Insights into Consumer Behavior* (Boston: Allyn and Bacon, Inc., 1968), pp. 41–53.

[14] Same reference as footnote 3, pp. 84–91.

[15] Leon Festinger and James M. Carlsmith, "Cognitive Consequences of Forced Compliance," *Journal of Abnormal and Social Psychology*, Vol. 58 (March, 1959), pp. 203–210.

compliance experiment is that the subjects were induced to comply and those who did, in fact, comply reduced dissonance in a variety of ways as predicted by the experimenters. Even in the artificial experimental situations, however, experimenters have been plagued by a loss of subjects who refused to comply. In the Festinger-Carlsmith experiment, 11 out of 71 subjects had to be discarded because of their refusal to comply. In another experiment, only 72 of the original sample of 203 subjects could be used.[16]

Experimenters must strike a balance between exercising too much force and not exercising enough. The implication of this methodological problem to marketing is that, in a natural setting, consumers are not likely to experience post-purchase dissonance via forced compliance because they will not behave in ways which they know will later arouse dissonance.

Exposure to Discrepant Information

Another set of circumstances under which dissonance may occur is when the consumer is exposed to *new* information not available to him at the time of decision making and which is obverse to the information he already has. This condition is called cognitive intrusion because new dissonant cognitions "intrude" upon one's cognitive structure.[17]

For example, suppose a consumer studied extensively and carefully the attributes of different makes of automobiles and purchased a particular make which he judged to be the best. Will he experience dissonance when he is later exposed to new information describing unfavorable attributes of the chosen make and/or favorable attributes of unchosen makes?

Whether exposure to discrepant information will arouse dissonance depends upon a variety of factors. The most important of these is the degree of commitment and ego-involvement.

The findings of several experiments suggested that when the discrepant information is not salient and the degree of public ego-involvement is small, dissonance will not oc-

cur. For example, Rosen found that when students made decisions individually *without* announcing publicly, more (67%) sought dissonance-*producing* information regarding the decisions made and less (33%) sought dissonance-reducing information.[18]

On the other hand, dissonance may be provoked because the consumer has publicly committed himself to the position that the choice he made is a good one. Public commitment results in ego-involvement which in turn increases the importance of that cognitive element on which one has committed himself.[19] "The magnitude of dissonance is a function of the ratio of dissonant to consonant cognitions, where each cognitive element is weighted for its importance to the person."[20] Consequently, public commitment tends to increase the magnitude of dissonance by increasing the relative weight of the dissonant cognitions.

Relating the above discussion to the Ehrlich *et al* study, it should be noted that most automobile purchasers are not put in a position to publicly defend the adequacy of their purchase decision, and discrepant information which they read in the newspaper will not arouse strong enough dissonance to make them resort to a dissonance-reducing behavior.

ALTERNATIVE THEORY SUPPORTED. To test if dissonance theory can be applied in a more natural situation where individuals do not commit themselves publicly, this writer conducted an experiment and examined whether, after being exposed to dissonant information, strong dissonance leads individuals to convince themselves that the original decision was correct.[21] Students were given the choice of essay type, objective type or any combination of both tests for midterm and final examinations.

---

[16] Chapanis and Chapanis, same reference as footnote 10.

[17] Bruce C. Straits, "The Pursuit of the Dissonant Consumer," *Journal of Marketing*, Vol. 28 (July, 1964), pp. 62–66.

[18] Sidney Rosen, "Postdecision Affinity for Incompatible Information," *Journal of Abnormal and Social Psychology*, Vol. 63 (July, 1961), pp. 188–190.

[19] A. R. Cohen J. W. Brehm, and B. Latane, "Choice of Strategy and Voluntary Exposure to Information under Public and Private Conditions," *Journal of Personality*, Vol. 27 (March, 1959), pp. 63–73; same reference as footnote 3.

[20] Same reference as footnote 6.

[21] Sadaomi Oshikawa, "Consumer Pre-decision Conflict and Post-decision Dissonance," *Behavioral Science*, Vol. 15 (March, 1970).

After indicating their preference, some were exposed to consonant information which supported their original choice while others were exposed to dissonant information.

They were also told either that they were committed to their original preference or that they could change their preference after reading the information. Dissonance theory predicts that those who were committed to the original preference and were exposed to discrepant information would try to reduce dissonance by becoming more convinced of the wisdom of their original decision. Kurt Lewin's field theory asserts, on the other hand, that discrepant information reduces the desirability of the chosen test and increases that of the rejected test and predicts the opposite outcome from dissonance theory.[22]

Experimental evidence supported Lewin's theory, showing that the students were positively influenced by both the discrepant and the consonant information regardless of their commitment. It appears that, under a natural circumstance, individuals do not respond to discrepant information in the way dissonance theory predicts.

Evaluation of the Theory and Applicable Circumstances

An attempt has been made to examine the experimental findings on the theory of cognitive dissonance. Many findings concerning exposure to discrepant information and post-decision dissonance arousal have been shown to be equivocal. In the forced compliance experiments, the artificial conditions under which compliance was obtained and some subjects' refusal to comply have reduced the usefulness of the experimental findings to the analysis of consumer behavior. It was shown, however, that if the subjects did comply, they attempted to reduce dissonance in a predicted manner.

Analysis of the theory and experimental findings suggested that the necessary condition for provoking dissonance strong enough to motivate dissonance-reducing behavior is that one be *committed on his own volition* to an undesirable product, position, or behavior and

be unable to retract this commitment. However, consumers are unlikely to experience strong dissonance since they will not knowingly commit themselves to undesirable or inferior products in a natural market setting.

ROLE OF ADVERTISING AS DISSONANCE REDUCER. Dissonance theory sheds new light on the role of advertising by increasing the repurchase probability of the advertised product. A seller's product advertisement reassures the consumer as to the wisdom of the purchase by emphasizing its desirable features and therefore helps to reduce post-purchase dissonance. Dissonance reduction, in turn, reinforces his purchase. It may increase the probability of his purchasing the same brand.

Dissonance reduction may not operate as a strong reinforcer in the case of frequently-purchased merchandise. The more frequently the product is purchased, the less important becomes the question of which brand is purchased at any one time, and the less the post-purchase dissonance. The consumer who has purchased a convenience good usually would not experience strong dissonance because he knows that he is not irrevocably tied to that particular choice, but can easily switch brands. Since his dissonance is not strong, advertising's role in reinforcing the purchase is diminished.

On the other hand, the consumer who has just purchased an expensive specialty good is likely to experience strong dissonance if his purchase is irrevocable and if it is important in some psychological sense. For example, if a substantial financial outlay is involved or if his taste and intelligence are judged by the purchase, strong dissonance may be present. Under these circumstances, an advertisement which emphasized the desirable features of the chosen brand can reduce the dissonance which may lead the consumer to form a more favorable attitude toward the brand.

WEARING-OUT OF REINFORCING EFFECT. However, the longer the time lapse before product replacement, the less reinforcing will be the effects of the advertising. In the meantime, the seller's advertising must compete with that of his competitors, and it may not operate effectively as a reinforcing agent long after the purchase. By the time he is ready to replace the product, the effect of the firm's original advertising may have worn off and the

---

[22] Kurt Lewin, *Field Theory in Social Science* (New York: Harper & Brothers, 1951), p. 274; same reference as footnote 3. p. 234.

attitude and preference of the purchaser may have been influenced by the more recent advertising efforts of the firm's competitors. Since dissonance is reduced over time,[23] it is reasonable to expect that the greater the post-purchase dissonance, the longer the period during which the seller's advertisement operates as a reinforcer.

Thus, for the consumer who purchased an expensive product, advertising can act as a reinforcement for some period of time following the purchase. This reinforcing effect, however, does not necessarily insure a repeat purchase because of the counteracting effects of competitive advertisements.

In summary, the theory of cognitive dissonance is designed to explain and predict post-decisional behavior, but in most instances it is not adequate to explain consumer behavior *before* a purchase decision.

[23] Same reference as footnote 6.

10 / Traits and Attitudes

A. BACKGROUND AND THEORY

This section begins with a discussion (Sherif and Sherif) of what is meant by an attitude. This is followed by an explanation (Bonner) of man's attitude-value complex.

10-A   CRITERIA OF ATTITUDE

Muzafer Sherif (Psychologist) and Carolyn W. Sherif (Psychologist)

When an attitude is discussed we are not talking about something that can be observed directly. We are speaking of a psychological concept designating something *inside* the individual. Just as we can never directly observe pain, psychological tension, or an unspoken idea, we cannot see an attitude. Nevertheless, the concept of attitude has several characteristics that differentiate it from other concepts referring to internal states of the individual.

Attitudes are not innate. They belong to that domain of human motivation variously studied under the labels of "social drives," "social needs," "social orientations," and the like. It is assumed that the appearance of an attitude is dependent on learning.

Attitudes are not temporary states but are more or less enduring once they are formed. Of course, attitudes do change; but once formed they acquire a regulatory function such that, within limits, they are not subject to change with the ups and downs of homeostatic functioning of the organism or with every just-noticeable variation in the stimulus conditions.

Attitudes always imply a relationship between the person and objects. In other words,

attitudes are not self-generated, psychologically. They are formed or learned in relation to identifiable referents, whether these be persons, groups, institutions, objects, values, social issues, or ideologies.

The relationship between person and object is not neutral but has motivational-affective properties. These properties derive from the context of highly significant social interaction in which many attitudes are formed, from the fact that the objects are not neutral for other participants, and from the fact that the self, as it develops, acquires positive value for the person. Therefore, the linkage between self and the social environment is seldom neutral.

The subject-object relationship is accomplished through the formation of categories both differentiating between the objects and between the person's positive or negative relation to objects in the various categories. The referent of an attitude constitutes a set that may range, theoretically, from one to a large number of objects. However, in actuality the formation of a positive or negative stand toward one object usually implies differential attachment to others in the same domain. For example, a singular attraction to one person typically involves a comparison with other persons who are similar and different. The attitude toward the person, therefore, necessarily includes the views toward others with

SOURCE: Carolyn W. Sherif and Muzafer Sherif, *Attitude, Ego-Involvement, and Change* (New York: John Wiley & Sons, 1967), pp. 112–113.

121

whom he is compared. Needless to say, this process need not be a conscious and deliberate one.

The referents of an attitude, as differentiated from other internal states by the above criteria, may be objects in the person's environment that are nonsocial, in addition to social objects.

As the above criteria imply, the formation of attitudes is integral to the process of forming a self concept. In fact, through the establishment of a constellation of subject-object relationships, the self concept is delineated. Through this process, the groups in which the child is born become not merely external realities to which he must adapt but *reference groups* with which he identifies or strives to identify himself.

Because the criteria for attitude include the person's relatedness to relevant objects on a conceptual level, the present approach is a cognitive approach. However, it is also a motivational-affective approach, for attitudes are not neutral affairs. Finally, it is a behavioral approach because the only possible data from which attitude can be inferred are behaviors, verbal or nonverbal. Attitudes are necessarily cognitive-motivational-behavioral. Any sharp separation of these is bound to be arbitrary and to distort the nature of the phenomena. In actual research practice, treatment of these aspects as "components" typically amounts to using samples of *behavior* in different tasks or situations assigned at different points in time. Although this is legitimate research practice, we should not let our research techniques blind us to the undeniable blending of cognitive-motivational-behavioral in *any* specific situation or task that arouses an attitude.

10-B THE ATTITUDE-VALUE COMPLEX AND PERSONALITY

Herbert Bonner (Psychologist)

A man's attitude-value complex is his chief psychological instrument for understanding human reality—perhaps of physical reality, as well. Look deep enough into an individual's attitudes and values and you discover no mere fugitive beliefs, but an expression of his total personality. While the values and attitudes of an individual are many and even diverse, the personality which they help to mold is not fractionated except in deviant cases; and the more consistent they are, the more truly do they give coherence and unity to it.

Attitude-Value Complex and the Self

While the self is defined divergently in the literature of social psychology and the psychology of personality, a preliminary delineation of it will adequately serve our purpose. Even a brief analysis shows that the self is fundamentally an organization of attitudes and values.

ROLE-PERCEPTION. The self is most clearly seen in role behavior. In role behavior the individual acts as an object to himself. The child first perceives himself as an autonomous being when he introjects the role of his mother. He plays her role in his perceptions of her bodily gestures, her words, the sound of her voice. Later, in playing with other children he will play their roles in such a way as to stimulate himself and respond to his own stimulation. He enacts one role and responds to his own role-enactment. When he has reached adulthood he will have mastered the enactment of many roles in accordance with his perception of the world around him. In his perception and enactment of roles he is making choices among alternative ways of behaving. If he is truly socialized, he will be able to synchronize the various roles into a relatively consistent set of roles—the role of the "generalized other."[1]

The enactment of roles depends on the individual's perceptions, and these perceptions are, as we saw, bound up with his attitude toward himself and others. The variety of roles which he is called upon to perform differ, so

SOURCE: Herbert Bonner, *Psychology of Personality* (New York: The Ronald Press Company, 1961), pp. 386–389. Copyright 1961, The Ronald Press Company, New York.

[1] See G. H. Mead, *Mind, Self and Society* (Chicago: University of Chicago Press, 1934), pp. 135–51.

that every individual comes to perceive himself in different ways. Each of the roles represents a different aspect of the person, so that in reality a person is as many "selves" as there are roles for him to enact. However, since the need for integration is strong in everyone, every individual will, through learning and necessity, combine them into a relatively consistent and dynamic configuration. This dynamic pattern is what we are able to identify as the self of a person.

The human self is, thus, at once public and private. It is public in the sense that the roles which the individual plays are social expectations. He is what he is because others perceive him through the roles which he enacts. It is private in the sense that he plays his roles in keeping with his own perception of what others expect and anticipate. The public self is the totality of role-expectations; the private self is the individual's uniquely organized ways of regarding himself; it is the individual as he appears to himself. Stated differently, the public self is the pattern of roles imposed upon the individual by others, whereas the private self is that pattern of roles which is selected largely by himself. The integration of these selves into a coherent person is made possible by the frame of reference, or attitude-value complex, which we have already described.

It should be noted in the foregoing phrasing that the self is not an organization completely determined by the expectations of others, or by the culture demands of the group. The self as here described is different from both the current behavioristic accounts of reinforcement and the psychoanalytic view that man behaves because of fear of punishment. We have stressed the importance of individual choices on a "scale" of values. Man behaves as he does, not only in expectation of rewards and fear of punishment, but because of his own perception of the course of action he should take. From this point of view, then, it is a fallacy to attempt the reduction of selfhood and self-directed behavior either to allegedly more elementary functions, or to cultural imperatives. The self has a degree of autonomy which is largely denied by both psychoanalytic and behavioristic accounts of human behavior. Although the attitude-value complex, which serves as a framework for

every self, is culturally conditioned in part, it transmutes the anticipation of reward and the fear of punishment, which weaken or destroy autonomous behavior, into individual perceptions of right and wrong. The individual internalizes the values of his community, to be sure, but every internalization is unique, so that, in effect, culture can never compel a person to act rightly or wrongly. The choice between these important values is the individual's alone. The choice between good and evil are autonomous properties of the person who possesses the capacity to anticipate the proper course of action.[2]

THE INTEGRATED SELF. We have said that with the exception of deviant cases, or in cases of immaturity, the self is a dynamic pattern of roles. The unified self is the reference point for all attitudes and values; it is an organization of these psychological variables. Inasmuch as neither attitudes nor values live in isolation, and since persistence is a fundamental property of the attitude-value complex, they make for the continuity and identity of the self. The "feeling of selfhood" is maintained by the involvements of the self in abiding attitudes and values. When the attitudinal system in which the self is involved radically changes; or when the value system for whatever reason becomes dysfunctional; or when the frame of reference in which both attitudes and values are embedded collapses, as sometimes happens in extreme cases, the self becomes disorganized. A disorganized self, then, is one in which the attitude-value complex no longer serves as a dependable guide to action.

Attitudes, values, and the self, thus, cannot be separated. Descriptions of value-behavior in the language of reinforcement, and of attitudinal behavior in terms of the force of cultural imperatives, are not false but irrelevant. The fragmentation of attitudes into mea-

[2] *Gestalt* psychologists, like Wertheimer and Köhler, have described the capacity to prevision the right course of action by the idea of *requiredness*. Thus, a person's ethical behavior is a product of his ability to perceive the requirement of the situation. See M. Wertheimer, "Some Problems in the Theory of Ethics," *Soc. Res.*, 2 (1935), 353–67; W. Köhler, *The Place of Value in a World of Facts* (New York: Liveright Publishing Corp., 1938).

surable units, practiced by the methodologists, and the denigration of values to the dimension of reward-and-punishment, which the reductionists try to effect, have not helped to perfect self-psychology and the psychology of attitudes and values. They have weakened not only the study of personality, but the other areas of the science of psychology as well.

B. RESEARCH AND APPLICATIONS

This section consists of an example of research (Alpert) on behavioral life styles, and research (Jacobson and Kossoff) on attitudes toward small cars.

10-C DO YOU REALLY KNOW YOUR CUSTOMERS?

Lewis Alpert (Marketing Executive)

Analyzing "behavioral life styles" was born in the middle of a think tank session at D'Arcy Advertising, when I was head of research there. Several of us felt that although we were inundated with data, we were not making the best and the most use of the information and we talked at length about it.

From our researchers' gab session came the idea of analyzing consumer behavior. The analyses we wrought give the marketer a detailed painting of his customers, and his competitor's customers, unlike the Demby studies (Dr. Emanuel Demby, president of Motivational Programmers Inc.) of creative and passive consumers, which provide a research sketch of consumers.

With the rise or fall of a percentage point in share of market often meaning $1,000,000 in sales, the market flooded with equally good products and media costs soaring, the need to know everything about the customer is nothing less than vital.

In building a foundation for brand strategy and advertising copy direction, marketers must identify the specific factors that set product users apart from non-users, and users of one brand from users of a competitive brand. They must determine the attitudes of their customers —their behavioral life styles—to develop a total picture of the market. With such a profile, an advertiser can design a detailed creative advertising strategy to keep his own customer, identify the vulnerabilities of competitors and develop advertising and marketing goals.

SOURCE: Lewis Alpert "Do You Really Know Your Customers?" *Media Scope,* Vol. 13, No. 1 (January 1969), pp. 58–59 and 86.

Study Yields Fascinating Insights

How does the study of consumers' behavioral life styles work? In a recent study of 5,424 men, we determined 25 behavioral life style factors (some of which were admittedly difficult and arbitrary to name) and considered their relation to two popular premium beers sold nationally. Some of the factors are associated with only one product or two, but others are categories of behavior which go far beyond a single type of product. They yield some fascinating insights into consumer purchasing.

The first, the Hard Drinker factor, is associated with the men's use of hard liquor, highball mixers and beer. The Liquor and Wine Connoisseur factor (11) (see Table 1) appears distinctly separate from both the Hard Drinker and the Cocktail Drinker (14) factors. Our twentieth factor, the Soft Drinker, is associated with soft drinks. Our study unearthed the Candy Consumer (3); the Cosmopolitan Traveler (4)—the man who takes plane trips, rents cars, uses credit cards and travels abroad; and the Cigar and Pipe Smoker (6). Cigaret smoking did not emerge as relevant to any of the factors.

Our Dress-Conscious Man (7) is a heavy purchaser of dress shirts, sport shirts, shoes and suits, and the Well-Groomed Man (8) buys many articles of personal toiletry. The Cough and Cold-Conscious Man (9) is a clear-cut consumer factor, as is the Man with the Photographic Memory (10), named (whimsically) for consumer use of photographic supplies, presumably to preserve memories in the form of photos.

TABLE 1

Men's Behavioral Life-Style Factors in Purchasing Beer and Other Products[a]

Life-Style Factor	All Men	Beer Drinkers	Non-Beer Drinkers	Beer Brand Y		Beer Brand W	
				Heavy Drinkers	Light Drinkers	Heavy Drinkers	Light Drinkers
Number of Men in Sample	5424	2943	2481	188	316	99	153
1. The Hard Drinker	0	.59	−.71	1.44	.69	1.04	.20
2. The Car-Conscious Man	0	.02	−.02	−.17	.05	−.03	.24
3. The Candy Consumer	0	—	.01	.20	.07	.50	.17
4. The Cosmopolitan Traveler	0	.07	−.08	.36	.11	.48	.25
5. The Electric Shaver	0	.02	.03	−.16	−.13	−.25	−.04
6. The Cigar & Pipe Smoker	0	.09	−.10	−.09	.01	.28	−.06
7. The Dress-Concious Man	0	—	−.01	−.10	.13	−.11	.15
8. The Well-Groomed Man	0	.02	−.02	−.01	.01	.41	.17
9. The Cough & Cold Conscious Man	0	.08	−.09	.69	.06	.27	.13
10. The Man With A Photographic Memory	0	.01	−.01	−.42	−.04	−.33	.05
11. The Liquor & Wine Connoisseur	0	−.04	.04	−.42	.14	−.73	.06
12. The Old Man	0	−.11	.13	.06	−.32	.43	.20
13. The Hard Driving Man	0	.04	−.05	.28	.13	.07	−.22
14. The Cocktail Drinkers	0	.01	.01	−.45	−.05	.72	.16
15. The Regular Shaver	0	−.06	.07	.68	−.20	−.49	.07
16. The Deodorized Male	0	.02	.02	.35	−.02	.32	−.07
17. The Lather Shaver I	0	.05	.06	.33	.16	−.18	−.09
18. The Lather Shaver II	0	.07	.08	.15	.06	.04	.25
19. Light Drinkers of Beer Brand W	0	−.24	−.29	−.40	−.18	.69	5.17
20. The Soft Drinkers	0	.04	.05	.73	.39	−.86	.22
21. The Outdoorsman	0	.07	−.08	.60	−.04	.22	−.12
22. Light Drinkers of Beer Brand Y	0	.21	−.25	−1.97	3.01	.04	−.26
23. The Bellyachers	0	.07	.09	.99	−.09	−.30	.03
24. The Injector Blade Shavers	0	.08	−.10	.04	−.03	.20	.01
25. Drinkers of Beer Brand W	0	.04	.05	−1.76	−.02	5.56	−.18

[a] The 0 in the first column indicates the base from which the factor scores (relative weights) were tabulated. A score of .59, for example, reflects a much greater frequency of usage than a score of .02 does, while a −.71 score indicates much less frequency. The chart points out that the Hard Drinker is closely associated with the heavy beer drinker; and that heavy drinkers of Brand Y are more likely to be outdoorsmen than heavy drinkers of Brand W.

Differences in Life Styles

The Hard-Driving Man (13), who drives a car a great deal, is to be distinguished from the Car-Conscious Man (2), who buys many supplies to operate and care for his car. The study pointed up shaving habit differences, with an Electric Shaver factor (5), and a couple of factors associated with lather (17, 18) and razor (15, 24) shaving.

We found the Deodorized Male factor (16) denoting high usage of deodorants; and the Bellyacher (23), the heavy user of digestive remedies. Our studied Outdoorsman (21) takes camping trips and buys ammunition. We also separated out beer drinkers (2,943), and divided them according to brand and the amount quaffed.

When we examined the results of the study, we found very noticeable differences in the behavioral life styles of men who are heavy beer drinkers (287), and among those who drink Brand Y (5040) and Brand W (252) beer. The heavy beer drinker is especially associated with the Hard Drinker. Like hard liquor drinkers, heavy beer drinkers are not inclined to be liquor and wine connoisseurs, nor are they likely to consume many soft drinks.

How do drinkers of Brand Y and Brand W beer differ? It might seem safe to assume that the two brands appeal to the same sort of audiences. But we found that Brand Y drinkers are Outdoorsmen, and more inclined to be hard drinkers. Brand W drinkers are more associated with the Cosmopolitan Traveler and the Dress-Conscious Man, and their association with the Candy Consumer and the Cigar and Pipe Smoker labels them as oral satisfaction seekers. Among light-usage beer drinkers, roughly the same pattern was discerned, although there were fewer extreme differences between groups purchasing either of the two brands.

As a result of our beer study, one of the beer advertisers involved quickly changed its selection of media to reach consumers with the life style that the study showed favored that brand. The company's advertising copy is now also being changed to appeal to those particular consumers, and should be catching up with the new media schedules shortly. What happens to sales of that brand will tell the ultimate tale, of course, but we believe the new schedule will prove beneficial.

To be used effectively, individual behavioral life style analyses must be performed for different products. Knowledge of behavioral life styles can influence the overall formation of marketing strategy for a brand, and such knowledge can give immediate creative guidance in the preparation of advertising copy, since the advertiser can identify the consumer and thus know better how to appeal to him.

This sort of product-positioning knowledge adds insight to the straightforward and long-used measure of consumer attitudes and demographics. Alfred Politz Research now considers these analyses a major breakthrough in market research.

10-D SELF-PERCEPT AND CONSUMER ATTITUDES TOWARD SMALL CARS

Eugene Jacobson (Psychologist) and
Jerome Kossoff (Psychologist)

One of the important new objects of consumer behavior that has appeared in the past few years is the smaller automobile. It has emerged in the United States with relative suddenness and is the occasion for discussion, expressed preferences, and crystallization of attitudes.

Source: Eugene J. Jacobson and Jerome Kossoff, "Self-Percept and Consumer Attitude Toward Small Cars," *Journal of Applied Psychology*, Vol. 47 (August, 1963), pp. 242–245.

As an innovation, it is of interest to the student of consumer behavior from a number of points of view. Among these is the possibility of developing measures for relating a readiness to accept small cars with a readiness to accept other kinds of innovation. Perhaps some people are more likely to express favorable attitudes toward small cars simply because, in general, they consider themselves to be the kind of people who are ready to try something new and different.

In the study reported in the following paragraphs, an attitude questionnaire was administered to a random sample of adults in a metropolitan area to discover whether persons who consider themselves ready for challenge and innovation are also persons who express more positive attitudes toward the purchase of small cars. (The findings were that this was not the case but rather that those persons who saw themselves as being cautious and conservative were more likely to express a positive attitude toward the purchase of small cars. The data provides some understanding of why this alternative relationship was found.)

Method and Sample

The population sample consisted of 250 adults, all of the persons 21 years old or older in 116 households chosen at random from a predesignated area in Woodside, Long Island, New York. Interviewing took place from June through September, 1960.

As a measure of attitudes toward the self, respondents were asked to complete a 16-item Likert-type scale. The two items reproduced here are representative of the scale:

"Unless there is a good reason for changing, I think we should continue to do things the way they are being done now."

1. Agree Very Much
2. Agree Somewhat
3. Neutral
4. Disagree Somewhat
5. Disagree Very Much

"When new ideas are going around, I am usually among the first to accept them."

1. Agree Very Much
2. Agree Somewhat
3. Neutral
4. Disagree Somewhat
5. Disagree Very Much

On the basis of total scores, cutting points were established and three groups were identified and labeled as Cautious Conservatives, Middle-of-the-Roaders, and Confident Explorers. The total scale had a Spearman-Brown corrected estimated internal consistency of .84.

In comparing the three groups, the Cautious Conservatives were more likely than the others to give responses indicating that they saw

TABLE 1

Self-Percept and Attitude Toward Small Cars

Attitude	Cautious Conservatives	Middle-of-the-Roaders	Confident Explorers
Favorable	79	58	49
Neutral	10	8	9
Unfavorable	10	34	42
Total(%)	99	100	100
N	86	71	93
	$\chi^2 = 22.51$[a]		

Note. Total $N = 250$.

[a] $p < .01$.

themselves as unwilling to take chances, wanting to have proved methods, and preferring safety to adventure. Confident Explorers were more likely to see themselves as ready to challenge the unknown, to trust their ability to handle situations, and to be free in the use of their resources.

Results

All three groups expressed more favorable than unfavorable attitudes toward small cars. A significantly larger percentage of the Confident Explorers expressed unfavorable attitudes toward small cars, and correspondingly, Cautious Conservatives were more likely to be favorable (see Table 1).

The same relationship was found in preferences for a second car. Confident Explorers were more likely to want a big car, Cautious Conservatives to prefer a small car.

When we examine correlates of these attitudes, several factors having a bearing on our preference emerge. One important relationship is found in the difference in attitudes between men and women. Women are much more likely to have a favorable attitude toward small cars than men (see Table 2).

This led us to re-examine the data on attitude toward the self where the data showed how women were more likely to regard themselves cautious and conservative than men (see Table 3).

However, when we examined attitudes toward small cars, self-percept, and sex simultaneously, the importance of self-percept was confirmed. As would be expected, most of the women who saw themselves as Cautious Conservatives were favorable toward small cars.

TABLE 2
Sex and Attitude Toward Small Cars

Attitude	Men	Women
Favorable	48	77
Neutral	8	10
Unfavorable	43	14
Total (%)	99	101
N	130	120
$\chi^2 = 27.08$[a]		

Note. Total $N = 250$.
[a] $p < .01$.

TABLE 3
Self-Percept and Sex

Sex	Cautious Conservatives	Middle-of-the-Roaders	Confident Explorers
Men	40	48	67
Women	60	52	33
Total (%)	100	100	100
N	86	71	93
$\chi^2 = 15.1$[a]			

Note. Total $N = 250$.
[a] $p < .01$.

But the Cautious Conservative men had the same pattern of response (see Table 4).

Although there were only a handful of women who had unfavorable attitudes toward small cars, those who did were Confident Explorers or Middle-of-the-Roaders. Confident Explorer men were more likely than Cautious Conservative men to have an unfavorable attitude.

This general pattern of relationships is illustrated in a second analysis, that of attitudes toward American-made small cars as opposed to foreign-made small cars. Cautious Conservatives are more likely to prefer American small cars, and Confident Explorers tend to prefer foreign small cars. Women prefer American small cars.

Women's attitudes in this area do not differ significantly from age group to age group. However, among men there are some interesting variations. Men in the age group 20–29 show the most marked interest in small foreign cars. The strongest preferences for big cars among men is found in the 40–49 age group.

Among women, differences in education have relatively little bearing on attitudes toward themselves or small cars. Among men, those who have more education are more likely to prefer a foreign small car.

Income is a factor in car preference among men. Those reporting less than $5,000 a year income are more likely to prefer small American cars. Those in the higher income brackets are more likely to prefer big cars or foreign-made cars if a small type is considered.

Of the 130 men interviewed, 112 owned cars. Ninety-four owned big cars; 14, small cars; and 4, sports cars. All of the small-car owners had a favorable attitude toward small cars and a preference for American makes. Among the large-car owners, most preferred large cars and foreign small cars. Among the 120 women interviewed, only 36 owned cars, 29 large and 7 small. Those who owned big cars were much more likely to be favorable toward the small car than their big-car-owning male counterparts.

TABLE 4
Self-Percept, Attitude Toward Small Cars and Sex

Attitude	Cautious Conservatives		Middle-of-the-Roaders		Confident Explorers	
	Men	Women	Men	Women	Men	Women
Favorable	71	85	44	70	39	71
Neutral	6	13	9	8	10	6
Unfavorable	23	2	47	22	51	23
Total (%)	100	100	100	100	100	100
N	34	52	34	37	62	31
	Men: $\chi^2 = 8.7$*		Women: $\chi^2 = 10.20$*			

Note. Total $N = 250$.
* $p < .01$.

In our sample, Cautious Conservatives were likely to be in their late forties or early fifties with a high school education and an income in the $5,000 range.

Confident Explorers as a group are younger. Sixty-six per cent are in the 20–39 age group as compared to 8% of the Cautious Conservatives. But, within the Confident Explorer group, the men and women who prefer big cars are, on the average, 6 years older.

Confident Explorers, both men and women, are better educated than Cautious Conservatives and have a slightly higher income. They are likely to have a college degree or some college training. Highest income was reported by the male Confident Explorers who preferred large cars. This subgroup, upon further analysis of the components of the attitude scale, was found to have the most liberal attitudes toward the use of money.

Discussion

A coherent pattern of attitudes toward small cars can be constructed from these findings.

First, it is clear that there is a strong and meaningful relationship between expressed attitudes toward the self and expressed preferences among cars. The relationship, however, is not as simple as the one predicted. Apparently the Cautious Conservative prefers the small American car, accepting it as a recognizable, more convenient, scaled-down version of the vehicle with which she or he is already familiar rather than a challenging innovation.

There seem to be two major kinds of Confident. Explorers. First, there is the relatively high-income, not so young, fairly well-educated man who expresses a preference for the standard large American car. Although he can be challenged by opportunity for innovation and feels competent to handle new experiences, he does not react to the small American car as a challenging innovation. Rather, he sees it as a low-priced, less comfortable vehicle and he feels that he can afford to own a large car with more conveniences. Part of his attitude of confidence is based on his access to money that he can use freely.

Then there is the relatively young, relatively well-educated man or woman who prefers the small car. These people, who see themselves as Confident Explorers too, are perhaps the model the authors had in mind when they began the study. Although in relatively high income brackets, for most of them money is committed to basic family expenses. For them the small car is a creative alternative to more expensive standard size cars. But also in this group are the individuals with relatively large amounts of disposable income who prefer sports cars, foreign and domestic.

Predictions about the Cautious Conservatives, then, can be made with fair probability of accuracy. It is highly likely that they will choose small American cars. Predictions about Confident Explorers have to be conditioned by additional information about income, age, sex, family status, and education.

II / Perception

A. BACKGROUND AND THEORY

The first article (Engel) deals with the nature of perception; and then the relationship of motivation and emotion to perception is explored (Vernon).

11-A THE NATURE OF PERCEPTION

James F. Engel (Marketing Educator)

An unequivocal definition of perception is sidestepped by most authorities. Generally, the concept refers to the process by which a stimulus and a response are related. The nature of this assumed relationship can best be grasped by a diagram. (See Figure 1.) An individual is exposed to a stimulus of some sort which he receives through his five senses of taste, touch, smell, sight, and hearing. Something happens in his unseen mental mechanisms, or "black box," to give meaning to these inputs, and this reaction is translated into an output—either overt behavior or some other response. To explain this process an inference is necessary to what happened within the black box, and the literature of psychology abounds with theories of this type.

Much of contemporary perception theory is built on the assumption that each stimulus or information input is somehow checked against stored categories of meaning. Many of these categories function quite predictably from individual to individual. For example, a yellow pencil is usually perceived as a yellow pencil because of its distance and angle from the perceiver, its relationship to its surroundings,

and common individual experience with pencils among other reasons. Other times, however, the response is unpredictable and appears to depend upon unique individual predispositions such as physical needs, psychological needs, and attitudes. In the latter instance the person is said to perceive selectively. (See Figure 2.) Each of these factors (attitude, psychological need, or physiological need) can become dominant and affect the response, and it is also probable that they somehow work in combination.

SOURCE: James F. Engel, "The Influence of Needs and Attitudes on the Perception of Persuasion," in Stephen A. Greyser, Editor, *Toward Scientific Marketing*, (Chicago: American Marketing Association, 1964), pp. 18–29, at pp. 18–20.

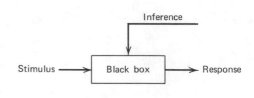

Figure 1.

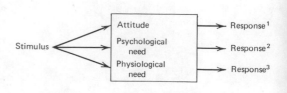

Figure 2.

11-B THE RELATION TO PERCEPTION OF MOTIVATION AND EMOTION

M. D. Vernon (Psychologist)

What general conclusions can we draw as to the effects of motivation on perception? These must necessarily be speculative, since few if any of the experiments described show with any certainty the type or degree of motivation or emotion which was actually experienced by the observers. Curiously enough, the effects of positive and pleasurable emotions aroused by the satisfaction of needs seem to have been less thoroughly investigated than the effects of frustrated needs and unpleasant emotions. This is unfortunate, since pleasurable emotions could be directly effective, and would not be repressed. However, it is possible that they are less easy to create in laboratory situations. In general, it seemed that those who were rewarded, or who had experienced success in a task, had some tendency to attend preferentially to the rewarded or successful situation, or related material such as pictures or words associated with reward or success, and to perceive them more readily. Positively valued material may also be perceived, apparently, in such a way as to accentuate certain irrelevant qualities of the material, such as size. This type of inaccuracy may occur to a small extent in everyday life. But it is doubtful if it would persist in any unambiguous situation in which the observer could check his judgments, since its inaccuracy might lead to the frustration rather than the satisfaction of need.

There does not seem to be much direct evidence as to whether need, satisfaction, and pleasurable emotion facilitate perception, making it more rapid or more accurate. One might suppose that perception would be facilitated in so far as it led directly to need satisfaction. Also, pleasurable feeling might produce a general state of elation which would stimulate the observer to perceive more efficiently. It seems possible that activity of the reticular formation would facilitate attention and discrimination in such circumstances. The experiment of Postman, Bruner, and McGinnies and other similar experiments, do suggest that in the furtherance of interests, which are undoubtedly highly motivated (even if the nature of the motive is not always clear), special knowledge is acquired which in itself facilitates perception of relevant material.

The most extensive data have been obtained from experiments in which unpleasant emotions have been aroused, by some form of painful experience, by frustration of needs and desires, or by arousal of emotional conflict over sex. There seems little doubt that with many people these states are liable to disrupt the process of perception, as they disrupt other activities, making it slower or more uncontrolled and inaccurate. However, some people appear to be stimulated by these experiences to try harder. In all probability, a severely painful experience is likely to have a prolonged disruptive effect. Indeed, we know that violent needs and emotions tend to monopolize attention completely, making the observer incapable of perceiving anything in his surroundings unless it, or some distorted perception of it, can be related to his need. A mild degree of pain or unpleasant emotion may make the observer more cautious and hence slower; or it may stimulate him to attend with greater concentration, hence producing in some cases more rapid and accurate perception. This latter result would be most likely to occur in situations in which rapid and accurate perception would enable the observer to avoid the pain or unpleasantness.

SOURCE: M. D. Vernon, *The Psychology of Perception* (Baltimore: Penguin Books, Ltd., 1962), pp. 217–219.

B. RESEARCH AND APPLICATIONS

The first selection in this section is a study (Laird) of "subconsciously received sensory impressions." The second selection (Birdwell) is an analysis of the effect of an individual's cognitive structure, self-image, and environment on his perception of automobiles.

11-C HOW THE CONSUMER ESTIMATES QUALITY BY SUBCONSCIOUS SENSORY IMPRESSIONS—WITH SPECIAL REFERENCE TO THE ROLE OF SMELL

Donald A. Laird (Psychologist)

It happens from time to time that an article which has excellent quality from the engineering point of view still does not impress the retail customer as possessing good quality, or that a poorly made article of poor materials impresses the customer as having excellent quality.

How is Quality Judged?

What are some of the factors which influence the customer's judgment of quality? Since the average purchaser has little technical skill in actually determining any real quality of manufactured articles, it is important to learn something about the factors which must be active in influencing these judgments of quality.

It is apparent that these influences reach the customer through some sense. The senses most actively and consciously used by the customer are sight and touch; the fingers are run through a cloth, it is held up to the light and the customer looks through it, the dyeing is inspected for uniformity, it may be wadded lightly and held to the cheek to determine softness. The sense of taste or the muscular senses are more rarely used consciously.

Testing the Role of Scents

The present experimental work is based upon the observation that the "general atmosphere" surrounding a product is often the determining element in the judgment of its quality. Packaging, store interior, prestige ad-

vertising are illustrations of this influence. The experimental work was done on the influence of faint scents upon the judgment of quality. Scents were chosen because competitive products vary markedly in this (due to different paints, finishing oils, etc.), because it was possible for us to vary the products in regard to their scent without altering their intrinsic engineering features and because observations of consumers suggested that the slight scent of a product was important in their selection of an article from a choice of several closely similar articles.

Women's silk hose were used for the experiment. They were bought in regular retail channels, were made by the same manufacturer, and were the same style, color, and design. So far as it is possible for textile machinery to make them, they were identical hose. Each pair of hose was packed in a separate box, and the boxes were identical.

A test set consisted of four pairs of these identical hose, packed in identical boxes. One pair was left with the natural slightly rancid scent which comes from the mixture of castor oil and sulphates which is used in lubricating the fibers of the yarns to facilitate weaving and to yield softness. A second pair of hose was given a very faint scent by a compound of synthetic aromatic chemicals; the narcissus note predominated in this scent. A third pair of hose was given a complex fruity type of scent, and the fourth pair was given a sachet type of scent.

All these scents were very faint, and it was attempted to have them no more intense than the natural rancid smell of the pair that was not re-odorized; the aim was to change the quality or type of the scent rather than to change the strength of the scent. The re-

Source: Donald A. Laird, "How the Consumer Estimates Quality by Subconscious Sensory Impressions—with Special Reference to the Role of Smell," *The Journal of Applied Psychology*, Vol. 16 (June, 1932), pp. 241–246.

odorization was brought about by pinning a small card of perfumer's blotting paper to which a drop of aromatic compounds had been touched to each pair of hose; the aromatics could have been added to the finishing oils in the manufacture of the yarns, but since the synthetic aromatics had been compounded to blend with rather than to be stronger than the natural rancid smell, the use of the scented blotter produced the same aromatic results.

The scents on the re-odorized hose were so faint that only six out of the 250 housewives tested noticed the scents. But the aromatic particles were present in the air entering the olfactory apparatus of the housewives and the data obtained show that through some subconscious channels their judgments of quality were influenced by this subconscious impression.

How the Data Were Obtained

Men from the laboratory made a house-to-house survey of 250 housewives in Utica, New York, using a set of the four hose as described. Middle class and upper strata homes were visited. The men were instructed to use the following presentation:

"Good morning. I want you to help us find the best quality of silk stockings. I do not have a single thing to sell. Women who have had experience in selecting silk hosiery, who know quality, are helping us size-up quality in hosiery. Here are four pairs of hose that are very much alike. They are the same color, and all are made in exactly the same pattern and style. Which pair do you judge to be the best quality? Feel them in your fingers, look through them, stretch them, look at the seams. Do anything you would ordinarily do to pick out the best for your own use."

Do *not* tell or suggest to the lady that she smell the hose. Scatter the four opened boxes three or four feet apart, so that the scent on one pair does not spread to the others. The boxes can be opened and the covers placed beside them.

The blotter that is pinned to each pair should be kept with that pair, although the woman may want to take it off in order to run her fingers through the leg of the stocking. Watch closely to see that the hose and pinned cards are kept in the right box. The number, or letters, on the card and on the box should agree exactly.

Observe closely to note whether or not they smell the hose, and record this as well as other observations on the data blank *after* you are out of the house.

Any woman who will cooperate in the test can be used.

Be careful not to get tobacco smoke over the hose, or other smells mixed with the ones already placed in them.

In case the lady asks which *is* the best hose after her test is done, tell frankly that you do not know, and that the test is actually to find out which women judge to be the best. "Factory engineers' judgment is not to be counted, you see, madam, when the important thing is the experienced judgment of women themselves."

There was little difficulty in obtaining the cooperation of 250 housewives; but the experiment was discontinued due to the publication of the following truthful news item in a local paper:

A scientific experiment in South Utica this forenoon alarmed a housewife and led her to telephone for the police.

The scare was caused by a group of Colgate University students posing as hosiery salesmen and bent on finding out whether or not a perfumed article of merchandise could be sold more readily than one that lacked the pleasant odor.

A student rang the bell of a home on Amy Avenue. No, the woman who responded did not care to inspect the hosiery. Too busy.

"But would you just look at these stockings and tell me what you think of the quality," he persisted. Reluctantly she looked at the materials in two or three boxes and declared them all about the same.

The student was insisting that she should determine the quality, when the doorbell rang, indicating someone was at the rear door.

"Say, what's your racket?" asked the impatient housewife. "You get out of here, or I'll call the police." The young man left. "I'll answer one door at a time," said the woman and closed the door.

Going to the rear of the house she could find no one at the door. She became suspicious and called Lieut. James V. Felitto of the detective bureau. Detective Felitto soon had Detectives Thomas Ferrar and Chris McDermott on the way to the house. They heard the story and started after the suspects.

In the Roosevelt Drive-Sunset Avenue section they came upon some Colgate students testing theories of salesmanship in the study of psychology.

Police learned the efforts were made at the suggestion of Prof. Donald Laird, professor of psychology at Colgate. They reported that the experimenters carried a box of three pairs of stockings which were perfumed and another with stockings that were without the artificial odor and their errand was to learn whether the housewives would consider the perfumed article more attractive than those without perfume.

The work was discontinued after the publication of this item, since it revealed to Utica housewives the purpose of the experiment and further data would have shown which scent they preferred rather than the rôle of subconscious sensory impressions upon the judgment of quality.

How Housewives Say They Judged the Best Quality

In the order of the occurrence, housewives thought they were determining the quality of the four identical pairs of hosiery by: texture, finer weave, feel, better wearing qualities, no sheen, heavier weight, and firmer weave. Although all pairs were the same, the housewives found no difficulty in telling why one pair was the best, although some of them did have difficulty in finding out *which* pair was the best.

How the Housewives Were Influenced by Scents in Judging Quality

Each pair of hose should have received the same number of judgments as being the best quality, if the scents played no part in

TABLE 1

Judged the Best Hosiery

Scent	1st 72 House- wives	Next 83 House- wives	All 250 House- wives
"Natural"	8.3%	8.4%	8%
Sachet	16.6	18.0	18
Fruity	24.9	22.8	24
Narcissus	49.8	50.6	50

subconsciously influencing the judgment of quality. The data in Table 1, which show that the scent played an important part in judging quality, have been arranged to show the reliability of the findings as well as the trend of the results.

The statistical reliability of the data is shown by the close agreement of the first two columns with each other and with the records for the total group.

Had the data been gathered by one man we might justly suspect some forcing of the judgments in favor of the narcissus type of scent, but this is ruled out by the fact that more than a dozen men took about equal part in the data gathering, as well as by the fact that the men were prejudiced in advance by their personal favor for the sachet type of scent.

Conclusion

Two things are plainly indicated by this experiment: (1) Subconsciously perceived sensory impressions received through the olfactory apparatus are potent in determining the housewife's judgment of quality in silk hosiery. (2) Scents of one type are more influential in determining this judgment of quality than are scents of another type.

11-D INFLUENCE OF IMAGE CONGRUENCE ON CONSUMER CHOICE

Evans Birdwell (Marketing Executive)

The primary objective of this study was to relate, empirically, an automobile owner's perception of himself to his perception of his car. A second objective of the study was to

Source: A. Evans Birdwell, "Influence of Image Congruence on Consumer Choice," in L. George Smith, Editor, *Reflections on Progress in Marketing*, (Chicago: American Marketing Association, 1964), pp. 290–303.

show that between ownership classes the average owner's perception of several brand and car types was significantly different. In other words, to show that the average Buick owner, for instance, holds a different image of the Ford than does the average Ford owner.

With these objectives in mind, the hypotheses of the study were formed. First, *that an automobile owner's perception of his car is essentially congruent with his perception of himself.* And second, *that the average perception of a specific car type and brand is different for owners of different sorts of cars.*

The Research Design

While the semantic differential as a measuring instrument will not be discussed in detail, the research design as finally conceptualized will be more clear if the salient principles of the technique are explained.

First, it must be remembered that the semantic differential is a technique of measurement which is highly capable of providing generalizations and which must be adapted to each research problem to which it is applied. There is no single set of standard scales and hence the development of these becomes an integral part of the research which is to use them.

In essence, the method involves repeated judgments of a concept or object (or a number of concepts or objects) against pairs of descriptive polar adjectives along a seven point scale, like this:

Good__:__:__:__:__:__:__Bad

Progressing from left to right on the scale, the positions are described to the subjects as representing extremely good, very good, slightly good, neither good nor bad, or both good and bad, slightly bad, very bad, extremely bad.

With these factors and our hypotheses well in mind, the following experimental plan was decided upon, modified, and then carried out.

SELECTION OF POLAR TERMS. A master list from which to select polar adjectives to describe automobiles was first derived. From this master list of terms developed for this study, a group was selected that were: (a) adjectives or could be put in adjectival form; (b) reasonably understandable; (c) possible to provide with antonyms; (d) could be used to describe either an automobile or the person who owned it; and (e) not obviously reduplicative of terms already employed. The terms finally selected are shown in Figure 1.

CONCEPTS MEASURED. The automobiles to be judged were selected on the basis of color and model type from all the several hundred American and foreign cars manufactured in 1963. From this group of possible concepts a smaller number were selected that were: (a)

Scale
Number

1	Sophisticated	___:___:___:___:___:___:___	Unsophisticated
2	Exciting	___:___:___:___:___:___:___	Dull
3	Husky	___:___:___:___:___:___:___	Weak
4	Happy	___:___:___:___:___:___:___	Sad
5	Eccentric	___:___:___:___:___:___:___	Conventional
6	Bold	___:___:___:___:___:___:___	Shy
7	Young	___:___:___:___:___:___:___	Old
8	Nimble	___:___:___:___:___:___:___	Clumsy
9	Simple	___:___:___:___:___:___:___	Complex
10	Sporty	___:___:___:___:___:___:___	Businesslike
11	Obvious	___:___:___:___:___:___:___	Subtle
12	Stale	___:___:___:___:___:___:___	Fresh
13	Robust	___:___:___:___:___:___:___	Fragile
14	Swift	___:___:___:___:___:___:___	Slow
15	Elegant	___:___:___:___:___:___:___	Plain
16	Lively	___:___:___:___:___:___:___	Calm
17	Indulgent	___:___:___:___:___:___:___	Thrifty
18	Reliable	___:___:___:___:___:___:___	Unreliable
19	Safe	___:___:___:___:___:___:___	Dangerous
20	Impulsive	___:___:___:___:___:___:___	Deliberate
21	Masculine	___:___:___:___:___:___:___	Feminine
22	Spacious	___:___:___:___:___:___:___	Cramped

Figure 1. Scale Format.

as diverse as possible; (b) recognizable and representative of domestic and foreign cars; (c) most likely to evoke significant responses; (d) reasonably appealing to all ages and income levels; and (e) not obviously repetitious of other concepts in the series. The automobiles finally selected were: Renault, Thunderbird, Chevrolet, Oldsmobile, Corvette, Cadillac, Ford and Rambler.

DEFINITION OF THE UNIVERSE. Twenty-five car owners were selected at random from four groups of all the new car purchasers in the universe.

The four groups were defined as follows:

Group 1—Owners of 1963 Cadillac, Lincoln, and Imperial.

Group 2—Owners of 1963 Oldsmobile, Chrysler, Buick, and Pontiac.

Group 3—Owners of 1963 Ford, Chevrolet, and Plymouth.

Group 4—Owners of 1963 Volkswagen, Falcon, Renault, Rambler, Corvair, and Volvo.

Each of the groups were sampled systematically using a random starting point and beginning with the most recent purchaser until twenty-five interviews were secured. Using the chosen adjectival scales, the respondents were asked to judge their own car, the cars selected for the study, and finally, to judge themselves.

Results: Part I

The "D-measure" between the respondent's evaluation of himself and all the other cars, including his own, was computed. These D-values were then ordered from smallest to largest. A D-value of zero would indicate complete congruity or complete perceptual agreement. The larger the D-value becomes, the more divergence there is from congruity and the smaller the D-value, the greater the congruity between concepts. The D-values were individually ranked for each ownership group so that the criteria of replication over different individuals would be met and one of the usual tests of significance might be used to test the first hypothesis. As a result of chance, one would expect a D-value between the owner's car and himself which ranked as small as one, two, three, or four, as often as a D-value which ranked as large as six, seven, eight or nine.

Discussion

Table 1 shows the distinctly close relationship between automobile owners' perceptions of themselves and their cars. The marked concentration of number one D-rankings in the Cadillac, Lincoln, Imperial category indicate a high degree of self-identification with their automobile for individuals in this group. Although there are fewer number one D-rankings in the medium-priced and economy compact ownership group respectively, very significant statistical relationships are present. Interestingly, there is a noticeable trend to less conceptual agreement between ownership group one and group four. While the overall degree of self identification is statistically high, the tendency toward fewer number one D-rankings for the owner's automobile is particularly noticeable.

In general, this is the expected result. In-

TABLE 1
Rank of D Between Owner's Evaluation of Himself and His Car

Ownership Group	Rank									Total of Those Ranking Less than 5
	1	2	3	4	5	6	7	8	9	
1. Prestige cars	12	5	4	2	2					23[a]
2. Medium-priced	11	3	4	3	2	2	1			21[a]
3. Low-priced	9	7	0	6	2	1				22[a]
4. Economy compacts	8	4	2	3	1	3	2		2	17[b]
										83[b]

[a] Significant at the 1% level.
[b] Significant at the 5% level.

dividuals in ownership group one are social and stylistic pace setters and most likely are not particularly limited in their purchasing power. As a result, they most often purchase to please themselves. As one moves down the social and economic ladder, the consumer is more often restricted in his ability to buy a car that is truly expressive of himself. While a young physician might readily identify with a Corvette or Porsche, the social pressure of the community virtually commands his purchase of an automobile befitting his position. On the other hand, the thirty-year old laborer might feel that an Oldsmobile convertible was most self-expressive, yet his economic situation demands that his automobile purchase be a more rational one. While both the physician and laborer feel their cars are right for them, there are other considerations besides self-expression which have influenced their choice.

For ownership group one, the results of a standard t-test between each concept's average D-rank and the expected mean rank of five show statistically significant congruency for Oldsmobile and Thunderbird as well as the Owner's Car (see Table 2, Part A). The fact that the t-value for the Owner's Car is

TABLE 2

Average of a Concept's D-Rank and Results of t-Test for:

Part A
OWNERSHIP GROUP 1—PRESTIGE CARS

Concept	Average Rank	s	t-value
Owner's car	2.12	1.296	10.87[a]
Oldsmobile	3.08	1.590	5.91[a]
Thunderbird	3.48	1.769	4.21[a]
Cadillac	4.64	2.260	.78
Ford	4.96	2.133	.09
Chevrolet	5.84	1.752	2.35[d]
Renault	6.96	1.979	4.85[a]
Corvette	7.20	1.356	8.30[a]
Rambler	7.28	2.144	5.20[a]

where: $t = \dfrac{\overline{X} - m}{S\sqrt{N-1}}$

and $\overline{X}$ = the average rank of D-values
  m = the expected mean rank, 5
  S = the standard deviation of the average rank of D-values
  N = the size of each sample group, 25

Part B
OWNERSHIP GROUP 2—
MEDIUM-PRICED CARS

Concept	Average Rank	s	t-value
Owner's car	2.76	1.86	5.90[a]
Chevrolet	3.52	2.32	3.12[b]
Ford	4.00	2.02	2.43[d]
Oldsmobile	4.40	2.09	1.41
Cadillac	4.88	2.05	.28
Thunderbird	4.88	1.76	.33
Rambler	6.40	2.87	2.39[d]
Renault	6.68	9.96	4.20[a]
Corvette	7.20	1.90	5.65[a]

Part C
OWNERSHIP GROUP 3—
LOW-PRICED CARS

Concept	Average Rank	s	t-value
Owner's car	2.52	1.55	8.85[a]
Chevrolet	2.92	1.56	6.65[a]
Oldsmobile	3.44	1.75	4.37[a]
Rambler	3.64	2.36	2.81[b]
Thunderbird	6.00	1.77	2.77[c]
Cadillac	6.12	1.75	3.14[b]
Ford	6.20	1.81	3.25[b]
Renault	6.60	2.10	3.73[b]
Corvette	7.80	1.16	11.81[a]

Part D
OWNERSHIP GROUP 4—
ECONOMY COMPACTS

Concept	Average Rank	s	t-value
Chevrolet	3.24	1.84	4.69[a]
Owner's car	3.56	2.57	2.75[c]
Oldsmobile	4.36	2.20	1.43
Rambler	4.56	2.49	.72
Ford	4.92	2.23	.17
Thunderbird	5.24	2.25	.52
Renault	5.64	2.24	1.40
Cadillac	6.56	2.09	3.65[a]
Corvette	6.80	2.33	3.78[a]

[a] Significant at the 0.1% level.
[b] Significant at the 1.0% level.
[c] Significant at the 2.0% level.
[d] Significant at the 5.0% level.

approximately double that of each of these concepts shows a much stronger degree of overall self-expression in the Owner's Car. It should be remembered that the D-value measures the degree of congruency between concepts on all the scales, so while these two concepts were self-expressive for persons in this category, the degree of their expressiveness was not nearly so intense.

The results of this same t-test for ownership group two show statistically significant average D-rankings for the Owner's Car, Chevrolet, and Ford, the degree of significance being smaller for each concept respectively. Again, this indicates that the degree to which these concepts were self-expressive was less intense than that of the Owner's Car. In ownership group three, the Owner's Car, Chevrolet, Oldsmobile, and Rambler show significant average D-rankings with Chevrolet showing very close conceptual agreement to the owner's perception of self.

As applied to the hypothesis which the experiment was designed to test, the results suggest that the hypothesis be accepted: *That an automobile owner's perception of his car is essentially congruent with his perception of himself.*

Two other pertinent facts were uncovered by averaging the D-rankings by ownership group and are worth mentioning at this point. First, the average D-rankings of the concept of Owner's Car was higher for each ownership group from one to four respectively, lending further weight to the conclusion that factors other than expression of self are important determinants of purchasing behavior, particularly in the lower socio-economic groups. Second, the noticeable shifts in the positions of concepts in the average D-rankings tend to indicate differing perceptions of different cars between ownership groups, and this is the subject matter of the second part of the experiment.

12 / Rational and Nonrational Thinking

A. BACKGROUND AND THEORY

This section begins with a discussion (Wasson and McConaughy) of selective attention and selective perception. The meaning of "meaning" is next discussed (Stewart). The third selection (Parry) deals with the communication of affective experience.

12-A TUNING IN THE SIGNAL: SELECTIVE ATTENTION

Chester R. Wasson (Marketing Educator) and David H. McConaughy (Marketing Educator)

The customer would get nothing else done if he paid attention to every incoming bit of information impinging on him. The number of possible stimuli to which anyone outside a soundproof isolation cell is subjected is astronomical. Even the marketing stimuli alone, in today's affluent culture, are far beyond any man's capacity to absorb. Each of us is exposed to an estimated 1,500 advertising messages alone each day and these are but a small fraction of the total marketing knowledge besieging our beleagured psyches. A mass of 8,000 items clamor for attention the moment we step through the automatically opened door of the nearest supermarket, displays of three times that many confront us when we enter a department store.

Nor are advertising, salesmen, and product displays the only claimants for our attention. The media in which the ads are embedded contain an even greater volume of editorial matter—news stories, discussion, soap operas, folk tunes, symphonies, recipes, and much more that may be of more immediate interest

SOURCE: Chester R. Wasson and David H. McConaughy, *Buying Behavior & Marketing Decisions.* Copyright 1968 by Meredith Corporation. Reprinted by permission of Appleton Century-Crofts, pp. 34–36.

than the ads. Nor does the outside world around us let up. Mother must get Johnny off to school and he wants to voice some complaints about the teacher or he wants her ear about a new craze which will require an advance on his allowance. Supper must be planned. Father, on his way to work, must pay close attention to all that traffic weaving around him on the freeway at 60 miles per hour and at the traffic jam that seems to be building up ahead, if he is to get to the office safely. With a contract proposal on his mind and thoughts of organizing a bowling team, he barely hears the weather report for which he purposely tuned in the car radio. Our senses are truly besieged with more stimuli than we ever could afford to heed. From the moment our ancestors became sentient beings, we have known the full meaning of the word competition.

How do we manage? The same way every organism does which continues to survive: we never tune in on most of it. We exercise selective attention as part of the process of selective perception. We select out those elements, of all the infinity of goings-on around us, which we have learned will attain the personal goals toward which we are driven.

The bullfrog, sitting immobile on that lily pad, exercises selective perception to enable him to appease his hunger drive with a belly full of the insects zipping through the evening air. Biologists tell us he is able to flick out his long tongue in time for the appetizing snatch because he sees only two aspects of everything around him: shape and velocity. He does not wait to take in all of the details which identify the species—the hair, color, wings, legs and the like—but concentrates on finding convex shapes moving in his direction, notes the speed, and makes the intercept. Likewise, when we check over the Wednesday evening food ads, we do not compare in detail the hundreds of items listed by all the stores in the area. We look only at the ads of the Full Basket Markets and of Oscars, the stores which are near us, and note only the rump roast and strawberry specials which fit into our Sunday dinner plans. The artichokes may be really a buy, but our family does not like them, so we do not even see the artichoke listing. For the frog, shape and motion are the only *cues* to which he responds to attain his goal of hunger appeasement. To us, the roast and the strawberries are the cues which get our attention, for much the same purpose.

The seller must first get the customer's attention with something the customer feels is important to his own ends. The message he uses is not received in all of its details even when successful. The customer interprets what he hears, omits many details, *amplifying* and *sharpening* what remains, so that it assumes greater importance to him, with more motive force.

Selective Perception

Most of us are familiar with the parlor game "gossip." A message is whispered to the first person, who whispers it to his neighbor as he heard it, and so on through the group. The last person makes known the story as he received it, which seldom resembles the original. It has been selectively perceived by each person according to the points in it that appealed to his interest, interpreted in terms of his own interests, then repeated in the assimilated form

to the next person who interprets it differently, according to those points he perceived as being important, and so on to the end distortion.

What we admit to our senses, what we perceive, is a product of two different forces: the physical stimulus itself and both our ability to discern it in detail and the interpretation we put on it because of our attitudes, values, and interests.

Even the sensing itself is a learned skill— the ability to discriminate among similar but slightly different stimuli. A brewmaster can taste differences among individual batches in his own plant. Few beer drinkers can distinguish between brands on a blind test or recognize their favorite brands. The artist sees no real blacks, but many kinds of near black; to most of us, they all look alike—black. The wine-tasting connoisseur is said to be able to distinguish not only the vintage, but also the estate of origin. Most of us can do little more than discern the quality difference between the poorest third pressing, an ordinary wine, and a vintage one. We cannot perceive the added sensory information denoting the real difference because we have not learned to discriminate the subtle differences that are there. The well-known tendency of experts to overdesign products in terms of the average buyers' tastes is partly due to their better-educated discrimination.

Whatever sensory information we do admit to our senses is given a specific interpretation in the context in which we view it, and we add to it associations built out of past experience. The items we choose to perceive are those which are important to our inner needs at the time. We interpret them in relation to the social role we are playing at that moment, according to expectations built up out of past experience which the stimuli bring to mind. These expectations lead us to affix meanings, feelings, and impressions to the original cue stimulus, organizing the whole into some meaningful relationship to our needs at the time.

12-B THE MEANING OF "MEANING"

Daniel K. Stewart (Marketing Executive)

Discourse on the nature of meaning is really discourse on the nature of reality, truth, or being—whichever synonym is preferred. And the search is an inductive or dialectical procedure. It is going to the first principles.

Thus, the task is not one of deductive or logistic argument because the meaning of the propositions of such arguments depends upon what you have already assumed the nature of meaning to be. Such propositions are asserted in the argument *because* they are *assumed* as being meaningful. And, thus, if the proposition to be arrived at is one asserting something about the meaning of "meaning," any deductive argument would be circular because its propositions would require this in the establishment of its conclusion. In other words, the meaning of the premises, as determined by an unstated antecedent condition, cannot be assumed where the nature of *meaning* is the declaration in the conclusion to be proved.

Therefore, we cannot make this assumption on the nature of meaning here because it is precisely this nature that it is our task to investigate. Once we feel we know something about its nature, we may then, upon assuming this extralogically, present deductive arguments on its manifestations.

Moreover, it is not the case that there can be a multitude of meanings of "meaning" that are equally correct. There can be only one

true explanation, *i.e.*, one that is true of reality, and it is our task as researchers to find out which one it is. To paraphrase Aristotle: "Where there is not one meaning [of "meaning"], there is no meaning."

The primary objective of communication is the elicitation of intended meaning. The measurement of this objective demands the existence of norms or standards (criteria) against which given symbol complexes are judged to have fulfilled their function. Thus, in research that purports to deal with communication, attention must be given to that which is explicated in the objective and for which all such criteria exist: the meaning of "meaning." This fact, of course, constitutes the heart of the communication problem in that it has to do with the "mind" side of the mind-body problem.

Communication is basically a $mind_1$-to-$mind_2$ process that requires a vehicle for the physical presentation of some symbol complex. (What is popularly described as "mass communication" is simply the generalized explication of this basic relation.) Symbol complexes, therefore, are, in fact, the physical representations of those meanings within $mind_1$ that are to be interpreted as the intended meanings by $mind_2$. Since a given unit of meaning does not usually stand in isolation, we speak of its system of thought and its system of explanation. And it is these systems which provide for a richness of understanding. Meaning, to have depth, thus seems to require some system of ideas—a compound sphere of relevancy—of which a given idea is but a participant.

12-C THE COMMUNICATION OF AFFECTIVE EXPERIENCE

John Parry (Marketing Educator)

In talking of affective experience, the intention is to include all messages meant to convey the quality of moods, preferences,

values, emotions, hedonic tones, strivings, pleasant and unpleasant conditions (physical or mental), volitions and attitudes. If it is said that attempts to convey the quality of some of these conditions are not normally regarded as the transmission of information, the answer is that the transmission of affective content frequently interferes with the reception of cognitive content.

The affective message is bound to be subjectively tinged, and it will help to start by seeing how far this is in itself a complicating factor. We will explore by easy stages, moving from disinterested transmission to messages whose *raison d'être* is the need to find expression for some private experience.

Let us assume first that somebody asks a factual question and is given the information required. In this situation the response, if concise and accurate, approaches the upper limit of cognitive utterance; that is to say, the speaker transmits information without distorting it, adding to it or overlaying it with emotional tone. Despite the triviality of its subject matter, his message can hold its own with a proposition about the nature of right-angled triangles or whatever may be selected as a prototype of objective statement.

Next, the speaker imparts a piece of information which the recipient has not asked for. He says, "There was an earthquake in Nicaragua on Thursday." The giving of unsolicited information need differ from the reply to a question only so far as the first implies a selection and so presumably some kind of interest by the speaker. He might have chosen to give other information or to have transmitted none at all; he did choose to mention Nicaragua. There is, however, no ground for saying that selective interest necessarily distorts the content of a speaker's message, that it adds to or detracts in any way from the information as it existed before this particular communication. It would, in fact, be unfortunate if this were so; it would imply, among other things, that disinterest was a condition of sound research, a view which not even the most rigorous metalinguist has yet propounded.

Then there is information concerning the speaker himself; for example, "I've caught a cold." Here the speaker is obviously the source of the information and there may be no way of confirming the truth of what he says. What he takes to be the onset of a cold may be a psychogenic symptom. But possibilities of this sort merely mean that it may be difficult to find an objective criterion for such a statement; they do not demonstrate that the statements are necessarily unreliable or distorted. Our concern is not with how the speaker comes by information, but with how he transmits it, whether he adds to or detracts from its content in doing so. The answer is that he need not.

So far we have argued that a human being may transmit information objectively even when he has reached it by self-communication. But it is equally obvious that he can, if he chooses, charge the simplest message, even a conventional greeting, with affective tone:

Conder: Good morning, Mr. Whistler. I'm Conder.
Whistler: In that case, Mr. Conder, good morning.

One does not need a diploma in method acting to know that any sequence of words can become the vehicle for an indefinite number of affective messages and that where there is dissonance between content and affective tone, it is the latter that is likely to get through, a point made forcibly by a music hall actress last century in her rendering of "Abide with me."

In the oblique affective message there are two cognitive elements running in parallel. If a man says "I see ICI dropped 1s 6d yesterday," he may be giving the recipient distasteful news about a favored investment and at the same time conveying his pleasure at the other's distaste. Every affective message contains a cognitive element. A scream of pain or a howl of mirth has its cognitive nucleus: someone has been hurt, someone is amused. How much more is conveyed depends on the expressive powers of the sender and the sensibility of the receiver.

B. RESEARCH AND APPLICATIONS

The research report (Wells) in this section deals with the effects of "yeasaying" and "naysaying" on research results.

12-D THE INFLUENCE OF YEASAYING RESPONSE STYLE[1]

William D. Wells (Psychologist)

It is sometimes convenient to think of answers to questions as being determined by information, role and style. "Information" refers to all the knowledge the answerer can bring to bear when making his reply. It determines answers because different respondents have different information at their disposal and therefore answer differently. "Role" refers to the way the respondent is trying to portray himself to the questioner. It is important because some roles encourage accurate responses and some encourage falsification. "Style" refers to the way the respondent reacts to questions as stimuli. It influences answers because some people express themselves in one way, some in another.

This report is concerned with style, and with the effects of a particular kind of response style on research results. It will show that style can be an important factor in studies which count on attitude scales, rating scales, personality inventories, survey questionnaires, "open-end" interviews, or projective tests to supply basic data.

DESCRIPTIVE DEFINITION OF TERMS. "Yeasayers," as described by Couch and Keniston and, as exemplified in the research summarized below, are perhaps best described as *impulsively over-expressive.* On personality inventories, attitude scales, and survey questionnaires, they tend to say "yes," to agree, to be enthusiastic and uncritical, to give high ratings to objects which impress them favorably.

SOURCE: William D. Wells "The Influence of Yeasaying Response Style, *"Journal of Advertising Research,* Vol. 1 (June 1961), pp. 1–12, at pp. 1–5. © 1961 by the Advertising Research Council, Inc.

[1] The research described in this report was conducted by the research department of Benton & Bowles, and at Rutgers University with the aid of a Benton & Bowles research grant.

"Naysayers," by contrast, are *cautiously underexpressive.* They are more apt to be controlled in their responses, careful, conservative and critical. They are more likely to say "no," to be moderate rather than enthusiastic, to avoid committing themselves unless they are sure of what they are doing.

OPERATIONAL DEFINITION. In the present research, response style was measured by paper-and-pencil questionnaires designed to give short reliable measures of yeasaying and naysaying tendencies. One of these questionnaires and some data on its development are given in Table 1.

This scale is the second of two scales used to measure yeasaying tendencies in the general population.

The first scale, YN-1, consisted of twenty items from Couch and Keniston's Tables 8 and 9 (Couch and Keniston, 1960). Reports by interviewers indicated that some respondents had difficulty understanding the reverse-scored items, that some of the vocabulary was not understood by respondents with little education, and that some of the item content was too personal. These reports, and an internal-consistency item analysis of YN-1, led to YN-2.

The best YN-1 items were retained practically unchanged. Some of the reverse-scored items were reworded so that they could be scored in the positive direction. The vocabulary was simplified, and a few new items were added. In making these changes, every effort was made to stay as close as possible to the original items, so that information obtained with YN-2 could form a feed-back loop with basic theory.

YN-2 is scored by summing the numerical responses to the twenty items. Omissions are counted as 4's. The lowest possible score therefore is 20, the highest possible score is 140,

Individual Influences

TABLE 1

The YN-2 Scale

You can rate the following statements on a seven point scale as follows:

(1) Strongly Disagree	(2) Disagree	(3) Slightly Disagree	(4) Neither Agree nor Disagree	(5) Slightly Agree	(6) Agree	(7) Strongly Agree

_____ 1. Novelty has a great appeal to me.

_____ 2. Let us eat, drink and be merry for tomorrow we die.

_____ 3. There are few things more satisfying than to really splurge on something.

_____ 4. I often make decisions on the spur of the moment.

_____ 5. I really enjoy plenty of excitement.

_____ 6. I'm apt to really blow up, but it doesn't last long.

_____ 7. It's great fun just to mess around.

_____ 8. I often say the first thing that comes to my mind.

_____ 9. Here today, gone tomorrow . . . that's my motto.

_____10. When I talk, I tend to bounce from topic to topic.

_____11. I often change my feelings about others.

_____12. There is nothing so satisfying as to really tell someone off.

_____13. I like to see people express their emotions.

_____14. I crave excitement.

_____15. My mood is easily influenced by the people around me.

_____16. It's a wonderful feeling to sit surrounded by your possessions.

_____17. I tend to act on impulse.

_____18. I would like to have breakfast in bed every morning.

_____19. I often lose my temper.

_____20. Movement, travel, change, excitement . . . that's the life for me.

and 80 is the midpoint of the possible range. Average scores have varied from group to group; most have been between 75 and 79. Most distributions have been approximately normal.

YN-1 had a (corrected) split-half reliability of .63. Similar coefficients for YN-2 have ranged from .82 to .92.

YN-2 is presented here as an interim measure, not as a finished product. It was an improvement over YN-1, and there are many reasons to believe it can be improved still further.

It should be noted that the terms "Yeasayer" and "Naysayer" are not intended to imply a strict dichotomy. Like the terms "short" and "tall," "Yeasayer" and "Naysayer" refer to alternate sides of a continuous distribution. There are degrees of "yeasayingness" and "naysayingness," just as there are degrees of "shortness" and "tallness;" and where one merges into the other is largely a matter of arbitrary definition. The answer to the question, "How many Yeasayers and how many Naysayers are

there in the general population?" therefore depends entirely on where one sets the point of separation.

In much of the research reported here the respondents were divided into two groups at the middle of the possible range of scores on YN-2. With this division 40 to 50 per cent of those interviewed fell above the cutting-point, and 50 to 60 per cent fell below it.

Instead of adopting an arbitrary cutting-point, it would have been possible to have split each sample 50-50 by dividing at the median, but then some respondents classified as Yeasayers in one set of data would have been classified as Naysayers in another. This was considered undesirable. An additional consideration in favor of the arbitrary cutting-point was that it separates respondents who gave predominantly positive responses from respondents who gave predominantly negative responses. In other words, above-midpoint scores on YN-2 represent "yeasaying" in fact as well as by definition.

It would also have been possible to have

applied the terms "Yeasayer" and "Naysayer" only to individuals at the extremes. This procedure would have sharpened Yeasayer-Naysayer differences in many instances, but it would also have reduced the number of persons classified in one group or the other. When samples were small it seemed wiser to accept the smaller difference between groups in order to gain the increased stability of results computed on broader bases.

It is important to re-emphasize the premise stated earlier that behaviors influenced by yeasaying—ratings, questionnaire responses, answers in open-end interviews, etc.—are always influenced by information and role, as well as by style. Because information and role sometimes combine to counteract the effects of style, Yeasayers do not always say "yes," and Naysayers do not always say "no;" Yeasayers do not always give high ratings, and Naysayers do not always give low ratings. Yeasaying and naysaying are tendencies, not ironclad regulations.

In spite of the fact that yeasaying and naysaying are not absolutes, the work reported here suggests that response style is a potential problem whenever answers to questions supply research data. When conditions are right response style can be decisive.

Rating Scales

TENDENCY TO TAKE EXTREME POSITIONS. Yeasayers differ from Naysayers in the way they use rating scales. Yeasayers are more inclined to take extreme positions, to avoid caution and qualification, to avoid neutrality. Their high ratings, therefore, tend to be higher, and their low ratings tend to be lower. This

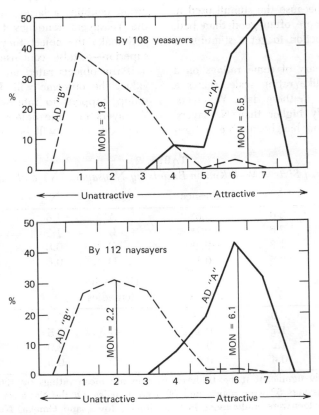

Figure 1. Rating of two advertisements. (Respondents were adults interviewed in Newark and vicinity. Scale was YN-2. Yeasayers defined as 80 and above; Naysayers as 79 and below. Significance of difference between Yeasayers' ratings and Naysayers' ratings tested by casting data into two-by-two tables (7 vs. 6 and below for Ad A, 1 vs. 2 and above for Ad B) and applying Chi Square. Differences were significant at .05 level.)

tendency is exhibited in Figure 1, which shows how Yeasayers and Naysayers evaluated two especially selected advertisements on a simple "unattractive-attractive" rating scale. Ad A, selected to elicit favorable reaction, was a four-color food ad with obvious appetite appeal. Ad B was a black and white patent medicine advertisement with a grim and graphic illustration of infected sinus cavities. As Figure 1 shows, both Yeasayers and Naysayers liked ad A and disliked ad B, but Yeasayers' ratings were more extreme in both directions. The rating differences were not large in this instance, but in routine testing differences of this magnitude frequently carry the decision.

Figure 1 shows that Yeasayers can react negatively if the stimulus is negative enough. Negative ratings from Yeasayers are rare, however, partly because Yeasayers tend to avoid giving low ratings unless the stimulus is odious, and partly because the stimuli used in rating studies are more often good than bad. It takes careful selection to get a stimulus as negative as this one.

Table 2, a summary of some ratings on a +5 to −5 like-dislike rating scale, shows a more usual pattern: in these data, Yeasayers' ratings are generally higher than Naysayers' ratings. This reaction has been observed re-peatedly—in ratings of popular brands, in like-dislike ratings of foods and beverages, in ratings of the desirability of various personality traits, in ratings of well-known political figures, in ratings of books, magazines and television programs. The pattern appears to be quite general: ratings made by Yeasayers are likely to be higher than ratings made by Naysayers if the rated object is not obnoxious.

Implications. Yeasayers' fondness for the high favorable rating can be worrisome when it is necessary to compare ratings made by a group containing large numbers of Yeasayers with ratings made by a group containing large numbers of Naysayers. The consequences of such mismatching are complex, because they depend at least in part on the real relationship among the objects being rated.

If the objects rated are in fact *of equal value*, and if one rating group contains a large number of Yeasayers while the other rating group contains a large number of Naysayers, the Yeasayers' tendency to give high ratings will make the object they rate appear to be superior—a false conclusion.

If the objects rated are in fact *different* in value, the outcome will depend upon which group happens to rate which object. If the Yeasayers rate the *better* of two objects, the rated difference will be in the right direction

TABLE 2

Like-Dislike Ratings of Sixteen Well-Known Brands by Naysayers (N) and Yeasayers (Y)

Gasolines	N	Y	Difference	Cameras	N	Y	Difference
A	2.0	2.6	0.6[a]	A	1.8	2.5	0.7[a]
B	1.9	2.6	0.7[a]	B	1.5	2.4	0.9[a]
C	1.7	1.3	−0.4[a]	C	0.8	1.3	0.5[a]
D	0.4	0.5	0.1	D	0.6	0.8	0.2

Coffees	N	Y	Difference	Headache Remedies	N	Y	Difference
A	3.3	3.0	−0.3[a]	A	2.9	3.5	0.6[a]
B	1.3	1.7	0.4[a]	B	2.5	3.0	0.5[a]
C	0.9	1.2	0.3	C	2.0	2.5	0.5[a]
D	0.2	0.4	0.2	D	0.6	1.4	0.8[a]

[a] Difference statistically significant at the .05 level. Figures are mean ratings by 166 Naysayers and 112 Yeasayers. Of the Yeasayers 52 were males, and 60 were females. Of the Naysayers, 86 were males and 80 were females. All raters were adults living in Des Moines, Iowa, and Omaha, Nebraska. Steps in the rating scale were designated by numbers only, with +5 defined as "like very much" and −5 defined as "dislike very much." The scale used to measure yeasaying was YN-2. The separation point between Yeasayers and Naysayers was a score of 80. If only extreme groups had been used (for example only Yeasayers scoring above 90 and only Naysayers scoring below 70), the entries in the *Difference* columns would have been approximately doubled.

but somewhat inflated, because Yeasayers rate things up and Naysayers rate things down. If the Yeasayers rate the *poorer* of the two objects, the real difference between the objects will be obscured. When the real difference between objects is small, and when the response style difference between rating groups is large, real differences can be reversed.

The ratings in Table 2 provide an illustration of such reversals. In these ratings, Yeasayers and Naysayers agreed on the rank order of the rated brands, but in three of the four product categories the Naysayers' rating of their favorite brand was lower than the rating assigned by the Yeasayers to the brand they liked second best. The consequences of this difference can be understood by imagining that conditions had made it necessary to assign brand A to one group for rating, and brand B to the other. If brand A had been assigned to the Yeasayers and brand B to the Naysayers, the apparent difference between the brands would have been in the right direction but inflated. If brand B had been assigned to the Yeasayers and brand A to the Naysayers, brand B would have (incorrectly) received the higher rating, just because it was the Yeasayers who rated it. Reversals of this kind have been observed often enough to make them appear to be fairly common.

13 ☒ Personality and Personality Differences

A. BACKGROUND AND THEORY

This section begins with a description (Bonner) of some characteristics of personality. This leads to a brief discussion (Levy) of contrasting styles of life.

13-A SOME CHARACTERISTICS OF PERSONALITY

Hubert Bonner (Psychologist)

It is easier to describe personality than to define it. In our description personality is the organized needs and abilities of an individual, or the characteristic manner in which he satisfies his needs and actualizes his potentialities. It is characterized by stability in change. A strain of consistency gives direction to man's behavior and sustains the individual in the face of shifting experience. Consistency refers to the enduring, but not unchanging, qualities of personality. Consistency gives to the behavior of a person a measure of predictability. The individual is thus seen to be a dynamic agent in the sociocultural process. He is not only conditioned by the customs and institutions of his culture but he transcends them and creates new ones. He is an active force in his own development. He sets up his own goals and either fails or succeeds in achieving them.

Furthermore, personality is not a thing possessed but a process of growth and experience. For this reason it cannot be measured like a physical object. What we measure is its flux, its change, its successive approaches to an end. It cannot always be described in terms of the organism's response to stimuli, although this formulation gives us knowledge of its elemental habit structure. For a penetrating understanding of personality a knowledge of the

individual's responses to stimuli is not only inadequate but intellectually destitute. Learning is only a slender portion of the total person's behavior. What we need to know in trying to understand any person is the degree of his self-awareness, the intensity of his striving for self-actualization, and the self-consistent intentions and values which serve to guide his conduct.

This general description of personality has several merits. It recognizes the place of learning, habit formation, problem-solving, motivation, and adjustment in individual behavior. Since these properties have been extensively investigated on an empirical and experimental level their use in personality theory is compatible with the scientific enterprise in psychology. To this extent our view of personality is in accord with the desideratum of making the study of personality scientific. On the other hand, our definition of science in the broad or open sense opens the door to an unbiased consideration of those creative aspects of personality which elude exact measurement. Purely empirical descriptions of personality do not come to grips with the complexity of individual behavior. Learning theory tends to be indiscriminate. It squeezes behavior into a narrow mold wherein all stimulations and reinforcements have an equal status in the organization of personality. The learning process has, of course, as we shall see, an important place in the structuring of personality. However, while learning tells us

SOURCE: Hubert Bonner, "Some Characteristics of Personality," in Hubert Bonner, *Psychology of Personality* (New York; The Ronald Press Company, 1961), pp. 36–40.

148

much about an individual's adjustment and survival, it sheds only a dim light on his persistence in a chosen direction even in the face of unbelievable obstacles. If the learning psychologist is all too eager to describe the person's determination as an index of unadaptability, or of learning deficiency, he is, of course, free to do so; but he is thereby devaluating the very essence of personality: its thrust into the future. We live not by habits only, but even more by presuppositions and intentions. We seek not only the satisfaction of our needs or the reduction of our tensions, but even more a steady growth toward maturity.

SOME WORKING PROPOSITIONS. To help the reader to form a clearer image of personality at the outset and to acquaint him with some of the guiding principles which make up the conceptual scheme for the study of personality, we present in the following few paragraphs some provisional assumptions or propositions in the study of personality. If, because of what we have already asserted in this chapter, some of these propositions now appear obvious through repetition, their importance is not, however, diminished.

1. Human behavior consists of acts. In our criticism of the atomizing tendency in psychology we argued that the stimulus-response couplet is inadequate to account for complex behavior. Consequently we posit the total act of the individual as the fundamental "unit" of behavior. Our object of investigation is the total personality, not an isolated modality, be it learning, motivation, cognition, or whatever. The modalities in themselves have no meaningful place outside the whole of which they are integral parts; they are derived from the whole by a process of differentiation; they are episodes, albeit important ones, in the total act called the personality.

2. Personality conceived as a whole actualizes itself in a determinate environment. Just as the separate acts of an individual cannot be understood apart from the whole person, so the total person cannot be fully understood if he is abstracted from his environment. Some of the most important characteristics of the total individual are derived from his environment, especially from the sociocultural matrix of customs and institutions. Differences in personality are expressions not only of inherent tendencies but even more of events in the social environment. The individual and his environment form a more or less coherent structure, namely, the person-in-his-environment.

Because of its familiarity this principle appears to be less vital than it is. However, it helps us to bridge the artificial gap between the subjective and the objective which the history of psychology has needlessly established. In our view, what was once outside the organism has been internalized and transformed by the intentions of the individual, and what was once inside it has been extraverted or actualized in response to the need for growth and self-realization. Internal and external, the organism and the environment, together constitute an indivisible whole of human experience.

3. Personality is characterized by self-consistency. We are quite aware of the strong tendency in some quarters to exaggerate the unity of the personality. This exaggeration appears to be a reaction against the molecularization of behavior which we already have noted. It is also partly based on a misunderstanding of the nature of self-consistency, on the erroneous belief that it means rigidity and freedom from change. It rests, finally, on the disproportionate concern of many psychologists with the pathological features of personality, such as mental and emotional conflicts, hysterical phenomena, neurotic ambivalence, and schizoid behavior.

Nevertheless, there is much confirming evidence for the principle of consistency. There is a strong tendency in every healthy individual to react similarly in corresponding situations. To say this is not to affirm the regnancy of habits merely, but to stress the driving forces of self-integrity. A mark of the mature yet growing person is the strong tendency to organize his behavior into a changeable but consistent pattern called the self.

4. Personality is goal-directed behavior. This principle is logically related to the preceding one. Self-consistency is not only the determination to maintain one's self; it also implies and involves the direction of acts toward a goal set up in advance. The unity of the personality is derived in large measure from the persistence of effort toward the attainment of a system of ends. Indeed, it is the properties of

goal-integration and purpose that lend personality its distinguishing mark of identification. Were it not for the individual's constant choice among a variety of means toward previsioned ends, we could not distinguish one person from another; for general behavior, such as learning, is very much the same in all people. Individual behavior, in short, is *intentional*.

5. Personality is a time-integrating structure. In traditional behavioristic psychology man is largely a creature of habit. Having been conditioned to respond in a given way the individual tends to persist in a mode of behavior until he has been "reconditioned," or until rewards and punishments compel him to surrender to a newly conditioned response. Psychoanalysis says very much the same thing. After the child's ego is fully structured in adolescence he largely recapitulates earlier forms of conduct in a contemporary setting. That this is true is not disputed, but the description is woefully incomplete. From our point of view, although the individual conserves much of the past and is deeply bound to the present, he foreshadows and anticipates the future. It is this future

orientation that we define as growth, self-enhancement, and creative conduct. The psychologist who ignores this aspect of personality because it eludes his demand for operational rigor and experimental validation is capitulating to a sterile principle.

6. Personality is a process of becoming. Personality is not, we have said, a mechanical process; it is not even a system of energy, merely, as one might be tempted to say. Rather, personality is an organization of potentialities striving to actualize themselves. The extent of this actualization will be helped or hindered by obstacles or facilitating conditions in the individual's social environment. This view of personality as becoming is reminiscent of the philosophical idea of *potentia*, without its mystical overtones. Like the tendency for becoming which has been posited in the quantum theory of modern physics, personality is a process standing halfway between the idea of an event and the event itself; a kind of reality "just in the middle between possibility and reality."[1]

[1] W. Heisenberg, *Physics and Philosophy* (New York: Harper & Bros., 1958), p. 41.

13-B CONTRASTING STYLES OF LIFE

Sidney J. Levy (Psychologist)

In expressing their values, in describing the kinds of roles they play in life and how they think those roles should be fulfilled, people reveal both real and ideal life styles. In one marketing study in Montana, life was described as slow-paced, with the people geared to the rigors and virtues of frontier life where it is cold and demanding; where the skills and rewards of hunting and fishing loom large; where men are rugged, touched with the nobility of the natural man and superior to the wan and tender Eastern city man. A man's life style was generally conceived as one of good fellowship, whether with a gun, a rod, or a drink. This may sound like parody; to show the reality of these views, I quote the com-

ments of some of the men describing the people and life style of Montana.

- The men here are real good, you can trust them. Most of them are outdoor men; they have to be or else they wouldn't live here. Most of them are honest.

- The men here are true Westerners; big, tough and rugged.

- Men are men here, and they are manly. Somewhat more honest and less sharp dealing than in the more civilized parts of the country.

- It's wonderful here. It's God's country. I like the frontier atmosphere. Life is casual and leisurely here, no frantic big city pace.

This contrasts with the kinds of life style men in metropolitan environments offer to sum up who they are. Here we find the familiar tunes of urban-suburban people, where

SOURCE: Sidney J. Levy, "Symbolism and Life Style," in Stephen A. Greyser, Editor, *Toward Scientific Marketing* (Chicago: American Marketing Association, 1964), pp. 140–150, at pp. 143–144.

men are first husbands and fathers, and run to the ragged rather than the rugged.

- The men here are very nice, a well-educated group of men who have many outside interests and are very congenial. They're home-loving and conscientious.

- Most of my neighbors are young families and pretty well child-oriented. The men are typical suburbanites, very much concerned with crab grass and PTA. They all work hard and bring home brief cases.

To grasp these life styles and how they are exemplified in individual lives requires an orientation to configurations, to patterns of ideas, feelings, and actions. We need to sense the man at work; to feel with him the peculiar flavor with which he invests his work or draws from it joy, irritation, monotony, impatience, anticipation, anxiety about today or tomorrow, comfort, competence, pride, a restless urge to succeed visibly, or a restless urge to reach five o'clock. We can think about what kind of motivation is useful in distinguishing the achieving executive from the adequate one, the upward striving white collar worker from the man who just wants to make a living. *To explore this large, complex symbol in motion that is a man's grand life style is to seek to define his self-concept*, to describe the central set of beliefs about himself and what he aspires to, that provide consistency (or unpredict-

ability) to what he does. Information about such self-concepts may come from various directions. Two students writing class autobiographies conveyed the contrasting sense of focus each felt about what he sought to achieve in life—one summing up that he wanted to live in accordance with "intelligence, truth, and justice," while the other said his aims boiled down to "thrift, security, and cleanliness." Presumably, the former young man represents a better potential market for books, the latter is possibly more geared to soap.

Such self-definitions can help us perceive the coherence of behavior in housewives who relentlessly pursue antiseptic cleanliness, in children accomplishing characteristically in school, as well as in doting or dismal fathers. This idea of one's self as "naturally" following its bent, accompanied by the feeling "doesn't everyone?" is the core personal symbol. When we understand this about a person, we can start to trace out the intricate pattern of his actions, to see how it affects the handling of money, choice of clothes, food preferences, interest in shopping, cooking, giving gifts, home workshopping. We can see how the persisting needs of one man to bend people to his will can make him a topnotch salesman, or where the urge to resist produces an obdurate purchasing agent.

B. RESEARCH AND APPLICATIONS

The one article (Bell) in this section is a report of research done concerning self-confidence and persuasion in automobile buying.

13-C SELF-CONFIDENCE AND PERSUASION IN CAR BUYING

Gerald D. Bell (Marketing Educator)

The study was conducted in a large urban area in western United States. One Chevrolet dealer was chosen to obtain people who had just bought a new car. Since there were over 50 Chevrolet dealers in this metropolitan area, customers had a wide range of choice. The dealer chosen for study had a good reputation

SOURCE: Gerald D. Bell, "Self-Confidence and Persuasion in Car Buying," *Journal of Marketing Research*, Vol. 4 (February, 1967), pp. 46–52.

in the area and with General Motors, and had a good sales and service record. Many of the 18 salesmen and other employees had worked for the dealer for many years with high morale. Salaries and benefits were good. Customers were mainly from suburbs close to the showroom and were primarily from the middle and upper class. Consequently, any generalizations from this study must be limited.

THE SAMPLE. Data were collected during June, July, and August, 1965, when 289 new cars were sold.) Attempts to interview the buyers of these cars were successful with 234 people (81 percent response). Respondents were predominantly Protestants between 26 and 45, high school graduates, and earned between $8,600 and $12,500 a year.

DATA COLLECTION. (Personal interviews were made up until eight days after the purchase. Interviewers waited at least one day after the purchase to allow the buyers time to reflect on their decision.) No more than eight days were allowed to pass before the interview so that the remorse or cognitive dissonance subjects were experiencing could be measured accurately before dissonance reduction was tried.

Fifty customers were interviewed between one and four days before they made their final purchase, to check the validity of the measures of general and specific self-confidence, persuasibility, and several additional variables. Comparisons between these 50 customers and the remaining respondents suggest that answers given on these factors differ only slightly before or after purchases. It might be noted, however, that people who were interviewed before their purchase had spent much time making a final decision and consequently were already influenced in the purchase situation.[1] Pretests of the questionnaire, hypothesis, and interview techniques were conducted for six weeks before the major study was begun. This aided greatly in the improvement of our hypothesis and research design.

MAJOR CONCEPTS. Generalized self-confidence was measured by the items used by Day and Hamblin and others [3]. Subjects were asked how much they agreed or disagreed with the following questions:

1. I feel capable of handling myself in most social situations.
2. I seldom fear my actions will cause others to have a low opinion of me.
3. It doesn't bother me to have to enter a room where other people have already gathered and are talking.
4. In group discussions, I usually feel that my opinions are inferior.
5. I don't make a very favorable first impression on people.
6. When confronted by a group of

strangers, my first reaction is always one of shyness and inferiority.
7. It is extremely uncomfortable to accidentally go to a formal party in street clothes.
8. I don't spend much time worrying about what people think of me.
9. When in a group, I very rarely express an opinion for fear of being thought ridiculous.
10. I am never at a loss for words when I am introduced to someone.

Individual scores on these questions were summed, and then respondents were ranked into three categories from high to low according to where the largest breaks in ranks occurred. Those who agreed with Questions 1, 2, 3, 8, and 10 but disagreed with the remaining questions were considered to have high self-confidence.

Specific self-confidence in buying a car was measured by asking questions about the purchase: (a) In general, how much experience have you had in purchasing a car? (b) Is buying a new car an area in which you have good ability? (c) How confident are you in your efforts at buying a new car? (d) To what extent have you not had the chance to learn about buying a new car?

Five response categories were established for each of these questions. Respondents who gave favorable answers to Questions a, b, c, and a negative reaction to d were considered to have high specific self-confidence. Subjects' total scores to these questions were summed and then were ranked into three categories where the largest breaks in rankings occurred.[2]

The use of a purchase pal was measured by asking respondents questions such as: (a) To what extent did you ask other individuals for their opinions and aid in buying your new car? (b) Did anyone ever go with you to the dealer to help with your purchase? (c) If so, how often did he go?

Salesmen were also asked to rate the customer on his use of a friend to help in his purchase. (The salesmen and customer ratings were highly correlated; Kendall's Tau rank-order correlation was $r_c = .66$, $P < .001$.) Those who asked others for their opinions and

---

[1] Michael Halbert refers to this process as "creeping commitment." This idea was developed by him at the Symposium on Consumer Behavior.

[2] All questions were intercorrelated, with Kendall's Tau rank-order correlation (r_c) being .71, $P < .001$.

aid in buying a car to a great extent, and who took a relative or friend to the dealer two or more times during the purchase, were ranked high on use of a purchase pal. Those who asked for advice to a moderate extent and took someone to the dealer at least once, were ranked medium on purchase pal usage. Finally, those who seldom asked for advice and did not take anyone to the dealer to purchase a car, were considered to be low on purchase pal usage.

Persuasibility was defined by asking respondents to what extent they were influenced by the salesman on the price, payments, particular car (color, style, size, etc.), accessories, delivery, and service. The answers to these questions were totaled and respondents were placed in one of five ranks on persuasibility. Immediately after the purchase the salesman was interviewed and asked to rank the customer on how easy he was to persuade on the above items. Response categories ranged from: He was very easy to persuade, quite easy, easy, average, not too easy, difficult, and very difficult to persuade. Combining these two measures led to ranking respondents in five categories. Salesmen's rankings were significantly correlated to customer self-ratings. (Kendall's Tau rank-order correlation was $r_c = .74$, $P < .001$.)

It should be noted that our measure of persuasibility differs from that used by Cox and Bauer. They measured the actual change in consumer decisions after being exposed to persuasive communications. Our measure is based on a combined index of customer and salesmen judgment of how much of a "fight" or how much resistance the customer put up in buying.

It might be noted that a customer who had shopped widely might enter the showroom knowing exactly what he wanted. The salesmen could possibly take him for one who was easily persuaded. However, since the customer himself would probably have a more accurate estimate of his persuasibility in this situation, such problems were reduced by combining the two indicators.

Furthermore, when salesmen were asked if it were possible to confuse those who had made up their minds with those who were easy to persuade, they were quite articulate on how to distinguish the two types. Even if a customer knows what he wants, the salesman may try to persuade the buyer to pay more, buy more insurance, select a car in stock slightly different from the one wanted, etc. Opportunities for influence, therefore, exist even though a customer has shopped extensively.

Findings

SPECIFIC SELF-CONFIDENCE AND PERSUASIBILITY. In past research, relationships between a person's general self-confidence and his persuasibility have been emphasized. Here, however, it seems important to analyze the effects of a person's specific self-confidence in car buying on his persuasibility. If an individual knows a lot about automobiles, has had much experience in buying and trading cars, and has much confidence in his ability to purchase a new car, he ought to be less susceptible to the influence of the salesman regardless of his general self-confidence. (His specific self-confidence in automobile purchasing seems to be more relevant than his overall confidence to his receptivity to influence attempts.)

London and Lim suggest that the more a person views a problem as complex, the more he will depend on his peers [5]. Correspondingly, Hochbaum points out that the less confidence a person has in his ability in a specific area, the more he will depend on social referents such as family or friends.[3] (These investigations suggest that people who have much specific self-confidence will be difficult to persuade. The data, however, do not support this conclusion. The findings shown in Table 1 (see page 154) indicate that there is no association between specific self-confidence and persuasibility.) This applies to both males and females under controls for age, social class, religion, marital state, salesmen used, and amount of shopping before the purchase. To explain the lack of association between these variables, the relationship between specific and general self-confidence is analyzed.

SPECIFIC AND GENERAL SELF-CONFIDENCE.

---

[3] Hochbaum asked male and female college students to predict the behavior of a person described in a case history. When the students were told they were good at performing this task, they were less likely to alter their judgment in favor of group opinion [4].

TABLE 1
Specific Self-Confidence and Persuasibility

Specific Self-Confidence	Persuasibility (percent)				
	High	Me-dium	Low	Total	Base
High	44%	25	31	100%	91
Medium	49	21	30	100	75
Low	50	26	24	100	68

$\chi^2 = 1.19, P < .45.$

The lack of an association between the above two factors leads to the question, "What is the relationship between specific and generalized self-confidence?" Is the association between specific self-confidence and persuasibility neutralized by the effects of a person's generalized self-confidence?

Table 2 indicates that these two variables are highly related for men and moderately related for women. The higher a person's general self-confidence is, the higher is his specific self-confidence. Evidently, an individual with generalized self-confidence develops skills or relies on his overall competence for decision making in specific situations such as car purchasing. The differences between males and females are probably due to variations in exposure to information about automobiles. Men, of course, are much more familiar with automobile operation and buying than are women.[4]

It might be pointed out that a relatively large number of women (40 percent) were high on specific self-confidence. This is probably because over 70 percent of the females were single, widowed, or divorced, suggesting that they were relatively independent compared with married women. They probably were used to supporting themselves and consequently had acquired automobile buying experience.

Use of Purchase Pals

Interaction of general and specific self-confidence might affect a customer's persuasibility by the type of information or help that he uses in car buying. A large number of customers asked a friend or relative to help buy a car. The use of purchase pals varied from

[4] Controls for age, social class, religion, marital status, salesmen used, and shopping behavior did not alter this association.

TABLE 2
Generalized Self-Confidence and Specific Self-Confidence by Sex

Specific Self-Confidence	General Self-Confidence (Percent)				
	High	Me-dium	Low	Total	Base
	Men				
High	51%	34	15	100%	71
Medium	30	45	25	100	59
Low	19	32	49	100	50

$\chi^2 = 21.6, P < .001.$

	Women				
High	42%	39	19	100%	20
Medium	24	60	16	100	16
Low	20	50	30	100	18

$\chi^2 = 4.48, P < .10.$

merely asking others for advice in a kind of car, to taking the friend to the dealer and letting him bargain for the car.[5]

The interesting point is that different kinds of customers used purchase pals to varying degrees. Depending on their combination of general and specific self-confidence, some customers sought the help of friends to a great extent while others did not.

One customer type had high general self-confidence but low specific self-confidence. A large number of both men and women in this category sought the help of a friend or relative who supposedly knew something about automobile buying.[6] Evidently, as the data in Table 3, Row A suggest, people with high general and low specific self-confidence realize that buying a new car is a relatively complex process which they know very little about. Since their general self-confidence allows them to face this weakness without being defensive, they ask for a friend's help.

[5] When the salesmen see a customer who is actively using a purchase pal, they refer to the purchase pal as a "cabbie." They imply that the customer is being "driven around" by the purchase pal. Often, the presence of a purchase pal makes the sale more difficult and thus less pleasant for the salesmen.

[6] These factors were first related for those high, medium, and low. Since the associations were the same as reported in Table 3, the categories were collapsed into high and low.

TABLE 3

General and Specific Self-Confidence and Use of Purchase Pals

General Confidence	Specific Confidence	Use of Purchase Pals (Percent)					Significance Level of χ^2
		High	Medium	Low	Total	Base	
A High	Low	74%	17	9	100%	57	P < .001
B High	High	29	36	35	100	60	< .35
C Low	Low	25	48	27	100	65	< .01
D Low	High	41	34	25·	100	52	< .06

Table 3, Row B indicates, however, that people with high general and specific self-confidence infrequently use a purchase pal. They probably have faith in their ability in most activities, particularly in automobile purchasing, and therefore rely little on others' help.

A rather unusual finding, Row C, appears for those who were low on both general and specific self-confidence. These individuals used purchase pals to a moderate degree. This was contrary to our expectations. We assumed they would be sensitive to lack of confidence in car buying skills since they have little general or specific self-confidence. Consequently, it was expected they would not use friends to help them buy a car. In seeking an explanation for this finding, interviewers asked respondents whom they used as their purchase pals. Those who used a purchase pal indicated that they used a close friend or relative, much more than a casual acquaintance (Table 4). If these persons felt inadequate in buying a car but were threatened by suggestions from others, the selection of close friends or relatives would not be so threatening. Another possibility is that these persons were unskilled in social relationships and thus had fewer friends to turn to.

Finally, the data in Row D suggest that those low on general and high on specific self-confidence use purchase pals quite often, although not as frequently as those in Row A. Possibly these persons ask friends to accompany them to the showroom to demonstrate their skills in car buying rather than to seek their advice. Their lack of general self-confidence would predispose them to attach special significance to areas in which they felt comfortable such as in car buying. Another explanation might be that their high specific self-confidence might lower their anxieties to the point where they could ask for help in buying a car.

In seeking an explanation for differences in the use of purchase pals, it is important to note the theory of Cox and Bauer that consumer decision making is a form of problem solving that consists of (a) identifying one's goals and (b) buying the products that will best satisfy these goals. Generally, a person's goals are performance or psychosocial buying goals. Performance goals are the functional characteristics of the product, while psychosocial goals are the personality and social needs involved in consumption such as status, sex appeal, etc.

Cox suggests that people interested in pur-

TABLE 4

Relationship of Customer Self-Confidence to Purchase Pal Used

General Self-Confidence	Specific Self-Confidence	Purchase Pal Used (Percent)						Significance Level for χ^2
		Spouse	Close Relative	Close Friend	Acquaintance or Friend	Total	Base	
A High	Low	12%	19	30	39	100%	52	P < .05
B High	High	16	26	32	26	100	37	< .38
C Low	Low	24	16	53	7	100	49	< .001
D Low	High	18	23	45	15	100	42	< .01

chasing a product primarily for psychosocial goals will seek information from sources that provide knowledge about the psychosocial aspects of the product [1]. Similarly, they will attempt to satisfy performance goals by seeking such information from performance sources. Furthermore, as the accuracy and quantity of the information obtained increase, the less a person will see risk in the purchase and, consequently, the more likely he will be to buy.

The data presented in Table 4 offer tentative support for these hypotheses. If we assume that an acquaintance or casual friend as a purchase pal, rather than a close friend or relative, is more a source of information on the performance or technical aspects of car operations than on the psychosocial aspects, the following analysis can be made. For the A group in Table 4, those who are quite confident in most areas of their lives but are uneasy about their car buying abilities, the most frequently used purchase pal are casual friends or acquaintances. This is consistent with Cox's theory.

We would expect these individuals to be able to solve most problems about the psychosocial appeal of the automobile since they presumably have confidence in their own judgment, self-image, and successful personal relationships. On the other hand, since they have little confidence in their car buying talents, we expect them to turn to sources for performance information to reduce the risk they see in this part of their purchase. In contrast for Group C in Table 4, only seven compared with 39 percent for Group A used a friend or acquaintance as a purchase pal. On the other hand, 53 percent used a close friend as a purchase pal. Since these individuals have low general self-confidence and low specific self-confidence, we expect them to have high needs for information on both the performance and psychosocial aspects of purchasing. The data indicate, however, that psychosocial needs appear to outweigh the performance needs. Evidently, the perceived risk of buying an automobile that is inappropriate for a person's personality and social relationships is of first importance. The objective performance of the car is not as important as the expected acceptance of the automobile to a person's significant reference groups.

Individuals in Group B select purchase pals from all categories. They are just about as likely to choose a close relative as a close friend, and so forth. One feature of importance is that they select casual acquaintances at a high rate compared to Groups B and D. Evidently, even though people in this group have faith in their car buying ability, many seek information from sources that might be more accurate as to performance than close friends or family.

Group D uses close friends and relatives most frequently. People in this group evidently know a lot about automobile purchasing and operations and use the performance expert less frequently than do customers who are low on specific self-confidence. Yet, these people have low general self-confidence and, therefore, higher needs for psychosocial support and information.

This analysis suggests then that customers use purchase pals to a different degree and for different purposes, depending on their particular combination of general and specific self-confidence. It should also be noted that a relatively small percentage of the total sample (only 16 percent of the married sample) used its spouses to a moderate or high extent as purchase helpers.

The Buying Team

The use of purchase pals by many respondents appears to be part of the reason for finding no relationship between specific self-confidence and persuasibility. Customer self-confidence was enhanced by the pal. The customer and his friend were, in effect, buying as a team. Where a customer was ranked high on the use of a purchase pal, the pal actually came to the dealer and bargained for price, car, accessories, payments, etc. It was not just the customer buying the car; it was a pair. Consequently, to accurately examine the relationship between specific self-confidence and persuasibility, it was thought necessary to measure the specific self-confidence of the buying pair and then relate this to persuasibility.

To do this the purchase pal's specific self-confidence was first measured. This score was weighted by the degree to which the customer used the friend, and then this score was added to the customer's ranking on specific self-confidence, yielding a combined index. The same questions as those used for customers were used to measure the purchase pal's specific self-confidence. The scores of purchase pals who were used most were given a weight of 3; those used moderately, 2; those used very little, 1. By adding these scores to the customer ranks on specific self-confidence, it was possible to establish a combined buying score for specific self-confidence.

The buying units that had high and low specific self-confidence were relatively low on persuasibility. Those medium on specific self-confidence were high on persuasibility. Hence, although there were fewer individuals in the low category of buying unit specific self-confidence because of the enhancement effect of the purchase pals, this finding corresponds with the association found by Cox and Bauer between general self-confidence and persuasibility [2]. This association held for both males and females and for the controls for age, social class, religion, marital status, shopping behavior, and salesman used.

REFERENCES

Donald F. Cox, "Consumer Decision Processes—Risk Taking and Information Handling in Consumer Behavior," forthcoming.

Donald F. Cox and Raymond A. Bauer, "Self-Confidence and Persuasibility in Women," *Public Opinion Quarterly*, 28 (Fall 1964), 453–66.

Robert C. Day and Robert L. Hamblin, "Some Effects of Close and Punitive Styles of Supervision," *The American Journal of Sociology*, 69 (March 1964), 499–511.

Godfrey M. Hochbaum, "The Relation Between Group Members' Self-Confidence and Their Reactions to Group Pressures to Uniformity," *American Sociological Review*, 19 (December 1954), 678–87.

Perry London and Howard Lim, "Yielding Reason to Social Pressure: Task Complexity and Expectations in Conformity," *Journal of Personality* (Spring 1964), 75–89.

14 / The Self

A. BACKGROUND AND THEORY

The first selection is a presentation (Douglas, Field, and Tarpey) of a self-image theory. Next the semantic barrier is explored (Hayakawa); and then a theoretical approach to the consumer's self-concept and market behavior (Grubb and Grathwohl) is presented.

14-A SELF-IMAGE THEORY

John Douglas (Marketing Educator), George A. Field (Marketing Educator), and Lawrence X. Tarpey (Marketing Educator)

Some of the most valuable contributions to the understanding of human motivation have come from a growing body of theory about the self, or self-image. The self is the individual as he sees himself; in other words, the self-image, self-conception, or self-perception is generally considered as synonymous with the term *self*. The self has several components, as can be seen from the diagram in Figure 1. First, there is the actual self, or the way the individual sees himself. Second, there is the way he thinks others see him, or "looking-glass self," so called because it is the way he sees himself through others (of course, his notion of the way others see him may be quite distorted). Third, there is the ideal self, or the way the individual would like to be (not necessarily the way he thinks he should be, however).

The self is believed by most psychologists to be largely the product of social interaction, though this is not the only factor. The child learns from interacting with others what type of person he is and what he would like to be; he also learns what possibilities are open to

SOURCE: John Douglas, George A. Field, and Lawrence X. Tarpey, *Human Behavior in Marketing* (Columbus, Ohio: Charles E. Merrill Books, Inc., 1967), pp. 64–67.

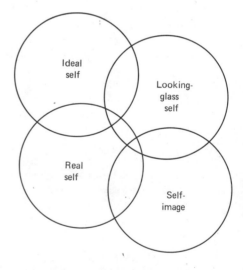

Figure 1. Components of self-concept. (Real Self —you as you are; Self-Image—the way you see yourself; Ideal Self—the way you'd like to be; Looking-Glass Self—the way you think others regard you.)

him and what his abilities and shortcomings are. He imitates his heroes, plays at various roles in an experimental way (he plays the father role, the role of policeman, etc.) as he grows up. Later he experiences a variety of real roles, which he internalizes to the point that some psychologists have come to regard the self as a collective internalization of his roles. But internalized roles, while closely related to the self-image, do not constitute the core of the self. Much more basic is the identification with a variety of reference groups with which a person's aspirations and self-picture have become enmeshed. Experiments have shown that when an individual is asked, "What are you?" his first identification is more likely to be with a reference group than with a role. He might say, "I am an American." "I am a Baptist," rather than "I am a father," "I am a thimble-maker."[1]

It is evident that the self is a percept, since it is the individual's perception or image of himself. Thus perception is at the core of identity or self; the individual's behavior depends greatly on how he sees himself in relation to his environment. And he tends to perceive the environment in ways that are acceptable to his self-image, even if he must interpret or "edit" the environment to make it fit his self-needs.

Within the self is a variety of motives, some more or less peripheral to the self and some more central. The latter are sometimes called ego-integrative motives and include any which help to enhance the self-image. Under this heading we could list a number of wants, such as the desire for love, power, achievement, status, recognition, group membership, or acceptance, as well as the desire for anything that directly or indirectly contributes to the self-image (wealth, possessions, skills, beauty, virtue, wit, etc.).

The self-image is man's most valuable possession and is the key to most of his behavior. The search for identity—to know what kind of person one is and can become—is a lifetime process, and the urge to preserve a relatively stable, somewhat flattering, and steadily more satisfying self-image is the driving and organizing force behind a large share of human activity. The self selects and evaluates

goals and motives and organizes the individual to implement this selection, so that goals are achieved or discarded. The self establishes intermediate goals as steppingstones to the long-range ones and is enhanced by reaching each step.

While self-image theory has made little impression on marketing education, it has played an important role in successful marketing for some time. Sophisticated marketers have long recognized that a very basic purchase and patronage motive is the support of the self-image. The individual buys the products and brands that match his self-image, particularly (insofar as he dares) his ideal self-image. This process applies equally to clothing, automobiles, homes and neighborhoods, cigarettes (e.g., the masculinity appeal popularized by Marlboro), liquor, and sports (since sports differ in acceptance by reference groups which help form the self). To a lesser extent, perhaps, food purchases are self-image oriented (e.g., the gourmet, the steak and potatoes plain-folks personality, the person who eats at the expensive restaurant versus the man who would feel out of place except at Joe's Greasy Diner). Thus stores are selected by the way in which they fit the self-image ("This is my kind of store; I feel at home here; they sell my kind of product and treat me the way I am used to being treated—or would like to be treated.")[2]

There are two significant aspects to this basic self-image factor in purchasing. First is the cognitive dissonance principle applied to the self-image; the individual strives to achieve a consistent self-image, by buying the right products from the right companies in keeping with his self-image. Thus he achieves cognitive consonance (a consistent self-image) and avoids cognitive dissonance (in this case, an inconsistent self-image). This results in reduction of internal tensions and produces satisfaction.

The second factor is the dramaturgic one. It has been pointed out that a fundamental part of human behavior is the individual's constant attempt to radiate or project the type of self-image he wants people to accept; this is akin to the role of an actor, and it is there-

[1] Helen Merrell Lynd, *On Shame and the Search for Identity* (New York: Science Editons, 1961), p. 170; M. H. Kuhn and T. S. McPartland, "An Empirical Investigation of Self-Attitudes, *American Sociological Review*, **19** (1954), pp. 68–76.

[2] Pierre Martineau, *Motivation in Advertising* (New York: McGraw-Hill Book Company, Inc., 1957).

fore dramaturgic in nature. Each person in his daily interaction with others, in addition to focusing on the task at hand, is attempting to act out a role and at the same time to project a personality or image consistent with both his self-image and the situation. This outer image he projects has been called the *persona*, after

the masks used in Greek plays to depict the character of the actor.

The marketer capitalizes on his knowledge of self-image theory by designing product and promotion to produce a product image that fits the self-image of the purchaser, which in turn influences his tastes and buying habits.

14-B PERSONALITY AND COMMUNICATION

S. I. Hayakawa (Semanticist)

What we call the symbolic self is pretty much the same as what Carl Rogers calls the self-concept and what Andreas Angyal calls self-organization. So let me state my suggested modification of the Darwinian law of self-preservation: The basic purpose of all human activity is the protection, the maintenance, and the enhancement, *not of the self, but of the self-concept, or the symbolic self.*

Next, let me give a definition of the self-concept. "The self-concept or self-structure may be thought of as an organized configuration of perception of the self which is admissible to awareness" (Rogers). Human beings perceive, are hopelessly addicted to the process of abstraction, symbolization, and of talking to themselves, not only about the universe around them, but about themselves. Hence, human beings, in addition to abstracting from and symbolizing the data of their environment, abstract and symbolize about themselves. And each of us, therefore, possesses not only a self, but a concept of self.

In the "Autocrat at the Breakfast Table" by Oliver Wendell Holmes, Holmes says that in any encounter between two individuals, there are six persons present. First, there are John and William. Then there are John's idea of John and William's idea of William, which may be entirely different from John and William. And then, third, there are John's idea of William and William's idea of John, which amounts to six "persons" altogether. This is a perceptive idea. Notice that John, therefore, acts not in his own interests, but his interests

as he sees them in terms of his self-concept, which may not be the same thing as his own interest. And William, too, acts in the interests of his self-concept, but possibly not of his actual self.

In the work of people in Perceptual Psychology, like Hadley Cantril, F. P. Kilpatrick, and others, you come across the idea quite frequently that the self-concept is the fundamental determinant of all of our behavior. Let me give you an illustration of this: Our environment is not a given, obvious fact. When ten of us walk down the same street, we actually see ten different environments, because each of the ten men have different sets of values, different ideas and different interests and, therefore, we do not actually inhabit the same environment. The self-concept, in a sense, creates the environment around it to which we react.

Here is another way of understanding what is meant by the self-concept. If we are Catholics, why don't we subscribe to Protestant magazines? If we are Protestants, why don't we subscribe to Catholic magazines? Why do we all tend to subscribe to magazines we agree with? Now, notice that from the point of view of information, this is a very silly thing that we do—subscribe to magazines that tell us what we already believe. But, from the point of view of self-concept, it makes perfect sense because the magazines that you don't agree with constantly imply that you are some kind of misguided fool, or possibly wicked, to believe the way you do; whereas the magazines that agree with you keep saying to you, in one way or another, that you are right; you are a swell guy; you're the intelligent man; and then they give you even more reasons for thinking what you already have been thinking and this strengthens and enhances the self-

SOURCE: Dr. S. I. Hayakawa, *The Semantic Barrier* (Providence, R.I.: Walter V. Clarke Associates, Inc.); a speech by Dr. Hayakawa at the 1954 Conference of Activity Vector Analysis at Lake George, New York.

concept. Let us say that a family you have met has invited your family to dinner. Whether you accept or don't accept revolves around the self-concept. You say to yourself, "we are the kind of family that doesn't associate with that kind of family" and then you find reasons to decline. If, however, it enhances your self-concept to

be seen at the home of these new acquaintances of yours, then of course, you accept. But, notice whether you accept or decline rests upon your perception of them and even more fundamentally, upon your perception of your own social position and the kind of person you are.

14-C CONSUMER SELF-CONCEPT, SYMBOLISM AND MARKET BEHAVIOR: A THEORETICAL APPROACH

Edward L. Grubb (Marketing Educator) and Harrison L. Grathwohl (Marketing Educator)

Self-theory has been the subject of much psychological and sociological theorizing and empirical research with the accompanying development of a rather large body of assumptions and empirical data.[1] The available knowledge strongly supports the role of the self-concept as a partial determinant of human behavior and, therefore, represents a promising area for marketing research.

Current theory and research places emphasis on the concept of the self as an object which is perceived by the individual. The self is what one is aware of, one's attitudes, feelings, perceptions, and evaluations of oneself as an object.[2] The self represents a totality which becomes a principal value around which life revolves, something to be safe-guarded and, if possible, to be made still more valuable.[3] An individual's evaluation of himself will greatly influence his behavior, and thus, the more valued the self, the more organized and consistent becomes his behavior.

The Self and the Interaction Process

The self develops not as a personal, individual process, but it evolves through the process of social experience. From the reactions of others, man develops his self-perception. According to Rogers:

A portion of the total perceptual field gradually becomes differentiated as the self . . . as a result of the interaction with the environment, and particularly as a result of evaluational interactions with others, the structure of the self is formed—an organized, fluid, but consistent conceptual pattern of perceptions of characteristics and relationships of the "I" or the "me" together with values attached to these concepts.[4]

Since the self-concept grows out of the reactions of parents, peers, teachers, and significant others, self-enhancement will depend upon the reactions of those people. Recognition and reinforcing reactions from these persons will further strengthen the conception the individual has of himself. Thus, the individual will strive to direct his behavior to obtain a positive reaction from his significant references.

Context of the Interaction Process

The interaction process does not take place in a vacuum; the individuals are affected both by the environmental setting and the "personal attire" of each involved individual. Therefore, the individual will strive to control these elements to facilitate proper interpretations of his performance.[5] Items of the environmental set-

SOURCE: Edward L. Grubb and Harrison L. Grathwohl, "Consumer Self-Concept, Symbolism and Market Behavior: A Theoretical Approach," *Journal of Marketing*, Vol. 31 (October, 1967), pp. 22–27, at pp. 24–26.

[1] See, for example, Ruth Wylie, *The Self-Concept* (Lincoln, Nebraska: The University of Nebraska Press, 1961).
[2] Calvin S. Hall and Gardener Lindsay, *Theories of Personality* (New York: John Wiley and Sons, Inc., 1957), pp. 469–475, or David Krech, Richard S. Crutchfield, and Egerton L. Ballachey, *Individual in Society* (New York: McGraw-Hill Book Company, 1962), pp. 495–496.
[3] Theodore M. Newcomb, *Social Psychology* (New York: The Dryden Press, 1956), p. 319.

[4] Hall and Lindsay, same reference as footnote 2.
[5] Erving Goffman, *The Presentation of Self in*

ting or the personal attire become the tools or a means of goal accomplishment for individuals in the interaction process.

Goods as Symbols

A more meaningful way of understanding the role of goods as social tools is to regard them as symbols serving as a means of communication between the individual and his significant references. Defined as "things which stand for or express something else," symbols should be thought of as unitary characters composed of signs and their meanings.[6] If a symbol is to convey meaning it must be identified by a group with which the individual is associated whether the group consists of two people or an entire society, and the symbol must communicate similar meaning to all within the group.

Symbols and Behavior

If a product is to serve as a symbolic communicative device it must achieve social recognition, and the meaning associated with the product must be clearly established and understood by related segments of society. This process is in reality a classification process where one object is placed in relation to other objects basic to society.

> The necessity for any group to develop a common or shared terminology leads to an important consideration; the direction of activity depends upon the particular way that objects are classified.[7]

Classification systems are society's means of organizing and directing their activities in an orderly and sensible manner.

A prime example of symbolic classification and consumer behavior is fashion. If a particular style becomes popular, behavior of a segment of society will be directed toward the purchase and use of items manifesting this style. As the fashion declines in popularity, the group will discontinue purchase of these items and may reject the use of the remain-

Everyday Life (Garden City, New York: Double-day and Co., Inc., 1959), p. 22.
[6] Lloyd Warner, *The Living and the Dead* (New Haven: Yale University Press, 1959), p. 3.
[7] Anselm Strauss, *Mirrors and Masks: The Search for Identity* (Glencoe, Illinois: The Free Press of Glencoe, 1959), p. 9.

ing portion of previous purchases. Thus, an act of classification not only directs action, but also arouses a set of expectations toward the object classified. Individuals purchase the fashion item because of their feelings about what the item will do for them. The *essence* of the object resides not in the object but in the relation between the object and the individuals classifying the object.

Classification and symbolism become means of communication and of directing or influencing behavior. If a common symbol exists for two or more people, then the symbol should bring forth a similar response in each, and therefore members of a group can use the symbol in their behavior pattern. Further, the symbolic social classification of a good allows the consumer to relate himself directly to it, matching his self-concept with the meaning of the good. In this way self-support and self-enhancement can take place through association with goods which have a desirable social meaning and from the favorable reaction of significant references in the social interaction process.

Goods and Self-Enhancement

The purchase and consumption of goods can be self-enhancing in two ways. First, the self-concept of an individual will be sustained and buoyed if he believes the good he has purchased is recognized publicly and classified in a manner that supports and matches his self-concept. While self-enhancement results from a personal, internal, intra-action process, the effect on the individual is ultimately dependent upon the product's being a publicly-recognized symbol. Because of their recognized meaning, public symbols elicit a reaction from the individual that supports his original self-feelings. Self-enhancement can occur as well in the interaction process. Goods as symbols serve the individual, becoming means to cause desired reactions from other individuals.

These two means of self-enhancement are represented in diagrammatic form in Figure 1.

Individual A purchases and uses symbol X which has intrinsic and extrinsic value as a means of self-enhancement. (Symbol X could include a purchase of a certain product type such as a swimming pool; purchase of a specific brand such as a Pontiac GTO; or a pur-

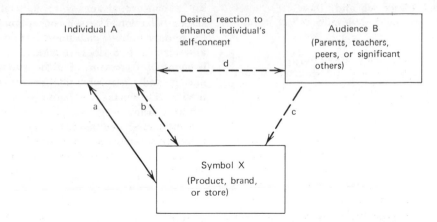

Figure 1. Relationship of the consumption of goods as symbols to the self-concept.

chase from a specific store or distributive outlet.) The intrinsic value is indicated by the double-headed arrow a, while the extrinsic values are indicated by the arrows b, c, and d. By the use of symbol X, an individual is communicating with himself; he is transferring the socially attributed meanings of symbol X to himself. This internal, personal communication process with symbol X becomes a means of enhancing his valued self-concept. An example of this situation is the individual who owns and uses a standard 1300 series Volkswagen. He may perceive himself as being thrifty, economical, and practical; and by using the Volkswagen, which has a strong image of being thrifty, economical, and practical, the individual achieves internal self-enhancement. This private and individual symbolic interpretation is largely dependent on one's understanding of the meaning associated with the product. Though the individual may treat this process in a private manner, he has learned the symbolic meaning from public sources.

By presenting Symbol X to Audience B, which may consist of one or more individuals from parents, peers, teachers, or significant others, the individual is communicating with them. Double-headed arrows b and c indicate that in presenting Symbol X to Audience B, Individual A is attributing meaning to it, and that in interpreting Symbol X, the relevant references in Audience B are also attributing meaning to the symbol. If Symbol X has a commonly-understood meaning between Indi-

vidual A and the references of Audience B, then the desired communication can take place and the interaction process will develop as desired by A. This means the behavior of the significant references will be the desired reaction to Individual A (as shown by arrow d) and, therefore, self-enhancement will take place.

A Model of Consuming Behavior

The following qualitative model is proposed to clarify the systematic relationship between self-theory and goods as symbols in terms of consumer behavior.

Consumption of Symbols: A Means to Self-Enhancement

1. An individual does have a self-concept of himself.
2. The self-concept is of value to him.
3. Because this self-concept is of value to him, an individual's behavior will be directed toward the furtherance and enhancement of his self-concept.
4. An individual's self-concept is formed through the interaction process with parents, peers, teachers, and significant others.
5. Goods serve as social symbols and, therefore, are communication devices for the individual.
6. The use of these good-symbols communicates meaning to the individual himself and to others, causing an impact on the intra-action and/or the inter-

action processes and, therefore, an effect on the individual's self-concept.

Prediction of the model:

7. Therefore, the consuming behavior of an individual will be directed toward the furthering and enhancing of his self-concept through the consumption of goods as symbols.

This model becomes the theoretical base for a conceptual means to understand consumer behavior. The self-conception approach to understanding consumer behavior is not all-inclusive but does provide a meaningful conceptual framework for the systematic ordering and comprehension of consumer behavior. Of further importance is that this model, although general, can be an aid to the marketing decision-maker and a guide for future research.

B. RESEARCH AND APPLICATIONS

The selection in this section (Krech, Crutchfield, and Ballachey) presents a concise statement as to the organization of wants and goals around the self.

14-D WANTS AND GOALS BECOME ORGANIZED AROUND THE SELF

David Krech (Psychologist), Richard R. Crutchfield (Psychologist), and Egerton L. Ballachey (Psychologist)

The human being responds not only to objects and persons in the outer environment but to his own body, his own thoughts, his own feelings. In so doing he develops cognitions about the *self* as a central and valued object. Important wants and goals emerge which have to do with the enhancement and defense of the self. And the self becomes a nucleus around which the many diverse wants and goals of the individual become organized.

The understanding of motivation requires that we take account of the crucial role of the self, and in understanding these relations of the self to motivation, we must first clarify the nature of the self.

The Nature and Development of the Self

The self is a product of social interaction. The infant does not distinguish between the self and the not-self. Only as he interacts with objects and persons in interpersonal behavior events does he come to perceive himself as an object separate and distinct from other objects and other persons.

This description may be made clear by a simple example. The child plays being mother or father, for instance. In his play, he talks to himself as his mother and father have talked to him, and he responds to this imaginary talk of his mother and father. The end result of speaking to himself as others have spoken to him is that he comes to perceive himself as a social object to which other people respond. And he learns to conceive of himself as having characteristics which are perceived by others: "I am heavy," "I am bright," "I am lazy," "I am shy."

THE SELF AND GROUP MEMBERSHIP. A study by Kuhn and McPartland[1] suggests that the conception of the self as a member of groups and classes takes priority over other self-conceptions. A group of 288 college students was asked to write 20 answers to the question, "Who am I?" The responses were classified into two categories: (1) those which refer to groups and social classes, e.g., girl, student, husband, Baptist, premedical student, daughter; (2) those which are evaluative, e.g., happy, bored, pretty good student, too heavy. One of the principal findings was that when subjects are limited to 20 responses they tend

SOURCE: David Krech, Richard S. Crutchfield, and Egerton L. Ballachey, *Individual in Society.* Copyright 1962 by the McGraw-Hill Book Company. Used with permission of the McGraw-Hill Book Company, Inc., pp. 79–83.

[1] Kuhn, M. H., and McPartland, T. S. "An Empirical Investigation of Self-Attitudes." *Amer. Social. Rev.*, 1954, **19**, 68–76.

to describe themselves as members of groups and classes before they describe themselves in evaluative terms. In other words, a student described himself as a husband, Baptist, or premedical student before he described himself as a good husband, happy, or too heavy. If we accept the assumption of the investigators that this ordering of responses is a valid reflection of the individual's self-concept, it appears that the self-concept is heavily infused with group membership.

Self-Evaluation

In seeking to understand the process of self-evaluation, we face three related questions: (1) What determines the values which the individual aspires to realize? (2) What defines for him a successful degree of realization of these values? (3) What social cues does he use in assessing his achievement?

Determinants of Values

The values of a society change, and they change because of the actions of individuals. Men are not mere carbon copies of their groups. Because of his particular life experiences, an individual may acquire new values and goals which dominate his life. And the accomplishment of these goals may result in a major social change. In a complex society, individuals are members of many different groups and the values of these different groups may conflict. In resolving this conflict, a synthesis of the conflicting values may be arrived at, resulting in a new value. This new value may then become accepted by the other members of the society. When this happens, a whole new complex of socially valued self-characteristics has been set up. For example, the early merchants who waxed rich synthesized their conflicting spiritual and temporal values by achieving an ethic which combined the virtues of the shrewd businessman and the pious churchgoer. Now the "good" man was one who walked in fear of poverty as well as of God. The "godly" man was the rich man.

LEVEL OF REALIZATION. We have seen that the individual tends to accept the values of his reference groups as his goals and that he judges himself in terms of his success in accomplishing these group-defined goals. What level of achievement defines for him whether he is a "success" or a "failure," a "good" man or a "bad" man?

There are at least four sets of important factors which determine the acceptable level of achievement of these goals. In the first place the individual's *understanding of his capacities and limitations* helps set these levels. The man who sets as his goal success as a scholar, but who thinks of himself as possessing only a "fair" intellect, will not seek to become the top scholar in his field. He will feel that he has realized his goal when he is accepted as merely another scholar among the vast company of scholars.

A second factor is the *awareness of what levels of achievement are possible*. Thus the rustic who values wealth, and believes that no man ever has amassed more than a house, a pig or two, and forty acres of farming land, will accept a much lower level of achievement as "success" than will the cosmopolite who knows that others have amassed millions and billions of dollars in wealth.

The third factor is an experiential one—the *individual's own history of success and failure*. The chronically successful man will demand of himself higher and higher levels of achievement before he will consider himself "successful"; the chronically failing man will progressively reduce his level in order to defend himself against further failures.

Finally, we have the social factor—*the status of the individual in his group*. An evaluation of the self, like any other evaluation, requires a comparison with something else. In the judgment of the self, the "something else" consists of comparative reference individuals and reference groups. In Hyman's[2] pioneering study of subjective status (the individual's conception of his own position relative to other individuals) 31 adult subjects were asked whether they had ever thought their standing was higher or lower that that of other individuals and in what different ways they had thought of their status, e.g., economic, intellectual, looks, etc. For each of the different status dimensions which the subjects reported, they were then asked with what group or individual they compared themselves. Hyman found that the individual's evaluation

[2] Hyman, H. H. "The Psychology of Status." *Arch. Psychol.*, 1942, No. 269.

of himself is primarily determined by his perception of his relative position or standing in two different kinds of reference groups: (1) membership groups, i.e., those groups to which he actually belongs, and (2) groups of which he is not a member but in which he aspires to membership. A premedical student may, for example, sometimes evaluate his intelligence by comparing himself with his fellow college students (a membership group); at other times he may evaluate his intelligence by comparing himself with "great physicians," a group to which he aspires to belong.

One particular way in which status in the group helps govern self-evaluation has been studied by Harvey.[3] Ten three-person groups were used, each group consisting of the leader, a middle-ranking member, and the lowest-ranking member of junior high school clique groups. Each subject performed on a dart-throwing test with his two clique mates present. After ten practice trials, the subject, before each trial, called aloud the score he actually expected to make on the next trial. His two clique mates wrote down their estimates of his performance before the subject called his estimate aloud. The results of this study are conclusive. The higher an individual's status in his group, the more he will overestimate his future performance; the lower his status, the less he will tend to overestimate. Indeed, three of the ten lowest-ranking subjects *under*estimated their future performance. None of the leaders or middle-ranking members gave underestimates. Harvey also found that the higher-status members not only set higher goals for themselves but were *expected* by their clique mates to perform at a higher level. The performance of the lowest-status members was, on the average, underestimated by both the leaders and the middle-ranking members. The lowest-status members were expected to perform more poorly than they actually did.

An observation by Whyte[4] suggests a further consequence of the underestimation of

[3] Harvey, O. J. "An Experimental Approach to the Study of Status Relations in Informal Groups." *Amer. Sociol. Rev.*, 1953, **18**, 357–367.
[4] Whyte, W. F., *Street Corner Society: The Social Structure of an Italian Slum.* Chicago: Univ. of Chicago Press, 1943.

performance observed in low-status persons. Among the Nortons (one of the clique groups he studied) bowling was a favorite sport. Alec, a low-ranking member of the group, was a skilled bowler in individual matches. But when he bowled with the entire group, his performance deteriorated. He was *expected* to do poorly, and he did poorly. He had several opportunities to prove himself, but each time he had an "off" night and failed.

SOCIAL CUES FOR SELF-EVALUATION. We now turn to the third question we face in seeking to understand the process of self-evaluation: what social cues does the individual use in evaluating himself as successful or unsuccessful? What cues does he receive from the reactions of others in interpersonal behavior events?

High-status persons tend to get cues from others that further enhance their high status; low-status persons tend to get cues from others that further depress their low status. The self of a high-status person is reflected from a magnifying looking glass, that of a low-status person from a reducing looking glass.

> Each to each a looking glass
> Reflects the other that doth pass—
> But in terms of social class!

We see here, in the process of self-appraisal by the individual, the importance of his accurate perception and interpretation of the reactions of other persons to him.

Wants, Goals, and Self-Conception

We can now see more clearly the ways in which the specific characteristics of the individual's self-conception and self-evaluation help account for the particular wants and goals he develops. For one thing, there are important wants and goals which have directly to do with achieving and maintaining feelings of self-esteem. For another thing, there is a selection of and emphasis on certain wants and goals in terms of their relevance for a particular self-picture of the individual.

SELF-ESTEEM AND IDEAL SELF. The child is early told by his parents and other adults what he should and should not be like. He is told what are desirable, or "good," personal characteristics and what are undesirable, or "bad," characteristics. As a result of these teachings in the values of his culture, the child comes to develop a conception of what he ought to be—the *ideal self.*

For most persons it becomes a major goal to achieve an "actual" self which is as similar as possible to the ideal self. To the extent that the gap between actual-self and ideal-self pictures is small, the individual feels a sense of enhancement of self-esteem. (There is, however, clinical evidence to suggest that an *ex-tremely close* correspondence between self and ideal self is really indicative of a precarious self-esteem, being based as it is on a blanket denial by the person of all shortcomings.) To the extent that his actual self falls far short of his ideal self, he experiences a diminished self-esteem. A great deal of the action and thought of the individual is driven by the want to enhance self-esteem and to remove threats to self-esteem.

15 / Individual Differences

A. BACKGROUND AND THEORY

The one article (Carey) in this section is a discussion of individuals and their responses to persuasive communication.

15-A INDIVIDUALS AND PERSUASIBILITY

James William Carey (Educator)

If a group of people is exposed to a persuasive communication, a full range of responses, a variety of attitude changes would result. Individual responses might vary along a scale from complete acceptance of the message to a negative reaction wherein an attitude completely opposite to that advocated in the message—the so-called boomerang effect—is adopted. How can this variety of responses be analyzed?

Janis has argued that intervening between the message and the response there is a set of predispositional factors that structure the relationship between the message and the attitude change. One class of predispositional factors can be labeled *communication-bound*. For example, individuals will respond differently to various types of appeals—negative vs. positive, social vs. individual; media may have differential appeals, some people being more readily influenced by broadcast or print; people will respond differentially to different types of arguments, arguments where the major conclusions are first or last, or both sides are presented, or one side; people will respond differently to group pressures, to sanctions, rewards, and punishments, hence the social situation will induce differential responses.

There is, in short, a whole class of factors related to the message—its content, style, appeals, the media, the communicator, and the situation that will induce a variety of responses.

It is also plausible that there are *individual differences in susceptibility* to persuasion, independent of message factors and situational factors. In other words, for any given set of messages, for any given set of situations, individuals could be ranked along a continuum from high to low persuasibility. Such an idea only recognizes what we know from our own experience with social life: some people are consistently difficult to convince of anything, whereas others are relatively plastic and malleable.

The major focus of the work on personality and persuasibility has been the enumeration of these communication-free factors, i.e., those personality states which determine a person's general level of persuasibility for all messages, in all situations.

In an early experiment Janis established that some persons are consistently resistant to all types of persuasive communications, whereas other persons consistently tend to be highly persuasible.[1]

SOURCE: James William Carey, "Personality Correlates of Persuasibility," in Stephen A. Greyser, Editor, *Toward Scientific Marketing* (Chicago: American Marketing Association, (1964), pp. 30–43, at pp. 31–34.

[1] Irving L. Janis and Peter B. Field, "A Behavioral Assessment of Persuasibility: Consistency of Individual Differences," *Personality and Persuasibility*, Irving L. Janis et al. (eds.), New Haven: Yale University Press, 1959, pp. 29–54.

In the experiment Janis presented a packet of materials to a group of high school students. The packet contained an initial questionnaire containing fifteen opinion questions, a booklet containing five persuasive communications on varying topics, another booklet containing five persuasive communications on the same topics but taking diametrically opposite positions. After exposure to each of the messages, the subjects were asked the same opinion questions as in the initial questionnaire.

A general persuasibility score was calculated for each subject on the basis of the amount of attitude change that occurred as a result of reading the two booklets. The highest score went to the subject who changed his initial opinion after reading the first booklet and then changed it all the way back after reading the second.

The experiment demonstrated consistent individual differences in persuasibility. A factor analysis was computed from the intercorrelations between persuasibility subscores on each communication. The result supported the hypothesis of a general factor of persuasibility which exists independent of topics and appeals.

But what specific personality traits determine a person's general level of persuasibility? What are the personality characteristics of persuasible and non-persuasible individuals?

It would seem likely that communication-free personality factors would cluster in two groups: (1) factors relating to intelligence and (2) factors relating to motivation and emotion. In the first case, it is obvious that a certain minimal level of intellectual ability is necessary to be able to comprehend a message and to decide whether to accept it or not. However, intelligence, by itself, is not a reliable predictor of attitude change. Intelligence, it turns out, is a communication-bound factor because its effect depends upon characteristics of the message. Following are some of the propositions relating intelligence to persuasibility. Note that in each case intelligence is related to attitude change only in terms of certain message characteristics.

"Persons with low intellectual ability and little education tend to be more influenced if the communication contains a one-sided presentation, limited solely to the arguments favoring the communicator's conclusions, whereas better educated people with high intellectual ability tend to be more influenced if the communication is two-sided—presenting both sides of the argument."[2]

"Persons with high intelligence will tend—mainly because of their ability to draw valid inferences—to be *more* influenced than those with low intellectual ability when exposed to persuasive communications which rely primarily on impressive logical arguments."

"Persons with high intelligence will tend—mainly because of their superior critical ability—to be *less* influenced than those with low intelligence when exposed to persuasive communications which rely primarily on unsupported generalities or false, illogical, or irrelevant argumentation."[3]

Researchers have been more successful in isolating communication-free factors bound up with motivation and emotion. In his most recent statement, Janis has argued that the following propositions have been, to an extent, verified:

- Men who display social withdrawal tendencies are predisposed to remain relatively uninfluenced by any form of persuasion.
- Men who openly display overt hostility toward the people they encounter in their daily life are predisposed to remain relatively uninfluenced by any form of persuasion.
- Men who respond with rich imagery and strong empathic responses to symbolic representations tend to be more persuasible than those whose fantasy responses are relatively constricted.
- Men with low self-esteem as manifested by feelings of personal inadequacy, social inhibition, and depressive effect are predisposed to be more readily influenced than others when exposed to any type of persuasive communication.
- Men with an "other-directed" orienta-

[2] Irving L. Janis, "Personality as a Factor in Susceptibility to Communication," *The Science of Human Communication,* Wilbur Schramm (ed.), New York: Basic Books, Inc., 1963, pp. 57–58.
[3] Carl I. Hovland, Irving L. Janis, and Harold H. Kelley, *Communication and Persuasion,* New Haven: Yale University Press, 1953, p. 183.

tion are predisposed to be more persuasible than those with an "inner-directed" orientation.

Notice that these conclusions are stated for males and not for females. It is not that females are beyond persuasion. In fact, in all the studies women have turned out to be more persuasible than men; but while it has been possible to predict on the basis of personality characteristics which males will be persuasible, it has been impossible to predict which females.

B. RESEARCH AND APPLICATIONS

The section begins with a report of research (Sieber and Lanzetta) on some determinants of individual differences in predecision information-processing behavior. This is followed by a study (McClure and Ryans) that investigated the differences between retailers' and consumers' perceptions of various product attributes.

15-B SOME DETERMINANTS OF INDIVIDUAL DIFFERENCES IN PREDECISION INFORMATION-PROCESSING BEHAVIOR

Joan E. Sieber (Psychologist) and John T. Lanzetta (Psychologist)

HYPOTHESES. The objective of the present research was to determine whether the two hypothesized variables underlie some of the observed individual differences in predecision behavior. This was determined in two ways: (*a*) Two groups of individuals categorized on the basis of a test of conceptual structure as having complex or simple conceptual structures were given decision problems and compared with respect to the following measures—self-ratings of degree of subjective uncertainty and number of response alternatives initially generated, and number of problem components differentiated and encoded, and number of controlled associates generated; (*b*) groups of structurally simple and complex persons were given training similar to that described above, designed to increase subjective response uncertainty, and degree of stimulus differentiation, encoding, and controlled association. Then, subsequent decision behavior was examined to determine whether persons categorized as having simple conceptual structures had learned to respond like the structurally

SOURCE: Joan E. Sieber and John T. Lanzetta, "Some Determinants of Individual Differences in Predecision Information-Processing Behavior," *Journal of Personality and Social Psychology,* 4, (November, 1966), pp. 561–571.

complex group following training. The following hypotheses were advanced:

1. When confronted with a decision task, structurally complex persons as compared to structurally simple persons will generate more response alternatives, report greater subjective uncertainty, differentiate more aspects of the decision problems, and generate more controlled associates to such differentiated problem components. As previously found, structurally complex subjects will take relatively more information before making decisions than structurally simple subjects.

2. After having reached a training criterion for the production of original responses (uncertainty training), or the discrimination and verbal encoding of many problem components, and producing of controlled associates (mediation training), structurally simple persons will exhibit more "complex" predecision behavior; that is, their level of information acquisition and subjective uncertainty will approximate that of untrained structurally complex persons.

Two additional dependent variables were examined: number of correct responses and time taken per query. Since the frequency of obtaining a correct solution to decision problems may be expected to covary with the amount of information acquired, structurally complex and trained subjects should have a higher probability of obtaining correct answers than structurally simple subjects, especially in difficult choice situations such as the present one. An "optimal" level of information acquisition and processing (i.e., a level at which persons process enough information to obtain a sufficiently comprehensive understanding of the problem to make a good decision) is assumed to exist for each type of choice situation, and structurally complex persons are assumed to operate closer to this optimal level in complex choice situations than structurally simple persons. Uncertainty and mediation training are therefore likely to bring the level of information acquisition and processing of structurally simple persons closer to the optimal for complex decisions.

It is difficult to predict the effects of training upon the information-processing behavior of structurally complex persons. If they are, in fact, processing information at an optimal level, training may consist of exercises which they have mastered, and may therefore leave their cognitive processes unaltered, or it may cause them to acquire and process information at a level of complexity beyond the optimal, perhaps resulting in an information overload, lowered efficiency and fewer correct decisions. In the absence of data on structurally complex subjects' level of information processing relative to the optimal, and relative to that level which is induced by training, no specific predictions can be made about the effects of training upon their information-processing behavior.

Although time per information query did not differ as a function of conceptual structure in a previous study (Sieber & Lanzetta, 1964), it is again examined to determine the effects of prior training.

Method

DESIGN. Five subjects were assigned to each of the 12 cells of a $2 \times 2 \times 3$ factorial design using conceptual structure, sex, and training as independent variables. Subjects were persons who had yielded test scores indicative of high structural complexity or low structural complexity. Prior to performing in a decision task, subjects received either no prior training (control group), training in generating response alternatives designed to increase re-sponse uncertainty (uncertainty training), or training in verbal encoding of visual stimuli, and generation of controlled associates to the encoded information (mediation training). Then, subjects were presented with 10 difficult decision problems, which consisted of identifying the objects depicted on slides which subjects presented to themselves tachistoscopically for 1/100 second durations. Subjects were free to observe the slide as often as they chose prior to making their decision. Data were gathered on amount of information acquired, time per query, correctness of decisions, amount of information given with decisions, and number of qualifying remarks accompanying decisions. For the control group data were gathered after participation in the decision task, to determine how much predecision uncertainty they experienced in an ambiguous decision situation, and how much verbal encoding and controlled association behavior accompanied their process of identifying the tachistoscopically presented slides.

PROCEDURE. Subjects were men and women at the University of Delaware who had yielded extremely high or low scores on the Sentence Completion Test (Schroder, Driver, & Streufert, 1966) and the Essay Problem Test.[1]

---

[1] The Essay Problem Test is an unpublished instrument devised by Howard Lamb and Carl Weinberg, University of Delaware.

The Sentence Completion Test consists of stems (words and phrases) which the subject uses in writing several sentences. These stems concern areas of interpersonal relations and situations involving uncertainty and the possibility of alternative decision, for example, Parents . . . , When I am in doubt . . . , Confusion . . . . Responses are scored in terms of the amount of differentiation and the number and complexity of alternative integrations of information exhibited. Interjudge reliability for the Sentence Completion Test is usually in excess of .85 after 1 day's training (Schroder, Driver, & Streufert, 1966). The Essay Problem Test consists of a set of directions for writing an essay on "Rules." The subject is instructed to discuss this topic at five different levels of complexity. These levels correspond to the criteria used in assessing complexity of conceptual structure in the scoring of the Sentence Completion Test. The Essay Problem Test is then scored according to the Sentence Completion Test scoring criteria, on the assumption that persons of low conceptual complexity are unable to discuss a topic

A total of 489 persons were tested in one of their regular classrooms, and of these 15 men and 15 women who yielded the highest scores and 15 men and 15 women who yielded the lowest scores were selected for this experiment. Structurally simple subjects were those who scored 2.0 or below on both instruments, and structurally complex persons were those who scored 2.5 or above on the Sentence Completion Test and 4.5 or above on the Essay Problem Test. (The maximum possible score on each instrument was 7.0.) These 60 subjects were later contacted and asked to participate in a study; no connection between the prior testing and this study was mentioned. Subjects were paid $1.25 for participation which lasted approximately 1 hour.

Stimuli consisted of 20 35-millimeter slides which had been photo-copied from photography magazines. These slides were designed to present ambiguous information; this was accomplished through the use of unusual and touched-up pictures. Lighting was constant for all subjects and was sufficiently bright to limit the amount of dark adaptation which occurred between tachistoscopic exposures of the slides. The illuminance of the screen on which stimuli were presented was .0748 footcandle, as measured with a Leeds and Northrup Macbeth Illuminometer, No. 1188202, using a .011 filter. The projector was located 9 feet from the screen.

Subjects were seated 9 feet from the screen. A response box was located beside the subject's chair with which he presented and changed slides by pressing the appropriate buttons, causing a microswitch to close which permitted the response to be recorded on an Esterline Angus Pen Recorder. Continuous recording yielded frequency and time data. A microphone was placed beside the subjects during the decision task, and their verbal responses were recorded on tape. The experimenter was absent from the room while the subjects participated in the decision task.

Control-condition subjects were told they were participating in a study of problem solving in which they would be asked to try to identify some pictures that could be projected

in a highly integrative fashion when instructed to do so. Reliability data are not available for the Essay Problem Test.

upon the screen. They were shown how to operate the projection equipment. It was explained that since each picture is projected for only 1/100 second, their task would be difficult, but that they could look at each slide as frequently as they wished before making a decision. They were asked to state their decision into the adjacent microphone only when they felt they could comfortably name the main object depicted. They were told that their statement need only be brief, for example, if the object were a car, they need only say "car," the requirement being simply to state what were the main thing or things in the slide, in whatever detail the subject deemed adequate. After two practice trials, the experimenter left the room, and the subject proceeded to view the stimuli and state his decisions into the microphone. After completion of the decision task, control subjects were required to look at five more tachistoscopically presented slides, once each, and to report after each viewing their decision as to the identity of the object depicted in the slide, and to indicate on a 9-point uncertainty rating scale how uncertain they felt about each identification; look at five additional tachistoscopically presented slides, five times each, and report after each viewing what things were seen in the slide and what hypotheses were formulated about the identity of the perceived object.

Uncertainty training condition subjects were told they were to participate in two experiments, the first in learning, the second in problem solving. They were shown how to operate the equipment and were then trained to generate many guesses as to the identity of the thing(s) depicted in some tachistoscopically presented training slides, in a manner similar to Maltzman's originality training technique: the subject was instructed to take one look at a slide and to then try to give at least 10 different guesses as to its identity as rapidly as possible, and to be as original as possible. It was pointed out that as long as he produced different guesses each time, with no more than 25 seconds between guesses, a signal light would remain on, but would go out following long delays or repetitions, and would remain out until the subject resumed guessing as instructed. The subject was told that the training would be terminated as soon as he had become sufficiently fluent in producing guesses. The subject was then shown a sample slide and allowed to hear a tape recording of the guessing of "a person who has participated in the training you are about to receive, and who became very fluent in generating guesses." The recording contained a preplanned running commentary of a man describing 10 possible things that the slide may have depicted. The subject was assured that this was only an example and not to be strictly imitated. However, it was pointed out that the recording contained some hints on the production of many ideas, for example, not to restrict oneself to only a few categories of topics, and not to be afraid to give unusual guesses. The subject was encouraged to guess similarly. He was then allowed to see the first training slide and commence guessing. The reinforcing light remained on as long as the subject generated different responses within 25-second intervals. In addition, the experimenter said "good" after each guess which was not a close associate of the previous one. The criterion for completion of training was production of 10 or more guesses to each of three different slides. Subjects who had failed to produce 10 guesses to a slide by the tenth trial were again read the cues described above on how to guess fluently and were encouraged to try harder. Subjects who had not reached criterion by 15 trials were automatically allowed to go on to the decision-making task. Only one subject failed to reach criterion. In most cases, once a subject gave more than 10 guesses for a given slide, he was able to exceed 10 guesses on all or most subsequent slides. The number of trials to criterion and mean number of guesses per trial during training were recorded. When subjects reached criterion, they were told that they could then go to the second task and were given the same instructions for the decision task that control subjects received.

Mediation training condition subjects were told that they would participate in two experiments, in the first they would learn how to notice and evaluate relevant information, and in the second they would be asked to solve some problems. They were shown how to operate the equipment and were then instructed to look at a slide which was exposed for a 1/100 second duration and to try to notice as many facts and details as possible and

report these to the experimenter. After the subject had looked at Slide 1, and stated the first thing he had seen, the experimenter reinforced the response with "good" and asked, "What else did you see?" This pattern of responding and reinforcement continued until the subject could report nothing more. After the subject had given all the facts he could about a given slide, he was asked, "On the basis of these facts, what hypotheses do you have about what is depicted in this slide?" All hypotheses were reinforced with "good," and after each hypothesis the subject was asked, "What else do you think it could be?" When no more hypotheses were forthcoming, the subject was told to look at the slide again and to name once more everything else he could discern. The same reinforcement and prompting followed each response. Hypotheses were again asked for, reinforced, and prompted. This was continued for a given slide for however many trials were required for the subject to generate 10 pieces of information and three hypotheses. Training continued until subjects had given 10 facts and three hypotheses within three looks for three slides. Data were recorded on the number of trials to criterion and the mean number of pieces of information and hypotheses given per trial during training. After subjects reached criterion in this training, they were given the same instructions and decision task that subjects in the control condition received.

Results

CONCEPTUAL STRUCTURE. Consistent with previous findings (Sieber & Lanzetta, 1964), the decision-making behavior of untrained subjects in the present experiment was observed to vary as a function of conceptual structure: Structurally complex subjects acquired more information prior to decision making and expressed greater uncertainty about the correctness of their decisions than structurally simple subjects. Complex subjects also gave relatively more information with their decisions, but the difference did not reach significance.

Discussion

Some persons consistently handle decision situations by acquiring a greater amount of relevant information with which they presumably evaluate the feasibility of their exist-ing choice alternatives or discover other more satisfactory alternatives. They possess con-siderable knowledge about the problem and express awareness of the existence of good choice alternatives other than the one which they choose. In contrast, other individuals acquire little information prior to making de-cisions, arrive at their decisions rapidly, and indicate that they have given little or no attention to other choice alternatives.

The present research was aimed at discover-ing some differences between the cognitive processes underlying these two styles of deci-sion making, and determining whether these cognitive processes may be modified by train-ing. Since previous research has shown that the amount of information that is acquired prior to arriving at decisions is a function of degree of response uncertainty, the following two processes (which produce response un-certainty) were hypothesized to underlie com-plex predecision information-processing be-havior: availability of many associative responses in response hierarchies, hence fluency in generating response alternative; and fluency in observing and encoding problem-relevant information and producing many al-ternative solutions based upon the information gained from the stimulus. The second process resembles the first in that it also produces high response uncertainty, but differs in that it stresses prior acquisition of facts about the problem and generation of hypothetical al-ternatives based upon these facts, rather than upon the subject's first impressions of the stimulus problem. The second process specif-ically includes those cognitive activities as-sumed to be produced by the first, namely, the acquisition of information on the basis of which choice alternatives are created and evaluated.

In the present experiment, training was directed at increasing subjects' facility in these two processes. As predicted, structurally sim-ple subjects (typically low information pro-cessers) who received prior training displayed a level of predecision information acquisition, information output when stating their deci-sions, awareness of other alternatives, and uncertainty about the correctness of their decisions which was greater than that of con-trol structurally simple subjects and not differ-ent from that of untrained structurally complex subjects. One may question, however, whether the training procedures could have directly reinforced these specific responses, resulting only in a learned increase in rate of responding, rather than a change in response uncertainty, which was assumed to have mediated the ob-served behavioral effects. Uncertainty training consisted of operantly conditioning subjects to name many possible solutions to given prob-lems, after making one information acquisition response. Mediation training consisted of con-ditioning subjects to give descriptive responses to the stimulus and later to give association responses to their descriptive data. Since sub-jects received social reinforcement for each acceptable verbal response, the two verbal output indexes could possibly have been facilitated if the reinforcement effects had generalized to all forms of verbal behavior. However, it is difficult to argue that this reinforcement could have directly facilitated the information-acquisition responses, since the procedure in no way reinforced or encouraged external stimulus seeking, but rather reinforced internal processing of information that had been obtained in a single viewing.

REFERENCES

Birge, J. S. The role of verbal responses in trans-fer. Unpublished doctoral dissertation, Yale University, 1941.

Caron, A. J., Unger, S. M., & Parloff, M. B. A test of Maltzman's theory of originality training. *Journal of Verbal Learning and Ver-bal Behavior*, 1963, 1, 436–442.

Driscoll, J. M., & Lanzetta, J. T. Effects of two sources of uncertainty in decision making. *Psychological Reports*, 1965, 17, 635–648.

Driscoll, J. M., Tognoli, J. J., & Lanzetta, J. T. Choice conflict and subjective uncertainty in decision making. *Psychological Reports*, 1966, 18, 427–432.

Driver, M. G., & Streufert, S. A. The general in-congruity adaptation level (GIAL) hypoth-esis: An analysis and integration of cognitive approaches to motivation. (Institute for Re-search in the Behavioral, Economic and Management Sciences) Lafayette: Purdue University Press, 1965.

Harvey, O. J., Hunt, D. E., & Schroder, H. M. *Conceptual systems and personality organiza-tion*. New York: Wiley, 1961.

Jenkins, J. J. Mediated association paradigms and situations. In C. N. Cofer (Ed.), *Verbal behavior and learning: Problems and processes.* New York: McGraw-Hill, 1963, pp. 210–244.

Kendler, T. S., & Kendler, H. H. Inferential behavior in children as a function of age and subgoal constancy. *Journal of Experimental Psychology*, 1962, 64, 460–466.

Kuenne, M. R. Experimental investigation of the relationship of language to transposition behavior in young children. *Journal of Experimental Psychology*, 1946, 36, 471–490.

Laffal, J. Response faults in word association as a function of response entropy. *Journal of Abnormal and Social Psychology*, 1955, 50, 265–270.

Lanzetta, J. T. Information acquisition in decision making. In O. J. Harvey (Ed.), *Motivation and social interaction.* New York: Ronald Press, 1963, pp. 239–265.

Maltzman, I. On the training of originality. *Psychological Review*, 1960, 67, 229–242.

Maltzman, I., Bogartz, W., & Breger, L. A procedure for increasing word association originality and its transfer effects. *Journal of Experimental Psychology*, 1958, 56, 392–398.

Mednick, S. A. The associative base of the creative process. *Psychological Review*, 1962, 69, 220–232.

Osborn, A. F. *Applied imagination.* New York: Schelinus, 1957.

Perin, C. T. A quantitative investigation of the delay of reinforcement gradient. *Journal of Experimental Psychology*, 1943, 32, 37–51.

Schroder, H. M., Driver, M. J., & Streufert, S. *Human information processing.* New York: Holt, Rinehart & Winston, 1966.

Shannon, C. E., & Weaver, W. *Mathematical theory of communication.* Urbana: University of Illinois Press, 1949.

Shepard, W., & Schaeffer, M. The effect of concept knowledge on discrimination learning. *Child Development*, 1956, 27, 173–178.

Sieber, J. E. Problem solving behavior of teachers as a function of conceptual structure. *Journal of Research in School Teaching*, 1964, 2, 64–68.

Sieber, J. E., & Lanzetta, J. T. Conflict and conceptual structure as determinants of decision making behavior. *Journal of Personality*, 1964, 32, 622–641.

Spiker, C. C. Stimulus pretraining and subsequent performance in the delayed reaction experiment. *Journal of Experimental Psychology*, 1956, 52, 107–111.

15-C DIFFERENCES BETWEEN RETAILERS' AND CONSUMERS' PERCEPTIONS

Peter J. McClure (Marketing Educator) and John K. Ryans, Jr. (Marketing Educator)

By definition, a purchase transaction involves a buyer and a seller. Yet, consumer market researchers have tended to focus on the buyer by exploring such phenomena as attitude formation and behavior within and among decision-making units as well as developing a variety of demographic, socioeconomic, and psychological variables for use in segmenting markets. In these studies the seller, though playing an important role, is seldom considered in the analysis of purchase decision making in more than a peripheral manner.

Despite the lack of research, manufacturers have tended to consider retailers as an important source of information about consumers and have sought their help to gain a greater understanding of the marketplace. In such

SOURCE: Peter J. McClure and John K. Ryans, Jr., "Differences between Retailers' and Consumers' Perceptions," *Journal of Marketing Research*, Vol. 5 (February, 1968), pp. 35–40.

instances manufacturers often feel that if they could only be as close to consumers as retailers, many of the roadblocks to more successful marketing would be substantially reduced. They assume that because of the retailer's familiarity and frequency of contact with consumers, his observations of their behavior are more accurate than people more removed from retailing.

Yet investigation suggests retailers' perceptions frequently differ from those of consumers, particularly about the relative importance of certain product attributes in the purchase decision. Furthermore, the retailers' ratings of competitors' brands differ significantly from consumers' on various products produced by these manufacturers.

In this article some differences between consumers' and retailers' views are developed in terms of:

1. importance to consumers of selected

product attributes, such as price in the purchase decision for refrigerators, ranges, and automatic clothes washers;

2. retailers' opinions about competitors' brands (Frigidaire, General Electric, and Sears) and the consumers' images of various appliances of these three firms.

Research Design

The data for this discussion were generated in two studies, conducted simultaneously in Indianapolis in the Spring, 1964 (See [2 and 3]). One study dealt with consumers' images of selected appliance attributes and other aspects of consumer behavior. The other focused on appliance retailers' perceptions of how customers rate product attributes and their perceptions of other aspects of consumer behavior, brand attributes, and retailer-manufacturer relations.

SELECTION OF RESPONDENTS. The respondent in the consumer study was the female household head. A random sample was drawn from those 1960 census tracts of Indianapolis (updated for new dwellings) in which more than half of the dwelling units had $5,000 or greater annual income. This process yielded 282 interviews. The definition of the population reduced, but not eliminated, the number of low income respondents in the study, the desired effect. One quarter of the respondents represented households with annual incomes of $10,000 and over, 63 percent with incomes between $5,000 and $10,000, and 12 percent with incomes under $5,000.

The respondent in the retailer study was the person in charge of merchandising major appliances in the firm. He was typically the owner or manager (of store or department), depending on the kind of firm. The retailer study involved a virtual census of appliance retailers in Indianapolis. From an initial listing of 123 retail outlets representing 99 separate firms with 24 branch locations, 89 successfully completed interviews represented 113 outlets. Of these 29 percent were appliance stores, 36 percent furniture stores, 12 percent department stores, and 23 percent tire and miscellaneous stores. All major retailers participated in the study.

DATA COLLECTION. The interviews for the consumer study lasted about one hour and

were done in the home. The retailer interviews were conducted at the respondent's place of work and varied from one and a half to three hours. Although the consumer and retailer interviews had different settings and contained several questions not common to both, care was taken to coordinate the particular questions and scaling devices generating the data discussed here.

Product Attributes. To measure the relative importance of price, style, service and warranty, extra gadgets, and ease of use in the purchase decision for refrigerators, ranges, and automatic clothes washers, consumers were asked "In purchasing a ———, the following characteristics are: . . . ." Each response was then given by the housewife on a seven interval scale ranging from zero (no importance) to six (very important). On the same scale appliance retailers were asked to rate how important they thought the same features were to customers for the respective appliances.

Brand Attributes. A ten interval scale ranging from one to five (agree) and minus one to minus five (disagree) was used to measure consumers' images of attributes of particular brands of appliances (adapted from [1]). For example, consumers were asked, "Do you think that Frigidaire refrigerators are high-priced?" The procedure was repeated using the phrases: "have good-looking styles," "are trouble-free," and "have extra gadgets" for Frigidaire refrigerators, General Electric, and Sears refrigerators, ranges, and automatic clothes washers. Housewives were permitted to rate the products even if they used these particular brands since the objective was to obtain an indication of consumers' images regardless of their viewpoint.

Retailers given comparable scales and phrases were asked to rate the three brands used in the consumer study but not specific appliances. They were asked not to rate the major brand they carried if it was one of these. It was felt that less response bias would be introduced this way. Unfavorable responses about their own supplier would be an indirect criticism of themselves, whereas a favorable rating of the other brands would not necessarily imply an unfavorable image of their own suppliers.

Retailers' and Consumers' Ratings, Importance of Given Attributes in Three Major Appliances

Attribute	Appliance	Respondent[a]	Ratings (percent)					Ratings More Positive		Significance Level for Mann-Whitney U
			Of No Importance 0–2	3	4	Very Important 5	6	Retailers	Consumers	
Price	Refrigerators	Retailers	6	16	12	23	43			
		Consumers	16	10	14	7	53		x	.85
	Ranges	Retailers	3	16	18	24	39			
		Consumers	18	7	13	5	57		x	.36
	Automatic clothes washers	Retailers	5	13	12	20	50	x		
		Consumers	18	8	16	6	52			.30
Style	Refrigerators	Retailers	5	27	24	21	23			
		Consumers	18	10	16	15	41		x	.11
	Ranges	Retailers	6	13	28	22	31			
		Consumers	17	9	17	13	44		x	.64
	Automatic clothes washers	Retailers	25	29	21	5	20			
		Consumers	29	16	15	9	31		x	.34
Service and warranty	Refrigerators	Retailers	3	7	12	15	63			
		Consumers	1	2	7	8	82		x	.001
	Ranges	Retailers	7	10	11	18	54			
		Consumers	2	1	7	8	82		x	.001
	Automatic clothes washers	Retailers	0	6	8	18	68			
		Consumers	2	2	6	9	81		x	.02
Extra gadgets	Refrigerators	Retailers	52	27	12	3	6			
		Consumers	44	16	14	8	18		x	.30
	Ranges	Retailers	25	33	23	9	10	x		
		Consumers	49	15	14	5	17			.01
	Automatic clothes washers	Retailers	34	42	11	5	8	x		
		Consumers	48	13	16	8	15			.66
Ease of use	Refrigerators	Retailers	8	11	23	28	30			
		Consumers	5	4	10	14	67		x	.001
	Ranges	Retailers	1	10	19	30	40			
		Consumers	7	3	10	13	67		x	.001
	Automatic clothes washers	Retailers	0	7	15	27	51			
		Consumers	4	4	10	14	68		x	.02

[a] *n* equals 82 for the retailer ratings and 280 for the consumer ratings.

TABLE 2

Retailers' and Consumers' Ratings of Brand Attributes of Three Major Appliances

Attribute and brand / Respondents	Appliance	Ratings (percent) Disagree −5 to −4	−3 to −1	Agree +1 to +3	+4 to +5	Base	Ratings More Positive Retailers	Consumers	Significance Level for Mann-Whitney U
High-priced									
Frigidaire									
Retailers	Refrigerators	3	8	62	27	75			
Consumers		7	27	51	15	257	x		.001
General Electric									
Retailers	Refrigerators	3	16	65	16	68			
Consumers	Refrigerators	6	28	50	16	257	x		.08
	Ranges	5	27	51	17	248	x		.19
	Automatic clothes washers	4	30	32	14	247	x		.08
Sears									
Retailers	Refrigerators	28	41	26	5	78			
Consumers	Refrigerators	17	51	30	2	256		x	.06
	Ranges	11	45	38	6	244		x	.001
	Automatic clothes washers	17	49	28	6	261		x	.05
Good-looking style									
Frigidaire									
Retailers	Refrigerators	1	5	52	42	76			
Consumers	Refrigerators	1	2	42	55	257		x	.02
General Electric									
Retailers	Refrigerators	1	7	52	40	68			
Consumers	Refrigerators	1	3	46	50	258		x	.04
	Ranges	0	2	50	48	251		x	.11
	Automatic clothes washers	0	4	52	44	250		x	.41

Table 2 (Continued)

| Attribute and brand | Respondents | Appliance | Ratings (percent) | | | | | Ratings More Positive | | Significance Level for Mann-Whitney U |
| | | | Disagree | | Agree | | | | | |
			−5 to −4	−3 to −1	+1 to +3	+4 to +5	Base	Re-tailers	Con-sumers	
Sears	Retailers	Refrigerators	2	23	50	25	80			
	Consumers	Refrigerators	0	7	55	38	256		x	.001
		Ranges	0	6	60	34	244		x	.01
		Automatic clothes washers	1	7	53	39	261		x	.001
Trouble-free										
Frigidaire	Retailers	Refrigerators	4	20	56	20	66			
	Consumers	Refrigerators	2	13	45	40	257		x	.01
General Electric	Retailers	Refrigerators	10	25	42	23	60			
	Consumers	Refrigerators	5	16	47	32	258		x	.01
		Ranges	1	17	52	30	250		x	.01
		Automatic clothes washers	5	23	45	27	250		x	.19
Sears	Retailers	Refrigerators	22	29	41	8	69			
	Consumers	Refrigerators	4	23	45	28	255		x	.001
		Ranges	1	19	53	27	243		x	.001
		Automatic clothes washers	4	23	41	32	260		x	.001

Table 2 (Concluded)

Attribute and brand / Respondents	Appliance	Ratings (percent) Disagree −5 to −4	−3 to −1	Agree +1 to +3	+4 to +5	Base	Ratings More Positive Re-tailers	Con-sumers	Significance Level for Mann-Whitney U
Extra gadgets									
Frigidaire									
Retailers	Refrigerators	1	14	66	19	73			
Consumers		0	13	55	32	255		x	.31
General Electric									
Retailers	Refrigerators	3	11	63	23	64			
Consumers	Refrigerators	1	11	57	31	257		x	.22
	Ranges	0	11	50	39	250		x	.11
	Automatic clothes washers	2	10	59	29	250		x	.73
Sears									
Retailers	Refrigerators	1	25	54	20	75	x		.63
Consumers	Refrigerators	2	20	61	17	255			
	Ranges	0	14	57	29	245		x	.02
	Automatic clothes washers	1	19	53	27	258		x	.26

Relative Importance of Product Attributes

Though the retailers' ratings of the relative importance consumers put on various product attributes in the appliance-purchase decision were generally consistent—in rank order—with the ratings given by the consumers, they tended to understate the degree of importance consumers attach to such attributes. The retailers underestimated the importance consumers attributed to the various product attributes in all cases except price of automatic clothes washers and extra gadgets on ranges and automatic clothes washers (see Table 1).

Among the three major appliances investigated, the appliance retailers and consumers were least similar in their responses on ranges. These differences were exhibited especially for service and warranty and extra gadgets. Considering the saturation of this product relative to automatic clothes washers, for example, such a finding is unexpected and is apparently inconsistent with the commonplace assumption that retailers are knowledgeable about consumers (see Table 2).

Retailers were best able to perceive the importance consumers placed on various product attributes for automatic clothes washers. This may reflect the greater usefulness of automatic clothes washers when compared with refrigerators and ranges, and consequently, the more intense response of retailers to the consumers' concern for service and ease of use.

The least difference was shown between the importance retailers and consumers attributed to the price of refrigerators, extra gadgets on automatic clothes washers, and style of ranges.

PRICE: THE RETAILERS' DEMON. Retailers generally reacted strongly on all questions about price, whether they related to the importance of price to consumers, the use of price as a strategy element, or the need for resale price maintenance. The reaction was noticeable regardless of whether open-end questions or rating scales were used. In response to structured questions, more than 88 percent of the retailers felt that price was an important consideration in the purchase of major appliances and that consumers were price-conscious. In some other instances, the retailers conceded the importance of other factors in consumer decisions about particular products, as reported in Table 1.

During the interviews the topic mentioned most frequently by retailers was price. For example, often when an apparently unsuccessful appliance retailer tried to explain his predicament, he would blame the pricing practices of competitors or the "bait advertising" of the "big store downtown." Other retailers complained that customers visited their store only to compare prices and then bought elsewhere, or that the discount store prices were forcing them out of business. However, despite such findings, price was not the only appliance attribute considered important by the consumer (see Table 1).

Store Owners. Although nearly all appliance retailers thought price was an important consideration, many felt that factors such as brand preference or product quality offset price considerations. However, store owners, particularly the small store owners rather than store or department managers, tended to feel that price considerations override all other customer considerations. Furthermore, it was the store-owner group that generally rated price as especially significant to consumers purchasing refrigerators, ranges, and automatic clothes washers. For example, more than 81 percent of the owners, as compared with 47 percent of the managers, rated price as extremely important (five or six) to the consumer in the purchase of refrigerators. The owners also consistently ranked price high as a strategy element and considered haggling over price basic to the retail transaction. Certainly, smaller retailers would be expected to find it difficult to compete with larger, more aggressive stores on price; it is not surprising that this attribute would be used to explain their current plight. Yet the consumers' replies did not support the retailers' assumption that price is all-important.

Competition Misconceptions

The retailers frequently perceived competitive brands (carried by competitive retailers) much differently than consumers did. For example, a retailer may view a competitor's brand as substantially lower in price and also much less trouble-free than consumers do. As a result, he may stress the trouble-free performance of his brand and quietly worry about price. Unfortunately for this retailer and this brand's manufacturer, consumers may not share his views and instead may feel there is not as much price differential as the retailer believes and the products of the competitive brand have much better quality than he judges.

Conclusion

Though there are undoubtedly exceptions to these findings, especially among other products and kinds of retailers, these observations are indicative of appliance retailers and consumers in a major market area.

If so, why are retailers not better informed of their customers and their customers' views; how they can be made more aware? Their familiarity and frequency of contact with customers make them the envy of many manufacturers operating from remote corporate offices. Yet this familiarity and frequency of contact do not seem to give retailers a highly accurate understanding of consumers. Thus:

1. Retailers consistently underestimate the strengths with which consumers view the importance of service and warranty, ease of use, and style in the appliance purchase decision. (Retailers are most accurate in their portrayal of consumers' views on automatic clothes washers and least accurate on ranges.)

2. Price is the special concern of appliance retailers who own their stores as contrasted with buyers or managers of larger stores.

3. Retailers tend to view attributes of competitive brands differently from consumers. These images are either over-sensitive or under-sensitive to specific attributes and seem to reflect historic stereotypes rather than current consumer brand images.

This study dealt with retailers in the aggregate. If each retailer is considered individually, the identification of that retailer's market in terms of current and prospective customers becomes vague for all but retail giants. Even so, the interested retailer can investigate his misconceptions of his market. Manufacturers faced with the problems of centralizing more of their production operations, yet who are dependent on thousands of small and middle-sized retailers for distribution, are especially vulnerable. The national manufacturer must develop marketing programs suitable for hundreds of retailers; consequently, his research should be aimed at developing propositions suitable for generalization over large categories of retailers.

REFERENCES

1. Irving Crespi, "Use of a Scaling Technique in Surveys," *Journal of Marketing*, **25** (July, 1961), 69–72.
2. Peter J. McClure, "An Analysis of Consumers' Images of Major Appliances and Brands of Appliances in Terms of Four Forms of Segmentation," Unpublished D.B.A. dissertation, Graduate School of Business, Indiana University, 1966.
3. John K. Ryans, Jr., "An Analysis of Appliance Retailer Perceptions of Retail Strategy and Decision Processes," Unpublished D.B.A. dissertation, Graduate School of Business, Indiana University, 1965.
4. Sidney Siegel, *Nonparametric Statistics for the Behavioral Sciences*, New York: McGraw-Hill Book Company, Inc., 1956, 116–27.

GROUP INFLUENCES

16 / Imitation and Suggestion

A. BACKGROUND AND THEORY

This section consists of a discussion (Bandura and Walters) of the role of imitation, and a definition (Sargent and Williamson) of suggestion.

16-A THE ROLE OF IMITATION

Albert Bandura (Psychologist) and Richard H. Walters (Psychologist)

Imitation plays an important role in the acquisition of deviant, as well as of conforming, behavior. New responses may be learned or the characteristics of existing response hierarchies may be changed as a function of observing the behavior of others and its response consequences without the observer's performing any overt responses himself or receiving any direct reinforcement during the acquisition period. In some cases the amount of learning shown by the observer can, in fact, be as great as that shown by the performer.

Relevant research demonstrates that when a model is provided, patterns of behavior are typically acquired in large segments or in their entirety rather than through a slow, gradual process based on differential reinforcement. Following demonstrations by a model, or (though to a lesser extent) following verbal descriptions of desired behavior, the learner generally reproduces more or less the entire response pattern, even though he may perform no overt response, and consequently receive no reinforcement, throughout the demonstration period. Under such circumstances, the acquisition process is quite clearly not as piecemeal as is customarily depicted in modern behavior systems.

SOURCE: Albert Bandura and Richard H. Walters, *Social Learning and Personality Development,* Copyright © 1963 by Holt, Rinehart and Winston, Inc. Reprinted by permission of Holt, Rinehart and Winston, Inc., pp. 47 and 106–108.

The role of models in the transmission of novel social responses has been demonstrated most extensively in laboratory studies of aggression. Children who have been exposed to aggressive models respond to subsequent frustration with considerable aggression, much of which is precisely imitative, whereas equally frustrated children who have observed models displaying inhibited behavior are relatively nonaggressive and tend to match the behavior of the inhibited model. There is some evidence from field studies that dependency responses and anxiety about sexual behavior can also be transmitted from parents to children. Moreover, cross-cultural and clinical observations provide examples of the shaping of antisocial, autistic, and other forms of grossly deviant response patterns through modeling.

In addition to teaching observers entirely novel patterns of response, the presentation of models may have inhibitory and disinhibitory or eliciting effects. For example, exposure to an aggressive model may result in the observer's displaying pain-producing responses, which, although not precisely imitative, have social effects that are in some respects similar to those that result from the model's behavior. Nonspecific imitation of this kind is perhaps most likely when the responses involved are already present in the observer's behavioral repertoire but are infrequently manifested because of the social disapproval they elicit.

The influence that the behavior of a model will exert on an observer is partly contingent on the response consequences to the model. Children who observe an aggressive model rewarded display more imitative aggression than children who see a model punished for aggression. Similarly, rewarding and punishing consequences to a model who violates a prohibition influence the extent to which his transgression will be imitated. In addition, models who are rewarding, prestigeful, or competent, who possess high status, and who have control over rewarding resources are more readily imitated than are models who lack these qualities. Such factors also determine in part which models will be selected as major sources of exemplary social behavior patterns. While immediate or inferred response consequences to the model have an important influence on the observers' *performance* of imitative responses, the *acquisition* of these responses appears to result primarily from contiguous sensory stimulation.

Characteristics of observers—for example, the degree to which they have previously been rewarded or punished for compliant behavior—also influence the extent to which imitative responses will occur. Moreover, susceptibility to the social influence of models is increased by temporary or transient states of the observer, such as emotional arousal of a moderate degree of intensity or the intensified dependency that can be induced through hypnotic procedures.

The same classes of events and the same model and observer characteristics that enhance or reduce the extent to which a model influences an observer contribute to the development of adult-child similarities of behavior, which in psychodynamic theories have usually been categorized as instances of identification. Since, however, this latter term is highly elusive and carries many surplus meanings, the behavioral phenomena to which it refers were conceptualized in terms of social-learning principles. It was consequently possible to apply a large body of research concerning observational learning to the understanding of the development of parent-child similarities and to suggest alternative interpretations of the genesis of certain forms of matching behavior that, in psychodynamic theories, have usually been considered to be the outcome of defensive processes.

It is evident, however, that the social-influence process cannot be accounted for entirely in terms of the effects of the presentation of parent and other models. Once imitative responses occur, the consequences to the agent will largely determine whether these responses are strengthened, weakened, or inhibited. Direct training through reward, aversive stimulation, and other disciplinary procedures undoubtedly play a large part in shaping and in maintaining patterns of social behavior.

16-B SUGGESTION

S. Stansfeld Sargent (Psychologist) and Robert C. Williamson (Psychologist)

Suggestion signifies inducing uncritical acceptance in others, or touching off responses in others almost automatically. However, only responses that previously have been learned can be produced in this automatic way. Thus suggestion evokes behavior by a kind of short-circuiting process. Many examples can be given: the embarrassing epidemic of yawning that occurs in a social group in response to

SOURCE: S. Stansfeld Sargent and Robert C. Williamson, *Social Psychology* (New York: The Ronald Press Company, 1966), pp. 326–327. Third edition, coypright © 1966, The Ronald Press Company, New York.

one person's yawn; the allergic individual who sneezes when presented with a beautiful but artificial rose; the children at a ventriloquist's show who are sure the dummy really talks; or the chemistry students, in a well-known experiment, who reported they smelled fumes from an odorless liquid ostentatiously uncorked at the front of the lecture hall.

Suggestion seems most effective when the recipient's attention is fixed elsewhere. Suggestibility is greatest during hypnosis, when the subject is in a dissociated state. There are tremendous individual differences in susceptibility to suggestion, for reasons not entirely clear. One investigator found that, in general, children at the age of seven or eight are more suggestible than at any other age.[1] Considerable controversy has centered about the question whether or not "suggestibility" should be considered a personality trait. Probably it should not be, since acceptance of suggestion seems to be affected by many temporary and situational influences. On some occasions everyone is suggestible; at other times, no one. A few individuals, though, do seem rather generally responsive or unresponsive to suggestion.

The part played by suggestion in human social behavior is hard to assess, but it is very significant. Parents know that subtle suggestion is a much better way to manage youngsters than commands or threats. Suggestion is a powerful means of social control, as is shown in advertising and propaganda. Historically, the suggestion-imitation hypothesis dominated social psychology at the turn of the century and for some time afterward.[2] Le Bon made it the basis of his "crowd mind." Although later psychologists took issue with his extravagant version of suggestion, it still retained its pre-eminent position. As with the process of imitation, neither the *how* nor the *why* was adequately answered.

The term *social facilitation* for the interactional process by which one individual influenced another gradually replaced "imitation" and "suggestion." In a number of experiments Allport demonstrated the intensification of experience that accompanied the presence of other people; there were higher scores for vowel cancellation, word associations, and analyses of excerpts from the reading of Marcus Aurelius in a group. Although there was an increase in the *quantity* of the performance, the *quality* suffered.[3] Unlike LeBon's mystical approach, which fused separate individuals into a group superconsciousness, Allport perceived the group as simply the totality of a number of individuals.

Although we cannot agree with the older viewpoint that somehow a group mind develops as a blending of separate nervous systems into one organic unity, the group does affect the thinking and behavior of individuals, so that an entirely different set of responses is possible in the group setting from what was possible before. In other words, the group is something more than the sum of its members. Whatever the theoretical and methodological arguments may be, there is ample evidence of the facilitating affects of other people. We eat more when others are around, and project more into emotional experiences when there is a fellow participant. Few things seem as pathetic as a play acted in an almost empty theater. Social facilitation remains a fundamental type of human interaction.

[1] R. Messerschmidt, "Suggestibility of Boys and Girls . . . ," *J. Genet. Psychol.*, XLIII (1933), 405–37.

[2] For a discussion of the background of this and related processes, see G. W. Allport, The historical background of modern social psychology, in G. Lindzey (ed.), *Handbook of Social Psychology* (Reading, Mass.: Addison-Wesley Publishing Co., Inc., 1954), Vol. I, pp. 3–56.

[3] F. H. Allport, "The Influence of the Group Upon Association and Thought. *J. Exp. Psychol.*, III (1920), 159–82. See also his *Social Psychology* (Boston: Houghton Mifflin Co., 1924).

B. RESEARCH AND APPLICATIONS

This section consists of a discussion (Barber and Lobel) of the "trickle-down" theory, and of a report of a study (Engel, Kegerreis, and Blackwell) of word-of-mouth communication by the innovator.

16-C "FASHION" IN WOMEN'S CLOTHES AND THE AMERICAN SOCIAL SYSTEM

Bernard Barber (Sociologist) and Lyle S. Lobel (Sociologist)

In social science usage, "fashion" is still an over-generalized term. One writer lists the following "fields of fashion": values in the pictorial arts, architecture, philosophies, religion, ethical behavior, dress, and the physical, biological, and social sciences. "Fashion" has also been used in reference to language usages, literature, food, dance music, recreation, indeed the whole range of social and cultural elements. The core of meaning in term for all these different things is "changeful," but it is unlikely that the structures of behavior in these different social areas and the consequent dynamics of their change are all identical. "Fashion," like "crime," has too many referents; it covers significantly different kinds of social behavior.

The description of "fashion" behavior suffers also from treating "fashion" as socially "irrational." "Fashion" is usually grouped with "fads" and "crazes." Robert Merton has shown how many kinds of patterned social behavior have latent, or unintended, as well as manifest, or purposed, consequences for the social systems in which they exist. This distinction, he says, often "clarifies the analysis of seemingly irrational social patterns." We shall confine ourselves to "fashion" in American women's clothes and show that this behavior is not at all socially "irrational" when seen in relation to the American class structure, age-sex roles, and economic system.

The field of "fashion" in American women's clothes is an area of rich, accessible, but still largely unexploited empirical materials. Our data have been taken primarily from a rough content analysis of "copy" in several women's "fashion" magazines. "Fashion copy" is part successful social analysis, part unexamined social sentiment; and its dual nature reflects and successfully affects, all at the same time, the social structuring of "fashion" behavior.

1. THE SOCIAL FUNCTIONS OF CLOTHES AND THE MEANING OF "FASHION." In all societies, the clothes which *all* people wear have at least three (mixed latent and manifest) functions: utilitarian, esthetic, and symbolic of their social role. In all societies, clothes are more or less useful, more or less handsome, and more or less indicative of their wearer's social position.

We may now give a preliminary definition of "fashion" for present purposes, a definition which will be expanded by the rest of our analysis. "Fashion" in clothes has to do with the styles of cut, color, silhouette, stuffs, etc., that are socially prescribed and socially accepted as appropriate for certain social roles, and especially with the recurring changes in these styles.

2. "FASHION" IN WOMEN'S CLOTHES AND THE AMERICAN CLASS SYSTEM. A. *The functions of consumption in the American class system.* The American social class system approximates the open-class "ideal type" of institutionalized class structure, in which moral approval is placed on mobility from lower to higher social class. The primary criterion of a man's social class status (and that of his wife and dependent children) is his occupational position. Occupational achievement is the primary determinant of social mobility. One of the chief, but by no means the only, index of relative rank of occupational posi-

SOURCE: Bernard Barber and Lyle S. Lobel, " 'Fashion' in Women's Clothes and the American Social System," *Social Forces*, Vol. 31, (December, 1952), pp. 124–131; reprinted by permission of the author and publisher. (Copyright, 1952, by University of North Carolina Press.)

tion and achievement is money income and capital wealth. Hence the great symbolic significance of *all* consumption in American society. At least on first glance we all apply the following social equation: consumption equals wealth or income, wealth or income equals occupational position, occupational position equals social class position, and, *therefore*, consumption equals social class position. Even when this consequence is not intended by any particular consumer, his consumption has this latent function. The kind of house a man owns, the kind of car he drives, where he sends his children to college, etc., etc., all have symbolic significance for his social class status.

In the American class system, women take their class status, by and large, from their relationship to men: unmarried young women from their fathers, adult married women from their husbands. Hence the symbolic significance of women's consumption.

B.   The dilemma of equality and difference in the class system. In concrete social fact, American society has been a relatively close approximation to the "ideal type" of an open-class system. A great deal of social mobility actually exists, so that social class boundaries, especially as between any few adjacent social classes, are somewhat vague. The American class system is a finely-graded continuum of strata rather than a series of sharply separated ranks with little mobility between them. The result of this kind of class structure, in combination with American egalitarian values, has been the possibility of asserting the equality and similarity of everyone in the society, despite the actual class differences which exist. The ideology of equality and the social fact of difference are not so obviously inconsistent that they cannot seem to square with one another.

As the new styles, set by Paris and first imitated by the designers of expensive "limited editions," gain wider favor, the designers of each lower price range include the new "fashion" points as best they can in the lines they create, in response to actual or anticipated demand from those on lower class levels. As the "fashion" trickles down, fabrics become cheaper and mass production necessary. But even at the lower price and lower social levels, there is an attempt to avoid complete uniformity. Manufacturers try to distribute their job lots over a wide geographical area, including only a limited number of dresses of the same style, fabric, and size in a shipment to any one city, any one retailer. When a general style has "trickled down" through all levels, the "fashion" must change. The universalization of what started out as distinctive cheapens its symbolic value. A new change, a new "fashion" symbol, is necessary.

For the most part, the "trickle" system does not result in a progressive imitation of exact models in all the strata of ready-to-wear. There are real differences. The "trickle" system is perpetuated because the American class system makes some women continually seek for symbols of their difference from those just below them in the class system and at the same time makes other women continually seek for symbols of their equality with those just above them in the class system.

C.   Social class differences in definitions of "fashion." We must abandon the stereotype of complete standardization in American women's "fashions." Although there is a certain similarity at all class levels, there are also important differences. Let us consider some of the different phrasings of the "fashion" theme that are used in "fashion copy."

At the top of the American social class system are those families where lineage, or family connections extending back one or more generations, counts in addition to present occupational position. These are the "old money" families with established preeminence of social status. At this top-most level, where there is little need to compete for status through consumption, women may even maintain a certain independence of current changeful "fashion." Their quality clothes can remain roughly the same for several years. They can stress the esthetic functions of clothes somewhat at the expense of "fashion's" dictates.

"Fashion," we may now say in summary conclusion, is not socially "irrational." It means several different things, even in regard to women's clothes alone; and all its different meanings are socially and culturally structured. "Fashion" behavior has functions, latent as well as manifest, for many different aspects of the American social system.

16-D   WORD-OF-MOUTH COMMUNICATION BY THE INNOVATOR

James F. Engel (Marketing Educator), Robert J. Kegerreis (Marketing Educator), and Roger D. Blackwell (Marketing Educator)

New products, new ideas, are standard conversational ingredients. They make news. Hence, in an era characterized by a continual stream of innovation, it is not surprising to find a renewed emphasis on the old adage that "your best salesman is a satisfied customer." The assumption, of course, is that the satisfied buyer will tell others about his experience and thereby add mileage to a manufacturer's promotional investment.

There seems to be no question that the first users of a new product or service are active in the word-of-mouth channel. King found, for example, that nearly two-thirds of those interviewed told someone else about new products they had purchased or tried.[1] What, however, is the motivation for this communication activity? There are several possible explanations.[2] Product involvement can motivate the new user to talk about his purchase and the pleasure and excitement resulting from it. Self-involvement can play a role in a conversation about a product or service or may serve to gain attention, suggest status, or assert superiority. Concern for others may precipitate talk by the innovator because he can thereby share his satisfactions resulting from use of the product or service. Finally, there is the possibility that the innovator feels doubts and anxiety and talks to others in *"such a way as to enhance the probability that more units will be sold."*[3]

The last hypothesis has recently been advanced but without firm evidence. The assumption is that the innovator attempts to win friends or relatives as customers and thereby reduce post-decision dissonance by reinforcing the wisdom of his purchasing act. There is only limited support in the marketing literature, however, for the assertion that doubts of this type follow buying decisions.[4] Much of the research generated by the theory of cognitive dissonance has been challenged in recent years,[5] and experience has demonstrated the methodological difficulties which are presented.[6]

Nevertheless, it is worthwhile to investigate whether doubts do exist after the innovation is used. One study demonstrates that those who received unfavorable word-of-mouth comments were far less likely to purchase a new product than those who received no communication, whereas those given favorable information were more likely to buy.[7]

This article reports the results of a recent study on the post-trial behavior of the first users of a new automotive diagnostic center in Columbus, Ohio. This is part of a broader study focusing on the decision processes of the triers of this new concept.[8] Among the ques-

SOURCE: James F. Engel, Robert J. Kegerreis, and Roger D. Blackwell, "Word-of-Mouth Communication by the Innovator," *Journal of Marketing*, Vol. 33 (July, 1969), pp. 15–19, at pp. 15–18.

[1] Charles W. King and John O. Summers, "Technology, Innovation, and Consumer Decision Making," research paper, Herman C. Krannert Graduate School of Business Administration, Purdue University, 1967, p. 21.

[2] Ernest Dichter, "How Word of Mouth Advertising Works," *Harvard Business Review*, Vol. 44 (November-December 1966), pp. 147–166.

[3] John R. Stuteville, "The Buyer as a Salesman," *Journal of Marketing*, Vol. 32 (July 1968), p. 16.

[4] For a thorough review of the relevant literature see James F. Engel and M. Lawrence Light, "The Role of Psychological Commitment in Consumer Behavior: An Evaluation of the Theory of Cognitive Dissonance," in Frank M. Bass, Charles W. King, and Edgar M. Pessemier, eds., *Applications of the Sciences in Marketing Management* (New York: John Wiley & Sons, Inc., 1968), pp. 39–68.

[5] A. Chapanis and N. P. Chapanis, "Cognitive Dissonance: Five Years Later," *Psychological Bulletin*, Vol. 61 (1964), pp. 1–22.

[6] Jack W. Brehm and Arthur R. Cohen, *Explorations in Cognitive Dissonance* (New York: John Wiley & Sons, Inc., 1962).

[7] Johan Arndt, "Role of Product Related Conversations in the Diffusion of a New Product," *Journal of Marketing Research*, Vol. 4 (August 1967), pp. 291–295.

[8] Robert J. Kegerreis, "Innovative and Diffusive Characteristics of the Earliest Adopters of a New

tions investigated in this part of the study were: "Are innovators prone to diffuse information through word-of-mouth?" "Are these innovators also 'opinion leaders' and thereby likely to influence the recipient?" "Are positive experiences diffused more rapidly and to a greater extent than negative experiences?" "What are the most likely motivations for post-trial communication?"

Methodology

It was necessary at the outset to establish some operational definitions because of the present state of confusion in terminology used in diffusion research:[9]

1. *Diffusion* is the process by which meaningful communications about an innovation are exchanged among members of a society.
2. An *innovation* is anything perceived to be new by the potential trier and whose adoption would tend to alter significantly the trier's patterns of behavior.
3. *Innovators* were the patrons of a new automotive diagnostic center during its first three months of operations.
4. *Adoption* of the innovation was considered to be trial of the service by innovator patrons.

The diagnostic center is a genuine innovation; it was a totally new concept in the Columbus, Ohio, market. An electronic diagnosis of an automobile gives the owner an objective analysis of its mechanical condition and clearly changes usual patterns of behavior in automobile maintenance and repair.

Personal interviews were conducted at the diagnostic center from the first day it opened; completed interviews totaled 249. One week after the interview a follow-up telephone interview was undertaken with each respondent to assess his satisfaction with the service and the extent to which he communicated with others. Then the same questions used in the on-site interview were asked of a sample of

173 persons listed in the Columbus Telephone Directory, using a random number generator. Thus, it was possible to compare innovators and noninnovators on a number of characteristics.

The personal interview lasted approximately 30 minutes. It encompassed a series of questions on the decision-making process, search for information, personality attributes, image and attitude scales, and socioeconomic questions.[10]

The following hypotheses were established relative to the subject matter here:

1. Compared with the population as a whole, innovators
   a. are significantly more frequently asked for their opinion about new things.
   b. are significantly more prone to relate unprompted experiences about innovations to others.
2. Innovators use the word-of-mouth channel to diffuse information about negative experiences to a significantly greater extent than positive experiences.

GENERAL REQUESTS FOR NEW PRODUCT OPINIONS. Using the five-point scale shown in Table 1, interviewers asked respondents how frequently their opinions were solicited about new things. Well over half of the innovators (59%) felt they were asked their opinions on new products more often than average, compared with only 32% of the general population. At the opposite end of the scale, only 7.5% of the innovators felt their opinions were asked less frequently than average, compared with 19% of the population. These differences are statistically significant, so the first hypothesis is accepted.

PERCEIVED FREQUENCY OF TRANSMITTED OPINIONS ABOUT NEW PRODUCTS. The second hypothesis stated that innovators are more prone to relate unprompted experiences about new products than their counterparts in the general population. Again a five-point rating scale was used. As the data in Table 2 indicate, about half of the population see themselves as initiating this kind of conversation more often than average, whereas 67% of

---

Automotive Service," doctoral dissertation, The Ohio State University, 1968.

[9] For a detailed review of these issues, see James F. Engel, David T. Kollat, and Roger D. Blackwell, *Consumer Behavior* (New York: Holt, Rinehart and Winston, Inc., 1968), Chapter 25.

[10] For details on the methodology see same reference as footnote 8.

TABLE 1
Relative Frequency of Requests for a Personal Opinion About New Things

Response	Innovators		Population	
	Number	Percent	Number	Percent
Much more often than average	60	24.9	17	10.0
Slightly more often than average	82	34.0	37	21.8
About average	81	33.6	84	49.4
Slightly less often than average	10	4.2	19	11.2
Practically never	8	3.3	13	7.6
Total[a]	241	100.0	170	100.0

[a] Frequencies in the "no answer" category are not included.

$\chi^2 = 28.28$, d.f. $= 1$, $p < .0005$ (χ^2 computed by collapsing rows into: [1] requests more than average and [2] average or lower).

TABLE 2
Relative Frequency of Transmission of Personal Opinions About New Things

Response	Innovators		Population	
	Number	Percent	Number	Percent
Much more often than average	82	34.5	38	22.3
Slightly more often than average	77	32.3	51	30.0
About average	67	28.1	56	32.9
Slightly less often than average	8	3.4	13	7.6
Practically never	4	1.7	12	7.2
Total[a]	238	100.0	170	100.0

[a] Frequencies in the "no answer" category are not included.

$\chi^2 = 8.098$, d.f. $= 1$, $p < .005$ (χ^2 computed by collapsing rows into: [1] requests more than average and [2] average or lower).

the innovators place themselves in this class. Conversely only five in every 100 innovators rate themselves as less than average in this respect, compared with 15 out of every 100 in the population. This difference is statistically significant, and the hypothesis is accepted.

POST-PURCHASE EVALUATION OF THE SERVICE. Before evaluating actual incidences of reported post-trial communications, it is necessary to evaluate the extent of satisfaction with the diagnostic center experience. If dissonance or anxiety was present, it should have been detected in a series of questions asked in the follow-up telephone interview with the innovators. These data appear in composite form in Table 3.

The bulk of the early triers (40.7%) found the innovation to be about what they had anticipated. Another 38.3% were more pleased than they had expected, while the remaining 19% were disappointed. The generally favorable evaluation is further confirmed by the

TABLE 3
Post-Trial Attitudes of Earliest Adopters of the Diagnostic Center

Response	Number[a]	Percent
General Evaluation		
Much more pleased than expected	33	15.3
Somewhat more pleased than expected	54	25.0
About as expected	88	40.7
Somewhat disappointed	29	13.4
Very much disappointed	12	5.6
Total	216	100.0
Reuse Intentions		
Intend to use again	175	84.3
Will not use again or unsure	35	15.7
Total	210	100.0
Evaluation of Price		
Price is "about right"	163	77.3
Service is underpriced	33	15.6
Service is overpriced	15	7.1
Total	211	100.0

[a] Frequencies in the "no answer" category are not included.

fact that 85% intended to repeat their use of the diagnostic center as the need arose.

Another measurement was made of post-purchase satisfaction by asking respondents to indicate their comparisons of the value of the service with its price. Three of every four said that the service was worth its price ($9.95), while 15.6% felt it was underpriced. Only 7% said it was overpriced. (Clearly the great majority were satisfied users.) If doubts existed, they were not detected from these questions. Obviously reuse of the service is the final measure of satisfaction, but the long time lapse between initial and subsequent use prohibited such a measurement here. The probability of many repeat customers, however, is indicated by the 85% stated intention of repeated use.

POST-TRIAL INFORMATION TRANSMISSION. Respondents were asked in the follow-up telephone survey whether or not they had told anyone of their experiences. The results in Table 4 are impressive. Within a few days after trial, 90% had told at least one other person about it, and 40% had told two or more.

TABLE 4

Post-Trial Information Transmissions by Innovators

Number of Persons Told	Number	Percent
Four or more	6	2.8
Three or more	20	9.4
Two or more	61	28.7
At least one	105	49.1
None	21	10.0
Total[a]	213	100.0

[a] Frequencies in the "no answer" category are not included.

TABLE 5

Types of Recipients of Word-of-Mouth Communication from Innovators

Recipient	Number	Percent
Friend	48	45.8
Relative	40	38.1
Business related	15	14.2
Other	2	1.9
Total[a]	105	100.0

[a] Frequencies in the "no answer" category are not included.

Note. These data were provided by those respondents who told only one person about the innovation during the specified period. Responses for those who made multiple contacts could not be separated by type of recipient.

It is possible, of course, that questions in the initial interview focusing on frequencies of discussions with others (Tables 1 and 2) conditioned respondents to share their experiences more frequently. It seems unlikely, however, because of the length of the initial interview and the variety of other topics covered. In addition, the high use of word-of-mouth reported here is quite consistent with the general communication patterns appearing in Tables 1 and 2.

The four categories of "recipient of information" are shown in Table 5. As one might expect, the great majority were friends or relatives.

The 40 dissatisfied customers showed no greater use of word-of-mouth than the satisfied customer. Therefore, the hypothesis that negative experiences are diffused to a greater extent than positive experiences must be rejected. Nearly all of those interviewed used the word-of-mouth channel.

17 / The Family

A. BACKGROUND AND THEORY

The first article (Baughman and Welsh) deals with the impact of changes in family structure. The second article (Kildegaard) explains the differences between a household and a family.

17A THE IMPACT OF CHANGES IN FAMILY STRUCTURE

E. Earl Baughman (Psychologist) and
George Schlager Welsh (Psychologist)

Families indoctrinate their children with basic approaches to living in a world with other people, approaches that may be only partially related to specific role-behavior. Perhaps if we examine, very briefly, how family structure has *tended* to change during the past 100 to 150 years, the meaning of this statement will become clearer.

Patriarchal Families

The patriarchal family, wherein the father—because of his strength and skills—is the only source of support, characterized Western society before the Industrial Revolution. Children grew up in these families expecting to remain in the same geographical area when they married, working at jobs in keeping with the family's class level, and lending support to relatives when they needed it. A family's place in the larger social group was usually well defined, as were the expectations placed on the individual members of the family. A person was expected to do his work, to be loyal to the clan, and to know his place in the community. Perhaps, above all, respect for authority was demanded.

SOURCE: E. Earl Baughman and George Schlager Welsh, *Personality: A Behavioral Science.* © 1962, Reprinted by permission of Prentice-Hall, Inc., Englewood Cliffs, New Jersey, pp. 211–213.

Companionship Families

The Industrial Revolution, of course, dealt many massive blows to the long-established social order, the reeling of which is still apparent. For the family, one significant result was certainly a weakening of the father's position. Other members of the family were no longer so completely dependent on him for their support, for many of the machines could be operated by children as well as by women. Another effect was that as families began to move away from rural areas (where they lived close to relatives with whom they had many social interactions) into urban areas, each family unit was much more on its own. As for individuals, they began to see that they could improve their lots in life by taking advantage of the new opportunities—that is, social mobility became a more realistic possibility than had traditionally been the case.

Within the family one result of all these changes was a *partial* redefinition of what was man's work and what was woman's work. Along with this redefinition followed a more equal sharing of work and responsibility between the sexes. This increased equality has led some observers to label the families of that period *companionship families*. These families ordinarily stressed individual initiative, self-control, independence, and active manipulation of the world. Faith in free enterprise seemed almost unlimited, and children were imbued with the belief that they were masters of their own destinies. Opportunities were at every corner; one only had to take advantage of them. In short, these families seemed to have a sense of moral obligation to go out, compete, and subdue both persons and things.

Colleague Families

The continued growth of the industrial plants, however, resulted in the establishment of tremendous bureaucratic structures. In these bureaucracies persons seldom do "complete" jobs; instead, they contribute a small bit to the total process. Indeed, as in the preindustrial period, each person tends to have his "place," yet the setting is quite different, for, among other things, now there are ladders to scramble up and considerable freedom to withdraw from one rung and try to climb up to another spot if one so chooses.

Daniel R. Miller and Guy E. Swanson, after studying families in the Detroit area, conclude that our bureaucratic society is spawning a new type of family structure that emphasizes developing interpersonal relationships, doing what is socially proper, and being flexible. They use the term *colleague family* to describe this new emphasis:

> The specialization on the job has entered the home, and the equal partners [of the companionship family] have been able to see that differences in talent, interest, and functions, as long as they are complementary, do not threaten equality. Instead they may enrich and promote the common life. For

this reason we call this type of family the "colleague" family. And, [like specialists at work, marriage partners] may defer to one another's judgment on the grounds of differing competence without feeling that they have personally lost in prestige.

They also point out some other effects of specialization—for instance, the wife's functions are being professionalized: witness the rise of study groups for child care, cooking, and homemaking.

What about a child, then, who must grow up in a colleague-type family? Miller and Swanson suggest that "he must learn to be a 'nice guy'—affable, unthreatening, responsible, competent, adaptive. It is this kind of skill in which the parent must train him."

The trend away from strictly patriarchal families to, first, companionship families and, more recently, colleague families appears to be real enough, yet we should clearly recognize that it is a broad social change rather than a process that has penetrated into every family. We can easily locate patriarchal and companionship families as well as colleague families in the America of today, and we can find them at every social-class level. Besides, for ease of exposition, we have been talking about relatively pure types. Clearly, though, many modifications of these relationships can be found. Yet we should not let these qualifications cut away certain basic facts: Families today are more "adjustment" conscious than in the past, and father's autocratic control is not quite what it was two or three generations ago.

17-B A HOUSEHOLD IS NOT A FAMILY

Ingrid C. Kildegaard (Marketing Executive)

One in sixteen of all persons living in households are nonfamily members. These "unrelated individuals" receive over 30 billion dollars in household income, nearly one tenth of all household money income. One sixth of the nation's households are headed by unrelated individuals, most of whom live alone.

Recent years have seen a sharp rise in the

SOURCE: Ingrid C. Kildegaard, "A Household Is Not a Family," *Journal of Advertising Research*, Vol. 7 (June, 1967), pp. 44–46. © 1967 by the Advertising Research Foundation, Inc.

number of nonfamily households. As the gap between household and family counts has widened, advertisers of home products and appliances have changed their marketing units from families to households. The following figures help explain their preference for households:

Year	Households (000)	Families (000)
1940	34,949	32,166
1950	43,554	39,303
1955	47,788	41,934
1960	52,610	45,602
1966	58,092	48,278
1985	84,421	68,282

Since 1940, the household count has gone from 35 to 58 million, a 66 per cent increase. Meanwhile the number of families has grown by 50 per cent. If all families were households, there would have been three million nonfamily households in 1940, compared with 10 million in 1966 and a projected 16 million in 1985.

How They Are Defined

But not all families are households. A family need not live in a housing unit. On the other hand, some households may contain more than one family. A family is defined by the Bureau of the Census as two or more persons related by blood, marriage, or adoption *and* living together. A young married couple sharing the home of the wife's parents is considered part of the parents' family. But if the couple are lodgers or live-in employees of the household, they are counted as a separate family, making two families in one household.

In contrast, a household is determined by where people live without regard to their relationships. The count of households is identical to the count of occupied housing units. A housing unit may be a house, an apartment, a house trailer, a single room or other "separate living quarters." The household consists of all persons who live in the unit, whether or not they are related. Boarding houses, dormitories, and other institutions classified as "group quarters" are excluded from the household count.

Chart I shows how households and household populations compare with those of families. Both include all *primary* families, those where the head of the family is also head of the household. This group accounts for virtually all families but only 83 per cent of the households. *Secondary* families are those where the family head is not head of a household. Most of these are young married couples or widows with young children. All are included in the count of families and in the family population. While not separate households, those members of secondary families who live in households are included in the household population. Those living in dormitories or other group quarters are excluded.

Like families, unrelated individuals are classified according to their household status. Primary individuals are heads of households while secondary individuals are guests, lodgers, or servants in households headed by nonrelatives. None of these 12 million individuals are included in the family population, though

CHART 1

Comparison of Household and Family Populations, March 1966

Number (000)			Population (000)	
Households	Families	Component	Households	Families
48,169	48,169	*Primary Families* (Two or more persons related by blood, marriage, or adoption, where the head of the family is also head of the household)	179,138	179,138
—	84	*Secondary Families in Households* (Two or more related household members, living in a household headed by a nonrelative)	200	200
—	25	*Secondary Families in Group Quarters* (Two or more related individuals living in rooming houses, dormitories, etc.)	—	68
9,923	—	*Primary Individuals* (Household heads living alone or with nonrelatives)	9,923	—
—	—	*Secondary Individuals* (A lodger, maid, or other individual living with nonrelatives)	2,166	—
58,092	48,278	Total	191,427	179,406

some of the families may belong to households headed by a primary individual. Of the 9.9 million primary individuals, about one in eleven shares his home with nonrelatives.

In all, the household population includes 99 per cent of the resident population. It excludes inmates of institutions, residents of group quarters, and members of armed forces living in barracks. At the same time, family population represents only 92 per cent of U. S. residents, excluding unrelated household members but including some of those persons residing in group quarters.

How They Differ

As might be expected, households tend to be smaller than families. In 1966 the median number of members was 3.30 for households and 3.72 for families. This is mainly due to one-person households which do not qualify as families:

Size	Households	Families
One person	9,044	—
Two persons	16,580	16,230
Three persons	9,939	9,774
Four persons	9,414	9,340
Five persons	6,223	6,165
Six persons	3,446	3,412
Six or more persons	3,446	3,357
Total	58,092	48,278

One in five households have female heads, versus one in ten families. The husband, happily, is considered the head of all husband-wife households:

Type of Unit	Households	Families
Husband-wife	42,060	42,107
Others with male heads	4,457	1,179
Others with female heads	11,575	4,992
Total	58,092	48,278

As might also be expected, there are more childless units among households, than among families:

Related children under age 18	Households	Families
None	30,056	20,178
One	8,688	8,721
Two	8,377	8,395
Three	5,385	5,388
Four or more	5,595	5,597
Total	58,092	48,278

The median age is higher for household heads than for family heads (48.1 versus 45.7). The difference is due to the large number of older one-person households who no longer qualify as families since losing their mates:

Age of Head	Households	Families
Under 25	3,552	3,049
25–29	4,964	4,553
30–34	5,059	4,738
35–39	11,880	11,094
45–54	11,743	10,459
55–64	9,693	7,490
65–74	7,185	4,651
75 and over	4,016	2,244
Total	58,092	48,278

Household heads are much more likely to be single, widowed, or divorced than are family heads:

Marital Status of Head	Households	Families
Negro		
Male	4,164	3,561
Female	1,790	1,131
White		
Male	42,352	39,636
Female	9,783	3,860
Total	58,092	48,278

Median family income in 1962 was $5,956, somewhat higher than the $5,532 median household income. Though the large number of households in the lowest income group lowered the average, all groups showed more households than families:

Total Income	Households (000)	Families (000)
Under $3,000	14,238	9,320
$ 3,000 to $ 3,999	4,912	4,325
4,000 to 4,999	5,188	4,669
5,000 to 5,999	6,016	5,424
6,000 to 6,999	5,408	5,100
7,000 to 7,999	4,305	4,023
8,000 to 9,999	6,071	5,804
10,000 to 14,999	6,402	6,019
15,000 to 24,999	2,152	1,889
25,000 and over	497	425
Total	55,189	46,998

New Reporting Plans

Household income data have not been part of the Census reporting program. Its 1962 income data were a special tabulation done for the Advertising Research Foundation. The other data summarized here represent the extent of household information published on an annual basis.

Every five years the Census publishes household estimates for states. Otherwise marketers have had to wait for decennial Censuses for more area and detailed data.

Largely due to the efforts of the Federal Statistics Users' Conference, the Bureau of the Census is planning to expand its annual publication series on households. To the characteristics already reported, they expect to add tables showing:

- Household income distributions.
- Education of household head.
- Relationship to household head.
- Employment status of household head.
- Occupation of household head.
- Presence of children by age.

Many of these data will be cross-tabulated, permitting an intensive analysis of one of the most important statistical series offered by the Bureau of the Census to marketers.

Where the Data Come From

Studies of household characteristics are conducted each spring by the Bureau of the Census in connection with the Current Population Survey. Reprints from their 1966 study appear in *Current Population Reports*, Series P-20, No. 164. Household estimates from previous years are published in earlier reports in this series.

The latest household estimates by state are for 1965 and were released in 1967. The estimates were based on 1960 Census household figures and on current state population estimates. These are published in *Current Population Reports*, Series P-25, No. 356.

Projections of the numbers of families and households through 1985 are made by the Bureau of the Census. Two series are reported, along with the underlying assumptions. These appear in *Current Population Reports*, Series P-25, No. 360.

Information on current plans for future household reports come from meetings and correspondence between the Federal Statistics Users' Conference and the Bureau of the Census. More details on this activity may be obtained from John Aiken, Executive Director, Federal Statistics Users' Conference, 1523 L Street, N. W., Washington, D. C. 20005.

All other reports are available from the Superintendent of Documents, U. S. Government Printing Office, Washington, D. C. 20402.

B. RESEARCH AND APPLICATIONS

The second section begins with a discussion (Zober) of the determinants of husband-wife buying roles, and concludes with an article (Patterson) that deals with the working-class family and its marketing behavior.

17-C DETERMINANTS OF HUSBAND-WIFE BUYING ROLES

Martin Zober (Marketing Educator)

P. D. Converse has found that the gender of the purchaser depends on the economic bracket in which the family falls and also whether the family is a rural or urban one.[1] In higher-income groups men incline to shop for their own clothing. In middle- and low-income

SOURCE: Martin Zober, *Marketing Management* (New York: John Wiley & Sons, Inc., 1964), pp. 353–356.

[1] Paul D. Converse and Harvey W. Huegy, *The Elements of Marketing*, 3rd ed., Prentice-Hall, Englewood Cliffs, N.J., 1946, pp. 31–32.

groups husband and wife shop jointly for clothing. If a family resides on a farm, the chances are that the farmer will do most of the household's buying. Generally, he shops at the same time that he sells his produce or conducts business transactions. In cities most of the shopping is undertaken by women. Even though more and more men have begun to shop for groceries where grocery stores and supermarkets remain open in the evening, women still predominate.

Ferber has studied the relative influence of husbands and wives in purchasing by inviting both to rate their spouses on the other's impact in buying a list of items.[2] He stated that the reliability of ratings of the relative influences of different family members or of different sexes was highly limited. Not only did the ratings of the same individual by two or more members of the family bear slight relationship to one another, but also the numerical values of the ratings and their distribution differed according to whether the husband or the wife was responding. Family members generally tend to deprecate their own influence relative to the influence ascribed to them by other members of the family. As a rule, Ferber found, wives seem to be more uniform in their ratings than husbands.

The ratings point in a general way to which family members or sex wields the lion's share of influence over the purchase of an item. Yet the usefulness of ratings for planning marketing campaigns is limited by their variability. Moreover, the basic reliability of these ratings remains in doubt. There is not much evidence of how far the responses agree with actual behavior. Ferber suggested that better results should be obtained by other approaches, such as by indirect questioning and the case history method.

ROLES OF SPOUSES. An experiment explaining the roles of husband and wife in decision making was conducted at Iowa State University.[3]

The object of this experiment was to ascertain how much influence each spouse wielded in the decision-making process and to learn whether each could predict his or her actions. Analysis of the influence was restricted to three variables: the total number of actions performed by each spouse; those actions that consisted of giving ideas and suggestions; and those that contributed to the functioning of the group. The measure of self-prediction was the question posed before and after the experimental session against what actually occurred.

The study disclosed that the husband did most of the talking and had the greatest influence on the decision. The wife was the peacemaker. In most cases, however, neither husband nor wife could predict the roles each would play in making the decision, even after the completion of the experimental session.

The experiment showed the difficulty of obtaining information about the respective roles of husband and wife in decision making. Perhaps depth interviewing might have been more fruitful on specific purchase situations to determine the respective influences of husband and wife. Decision making varies with convenience items as compared with shopping for specialty goods. Certain items necessitate more deliberation and planning than others.

INTERACTION OF SPOUSES. In an effort to determine the interaction of husband and wife through depth interviews, it was noted that the housewife was the principal purchasing agent of the family, albeit influenced by other members of her household.[4] She normally wishes to buy things which will please the members of the family provided this does not conflict with her own views of what is right, proper, healthy, and esthetic. Through their behavior, however, the other family members exert pressure to cajole her to buy the things that satisfy their own desires. That both influences are often exercised subconsciously and manifested in camouflaged form does not reduce their importance.

In shopping for major products such as ap-

[2] Robert Ferber, "On the Reliability of Purchase Influence Studies," *Journal of Marketing*, Vol. 19, No. 3, January 1955, pp. 225–232.

[3] William F. Kenkel and Dean K. Hoffman, "Real and Conceived Roles in Family Decision Making," *Marriage and the Family*, Vol. 17, No. 4, November 1956, pp. 311–316; William F. Kenkel, "Influence Differentiation in Family Decision Making,"

Sociology and Social Research, September–October 1957, Vol. 42, No. 1, pp. 18–25.

[4] *Basic Research Report on Consumer Behavior*, published by Alderson and Sessions, Philadelphia, April 1957, mimeographed, pp. 602–605.

pliances or automobiles, the wife rarely acts alone. These products are purchased jointly. The interviews suggested that answers on major purchase decisions tended to be governed by the buyers' notions of the right and conventional things to do. For example, the husband was often credited for judgment on mechanical details and operation of equipment, although further searching indicated but little basis in fact for this at times and observed that it was asserted largely because it represented the respondent's view of the proper masculine role. The amount of cooperation taking place between husband and wife is also an outgrowth of their social and economic status.[5] Among lower-income families the purchase of an automobile is a combined decision, whereas the upper-class husband makes the decision alone. Yet this is not necessarily the pattern for other economic decisions.

There is greater autonomy in the spending of money and handling of bills at the top and bottom of the economic hierarchy than among the middle class. At the bottom most of the available income is spent on necessities. At the top there is less disposition to debate expenditures because there is enough economic leeway. What is broadly defined as the middle class may be expected to show the greatest cooperation in making economic decisions because of aspirations to advance its status. Among these middle-class families, particularly the intellectual and professional classes with

moderate rather than high incomes, there is a particularly high frequency of cooperation in making buying decisions because of the need to weigh alternatives.

Conflicting values of husband and wife also influence the purchase decision.[6] While husbands are usually the first to mention buying a new car for the family, wives may often try to talk them out of it. Wives generally place less value on having a new car than do their husbands. As a result they may argue against buying a new model, or failing that, may persuade their husbands to buy a lower-priced one. This resistance reflects a difference between husband and wife over the scale of values rather than opposition to a new automobile on the basis of safety or some other inherent characteristic. Furnishing the home, saving money, providing for the children are objectives in the hierarchy of values usually regarded more highly by the wife than by the husband.

Yet when the make-model preferences of husbands and wives are compared with purchases, the husband usually wins. The family usually buys the car he prefers or that he and his wife agree is best. One-third of the nation's families purchase makes that neither the husband nor the wife prefers. This may result from lack of knowledge of trading in for a new model; the family may be compelled by the trade-in allowance to buy a lower-priced car. The lower valuation placed by women on cars suggests, moreover, that they would lean toward the lower-priced makes.

[5] "Family Buying Decisions: Who Makes Them, Who Influences Them," *Printer's Ink*, Sept. 19, 1958, p. 21 ff.

[6] *Ibid.*

17-D MARKETING AND THE WORKING-CLASS FAMILY

James M. Patterson (Marketing Educator)

One of the striking characteristics of the modern market is the basic similarity between the ways high-income families and low-income families distribute their expenditures over broad budget categories. Except for food and

SOURCE: James M. Patterson, "Marketing and the Working-Class Family," in Arthur B. Shostak and William Gomberg, Eds., *Blue-Collar World: Studies of the American Worker.* © 1965. Reprinted by permission of Prentice-Hall, Inc., Englewood Cliffs, New Jersey, pp. 76–80.

tobacco and, to a lesser extent, clothing, home furnishings and appliances, and automobiles, the high-income family and the low-income family handle their budget problems in much the same way. Consequently, income is no longer the important explanation of differences in family spending behavior that it once was. On the other hand, it must be remembered that, although the rich families and the poor families allocate their expenditures among broad budget categories in much the same way, this does not mean that the same specific products are always bought, or that, when the same specific products are purchased, they are similar in quality. The fact is that they are not. Still, it would be a mistake to assume that the high-income family invariably purchases the high-quality product and vice versa, for it simply is not true.

A striking example of how important it is to divide markets into segments along behavioral rather than along straight economic lines is found in the recent research on the "blue-collar" segment of the market. This is, of course, a very important market for most consumer goods, because it contains some 25,000,000 families and in many specific markets represents up to 60 per cent of the market potential. (It is also the market segment that is most removed from the typical middle-class marketing executive's experience.) As a paradoxical segment in its marketing behavior, the "blue-collar" segment contains a great many surprises for the unwary observer who may try to understand it in terms of his middle-class values. Consider, for example, the following items from the trade press:[1]

- In 1961 52.2% of all outboards were sold to blue-collar families.
- The working-class wife buys 40% of all *top-priced* refrigerators; 38% of the *most* expensive washing machines and 37% of the *best* sewing machines.
- In spite of a price differential between a premium coffee and other brands (private and national) working-class families accounted for 20% more of the premium brand's sales than did white-collar families in a special analysis based on reports from leading chains.
- In an analysis of sales of recent buyers of 20 different products and services, in 11 of the 20 categories, more sales were made to working-class families than to Chicago's middle- and upper-class population.

The Working-Class World[2]

The working-class world is a simple world. Meager education, routine and relatively sim-

ple workaday roles, limited information about diverse and remote events, coupled with the fact that close associates on and off the job are people very like themselves, apparently serve to foreshorten the working-class family's world view. Because both direct and vicarious experience with other or contrasting world views is limited and narrow, the working-class family's perspective is, in general, severely truncated and quite unsophisticated. Situations and alternatives typically are seen in black-and-white terms and people are classified as either "in" or "out" in "we" and "they" terms.

This overly simplified world view, in turn, seems to produce certain other behavioral traits which characterize the working class. The first is a sense of fatefulness—a sense that the events that occur are caused by luck or chance. When the simple model of the situation fails to work (which is quite often), "fate" —not the model—is presumed to be the cause. This attitude, in turn, tends to create a sense of powerlessness and of insecurity. Furthermore, limited education and narrow social and cultural experience, combined with the absence of a rich and sophisticated variety of perspectives, seriously restrict the working-class member's ability to achieve his goals in the impersonal competitive sectors of society where it is "what you are" and "what you can do" that counts. Consequently, the working-class family tries to evolve a way of life that will both reduce its felt insecurity and allow it to achieve its goals in a personal and noncompetitive way. The general tendency is to seek out the routine and familiar and predictable and to avoid the uncertain. And because members of the working-class family frequently lack both the confidence and the ability to do and say the right thing in new situations, they try to avoid situations where new roles must be improvised and new relationships established. Furthermore, because they frequently are not able to compete effectively in the impersonal social world, they tend

---

[1] Reported in *The New York Times,* December 20, 1961; March 7, 1962; and May 16, 1962.

[2] This section is based on the findings of: Albert K. Cohen and Harold M. Hodges, "Lower-Blue-Collar-Class Characteristics," *Social Problems,* Vol. X, No. 4 (Spring, 1963), pp. 303–34; Lee Rainwater, Richard P. Coleman, and Gerald Handel, *Workingman's Wife* (New York: Oceana Publications, Inc., 1959); and Bennett M. Berger, *Working-Class Suburb* (Berkeley: University of California Press, 1960).

to fall back on an elaborate network of highly personal relationships with people similarly circumstanced—primarily, neighbors and kin who help each other in time of trouble. This heavy reliance on personal relationships as a means of goal achievement and security, in turn, means that the working-class family is overly concerned about what others think of them and, therefore, subjected to tremendous pressure to conform to accepted working-class norms and standards.

In sum, the working-class family tends to be a family of limited social activity and experience which emphasizes personal, noncompetitive bases of status and social identity. Typically, they don't know the middle-class Joneses, and, because there is always a chance that they will be socially downgraded, they seldom risk trying to keep up with them. Their world view is one of pervasive anxiety. They tend to prize the present, the known, the personal. They avoid the competitive, the impersonal, and the uncertain. They tend to indulge rather than invest—they are overly preoccupied with the stability of basic, human relationships and they are in large measure "other-directed." Furthermore, because most working-class families see themselves severely restricted in their ability to rise in social status, the "others" with whom they identify, that is, the frames of reference which govern their behavior, are largely chosen from within their own class. Perhaps more than in any other class, the working-class family looks horizontally for its norms and standards rather than outside or up to the next class.

Implications for the Working-Class Family's Marketing Behavior

A number of possible relationships between behavioral characteristics and patterns of market behavior readily suggest themselves and are worthy of note.

1. The limited-experience world, limited in experiences both direct and vicarious, tends to cause working-class family expenditures to be concentrated into fewer categories of goods and services and more in terms of immediate consumption than is true of middle-class families, where the experience world is much broader.

2. The inordinate concern for enhancing their working-class position and stabilizing their interpersonal relations apparently causes the working-class family to avoid spending their money in ways that are not regarded as respectable or that are "out of place." Consequently, they merely seek to achieve the "common man's" level of recognition and respectability with their spending; they seldom try for more. They know that to try to keep up with the middle-class Joneses is doubly risky, because they typically are not very good at playing this game, and at the same time doing so might weaken or alienate certain important personal relationships which they had formed as a hedge against the proverbial "rainy day."

3. Given this much less ambitious goal of merely keeping up with the Cassidys rather than the Joneses—that is, to strive only for a "common man" level of recognition and respectability—certain contrasts with middle-class marketing behavior seem to take on a new meaning. For example, the emphasis on the contents of the house rather than the house itself. For the middle-class family, the house is the status symbol par excellence. Perhaps even more, it is a symbol of upward striving and of collective self. But for families whose upward mobility is restricted by limited social skills and perspectives, the house apparently symbolizes something much more practical and utilitarian. Consequently, working-class housing tastes run to "decent," "clean," "new," "safe," and the like. And, with the exception that they seek to avoid slums or checkerboard neighborhoods, the socially significant address has little or no meaning for them.

It is the contents rather than the house that becomes the center of spending interest for the working-class family. In fact, within the working class itself, there are striking differences between the dark-blue- and light-blue-collar families. Albert Cohen and Harold Hodges[3] recently found that the prevailing market value of the so-called "lower-lower class" family's car, TV, and basic appliances averages almost 20 per cent higher than the average value of equivalent "upper-lower"-class family's possessions, despite a median family income that is fully one-third lower. They would hold that this is due, in part at least, to the fact that the lower-lower-class member's basic pessimism causes him to spend

[3] Cohen and Hodges, *op. cit.*, p. 330.

in ways that promise immediate gratification. Also, because the lower-lower-class conjugal family is a precarious entity at best, its members are apparently reluctant to invest heavily in a house whose principal function is to serve as a presentation of the "collective self" and to demonstrate the common identity of the conjugal family: their house serves other ends.

4. The observed tendency to buy an unexpected share of nationally advertised brands and top-of-the-line models can in part be explained as a consequence of the pervasive anxiety that characterizes the working class. Apparently the working-class family reduces their insecurity about value and quality when they buy a known brand or premium model. In fact, there seems to be a widespread feeling around working-class families that "you only get what you pay for."

5. The working-class family's tendency to "trade" along local, known, and friendship lines can perhaps be explained by their overriding concern with personal relationships.

6. And finally, the tendency of the working-class family to shop in certain stores and not in others can be explained in part by their reluctance to chance being socially downgraded by either the sales clerks or the middle-class customers whom they think they will find there. Also, this shopping pattern can perhaps be explained in part by their discomfort at being surrounded by a "foreign" symbol system. Thus, the advertisements, décor, location, type of sales personnel, and class of clientele all combine to give a store a class identification which is widely understood.

18 / Social Influences

A. BACKGROUND AND THEORY

The determinants of group identity are discussed in the first section (Zaleznik and Moment), and group influence on purchase behavior in the second selection (Wasson, Sturdivant, and McConaughy).

18-A DETERMINANTS OF GROUP IDENTITY

Abraham Zaleznick (Marketing Educator)
and David Moment (Marketing Educator)

The experiences of individuals in and through a culture determine member behavior in groups. At the same time, groups create new forms of behavior that over time result in cultural change. We cannot, therefore, be completely deterministic, otherwise it would be difficult to account for change in individuals, groups, and society as a whole.

All the elements of group identity are culturally derived. The fact is, however, that no two individuals experience a culture in quite the same way. Nor are cultural experiences alike. The United States, for example, is a pluralistic society in which regional, ethnic, and socio-economic class differences permit variations in style of life and in sets of values.

Group Purpose

A second set of forces determining the identity of a group stems from the purpose of the group. A work group, like many factory groups with a fixed purpose set externally, will develop relationships by superimposing its cultural outlooks on the purpose of the group. For work groups whose purpose is somewhat more vague, such as committee and task groups dealing with abstract problems,

SOURCE: Abraham Zaleznik and David Moment, "Determinants of Group Identity," *The Dynamics of Interpersonal Behavior* (New York: John Wiley & Sons, Inc., 1964), pp. 56, 57–58, and 62–63.

the purpose of the group as it defines the status and role of members is less rigid. Here emergent behavior is potentially more significant than past behavioral patterns. The tendency for members to seek definitions of the situation quickly leads them, however, to use group purpose to create structures that may be psychologically comfortable, but of negative value in the work of the group. We tend to find, therefore, a persistent tendency to detail tasks beyond the limits we consider functional, to invoke authority to define the group in terms of its task, particularly in those cases where ambiguity is intolerable to individual group members. Although group purpose as a means for defining the situation is readily available, we need to recognize the dangers inherent in overly rapid definition and over delineation of tasks especially where group tasks demand creative solutions.

Identification with the Leader

The classic statement of the function of the leader in the emotional life of the group has been presented by Freud in *Group Psychology and the Analysis of the Ego*. Freud viewed the leader as the source of cohesion among group members in their common identification with him. Their emotional attachment to him becomes a common element in the psychic experience of group members and becomes the source of the tie binding members to each other. The withdrawal of the leader figure, or the abandonment of him as an object for identification, breaks the attachment among group members and induces anxiety. Where group members succeed in identifying with their leader, their loyalties toward him, as well as their fear of him, serve to establish the definition of the situation. All relationships are bound in his activity. His values are adopted by group members and his behavior becomes unconsciously, at least, a model for them.

The powerful position of a leader figure is, of course, subject to abuse. It can result in extreme dependency on the part of members as well as chaotic behavior when the leader's position is challenged or undermined.

Freud's position should not be taken to define how a leader should behave in a group or his role in its identity. But the position of the leader does indicate the exceptionally crucial problem leadership poses in and for groups.

18-B GROUP INFLUENCE ON PURCHASE BEHAVIOR

Chester R. Wasson (Marketing Educator), Frederick D. Sturdivant (Marketing Educator), and David H. McConaughy (Marketing Educator)

The Group as the Source of Learning Content

Learning theory helps us understand how we form consumption habits but not why we develop the specific habits we do. It helps us to understand why we tend to satisfy hunger at breakfast with one kind of food or see a different menu as the cue to hunger satisfaction in the context of the evening meal. But learning theory does not by itself explain why Midwestern children eat a cold or hot cereal for breakfast, Hawaiian children eat poi, and Southern children, grits and gravy. The anthropologist recognizes such regional, class, and other uniform differences as cultural patterns which the sociologist shows are transmitted to us through our group memberships. The specific content of our habits originates in the cues first suggested as sources of possible satisfaction by these groups, and the behavior patterns suggested by them derive from the larger culture of the social classes of which they are a part, in the regions in which they are found.

The other members of the group with which we are in relatively direct contact help us short-cut the learning process by passing on

SOURCE: Chester R. Wasson, Frederick D. Sturdivant, and David H. McConaughy, *Competition and Human Behavior.* © 1968 by the Meredith Corporation. Reprinted by permission of Appleton-Century-Crofts, pp. 42–44.

suggestions out of their experience as to the best ways of satisfying our drives. From infancy onward, we learn to look to those around us for possible answers to needs problems. The groups thus become the trusted sources for perceivable cues to drive fulfillment. They save us much frustrating trial and error by furnishing decisions concerning which behavioral solutions are acceptable and which not acceptable. Because such suggestions and rulings lead to satisfaction so dependably, we come to accept group behavioral standards, to refer to group experience and norms, when deciding on the right ways to satisfy our drives.

The "right" solutions suggested by our groups for most of our needs are only a small part of those which could, objectively, satisfy them. No culture encompasses more than a fraction of the possible sources of nutrition as acceptable sources. There are many more ways of keeping warm and gaining personal enjoyment of any kind than suggested by the limited experience of any one group. Hence, different groups will develop varying norms of behavior, even opposite ones.

There are also internal variations in the standards of right conduct within the group, dependent upon the place of the individual within the group structure, upon the role of the individual within the group. All groups have some organizational structure with an assigned role for each member. For any of us past childhood, the role will differ in each group to which we belong.

Such a multiplicity of memberships and roles creates problems of choice for each of us. Each of us must solve problems in terms of his own temperament. Consequently, some individual differences in behavior arise from the varying impact of group standards on each of us.

Initially, we have no problem in the choice of our reference group—the family is the only group we know in early childhood. As we mature, however, we join other groups of necessity or by choice, and these groups become added sources of experience and thus also become reference points to acceptable behavior. As our social contacts widen, the probability that our reference norms of behavior will conflict comes close to being a certainty. At such points, we must and do make choices as to our preferred reference groups.

The most common reference group choice is some membership group with which most of our daily routine is associated. Sometimes, however, some of us make a choice outside our actual membership groups because of ambitions and aspirations communicated to us by the larger culture around us. We then attempt to pattern our behavior on the basis of perceptions of the proper mode gained from observation and from information sources other than the direct communications from people in our membership groups. For the most part, our conformity to the conduct of external reference groups has to be limited to

acquisition of the material symbols we perceive as identifying us with such aspirational groups. Most of the remainder of our behavior will still be shaped by family and other background membership groups, although sometimes in a negative manner.

All group standards tend to be conservative by the very fact of being based on experience. The influence of the group tends to deter the acceptance of innovations which are the heart of progress and of marketing profit. Groups vary in their degree of resistance to change. Some cultures are monolithic; tradition-bound, they allow little variability in behavior in any sphere. The multiplicity of group memberships in an urban industrial society creates considerable freedom within a range of behavior and thus permits ready acceptance of some kinds of innovation. But even in such a society, innovations requiring much new learning take hold slowly at first, and must come into group acceptance through members who play the special role of tastemakers and opinion leaders.

Understanding the content of purchase behavior thus involves a grasp of the dynamics of *reference group* influence—both of *face-to-face* groups (especially the family), and of *aspirational groups,* and the influence on behavior of the *role* the individual plays within the group. Comprehension of the process of innovation acceptance involves an understanding of the social process involved and of the special role played by the *tastemaker.*

B. RESEARCH AND APPLICATIONS

The first article (Lopata) discusses the "conformity" to be found in suburbia. It is followed by a consideration of the myth of the wife of the "happy worker" (Sexton). The final selection (Stafford) gives us a sociometric analysis of group influences on consumer brand preferences.

18-C CONFORMITY IN SUBURBIA

Helena Znaniecki Lopata (Sociologist)

Dramatically interwoven images of mass-produced homes inhabited by uniformly over-protected suburban children who throw around $50 bills given to them by domineering "moms,"—while identically dressed and weak-willed fathers slave in faraway places until removed by untimely death—are not the products of cartoonists, but of supposed objective analysts.

Such images are terrifying, especially when they are applied to millions of people. One-third of the population of metropolitan Chicago now lives in the suburbs. More millions encircle the other major cities of the U.S. and Canada. Can all these people be alike? If they are, how and why did they get that way? How long did it take?

In order to find answers to these questions, I selected for investigation a random sample of 300 suburban housewives living in socio-economically divergent communities in the Chicago area.

Women with certain common characteristics were selected for the study. They were home owners. They lived in suburbs around Chicago—either in new suburbs or in new areas of established communities. They were full-time homemakers. They had children—all but two had pre-high school youngsters. All the women were approached without previous warning by interviewers.

If these women were all conforming to the same patterns of behavior and the same models, as they are assumed to do, then we must hypothesize either that they were alike or models, as they are assumed to do, then we must hypothesize either that they were alike

SOURCE: Helena Znaniecki Lopata, "Conformity in Suburbia," *Advertiser's Digest*, **29** (July, 1964), pp. 9–12, condensed from *Free*, published by Roosevelt University.

because the suburb made them so or that they were alike before they moved into their present homes.

If we assume that the suburbs do produce "suburban type" people, the question arises: How long does it take suburbanites to be molded? The study revealed that it could not have taken a lifetime for the majority of women interviewed because only 13% spent most of their lives in other suburbs, and only 3% in the suburbs in which they now reside.

Going further, the study revealed that the average length of residence of the women in their present homes was 24 months, and that most of them had moved from apartments in Chicago. Such facts tend to cloud the popular image of uniformity and they are probably representative for most suburbanites.

Now, if the picture of conformity were true, that fact that this group moved to the suburbs as adults and had been there only a relatively short time, means that either its past must have been homogeneous or the suburb is so powerful an influence that it negates all past heterogeneity.

The latter hypothesis can be debated and disproved by any intelligent social scientist. People do not shed so easily all past differences, even when they so desire. The assumption that people in identical houses must be identical in personality comes, I think, from the magical assumption that the face of the house represents the soul of the owner.

Furthermore, the occupational, religious and economic divergences, and the differences in size of family, group membership and community participation are so great even within the same suburb, that suburban families simply cannot live identical lives. To generalize about suburbanites as if they were all uniform is simply to ignore the facts of life in our society.

Our other hypothesis—that suburbanites are alike because of similarity of background—can be supported only by showing either that the city from which most of them came is homogeneous or that the suburbs attract elements of the city which are already alike.

We know that the city is not homogeneous. In fact, the critics of the suburbs constantly remind us of this. The idea that the millions of people in suburbs had identical backgrounds is on its very face questionable. Even our small sample of 300 women shows a great divergence in past life-circumstances.

What brings people to the suburbs? We asked them why, and why they chose a particular community, and what are the advantages and disadvantages of suburban living which they discovered after moving. Their answers showed that they moved primarily to obtain a home and to get away from the many problems of rearing children in the city.

Why did they choose a particular suburb? The price of the house and the convenience of location were the most frequently stated reasons. However, when we asked what they liked about their suburb, they answered in terms of human relations and "the way of life." In fact, most of them were happy in their daily lives and their roles and felt that the suburbs contributed to making these enjoyable.

In fairness to the critics of suburbia, we must admit that, in spite of past variations and diversifications, some suburbanites do display some forms of outward conformity. But is it any greater than the conformity of the urbanites?

We cannot say that this conformity involves all suburbanites, nor do we have any proof that it is anything but outward. If there is such outward similarity among some suburbanites, then we must assume that it is purposely and consciously induced.

Indeed, we may pose the hypothesis that it is the urban background which has produced the insecurities of the suburbanites and their lack of feeling of competence in furnishing a home, disciplining a child, serving a meal, walking and dressing. If other-directedness exists in the modern suburbs perhaps it is be-cause previous training failed to provide effective models of behavior.

Many of our suburban housewives had experienced upward mobility. Their husbands have higher status jobs than their fathers, and have higher incomes. They own homes, whereas they had been brought up in apartments. They are successful in the American society, although they come from immigrant and/or lower-class backgrounds.

Since many suburbanites are the children or grandchildren of lower-class urban dwellers, some other-directedness must be expected of them. If our society has an open and fluid class system, as we pridefully state it has, we should not be surprised if persons with immigrant, minority or lower-class backgrounds become more middle-class in their outward behavior as they move up the ladder.

We know from many studies that those lacking a background of class stability will display a greater tendency to conform to outward symbols of class status than those who have been secure in their class identification over generations. Still it is amazing that so many people are able to live in the suburbs, and that so many can now afford to adapt a previously restricted form of behavior.

While criticizing suburbanites in round generalizations for using each other as models of some forms of external behavior, we tend to minimize the actual heterogeneity of suburban residents. Next we jump to an illogical conclusion that the type of life suburbanites are trying to give to their children will have dire consequences.

Perhaps this is because we use our own system of values in judging other people. We laugh at a person who places a lamp in a picture window, instead of rejoicing that so many people have lamps and windows. We criticize the suburbanite for not being individualistic in the treatment of his children, and in our next breath we tell him to get together with others to draw up uniform rules for teen-age behavior. We state that he is over-protecting his children, while accusing his urban friends of not caring enough for their children to supervise them properly.

We blame the suburbanites for being unconcerned with problems of the larger society; on the other hand, we complain they are too much involved in "outside activities." We want a democratic society inhabited by people capable of making decisions, yet we criticize the suburban family for allowing their children to participate in the decision-making process. We praise success, but label the desire to own a home and a car as "conformity." In so doing we often confuse a convergence of individual decisions with a compulsion to lose individuality.

All homes in the suburbs are not alike. They are inhabited by people with heterogeneous backgrounds who, in spite of a superficial convergence of minor aspects of life and purposeful conformity in other aspects, are not all living in the same way.

These people cannot possibly rear their children in an identical manner. On the contrary, they may be giving these children sufficient stability to enable the next generation to become more secure and autonomous in its behavior than its predecessors.

18-D WIFE OF THE "HAPPY WORKER"

Patricia Cayo Sexton (*Educator*)

The myth of the American woman casts her as a cheery magazine portrait, presiding over the succulent roast, with smiling offspring reaching for their portions while the husband watches benevolently from the head of the table. The myth is pleasant but totally false when applied to the wife of the average worker.

No more accurate is the European male-inspired myth of the American woman as super-privileged, pampered by luxury and attention, dominating her husband and family, and spending most of her day flitting through the cocktail-club circuit. This may be a faithful portrait of some strata of American womanhood, but not of the worker's wife.

Her day's circuit is rarely concentric with the club and social rounds traveled by her middle-class counterpart. Instead of the Junior League, her concern is mainly with Junior and his unceasing demands on her energies. Instead of presiding over a PTA meeting, arranging a charity ball at the local yacht club, entertaining week-end guests, or even collecting signatures for Adlai Stevenson, she is busy with Junior's whooping cough, the week's ironing, the plugged sink, the wet pants, the runny nose, the pay check that can't cover expenses, the kids who won't stop yelling and

fighting—and the husband who offers little affection or attention in payment for her drudgery.

In observing that "the mass of men lead lives of quiet desperation," Thoreau used the traditional masculine gender to submerge the feminine. Today even those intellectuals who believe in the myth of the Happy Worker will have to admit that "quiet desperation" aptly describes the life of his wife.

The workingman's wife has no collective voice. Indeed, there is nothing "collective" about her; she is basically unorganized, a central quality of her life. She is neither a joiner— nor a participant. Though deeply religious, she is much less likely to attend church regularly than her middle-class counterpart, and still less likely to take a more than menial role in church affairs. Similarly, her PTA activity is relatively limited, and—most tragically—she is usually a stranger, sometimes suspicious and hostile, to her husband's union, the one organization that ought to have a natural interest in her potentialities.

She is, typically, a harried housewife, lonely, worried about everything from the diaper wash to world cataclysm; and—above all— she is virtually isolated from life outside the confines of her family and neighborhood. In the sociologist's language, she is a "primary" group person living in a "secondary" group society.

She does not have time or money for club life and "entertaining"; worse, she seems to lack the inner resources—the self-direction, the confidence, the assertiveness, the will—to

SOURCE: Patricia Cayo Sexton, "Wife of the 'Happy Worker,'" in Arthur B. Shestak and William Gomberg, *Blue-Collar World: Studies of the American Worker.* © 1965 Prentice-Hall, Inc. Reprinted by permission of Prentice-Hall, Inc., Englewood Cliffs, New Jersey and *The Nation*, pp. 81–85.

move about freely in the larger world. Though deeply resourceful in organizing her own household with limited means, she usually doesn't have the impulse, much less the know-how, to go outside her home for help—to set up neighborhood nursery groups, for example, in order to reduce her work load. She is almost helplessly dependent on the neighborhood folkways and mores—what "other people would think" and, especially, her husband.

The lack of resources—financial, psychic and social—of the workingman's wife may account for the discovery recently made by a mental-hygiene survey (*Americans View Their Mental Health*) that she belongs to one of the two most discounted groups in our society—the other group being male clerks.

Vitally dependent on her husband, emotionally and financially, the workingman's wife is inclined to see him as "insensitive and inconsiderate, sometimes teasing, sometimes accusing, sometimes vulgar, always potentially withholding affection." In their sexual relations, she often feels he treats her as an "object for his own personal gratification without the kind of tenderness she so much wants."

18-E   A SOCIOMETRIC ANALYSIS OF GROUP INFLUENCES ON CONSUMER BRAND PREFERENCES

James Ellis Stafford (Marketing Educator)

A major question facing marketing today is exactly how, in what way, and to what extent social factors influence consumer behavior. It has been shown, for example, that consumer brand preferences are related to economic considerations such as price. But are there other forces, both psychological and social, at work which also influence the consumer in his brand selection? The basic problem of this dissertation, therefore, was to determine experimentally if one type of social factor—informal membership groups—influenced brand preferences, and then to analyze and describe in detail the process of this influence.

The design of this experiment consisted of sociometrically selecting and analyzing ten groups of women from Austin, Texas, who were neighbors, close friends, or relatives; who enjoyed shopping together; and who were given a common experimental task to perform—the selection of a loaf of bread from four previously unknown brands twice a week for eight weeks.

Each of the ten groups were sociometrically analyzed to determine internal leadership patterns, communication networks, and degree of cohesiveness. Similarly, the actual brand choices of the women were observed, recorded and analyzed on an individual basis to deter-

mine the degree of brand loyalty, and on a group basis to determine whether group influences existed, how they functioned, and what impact they had on particular brand preferences and brand loyalty. Analysis of variance and chi square were the primary statistical techniques employed in the testing of the following general hypotheses:

1. Small, informal social groups exert influences toward conformity on member brand preferences.

2. The degree of influence exerted on a member toward certain brand preferences by the group is related directly to the "cohesiveness" of that group.

3. Within a group, the "leader" is the most influential member with respect to member brand preferences.

The study led to the following tentative conclusions. First, hypothesis 1 was supported. While no significant preference was shown for any one of the four brands used in the study, there was a definite indication that the groups influenced the members toward conformity of brand preference. Second, hypothesis 2 was partially rejected. No statistical significance was found between the level of cohesiveness and member brand loyalty. Only when cohesiveness and leadership patterns were combined was any relationship with member brand loyalty uncovered. In more cohesive groups, the probability was much higher that the members would prefer the same brand as the group leader. Third, the

Source: James Ellis Stafford, "A Sociometric Analysis of Group Influences on Consumer Brand Preferences," in Peter D. Bennett, Editor, *Marketing and Economic Development* (Chicago: American Marketing Association, 1965), pp. 459–460.

results gave significant support to the third hypothesis. Leaders were found to influence group members in two ways. First, the higher the degree of brand loyalty exhibited by a group leader, the more likely were the other members to prefer the same brand. Second, the greater the degree of leader brand loyalty, the higher was the percentage of his group becoming brand loyal also.

With respect to the concept of brand loyalty per se, it was found, for example, that many consumers became brand loyal even where there was no discernable difference between brands. In most cases, however, this loyalty developed only after a period of search or exploratory behavior among the test brands. Once each brand had been tried, then the probability of brand loyal behavior increased appreciably beyond the level expected by chance. Similarly, each time an individual repeated a brand choice, the probability was much higher that he would select the same brand again. Finally, an individual's degree of "suggestibility" was found to be closely related to a "readiness" to become brand loyal. The more suggestible individuals became brand loyal significantly quicker than less suggestible individuals.

In conclusion, while an exploratory experiment of this nature is more often suggestive than conclusive, it appears that there is sufficient evidence to conclude that small, informal social groups do influence member brand preferences.

19 / Ethnic and Religious Influences

A. BACKGROUND AND THEORY

A brief statement (Faber) about ethnic and religious differences plus a short discussion (Gibson) of the Negro market constitute the first section of this chapter.

19-A VARIATIONS ASSOCIATED WITH RELIGIOUS AND ETHNIC DIFFERENCES

Bernard Faber (Sociologist)

The influences of religion and ethnic-group connection are frequently highly intertwined so that we cannot be certain whether the cultural factor in socialization is primarily religious or mainly ethnic. There are wide variations in child training among different groups. In her study of immigrant parents in America, Wolfenstein found variations in the use of punishment among different ethnic groups. She reported that Chinese and Jewish parents tended to be moderate in their punishment. The Syrians, however, do not as a rule hesitate to apply punishment.[1]

Similar results can be found in cross-nation comparisons. Rapp found that mothers in Germany tended to favor dominating and ignoring techniques in controlling children and to be more possessive of children than American mothers.[2] Hence, distinct family practices related to ethnic groups can be discerned.

Findings on religious and ethnic differences in socialization suggest that where parents sponsor activities related to independence and achievement of children, interpersonal competence is enhanced. Rosen has shown that Protestant, Jewish, and Greek mothers in the United States place a greater emphasis upon independence and achievement in children than do mothers with a Southern Italian or French-Canadian background. This sponsorship is reflected in the high motivation for achievement of children from Jewish and Greek homes.[3]

The discussion which follows is concerned only with the Jewish and Italian families. Strodtbeck compared the interaction process of Jewish and Italian families. He found that, in the Italian families, the father had very high power in contrast to both the mother and the son, in Jewish families, the differences were much less. There was more equality in Jewish families. The emphasis upon sponsored independence and achievement was maintained by minimizing status and power differences in the Jewish family. The lessening of power differences provided an opportunity for (a) increased interaction on the part of the Jewish son, and (b) with that interaction, practice in

SOURCE: Bernard Faber, "Variations Associated with Religious and Ethnic Differences," *Family Organization and Interaction* (San Francisco: Chandler Publishing Company, 1964), pp. 471–473.

[1] Martha Wolfenstein, "Some Variants of Moral Training in Children," in Margaret Mead and Martha Wolfenstein, eds., *Childhood in Contemporary Culture* (Chicago: University of Chicago Press, 1955), pp. 439–468.

[2] Don W. Rapp, "Childrearing Attitudes of Mothers in Germany and the United States," *Child Development*, 32 (1961), pp. 669–678.

[3] Bernard C. Rosen, "Race, Ethnicity, and the Achievement Syndrome," *American Sociological Review*, 24 (1959), pp. 47–60.

active participation in making decisions in a group situation.[4]

The findings by Strodtbeck are supported in a study reported by Maurice L. Farber in which differences in the socialization of English and American boys were investigated. Farber found that, whereas American boys stressed the adjustment of the child to other children (equalitarian interaction), English

[4] Fred L. Strodtbeck, "Family Interaction Values and Achievement," in D. McClelland, A. Baldwin, U. Brofenbrenner, and F. L. Strodtbeck, *Talent and Society,* Princeton: Van Nostrand, 1958, pp. 135–194.

boys focused upon conforming behavior toward adults. The English boys appeared to be attuned to suppressing activities opposed by the adult world, the American boys were oriented to courting actively the approving attention of parents.[5] The American boys emphasized *congeniality* rather than merely *conformity* in relations with both adults and peers. Hence, the American boys would give greater attention to competence in interpersonal relations and to achievement.

[5] Maurice L. Farber, "English and Americans: Values in the Socialization Process," *Journal of Psychology,* 36 (1953), pp. 243–250.

19-B WHY THERE IS A NEGRO MARKET

D. Parke Gibson (Marketing Executive)

Imagine a country with a per-capita income slightly more than the per-capita income of western Europe as a whole and considerably higher than the per-capita income in Asia, Africa, and Latin America combined.

Further, imagine this country with six million families or households, of which more than half own automobiles, which is thirty times more passenger cars than there are in the Soviet Union and more than in all of Asia, Africa, and Latin America. One of these families out of every sixteen has two automobiles, and one out of every one hundred has three or more autos.

In this country 40 percent of all the families own homes, and 75 percent of the homes have television, which is twice as many television sets as in all of France or Italy and four times as many as in East Germany or Sweden. Half of these households have automatic clothes washers, 8 percent have food freezers, and 4 percent of the dwellings of these families are air-conditioned.

These families have more of their members studying in colleges than the total enrollment in Britain or Italy and slightly less than in West Germany or France.

This "country" does exist—it is the Negro market in the United States. From the standpoint of selling goods and services, the coun-

tries abroad and their peoples are often better understood by American business than is the Negro consumer in America.

The American society today is divided into two basic groups, the white and nonwhite populations, and as a result the two groups, for the most part, operate separately in the patterns of human activity in the basic areas of economics, housing, and social activity.

There are four reasons why the Negro market exists: (1) forced identification of the people comprising this market, (2) definable purchase patterns by this group of consumers, (3) the size of this market, and (4) the location of this market within the United States.

American Negroes constitute over 92 percent of the nonwhite population in the United States and 11 percent of the total population. The term nonwhite, therefore, is often used interchangeably with the term Negro.

Eleven percent of the nation's population spread out on an even basis throughout the fifty states would, of course, not constitute a factor. Yet, when one considers that the nation's twenty-two million Negroes are concentrated in seventy-eight cities and that in these markets they become 25 percent of the population, the percentage factor takes on prime importance, since this means that *one person in four is a Negro.*

Negroes, as 11 percent of the total population in the United States, consume over 50 percent of the Scotch whiskey imported into

SOURCE: D. Parke Gibson, *The $30 Billion Negro* (London: The Macmillan Company: Collier-Macmillan Ltd., 1969), pp. 7–10.

the nation, consume more than 70 percent of the entire output of the Maine sardine industry, consume more than 49 percent of all the grape soda produced in America, spend 23 percent more for shoes than does the majority white population, and spend up to 12 percent more for food sold in supermarkets to be consumed at home.

B. RESEARCH AND APPLICATIONS

The first article (Alexander) is a report of research done on the significance of ethnic groups in marketing new-type packaged foods. The second article (Van Tassel) is a discussion of what we know and what we need to know about Negroes as consumers.

19-C THE SIGNIFICANCE OF ETHNIC GROUPS IN MARKETING NEW-TYPE PACKAGED FOODS IN GREATER NEW YORK

Milton Alexander (Marketing Educator)

To manufacturers and distributors of new-type packaged foods, Greater New York ranks first as a market and as a marketing enigma. On the one hand, it is easily the largest spender for foods among the 168 standard metropolitan areas. On the other, it is most unyielding to product innovations.

Hence, the perennial question of food marketers: What is it that makes New York so different from other marketing areas? And what, if anything, can and should be done to adjust for the difference? According to a traditional hypothesis, the area's atypical pattern of consumer behavior stems from the heterogeneous nature of its population. New York is said to comprise a melting pot of several fairly distinct ethnic markets in one.

Based on a pilot study, this hypothesis oversimplified local food marketing problems. Furthermore, assumptions of ethnic difference were found to rest on long-established hunch rather than current fact. As such, they were largely unrelated to the present-day ethnic setting and to the new-type products which represent an ever-increasing share of consumer expenditures for food. In short, there was an evident need to modernize the traditional hypothesis and to establish guideposts for mar-

SOURCE: Milton Alexander, "The Significance of Ethnic Groups in Marketing New-Type Packaged Foods in Greater New York," in Lynn H. Stockman, Editor, *Advancing Marketing Efficiency* (Chicago: American Marketing Association, 1959), pp. 557–561.

keters in this and other heterogeneous areas. This study represents a beginning attempt to fill both needs. It brings up to date the food habits of four major ethnic groups—Italian, Jewish, Negro, and Puerto Rican. More pointedly, it explores the impact of inter- and intra-group differences on acceptance of six "model" new-type products—frozen food dinner, frozen red meat, frozen fruit pie, instant coffee, cake mixes, and dehydrated soups.

Despite all countervailing socio-economic pressures, ethnic food habits continue to prevail in Greater New York. The ethnic setting, therefore, remains a necessary basis for local food marketing strategy and practice. This is particularly so with regard to new products. Further, an awareness of ethnic differences and of dynamic internal changes (both socio-economic and dietetic) may lessen the marketer's acceptance of behavioral myths regarding ethnic groups.

From the marketer's point of view, the residual ethnic influence in food consumption is variously affected by demographic trends. In the case of Negroes and Puerto Ricans, by an accelerated rate of in-migration; a clustering in the inner city; and an apartness from the general population. In the case of Jews, by conflicting drives toward cultural assimilation and continued clustering even in the adjacent suburbs. And, finally, among Italians, by the increased incidence of intermarriage with "outsiders."

Meanwhile, ethnic food habits have shown

a remarkable resilience even under pressure for conformity. Consumption patterns are still evolving. The following is a sampling of significant ethnic attitudes toward foods new and old.

Beginning with typical second-generation Italian housewives, there appears to be a marked residual antagonism toward processed-packaged foods which, incidentally, fail to appear in 80 per cent of the group's lunches, 64 per cent of its suppers, and 95 per cent of its breakfasts. Also, freshness remains the dominant appeal in Italian usage of coffee, vegetables, and meat. At the same time, more housewives are being swayed toward product innovations by the convenience of new-type packaged foods.

The same is true of second-generation Jewish housewives. Thus, 90 per cent of Jewish families were found to prefer fresh to canned or frozen alternatives. And about one of three of their breakfasts and one of five of their suppers featured one or more traditional delicacies.

Many young Negro housewives also tend to adhere to their traditional diets. For example, the use of meat at breakfast; the preference for starchy products; and the aversion for "raw foods." On the other hand, many ethnic traditions are weakening. By and large, young Negro housewives are found to rebel against the low-income meat-meal-molasses or rice-beans-plantain diets. And in growing numbers, they adopt processed-packaged foods as symbols of social status.

The Puerto Rican diet represents a unique blend of traditional and new-type food preferences. So strong is the ethnic effect, however, that the low-income tropical diet generally prevails. New-type foods, therefore, are supplements to, rather than substitutes for, traditional favorites. Nevertheless, almost every type of packaged food innovation has breached the group's ethnic loyalties.

Now, specifically, how does this dynamic ethnic setting, for some 55 per cent of New York's population, affect the acceptance of new-type packaged foods? In partial answer, let us review the major findings for each of the six "model" foods featured in this study.

First, frozen food dinner. Italian acceptance is apparently hampered by deep-seated ethnic preferences for fresh meat and vegetables. Sales prospects are brightened only by two relatively minor offsets in the ethnic diet. First, by the continued simplicity of Italian meals. And second, by the group's traditional liking for processed-packaged fish. In any event, Italians place last in rate of consumption. In the Jewish group, a residual ethnic influence seems to militate against large-scale acceptance. The net upshot: Jews rank last in most indices of acceptance. Product convenience is recognized. But this "like" is outweighed by the "dislike" of product taste and expense. Negroes also tend to resist frozen food dinners—seemingly on traditional grounds. The net result is widespread use but in limited quantities. At the other end of the acceptance scale, Puerto Ricans are found to lead all other groups in rate of consumption, presumably due to the high incidence of working housewives within this group.

Italians rank at least second in ethnic acceptance of the second "model" product—frozen red meat. But consumption by Jews is obviously discouraged by the dietary laws—especially in the case of pork. Regardless of variety, however, Jewish consumers resist the product's taste and price. Frozen red meat is also opposed to the Negroes' traditional preference for fresh and fatty cuts. Their resistance is further hardened by the prevailing inadequacy of refrigeration in Negro homes. In the case of Puerto Rican housewives, ethnic distaste for the product is at least partly offset by the working housewives' need for convenience. Puerto Ricans lead in all indices of acceptance. This showing, however, is almost entirely confined to the more economical luncheon cuts.

Frozen fruit pie, the third "model" product, seems to hold but little interest for Italians. At any rate, they rank last in per-capita consumption—avowedly due to a marked dislike of flavor. Jewish consumers do relish sweet goods, but of a distinctive type—either baked at home or available in the many specialty bakeries throughout the area. Principally for this reason, they rank last in regular usage of the frozen product. Also, as per tradition, Negroes still do not "take to" fruit pies. Hence, their bottom score in rate of consumption. In contrast, the Puerto Ricans' craving for sweets is so intense that it seems to overcome the group's dislike of product taste and expense. Usage of the product is still spotty, however.

A strong residual preference for their special

blend sharpens Italian resistance to instant coffee—the fourth "model" food. As a result, Italians trail other ethnic groups (excepting Negroes) in rate of consumption. In contrast, instant meets with a favorable response from Jewish consumers. Due to the group's tea-drinking tradition, the rivalry of regular coffee is minimized. Instant, however, is found to be an addition to the group's cultural inventory rather than a replacement for an established item. While the Negroes' ethnic diet also favors acceptance of instant, countervailing socio-economic forces tip the balance against heavy consumption. Actually, Negroes are found to rank last in terms of actual purchases. As with Italians, the Puerto Rican's traditional diet also features a distinctive type of coffee. Here, however, opposition to instant is tempered by light coffee-drinking habits. And according to the indices of acceptance, Puerto Ricans rank second in per-capita consumption.

Similar implications may be read into the acceptance ratings of cake mix. Here, for reasons already cited in connection with frozen fruit pie, both Italians and Negroes are found near the bottom of the acceptance index, but just a notch above the Jewish group, which is in last place. Puerto Ricans (for all their difficulty in deciphering package directions) seemingly lead the other ethnic groups.

The sixth "model" food—dehydrated soup—also fares rather badly in the Italian diet, at least in comparison with the sales potential of the generic product. Thus, while Italians rank first in usage (vs. non-usage), users in the group rank only fourth in per-capita consump-tion. In the Jewish group, non-usage still appears to be the rule. Typically, Negroes seem to use dehydrated soup in limited amounts; and they trail all other groups in the indices of acceptance. In rather familiar contrast, the elastic food habits of the young Puerto Rican group have also yielded to this new-type product in large measure.

Now, one may ask: How can manufacturers and retailers implement these varying manifestations of the ethnic effect? There is no simple answer because there is no pat formula for "segment selling"—one that would cover all products and all groups across the board and regardless of time period. An ethnic marketing approach, therefore, demands a separate and distinct adjustment for each combination of ethnic group and new-type packaged food.

For the manufacturer, this selective approach would find useful application in the formulation of marketing strategy and in estimating sales potentials—even if only as a qualitative guide. It would also help him capitalize on opportunities for sectional listing of new products in the large food chains, in in-store promotion, in couponing, and in the deployment of missionaries. At the very least, a fact-based approach to ethnic groups could reduce losses due to a misdirection of promotional efforts. Similar benefits would accrue to supermarket operators in developing new store locations and in making optimum adjustments, in their merchandising, for significant ethnic differences.

19-D THE NEGRO AS A CONSUMER—WHAT WE KNOW AND WHAT WE NEED TO KNOW

Charles E. Van Tassel (Marketing Executive)

During the past few years, there has been a substantial increase in interest and in research effort on the part of marketing management regarding the Negro as a consumer. More and

SOURCE: Charles E. Van Tassel, "The Negro as a Consumer—What We Know and What We Need to Know" in M. S. Mayer and E. S. Vosburgh, Editors, *Marketing for Tomorrow . . . Today* (Chicago: American Marketing Association, 1967), pp. 166–168.

more companies are paying more and more attention to the Negro as they search for market expansion opportunities, and their action is prompted primarily by four factors.

First of all, there has been an increased economic awareness of the Negro in recent years. The sheer size of the Negro population and the magnitude of its purchasing power have certainly heightened the businessman's interest in what is commonly referred to as "the Negro market." Second, there is an ever-increasing social awareness of the Negro. Organized efforts ranging from local neighborhood demonstrations against various forms of discrimination to relatively large and powerful national groups such as the NAACP and CORE have been quite effective in increasing the awareness of the Negro by American industry. A third factor pertains to increased political involvement. The most obvious example of this, and one which has profound implications for the business community is the passage of the Civil Rights Bill. Government action, then, has been in part responsible for business being more attentive to the Negro. The fourth factor which has been instrumental in spurring business interest in the Negro relates to the increased availability of market information about Negroes.

While the economic, social, and political dimensions are certainly of profound importance, it is the fourth element, the nature and extent of market information currently available about Negroes, which is of prime importance to the marketer.

Negro Market Demographic Information

Most of the data available now on the Negro market are of a demographic or descriptive nature. For example, it is known that:

1. The Negro population rose from 13 million in 1940 to approximately 21 million today—an increase of over 60 per cent. By comparison the white population increased in size by about 45 per cent during the same period.
2. Negro median family income is approximately one-half that of white median family income.
3. Negroes have an aggregate annual purchasing power of between $25 billion and $30 billion—about 7 per cent of the U.S. total.
4. Negro consumers represent a rather compact sales target. While about one-seventh of the white population lives in the 25 largest cities in the U.S., one-third of all Negroes are concentrated in these 25 cities.
5. The Negro market is relatively young. Median age for whites is about 30. Median age for Negroes is around 23.

Additionally, there is a wide range of data available concerning such areas as geographic location, population mobility, job status and employment stability, educational levels, and family life, including such details as divorce, death, and illegitimacy rates.

This sort of factual knowledge is, of course, fundamental to an understanding of the basic dimensions of any market. It is not enough, however, to serve the purposes of management in setting policy relative to the Negro market.

Negro Market Purchasing Patterns

In terms of relative purchase quantities, it is known, for example, that:

1. Negro families tend to buy substantially more cooked cereals, corn meal, household insecticides, cream, rice, spaghetti, frozen vegetables, syrup, and vinegar, among others, than do their white counterparts.
2. The average Negro male supposedly buys 77 per cent more pairs of shoes during his lifetime than the average white male and pays more for them.
3. Reportedly, Negroes purchase as much as one-half of all Scotch whiskey consumed in the U.S.
4. Negroes also apparently consume somewhat more flour, waxes, toilet and laundry soap, shortenings, salt, peanut butter, fruit juices, and canned chili than whites.

While Negro purchase habit information is not as readily available as descriptive market data on Negroes, a fund of knowledge is being developed in this area which should serve marketers well in the future. But the combination of information in these two areas is still not sufficient upon which to base a rational approach toward this market.

Negro Market Attitudes and Motivations

One area remains to be explored: attitudinal and motivational dimensions of Negro consumer behavior. And it is here that the greatest void of knowledge exists.

Of course, some reliable information, some hypotheses, and some plausible suggested explanations are available regarding why Negroes act and react as they do in the market place. For example, many marketers have suggested that Negroes frequently attempt to emulate white society through purchases of products with high quality images. If this is true, it would at least partly explain the Negro's relatively higher expenditures on well known brands of Scotch, expensive clothing, quality furniture, appliances, and the like.

Another thesis is that Negroes as a group have accepted the values of white middle-class society, but, at the same time, experience difficulties in purchasing products which represent some of these values. A basic dilemma arises where the Negro must choose whether to strive, frequently in the face of formidable odds, to attain white middle-class values, and the products which are associated with these values, or simply give up and live without most of them.[1]

There are a variety of other explanations regarding why Negroes behave as they do in their roles as consumers. There is one major area, however, where relatively few explanations are available. This is also the area which probably provides the single greatest opportunity to influence the purchase behavior of Negroes—communications.

COMMUNICATIONS RESEARCH. Probably the most frequently raised and most perplexing issue relates to the advisability of adopting an "integrated" approach toward advertising. Some questions frequently asked by companies regarding how to communicate most effectively with Negroes are:

1. Should our advertisements be integrated or segregated; that is, should we use all white, all Negro, or white and Negro models?
2. Should we attempt to reach the Negro consumer by placing our traditionally "white" advertisements in Negro media, or should we have specially designed advertisements for Negro media?
3. If we produce integrated advertisements, should these advertisements be restricted to Negro media, or should they be exposed through general media?
4. If Negro media are used, which media in particular are best?
5. Does the Negro feel complimented or honored when he sees an advertisement specially designed to attract his attention and interest, or does he view this sort of

thing as just one more reminder that he is different?
6. How would our white customers react to integrated advertisements in general media?

A certain amount of research has, of course, been completed in this general area. Something is known, for example, about viewing, reading, and listening habits. It has been established that radio is the major medium for Negroes, followed by television, newspapers, and magazines. And this pattern is known to be different than that for whites. Studies have shown that radio stations employing rather tasteless music and advertising programming appeal to the Negro working class and frequently offend and alienate middle and upper class Negroes. Evidence is available to show that advertisements which are apparently designed to appeal to Negro buyers, but which show Negroes in a situation which the Negro viewer recognizes as unrealistic can do more harm than good.

Some work has also been done on Negro reactions to various advertising stimuli. It was found in one fairly recent study that when people were presented with a series of general concepts, such as integrated advertisements, segregated advertisements, and various media alternatives, there was a great similarity in responses by Negroes and whites. Whereas advertising strategies of many large companies would lead one to expect sizeable differences in reactions of Negroes and whites to these alternatives, they were surprisingly alike.[2]

Other research studies indicate that the use of Negro models can be quite favorable, as long as the advertisements are presented in a dignified, meaningful, and realistic way. And, importantly, it has been determined that Negroes frequently view companies which run integrated advertising campaigns as more progressive, more friendly, more desirous of the Negro's business, a fairer employer, and more anxious to work out today's social problems than companies which do not participate in integrated advertising.

Reactions of white respondents are also frequently more favorable than might be ex-

[1] Raymond A. Bauer, Scott M. Cunningham, and Lawrence H. Wortzel, "The Marketing Dilemma of Negroes," *Journal of Marketing.* Vol. 29, July, 1695, pp. 1–6, at p. 2.

[2] Arnold Barban and Edward Cundiff, "Negro and White Responses to Advertising Stimuli," *Journal of Marketing Research,* November, 1964, pp. 53–56.

pected. They often view integrated advertisements which are tastefully presented as pleasant, appealing, meaningful and dignified. In addition, they too view a company which runs integrated advertising as generally more friendly, more progressive, and a fairer employer.

Research efforts of these types, however, are infrequent. Too little effort has been extended to date, in terms of uncovering Negro attitudes and motivations in the market place. The widely varying approaches taken by so many companies in an attempt to communicate with the Negro consumer strongly suggest that the answers to fundamental marketing questions simply are not available. It has been stated that, "Insufficient knowledge of the Negro consumer's motivations has led to sharp controversy over the direction advertisers should take to reach this market."[3]

While opportunities for the future lie partly in continuing to develop descriptive data and actual purchase behavior information on Negroes, significant gains will be primarily dependent upon ability of marketers to develop and properly interpret attitudinal data such that a sound basis can be established for understanding and communicating with the Negro as a consumer.

A Look at the Future

In addition to reviewing past and present strengths and weaknesses regarding marketing to the Negro, it is useful to consider some expected future developments which will likely affect the approach taken by marketers in reacting to the ever-changing composition and requirements of the Negro market.

First, it is reasonable to expect a continued growth in the size and importance of the Negro market. It is expected that by 1970 Negroes will number somewhere around 25 million, and personal income should rise to about $45 billion. The influence of Negroes as consumers will be increasingly felt.

Second, geographic shifts will continue as the Negro becomes increasingly more urban. During the 1970s there will likely be a trend away from the central city to the suburbs as

[3] "Ad Men Straddle the Color Line", *News Front*, Vol. 10, No. 1, February, 1966, pp. 10–15 at p. 10.

social barriers fall and as income and educational levels rise for the Negro. Those developments will certainly affect consumption patterns.

Third, there will be increased pressure applied by special interest groups and by the government for a speeding up of the aggregation of Negroes into the mainstream of American life, which will, in turn, influence purchase behavior.

Fourth, basic social and economic forces will serve to radically change Negro expenditure patterns. For as incomes increase, and as intellectual and social horizons are broadened for Negroes and whites alike, expenditures of Negroes will shift in favor of goods and services which will upgrade their levels of living. Many products which have long received a disproportionately large share of the Negro's income, such as food, clothing, liquor, and entertainment will probably realize much slower growth in the future. A higher percentage of the Negro's income will be channeled toward such items as education, housing, medical care, automobiles, furniture and appliances, travel, insurance, and banking and credit facilities—that is, forms of consumption which have heretofore been unattainable.

Finally, substantial changes will be required in corporate policies directed toward the Negro in the future. Companies which have avoided meeting this problem and this challenge will be forced to become actively involved. This, in turn, will place added emphasis upon the need for collecting, and properly interpreting data on the Negro as a consumer. Companies which have been actively involved in recruiting Negroes as customers will find a need to change their strategies and upgrade their abilities. For whereas the Negro may react favorably to an integrated advertisement now, no matter how ill conceived and how poorly presented, simply because it does finally represent a step forward, he will become more discriminating in his tastes over time and less tolerant of marketing programs borne out of inadequate knowledge on the part of management.

Conclusion

If one general observation can be made from this brief analysis, it is that the Negro market is in a perpetual state of change, and that the change is of a more revolutionary than evolutionary nature.

The challenge of keeping pace with this change is based upon the recognition of two prerequisites which must be accepted in order to establish effective marketing policies directed toward the Negro. First, a complete understanding of the Negro as a part of American life is required. One must be aware of the deep-rooted social and economic forces which are changing the Negro's role in society. For these forces will, in turn, shape the Negro's role as a consumer. Second, marketers must develop more and better information regarding the true attitudes, experiences, and motivations which influence the Negro's behavior in the marketplace.

Until these two things are accomplished, companies will be placing themselves in the dangerous position of taking action based upon hunch and intuition. For only when a true understanding of the Negro is reached regarding his emerging role as a member of society, as well as the forces which specifically influence his purchase activities, will it be possible to develop intelligent programs designed to optimize the opportunities presented by this important segment of the ethnic market.

20 / Influences of Social Class

A. BACKGROUND AND THEORY

This section begins with a delineation (Kahl) of social classes, and is followed by a look at the effects of social stratification on market behavior (Rotzoll).

20-A CLASSES AS IDEAL TYPES

Joseph A. Kahl (Sociologist)

Although there is a great deal of controversy over details, and considerable variation from one part of the country to another and from small towns to large cities, many researchers agree that contemporary American urban society can usefully be described as having five social classes. No single variable defines a class; instead, the interaction between several variables creates the total way of life which characterizes a class. Value orientations emerge from, integrate, and symbolize the class way of life. The classes can be labeled as follows:

1. *Upper Class.* Wealthy families who strive for a stable pattern of refined and gracious living. In its ancient form an upper class is based on inherited property and fixed traditions, and the earning of more money takes second place to the spending of income from property. But our upper class is mixed, and contains many newly successful persons who learn the gracious way of life and become accepted by their peers.

2. *Upper-Middle Class.* The successful business and professional men (but not those at the very top), and their families. Income is mostly from current occupation, thus the emphasis is on long-term careers. These people live in large houses in good suburbs or

SOURCE: Joseph A. Kahl, "Classes as Ideal Types," *The American Class Structure* (New York: Holt, Rinehart and Winston, Inc., 1959), pp. 215–217.

in the best apartment houses; most are college graduates; they dominate industry and community organizations.

3. *Lower-Middle Class.* The less successful members of government, business, and the professions, and the more successful manual workers. This is the least clearly defined level, shading imperceptibly into the working class. These people live in small houses or in multiple-family dwellings. Most are high-school graduates, and some have had a little additional training. They are the model for the popular stereotype of America's "common man." They emphasize respectability.

4. *Working Class.* Factory and similar semiskilled workers. These are the people who work from day to day; they live adequately but on a small margin, have little hope of rising, aim at getting by. They are gradutes of grammar schools, with often some high-school training.

5. *Lower Class.* People who have the lowest paid jobs, work irregularly (especially in bad times), live in slums. They usually have not gone beyond grammar school (and often have not finished it), their family life is unstable, their reputations poor, and their values are based on apathy or aggression, for they have no hope.

These ideal-type classes are helpful abstractions, but cannot be used without practical judgment; they will help us order our thinking about the complexities of social reality, although they may encourage us to assume falsely that a community can be neatly divided with each family tagged and placed in its niche.

Flexibly interpreted, the ideal types imply that the majority of families in most communities can be placed in one of the five categories. These families will have scores on the several key stratification variables that fit into a pattern; their occupations will provide incomes that permit a style of life and a network of associations that bring them prestige, and they have a class identification and a set of values that harmoniously integrate their social lives—they know who they are and their neighbors know who they are, and they have beliefs that are "appropriate" to their position.

But many families would not fit. One or two of the index scores they would receive would be out of phase with the others. Does this mean that the ideal types are useless in understanding these families? On the contrary, the discrepancy of one or two variables from the expected pattern is usually best understood by considering it as a deviation from the typical. Often the discrepancy indicates that the family is mobile. Their values may

be typical of the next higher class; in order to live according to their values, they are likely to be ambitious people who are striving to increase their incomes so as to achieve a style of life they consider appropriate to their values, and one that will bring them contact with and approval from the people they consider suitable for friends.

Or they may be people who are slipping down in the hierarchy. They will cling to old values, and will feel squeezed because they no longer can buy the prestige they believe they are entitled to. Such people are often miserably unhappy; they think of themselves as failures, and believe the world to be a hard and vicious one.

Or they may be young people who are at the beginning of their careers. They may have high occupations but low beginning salaries. They need time to get into their appropriate niche.

Or they may be people who take a certain pride in being "different." If there were not some standard in their minds of what is typical, how could they enjoy being different? Many intellectuals and artists are, in this special sense, "outside the class system."

20-B   THE EFFECT OF SOCIAL STRATIFICATION ON MARKET BEHAVIOR

Kim B. Rotzoll (*Advertising Educator*)

There seems to be general agreement among sociologists that class-inspired market behavior is closely related to the breakdown of the high degree of inter-personal communication that typified the early American community. Indeed, as Veblen has suggested, in lieu of the "subtle means of appraisal" typical of the small town, there is a tendency as a community grows "for its citizens to put relatively more of their possessions 'on their backs,' into cars and other seeable goods."

A FRAME OF REFERENCE. It seems practical to utilize the Warner class structure as a frame of reference. This is undertaken with full knowledge of the relativity of the structure as well as some of the conceptual problems that

SOURCE: Kim B. Rotzoll, "The Effect of Social Stratification on Market Behavior," *Journal of Advertising Research,* Vol. 7 (March, 1967), pp. 22–27. © 1967 by the Advertising Research Foundation, Inc.

plague it. It is, however, still widely used as a standard both inside and outside the field of sociology.

I have attempted to synthesize material on the four lower classes of the six-class framework. It is generally conceded that these classes include more than 90 per cent of the American population and they have been extensively investigated.

All investigations are cursed with working definitions of one form or another. Mine are these:

Lower-lower class—the unskilled labor group.

Upper-lower class—the wage earner, skilled worker group.

Lower-middle class—the white collar, salaried group.

Upper-middle class—mostly the professionals and successful businessmen.

Three facets of market behavior will be considered for each class:

1. Consumption patterns.
2. Shopping patterns.
3. Spending and saving patterns.

Lower-Lower Class

CONSUMPTION PATTERNS. There is considerable evidence to suggest that social factors affect the purchasing behavior of low-income families. Caplovitz[1] in his study of consumer practices in three Manhattan public housing developments, makes early reference to the fact that low-income families are consumers of many major durables, predominately new, and often the more expensive models. It was also observed that the scarcely utilitarian symbol of modern living—the color telephone—was present in 23 per cent of the apartments with telephones.

It is interesting to speculate about how consumption "standards" for the lower income groups are set. Television may be a major factor here, given the oft-observed inverse relationship between television viewing and income level.[2]

Vidich and Bensman[3] add a significant dimension to the study of the consumption patterns of this group by observing the rejection of the traditionally middle class "deferred gratification" ethic. They observe that Springdale's "Shack People" tend to reject middle class standards in such areas as housing and prefer instead to spend their money on immediate needs and fancies such as sporting equipment.

SHOPPING PATTERNS. It seems apparent that if the lower income groups are increasingly trying to bridge the gap between their levels and standards of living, that some form of credit must serve as the span. Yet these families by their low-income status are often the poorest of credit risks. Caplovitz observes that this paradox is solved with the personalized services offered by local merchants. By avoiding the more bureaucratic credit contacts, the merchant (and the flourishing door-to-door peddler) is often able to offer credit by applying social rather than legal pressure to assure payment. This, of course, literally forces the consumption-oriented family to deal with local merchants who offer this financing service tailor-made for low-income areas. Martineau (1958) offers similar observations concerning the provinciality of the shopping patterns of lower-income families.

SPENDING AND SAVING PATTERNS. The precarious nature of saving activity in low-income families is summarized by this finding from the Martineau Chicago study:

The aspirations of the Lower-Status person are just as often for spending as they are for saving. The saving is usually a non-investment saving where there is almost no risk, funds can be quickly converted to spendable cash, and returns are small. When the Lower-Status person does invest his savings, he will be specific about the mode of investment, and is very likely to prefer something tangible and concrete—something he can point at and readily display.

Upper-Lower Class

CONSUMPTION PATTERNS. Technological mobility has clearly been an important influence on this wage earner/skilled labor group. Rainwater, Coleman, and Handel's[4] major study of working class wives suggests that one of the strongest motivations operating within this group is a desire to put "distance" between themselves and those in lower socio-economic positions; that is, to acquire "respectability." There is, thus, far more emphasis on the home than is found in the lower stratum. Indeed, Martineau observes:

The Upper-Lower Class man sees his home as his castle, his anchor to the world, and loads it down with hardware—solid heavy appliances—as his symbols of security.

The evidence suggests that the aspirations of this group seem focused first on the desire to achieve a "decency level" of housing and then on a drive toward the oft-sought "level

[1] Caplovitz, David. *The Poor Pay More.* New York: The Free Press of Glencoe, 1963.
[2] *Advertising Age.* New Simmons Report Pits Magazines vs. TV. *Advertising Age,* August 5, 1963, p. 1 ff.
[3] Vidich, Arthur J. and Joseph Bensman. *Small Town in Mass Society.* New York: Anchor Books, 1960.

[4] Rainwater, Lee, Richard P. Coleman, and Gerald Handel. *Workingman's Wife.* New York: Oceana Publications, Inc., 1959.

of the Common Man" in the consumption sphere. Thus, purchases tend, as Martineau has observed, to be more "artifact-oriented" than "experience-oriented."

It is interesting to note evidence of a certain degree of class loyalty regardless of economic condition. Martineau, in the *Tribune's* study of the class structure of Chicago, notes the emergence of the upper-lower "Stars" or Light-blue Collar Workers described as "high-income individuals who have the income for more ostentatious living than the average factory worker but who lack the personal skills or desire for high status by social mobility."

SHOPPING PATTERNS. There is general agreement between studies in this area that Upper-Lower families are somewhat less provincial in their shopping habits than Lower-Lower, but are still relatively limited compared to middle class standards.

Martineau suggests that this can be partially explained by familiar social "clues" offered by the local stores being more harmonious with the values shared by the class members, than those of the more "impersonal" establishments of the downtown areas and, less so, the suburban shopping centers.

Lower-Middle Class

CONSUMPTION PATTERNS. Kahl[5] holds that lower echelon White Collar Workers and small businessmen are at the bottom of the white collar status ladder while their manual counterparts are at or near the top of theirs. He adds, however, that many members of this class are children of immigrants and feel their status is highly cherished by comparison.

These studies, then, suggest an essentially horizontal orientation rather than an emphasis on "anticipatory socialization" that might appear characteristic of a class at the "bottom of the white collar status ladder."

SHOPPING PATTERNS. The social consciousness evidenced in the foregoing examination of Lower-Middle consumption patterns is generally reflected in shopping habits. An illuminating sidelight on the emphasis of what is "socially acceptable" is offered by this excerpt from the *Tribune* study of Park Forest.

[5] Kahl, Joseph A. *The American Class Structure.* New York: Rinehart & Company, Inc., 1959.

Middle-Class people had no hesitancy in buying refrigerators and other appliances in discount houses and bargain stores because they felt they could not "go wrong" with the nationally advertised names. But taste in furniture is much more elusive and subtle because the brand names are not known; and therefore, one's taste is on trial. Rather than commit a glaring error in taste which would exhibit an ignorance of the correct status symbols, the same individual who buys appliances in the discount house generally retreats to a status store for buying furniture. She needs the support of the store's taste.

The Lower-Middle class woman's shopping sphere thus appears considerably greater than her working class counterpart. The symbolic nature of her purchases apparently forces a certain degree of shopping flexibility.

SPENDING AND SAVING PATTERNS. The desire for social "correctness" implies a certain willingness to "play the game" and a corresponding emphasis on high family expenditures. This stands in reasonably sharp contrast to the Upper-Lower "dilemma" of cash-orientation and the desire for purchases that can be made with credit. There is little evidence that Lower-Middle families experience the same conflict.

This stratum's attitudes toward savings again reflect certain symbolic implications. Martineau observes:

Middle-Class people usually have a place in their aspirations for some form of savings. This saving is more often in the form of investment, where there is risk, long-term involvement, and the possibility of higher return. Saving, investment saving, and intangible investment saving—successively each of these become for them increasingly symbols of their higher status.

Upper-Middle Class

CONSUMPTION PATTERNS. The Upper-Middle class is composed of family units headed by individuals who have achieved success in their respective endeavors. With high education levels and the assurance of occupational competence, there seems a marked lack of adherence to group norms of consumption above a certain accepted level. Indeed, some of the more prominent consumption patterns seem to reflect the emulation of higher strata. There seems, in short, apparently somewhat more of a reliance on one's *own* taste than has been found at any of the previous levels. These factors combine to thwart any attempt to comfortably pigeon hole consumption patterns associated with this stratum. There are, however, some emerging patterns.

Warner's *Jonesville*[6], for example, paints a disturbing picture of an upper-middle class that is "desperately" trying to separate itself from what Martineau has called, "the middle majority." Bergel[7] adds support to this observation.

The most ambitious people are in the upper-middle and lower-upper classes. In these groups, talents, achievement, and success are concentrated. Yet in many respects these are also marginal groups, always in danger of losing status, of being overtaken by others with more talent and more impressive achievements. Here are not only the "status seekers" but also the "status clingers." If their prestige is high, they will lose it unless they can keep their performance on a high level. If their income is substantial, their expenditures are even more so if they hold positions requiring "conspicuous consumption."

SHOPPING PATTERNS. There is, predictably, an apparent emphasis on the environment of the selling situation as revealed in the *Tribune* studies. The store must be clean, orderly, reflect good taste, and be staffed with clerks who are not only well versed in their particular merchandise line, but also appropriately aware of the status of the customer. This clearly favors the specialty stores both in the suburbs and the urban areas with a corresponding distrust of the more general outlets.

SPENDING AND SAVING PATTERNS. Warner and Lum[8] have observed:

. . . the budget of an individual or family is

[6] Warner, W. Lloyd. *Democracy in Jonesville.* New York: Harper & Brothers, 1949.
[7] Bergel, Egon Ernest. *Social Stratification.* New York: McGraw-Hill, 1962.
[8] Warner, W. Lloyd and Paul S. Lunt. *The Social Life of a Modern Community* (Yankee City Series, Vol. 1). New Haven, Conn.: Yale University Press, 1941.

a symbol system, or a set of collective representations that expresses the social values of a person's membership in group life.

It is, as we have seen, difficult to determine precisely what is meant by "group life" in terms of this stratum. The budget, however, clearly reflects the necessity for expenditures in terms of their symbolic as well as their functional value. In addition, however, class members seem strongly oriented toward financial sacrifice for "good" schooling for their children.

It has already been observed that increased income enhances the opportunity for increased savings. It is simply not clear on the basis of the sources studied whether this pattern holds true for this stratum. Their allocation of resources covers a considerable breadth of endeavors. We can, however, assume with some certainty that the oft-observed credo of "spending money to make money" results in more of a strain on the spending:saving ratio than would prevail at a somewhat more secure social plateau.

Some Conclusions

Consumption standards of the four American social classes studied appear to rest at two loci. The first, the so-called "level of the Common Man," seems essentially the consumption standard of the Lower-Middle class. As such, it becomes the goal of those classes below it and a norm for the Lower-Middle. It is, however, essential to remember that the interpretation of this "American standard" is formed through class value systems which are, in turn, related to the stratum's "world view." Thus, distinctive interpretations of essentially identical consumption goals will persist. These deviations commonly form the differences in life styles that characterize the various strata.

The second locus apparently lies in the Upper class and serves as a consumption reference to the Upper-Middle class of our investigation. Distinctively horizontal reference thus seems to diminish with this stratum of predominately achieved status and resultant self-esteem.

B. RESEARCH AND APPLICATIONS

The first article in this section is a research report (Rich and Jain) on social class and life cycle as predictors of shopping behavior. Questions are raised in the next selection (Wasson) as to the relevance of income classes when studying social classes.

20-C SOCIAL CLASS AND LIFE CYCLE AS PREDICTORS OF SHOPPING BEHAVIOR

Stuart U. Rich (Marketing Educator) and Subhash C. Jain (Marketing Educator)

The traditional distinctions between the various social classes and stages in the family life cycle seem to be quickly diminishing. The main objective of this article is to report the findings of a study done to test the usefulness of social class and life cycle in understanding consumer behavior during changing socioeconomic conditions.

Method

The data used in this study were originally collected by one of the authors for a comprehensive work in 1963 on shopping behavior of department store customers [12]. The data consisted of about 4,000 personal and telephone interviews in Cleveland and New York. For this article part of the data was reanalyzed, namely the results of 1,056 personal interviews with a probability sample representing all women 20 years of age and older residing in the Cleveland standard metropolitan statistical area. In collecting the original data, a random procedure divided this Cleveland area into 19 zones and selected a sample of places—one place in each zone. This random procedure was repeated and a second, independent sample was drawn, providing a replicated probability sample.

The two major variables used here were social class and family life cycle. Social class was stratified by a multiple-item index, Warner's Index of Status Characteristics [17], widely used in social research. In this index Warner had four variables, source of income, occupation, dwelling area, and house type.

SOURCE: Stuart U. Rich and Subhash C. Jain, "Social Class and Life Cycle as Predictors of Shopping Behavior," *Journal of Marketing Research,* Vol. 5 (February, 1968), pp. 41–49.

This index was modified and source of income and house type were replaced with the amount of income and education of family head. Warner originally used source of income only because of the difficulty in obtaining income amount. It has been found that house type, which is mainly a reflection of house value is mainly dependent on occupation. If house type and occupation were used, occupation would have been weighed very heavily. Therefore, education—also an important determinant of social class—was substituted for house type.

To measure life cycle, the following breakdown was used: under 40 without children, under 40 with children, 40 and over without children, 40 and over with children. This gave a measure of the effects of age, married status, and children in the household—all important determinants of shopping behavior. Using 40 as the dividing point for age indicated whether there were preschool children in the household, another important factor influencing shopping habits. [12].

Highlights of the differences in shopping behavior of women in various social classes and stages in the life cycle are described here. Chi-square tests were used to ascertain which of these differences were significant at the .05 level and to determine, for instance, whether social class affected women's interest in fashion and choice of shopping companions.

Factors Affecting Shopping

INTEREST IN FASHION. If traditional distinctions between the women in various social classes and stages of the life cycle are disappearing an indication would be expected in women's interest in fashion. Respondents' interest in fashion was measured from these five statements, each printed on a separate card and handed to the respondent. She was asked to state her preferences, which were noted by the interviewer.

1. I read the fashion news regularly and try to keep my wardrobe up to date with fashion trends.
2. I keep up to date on all fashion changes although I don't always attempt to dress according to these changes.
3. I check to see what is currently fashionable only when I need to buy some new clothes.
4. I don't pay much attention to fashion trends unless a major change takes place.
5. I am not at all interested in fashion trends.

In Table 1, the fashion interests of the women belonging to various social classes are compared. Fashion plays an important part in the lives of all women regardless of class. Except for the lower-lower class, in which a slightly higher percentage of women than in other classes showed no interest in fashion at all, very small percentages of women among all other classes found fashion uninteresting.

Table 2 summarizes the methods that women in various social classes used for following fashion trends. Except for watching television and listening to the radio, where the differences between social classes were not significant, the helpfulness of the various methods shown in keeping women up to date on fashion changes increased with social class level. The rate of increase varied, however, with different methods. For example, in the category "discussing fashion with others," there was relatively little difference between the lower and middle classes. In "looking at newspaper ads," there was a sharp rise in helpfulness from the lower-lower class to the upper-lower class, but the difference is not particularly significant until the upper-upper class. In summary, the traditional view of greater fashion interest for higher social classes generally holds true for particular methods used to keep informed of fashion although the increase in interest is seldom in any direct proportion to the increase in social level.

Unlike social class, life cycle did not affect fashion interest. There were no significant differences in the methods used by women in various stages of the family life cycle for being informed of fashion changes.

SOURCES OF SHOPPER INFORMATION. Newspaper ads are an important source of shoppers' information. The degree of helpfulness

TABLE 1

Interest in Women's Fashions by Cleveland Women Shoppers, by Social Class

	Social Class[a]					
Statement on Degree of Interest	L-L	U-L	L-M	U-M	L-U	U-U
Read news regularly and keep wardrobe up to date	14%	8%	9%	10%	19%	9%
Keep abreast of changes but not always follow	19	29	42	50	47	64
Check what is fashionable only if buying new clothes	15	22	15	17	17	9
Only pay attention to major fashion changes	22	23	19	14	14	18
Not at all interested in fashion trends	24	16	12	9	3	—[b]
Don't know	6	2	3	—	—	—
Total	100%	100%	100%	100%	100%	100%
Number of cases	132	346	265	206	36	11

[a] In this and subsequent tables, L = lower, M = middle and U = upper.
[b] In this and subsequent tables, a dash represents less than .5 percent.

TABLE 2
Methods Helpful to Cleveland Women on Fashion Trends, by Social Class

| | Social Class | | | | | |
Method	L-L	U-L	L-M	U-M	L-U	U-U
Going to fashion shows	5%	3%	7%	9%	22%	18%
Reading fashion magazines	14	13	11	23	36	27
Reading other magazines	17	18	26	31	28	46
Reading fashion articles in papers	22	34	46	45	56	64
Looking at newspaper ads	39	57	60	68	67	91
Going shopping	36	50	53	63	75	73
Discussing fashion with others	21	22	29	34	36	46
Observing what others wear	22	36	81	51	58	55
Watching television	32	28	25	26	25	46
Listening to the radio	2	5	5	2	8	—
Don't know	3	1	1	—	—	—
No interest in fashion	30	18	14	10	3	—
Total[a]	243%	285%	358%	362%	414%	466%
Number of cases	132	346	265	206	36	11

[a] Total exceeds 100 percent because of multiple responses.

which women attributed to newspaper advertising was analyzed. Women in various social classes seemed to find newspaper ads helpful to about the same degree, except a slightly greater percentage of women in the lower-lower class found them somewhat more helpful.

Another measure used to study the importance of newspaper ads was to analyze the regularity with which women in different social classes looked at newspaper ads. Here again, women of different status groups showed no significant differences in the regularity of their looking at newspaper ads. These results agreed with findings of a recent study reported in *Editor and Publisher:*

"The daily newspaper's coverage of the market place on the average day is nearly universal. Almost every household, 87%, gets a newspaper. . . . The mass exposure opportunity represented by this high percentage of page opening is remarkably consistent for men and women of all ages, incomes, educational attainments and geographical locations" [14].

Carman has reported a similar finding about the importance of newspaper ads as a source of information for members of different social classes [2, p. 29].

Among women in the various stages of the family life cycle, those with children con-

sidered the newspaper ads more helpful. For instance, 88 percent of the women 40 and over with children found ads helpful compared with 73 percent of those without children. Among the women under 40 with and without children, the percentages were 81 and 70, respectively. Further analysis showed that women with children looked at newspaper ads more often than those without children. Age itself had little effect on either the regularity of looking at ads in newspapers or the helpfulness attributed to these ads.

INTERPERSONAL INFLUENCES IN SHOPPING. Interpersonal influences play an important part in shopping decisions. For practical application to marketing, it is necessary to know who these influencers are for each segment of the market. The traditional view has been that upper classes interacted more with members of the immediate family and put great emphasis on lineage. The middle class, though, was generally considered self-directing, had initiative, and was dependent on themselves and their friends more than on relatives. Like the upper classes, the lower classes depended on relatives and family members more often [5, p. 286]. Our findings differed in some respects from this view.

Tables 3 and 4 present data on the impact of interpersonal influences on shopping decisions under two categories, helpfulness attri-

TABLE 3

Discussion of Shopping with Others, Cleveland Women, by Social Class

Consider it Helpful With	Social Class[a]		
	Lower	Middle	Upper
Friends	34%	37%	50%
Husband	13	18	24
Mother	5	5	6
Other family members	20	14	18
No one	36	39	32
Total[b]	108%	113%	130%
Number of cases	478	471	47

[a] Significant differences were noted even when we divided the respondents into six social classes. However, to save space here in some instances only three classes are shown.
[b] Total exceeds 100 percent because of multiple responses.

buted to discussing shopping with others and persons with whom respondents usually shopped. In both categories, women in various social classes showed no significant difference in the influence of friends on shopping. The husband was slightly more important as a shopping influence for the middle and upper classes than for the lower classes, and children were more likely to be taken on shopping trips by the middle and upper classes. However, mother and other family members were not mentioned to any large extent by the lower classes as traditional research would indicate.

Note also in Table 3 that the proportion of women who attributed no help to discussing shopping with others was not significantly different for the three classes. This does not agree with what Rainwater, Coleman, and Handel said, "the working class largely depended on word-of-mouth recommendation before making major purchases" [11, p. 210].

SHOPPING ENJOYMENT. Most women enjoyed shopping regardless of their social class. However, women in different social classes had varying reasons for enjoying shopping. Some reasons—such as the recreational and social aspects of shopping, seeing new things and getting new ideas, and bargain hunting and comparing merchandise—were mentioned by all social classes without any significant difference. Another reason, namely acquiring new clothes or household things, was more enjoyable for the two lower classes. However, a pleasant store atmosphere, display, and excitement were specified as reasons for enjoying shopping by a greater proportion of the women in the upper-middle, lower-upper, and upper-upper classes. Stone and Form found that enjoyment in shopping was not a function of social status [13]. This was in accord with our general finding on shopping enjoyment although, as just noted, the reasons for enjoyment sometimes varied among social classes.

Life cycle did not have any effect on the enjoyment of shopping for clothing and household items. For instance, 38 percent of the women over 40 with children enjoyed shopping for such reasons as pleasant store at-

TABLE 4

Persons with Whom Cleveland Women Usually Shop, by Social Class

Usually Shop With	Social Class					
	L-L	U-L	L-M	U-M	L-U	U-U
Friends	32%	31%	26%	34%	39%	46%
Husband	20	25	32	35	33	9
Mother	5	7	9	9	3	—
Children	10	15	22	23	28	—
Other family members	21	23	16	10	8	18
No one in particular	26	20	17	22	17	36
Never shops with others	—	2	1	2	—	—
Total[a]	114%	123%	123%	135%	128%	109%
Number of cases	132	346	265	206	36	11

[a] Total exceeds 100 percent because of multiple responses.

TABLE 5

Frequency of Shopping Trips of Cleveland Women, by Life Cycle

| | Stage in Life Cycle | | | |
| | Under 40 | | 40 and Over | |
Times Per Year	No Child	Child	No Child	Child
52 or more	30%	30%	25%	31%
24 to 51	33	25	17	20
12 to 23	23	28	18	21
6 to 11	2	4	6	7
1 to 5	12	12	27	21
Less than once	—	—	2	—
Never	—	—	1	—
Don't know	—	1	4	—
Total	100%	100%	100%	100%
Number of cases	66	474	240	276

mosphere, displays, and excitement compared with 36 percent in this age group without children. For women under 40 without children, the percentages were 37 and 41, respectively.

SHOPPING FREQUENCY. The frequency with which women shopped during the year was significantly associated with social class. For example, 38 percent of the women in the upper class and 34 percent in the middle class shopped 52 or more times a year compared with 24 percent in the lower class. These findings do not match those of Stone and Form. According to them, women in either the upper or the middle class shopped less often than women in the lower or working class.

Younger women shopped more often than older women, but presence of children did not make any significant difference within the two age groups (Table 5). Stone and Form found the frequency of shopping trips mainly dependent on children in the family.

IMPORTANCE OF SHOPPING QUICKLY. The higher the social status of a woman, the more she considered it important to shop quickly. Thus 39 percent of upper class women regarded it important to always shop quickly though only 30 percent in lower class and 34 percent in the middle class did. Only 10 percent of upper class women felt it was not important to shop quickly compared with 19 percent and 29 percent in the middle and lower classes, respectively.

BROWSING. Tendency to browse without buying anything was more prominent among the upper-lower (41 percent), lower-middle (44 percent), and upper-middle (42 percent) classes. Yet women in the lower-lower, lower-upper, and upper-upper classes mentioned it less often (Table 6).

DOWNTOWN SHOPPING. The lower the social status, the greater the proportion of downtown shopping (Table 7). Sixty-eight percent of lower-lower class women were designated as high downtown shoppers, only 22 percent of the lower-upper class and 18 percent of the upper-upper class were considered to be so.

This also suggests that suburban shopping centers are becoming increasingly more important for the upper classes. This has been noted in *Women's Wear Daily*, "It is a mistake to promote just $25 dresses in a suburban store. . . . We have found, from experience, that higher price clothes do sell in depth in the suburbs" [10, p. 40].

Cross tabulations by life cycle showed a

TABLE 6

Browsing of Cleveland Women, by Social Class

| Regularity of Occurrence | Social Class | | | | | |
	L-L	U-L	L-M	U-M	L-U	U-U
Regularly or fairly often	29%	41%	44%	42%	22%	18%
Once in awhile	30	37	35	36	31	27
Never	40	21	20	22	44	55
Don't know	1	1	1	—	3	—
Total	100%	100%	100%	100%	100%	100%
Number of cases	132	346	265	206	36	11

TABLE 7
Shopping Done Downtown by Cleveland Women, by Social Class

Proportion of Downtown Shopping[a]	Social Class					
	L-L	U-L	L-M	U-M	L-U	U-U
High	68%	50%	42%	33%	22%	18%
Low	19	33	37	50	59	64
None	11	15	19	15	16	18
Don't know	2	2	2	2	3	—
Total	100%	100%	100%	100%	100%	100%
Number of cases	132	346	265	206	36	11

[a] High downtown shoppers shop downtown half or more of the time; Low downtown shoppers, one-quarter or less of the time; None means women who do not shop downtown.

tendency for young people to patronize shopping centers more than older people, as suggested by other findings.

No significant differences on downtown shopping existed among the women in the various social classes living in the city. However, among the suburbanites, social class was inversely related to downtown shopping. For instance, among the city dwellers about 60 percent of the women in the two lower and two middle classes were ranked as high downtown shoppers. Yet, among the out-of-city residents 43 percent of lower-lower class women and 37 percent of upper-lower class were considered high in-town shoppers; only 32 percent in the lower-middle and 27 percent in the upper-middle class were high downtown shoppers. The percentages for the two upper classes further decreased to 22 percent and 18 percent, respectively.

In contrast, about 70 percent of the women in the two upper classes (living in the sub-urbs) were low downtown shoppers though the same percentage was 29 percent for the lower-lower class and 40 percent for the upper-lower class. However, when the high and low categories were considered together and compared with the "none" group, downtown shopping by suburbanites increased in each higher social class.

In general, a greater proportion of higher class women shop downtown, but women in the lower classes appear to shop more intensively in the central business district.

TYPE OF STORE PREFERRED. As seen in Table 8, higher class women more often named the regular department store as their favorite. The department store maintained a broad image as a favorite store since 51 percent of the lower-lower class women and 60 percent of the upper-lower class designated it their favorite store. A greater percentage of lower-lower (14 percent) and upper-lower (11 percent) women favored the discount

TABLE 8
Kind of Favorite Store of Cleveland Women, by Social Class

Kind of Store	Social Class					
	L-L	U-L	L-M	U-M	L-U	U-U
Regular department	51%	60%	77%	83%	88%	91%
Discount department	14	11	6	2	—	9
Variety and junior department	2	6	6	5	—	—
Mail order	9	14	5	2	3	—
Medium to low specialty	2	2	1	—	6	—
Neighborhood	11	2	1	1	3	—
Others	11	5	4	7	—	—
Total	100%	100%	100%	100%	100%	100%
Number of cases	132	346	265	206	36	11

TABLE 9
Kind of Department Store Favored by Cleveland Women

Kind of Department Store	Social Class					
	L-L	U-L	L-M	U-M	L-U	U-U
High fashion store	4%	7%	22%	34%	70%	67%
Price appeal store	74	63	36	24	19	18
Broad appeal store	22	30	42	42	11	15
Total	100%	100%	100%	100%	100%	100%
Number of cases	67	208	204	71	32	10

store than did women in either the middle or upper classes.

As shown in Table 9, the high fashion store became more important for each higher class. But, the price appeal store was inversely related to social class. The broad appeal store was mentioned by the two middle classes more often. These findings generally agreed with what Martineau discovered:

> The blue collar individual, as his family income goes up, proceeds from cars to appliances to home ownership to apparel. He and his family are candidates for almost any store, and the most successful stores which would traditionally appeal to them have held them by steadily trading up, both in merchandise, store facilities and their image. . . . The point again is that this person has changed. He is not the same guy. He has long since satisfied his needs and wants and now he is interested in satisfying his wishes. [9, p. 56].

The high preference of the lower class shoppers for the regular department stores is therefore not surprising.

TABLE 10
Kind of Favorite Store of Cleveland Women, By Life Cycle

Kind of Favorite Store	Stage in Life Style			
	Under 40		40 and Over	
	No Child	Child	No Child	Child
Department	65%	57%	83%	79%
Discount	9	13	2	2
Mail order	5	11	2	7
All others	21	19	13	12
Total	100%	100%	100%	100%
Number of cases	66	474	240	276

The kind of department store women in the various social classes mentioned most often was also analyzed for the following kinds of merchandise: women's better dresses; house dresses and underwear; children's clothing; men's socks and shirts; furniture; large appliances; towels, sheets, blankets and spread; and small electrical appliances and kitchen utensils. Here again the two upper classes specified the high fashion store as their favorite for the first five of these eight kinds of merchandise. Women in the two lower classes shopped at the price appeal store most of the time for all items.

Analysis of the favorite store of women in various stages of the life cycle showed that the regular department store ranked high among all women except that younger women with children showed somewhat less preference for it. Table 10 shows that 57 percent of the younger women with children and 65 percent of the younger women without children mentioned the regular department store as their favorite. Discount stores were preferred by the younger women a little more than by the older ones. No significant differences were revealed between the types of stores favored by women in various stages of the family life cycle for the eight kinds of merchandise individually.

Conclusion

Socioeconomic changes in income, education, leisure time, and movement to suburbia cut across traditional class lines and various stages in the life cycle. Some authors like Rainwater, Coleman, and Handel have found social class a significant factor in determining consumer behavior [11]. However, recent writings seem to indicate that social class distinctions have been obscured by rising incomes and educational levels [8, 9].

Our empirical findings tend to support the second viewpoint. The random sampling procedure used assured every Cleveland woman 20 years of age or older an equal chance of being selected, and interviewer bias was closely controlled. Hence we are able to generalize about shopping behavior in Cleveland. Admittedly, all findings cannot be applied to women in other cities. However in the original study, which included Cleveland and New York-northeastern New Jersey metropolitan areas, many patterns of shopping behavior for women in particular income or life cycle categories were almost identical in the two areas despite the contrasting patterns of size, geographical location, demography, and kinds of stores found in these two cities [12].

Spot checks made of Cleveland and New York women in the present study again produced similar results. For instance, among women under 40 with children in Cleveland, 30 percent shopped 52 or more times per year compared with 34 percent for this group in New York. For women 40 and over with children, the percentages were 31 and 30 for the two cities. On the importance of being able to shop quickly, 30 percent of the lower social class women in Cleveland felt this was always important, as did 34 percent of the middle class women and 39 percent of the upper class women. In New York these percentages were 29, 36, and 39, respectively. In other words, there seems to be evidence that many of the shopping behavior patterns of Cleveland women exist in other cities.

The findings thus question the usefulness of life cycle and social class concepts in understanding consumer behavior in view of recent changes in income, education, leisure time, movement to suburbia, and other factors. Students of marketing and store executives may need to reconsider how far these sociological concepts should be used for segmentation purposes and what their probable impact will be on marketing policies and programs.

REFERENCES

1. Bernard Barber and Lyle S. Lobel, "Fashion in Women's Clothes and the American Social System," *Social Forces*, 31 (December 1952), 124–31.
2. James M. Carman, *The Application of Social Class in Market Segmentation*, Berkeley, Calif.: University of California, 1965.
3. Lincoln Clark, ed., *The Life Cycle and Consumer Behavior*, Vol. 2, New York: New York University Press, 1955.
4. "Experts Set Youth Market Guidelines," *Women's Wear Daily*, 113 (October 18, 1966), 19.
5. August B. Hollingshead, "Class Differences in Family Stability," in Reinhard Bendix and Seymour Martin Lipset, eds., *Class, Status and Power*, New York: The Free Press, 1965.
6. David L. Huff, "Geographical Aspects of Consumer Behavior," *University of Washington Business Review*, 18 (June 1959), 27–35.
7. Subhash Jain, "A Critical Analysis of Life Cycle and Social Class Concepts in Understanding Consumer Shopping Behavior," Unpublished doctoral dissertation, University of Oregon, 1966.
8. Frederick C. Klein, "Rising Pay Lifts More Blue Collar Men into a New Affluent Class," *The Wall Street Journal*, 165 (April 5, 1965).
9. Pierre Martineau, "Customer Shopping Center Habits Change Retailing," *Editor & Publisher*, 96 (October 26, 1963), 16, 56.
10. Trudy Prokop, "Jack Weiss: No Gambler, But a Man of Decision," *Women's Wear Daily*, 113 (November 28, 1966), 40.
11. Lee Rainwater, Richard Coleman, and Gerald Handel, *Workingman's Wife*, New York: MacFadden-Bartel Corp., 1962.
12. Stuart U. Rich, *Shopping Behavior of Department Store Customers*, Boston, Mass.: Division of Research, Graduate School of Business Administration, Harvard University, 1963.
13. Gregory P. Stone and William H. Form, *The Local Community Clothing Market: A Study of the Social and Social Psychological Contexts of Shopping*, East Lansing, Mich.: Michigan State University, 1957, 20.
14. "Survey Proves High Exposure for Ads on Newspaper Pages," *Editor & Publisher*, 97 (October 3, 1964), 17–8.
15. Thayer C. Taylor, "Selling Where the Money Is," *Sales Management*, 91 (October 18, 1963), 37–41, 122, 124, 126.
16. ———, "The I AM ME Consumer," *Business Week*, (December 23, 1961), 38–39.
17. Lloyd W. Warner, M. Meeker, and K. Eells, *Social Class in America*, Chicago: Social Research, Inc., 1949.
18. Edward B. Weiss, "The Revolution in Fashion Distribution," *Advertising Age*, 34 (June 24, 1963), 104–5.

20-D IS IT TIME TO QUIT THINKING OF INCOME CLASSES?

Chester R. Wasson (*Marketing Educator*)

Pierre Martineau pointed out that social class is not income class in a widely reprinted article in the *Journal of Marketing* nearly a decade ago.[1] Despite the wide notice this article attracted, marketing texts and many marketing people still treat income level as synonymous with social class and as a sound guide to spending patterns. At the time Martineau had to base his argument on relatively fragmentary data. Today definitive proof exists that his thesis is correct. The tabulations of the Bureau of Labor Statistics 1960–61 Survey of Consumer Expenditures show clearly that the pattern of expenditure allocation has little relation to the income level and that effective market segmentation is primarily a result of such social class indicators as occupational classification and other measures of culture like region, locality, and stage in the family life cycle. Whatever validity income classification ever had was due to a very rough and now disappearing correlation with occupational status.

The *Chicago Tribune* studies of spending of the 1950s, on which Martineau based his thesis, were designed with the aid of W. Lloyd Warner and built on sociological analyses of Warner and his associates.[2] All of them showed that in any given community social class was the basic determinant of the cultural patterns and, therefore, of the pattern of expenditure priorities. Social class was defined originally on the basis of the relative prestige accorded a family by its neighbors, and it was established that the same ranking would be achieved by a rating scale calculated from occupation, source of income, and type of housing—the system used in the *Tribune* studies.

As a practical matter, however, such a

multi-factor measure can be costly to use, and little of the available data that must be used in marketing can be so tabulated. All that is usually available are single factor classifications by income, occupation, or occasionally such other social-class-related factors as educational level and housing. The tendency has been to settle on the use of income.

Income level was doubtless a fairly good approximation of social class when the housewife neither had nor sought many employment opportunities outside of the home and when manual labor was, relative to the demand, plentiful. Neither is the case today. Relatively large numbers of blue collar families, whose social status is manifestly well below that of white collar families in general, earn more income than substantial numbers of white collar families and even some professionals. Income reporting is never reliable, as anyone who has ever gathered family budget reports is aware, and its meaning changes over time with changes in the value of money, with changes in the composition of the family, and, for middle-class occupations, with promotions.

The occupational classification, by contrast, is not only related to the family's position in the social hierarchy, but, perhaps more important, is the main basis for it. Not only is occupation of the head one of Warner's three basic indicators, but it is also the main source of income (another indicator) for most families. It is very closely correlated with type of housing and neighborhood as well, of course, as with educational level. It also has the virtue of seldom changing during the life cycle of the family, being easily and reliably identifiable, and of always indicating the same general social station. Furthermore, most published studies rest on data which permit occupational classification, and much of it is so tabulated—including the BLS studies. As ordinarily handled, it has one flaw: all of the self-employed are grouped together whether they are rag-pickers or free-lance stock market analysts. As Figure 1 indicates, the self-employed do not constitute a homogeneous classification. The income distribution is

SOURCE: Chester R. Wasson, "Is it Time to Quit Thinking of Income Classes?" *Journal of Marketing*, Vol. 33 (April, 1969), pp. 54–57.

[1] Pierre Martineau, "Social Classes and Spending Behavior," *Journal of Marketing*, Vol. 23 (October, 1958), pp. 121–130.

[2] See, for example, W. Lloyd Warner and Paul Lunt, *Social Life of a Modern Community* (New Haven, Conn.: Yale University Press, 1941).

clearly U-shaped. For the rest, we can clearly distinguish the upper middle class in the category of salaried professionals and managers, the lower middle class in the group designated as sales and clerical. The three lower classes are easily recognized in the categories of skilled workers, semiskilled wage earners, and unskilled wage earners, respectively.

As Figure 1 indicates, the correlation between occupational class and income level is not close. Every income level separately tabulated in the BLS 1960–61 study contained a substantial proportion of families in every class from top to bottom of the occupational scale. And as Table 1 demonstrates graphically, it is occupational class, not in-

come, which determines the proportion of spending allocated to some of the most important categories. (The inter-occupational class comparisons made in this table were limited to incomes between $4,000 and $10,000 because these were the groups which contained substantial numbers of every occupational level and relative comparability of family size, with at least 370 families in every cell in the sample. The tabulated results in the other classifications were consistent with those in the groups depicted.) For example, a government survey indicated that food expenditures have a higher priority the further we go down the occupational scale, and that the middle class white collar workers value housing and quality of neighborhood

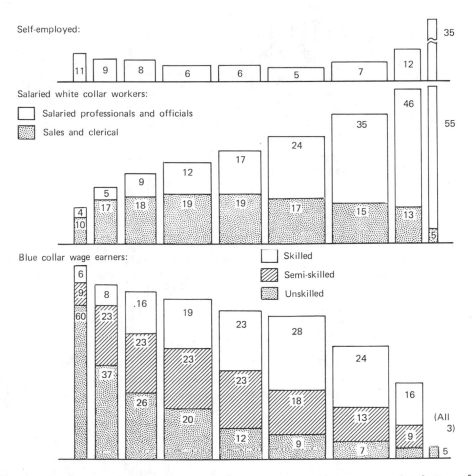

Figure 1. How occupational classes cut across income groups: The percentage distribution of occupational classes within each income group, urban employed families, U.S.A., 1960–1961.

TABLE 1

Average Percentage of Total Expenditure Allocated to Selected Categories at the Same Income Levels, Urban Employed Families, United States, 1960–61

Occupation of Head	Food Income Group ($000)				Shelter Income Group ($000)				Education and Reading Income Group ($000)			
	4–4.9	5–5.9	6–7.4	7.5–9.9	4–4.9	5–5.9	6–7.4	7.5–9.9	4–4.9	5–5.9	6–7.4	7.5–9.9
White Collar:												
Professionals	21	23	23	23	16	17	16	14	2.5	2.2	2.1	2.2
Clerical, etc.	24	24	24	24	16	15	14	13	1.7	1.7	1.8	2.0
Blue Collar:												
Skilled	25	26	24	25	14	13	12	11	1.3	1.4	1.5	2.0
Semi-skilled	27	26	26	25	14	13	12	11	1.1	1.4	1.7	1.5
Unskilled	28	27	25	24	14	13	13	11	1.2	1.5	1.9	1.7

Source: *Survey of Consumer Expenditures, Supplement 2, Part A, BLS Report 237–8, July, 1964, U. S. Dept. of Labor.*

TABLE 2

Percentage of Total Expenditure Allocated to Selected Classes of Items by Families in Different Stages of the Family Life Cycle, Urban United States, 1961

Stage of the Family Life Cycle	Average Age of Head	Percentage of Total Expenditure Which Is Devoted to:						
		Meals away from home	Clothing	Recreation	Education and Reading	Transportation	Home Furnishings and Equipment	Medical Care
Young single adults ("Single consumers under 25 years of age")	22	7	14	6	3.3	18	3	3
Early married couples (Husband-wife families with oldest child less than 1 year)	27	5	8	4	1.3	16	10	8
Older Husband-Wife Families with Children:								
Oldest child under 6	29	4	9	4	1.4	16	7	7
Oldest child 6–17	40	5	11	5	1.9	14	5	6
Oldest child 18 or more	52	5	12	4	4.0	17	4	6
Empty nest 2-person families (2-person families 55–64)	60	5	9	3	1.3	16	5	8
Retirees (2-person families 65–74)	69	4	7	3	1.2	14	4	10

Source: BLS Report 237-38, Supplement 2, Part A, July 1964.

more highly than do blue collar workers in the same income class.[3] Expenditures for education and reading also have a clear class bias, on the upward side.

When occupational class is held constant, on the other hand, there is no clear relationship between expenditure allocations and income. Although the aggregate tabulation for all occupations indicates some decline in the percentage allotted to food as we go from one income class to a higher one, white collar employees show a level percentage regardless of income, and salaried professionals a possible tendency to increase. Skilled worker families exhibit no clear tendency one way or another, and the two lowest occupational classes tend to exhibit a negative income elasticity of expenditure for food.

The pattern of differences in expenditure allocations are both too consistent and too large to be due to mere chance variation or sampling error. Therefore, it is difficult to perceive any logic in combining such disparate data into single income classifications.

Of course, occupation is not the sole cultural factor segmenting markets. Regional differences in needs are recognized even in the BLS standard budgets. But needs alone are not the full story. The tabulations hint at added real differences in taste and spending priorities which would come as no surprise to experienced marketers or to sociologists familiar with differing regional attitudes. The South, for example, has a total average income level about 10% below that of any other region, but the urban workers there spend a significantly lower proportion of the available income on food than in any other region and a much higher proportion on personal care items. Within-region differences between large cities exhibit interesting dis-

parities which would repay analysis of the BLS computer tapes. The author has analyzed these and some other differences, as shown in the final tabulation, in more detail than there is room for in this paper.[4] Table 2 shows the adaptation of the data to the family life cycle concept the author was able to develop from the BLS tabulations.

This analysis does not mean that income is unimportant, of course. It still obviously limits how much can be spent, given the culturally determined patterns of priorities. The artisan with a family income of $6,000 per year in 1961 would not spend as much for shelter as the $6,000 professional, but the $8,500 artisan would; he might even be a neighbor. Obviously, the 24% of his total spending which goes for food is much less for the clerk with a $4,000 income than the same 24% for the clerk earning $8,000. But the income amount does not influence the distribution of that expenditure, only the amount which can be spent, given the sub-cultural pattern.

These BLS data make clear, as no previously available information has, that market segmentation is influenced strongly by a complex of cultural influences, of which occupation and the other elements of social class are important components. Study of the BLS data alone would be of considerable value to many kinds of firms, and the tapes giving the original data are available for those who wish them. Beyond this, however, they demonstrate the need to look at our marketing studies in terms of occupation first, and only then at income level.

[3] *Survey of Consumer Expenditures,* Supplement 2, Part A, BLS Report 237–8 (Washington, D.C.: U.S. Department of Labor, July, 1964).

[4] Chester R. Wasson, Frederick D. Sturdivant, and David H. McConaughy, *Competition and Human Behavior* (New York: Appleton-Century-Crofts, 1968), pp. 52–54 and 114–142; Chester R. Wasson and David H. McConaughy, *Buying Behavior and Marketing Decisions* (New York: Appleton-Century-Crofts, 1969), Chapter 9.

21 / Influences of Role

A. BACKGROUND AND THEORY

This first section explores the concept of role: the meaning of role-taking (Turner); a paradigm for role analysis (Hare); and an examination of the nature of status (Douglas, Field, and Tarpey).

21-A ROLE-TAKING, ROLE STANDPOINT, AND REFERENCE-GROUP BEHAVIOR

Ralph H. Turner (Sociologist)

For decades sociologists have made reference to "taking the role of the other" ("role-taking" for short) as a basic explanatory concept in relating the acts of the individual to the social contexts of his actions.

The Meaning of Role-Taking

Role-taking in its most general form is a process of looking at or anticipating another's behavior by viewing it in the context of a role imputed to that other. It is thus always more than simply a reaction to another's behavior in terms of an arbitrarily understood symbol or gesture.

By *role* we mean a collection of patterns of behavior which are thought to constitute a meaningful unit and deemed appropriate to a person occupying a particular status in society (e.g., doctor or father), occupying an informally defined position in interpersonal relations (e.g., leader or compromiser), or identified with a particular value in society (e.g., honest man or patriot).[1] We

shall stress the point that a role consists of behaviors which are regarded as making up a meaningful unit. The linkage of behaviors within roles is the source of our expectations that certain kinds of action will be found together. When people speak of trying to "make sense" of someone's behavior or to understand its meaning, they are typically attempting to find the role of which the observed actions are a part.

Role will be consistently distinguished from status or position or value type as referring to the whole of the behavior which is felt to belong intrinsically to those subdivisions. Role refers to behavior rather than position, so that one may *enact* a role but cannot *occupy* a role. However, role is a normative concept. It refers to expected or appropriate behavior and is distinguished from the manner in which the role is actually enacted in a specific situation which is *role behavior* or *role performance*.[2] While a norm

SOURCE: Ralph H. Turner, "Role-Taking, Role Standpoint, and Reference-Group Behavior," *The American Journal of Sociology*, 61 (May, 1956), pp. 316–328, at pp. 316–317, by permission of The University of Chicago Press. Copyright 1956 by University of Chicago.

[1] Role is conceived more inclusively here than in Linton's famous definition (Ralph Linton, *The Study of Man* [New York: Appleton-Century Co., 1936], pp. 113 ff). The term "appropriate" in the

definition is purposely left without a further referent, since the particular content of the role (i.e., that which is regarded as appropriate) will vary depending upon the vantage point of the person or persons formulating the role conception. Cf. also Theodore R. Sarbin, "Role Theory," in *Handbook of Social Psychology*, ed. Gardner Lindzey (Cambridge, Mass., Addison-Wesley Publishing Co., 1954), I, 223–58.

[2] Cf. Theodore M. Newcomb, *Social Psychology* (New York: Dryden Press, 1950), p. 330.

is a directive to action, a role is a *set of norms,* with the additional normative element that the individual is expected to be consistent. The role is made up of all those norms which are thought to apply to a person occupying a given position. Thus, we return to our initial emphasis that the crucial feature of the concept of role is its reference to the assumption that certain different norms are meaningfully related or "go together."

21-B A PARADIGM FOR ROLE ANALYSIS

A. Paul Hare *(Sociologist)*

The content of role expectations can be visualized along the two axes in Figure 1. The behavior expected from others to the self and by the self to others can, in each case, extend from that which is *required* to that which is *prohibited*. These expectations include both the form and content of interaction. To some extent there are also expectations for the personal characteristics of the individual who will fill the role.

The central tendency of the expectations for a role in each area could be indicated by a point on a graph which has as its coordinates a measure of the extent to which behavior in that area is required or prohibited along each axis. Some typical roles in the control area would be those of the "authoritarian" who is required to control and be controlled, the "anarchist" who neither controls nor is controlled, the "dominator" who is required to control and cannot be controlled, and the

SOURCE: A. Paul Hare, *Handbook of Small Group Research* (New York: The Free Press of Glencoe, 1962), pp. 103–105.

"submitter" who is required to be controlled, but cannot control. The "democrat" would appear in the middle of the figure as one who is required to control or be controlled as the occasion demands.

In addition to these expectations for the content of interaction, a role can be seen as also including expectations for the frequency and duration (i.e., pattern) of interaction and the communication network involved for both output and input in each of the content areas. To continue the example in the control area, the expectations for the behavior of self to others would include a specified degree of control, carried out with a given frequency and duration, to specified group members. In the same way the control of the self by others would have a given interaction pattern, emanating from given members of the group.

Although this method of delineating the expectations for a role may prove too complex to be used in its complete form, it may prove relevant for some research problems. For example, one might wish to distinguish a role

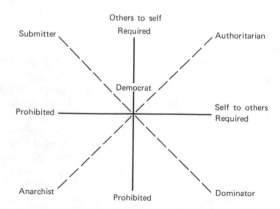

Figure 1. A paradigm for role analysis in the control area.

which required an individual to interact in a controlling way frequently but for a short duration, from one in which the individual was expected to act with the same degree of control infrequently but over a longer period of time. Or, in another case, two roles might be equal in power and similar in interaction pattern, and yet different in that an individual in one role might control only one other person, while in the other role he might control a dozen persons. Similar variations might occur in the interaction patterns and communication networks which govern the control of the self by others.

The concept of role as it is used in the literature does not generally involve all of the aspects of behavior which have been suggested here. Rather, each author tends to limit his description of role to some aspects which are particularly relevant to his experiment. In some cases the subject's position in a communication network (e.g., central person, member, or isolate) is seen as the most important aspect of the role, in others his position in the typical interaction rate or pattern (e.g., the person who talks most), and in others his position in the content area (e.g., task leader versus social-emotional leader).

21-C THE NATURE OF STATUS

John Douglas (Marketing Educator), George A. Field (Marketing Educator), and Lawrence X. Tarpey (Marketing Educator)

The individual in a social vacuum has no status. Let us observe the mechanisms of status as it evolves in a small group, first with animals and then with the more complex human systems.

Scientists have studied the pecking order of chickens. A chicken reared in isolation has no status. Introduce a second chicken into the yard, and the race for status is on. When the two are competing for a choice bit of food, they will peck each other until they determine which one can dominate the other; the less aggressive chicken soon learns her place. She can be pecked by the other chicken, but she dare not return the peck. The pecking order can be reversed by controlling the hormone supply—male hormones will make the submissive chicken more aggressive, and she will out-peck her former superior. If an entire flock of chickens is placed in the henyard, a pecking order will soon be established; each chicken will learn that she can peck the chicken below her but not the one above her in strength and aggressiveness. Thus we have a crude but clear-cut system.

Did Robinson Crusoe have status? Clearly he did not when he first occupied his island.

But when he encountered his man Friday, a status system quickly developed. Friday became his faithful servant, giving Crusoe the higher status.

In the same way, the student can observe status operating in small groups such as the family. In a patriarchal society, the father has top status; in a matriarchal society, the mother reigns. In a primogeniture system, the eldest son has higher status than subsequent siblings.

Because status tends to develop in every group in ways that assign to each individual a position entailing specific responsibilities and privileges, it has been called "an important kind of cement that binds an organization together."[1]

STATUS IS A RELATIVE CONCEPT. Since your status in a group is relative to that of the other members of that group, you may have a different status in each group to which you belong. For instance, at home you may be the third child in the family; your older siblings may have higher status by reason of seniority; your parents, in turn, have still higher status. Along with this status go responsibilities and privileges. Big brother must look after junior; but he can borrow dad's car,

SOURCE: John Douglas, George A. Field, and Lawrence X. Tarpey, *Human Behavior in Marketing* (Columbus, Ohio: Charles E. Merrill Books, Inc., 1967), pp. 152–159.

[1] Robert Dubin, *Human Relations in Administration*. 2nd ed. (Englewood Cliffs, New Jersey: Prentice-Hall, Inc., 1961), p. 283.

while junior must be content with a bicycle. Your position in your informal social group may differ from your intra-family status; nevertheless, it is very probably evident to the group members.[2] In college, you may have one status as student in the classroom, where the professor dominates, but quite another in the fraternity, where you are president. If you are married, you enjoy another status relationship in your own family, superior to the statuses of your children; in fact, it is precisely for the maintenance of this system that children address their parents as Dad or Father, rather than by name, just as they call other adults Mr. or Mrs. to preserve the basic status relationships. As captain of the baseball team, you have still another status. This set of status systems, that exists for each group in which you participate, involves everyone in that group.[3]

STATUS MAY BE ASCRIBED OR ACHIEVED. Ascribed status is acquired without having to be earned, often through inheritance or fortuitous circumstances. For instance, a king inherits top status in his country. The Dalai Lama of Tibet is chosen as spiritual ruler because he is born at the exact moment of death of the previous Dalai Lama and is presumed to be a reincarnation. In some preliterate tribes the albino is accorded special status. In India, birth in a specific subcaste determines an individual's status. In Western industrial society, it is beneficial to be born the eldest son into a family that owns a major corporation.

Achieved status is the result of the individual's own efforts. In the American dream, any average youth can become President, particularly if he was born in a log cabin in Illinois. In theory, any hard-working youth can become president of a large corporation. And, presumably, any youngster can determine, in his own lifetime, his own social status.

The facts are at variance with this rosy egalitarian outlook. Careful studies of social mobility (changes in status) have exploded a number of popular myths in America with regard to stratification systems. One of our favorite myths is the Horatio Alger legend. Horatio Alger is widely believed by those who have not read the stories to represent the typical hard working, frugal American boy who succeeds through sheer grit and ability. In fact, Horatio succeeded in the fictional accounts through luck; he would, for instance, just happen to be wandering down the street when the rich man's daughter charged by on a runaway horse. Her facile rescue by Horatio would lead to success.

The Horatio Alger myth is founded partly on wishful thinking and the American frontier tradition, partly on our inherited egalitarian philosophy traceable to 18th-century French thought, and partly to distortion of the data. It is true that outstanding examples of social mobility exist. We can easily locate shining examples of the self-made tycoon. or entrepreneur. These examples, however, are the exceptions. A number of studies of the careers of business leaders show that since the mid-nineteenth century the recruiting ground for the majority of our top businessmen has been the upper and upper-middle class. Moreover, at any level, the probability that a young man will enter his father's occupation is higher than for any other single possibility.[4]

Another myth is the high mobility of the Anglo-Saxon Protestant. While such a background may be useful in the inheritance of ascribed status, recent studies show that Jews exhibit the greatest upward mobility, probably because of cultural attitudes favoring education and motivation to achieve.[5]

Another myth is that upward mobility is more prevalent in the United States than in the older industrial societies of Europe. Recent analyses suggest that mobility rates are similar in industrialized societies; nor have they exhibited much change. Today it is neither harder nor easier to raise one's status than in the past, though this question has been the subject of much sociological debate.

[2] William Foote Whyte, *Street Corner Society* (Chicago: The University of Chicago Press, 1943).

[3] Dubin, *op. cit.*

[4] Seymour Martin Lipset and Reinhard Bendix, *Social Mobility in Industrial Society* (Berkeley and Los Angeles: University of California Press, 1959), Chapter III, esp. p. 203.

[5] Lipset and Bendix, *op. cit.*, p. 223.

The Elements of Status

An individual's status has a number of components, the nature of which are explored in this section. The main elements of status are attributes, situational aspects, evaluations, and systemic factors.

STATUS DEPENDS UPON ATTRIBUTES. Every individual has many attributes or characteristics, some of which relate to status and some of which do not. For instance, in the general American culture, the color of a person's eyes has no effect on his status, but the color of his skin may have important status connotations; high I.Q. has little direct effect on status, but high educational level, income, and occupational attainment are important status criteria. The criteria applied to status attributes differ according to the culture pattern; in China, prestige comes with age, while in Hollywood youth is worshipped, and the aging star is likely to be a falling one. Thus status represents the values attached by the group and the culture or subculture to various attributes of the individual.[6]

Sources of Attributes:

1. *Attributes may be given.* Given attributes are those which are part of the natural endowment of the individual, or which come to him, without effort on his part. Skin color is an example of this; so is birth into a prominent family. Neither of these is readily attained or achieved. True, one can marry into a prominent family, but that is not quite the same as having eminent forefathers.

2. *Attributes may be attained.* Sociologists have shown that churches, for instance, differ in their status levels; so do corporations. A status-hungry individual may change his religion to Episcopalian and accept employment with General Motors. This type of attained status is borrowed from the organizations that possess it.[7] Attained status may some-

times be the result of fortuitous circumstances—being in the right place at the right time.

3. *Attributes may be achieved.* The poor boy who achieves wealth or political stature through hard work and perseverance is a classic example.

STATUS EXHIBITS SITUATIONAL VARIABILITY. The situational context can effect temporary or even lasting changes in the status of an individual. For instance, a Second Lieutenant recently graduated from officers' training school may have three months' training and no actual military experience, yet his status is on a distinctly higher level than that of the Master Sergeant, who in battle may assume actual control to prevent the defeat or obliteration of the troops. His status may then rise suddenly—and be confirmed by the military organization. In wartime, many sergeants are commissioned and given responsible positions of command. If the newly commissioned sergeant is promoted more rapidly than the Second Lieutenant, he will become the latter's superior in status.

STATUS IS A PRODUCT OF EVALUATIONS BY OTHERS. Status, though real, is a subjective reality, since it is a ranking process. It is the group's evaluation of your attributes, more than the attributes themselves, that determines your status.[8] In a study of community or organizational status, each member of the community or organization may be asked to rank each person in the group, including himself; or the ranking may be performed by families.[9]

The methodological problem in determining status by this means inheres in the existence of deviant evaluators. For instance, in Figure 1, there are three group members—A, B, and C. All members of the group agree that C has higher status than A or B, and that A and B share equal status. No problem exists. Now suppose, as in Figure 2, that each thinks one other has higher status, but no two

---

[6] David Moment and Abraham Zaleznik, *Role Development and Interpersonal Competence* (Boston: Harvard University, 1963), p. 98.
[7] C. Wright Mills, *White Collar: The American Middle Classes*, Galaxy Book Edition (New York: Oxford University Press, 1956); See also Robert Presthus, *The Organizational Society* (New York: Alfred A. Knopf, 1962), p. 153.

[8] Dubin, *loc. cit.*
[9] George A. Field, "Cultural Classes in a Planned Community," (Ph.D. Dissertation, University of Pennsylvania, 1954), available from University Microfilms, Ann Arbor, Michigan.

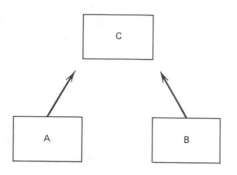

Figure 1. Perfectly structured status system; A, B, and C agree that A & B are equal and that C is superior. Group consensus with no deviant perceptions.

recognizing that it is a biased ranking without full group consensus. The problem would be more acute if it were a question of assigning each member to a specific bracket, such as upper, middle, or lower class.

One solution might be to discard the deviant rankings—that is, to disqualify the evaluators who disagree (this happens to the minority vote in a presidential election). Ignoring the deviant evaluators makes status a model average evaluation.[10]

Finally, it is important to recognize that status depends on the way attributes are *perceived* by the evaluators. It is not the possession of attributes, but the way they are effectively projected by the individual evaluatee and perceived by the evaluator, that determines the status. The attributes are the raw material; the projection and perception of the attributes are communications processes, and the evaluation by the evaluator as he perceives the attributes is the status-conferring process. Status, like beauty, is in the eye of the beholder.

agree. In other words, A thinks B has highest status, and B thinks C has highest status, while C puts A at the top. A true status system cannot be said to exist, because there is no consensus of rankings. Let us extend the rationale to a larger group, say twenty persons. Suppose eighteen agree that A has the highest status, but two of them disagree. In this case, we can take a statistical average,

[10] Field, *op. cit.* For a detailed analysis of this problem and some related conceptual and methodological problems, see pp. 22–30.

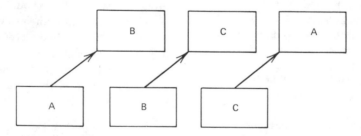

Figure 2. No group consensus; therefore, no status structure. A perceives B as higher than the rest; B perceives C as higher; and C accords A higher rank.

B. RESEARCH AND APPLICATIONS

The article (Alpert and Gatty) in this section represents an application of the discussion of role to marketing and to consumers. We learn about a method of product positioning by behavioral life-styles.

21-D PRODUCT POSITIONING BY BEHAVIORAL LIFE-STYLES

Lewis Alpert (Marketing Executive)
Ronald Gatty (Educator)

Many in marketing management realize that products which appear to be competitive products may actually be serving different segments of the consumer market, and serving them in somewhat different ways. In order to provide a basis for brand strategy, the specific factors that distinguish product-users from non-users, and users of one brand from users of a competitive brand need to be identified. The differentiation of brands by studying the ways in which their consumers differ as well as how consumer perceptions of various brands differ is termed "product positioning." Utilizing simple and direct survey questions, consumers have been described in terms of their usage and image of the brand as well as in terms of the standard demographics such as age, income, and size of family. However, more recent developments employing factor analysis have proved useful in identifying the differences between products related to consumer preferences and purchases.

This use of factor analysis goes well beyond the early brand-image studies in which the attitudinal variables were selected by subjective management judgments and motivational research. Factor analysis provides certain insights which assist in the development of hypotheses regarding which variables are important in "product positioning" and also in formulating brand profiles.

The availability of new data sources and the development of factor analysis as a guide for product positioning has enabled many major companies to use this method in studying their brand position and indentifying con-

sumer market segments on the basis of the benefits consumers are seeking. The present paper goes further, however, in demonstrating that consumer behavior as well as attitudes can be used in factor analysis for product positioning. The factors that form the basis of such product profile are referred to as "behavioral life-style" factors since they depend on behavioral patterns of purchasing and product-use. Further research effort is now being directed toward integrating multivariate measures over all aspects of the consumer, both behavioral and attitudinal, to provide a better total picture of consumer differences.

New Data Sources

Computer programs for factor analysis have now become a standard offering of several commercial research firms. Also of importance is the increasing availability of basic data on brand usage provided by syndicated research services.

Both W. R. Simmons Associates Research, Inc. and Brand Rating Research Corporation regularly conduct national probability surveys that provide a massive databank of information that can serve as a data base for studies of product positioning. In both services, extensive data are gathered through personal interviews and self-administered questionnaires or diaries on media exposure and brands purchased. This paper will show how brand position may be defined by using factor analysis and the concept of behavioral life-style factors, with data drawn from 1965 Brand Rating Index.

The approach developed can be followed for any product or brand covered by the syndicated services. The use of these concepts

SOURCE: Lewis Alpert and Ronald Gatty, "Product Positioning by Behavioral Life-Styles," *Journal of Marketing,* 33 (April, 1969), pp. 65–69.

and methodology will provide a foundation for understanding one's brand competition. They point the way to finding a framework for developing marketing and advertising goals, keeping one's own consumers, and taking advantage of the vulnerabilities of one's competitors.

The first phase of this study sets out to determine the general behavioral life-styles of men that could be inferred from consumer usage of 80 categories of products, brands, and services reported by the syndicated service. The second phase of the study will report the result of a research experiment

TABLE 1

Eighty Variables on the Use of Products and Services, Introduced as Input Data in a Factor Analysis of 5,424 Male Respondents From the 1965 Brand Rating Index Survey

1.	Car wax and polish	41.	Miles driven
2.	Regular double edge blades	42.	Pain reliever tablets
3.	Stainless steel injector	43.	Cold tablets
4.	Hair tonic	44.	Cough drops
5.	Pre-shave lotion	45.	Throat lozenges
6.	Suits	46.	Cigarettes
7.	Shoes	47.	Pictures
8.	Dress shirts	48.	Pictures without flash bulbs
9.	Sport shirts	49.	Gallons of gas
10.	Hats	50.	Regular soft drinks
11.	Rye whisky	51.	Diet soft drinks
12.	Canadian whisky	52.	After-shave lotion
13.	Bourbon	53.	Ale
14.	Scotch	54.	Miles driven in town
15.	Gin	55.	Miles driven on highway
16.	Vodka	56.	Movies
17.	Rum	57.	Hair shampoo
18.	Brandy	58.	Mouthwash
19.	Cordials or liqueurs	59.	Sleeping tablets
20.	Domestic wine	60.	Hemorrhoid remedy
21.	Imported wine	61.	Stomach remedy
22.	Bottled cocktails	62.	Headache remedy
23.	Bottled cocktail mixers	63.	Denture cream
24.	Soft drinks as highball mixers	64.	Shaving soap
25.	Airplane trips	65.	Long distance telephone calls
26.	Rented car in past year	66.	Candy bars
27.	Movie film used	67.	Packaged hard candies
28.	Motor oil	68.	Chewing gum
29.	Anti-freeze	69.	Deodorant cream
30.	Stainless steel blades	70.	Deodorant roll-on
31.	Gasoline credit cards	71.	Deodorant spray
32.	Travel credit cards	72.	Electric shave
33.	Foreign trips last year	73.	Shaving cream in cans
34.	Small cigars	74.	Shaving cream in tubes
35.	Cigarillos	75.	Lather shaving cream in tube
36.	Regular size cigars	76.	Beer
37.	Pipe tobacco	77.	Heavy drinkers, Brand Y beer
38.	Camping trips	78.	Light drinkers, Brand Y beer
39.	Ammunition	79.	Heavy drinkers, Brand W beer
40.	Three-inch tape	80.	Light drinkers, Brand W beer

TABLE 2

Factor Analysis of Product-Use Data: The First 16 Factors and Major Factor Loadings with 80 Variables

Factors and Variables	Loading Factor	Factors and Variables	Loading Factor
Factor I:		**Factor VIII:**	
The Hard Drinker		The Well-Groomed Man	
Rye whisky	.61	Hair tonic	.56
Canadian whisky	.62	After-shave lotion	.53
Bourbon	.60	Hair shampoo	.65
Scotch	.49	Mouthwash	.47
Gin	.62	**Factor IX:**	
Vodka	.59	The Cough- and Cold-Conscious	
Highball mixers	.72	Man	
Beer	.65	Cold tablets	.64
Factor II:		Cough drops	.68
The Car-Conscious Man		Throat lozenges	.71
Car wax and polish	.55	**Factor X:**	
Motor oil	.77	The Man with the Photographic	
Anti-freeze	.76	Memory	
Miles driven	.78	Unexposed movie film	.60
Gasoline	.87	Flash pictures taken	.85
Factor III:		Pictures taken without flashbulbs	.84
The Candy Consumer		**Factor XI:**	
Candy bars	.70	The Liquor and Wine Connoisseur	
Packaged hard candies	.72	Rum	.57
Chewing gum	.63	Brandy	.67
Factor IV:		Liqueurs	.66
The Cosmopolitan Traveler		Domestic wine	.53
Plane trips in past year	.67	Imported wine	.68
Car rental in past year	.68	**Factor XII:**	
Gas credit cards	.50	The Old Man	
Other credit cards	.50	Hats	.48
Foreign trips last year	.54	Denture cream	.55
Factor V:		**Factor XIII:**	
The Electric Shaver		The Hard-Driving Man	
Pre-shave lotion	.69	Miles driven in town	.83
Electric shaver	.82	Miles driven on highways	.81
Factor VI:		**Factor XIV:**	
The Cigar and Pipe Smoker		The Cocktail Drinker	
Small cigars	.71	Bottled cocktails	.81
Cigarillos	.75	Cocktail mixers	.73
Regular cigars	.67	**Factor XV:**	
Pipe tobacco	.57	The Regular Shaver	
Factor VII:		Regular double-edged blades	−.77
The Dress-Conscious Man		Stainless steel double-edged blades	.67
Suits	.54	**Factor XVI:**	
Shoes	.67	The Deodorized Male	
Dress shirts	.70	Roll-on deodorant	−.80
Sport shirts	.65	Spray deodorant	.67

illustrating the differences between specific brands of beer in terms of the purchasing patterns and behavioral life-style factors of the male consumers. Separate analyses were conducted for heavy and light users of two major brands designated as Brand W and Brand Y.

Men's Life-Style Factors for All Products

Eighty variables concerning consumer usage of products and services, as listed in Table 1, were drawn from the BRI 1965 survey data which is available on computer tape. All of the 5,424 male respondents were checked against each of the 80 categories in order to designate which of the categories are applicable to the various respondents. The original BRI data showed several degrees of frequency-of-usage so that some judgment had to be applied in determining the degree of usage that would qualify the respondent as a "user."

The factor analysis was programmed to draw out 25 factors in accord with the principal components method.[1] For each of the 80 variables the computer output lists a "factor loading" on each of the 25 extracted factors.

For purposes of illustration, 16 of these extracted factors are shown in Table 2, including the product-usage variables that are highly associated with each of the factors. The degree of usage is measured by the "factor loading." In order to determine the percentage of variation in the variable explained by that factor (that is, communality), the factor loading is squared.

Some of the factors which are associated with the use of only one or perhaps two products are designated as distinct product-use factors. Other factors, however, do suggest categories of behavioral life-styles that go well beyond the use of a single type of product and thus add to knowledge in providing a framework for identifying characteristics of people which are relevant to certain patterns of product usage.

Of the 25 extracted factors, ten seem to be associated not only with the use of a *group*

of products, but also with a pattern of purchasing a single product category. Thus factor analysis provides a characterization of the consumer that yields some interesting groupings of behavioral life-styles in purchasing which would not be apparent from simple tabulation and inspection.

Together the 25 factors yield an interesting picture of the behavioral life-styles in the purchasing patterns of the American male. The purpose here has been to contrast how these purchasing patterns differ between consumers and non-consumers of two competing brands of beer.

Life-styles of Beer Drinkers

The next step is to see how consumers of the product under study—in this case, beer —differ from non-consumers, and how consumers of one brand differ from the consumers of the major competitive brand. Tables 3 and 4 provide summarized data for drawing the contrasts.

In Table 2 beer drinking is shown to be particularly associated with the Hard Drinker. In addition, heavy beer drinkers are more clearly defined than light beer drinkers as can be seen from Table 4 where factor loading is generally higher for heavy beer drinkers. Thus, they are distinctly Hard Drinkers and not Soft Drinkers and are not inclined to be either Liquor or Wine Connoisseurs.

Brand distinctions are quite apparent among heavy beer drinkers. For example, Brand Y drinkers are Outdoorsmen, and thus more inclined to be Hard Drinkers; whereas the Brand W drinkers are more associated with the Cosmopolitan Traveler, The Dress-Conscious Man, The Well-Groomed Man, The Cocktail Drinker, and The Car-Conscious Man. Brand W drinkers seem to seek more oral satisfaction, being associated with the Candy Consumer and the Cigar and Pipe Smoker. Among light beer drinkers, approximately the same type of pattern can be discerned though with less extreme differences between the two brands.

The foregoing highlights the major differences in behavioral life-styles and product-use of the various groups of consumers, as suggested by the interpretation of the factor analyses. From this analysis come sound work-

---

[1] *Biomedical Computer Programs* (Los Angeles: School of Medicine, University of California, Revised 1965).

TABLE 3

Men's Life-Style Factors in Purchasing All Products and in Purchasing Beer[a]

Life-Style Factor	All Men	Beer Drinkers	Non-Beer Drinkers	Beer Brand Y		Beer Brand W	
				Heavy Drinkers	Light Drinkers	Heavy Drinkers	Light Drinkers
Number of Men in Sample	5424	2943	2481	188	316	99	153
1. The Hard Drinker	0	.59	−.71	1.44	.69	1.04	.20
2. The Car-Conscious Man	0	.02	−.02	−.17	.05	−.03	.24
3. The Candy Consumer	0	—	.01	.20	.07	.50	.17
4. The Cosmopolitan Traveler	0	.07	−.08	.36	.11	.48	.25
5. The Electric Shaver	0	.02	.03	−.16	−.13	−.25	−.04
6. The Cigar & Pipe Smoker	0	.09	−.10	.09	.01	.28	−.06
7. The Dress-Conscious Man	0	—	−.01	−.10	.13	−.11	.15
8. The Well-Groomed Man	0	.02	−.02	−.01	.01	.41	.17
9. The Cough- and Cold-Conscious Man	0	.08	−.09	.69	.06	.27	.13
10. The Man With A Photographic Memory	0	.01	−.01	−.42	−.04	−.33	.05
11. The Liquor & Wine Connoisseur	0	−.04	.04	−.42	.14	−.73	.06
12. The Old Man	0	−.11	.13	.06	−.32	.43	.20
13. The Hard-Driving Man	0	.04	−.05	.28	.13	.07	−.22
14. The Cocktail Drinkers	0	.01	.01	−.45	−.05	.72	.16
15. The Regular Shaver	0	−.06	.07	.68	−.20	−.49	.07
16. The Deodorized Male	0	.02	.02	.35	−.02	.32	−.07
17. The Lather Shaver I	0	.05	.06	.33	.16	−.18	−.09
18. The Lather Shaver II	0	.07	.08	.15	.06	.04	−.25
19. Light Drinkers of Beer Brand W	0	−.24	−.29	−.40	−.18	−.69	5.17
20. The Soft Drinkers	0	.04	.05	.73	.39	−.86	.22
21. The Outdoorsman	0	.07	−.08	.60	−.04	.22	−.12
22. Light Drinkers of Beer Brand Y	0	.21	−.25	−1.97	3.01	.04	−.26
23. The Bellyachers	0	.07	.09	−.99	−.09	−.30	.03
24. The Injector Blade Shavers	0	.08	−.10	.04	−.03	.20	.01
25. Drinkers of Beer Brand W	0	.04	.05	−1.76	−.02	5.56	−.18

[a] Average factor scores for each consumer segment, as a deviation from the total male segment, based on BRI 1965 data.

TABLE 4

Profile of Product Use and Behavioral Life-Styles of Beer Consumers and Heavy and Light Consumers of Major Beer Brands Y and W[a]

All Beer Consumers		Heavy Beer Consumers				Light Beer Consumers			
		Brand Y		Brand W		Brand Y		Brand W	
Hard Drinker	.88	Hard Drinker	1.40	Hard Drinker	1.33	Old Man	−.45	Cosmopolitan Traveler	.33
Old Man	−.24	Soft Drinker	−.78	Soft Drinker	−.99	Soft Drinker	.34	Car-Conscious Man	.26
Cigar & Pipe Smoker	.19	Cough- & Cold-Conscious Man	.78	Liquor & Wine Connoisseur	−.69	Cosmopolitan Traveler	.19	Cough- and Cold-Conscious Man	.22
Cough- and Cold-Conscious Man	.17	Outdoorsman	.68	Cosmopolitan Traveler	.52	Hard Drinker	.18	Well-Groomed Man	.19
Outdoorsman	.15	Liquor & Wine Connoisseur	−.46	Candy-Conscious Man	.49	Cough- & Cold-Conscious Man	.14	Soft Drinker	.17
Cosmopolitan Traveler	.15	Cocktail Drinker	−.46	Well-Groomed Man	.43	Dress-Conscious Man	.14	Hard-Driving Man	−.17
Electric Shaver	.15	Electric Shaver	.44	Cigar & Pipe Smoker	.38	Cigar & Pipe Smoker	.11	Candy-Conscious Man	.16
Hard-Driving Man	.09	Cosmopolitan Traveler	.42	Cough- & Cold-Conscious Man	.36	Liquor & Wine Connoisseur	.10	Dress-Conscious Man	.16
Liquor & Wine Connoisseur	−.08	Photographer	−.42	Photographer	−.32	Car-Conscious Man	.07	Deodorized Male	.09
		Hard-Driving Man	.33	Old Man	.30	Cocktail Drinker	−.06	Old Man	.07
		Deodorized Male	.33	Deodorized Male	.30			Photographer	.06
		Candy-Conscious Man	.19	Outdoorsman	.30				
		Car-Conscious Man	−.15	Hard-Driving Man	.12				
		Dress-Conscious Man	−.09						
		Not An Old Man	−.07						

[a] Factors are in rank order of differences from non-consumers of beer, measured in factor loadings.

ing hypotheses about consumers of a product and its major brands, which must be integrated into the overall on-going consumer research program in order to develop a fuller definition of market segments and product positioning with an expanded profile of the consumers in each segment.

A knowledge of behavioral life-styles should influence overall formation of marketing strategy for a brand, and it can also provide immediate creative guidance for advertising copy. Advertisers will be better able to identify the audience for their copy and the types of appeals which may interest them.

The development of product-positioning described in this article will add insight to the straightforward measures of consumer attitudes and demographics that have so long served as the basis of product positioning and brand positioning.

22 / Influences of Innovators and Leaders

A. BACKGROUND AND THEORY

This section begins with a look (Wasson, Sturdivant, and McConaughy) at the social process of innovation and product acceptance. Then there is a brief discussion (Zaltman) of how innovations are adopted.

22-A THE SOCIAL PROCESS OF INNOVATION AND PRODUCT ACCEPTANCE

Chester R. Wasson (Marketing Educator)
Frederick D. Sturdivant (Marketing
* Educator), and*
David H. McConaughy (Marketing
* Educator)*

Adoption of products or practices requiring new learning is usually a slowly accelerating process. Even when it can be shown that a major benefit will ensue, early adoption may meet stiff resistance. The steel plow was far from being welcomed by farmers struggling to break tough sod with clumsy wooden plows; they accused the steel plow of poisoning the soil. The modern American thinks he must carry his shower bath with him even in a camping trailer, but it took decades to get acceptance for the idea of bathtubs and regular baths. Hybrid corn was known to give a 25 percent better yield when first introduced in the 1920s, yet the Agricultural Extension Service and commercial firms both put in six years of intensive educational effort before the first 6 percent of the farmers adopted it.

Once the early adopters accept an innovation, however, the process accelerates as the neighbors and group associates see their success and discuss it with them. They thus gain

SOURCE: Chester R. Wasson, Frederick D. Sturdivant, and David H. McConaughy, *Competition and Human Behavior.* Copyright 1968 by Meredith Corporation. (Reprinted by permission of Appleton-Century-Crofts, pp. 55–59.

the assurance and any instruction needed to get them to pick up the idea and adopt it. The second six years of hybrid corn promotion ended with 80 percent adoption. We now know that any really new product which requires much ideational learning must come into use through just such a slowly accelerating process of group adoption. A reasonably solid body of research has established the general outlines of this process and of the nature of the social structures involved.[1]

All of the research indicates that the community divides into roughly five role groups with respect to such an adoption process:

1. *Innovators*—the first 2 to 3 percent of

[1] Everett Rogers. *The Diffusion of Innovations,* New York, Free Press, 1962. Herbert F. Lionberger, *Adoption of New Ideas and Practices,* Ames, Iowa, The Iowa State University Press, 1960. "America's Tastemakers No. 1 and No. 2," *The Public Opinion Index for Industry,* Princeton, Opinion Research Corporation, April, 1959, July, 1959. The Rogers and the Lionberger books are summaries of the primary studies which are available in the adoption of innovations, and they form the basis of the whole discussion of innovation in the latter part of Chapter 4, except where specific reference is made to the Opinion Research study.

the adopters. They seek out and pioneer products, often before released for general use.

2. *Early adopters* (sometimes labelled as opinion leaders, peer group leaders, key communicators, influentials, tastemakers)—the remainder of the first 12 to 15 percent of adopters. They are the earliest to try and then adopt a product idea after its general release. Until a revolutionary product gets this group's approval, it will not gain acceptance with the remainder of the group. The rest look to these early adopters for legitimation of the product. They learn of its utility and manner of use largely through face-to-face personal communication with them.

3. *Early majority*—the remainder of the first half of adopters.

4. *Late majority*—they lag behind the early majority in adoption, and their adoption tends to herald a slowdown in the adoption rate and impending market saturation.

5. *Late adopters* (also called laggards or skeptics)—the last 12 to 15 percent of adopters. They also tend to be the last to abandon a product in favor of its successor.

To this classification should be added two others: *change agents,* who are outside the group. Change agents are those professionals whose job is to influence the introduction of innovations into the group. They include such persons as technical-assistance workers in the less developed countries, agricultural-extension agents, the detail men who promote new drugs to physicians, salesmen and dealers for new products, public health officials, nurses, school administrators and teachers, and advertising and publicity people.

The gatekeeper is either a key member of the group or an expert outside advisor in a position to make decisions and choices for the spending unit. The housewife is usually the gatekeeper for the adoption of a particular brand of any household item or food. The physician is the gatekeeper for the use of a new drug. He does not consume it himself, but without his prescription we do not buy it.

The college teacher is the gatekeeper for new textbooks. A half-dozen consulting engineers design most utility plants, and products and product brands must be specified by them or they do not get introduced. The architect is the gatekeeper for many building industry applications of new materials and new products. The gatekeeper has no special place on the time continuum of adoption—he can be a gatekeeper among the late adopters as well as among the innovators.

Extensive research has demonstrated that the place of the individual group member on the time continuum of adoption is no mere accident of the timing of initial contact but reflects a true group role structure. Only selected group members can serve as effective early adopters; they have a special place in a specific structure of group interrelationships and communication.

Innovators, the very early adopters, are opinion leaders in the actual face-to-face group structure only in those situations in which the social norm is modernity and change, situations in which the element of change or progress itself has high prestige. The opinion leader must be the highest prestige member of the group, and we now know that the leader in any group must be one who conforms more closely to the norms of the group than any other member. Innovators also exist in some communities in which the norm is traditionalist, but they do not normally have a great deal of prestige. They are outside the local informal face-to-face groups and their own social contacts are with similar people in other areas. They are watched but not followed until a high prestige opinion leader only slightly ahead of his group adopts the change. This difference in the structure of two types of communities indicates converse sides of the same principle: *changes are adopted as a result of the personal influence of another member of the group who is of the same or only slightly higher degree of innovativeness.* The innovator can be the opinion leader in the modern community because the rest of the community is only a little behind him. In a traditionalist community, too great a gap of innovativeness exists between him and the rest of the community.

The adoption process itself can be diagrammed as a tree which can be conceived

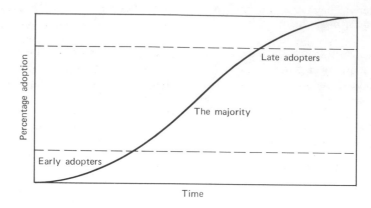

Figure 1. The adoption cycle, adopter characteristics, and information sources.

of as either a communication network or as a system of adoption. Information about the product comes to the group from the outside through an opinion leader, then passes through him to others who have a relatively early adoption tendency. The latter transmit knowledge of the benefits and methods of use to a larger number who are just a little slower to adopt, and so on. Lionberger has summarized what several scores of agricultural studies show about the characteristics of farm operators and the major sources of farm in-

formation used in the relation to the adoption curve as indicated in Figure 1.

Note the close relationship between social participation and time of adoption, and note also that the early adopters *are open to and do seek information sources outside the group,* whereas the early and late majorities depend heavily on local opinion leaders and other sources close to home. In the language of the sociologist the early adopter is more *cosmopolite* than later adopters—his orientation tends to be more with the external society

Early Adopters	The Majority	Late Adopters
Distinctive Characteristics*		
Large farms	Average farms	Small farms
High income	Average income	Low income
Take risks	Age 50 to 60	Security-minded
Usually under age 50	Receptive but not	Usually over age 60
Actively seeking	actively seeking	Complacent or skeptical
new ideas	Participate in some	Seldom participate
Participate in many	local groups	in formal groups
nonlocal groups		
Sources of Information Used**		
Colleges and other	Adoption leaders and	Other local farmers
research sources	other farmers nearby	and adoption leaders
Agricultural agencies	Farm papers, maga-	Farm papers, maga-
Mass media sources	zines and radio	zines and radio
Other highly competent	Commercial sources	Local dealers
farmers far and near	Agricultural agencies	Almanac
Commercial sources		

* In relation to characteristics of those in adjoining categories.
** Listed in estimated rank order of use.
SOURCE: Reproduced by permission from Herbert F. Lionberger, *Adoption of New Ideas and Practices,* © 1961 by The Iowa State University Press, Ames, Iowa, page 34.

and news sources than that of later adopters. It is he who picks up the idea from advertising, news and publicity articles, and commercial sources he trusts. Thus it becomes doubly important for the seller, who is always an outsider, to concentrate the introductory efforts on this early-adopter group. They are the only group open enough to perceive the potential importance of the benefit package the seller has to offer. They are the only ones who will respond immediately, if what he offers is a true innovation.

22-B ADOPTION OF INNOVATIONS

Gerald Zaltman (Sociologist)

It is important, therefore, that businessmen understand how people *learn to like*, for this will explain to some extent how they come to adopt objects and ideas. There are basically two types of learning involved: cognitive (or perceptual) learning and affective learning. *Cognitive learning* is the process by which an individual becomes consciously aware of a stimulus. Marketing men are interested in this type of learning because they are anxious to determine such things as how long the average consumer must listen to a jingle before it becomes "familiar" to him. *Affective learning* takes place when the consumer begins to "like" a product stimulus after he has become consciously aware of it. Knowledge of affective learning provides insights into the problem of how long it is necessary for a person to listen or look before he "likes" a product. There is an important interrelationship between these two concepts of learning.

Learning has been defined as:

> . . . the process by which an activity originates or is changed through reacting to an encountered situation, provided that the characteristics of the change in activity cannot be explained on the basis of native response tendencies, maturation, or temporary states of the organism [for example, fatigue, drugs].[1]

The most fundamental elements of the learning process are termed the drive, the cue, the response, and the reinforcement.[2] A *drive* is a strong stimulus such as great physical pain (primary drive) or a keen desire to succeed in a vocation (secondary or learned drive). The *response* is the effort made to satisfy the drive, to alleviate the pain, or to succeed in one's vocation. *Cues* are the stimuli that determine which response is made and when and where it is made. Stimuli also serve as cues. A traffic signal to "Stop" or "Go" is a stimulus functioning as a cue. Thus stimuli may vary in strength (in which case they are drives) and in kind and distinctiveness (in which case they are cues). Furthermore, "different strengths of stimulation may themselves be distinctive and hence serve as cues."[3] Hunger is a stimulus that functions both as a drive and as a cue. As a drive it motivates a person to try to locate food. The hungrier one is, the greater the drive. Yet hunger may also vary in kind as well as in strength. A person may be hungry ("have a craving") for Chinese food or he may have a sudden desire for something sweet. This more specific stimulus, indicating the kind of food a person is hungry for, is a cue that determines the response made (going to a Chinese restaurant, buying a candy bar) to satisfy the drive. Thus, a person may make one response when just a little hungry and another response when very hungry.

Reinforcement, or reward, occurs when a response is followed by a reduction in the strength of the drive. The effect of the reinforcement is to strengthen the relationship between a cue and the satisfying response. The next time the same drive occurs, the same response is more apt to be made. Reinforcement, or reward, is the basic prerequisite for habit formation; rewarding a response in-

SOURCE: Gerald Zaltman, *Marketing: Contributions from the Behavioral Sciences* (New York: Harcourt, Brace & World, Inc., 1965), pp. 19–22.
[1] Ernest R. Hilgard, *Theories of Learning*, 2nd ed. (New York: Appleton-Century-Crofts, 1956), p. 3.
[2] For an excellent discussion of the essential elements involved in learning, see John Dollard and

Neal E. Miller, *Personality and Psychotherapy* (New York: McGraw-Hill, 1950), pp. 25–61.
[3] *Ibid.*, p. 33.

creases the probability of its recurrence. *Learning occurs when the repeated reinforcement of a response triggered by a cue causes a more or less permanent change in an individual's behavior.*

A product or service that satisfies a physiological need (such as hunger) or a psychological need (such as prestige) thus becomes a reinforcing agent, or, as it is often called, a goal-object. Each time reinforcement occurs there is an increased likelihood that when the same drive is again experienced the same goal-object will be sought. Each time the same goal-object produces a reward, further reinforcement occurs. This will obviously bring about a change in behavior if the likelihood of reuse is increased with each successive satisfactory trial of the item. This type of behavior change is called learning. For example, a headache causes a certain *drive*, that is, a desire to reduce the headache. Having had a satisfactory past experience with a particular brand of aspirin containing a new ingredient (cue), the consumer will be apt (reaction potential) to repurchase (response) the same brand of aspirin. The brand of aspirin with the special ingredient is thus the goal-object.

There is an interrelationship among the fundamental learning factors. Cues are the distinctive characteristics of a product or innovation. If the value of these cues is highly esteemed, then the amount of reward perceived is correspondingly high. The customer perceives the cues of an innovation as a means of reducing the drive. This cue-response connection is the essence of learning. Cues may take the form of a brand name, a package design, a product category or a price-size relationship, a certain quality, or any other product attribute. For example, a desire for a particular type of food may be aroused by an advertisement or by observing others eating that food. A cue, in the form of a low price or well-known brand name, may encourage a favorable shopping response. If the consumer is rewarded to his satisfaction, he will continue to respond favorably to the same cues or goal-objects because of this gratifying past experience. The buyer has learned that this cue is a means of satisfying a drive. For this reason we say that cues are the stimuli that determine which response is made. The buyer may also learn that a competing brand does not satisfy the same need as economically or as quickly. This may result in a more or less permanent change in behavior; he may avoid the competing product. Thus, a continually rewarded response may result in *discrimination* among products. *Comparative shopping is an important part of the process whereby a consumer "learns" that the purchase of one product or brand is more rewarding than the purchase of another.*

One further point may prove useful. When learning has occurred there will usually be a hierarchy of responses. For example, suppose that a shopper has in mind certain price-quality-size relationships that must be met before his drive can be satisfied. Past results will have established that some brands just meet these requirements, some go beyond, and some brands fall short. A relatively consistent preference for brand A over brands B, C, and D is evidence that learning has occurred. Learning is also characterized by the consistent buying of brand B (rather than C or D) when A is absent, if B is known by the consumer to fulfill the minimum price-quality-size requirements of the drive. This can have a negative effect on brand A, of course. The greater the perceived similarity between A and B, the greater the chances that consumer will substitute B for A. If A and B were brands of aspirin, for example, with the same ingredients and the same price, they would be equally attractive goal-objects. This would cause a high degree of *generalization*. Generalization, in this instance, occurs when the consumer responds favorably to products that are similar to the one he preferred originally. The minimum differences between A and B perceivable to the consumer are known as the *differential threshold.*

B. RESEARCH AND APPLICATIONS

The material presented in this section deals with an analysis (Robertson) of the social factors in innovative behavior.

22-C SOCIAL FACTORS IN INNOVATIVE BEHAVIOR

Thomas S. Robertson (Marketing Educator)

HYPOTHESES. Innovators possess predispositional characteristics that distinguish them from noninnovators. Innovators are:

- More venturesome in their consumption behavior than noninnovators.
- More socially integrated within their communities.
- More cosmopolitan in outlook.
- More socially mobile.
- Overprivileged relative to fellow community members.

DESIGN. The empirical inquiry proceeded by selecting one particular innovation and examining its consumer innovators and noninnovators within a defined community. This chosen innovation was the Touch-Tone (push-button) telephone; the selected community was the middle-class, suburban Chicago township of Deerfield, Illinois. The Touch-Tone innovation was of general relevance to community members, and installation was available for all households.

Innovators were defined as the first 10% of the community's members to adopt. The sample consisted of 100 respondents, including 60 innovators and 40 noninnovators. This breakdown was deemed advisable to effectively investigate the predispositional factors and also to trace in detail the flow of communication which innovators utilized.

The Touch-Tone innovator population included all family units within the city of Deerfield who specifically requested Touch-Tone before November 1, 1965. For example, the purchase sequence was instituted at their volition and not at the initiative of the telephone company. This amounted to approximately 200 adopting units. (Excluded were unlisted telephone number households and households where Illinois Bell studies had been conducted within the previous year.) The non-Touch-Tone population included all family units within the city of Deerfield who did not innovate in Touch-Tone purchasing and who lived within a one-block radius of a Touch-Tone innovator.

PROCEDURE. The data-gathering approach was through an in-home personal interview with the female head of the household. She was chosen as the "spokesman" for the family consumption unit. Due to the complexity of the behavior being studied, depth interviews, administered by professional interviewers, were necessary. The philosophy was to probe the respondent's conception of herself and her family, their community role, and her configuration of thoughts toward innovative behavior. In this way, it was felt, the predispositional factors could be investigated most insightfully.

SAMPLING. The sample selection proceeded where Touch-Tone innovators were concentrated on a geographic basis within the sample location (Deerfield). Concentrated cluster sampling allowed the maximum opportunity for studying the interpersonal relationships of community members. These geographic concentrations were evidenced by plotting the Touch-Tone innovators on a city map. The street with the largest number of Touch-Tone innovators was chosen first and interviews arranged by phone with each innovator on that street. Noninnovator appointments were made with individuals living within a one-block radius. Streets with fewer Touch-Tone innovators were chosen next and the same procedure followed.

Analysis was conducted in line with the

SOURCE: Thomas S. Robertson, "Social Factors in Innovative Behavior," in Harold H. Kassarjian and Thomas S. Robertson, Editors, *Perspectives in Marketing* (Glenview, Illinois: Scott, Foresman & Co., 1968), pp. 361–370, at pp. 364–370.

TABLE 1

Predispositional Factor Results

	Group	Degree of Variable (%)[a]			Mean Variable Score (17.00)	Significance Level of Mean Difference
		High	Medium	Low		
Venturesome-ness	Innovators	69	53	15	4.88 ⎱	.01
	Noninnovators	31	47	85	4.12 ⎰	
Social integration	Innovators	63	44	50	4.13 ⎱	.05
	Noninnovators	37	56	50	3.78 ⎰	
Cosmopolitism	Innovators	10	48	58	2.77 ⎱	.10
	Noninnovators	90	52	42	3.03 ⎰	
Social mobility	Innovators	68	47	35	3.93 ⎱	.05
	Noninnovators	32	53	65	3.20 ⎰	
Privilege	Innovators	70	46	42	3.68 ⎱	.01
	Noninnovators	30	54	58	3.25 ⎰	

[a] All results are adjusted for the difference in innovator (60) versus noninnovator (40) sample sizes.

hypotheses, both quantitatively and qualitatively. Responses to open-end questions were coded by predispositional factor so that scores measuring each hypothesis were obtained. Analysis also proceeded on a qualitative level, taking advantage of the richness in response patterns.

Scoring

An example of the scoring procedure follows for the social mobility variable. A similar procedure was used for all other variables. Five questionnaire components yield the social mobility score. The answers to these components can be arranged on seven-point scales from high social mobility to low social mobility. The mean of the several components gives the social mobility score for the respondent.

The questionnaire components used were the following:

1. Questions measuring occupational mobility: "What is your husband's occupation?" "What position did your husband hold before this one?"

2. Questions measuring locational mobility: "How long have you lived at this address?" "How often have you moved within the last five years?"

3. Questions measuring friendship patterns in terms of continuity or change: "What about your friends and the friends that you and your husband have together? Where do you know them from and how long have you known them?"

4. Questions measuring organizational mobility: "How often do you give up one organization and join another?"

5. Questions measuring intended neighborhood mobility patterns: "What do you dislike about your neighborhood?" "If you move, what kind of neighborhood would you like to move to?" "Why?"

In total, these various components of mobility allow the assignment of a social mobility score. This score measures past mobility and also considers anticipated mobility.[1]

Results

Predispositional factor results are summarized in Table 1. The percentages of innovators and noninnovators falling within the high, medium, and low categories on each factor are indicated, as well as the mean scores obtained by each group and the significance level of the difference between the means. Percentages are adjusted for the difference in sample sizes—60 innovator and 40 noninnovator respondents. The mean scores are based on a maximum possible score of 7.0

[1] A factor not investigated in the present research is whether the effect of these five characteristics would change across different product categories.

(most venturesome, most socially integrated, etc.), while the minimum possible score is 1.0.

It is shown that the only refutation of the hypotheses occurs in the cosmopolitism variable. All other variables bear significant findings in the postulated direction.

VENTURESOMENESS. Innovators are significantly higher on venturesomeness. They more readily take new product risks. This is revealed in their actual purchases of innovations, in their stated willingness to buy hypothetical innovations, and in their self-conceptions in regard to new-product purchase behavior.

Innovators for the Touch-Tone innovation were more likely to have purchased other home-appliance innovations. In a list of 13 innovations, including the electric knife, electric broom, color television, and electric toothbrush, innovators adopted an average of 6.2 items while noninnovators adopted 4.5 (Table 2).

Self-conceptions of innovators and noninnovator respondents regarding new product purchases are revealed in the following responses.

Question: "How do you feel about buying new things that come out for the home?"

Innovator responses: "I'm very interested in trying them. The minute I see new things advertised I try to find them in the stores."

"I'm terrible for that. I try everything. If you don't have them you don't miss them, but if you have them you need them."

Noninnovator responses: "We're not real anxious to buy new things. We're quite conservative about what we buy and think a long time before we do."

TABLE 2

Adoption Rates of Thirteen Home-Appliance Innovations

Number of Innovations Purchased	Innovators (N = 60)	Non-innovators (N = 40)
10 to 13	7%	0%
8 to 9	20	10
6 to 7	33	25
4 to 5	31	30
2 to 3	7	25
0 to 1	2	10
Mean/13	6.2	4.5

"I am very conservative. I'm very slow when it comes to buying new things."

A foremost implication for marketers is that *innovators for a new product are likely to be drawn from past innovators for similar products.* First purchasers of a company's new product offering may well coincide with purchasers of its previous new product offerings.

Since innovators perceive themselves as first buyers, they perhaps should be advertised to in accordance with their self-conceptions. The sales appeals could be to "knowledgeable individuals who distinguish themselves by new product purchases to better fulfill their needs."

SOCIAL INTEGRATION. Innovators are more socially integrated within their neighborhoods. They interact with more people, perceive themselves to be more popular; perceive the neighborhood to be more socially oriented; and believe in formal organizations more, although they belong to somewhat fewer.

A primary implication here is that innovators are more in touch with other people and, therefore, more inclined to influence and be influenced by other people. This suggests that personal influence channels of communication are of particular importance in appealing to the innovator. It is further suggested that the innovator be encouraged to influence his peers.

Suggestions that marketers utilize personal influence are not new. The problem is how to implement a personal influence strategy. The major drawback has been the identification of "opinion leaders." In the present instance, however, innovators are identified by purchase of the product and are known to have high potential influence because of their many contacts with other people. Such innovators could be appealed to directly to "tell your friends" and could be provided with product ammunition such as catalogs and information releases. Rather than ceasing to appeal to innovators once they have purchased, communications might be increased.

COSMOPOLITISM. Innovators are less cosmopolitan; they are somewhat more oriented toward their local community. This is the only unconfirmed hypothesis. However, this finding may in fact make sense. If the innovator is socially integrated within his local neighborhood group, it would appear that he might also be more oriented toward that group.

In the studies of farmer and physician innovators, they were found to be more cosmopolitan in outlook. They looked beyond their communities to cosmopolitan sources of information on innovation. It may well be that consumer information sources are so diffuse that one need not look beyond the local community. How cosmopolitan does the individual have to be to learn of a new electric appliance? It will be advertised in his local newspaper or in national magazines, and there really is no cosmopolitan source of information.

For consumer products other than home appliances, however, a cosmopolitism hypothesis might again be in order. For products which have no mass appeal but are of specialized interest, the innovator might be cosmopolitan. The "tastemaker" study, for example, looked at auto rentals, credit cards, and traveler's checks, and here it might be hypothesized that the innovator was a cosmopolitan.

SOCIAL MOBILITY. Innovators are more socially mobile. They climb up the social class ladder and aspire to further advancement. This is nowhere better revealed than in the question relating to movement from the neighborhood.

Question: "If you move, what kind of neighborhood would you like to move to?"

Innovator responses: "My husband would like to move east of the tracks but this is very expensive. I would rather find something we could afford. [Where?] An upper-middle-class neighborhood—an older refined elegance, nicely maintained, with more conveniences."

"Older, more established homes, but they cost so much we just couldn't afford them. I mean like $100,000 homes . . ."

Noninnovator responses: "I'd like to move to a small town. I don't care for the pace. I don't want to have to watch the next guy, and I don't like to try to climb up the social ladder. We just like to be left alone."

"Just about the same. Maybe a little more stable people who won't be moving in and out quite so frequently."

Advertising and sales strategies and appeals should [deal] with the innovator who is moving up the status hierarchy. To him, the purchase of new products may signify his arrival or may be a means of conspicuous consumption. Perhaps the socially mobile person is going through new life experiences and is therefore more accustomed to newness and more drawn toward new product experiences. Whatever the underlying motivations, marketers must make their products meaningful to the socially aspiring consumer innovator.

PRIVILEGE. The privilege measure reveals that innovators are more financially privileged than other community members. They have higher discretionary income than their neighbors and perceive themselves to be richer. Thus, within one fairly homogeneous community, the innovators are relatively overprivileged.

Innovators are also found to be less concerned with cost. Only 42% knew the exact cost of the Touch-Tone innovation, while 32% had absolutely no idea. When noninnovators were asked reasons against adoption of the product, 33% mentioned cost. When asked what kind of information they would want before considering purchase, 40% expressed a desire for price information.

Innovators need not come from the highest income levels in society but may well come from the overprivileged sectors of each social class. Here again, the product category to which the innovation belongs would bear an influence. Innovators are less concerned with cost and should be appealed to accordingly.

ECONOMIC INFLUENCES

A. BACKGROUND AND THEORY

The first article in this section is a presentation of an economic model (Tucker). Next the topic of profit and its importance is explored (Homans).

23-A THE ECONOMIC MODEL

W. T. Tucker (Marketing Educator)

The primary economic model relevant to consumer behavior is as explicit but not so complex as the psychological. It adds few important constructs save those that make the essentially direct hedonic position somewhat more operational. It does stress an aspect of choice behavior that psychology generally pays little attention to: the scarcity of resources. The decision not to buy or not to save may be a concomitant of the resource level more than the drive level. Economists tend to disregard the drive level, except in such fairly crude terms as Keynes' propensity to spend, just as psychologists tend to treat resource levels as given.

There are suggestions in economic analysis that one *may* forgo an intense pleasure in order to—and here words fail. Almost anything that can be said suggests a greater desire of some sort simply because of English syntax and Anglo-Saxon predisposition. The closest approximation is to suggest that one does not choose what one wants so much as what one can choose. This statement does limited but important violence to the notion. In formal analysis, economists accept the distortion in order to deal rigorously with choices in terms of assortments of choices.

Imagine a child at an amusement park. He

has limited time; he has limited money; and he has a limited capacity for sensation. He might well take a fairly unexciting ride first, not because it offered the greatest return for his expenditure in any usual sense, but largely because it would not seriously deplete his ability to derive thrills from subsequent activities. In any case, his scarce resources might be more important in the process of choosing than any combination of drive states, stimuli, or reinforcement. Of course, this is not to say that choice behavior of any sort defies purely psychological explanation, even if one deals with only that restricted portion of psychological theory suggested earlier.

Economic theory is, in the analysis of consumer behavior (or consumer demand), as elegant as in other areas of analysis. With a limited number of assumptions it concludes that there is one, and only one, assortment of rides and exhibits in the amusement park that will maximize the child's satisfaction. The normal presumption is that the consumer knows the price and availability of all alternatives and can properly assess the satisfaction to be derived from each. Such an assumption is surely less acceptable for the child than for an adult, surely less valid in an amusement park than in the supermarket. It has a certain intuitive acceptability in either case.

The second assumption is that sequential rides on the carousel will each deliver less satisfaction than the last. This is the notion of marginal utility so thoroughly developed by

SOURCE: W. T. Tucker, *Foundation for a Theory of Consumer Behavior*, Copyright 1967, Holt, Rinehart and Winston, Inc. Reprinted by permission of Holt, Rinehart and Winston, pp. 8–9.

Marshall. Other assumptions state possible relationship of the carousel to the roller coaster. The child may prefer the roller coaster to the carousel, the carousel to the roller coaster, or he may have no preference between the two. And his preferences are transitive. If he prefers the carousel to the roller coaster and the roller coaster to the fun house, he must prefer the carousel to the fun house.

Given these assumptions it is possible to develop mathematically precise descriptions of the ways in which the child's choices of assortment will change when prices or any of the rides change or when he is given more money to spend. And, if one could measure the utiles (units of satisfaction) involved in the various rides, he could predict the specific assortment that would be chosen. But even

lacking this, he could, by observing the assortment actually chosen, draw some conclusions about the shape of the child's indifference curve. An indifference curve is one connecting all assortments that deliver equal satisfaction, for instance:

$$5 \text{ Carousel} + 3 \text{ Roller Coaster} =$$
$$10 \text{ C} + 1 \text{ RC} = 3 \text{ C} + 8 \text{ RC}$$

The one chosen will be whichever of these combinations (or of the other possible equal-utility assortments that lie on the curve) costs the least. When the cost of the roller-coaster ride is low compared with the cost of the carousel, the assortment chosen will be quite different from that chosen when the cost of the roller-coaster ride is high in comparison to that of the carousel.

23-B PROFIT

George Caspar Homans (Sociologist)

We define psychic *profit* as reward less cost, and we argue that no exchange continues unless both parties are making a profit. Even the pigeon, when it finds its rewards and costs nicely balanced, may try to get out of the situation or indulge in emotional behavior rather than continue its exchange with the psychologist. But our argument is more familiar in the field of human buying and selling, and we shall illustrate it from this field.

Suppose I go into a store to buy a can of coffee at the price of one dollar. From one point of view the value of what I get is a dollar, the cost of what I give is a dollar, reward and cost both equal price, and therefore in terms of accounting I have made no profit on the transaction. The same is true of the storekeeper: he makes no profit on this single transaction considered by itself. It takes at least two transactions to make an accounting profit, as when the storekeeper sells me the coffee for more money than it cost him earlier when he bought it from the wholesaler. In short, this point of view eschews any consideration of the psychological value of the

SOURCE: George Caspar Homans, *Social Behavior: Its Elementary Forms* (New York: Harcourt, Brace and World, Inc., 1961), pp. 61–64. © 1961 by Harcourt, Brace and World, Inc., and reprinted with their permission.

coffee and the money to the storekeeper and myself.

But we in this respect may not avoid psychological value, either positive or negative, and so we must take another look at the transaction. From this point of view the value of what I get is the value to me of a can of coffee. And what is its cost? In our terms it is not the dollar but the forgone value of the alternative uses I might have made of the dollar. Moreover, the value of what I get is greater than the value of what I have given up, for if at the moment I saw any better use for my dollar I should presumably not have bought the coffee. In our present terms, I have a profit. It may not be a great profit: I may be pretty evenly balanced between buying the coffee and not buying it. But a psychic profit for the moment I have.

Nor am I the only party to the transaction. How about the storekeeper? When he sells the coffee he has my dollar. That is his reward, but what is his cost? What has he forgone? Just as I have forgone the alternative uses of the dollar, he has forgone the alternative uses of the coffee; but in his position he has little use for it unless he sells it to someone. At the moment my dollar is more valuable to him than the coffee, and he too is making a psychic profit, even though later, when he balances his books, he may find that he has lost money, that he has no accounting profit, on this batch of coffee. The open secret of human exchange is to give the other man behavior that is more valuable to him than it is costly to you and to get from him behavior that is more valuable to you than it is costly to him.[1]

One further question: Why is it that the coffee is more valuable to me than the dollar, and the dollar more valuable to the storekeeper than the coffee? The reason is that, at the moment of the transaction, I am relatively—never absolutely, of course—long on dollars and short of coffee, and the storekeeper is relatively short of dollars and long on coffee and other groceries. Once dollars and coffee are established as reinforcers, it is the degree to which we are deprived of them that determines their value.

So far we have considered the profit on a single transaction, but what if the transactions continue? Let us think in terms of Person and Other. At the time of their first exchange both make a profit. Person badly needs help, and he does not give up much in self-respect in asking for help only once. Other is skillful and can well afford to give up a little time from his own work if he gets for it the warm approval of Person. Both having found the exchange profitable they repeat it, and what happens? Our propositions tell us that the more approval Other has gotten from Person in past transactions, the less valuable to him any further approval becomes; and the more help he has given Person, the more costly any further helping becomes in time lost from his own work. In the same way, the more help Person has gotten from Other, the less, for

the time being, he needs any further help and the more costly he finds any further confession of inferiority. A little inferiority may not cost much, but the cost of much conspicuous inferiority may rise disproportionately. The profits from exchange decrease with the number of exchanges, that is, with the time spent in exchange. And there probably will come a time in the course of a day in the office when Other begins to feel that the cost of helping Person any more is greater than its reward, and spends the rest of the day doing his own work. Something of the same sort is probably true of Person. In other words, the less a man's profit on a particular unit-activity, the more likely he is to change his next unit to the alternative.

Let us sum up what we have had to say so far about profit. Though we use the word because it suggests a difference between two values, our profit is not the profit of accounting. Accounting profit is measured by comparing two transactions, such as the money a merchant spent for a pound of coffee with the money he later sold it for. For us profit is a matter of a single transaction. Profit is the difference between the value of the reward a man gets by emitting a particular unit-activity and the value of the reward obtainable by another unit-activity, forgone in emitting the first. This we call the profit per unit. If it is true that the more valuable the reward of a particular activity, the more often a man will emit it, but the more costly, the less often he will do so, then the less his profit per unit, the less likely he is to make the next unit he emits another of the same kind. This further means that he is more likely to change his next unit to the alternative activity; and the point of zero profit comes where the probability of change between alternatives is greatest. If we are to explain a change from one activity to the next we badly need the notions of cost and profit.

[1] C. I. Barnard, *The Functions of the Executive* (Cambridge, Mass., 1938), pp. 253–55; N. W. Chamberlain, *A General Theory of Economic Process* (New York, 1955), pp. 80–85.

B. RESEARCH AND APPLICATIONS

This chapter ends with a report (Smith and Broome) of a laboratory experiment for establishing indifference prices between brands of consumer products.

23-C A LABORATORY EXPERIMENT FOR ESTABLISHING INDIFFERENCE PRICES BETWEEN BRANDS OF CONSUMER PRODUCTS

Edward M. Smith (Marketing Educator) and Charles L. Broome (Marketing Educator)

The traditional view in marketing is that quality is somehow related to cost, and that quality is a major determinant of the price which may be charged for a product. As an intrafirm concept this view is possibly valid. However, for interfirm comparisons the cost-quality relationships are less likely to hold true. Firms have different cost conditions arising from differences in managerial ability; differences in the quality of raw materials, labor, and supplies; differences in plant and equipment; and differences in marketing efficiency.

Absolute homogeneity, of course, is impossible. In nature no two things are ever exactly alike. Wheat grown in two different fields will never contain exactly the same mineral, vitamin, and protein content. Handmade products likewise vary in shape, quality of workmanship, etc., even when they are meant to be alike and are produced by skilled craftsmen. Machine-made parts also are only approximately alike, depending on the degree of tolerance permitted. Even if all products were carefully classified into numerous types and grades, differences would still be found within each group. The only kind of "commodity" which is truly homogeneous is the kind whose value lies in the privilege accorded to its owner of claiming some stipulated benefit—for example, postage stamps, railroad tickets, securities. Aside from these

exceptional cases, homogeneity is merely a convenient simplification, like the statistician's device of lumping different data into a single class.[1]

Just as quality-cost relationships are acknowledged as being basic in many types of pricing decisions for the firm, some writers have suggested that price may be a determinant of the consumer's perception of quality. For instance, Gabor and Granger cited some cases in which products met consumer resistance because the prices were initially set too low.[2]

Scitovsky suggests that inexpertness of the consumer as a shopper has led to the judging of quality by indices of quality, an important one of which is price. He further suggests that consumers often associate two prices with a commodity—the "normal" or "fair" price and the actual price which must be paid. The difference in the two prices suggests to the consumer how cheap or expensive the commodity is.[3] Scitovsky suggests that the situation is different for new products. "A new commodity has no traditional price, no past reputation; its quality, therefore, is likely to be appraised partly or wholly on the basis of its present price."[4]

Source: Edward M. Smith and Charles L. Broome, "A Laboratory Experiment for Establishing Indifference Prices Between Brands of Consumer Products," in Raymond M. Haas, Editor, *Science, Technology & Marketing* (Chicago: American Marketing Association, 1968), pp. 511–519.

[1] Lawrence Abbott, *Quality and Competition: An Essay in Economic Theory* (New York: Columbia University Press, 1955), pp. 14–15.

[2] André Gabor and Clive Granger, "The Pricing of New Products," *Scientific Business*, August, 1965, p. 143.

[3] Tibor Scitovsky, "Some Consequences of the Habit of Judging Quality by Price," *The Review of Economic Studies*, Vol. 12 (1944–1945), p. 101.

[4] *Ibid.*

A purchase is the end result of a consumer decision-making process. Uncertainty as to the criteria of quality to be used, the completeness and reliability of the information held on each criterion, and the uncertainty about the predictive value of each criterion may lead, in conditions of inadequate informational inputs, to a tendency to judge quality on the basis of price.[5]

Further, under conditions of uncertainty, other types of information, in addition to price information, may influence a person's evaluation and perception of a brand. Scitovsky has made reference to "indices of quality,"[6] and Tull, Boring, and Gonsior have referred to "a variety of informational inputs concerning a set of criteria . . . for judging the product."[7] Knowledge of a brand's position in its respective market, for example, might influence a person's evaluation and perception of the quality of a brand.

Unfortunately, we know too little about the kinds of information consumers desire about the products which they purchase, how actively they seek information, and precisely how the available information is used in buying decisions. Under certain conditions it is reasonable to believe that consumers do follow simplified decision rules based upon a belief that the higher the price, the higher the quality. It is possible, however, that these simplified decision rules are principally in high risk situations or only when better information is unavailable. This type of speculation leads to the possibility that the effect of price and market-standing information may not equally affect brands in all classes of products, or brands of varying degrees of familiarity.

Important questions for marketing management can be raised. What is the best price level at which a new product should be introduced? What type of informational strategy should a given firm use? (The informational strategy most certainly should be different for low price and high price firms.) What information do consumers use in judging quality and how are these criteria ordered?

This paper will describe an experiment conducted for the purpose of gathering data to test hypotheses about the effect of price and market-standing information on consumers' brand preferences. The study, of which this is a part, had three major purposes: (1) to test hypotheses about the effect of price and market-standing information on consumers' brand preferences, (2) to test hypotheses about consumers' consistency in expressing brand preferences, and (3) to develop an experimental methodology for collecting data of the type needed to test the hypotheses.

Hypotheses

The following two hypotheses were tested in the study:

1. Consumers' brand preferences will be the same with and without price information about the brands.
2. Consumers' brand preferences will be the same with and without information about brand market standings.

Subjects and Laboratory Facilities

The laboratory part of the study was conducted at the University of Alabama during the period February 23 to March 8, 1966. Wives of University of Alabama students were the subjects in the study. Letters were sent to 311 wives of University of Alabama students inviting them to participate in a brand preference study. These letters were followed up in from two to six days by a personal call by a student asistant who interviewed the potential subjects to obtain a commitment for a definite date and time. Of the 311 wives invited to participate, 196, or 63 per cent, took part in the study.

Laboratory sessions were scheduled so as to make it as convenient as possible for the subjects to participate. A total of twenty laboratory sessions were scheduled. No more than twenty-five subjects were to be scheduled for any one session.

Subjects were residents of two University of Alabama married student housing projects. Space convenient to the housing projects was obtained for conducting the laboratory part of the study. In order to minimize the in-

[5] D. S. Tull, R. A. Boring, and M. H. Gonsior, "A Note on the Relationship of Price and Imputed Quality," *The Journal of Business*, Vol. 37 (April, 1964), p. 186.
[6] Scitovsky, *op. cit.*, p. 100.
[7] Tull, *loc. cit.*

fluence of distractions at home and differences arising from the persons who administered the tests, central locations were used rather than conducting the sessions in the subjects' homes. Seventeen of the sessions were held in a classroom of an elementary school located near one of the student housing projects. The remaining three sessions were held in classrooms on the campus in a building adjacent to the second housing project.

The requirements for physical facilities were minimal for this study and consisted of individual work spaces for the subjects, work space for use by assistants in preparing the sets of decision forms, and display arrangements for the products and market-standing and price information. The laboratory facilities were far from ideal, but the high degree of participation due to the convenient locations more than offset any disadvantages.

Data and Experimental Methodology

The hypotheses regarding the effect of price and market-standing information on consumers' brand preferences were tested through an analysis of variance technique developed by Henry Scheffé for paired comparisons data showing degrees of preference.[8] The basic units of data were indifference prices determined for each subject between every possible pair of brands in every product class. The indifference prices between the pairs of brands were determined in cents.

TEST GROUPS. In order to determine whether or not the influence of price and market-standing information was different depending upon the type of product and the degree of familiarity with the brands, four different product classes of low-cost, consumer goods were selected and for each class of product both known and unknown brands were used. The following product classes were used: toothpaste, sweet peas, coffee, and aspirin tablets. For each product class six known and six unknown brands were selected.

Brand preferences were determined through the use of paired comparisons tests. For each group there was a corresponding

[8] Henry Scheffé, "An Analysis of Variance For Paired Comparisons," *American Statistical Association Journal*, Vol. 47 (September, 1952), pp. 381–400.

control group involving the same brands of the products. Each group of subjects was designated either a "price," "market-standing," or "control" group. Subjects in the price groups were given information about the brands, and those in the market-standing groups were given information about the market standings of the brands. Subjects in the control groups were given no additional information. The brands were displayed and were available for examination by all groups.

Each group of subjects made decisions involving six brands in each of four product classes. Brands in two of the product classes were well-known to the subjects, and the brands in the remaining two product classes were unknown to the subjects. For example, a group could have been given known brands of coffee and aspirin tablets and unknown brands of sweet peas and toothpaste. The unknown brands were, for the most part, dealers' brands selected from other sections of the United States.

PAIRED COMPARISONS TESTS. A paired comparisons technique was used to determine brand preferences. Since degrees of preference were desired, a two-step paired comparisons technique was used. The subjects were first given lists of the fifteen pairs of brands in each product class. The subjects were instructed to circle the brand in each pair of brands which they would prefer to receive as a gift. This procedure established simple preferences, such as Brand A preferred over Brand B.

After these simple brand comparisons were made, the subjects were then given decision forms containing, for each pair of brands, pairs of choices consisting of the preferred brand and the less preferred brand and varying sums of money. These sets of decision forms were prepared individually for each subject and were determined by the initial simple brand preferences. The indifference point in terms of money was established between the pairs of brands. This was the amount of money which would have to be given with the less preferred brand to force the subject to switch from her preferred brand. For purposes of illustration, assume that in the pair of Brands A and B, the subject chose Brand A. She was then given a decision form which contained pairs consisting of *Brand A* and *Brand B plus varying sums of money*. In every product class fifteen intervals were used, and the increments of money varied depending upon the retail price of the products involved. The following price intervals were used: two cents for sweet peas, four cents for toothpaste, six cents for coffee, and six cents for aspirin tablets. The highest monetary incentive offered with the less preferred brand exceeds fifty per cent of the regular retail price in every instance. An illustrative decision form is shown in Figure 1, where Brand A was originally preferred over Brand B.

SWEET PEAS (Known)
Brand A or Brand B + .02
Brand A or Brand B + .04
Brand A or Brand B + .06
Brand A or Brand B + .08
Brand A or Brand B + .10
Brand A or Brand B + .12
Brand A or Brand B + .14

Figure 1. Illustrative decision form for the hypothetical brands A and B.

For each pair of brands, the subject was given seven pairs of choices. The subject was asked to draw a line indicating the point at which she would switch from her preferred brand to the less preferred brand plus a sum of money. Since a subject with no preference, or a very low order of preference, might switch from her preferred to the less preferred brand for less money than the lowest amount shown, the subject was allowed to draw a line at the top of the list. This was treated as a no preference situation. A subject with a very high order of preference might not be willing to switch from her preferred to the less preferred brand for the largest sum of money offered, and, in these instances, the subjects indicated this by drawing a line at the bottom of the list.

TABULATION BY TEST GROUPS. The point at which a subject switched brands established the indifference point, or the amount of money by which one brand was preferred to another. Since the preference for A over B is equal to minus the preference of B over A, the indifference points for a pair of brands

were always expressed in one order only. A positive value indicated the amount by which the first brand was preferred over the second, while a negative value indicated the amount by which the second brand was preferred over the first. This provided the data in the form required for the method of analysis employed. The indifference points for each individual were determined and tabulated by test groups. An illustrative example is given in Table 1.

A total of sixteen sets of data were obtained. They are as follows:

Control, aspirin, unknown
Control, coffee, unknown
Control, sweet peas, known
Control, toothpaste, known
Control, aspirin, known
Control, coffee, known
Control, sweet peas, unknown
Control, toothpaste, unknown
Market-standing, aspirin, unknown
Market-standing, coffee, unknown
Market-standing, sweet peas, known
Market-standing, toothpaste, known
Price, aspirin, known
Price, coffee, known
Price, sweet peas, unknown
Price, toothpaste, unknown

The market-standing hypothesis was tested using known brands of toothpaste and sweet peas and unknown brands of aspirin tablets and coffee. For testing the hypothesis on the effect of price, known brands of aspirin tablets and coffee and unknown brands of sweet peas and toothpaste were used.

Ten of the groups included forty-eight subjects, while the remaining six groups were composed of fifty subjects. A total of sixty indifference points were established for each subject, and the study yielded a total of 11,700 indifference points.

Rewards

Subjects were rewarded for participating in the study. Rewards were used to encourage participation; and, in addition, the system of making the rewards was so designed to penalize a subject for making incorrect decisions.

The rewards consisted of a combination of merchandise and money representing a basic sum of money plus a number of their choices. The average value of the rewards, including

TABLE 1

Hypothetical Indifference Points for Control Group Using Known Brands of Sweet Peas

Indifference Points

AB	AC	AD	AE	AF	BC	BD	BE	BF	CD	CE	CF	DE	DF	EF	Subject and Group Identification
2	2	2	2	8	0	4	4	8	4	4	8	0	4	4	CSK1
8	4	8	6	8	−4	0	−2	0	4	2	4	−2	0	−2	CSK2
−2	0	2	6	2	2	4	8	4	2	8	2	4	0	−4	CSK3
0	−2	4	6	2	−2	4	4	2	6	6	4	0	−2	−2	CSK4
.															
.															
.															
8	0	6	8	4	−8	−4	−2	−6	6	8	4	2	−2	−4	CSK49
0	4	−4	2	4	4	−4	2	4	−8	−2	0	6	8	2	CSK50

the money and the retail value of the merchandise, was approximately $2.50. Prospective subjects were told that they would be rewarded for participating in the study, and the approximate value of the rewards was indicated. In order to insure care in making decisions, the subjects were informed during their instructions that their rewards could consist of a number of their choices. Prior to the beginning of the laboratory session the subjects were asked to write down two numbers for each product class from which rewards were to be made. The first number was used to identify an individual decision form, and the second identified a pair from which the subject received her preferred brand, or the less preferred brand plus the indicated sum of money. For a pair of brands, a subject could make certain of receiving her preferred brand only by selecting the preferred brand over the less preferred brand and all sums of money offered. Subjects with weak brand preferences were more likely to receive the less preferred brands and money than were the subjects with very strong brand preferences.

Evaluation and Conclusions

It was possible through the use of a controlled experiment to collect a large amount of data about the influence of selected kinds of information on consumers' brand preferences. A study of this type requires careful planning and execution of the experiment in terms of the objectives of the study, the method of analysis to be used, and the desired form of the data. Careful pretesting of forms, instructions, and procedures was critical, since the execution of the experiment was complex. As an illustration, this study

required, in addition to the instruction forms, a total of 248 different decision forms. Approximately 150 students assisted with two or more of the laboratory sessions.

The laboratory methodology described in this paper was subject to the usual limitations given for such experiments. The decisions were made in an artificial environment which ignored the influence of personal selling, promotions, shelf position, and space allocation. On the other hand, the ability to control the influence of variables other than the ones of interest was an advantage of the experiment.

Some frustration was evident in all groups of subjects when dealing with unfamiliar brands. Under these conditions, one might expect low indifference points between brands in a product group. The indifference points between the brands in a product group were somewhat higher than expected.

Fifteen intervals were used in this study to prevent clumping at the end of the scale. In spite of this, there was more clumping at the extremes than was expected. It may be that subjects tended to polarize their judgments and to think of brands as good or bad rather than in terms of precise degrees of goodness or badness. If preferences are strongly held, extreme values would be expected. The clumping of indifference points was found in the unfamiliar brand groups as well as in the familiar brand groups.

The preferences established in this study for unknown brands were initial ones only, and it is not possible to predict how a subject might choose in repeat situations after using the unknown products. In a market situation perceived quality differences and promotional activities could, no doubt, cause results quite different from the initial ones.

THE BUSINESS FIRM AND THE CONSUMER

24 / The Business Firm

A. BACKGROUND AND THEORY

The material in the first section relates to the composition of a business firm and the variables that influence decisions about the marketing of products. We look at a firm's organizational structure in the light of an underlying theory of buyer behavior (Howard).

24-A ORGANIZATION STRUCTURE AND ITS UNDERLYING THEORY OF BUYER BEHAVIOR

John A. Howard (Marketing Educator)

A company's organizational structure can be defined in terms of the flows of information that enable the company to operate. Specifically, these flows can be described by the usual paradigm of communications research: *Who* communicates *what* to *whom* and *when* through which *channel* with what *effect*. The central role of these information flows in a company is not at all obvious, however; and this is one of the reasons why the usual organization chart often hides more than it reveals about the real nature of a company.

Taking this view of company organization as a network of information flows as a background, one must analyze why these flows are what they are, which is another way of saying, "Why the organizational structure is what it is." Any company's organizational structure is the result of many forces, but one of the dominant forces is the way executives think. The way they think, in turn, determines the kinds and amounts of information they want in making their decisions. Normally it has been said that "An executive is a prisoner

SOURCE: John A. Howard, "Organization Structure and Its Underlying Theory of Buyer Behavior," in John S. Wright and Jac L. Goldstucker, Editors, *New Ideas for Successful Marketing* (Chicago: American Marketing Association, 1966), pp. 87–93, at pp. 87–92.

of his communication network." Now with the new computer technology his information network can be redesigned. Major organizational changes are in the offing.

One of the things that marketing executives obviously think much about is the buyer. The way they think about him determines the information they want about him. In fact, it seems that a greater emphasis upon thinking about buyers is the central characteristic of the marketing concept which has received so much attention.

Not only do executives think about buyers but they think systematically about buyers. Executives soon develop firm views about what causes buyers to behave as they do. These views imply that certain relationships exist. In other words, executives have a theory of buyer behavior. Anyone doing research on the executive decision process quickly finds, however, that executives do not generally articulate these beliefs with ease. The beliefs are implicit. Only upon repeated and insistent interrogation are they usually able to make their beliefs explicit.

Two developments have tended to place the executive in the position of having to articulate his theory of buyer behavior. One of these developments took place some years ago and the other is on the horizon. The first development is market research. It was adopted rapidly by industry after World War II. When they meet to discuss a market research report and they attempt to explain the findings, executives expose their beliefs about the nature of the buyers. The executive seldom has the time to participate in such meetings long enough to fully articulate his beliefs and his theory. By participating more in the original design of the study, however, he would be still more explicit. Unfortunately, one of the greatest weaknesses in rational decision in current marketing is that the executive who uses the report seldom participates in the study design where the decision is made as to what facts to collect.

Only when one looks to the future is it obvious how the executive's theory will shape company organization. Here we find that the second development which is a still more radical innovation than market—computer and its related paraphernalia—is clearly on the near horizon. First, the computer has removed some serious barriers to the use of normative decision models. In using normative decision models, General Electric is finding that automated marketing decisions are far more sensitive to errors in sales estimates than to errors in the other decision inputs such as production cost and the interest rate. Hence, in this way the computer is showing us how essential it is to reduce the error in our estimates of buyer behavior. Second, the computer has made possible the implementation of the concept of a *marketing information system*. What does one mean by a company marketing information system? It has at least two identifying characteristics: it is *centralized* and *continuous arrangement* for collecting market facts.

By examining these two characteristics of centralization and continuity, it will become more obvious why executives' theories of buyer behavior must now be laid bare. First, in the process of pooling the information collection activities of the marketing operation, each element of the operation such as advertising, distribution, market research, product development, sales and the like is placed in the position of having to defend why it wants some kinds of information and not others. The give and take of the negotiation process of working out this list of information requirements will inevitably give hints as to each executive's theory, and the more articulate executives will describe theirs in some detail. The executive's theory is probably most apparent when he is justifying the facts he wants than in most other circumstances.

Second, the continuity characteristic of a marketing information system requires that fact collection be far better planned than it now tends to be in the typical market research department which is so often deluged by *ad hoc* studies. If the system is to be useful, comparable data must be collected at regular intervals. Hence, a heavy investment is being made. In all areas of decision, the amount of money at stake strongly determines the amount of attention, thought and care given to the decision. Hence, the continuity characteristic will be a force requiring each executive to articulate his theory as best he can.

Theory of Buyers and Information Flows

The foregoing comments have implied that an executive's theory of buyers will shape the flows of information which are the structure of the company of organization. Let us now, however, be more explicit about the way in which this is so.

The implementation of a computerized marketing information system requires that all executives in the marketing operation of a company be willing to accept (to internalize psychologically) roughly the same theory of buyer behavior. Contemplating the installation of a marketing information system has a certain diagnostic value. For example, it implies that unless executives do have essentially the same theory the company cannot hope ever to *develop* and *execute* a coherent, unified marketing plan with or without a computer. A strong top executive may force the development of such a plan by sheer leadership; but unless his subordinates believe in it, they will not execute it as effectively. A corollary of this implication is that a company with a coherent, unified marketing plan is evidence that its executives do think alike and do hold to the same theory of buyer behavior.

The following illustrates the point of the consequences of a company's marketing executives holding different theories of buyer behavior. The example concerns the introduction

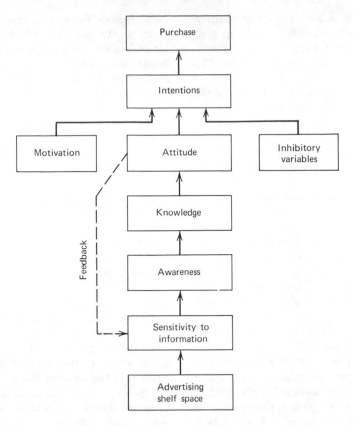

Figure 1. Buyer behavior.

of a new product in the package goods industry, e.g., General Foods, P. & G., or General Mills. Assume that the sales manager holds to the theory that the housewife has a simple information input system. For example, he believes that she is influenced simply in proportion to the brand stimuli that she is exposed to: the more shelf space devoted to a brand, the more likely she is to buy.

The advertising manager, on the other hand, having read some of the perception research holds to the theory that she has a very complex information input system. He believes that her attitude and values cause her to admit some information and simply not "see" (not perceive) other bits of information though they are directly in front of her on the shelf as she walks down the aisle of the supermarket.

A diagram will show the difference. Figure 1 presents a part of a theory of the process by which buying behavior is affected by mar-

keting.[1] Here is the traditional hierarchy of awareness, knowledge, attitude, intention to purchase and actual purchase. To make it a meaningful and comprehensive analytic framework, motivation, and such inhibitory variables as price, level of availability in the retail store and the like must be added.

More important for the purpose here is the variable, Sensitivity to Information, because it distinguishes the sales manager's theory from the advertising man's theory. The principle underlying this variable is that as a buyer's attitude toward a brand becomes more favorable there is a feedback from his attitude to the buyer's perceptual process. The effect

[1] For a complete theory of buyer behavior, see a forthcoming book by J. A. Howard and J. N. Sheth, *The Theory of Buyer Behavior*. For a summary of the theory see J. A. Howard, "The Theory of Buyer Behavior." Symposium on Consumer Behavior, University of Texas, April 18 and 19, 1966.

of this feedback is to increase the probability that she will "see" (perceive) anything associated with the brand, such as a verbal statement, an ad, or a box on the shelf. This feedback is shown in Figure 1.

The sales manager does not believe that this variable exists; the advertising manager believes that it does. As a consequence the salesman will be much less sanguine than the advertising manager about the effects of advertising. Because of his belief in the variable, the advertising manager will argue that advertising has two effects. The first is the traditional effect. It causes the buyer to have a more favorable attitude toward a brand, which will increase the buyer's probability of purchase if she is exposed to the opportunity to buy the brand. The second effect is the more interesting one. The buyer has a greater probability of being exposed to the brand, that is, a greater probability of perceiving the brand when she is confronted with it physically in the supermarket.

The advertising man as a consequence of his theory will argue in a rational manner that relatively more money should be allocated to advertising and less to getting the product in to the supermarket. On the other hand, if both executives hold the same theory, that is, they both believe there is a variable called Sensitivity to Information which operates as described, they are far more likely to agree on a common marketing plan and to execute that plan in good faith rather than with some feeling that they have had something "foisted off" on to them.

A number of implications follow from the analysis here. A company's marketing operation can be organized more simply and its parts can work together far more smoothly if all executives hold the same theory of buyer behavior. Above all, there will be less latent conflict between the executive and his market researcher because the executive will fulfill his true role of being the formulator of the problem and leave the market research department free to collect the data that best measures the variables implied in the executives formulation and free to develop the more basic theory that should underlie all of the company's market research. The elements of the marketing plan will be coordinated because all executives will be more inclined to think it is the sensible thing to do. There will be greater room for creativity. Finally, this common theory is essential to using the new information collection and processing technology most effectively.

B. RESEARCH AND APPLICATIONS

This section contains a study of corporate images and their importance to the firm (Martineau).

24-B SHARPER FOCUS FOR THE CORPORATE IMAGE

Pierre Martineau (*Marketing Educator*)

In one sense, the idea of a corporate image is certainly not new. Companies have done institutional advertising for many years, and sophisticated public relations people have long stressed the significance of many kinds of intelligent effort in building up a general reservoir of good will for a firm. But the concept of a corporate image has given much greater meaning to these efforts. Against the background of thinking about brand images and product-area images, it offers something new, distinct, and valuable.

Mirage or Reality?

Because the transition from brand image to corporate image has proceeded so fast, many of the component parts of the corporate image concept are still muddy and need to be overhauled in the light of other knowledge and experience. Businessmen are doing and saying things that do not make sense. For instance:

SOURCE: Pierre Martineau, "Sharper Focus for the Corporate Image," *Harvard Business Review*, Vol. 36 (November-December, 1958), pp. 49–58. © 1958 by the President and Fellows of Harvard College; all rights reserved.

• One current estimate of how much United States business spends each year to make itself better liked is $1 billion. But when the average president is asked what impression he is trying to create in the public mind, he emphasizes "selling good products at reasonable prices."[1] Is this all? Is this the way the public assesses corporations? Or is this a primitive kind of thinking on the subject of corporate images?

• For many years leading corporations such as American Telephone & Telegraph and Standard Oil Co. (New Jersey) have conducted public opinion surveys hoping to learn the climate of public feeling toward them. Are such studies measuring anything of significance? Are they measuring what they assert to be measuring? What does it mean when the index of negative reactions drops—a more favorable (less critical) image or a weaker (more apathetic) image?

• The literature on the subject implies that the task of molding a corporate image is essentially a public relations function. Is it? Is this the most important way for a company to convey meaning about its image?

• One study purporting to show the corporate image of the steel manufacturers asked the respondent which company he would recommend as a place for a young executive to start working and which company he would invest $5,000 in if he had $5,000 to invest. In defense of the study, it was asserted that the image of the company as a place to work would be indicative of its future growth possibilities. Is this plausible? Is there any such logical relation between the different aspects of the corporate image?

COMPANY PERSONALITY. In order to put the corporate image in perspective as a workable concept, we need to understand where companies are trying to go with it. And what started this line of thinking in the first place?

In a remarkably few years the goals of advertising and marketing in the consumer field have been broadened past the functional stages. Today sophisticated strategy embraces a conscious effort to create a distinctive and, of course, positive brand image. The successful brand invariably has psychological meanings and dimensions which are just as real to the purchaser as its physical properties, and in many instances the purely subjective attributes play a far more important role in the brand's fortunes than do the functional elements. But in every case the aura of the symbolic dimensions contributes to the value and the public estimate of the brand.

Often the scope of the problem becomes widened to include a whole product area. Furriers want to know why women buy fewer fur coats. Retailers in the men's clothing field are concerned about their decreasing share of the consumer dollar. Trade associations in the beer industry are asking themselves why per capita beer consumption is declining, whereas wine consumption is increasing. Obviously what is involved is essentially not price, not distribution, not the physical products, but the sets of attitudes which are bearing on and directing consumer behavior in a whole area.

To go a step further in the complexity of images, perceptive retailers everywhere are sensing the vital importance of the many nonprice components of their operations which contribute to their store character. Speakers at leading 1958 conventions in both the supermarket and the department store fields have urged the development of store personality as a primary objective of retailing today.[2] Theorists readily acknowledge that the decision maker in the department store relies more and more on nonprice factors as a major competitive weapon for building sales volumes.[3] In other areas of retailing, management is learning how to "sell the store" as a commodity, just as it learned how to sell products. For example:

• The Kroger grocery chain is launched on a major operating and advertising program specifically designed to project a favorable company image.

[1] Kenneth Henry, "Creating and Selling Your Corporate Image," *Dun's Review and Modern Industry*, July 1958, p. 32.

[2] Pierre Martineau, "The Personality of the Retail Store," HBR January-February 1958, p. 47.

[3] Perry Bliss, "Non-Price Competition at the Department Store Level," from *Marketing in Transition*, edited by Alfred L. Seelye (New York, Harper & Brothers, 1958), pp. 161–170.

• Jewel Food Stores, though operating in only one market, has become one of the largest grocery chains by marching under the banner of a pleasing store personality. What started out years ago merely as a promotional idea—"Shop at your friendly Jewel Store"—has long since become a religion for management.

The merchant is realizing that unless the prospective customer can consciously or unconsciously see a "fit" between her own self-image and the image of the store, she will not patronize it, no matter what price offerings are made. It is perfectly logical, therefore, for the manufacturer to inquire whether a similar attraction or repulsion may be taking place between the consuming public and his company's personality which would have tangible bearing on the sale of his products.

TOO MUCH TO FOCUS? Much of the confusion over the corporate image stems from somewhat conflicting sources. On the one hand, some people are likely to be uneasy over the fact that so little can say so much. On the other hand, a great deal of skepticism exists that such a conglomeration of activities as the modern corporation *can* lend itself to compact expression.

In the strictest sense, every company can be said to have a corporate image. Every bank, every railroad, every manufacturer has a personality or reputation consisting of many facets. The corporate image of American Airlines embraces infinitely more meaning than some airplanes flying in the sky; it symbolically projects associations of waiting rooms, stewardesses, type of equipment, excellence of meals, interior décor of the planes, how fast the baggage is unloaded, the extra fare flights, attitudes toward serving liquor, the company's color scheme and trademark, and so on. The vague generalized image behind the specific is called into mind by some specific facet. Yet it is the vague part, the set of many associations and meanings, which the image really refers to.

But, as if the subtlety of the problem were not enough to bother people, there is also its complexity. For example, I know of one consultant who questions that these complex images even exist. Why? He argues that the manufacturer, if a large one, operates in so many different areas that no one image is possible. The company is a workshop, a research laboratory, a training school for executives, a source of employment for hundreds of workers, a civic institution, a buyer, and, among these many other things, a maker of profit. The point is, he argues, that it has no one single image because it cannot have. It is far too complex.

Or, to use a more concrete illustration, what is the corporate image of the Chicago Tribune Company? It publishes newspapers. But also it operates radio and television stations; it is an office-building landlord in both Chicago and New York; it syndicates comic strips and feature articles to newspapers throughout the country; it operates a fleet of ocean-going boats; it is one of the largest paper manufacturers and one of the largest owners of timberlands; it has built and maintains an entire Canadian city; it has important hydroelectric developments; and it is part owner of a major aluminum-manufacturing project.

"LET THE PRODUCT SPEAK." In each particular product area, the buyer would generally be concerned only with the activities of the company as a manufacturer in that field, and give very little thought to the baffling complexities of the corporate image. This is why the particular consultant I have mentioned contends that management thinking should be solely about the product at the point of sale. What is important in organization thinking is what happens at this critical spot, he argues. Naturally he turns a jaundiced eye on institutional advertising. Not only is it ineffective, in his viewpoint, but it might give rise to misunderstandings about the company's motives. "Let the product speak for you," is his advice. If there is such a thing as a corporate personality, he does not feel that it is viable—that it will pass coin from one public to another.

There is still another problem. The multi-line company not only has to address a number of buying publics but also many other significant groups that have to be influenced in extremely diverse ways. For example, the labor unions who bargain with International Harvester are surely not impressed with its attractive "I H" design or the excellence of its machinery. And the investing public is probably only concerned with the dividend and earnings record, and the general character of management: whether it is progressive, competitive, and stockholder-oriented. May it not be, then, that there is not only too much for the modern corporation to say but also too many different people to say it to?

Direction & Indirection

In trying to unravel some of the misunderstandings about the corporate image, I must grant at the outset that much or even most institutional effort is ineffective and not communicating what the company hopes it will. It does not follow, however, that these meanings cannot be imparted with a different kind of communication.

I think that if advertising is viewed as a communication process, it will be seen that there are many other ways to convey and mold the corporate image besides the customary platitudinous messages to the effect that the company is visionary, honest, friendly, considerate, dependable, trustworthy, brave, with unbelievable resources, and so on and on. Certainly management should evolve advertising strategy which not only has such rigid meanings but particularly will cause us to like the corporate personality just as we like a person.

In the Westinghouse study previously mentioned, readers of strictly corporate advertising stated that Westinghouse is a very stable company, its stock is a good thing to own, it is a leader in research, the company's appliances are good and the new lines are greatly improved, and that Westinghouse is a good place to work. *Yet the advertising said none of these things.* All of these comments were provoked voluntarily by corporate advertising showing six applications of atomic reactors.

While I have deliberately pointed out the difficulties of abstracting one simple symbol for a complex corporate image, nevertheless that is the way the human mind tends to think. To pragmatic persons who say, "Why all of this bother about images? Let's just run our companies," I should like to refer to what is undoubtedly the best book on the subject: *The Image* by Kenneth E. Boulding.[4] The author points out that it is not mere knowledge and information which direct human

[4] Ann Arbor, University of Michigan Press, 1956.

behavior, but rather it is the images we have —not what is true but what we *believe* to be true. In any situation these patterns of subjective knowledge and value act to mediate between ourselves and the world.

The human mind can only handle so many complexities. It has to oversimplify and abstract a few salient meanings. We bundle up whole nations in simple cartoon figures like Uncle Sam or John Bull. The simple symbolic images act as a rough summation or index of a vast complexity of meanings. We personalize them and like them or dislike them because this is the only way we can interact with things—to endow them with the attributes of people.

BUILT-IN FILTERS. The business executive cannot afford to scoff at this subject of images because people are acting toward his company on the basis of them—not on the basis of facts and figures. Once these stereotyped notions are formed in people's minds, they are extremely difficult to change. They serve as emotional filters which are used by everyone in listening and seeing. Facts or no facts, these images cause us to reject what we do not agree with. On the other hand, we allow agreeable material to pour in unchallenged. The good image has a halo effect, so that it gets credit for all sorts of good things which might be quite contrary to truth.

Power of Stereotypes

I have pointed out that the image is a kind of stereotype. It is an oversimplification. In a sense, therefore, it negates the complexity of the modern diversified corporation. But this does not make it less workable as an operational tool. Far from it. In fact, it is the reality that creates the need for the illusion.

THE HIDDEN PERCEIVERS. To begin, I think it would be most fruitful to look a little closer at the notion that the corporation is addressing itself to many different publics, each of which is looking at the corporate image from behind a different set of lenses. Many public relations people who acknowledge this in theory behave in practice as if there were only one public to be addressed.

While it is certainly true that the various publics overlap and are not discrete, they all see the image differently because their perceptions, their expectations, and their wishes differ. Compare the viewpoints of the following groups:

1. *Stockholders—sophisticated people who determine the company's access to capital.*

2. *Consumers—relatively unsophisticated people who buy the company's products for any number of reasons.*

3. *Potential customers—people who could buy the company's products but do not.*

Whereas companies generally address consumers and nonconsumers alike, in our experience at the *Chicago Tribune*, they may be poles apart in their attitudes. Consumers like the products, they are familiar with them, they read the advertising to support their favorable opinions. But nonconsumers very often have negative stereotypes of the company which prevent them from learning anything about the products. Their negative attitudes in some way have to be altered; otherwise they will always act as a barrier to getting information through.

4. *Employees—top management, middle management and the rank and file of production workers.*

Here it is worth noting that each group will have very different perceptions of the company as a place to work. The perennial sin of employee publications and employee benefits is that they are conceived and remain embedded in the mental set of top management.

5. *Vendors in the distribution system—retailer's, wholesalers, manufacturer's agents.*

A very large part of so-called consumer advertising is really designed to influence the vendors. In the Antitrust Division's action to prevent the Procter & Gamble Company's merger with Clorox Chemical Company, considerable stress was placed on Procter & Gamble's ability to secure overnight retail distribution for its new products, such as Crest Toothpaste and Comet Cleanser. The retailer's image of the saleability of Procter & Gamble's products constitutes a very tangible factor in its greater resources.

6. *Suppliers—those who furnish credit, services, materials, and prices.*

The attitudes they form about a company can be very important. For example, if the bank believes the company will ultimately be successful, it allows much greater credit leeway. Thus, fabricators are (as they should be) deeply concerned with the attitudes of textile mills and steel mills that are their suppliers.

7. *Neighbors—the community where the company has plants or general offices.*

If a company operates stockyards or quarries or stream-polluting mills, or anything like that, obviously local opinion becomes very important. Local officials assess taxes and pass zoning ordinances. So of course such companies have to make themselves welcome to the communities where otherwise they would be regarded as a nuisance.

In a broader perspective, nearly all companies recognize the importance of a favorable public climate at the local community and plant city levels. Presidents speak at civic occasions, executives are active in local charities, educational scholarships are created, and many corollary activities are undertaken with the purpose of creating an image of a good neighbor and a responsible citizen. I think this aspect of the corporate image is extremely important in dealing with government functionaries. And also in lawsuits. Remember that railroads and public utilities constantly face the problem of excessive and unreasonable verdicts in personal injury cases because the judgment of the typical juror is swayed by his unfavorable images of these companies.

Between each of these publics and the company are surrogate groups that in reality act for them. For instance, the union is not really a public, but acts for the employees. Investment counselors, bond houses, and stockbrokers are the surrogates for the shareholders, and in most instances it is more important for them to perceive a favorable corporate image than for the shareholders; they are, after all, the "influentials." The retail dealer has wholesalers, distributors, and manufacturer's agents between him and the company. And the retail dealer finally is the ultimate link in the chain of surrogates between the consumer and the company.

Molding the Image

Let us turn now to the practical question of how to create a clear, persuasive corporate image. Let us consider such aspects of the question as what products the company should identify itself with, how one company can be distinguished from another, and the relative roles of public relations and advertising.

IDEALIZED IDENTIFICATIONS. The consumer is always asking: "What do they want me to do? Do they want me to clean my desk? Do I scrub floors, or do I enjoy myself?" As the woman looks at dishwashing compounds, she senses that the company not only wants to sell her something but asks her to do something unpleasant. A vacuum cleaner company is persuading her to perform a nasty, thankless chore. A scouring powder forces a woman to do hard, dirty work, and the subjective conclusion may be that any maker with such goals does not like women. By contrast, the maker of an electric toaster or a new gas range wants her to be happy and appreciated.

In advertising, therefore, the company has to be careful about which products it appears to "love" and which it just handles. Procter & Gamble just "handles" detergents and scouring powders. But it identifies with Zest and Camay soaps, which have significant emotional connotations as toiletries of beauty and scent, and with Ivory soap, which is identified with childloving.

Too often companies identify with products they like instead of products that the consumer finds pleasant. It is, of course, important to discern which products the consumer likes and to identify the company with those. It *does* make considerable difference whether the company identifies with products like meat or cosmetics as compared to items that force one to do disagreeable tasks. "Cooking is a chore, but my family will love me, will compliment me, will realize I am indispensable and very capable. Hand lotions, lipsticks, hair sprays will make me attractive. The company wants me to be beautiful. How nice! What a nice company."

The products and services that the consumer identifies a company with have a far more important bearing on the image than all the knowledge of economists and antitrust lawyers who know the "big picture." To illustrate:

• I think a primary reason why the government failed to whip up any public feeling toward Atlantic & Pacific Stores in its antitrust suit was because people did not see Atlantic & Pacific as some powerfully big corporation—the largest retailer. Rather, people knew individual A & P stores that trimmed lettuce, sold aromatic-smelling coffee, and accommodatingly carried out heavy bundles.

• How can the public dislike General Motors? In the public eye, it is not seen as a huge corporation dominating the automobile field. At the point of public contact, the GM image has filtered down to become one of pleasant people making and selling cars at retail, figuring out trades so the prospect can have a car with a radio, white sidewall tires, and blue windshield glass. "GM bargains with me; it wants me to be happy with a new car."

• Jersey Standard is not "the biggest oil company"; rather, it handles Flit and radiator cleaner, just like any small company handling small things. So people can like Jersey. "How can you hate a company that makes Flit?"

• United States Steel brought itself within public awareness by promoting a "White Christmas"; people like the notion of appliances for Christmas, and therefore U.S. Steel is simple and nice.

At the point where the consumer, the public, and the company all meet, the corporate image has to be uncomplicated so that it can be expressed quickly in feeling or logic. The public must accept the various deeds of the manufacturer so that it can fit them together logically or emotionally; if it cannot find a simple motive for some corporate activity, then it is liable to impute a wrong motive. Accordingly, Lever Bros. should not put out vitamins and Schenley should not manufacture penicillin, for these are illogical steps. They do not fit the pattern of the corporate image. But if a company should make a success of some such maverick enterprise, then the public reconstructs its logic to accept the company in this new field.

COMMON PITFALLS. Molding and shaping the corporate image is a highly positive, constructive job, which needs to be approached with vigor and enthusiasm. There are, however, several problems that management should frankly face up to—and some that it may have to live with.

First there is the problem of "living modern" in times of continuous change. It is quite true that, today as always, there is no substitute for the excellence of a company's products. But we have an economy which has emerged from the production and refinery stage. Unless all products in the market place are good in a functional sense, they die an immediate and unlamented death. Now we are in the era of promotion and merchandising, where the fortunes of a company depend far more on its abilities to advertise and merchandise and promote its products, because it is taken for granted that all products will perform their functions. But in my experience there are far too many mental "DP's" at the management level who cannot shift their perspective from the long-gone days when there were distinctive product differences to dramatize.

Take the case of an advertiser selling electric motors. One ½-horsepower motor performs exactly like another. Yet the maker typically has such a dearth of imagination and of communicative skills that his only recourse is to spell out ten or twelve points of superiority. The buyer knows that ½-horsepower motors are identical. Furthermore, he will recognize that all of the points the manufacturer alludes to are of such miniscule importance as to be valueless. I have heard my wife spontaneously object to dull TV commercials: "What are they telling me such nonsense for? Who cares?"

Generally when it dawns on the executive group that there is such a thing as a corporate image, it fails to distinguish between two general sets of meaning: (1) the functional meanings, which have to do with quality, reliability, service, price, and the like; and (2) the emotive meanings, which have to do with the subjective viewpoints or "feeling tone" of the various publics. In large measure we believe what we wish to believe. Modern communication theory recognizes that our feelings steer our senses.

If a company or a brand is saddled with a negative image, even the most realistic and functional qualities of its products will be colored and altered. We find reasons to reject what we do not like. And at the other extreme,

when the feeling tone is favorable to the corporate image, we persistently look for the good side of every experience with this company and its products. This is why any consideration of corporate images has to be concerned with feeling tone and emotive components as well as with the functional and intellectual meanings.

The extreme difficulty of changing a negative image stems from the fact that the individual's attitudes are embedded in a subrational matrix of feeling. He remains immune to logic. In our *Chicago Tribune* studies of nonconsumers in the newspaper field, these groups remained stubbornly oblivious to any changes or improvements in the newspapers they did not like. They will go on for years parroting the same attitudes which long since have ceased to have any basis in fact at all. For example, a newspaper, which had changed its name 13 years ago and had been sold in the meantime, was still associated with the same name and the same ownership as far as these nonconsumers were concerned. Their feelings simply would not let them accept reality.

In the task of molding a favorable corporate image, the public relations people can and should play an important role; there is an infinity of meanings and situations that cannot be approached with direct advertising. Public relations is a tool, however, that is little understood by management. For the most part, its use is still mired in the primitive notions of grinding out news releases or arranging for the president to speak. Public relations itself suffers from a poor image. Too many executives still characterize it as glib press-agentry. They associate it with some company frantically trying to get off the hot seat after particularly bad publicity. Rarely is it though of as a dynamic on-going program, like the company's advertising, which in its own way can mold public attitudes.

IMAGINATIVE IMAGERY. The most direct, overt way for the company to project its character to the public is by advertising. I do not mean traditional institutional advertising. Much of it, in my opinion, is too stilted, too impersonal, too management-oriented, and too much the same to be effective in achieving its goal of creating a favorable climate of public feeling. Certainly, sameness of approach will not build a sense of psychological uniqueness and richness for the corporate image in the public mind—and I think that is necessary. Fortunately, however, neither dullness nor conventionality is necessary. Advertising is a field for originality and imagination.

The style of advertising—literally how it is done—contributes enormously to brand and corporate images. Olivetti, for example, has used a unique style of abstract advertising to create a very distinctive quality image in the field of office machines. Any competitive manufacturer could duplicate whatever words Olivetti might choose to say about itself, but no one could retrace the corporate image created by this particular style.

The big department store has generally sensed this much better than the manufacturer. The astute store manager knows that all of his activities are acting as symbols to project to his public the store's inherent character, and therefore they should be expressive, distinctive, and congruent. In the manufacturer's terms, this means that his advertising style, his trademarks, his packaging, his stationery, his reception rooms, his general offices, his reports to stockholders, and his color schemes should be expressive—all saying the same things about the company.

The annual financial reports have become a meaningful and distinct channel of communication—and they say more than the words alone convey. For example, after looking at a Bell & Howell report, it is easy to understand the enthusiasm of investment counselors for the company. The format of the report eloquently conveys that this is a youthful, dynamic, years-ahead organization. All of this is totally apart from the content of the report. By contrast, the report of Pacific Gas & Electric unmistakably relays an image of a staid, old-fashioned management.

The retailer rarely uses straight institutional advertising. Rather, he sees every merchandise offering as institutional advertising. At the same time that he features timely merchandise, the tone and style of the advertising are proclaiming volumes of meaning about the personality of the store itself. This is why

the manufacturer should see his regular product advertising as contributory to the corporate image. Regardless of how little or how much it is conveying about the company as a maker of the product, it is saying *something*.

Conclusion

There is no one corporate personality. There cannot be because every firm has different publics, and the four primary ones—stockholders, employees, vendors, and buyers—will see different aspects of the corporate image.

Creating and selling a corporate image is far more than a task for the public relations staff. Every activity of the company adds some meaning to the public's picture of the management that is running the organization. Regardless of the complexity of the corporate structure, at the point where product and buyer come together the consumer also weighs in the balance some associations about the maker of that particular product. Many corollary meanings emerging from the corporate image can play a role in the actual purchase decision at the moment of sale.

Because any functional and price attributes of the product will be filtered through an emotional lens in the buyer's mind, it is important for the corporate image to be liked. This is why it is so necessary to consider what I call the "feeling tone" and the emotive meanings as well as the functional and rational dimensions of the corporate image.

Many channels of communication by which we humans customarily and believably convey meaning to each other are mostly overlooked by management. These avenues of meaning are particularly important in molding positive brand and corporate images. Creating a spectrum of meaningful intangibles is a dual responsibility. In advertising, for instance, the agency as the creative force has to propose symbols which will communicate successfully to the company's publics. And management has to allow such creative effort instead of holding to narrow rationalistic approaches.

25 / Segmentation of the Market

A. BACKGROUND AND THEORY

The section begins with a look at a "new" market—the child consumer (Mc-Neal). It is followed by an explanation of psychographics.

25-A THE CHILD CONSUMER: A NEW MARKET

James U. McNeal (Marketing Educator)

Marketers—retailers and manufacturers—employ a variety of demand factors to define markets. They commonly use income, size, location, education and many other criteria. For years one important means of segmenting markets has been the concept of life cycle. Essentially, the markets were divided into the following categories: (*a*) young single adults, (*b*) newly married couples with no children, (*c*) young married couples with young children, (*d*) married couples with adolescent children, (*e*) married couples whose children have moved from home.[1]

However, in recent years some marketers began to realize that the life cycle as a criterion for market definition was omitting an increasingly important market segment; namely, the youth market. Seemingly overnight, the marketer became aware that youth, in addition to adults, had desires for goods and money to back them up.

The result of this realization was a flurry of activities aimed at what was termed the "teen market."[2] Companies, and divisions of companies, cropped up to make products for the teens, advertisements to teens proliferated (often from a special division in an advertising agency concerned only with teens), and retail stores started setting aside areas termed as "teen-land" and junior shops.

Today, the teen market is a truism among marketers. There are copious facts and figures about it. And hundreds, perhaps thousands, of marketers are striving hard for their share of the 10–12 billion dollars spent annually by the nearly 20 million teens.

Now, the perceptive marketers is discovering still another new age-graded market even younger than the teen market—*the child market*. There has always been an awareness in modern marketing of the influence of the child on household purchases. And agressive marketers capitalize on this relationship, for example, with numerous advertisements that tell the child to encourage the *family* to buy cereals, soft drinks and even automobiles.

The new child market referred to here, however, does not mean the children that influence parental purchases. Neither does it mean items purchased by the child for the household such as milk and bread. And, neither does it include the billions of dollars spent on children by parents.

The term, child market, as employed here,

SOURCE: James U. McNeal, "The Child Consumer: A New Market," *Journal of Retailing*, Vol. 45 (Summer, 1969), pp. 15–22 and 84.

[1] For a discussion of life-cycle as a base for market segmentation see, William D. Wells and George Gubar, "The Life-Cycle Concept in Marketing Research," *Journal of Marketing Research*, 3 (November 1966), 355-63.

[2] See, for example, "Do Ad Men Understand Teen-Agers?" in James U. McNeal (ed.), *Dimensions of Consumer Behavior* (New York: Appleton-Century-Crofts, 1965), pp. 210–17.

refers to that group of children between the ages of 5 and 13 (roughly the elementary school age children) that make purchases of goods and services for personal use and satisfaction.

There have always been children just as there have always been teen-agers. But definitively speaking, in order for a group to be termed a market, it must be sizable, it must have desire and it must have ability to buy. As our affluence has grown it has backed down through the teen level and finally to the children. Consequently, there is now a large number of children in the United States with many desires and money to fulfill them.

In the case of children there is an additional requisite for being a market. There must be an understanding of money and the purchase act. As Reisman *et al.*, have noted, however, affluent Americans tend to give their children consumer training at a very early age.[3] Typically, an American youngster makes his first independent purchase around age five.[4] During at least a year prior to the solo, the parents were training him diligently in the art of consumption This training included such things as letting the youngster give the money to the supermarket cashier or retrieve a box of cereal from the shelf, and showing him how to give the squeeze-test to a loaf of bread.

Probably the consumer training was intensified after the solo act in order that the child might eventually relieve the parent of more menial purchase tasks such as the "bread and milk runs" or the returning of some product for exchange.

Size of Child Market

To measure the child market we need to ask two questions. How many children are there? How much money do they have to spend? The individual marketer, of course, wishes to know what portion of this total market wants his product and how much of it the youngsters will buy.

In 1967, there were an estimated 36,732,000 children in the United States ranging from age 5 to age 13.[5] By 1985 this group is forecasted to have a minimum growth of 17 percent (to 40,447,000) and a possible growth of 53 percent (to 52,719,000).[6] There is today an almost equal number of girls and boys among the 36.7 million children, and they are distributed among approximately 20,000,000 families

Stating how much money these youngsters have to spend is difficult. Their sources of purchasing power are numerous. They include earned income from odd-jobs, paper routes, etc., gifts from parents and relatives (particularly grandparents) and allowances which generally are perceived as a combination of earnings and gifts.

Yet those organizations that normally gather income data (government agencies, trade associations and universities) have not concerned themselves with this market, or in most cases, even recognized it as a market. Consequently, income data for this group is unavailable and only can be roughly estimated.

Even if income data were available, little is known about the children's saving habits. Lack of this information makes it still more difficult to estimate their expenditures.

With the assistance of some interested faculty members of the University of Georgia, an average weekly expenditure of $1.10 was determined.[7] It is believed that this is a conservative figure. Further, it is believed that this figure would not vary significantly over large numbers of children from most income groups but would vary directly with the age of the child.

If this "guesstimate" can be accepted, it means that this market has a value of approximately 2 billion dollars annually. This value is in agreement with verbal estimates

[3] David Riesman, Nathan Glazer and Reuel Denny, *The Lonely Crowd* (New York: Doubleday and Company, 1953).

[4] James U. McNeal, "An Exploratory Study of the Consumer Behavior of Children," in James U. McNeal (ed.), *Dimensions of Consumer Behavior* (New York: Appleton-Century-Crofts, 1965), pp. 190–209.

[5] *Current Population Reports*, Series P-25, No. 286 (Washington D.C.: Department of Commerce, July 1964), p. 6.

[6] *Ibid.*

[7] This figure consists of an estimated *average* of 50 cents per week received from parents and 60 cents per week from gifts and earnings.

made by some advertising agencies and businessmen.

While the $2 billion figure may seem small when compared with the expenditure of other age groups, it is a very significant amount when viewed in terms of various products such as gum, candy and frozen desserts. For example, assume that each member of this group chews two pieces of gum per week or approximately 100 pieces per year. This means consumption of 3,673,200,000 pieces of gum or approximately $36,700,000 in expenditures for this one product.

Demands of the Child Market

Basically the child consumer is no different from any other consumer—he wants things that satisfy his needs.[8] For this new consumer, the purchase act provides two levels of satisfaction. First, the obvious satisfaction is produced by the items purchased, consisting normally of a wide array of sweets and a few inexpensive toys. The second dimension of satisfaction stems from the purchase *act* rather than from *what* is purchased. In effect, the purchase act is evidence of "grown-upness." And, surely, at the top of the youngster's hierarchy of needs is the need to be considered mature by adults.[9]

Gradually the inherent value of the consumption act declines with maturity. The first type of satisfaction, that produced by possession and use of products, becomes increasingly important. This change in the value of the purchase act normally occurs between ages 5 and 12. Thus, this span of time might aptly be termed the apprenticeship period of consuming.

From the viewpoint of the two types of satisfaction, the new child consumer demands products, mostly sweets, to satisfy his present needs, and demands to obtain them in an independent manner.[10] He wants such items

[8] Much of the material in this section and the following sections is adapted from McNeal, *op. cit.*

[9] Arnold Gesell and Frances Ilg, *The Child from Five to Ten* (New York: Harper and Brothers, 1946).

[10] The degree of independence desired in the purchasing process appears to vary directly with ages. McNeal, *op. cit.*, pp. 195–96.

as candy, ice cream and gum constantly. He is inconsistent in his purchase habits at first, seemingly having little brand, or even product, preference. At one time he may spend minutes trying to make a candy purchase decision; yet, the next time he may purchase on impulse.

He usually disregards future needs, spending only for the present. Thus, saving money usually means saving it until he again is in a place of purchase. He gives no consideration to the source of funds. His demands are endless, and he expects money to be likewise. On the other hand, since he is just learning to understand the concept of money, he fortunately thinks in terms of pennies and nickels rather than dollars. And more fortunately, by the time he concerns himself with "dollar" purchases, he usually has learned respect for the source of funds and is willing to work for them.

As mentioned above, the child quickly seeks independence in his purchase behavior. He wants to give the money personally to the "store-man," put the coins in the vending machine and retrieve the products from their shelves and cases. And one of his greatest childhood thrills is his first trip to the store by himself. What an expression of independence! It is exciting, mysterious and self-rewarding. Usually he is quite nervous while he is in the store, particularly during the actual exchange. This uneasiness typically accompanies the trip back home, and he welcomes the sight of his house. Once home, there is a feeling of both relief and accomplishment. Henceforth, he demands to make the trip frequently, and his parents are usually willing to permit him to do so because he can also perform the "milk and bread run." Thus, there is recognition by both youngster and parents that he is now truly a consumer.

Development of Consumer Behavior Patterns

By age seven the child consumer has "soloed," and begins to perfect his consuming skills. He achieves this refinement in a variety of ways. Mainly, he copies the consumer behavior patterns of his parents. Bandura has noted that the child copies not only the general patterns of behavior but also "the mannerisms, voice inflections, and attitudes which the parents have never directly attempted to teach."[11] The youngster applies these patterns of behavior at every opportunity. He asks to make trips to the store, and during in-store shopping with his parents, he attempts to assist them.

At the same time that the child is copying parental behavioral patterns, the parents are usually trying to teach the child the procedures of purchasing. It the child cannot immediately implement some newly learned behavior, he often pretends to do so in his play. As one youngster stated, "I play store all time."

The child also copies the consumer behavioral patterns of his peers and seeks advice from them about consumption. This peer influence usually becomes strong at age seven. The nature of the influence typically consists of recommendations about flavors and brands of sweets.

The child also learns a great deal about consumer behavior from advertising, particularly that on television. From advertising the child learns about brands, types of stores and pricing. And even though there may be a dislike for television advertising that increases with age, the child readily admits that the advertising does influence his consumer behavior.

By the time the child reaches age nine or ten, he has a simple understanding of the marketing process. He can discuss the functions of stores, the sources of products and even the concept of profit. He even discusses such matters as sales, bargains and trading stamps. Some of this knowledge is acquired in the classroom under such terms as "social studies" and "the environment we live in."

By age nine the glow of the shopping process is wearing off, and if permitted, the child may show discrimination in making shopping trips. This reduction of interest in consumption can be expected as shopping begins to lose its problem character and the youngster develops a feeling of competence in it. By ritualizing those activities in which he

has developed competence, he can achieve freedom to meet new zones of experience.[12]

By the time the child reaches his last year of elementary school, his consumer behavioral patterns are much like those of an adult. He is assigning social value to many products, participating in family discussions about major purchases and is on a first-name basis with a number of "store people."

Marketing to the Child Consumer

The fact that there is a child market cannot be denied. The most obvious evidence is the large amount of marketing effort aimed at this market.

It is true, for example, that much advertising to children is attempting to get them to influence the purchases of their parents. But, increasingly, marketers are seeing children as a market, and are devoting attention to them from this viewpoint. Instead of saying, "ask your mother to buy so-and-so," advertisements to children often simply say, "buy so-and-so."

In supermarkets, for instance, products that appeal to children are placed at lower levels for their convenience. Only a few years ago these same products were displayed at a higher level so they could *not* reach them. These same supermarkets often have smaller shopping carts for the children as well as racks for parking bicycles. One supermarket chain, with the advice of a number of outstanding behavioral scientists, conducted studies of children's shopping behavior.[13] The study not only provided a wealth of information on children's attitudes toward shopping, but also furnished a great deal of insight into their actual purchase behavior patterns.

Manufacturers have been quick to recognize the potential of the child market and have provided it with a wide array of products ranging from fashions[14] to candies.[15] These

---

[11] Albert Bandura, "Social Learning Through Imitation," in Marshall R. Jones (ed.), *Nebraska Symposium on Motivation* (Lincoln, Nebraska: University of Nebraska Press, 1962), pp. 214–15.

[12] John E. Anderson, "The Development of Behavior and Personality," in Eli Ginzber (ed.), *The Nation's Children*, II (New York: Columbia University Press, 1960), 57.

[13] "A Study of the Child as a Consumer" (Cincinnati: The Kroger Food Foundation, 1954). (Mimeographed.)

[14] "Kid Stuff Swings to a Grownup Look," *Business Week* (April 17, 1965), pp. 66 ff.

[15] *The Avisco Candy Study* (Philadelphia: FMC Corporation, 1964).

same manufacturers heavily promote these products directly to children via television programs for children, comic books, the backsides of cereal packages and other media. Producers of children's products have even entered the school environment in order to promote the goods. They give the teachers such items as pencils and book covers which are, in turn, given to the children. In some cases the manufacturers are even furnishing books containing advertisements of their products.[16] One producer of food goods has developed a coloring book that can be purchased from magazine racks in supermarkets.[17] It appears to be an ordinary coloring book except that it contains some pictures of the manufacturer's products.

Marketing to children is not without its problems, however. To some parents the idea of selling to children conjures up visions of exploitation of the innocent and unknowing.[18] Consequently, marketers must be careful when "courting" the child consumer so as not to offend the parent.

Catering to children can be troublesome for

[16] The author's daughter used a supplementary geography book during the fifth grade which was furnished by a bakery. The bakery's bread was generously advertised throughout the book.
[17] *Grocery Store Coloring Book,* Bozell and Jacobs, Inc., and Skinner Macroni Co., 1965.
[18] Roy G. Francis, "Some Sociological Implications of Demographic Change," in William A. Mindak, *Proceedings of the 8th Biennial Marketing Institute of the Minnesota Chapter* (Chicago: American Marketing Association, 1961), p. II–y.

the retailer. He frequently claims that children damage goods or fixtures and make shopping unpleasant for adults.

Finally, there is the problem of finding adequate media through which to advertise directly to children. The marketer is normally limited to a few television programs, a small number of radio programs and comic books. Usually he is not allowed, for example, to place cards on school buses or sign boards near the schools.

Conclusions

A child market definitely exists in the United States. Like the teenager and adults, the child has wants and the means to satisfy them.

The specific desires of the child market differ from those of older consumers. Therefore, this new market must be treated differently by marketers who wish to serve it. Special advertisements in special advertising media must be employed. Merchandising at the retail level must take the nature of the child into consideration.

Marketing to this young group is difficult and troublesome. But the rewards may be great. Not only can marketers benefit profitably by serving this market now, but they may be ensuring themselves for future marketing as the youngster grows. If the child is served correctly in his early consumer years, he probably will develop store and brand loyalties that will remain throughout his life. Such a marketing strategy might be termed "growing customers for future use."

25-B PSYCHOGRAPHICS: "WE'VE FOUND THE FRIEND'S HOUSE"

Why is it that in today's neatly staked-out demographic landscape, where income, education, and job status are pretty much carbon-copy matters, only certain families live aggressive, consuming lives, buy with an adventuresome flair, and passionately pursue

SOURCE: "Psychographics: 'We've Found the Friend's House,'" *Sales Management,* 101 (*July 15,* 1968), pp. 58–64. Reprinted by permission from *Sales Management: The Marketing Magazine;* copyright, 1969, Sales Management, Inc.

the gracious, free-flowing life-style? If researchers could sift out the big spenders from their conservative and cautious neighbors, and identify them for advertisers, then the marketer, the copywriter, and the brand manager would be in clover. And what if certain magazines could link circulation to the families who, demonstrably, out-buy their demographic neighbors?

Although demographic studies abound, until now it has been almost impossible to predict—or even understand—differing prod-

In the affluent world of "upper demography," can good prospects be distinguished from bad? Indeed yes, say Dr. Emanuel H. Demby and Dr. Louis Cohen, of Motivational Programmers, Inc. Asked by Holiday magazine to prove the point, MPI now turns in its report which divides the nation into "creatives"—big spenders, and "passives"—not so big. Among the most sensitive barometers separating one from the other, MPI reports, are these:

Purchase or Activity	Creatives %	Passives %
Watch pro baseball on TV regularly	8	28
Professional sports instruction for self in past year	37	16
More than 10 round trips by air in lifetime	80	25
Four or more business trips by air in past year	49	7
Have rented auto at least once	83	39
Possess valid foreign passport	28	4
Visited museum in past six months	54	17
Now member of book or record club	44	19
Read five or more nonfiction books in past year	56	14
Read five or more fiction books in past year	55	15
Ever go fishing?	54 "yes"	63 "yes"
Hunting?	26 "yes"	33 "yes"
Skiing?	20 "yes"	7 "yes"

uct purchasing patterns and buying motives among families within the same demographic package. Now along comes Dr. Emanuel H. Demby, 48, president of Motivational Programmers, Inc., New York City, whose company has done major research for IBM, *Time,* and Celanese Corp., among others. He is out to prove that not only can life-styles be identified and classified for the marketer but that purchasing behavior can then be revealed and explained.

Money doesn't matter much, Demby says blithely. Rather, the "qualitative difference in new-product purchasing styles" differentiates between light- and heavy-purchase groups, between the grade A prospect and the dud— even though both make $10,000 a year. The poor prospect for premium-priced, quality products is the individual who favors status quo living and who seldom buys anything which will change deep habit ruts—the "passive" individual. His opposite, the "creative," whose orientation is highly social and outgoing, relishes change and is eager to buy and try new products that hint of zestful living: *imported* beer, not just "beer"; hot trays; blenders; jazz concerts.

The Creative Criteria

Significantly, Demby's creative-passive approach reached a supportable stage last year in Cleveland, where he meticulously probed the purchasing histories and patterns of life of 393 upper- and middle-income households. He found that of some 300 relatively new products and services "characteristic of an interesting, creative way of life," a checklist of just 37 could be used to segment the heavy buyers—the creatives—from the low-purchase passives, even though both groups were equally well-heeled. The Cleveland sample, in fact, split almost in half: 51 percent qualified as creative, and 49 percent, passive.

More than four times as many of Demby's Cleveland creatives bought Bitter Lemon, "the sophisticated drink mix," as passives, for example. On the other hand, the passives almost matched the creatives in room air conditioners because, says Demby, "You don't have to be creative to want to be cool." The creatives led, understandably, in the purchase of electric hot trays and electric food blenders: "No antecedent product; you need to be creative to understand how and when to use a blender." Thus, Demby concluded, after categorizing his Cleveland households, "There is obviously a powerful segmentation at work which goes beyond the demographic. Marketing men tend to see purchasing behavior as a person's central activity. In a way it is, for what you buy reflects what you are, your frame of reference to life."

B. RESEARCH AND APPLICATIONS

The discussion now turns to segmentation problems and the criteria that may be used to determine market segments, namely, the use of psychological classifications (Lunn).

25-C PSYCHOLOGICAL CLASSIFICATION

J. A. Lunn (*Marketing Educator*)

In both marketing and advertising strategy, there is a growing emphasis on the need for market segmentation. Researchers are not merely being asked such questions as, "How many people bought our product last week?" or "What do people think of our product vis-à-vis competitors'?"

Increasingly, they are also being asked, "What *kind* of people are our heavy buyers, how do they differ from light buyers, from nonbuyers?" or "Who are the best prospects?"

The assumption made is that people are not all equally likely to buy a given brand or product. Needs and circumstances differ, and, with them, so do purchasing patterns. Granted this assumption, it may be unwise to aim a product at the total population. The initial success of a new launch or the continuing success of a long-established brand, may hinge upon the precise identification of the best *target subgroup*—a group of people whose needs and circumstances predispose them towards purchase of the product.

For instance, it might be important to identify our target group for product testing, so that their preferences are not swamped by the irrelevant, possibly misleading, preferences of people for whom this kind of product has little appeal. The same considerations apply throughout the research process, for example

SOURCE: J. A. Lunn, "Psychological Classification," *Commentary: The Journal of the British Market Research Society* (July, 1966), pp. 161–173, at pp. 161–163.

in brand-image research, copy testing, and media allocation.

This growing wish to focus attention on specific population subgroups has led to a critical re-examination of market research tools for this purpose—that is upon the standard repertoire of consumer classifications. For years we have analyzed our data by such characteristics as age, social class, region, household size. These so-called demographic variables have an obvious value. They identify important differences in peoples' circumstances, which are often reflected in their buying behavior. For example, larger households often buy more and different kinds of products than smaller households; sheer size of disposable income obviously sets certain constraints on purchasing.

However, it is becoming increasingly realized that demographic classifications alone are inadequate for segmentation. Consequently, a demand has arisen for new forms of classification, both to provide a sharper description of present and potential buyers and at the same time, to increase our understanding of the market situation. And considerable interest has been taken in the possibilities of classification by psychological characteristics.

THE NEW CLASSIFICATIONS. We have developed a number of new attitude classifications. Some of these have been very specific, and mainly applicable to the product field in question. Others, however, have been of a more general nature, clearly applicable to a much wider span of consumer behavior. These latter we regard as the first steps towards our final objective; namely, the establishment of a small repertoire of consumer personality scales, each of proven value to several product fields.

I shall now outline some of these more general dimensions under three headings.

1. Firstly, the area of *economy*. Despite a certain amount of initial scepticism we have found it possible to develop measures reflecting a concern with economy that applies to a wide range of purchases. This does appear to be a general housewife characteristic. What we have found, however, is that there are at least two distinct facets between which it is important to distinguish. Firstly, there is what we call "economy-mindedness"—the tendency to buy cheap rather than expensive goods, to keep within a strict housekeeping limit, to deny oneself luxuries. This is quite different from what we call "bargain-seeking," which reflects the satisfaction of saving a few pennies by shopping carefully and comparing prices, and the relish of hunting for bargains. One way of putting the distinction is that whereas the economy-minded housewife abhors extravagance, the bargain-conscious woman may welcome it: but she looks for the cheapest shop to be extravagant in.

We have checked on this distinction a number of times, and found the two scales to have a quite distinct pattern of correlates. For example, the more *economy-minded* housewives tend to come from the lower social classes, but not from any particular family-size group. However, the more *bargain-seeking* housewives are found amongst all social classes, but tend to come from larger households. The two scales also identify separate patterns of consumer behavior.

2. Another area is that of *experimentalism*, which may be defined as a willingness to and relish in buying new and different things. This again appears to be a very general characteristic. It does, however, have two quite distinct opposites. On the one hand are the rigid people who have an almost compulsive need to do

and buy the same kind of things: on the other hand are the people who are afraid to buy something new or different, unless, say, it has been strongly recommended, and who are anxious in case a purchase turns out to be a mistake.

3. A third and quite different area is *conservatism*. Here we mean the people who have relatively old-fashioned tastes and habits. For example, in housework they relish doing things by hand, and enjoy cleaning and polishing the hard way; they abhor quick, easy methods and labor-saving devices: in cooking, they prefer the traditional methods and recipes.

HOW DO THE NEW CLASSIFICATIONS RELATE TO CONSUMER BEHAVIOR? Our first results have been very encouraging. We are identifying pronounced differences in patterns of usage and purchase for both products and brands.

I have only space for a few illustrations, and have chosen examples for scales mentioned in the previous section. I am unable in this paper to specify product fields.

Example 1—conservatism. The *conservatism* scale was tried in a field where there are two distinct types of product: A requires considerable effort in its usage, whereas B is very much a labor-saving product. (see Fig. 1)

Analyses by demographic breakdowns had shown no significant discrimination between regular buyers of the two products: analysis by conservatism showed quite marked discrimination. (Fig. 1).

Example 2—experimentalism. My second example is from a product field of fairly recent origin, but in which a high proportion of housewives purchase. There is a slight tendency for buying to vary with age and social class. But much sharper relationships were found between heaviness of buying and each of four psychological classifications. The most pronounced of these was experimentalism.

Analysis by product *type* proved even more illuminating. In Fig. 2, type A is a fairly recent launch, type B one of the earliest launches. It can be seen that A is achieving its sales chiefly to keen experimentalists. How-

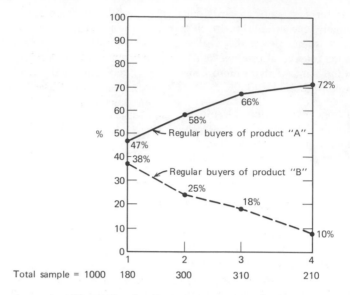

Figure 1. Score on conservatism scale.

ever, a disinclination to be experimental is no longer a barrier to buying *B*.

Incidentally, some analyses currently being performed are confirming the general value of the experimentalism scale. High experimentalists show much more brand-switching and, correspondingly, less brand-loyalty over a range of product fields. Moreover, there are indications that this scale may help to identify "new product buyers" or even "innovators,"[1] groups whose possible existence has intrigued

---

[1] The assumption is sometimes made that it is important, when launching a new product, to ensure that it appeals to a group of "innovators," at once experimental and influential whose acceptance of the product will do much to ensure its success. And that, consequently, we should focus upon them in all the research stages preparatory to the launch of a new brand or product. There may be a lot in this. But there are a number of other considerations. For instance, unless the product also satisfies some specific additional need, psychological or physical, the innovators, while happy to give it a trial will quickly transfer their allegiance elsewhere. Indeed, there may be a group of extreme experimentalists—"try anything once-ers"—whose purchasing is so fickle and changeable that their opinions should be isolated in new product research in order to be ignored: at least in the field of frequently purchased consumer expendables.

market researchers for some time. (See, for instance, the paper given by John Clemens at the 1963 M.R.S. Annual Conference.[2])

Example 3—"economy." The first two examples showed simple relationships between a single scale on the one hand and a measure of consumer behavior on the other. Clearly, the situation is more complex than this. And to give a more precise and, therefore, valuable picture, we need to interrelate those classifications, psychological, demographic, or whatever that are important for the aspect of consumer behavior under study.

Value for Marketing and Advertising

The kind of classifications I have discussed are quantitative: they enable us to divide people into groups in terms of their different positions along the dimensions concerned. And to a large extent they can be used throughout the market research process in the same way as demographic classifications.

Assume we have shown, or have reason to believe, that experimentalism is a key variable for our brand: our target group lies mainly among high experimentalists. We might select our sample for product testing and copy test-

[2] J. Clemens, "New Product Buyers," in *New Developments in Research* (London: The British Market Research Society, 1963).

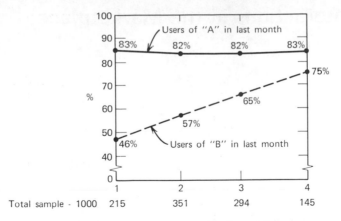

Figure 2. Score on experimentalism scale.

ing chiefly from among the high-priority group: we might use experimentalism as a breakdown in usership and brand-image studies: and, if high experimentalists are shown to have particular viewing or reading habits, we might give media instructions accordingly.

Moreover, being expressed in terms of motivations, psychological classifications increase our understanding of the market and suggest marketing action. Take the example shown in Fig. 1. Here, it seems that there are two distinct submarkets separately catered for by product types A and B. If our brand was an A type, we would focus attention upon the more conservative groups and stress one set of product benefits; if it was a B type, we would focus attention upon the least conservative groups and stress a quite different set of benefits. (There might, of course, be benefits common to the two types.)

At the same time, we might obtain leads for pack design; or even for a new or modified product to satisfy needs not at present fully catered for. We might also obtain leads for distribution, if we discovered that our target group say high conservatives favored a particular type of outlet, say counter-service stores.

This greater understanding of the consumer not only helps marketing decisions: it also helps advertising men, and in broadly two ways.

Firstly, we are able to provide copywriters with rich and detailed portraits of the kind of people on whom they should focus their advertising—and of the most persuasive copy themes, either to reinforce existing buyers or to win over fresh buyers.

Secondly, where psychological target groups can be shown to have particular viewing, reading, even travelling patterns, there may be an opportunity for more efficient media allocation.

26 / Interactions in the Marketplace

A. BACKGROUND AND THEORY

The first reading in this section (Marvin) points out some basic concepts that underlie a company's product strategies. We then turn to an analysis (Weiss) of consumer "rights" and their effects on corporate activities in marketing.

26-A   SOME BASIC CONCEPTS UNDERLYING COMPANY [PRODUCT] STRATEGY

Philip Marvin (Marketing Executive)

Those responsible for advancing technology and maintaining company operations provide leadership not only by exhausting inner-directed resources but also by borrowing the best from the experiences of others. A process that proceeds from observation to analysis, synthesis, testing, and evaluation and then begins all over again with more observation is fundamental to future growth and development.

Failure to capitalize on new concepts can be just as disastrous as failure to capitalize on growth opportunities. One is related to the other. Growth opportunities inherent in a changing business climate generate a need for new concepts. If the business is to take advantage of growth opportunities as they appear on the horizon, these needs must be met.

Industry leaders of the future, as in the past, will be those who have noted these new needs and acted to meet them as they arose. Keeping up with the Joneses isn't enough in business operations. "Firstness" can be an asset. Real leaders don't deal in averages—they set averages for others to achieve. Their acute aware-

SOURCE: Philip Marvin, "Some Basic Concepts Underlying Company [Product] Strategy," reprinted with permission from *Developing a Product Strategy* (Elizabeth Marting, editor), AMA Management Report No. 39, American Management Association, 1959, pp. 11–24, at pp. 11–13.

ness aids them in developing a sensitivity to situations and details. They detect ways and means of turning opportunities into profits.

There are no secrets of success in the sense that they are inscribed on a parchment and safely secured in the inner recesses of a vault owned by one of the more prosperous companies. Most successful executives will admit that many of the keys to prosperity for their organizations would only have unlocked doors to disaster in other businesses. The important thing to determine, these men add, is what's good for the individual company.

But one suspects that there are certain clues or guidelines having more or less universal applicability that will help management profit from the lessons learned by others in planning for growth. These guidelines are highlighted by synthesizing the experiences of executives that reveal the causal factors underlying success or failure. They disclose no new managerial concepts and no radically different techniques. Rather, they reveal common shortcomings that have cropped up when management's time and thought have been diverted by a myriad of matters demanding attention. Revealing, as they do, some serious pitfalls, they might justifiably be called secrets of success.

Some specific questions provide keys to these clues:

1. Are the basic ingredients of growth recognized?

2. Are profit-producing responsibilities clearly positioned?

3. Are performance-measurement areas known and understood?

4. How does the product plan fit into the risk spectrum?

5. Is size growing faster than earnings?

Basic Ingredients of Growth

In planning ahead, it is important to have a clear concept of the factors that contribute to business growth. Companies that have developed in size, strength, and income have capitalized on four opportunities for growth. These are (1) growth markets, (2) capital accumu-. lation, (3) technical advance, and (4) creative merchandising.

The first—growth markets—calls attention to opportunities that are created by population increases, bringing about the demand for different products as our way of living expands and develops new needs. Capital accumulation gives a business a resource to work with and the opportunity to multiply management's effectiveness as a profit producer. Technological advances reveal new directions that product and process exploitation can take. Creative merchandising provides the opportunity of acquiring a greater share of customers' dollars.

Each of these opportunities is open in varying degrees to every business man. All must be combined with the ability to turn opportunities into a profitable return on the investment involved.

26-B MARKETERS FIDDLE WHILE CONSUMERS BURN

E. B. Weiss (Marketing Executive)

It was in 1962 that President John F. Kennedy proclaimed the consumer's four-pronged Magna Charta:

1. The right to safety.
2. The right to be informed.
3. The right to choose.
4. The right to be heard.

These four "rights" symbolized—and heralded—consumerism. They became the basis for auto and tire safety legislation, the truth-in-packaging bill, and truth-in-credit regulations. And they will spawn six to ten additional consumer bills over the next several years.

In 1962, industry tended to shrug off consumerism as a political gambit that would soon fizzle out. During the six ensuing years, each industry affected by proposed legislation has tended, on balance, to oppose uncompromisingly each new legislative proposal on behalf of consumerism. The food industry fought truth-in-packaging bills for five years. Truth-in-credit legislation was opposed by the credit industry for seven years. The meat packers'

SOURCE: E. B. Weiss, "Marketers Fiddle While Consumers Burn," *Harvard Business Review*, Vol. 46 (July–August, 1968), pp. 48–53, at pp. 48–51. © 1968 by the President and Fellows of Harvard College; all rights reserved.

initial posture was one of confrontation; reluctant collaboration came only toward the end of the debate.

Clearly, industry has been unwilling to accept the philosophy that what is good for the public is good for business. That is why few corporate managements have directed the organizational changes necessitated by consumerism, why even fewer managements have charted an imaginative course to guide present consumer legislation to beneficial socioeconomic ends, and why few managements have ordered a study of impending consumer legislation so as to have an appropriate marketing program ready in advance.

In short, after six years of tuning up, Washington is literally racing toward additional consumerism legislation, regulation, and organization. State governments are doing the same thing, and so are many city governments. But industry's attitude tends to remain a mixture of confrontation, lamentation, and pious posturing. The marketing fraternity, especially, is almost united in its opposition. Marketing conventions resound with wails of anguish, of frustration, of bewilderment. Thunderous applause is reserved for the speaker who ties Communism and consumerism into an unholy alliance.

This is the road to a quasi-utility status for

marketing. I do not predict that corporate marketing departments will be supervised in the minute way that railroads or power companies are. But I do foresee a future in which, rightly or wrongly, marketing will be regulated by law far more than it has ever been before. Most marketing leaders have only themselves to blame if they do not like this prospect.

The 'Smugly' Americans

I will concede that at the very top management level, consumerism is tending to be accepted as part of the new dimensions of corporate social responsibility. But, at the marketing level, fanatical and tearful defense of the status quo remains typical. It is probable that the top managements of many companies will direct their marketing departments to adopt policies and practices more responsive to the public's desires. If this happens, it will help. But in view of marketing's abysmal record to date, I am dubious that it can save itself in time from substantial extensions of government regulation.

WHO NEEDS 1,000 EYES! The Chinese say the buyer needs a thousand eyes—the seller but one. Marketing wants to keep it that way. However, consumerism now says the *seller* needs a thousand eyes—the buyer but one.

The buyer will never be protected to that degree, but he will need fewer than 1,000 eyes in the future. Years ago, when the employer became legally responsible for reasonable diligence in providing safe working conditions for his employees, and when workmen's compensation laws emerged, both the incidence and the severity of on-the-job injuries were sharply reduced. Is it unreasonable to conclude that new legal concepts of the seller's responsibilities and liabilities could accomplish similar results for the general public?

Consumer exploitation has been replacing labor exploitation as the real problem of our times. *We would not permit the things to be done to people as workers that we allow to be done to them as shoppers!* A more intelligent society, especially its younger generation, insists this must change.

But the market is self-policing, argues the marketing man, because the shopper is sovereign. This is true in a legalistic sense, perhaps—and it may check with the precepts of clas-

ical economics. But to the U.S. public of today it sounds more and more like pure poppycock.

No marketing man hissed (but hundreds applauded) when the former president of a large publishing enterprise declared:

"Freedom of shopping decision is a fundamental prerogative—even the freedom to be wrong, to make a wrong choice. No one has to buy anything, at any price, at any time. . . . Some degree of responsibility must rest on and with the consumer. He cannot be regarded as a pitiable imbecile. He cannot be wholly protected in every move and every purchase he makes, every day of his life."

Bewildered Buyers

The fact is that technology is expanding at such an unprecedented rate and spawning such a torrent of new products that it is difficult for the trade, not to mention consumers, to keep fully informed about them. Should shoppers be expected to be able to differentiate between a latex foam mattress and a urethane foam mattress? How many consumers can be expected to understand the difference between a transistorized and a solid-state radio or TV?

Technology has brought unparalleled abundance and opportunity to the consumer. It has also exposed him to new complexities and hazards. It has made his choices more difficult. He cannot be chemist, mechanic, electrician, nutritionist, *and* a walking computer (very necessary when shopping for fractionated-ounce food packages)! Faced with almost infinite product differentiation (plus contrived product virtues that are purely semantic), considerable price differentiation, the added complexities of trading stamps, the subtleties of cents-off deals, and other complications, the shopper is expected to choose wisely under circumstances that baffle professional buyers. His job is not made easier by the fact that prices tend *not* to be uniform in different stores even of the same food chain, and may vary daily. Moreover, if he is like most of us, he has to decide in a hurry.

Let us suppose he stops to buy a can opener. He finds there are hand, wall, and table models, manually operated or electrically powered. Some are combined with knife sharpeners. They are finished with various materials. They come in a range of colors. Some differences are functional and practical; others are merely for appearance or for promotion. Moreover, he must usually choose the can opener without the aid of a salesclerk. (If a clerk is present, he is apt to be as confused and unknowing as the customer!)

CAVEAT VENDITOR. I am not arguing that prices should not fluctuate, that various package sizes should not be offered, or that different models, brands, and colors should not be displayed. My point is simply that the shopper is dazed—and understandably so. U.S. marketers should be taking far more responsibility than they have thus far to help the customer make decisions. Just how much protection does he or she need? That is a question about which reasonable and sincere men differ; but the need for offering *much more* than at present is, in my opinion, beyond dispute.

A free economy depends on rational consumer choice. If consumers cannot choose wisely, if they regularly reach their decisions in a state of wonder and perplexity, if they make their choices on the basis of meaningless and irrelevant claims, a free economy suffers.

Just as a rational voting procedure is necessary to a free political system, so a rational shopping system is necessary to a free market. The marketplace displays more irrationality than rationality. The better educated, more sophisticated shopper of today is beginning to rebel. Politicians are paying heed; marketers are not.

Can Self-Regulation Succeed?

Marketing men regularly advance the contention that the device of self-regulation should be attempted and exhausted before resorting to legislative remedies. It is beyond dispute that our whole political and economic system fares better if regulation of industry takes place voluntarily by business itself. The sad fact, however, is that marketing has an especially poor record of self-regulation, even in areas where its self-interest is most obvious. The list of consumer legislation (ranging from auto safety laws and product warranties to meat controls and truth-in-lending regulations) is obviously a damning indictment of the failure of marketing to regulate itself. So are the scores of fair practice codes voluntarily drawn up by industry under Federal Trade Commission supervision—and then blithely ignored by industry.

Dr. William Haddon, Jr., Administrator of the National Highway Safety Agency, reminded the auto industry of the inherent futility of self-regulation: "Voluntary standards failed to produce the degree of safety that could be well afforded through the more universal application of modern technology."[1] Because Detroit lacked the foresight to act with statesmanship on matters of the greatest public urgency, safety standards for automobiles are now being established by government.

'CAN WE GET AWAY WITH IT?' Some marketing men ask, "Wouldn't industrial self-regulation be a lot more effective if the antitrust laws were repealed to allow better enforcement of codes of ethics?" Unfortunately, nothing in the present or in the past history of business conduct in the face of competition justifies any real confidence that self-regulatory power would not be abused by business. Perhaps no function of business has indicted itself more severely in this respect than marketing. The marketing practices that are regulated in most consumer legislation seldom involve out-and-out fraud (which is susceptible to some degree of effective self-regulation). Instead, they embrace marketing practices in the gray areas. This is the crux of consumer legislation—not fraud, but dubious ethics, dubious morality.

There is a decided tendency in marketing to use the words "legal" and "honest" interchangeably. When the marketing executive says that most marketing programs are "honest," what he really means is that most marketing programs operate within the law. His too-common tendency is to ask, "Is it legal?" If the answer is affirmative, then he presumes he has demonstrated his responsibility to society. In short, the philosophy of the day, in considering borderline cases involving public taste, fair dealing, and full and accurate information, too often seems to be, "This is the deal: Can we get away with it?"

This attitude may have sufficed in a previous age, but a more sophisticated society, especially the younger and better educated segments, is now beginning to say, "That is

[1] Quoted in *Freedom of Information in the Marketplace* (Columbia, Missouri, School of Journalism, University of Missouri), December 1966.

not a modern concept of social responsibility."
It is saying that marketing must observe standards of morality and good taste. It is even
saying, at this very moment, that the business
community definitely and specifically has a
legal obligation to protect the user *against
his own carelessness!* It wants to hold the manu-

facturer accountable for harm to the careless,
as well as the careful, user.

The burden of proof will increasingly be on
the seller. The trend will be to hold him
strictly liable without requiring proof of negligence or culpability. This view has already
become law in several states.

B. RESEARCH AND APPLICATIONS

This section begins with a look at some new products that have succeeded
(Nielsen) and some of the reasons for their success. We then turn to a method
that uses consumer satisfaction as a measure of marketing effectiveness (McNeal).

26-C WHAT ARE THEY LOOKING FOR?

Arthur C. Nielsen, Jr. (Marketing Educator)

The old axiom that the word "new" is the
most exciting word in the English language
appears to be as true today as it always was,
in spite of incessant usage. It is, in fact, sometimes difficult to understand how a word used
as often as this one is could continue to have
any impact at all, but such seems to be the
case.

To the consumer it promises a product that
is different in either sight, smell, taste or function and thus "better"—at least in some small
but definable way. Just how well most new
products live up to this promise is a matter
of judgment by the individual consumer, but
it does appear that many products declared to
be "new" are found to be something less than
that by a majority of consumers. This naturally
leads to a high mortality rate for new products.

In the huge field of drug and grocery products—over $64 billion annually—where some
of the most inventive and aggressive manufacturers in the world compete, it is possible to
get a reasonably good estimate of the percentage of new products that succeed or fail because of the wide use made of Nielsen testmarketing facilities. Consider the results of 103

new or improved products that were tested.
(It should be pointed out that many new products "fail" before they ever reach the testmarketing stage.) Consumers found that 56
of them were new enough and different
enough to satisfy their desire for something
with which to feed their dogs, reduce their
waistlines, brush their teeth, spread on their
bread, or use in dozens of different ways. These
consumers proved their interest in the only
way that really counts, by buying the product,
using it, and then buying it again. "People"
proved just how much they wanted to buy
these 56 new products by spending over $550
million on them during a recent 12-month period, *even though nine of them had been on
the market less than a year.* (No attempt was
made to adjust their volume to equal a 12-
month total.)

But what were the circumstances regarding
some of the products individually? What, for
example, were some of the details surrounding
the success of these products?

Although we must refrain from identifying
the products by name, we can disclose some
of the background and action surrounding
the marketing of a few of these products in
order to better explain why consumers were
so obviously willing to invest money in the
satisfaction promised by these products. We
believe the following case histories help in
this regard.

SOURCE: Arthur C. Nielsen, Jr., "What Are they
Looking For?" Reprinted from *Printer's Ink,* Vol.
287 (May 29, 1964), pp. 58–62. Copyright 1964
by Decker Communications, Inc., 501 Madison
Ave., New York, N.Y.

DELTA BRAND. *Pertinent history:* The product group in this case is large (total national sales average around $50 million each bimonthly period based on consumer prices), and is split among many minor brands traditionally accounting for over 50 per cent of the market.

Leading national brands in this group seldom achieve a sales share of much over ten per cent, with most of them considerably under this figure. "Delta" brand was introduced into this product group by a manufacturer who already had the largest-selling brand in the field. Although Delta, as a finished product, was developed in the company's own research laboratories, the principle or discovery that led to its origin was the result of independent scientific investigation (university type) which was widely published in national magazines and newspapers.

In the initial promotion, the manufacturer of Delta used heavy couponing in all major markets and an advertising theme tied closely to the wide interest generated by the scientific disclosure. The introductory phase was successful—measured by any yardstick—but it took a year to prove that Delta's progress was something more than a successful promotion. It might be added that Delta's all-commodity distribution is now just three points shy of the leading brand in this product group; what's more, Delta's companion brand has maintained the competitive position it held prior to Delta's entry in the field.

PARK BRAND. *Pertinent history:* Despite the seemingly inexhaustible public demand for products of the type represented by "Park" brand, very few well-known manufacturers have ventured into the field for numerous reasons. Perhaps the foremost among these was the well-known fickleness of consumers for items of this type, which in turn had given companies producing these products somewhat of a reputation for hit-and-run tactics. That many other manufacturers had kept a covetous eye cocked in this direction can be gauged by the number of companies that entered the field, once the ground had been broken by Park brand, the product of a highly respected firm.

The introduction of Park to the national market was accomplished by advertising alone, with a rather noteworthy lack of free samples or any other type of consumer deal. Although advertising expenditures were heavy, the copy itself was soft-sell. This had the virtue of being a refreshingly new approach to the advertising of products of this type.

Starting from scratch, sales of Park increased with such velocity that they had already reached the multi-million-dollar stage by the time the first bimonthly measurement was taken. Distribution by then had also expanded to a level that could be considered almost perfect from the standpoint of exposure.

Perhaps most significant, in view of Park's monumental success, are the possible rewards inherent in providing not only a first-rate product, but also in recognizing the effectiveness a restrained advertising appeal can have in certain cases.

SIGMA BRAND. *Pertinent history:* "Sigma" brand entered a relatively new product group with a standard type product (A), but had also developed two specialty types (B and C) which were held in reserve.

Primarily due to the importance of Sigma's manufacturer, plus the strength of the introductory promotion, reasonably wide distribution was achieved for type A within a relatively short time. Share of consumer sales however, instead of rising as distribution expanded and consumer awareness of Sigma increased, actually declined.

After about six months, when it was definitely decided that A was not going to live up to its expectation, types B and C were placed on the market. In just ten months distribution of each surpassed that of A, as did share of total market sales.

This case seems to bear out once more the advantage of having more than a single string for one's bow. Instead of having to spend many months in developing new varieties or types, Sigma's manufacturer was ready to launch a new offensive with B and C as soon as A's indifferent success was apparent. These two new types, in less than a year's time, had taken over a fifth of the entire market.

Further evidence of the public's reaction to new products can be gained from a Nielsen study of 18 new and/or improved brands. On the chart we have compared the sales gain for all grocery products versus the composite trend for 18 brands over the same time period. Note that at the end of the second year, the 18 new products were up 51 per cent, com-

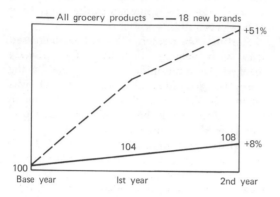

Legend: — All grocery products   — — 18 new brands

+51%

108   +8%
104
100
Base year   1st year   2nd year

Figure 1. Sales of new and/or improved products vs. all grocery products (two-year trend).

pared to an eight per cent gain for all products. An examination of the 18 individual brands reveals that they all had something *really new* to strike the consumer's fancy—a plus that was easily apparent to the user. Fifteen of the 18 brands were entirely new; three represented improved established brands.

And so the evidence could be piled higher and higher, revealing the consumer's desire for new products. Although each case presents a different set of circumstances, products and promotional methods, some basic similarities existed in all examples. A good new product—different in some demonstrable way —was an essential ingredient common to all. Intelligent promotion or advertising that developed wide distribution was also present in each case. Once these elements are coupled with proper timing and strong support, there is little doubt as to the reaction people have to new products: *They buy them!*

We can prove that people buy them—at least the good ones that are well-marketed, as stated above. But why people buy the first package—before they know whether it is good, bad, or indifferent—is another matter.

To begin with, it seems obvious that a variety of deep-seated psychological factors enters into the reasons why some people prefer one product to the other; or, why certain people

couldn't wait to buy their first television set, and others claimed they wouldn't have one in the house.

But these strong—and sometimes bizarre— reactions to new products seem much more pronounced when ownership implies an expression of personal taste or affluence. Clothing, automobiles, homes, etc., fall more easily into this category than most articles sold in food and drug stores. And the reasons why people buy new cake mixes, cold tablets, or detergents (or the thousands of other everyday products) usually reflect, I believe, different motivations.

Naturally, the most important single reason is knowing that the new product exists. Here, of course, advertising is playing a vital role in informing the public about new products. The second most obvious factor is the new products' easy availability. From then on, I believe the reasons tend to vary as to importance. It appears that curiosity must play a large part with some people, whereas others must be entirely convinced by advertising, or word-of-mouth recommendations. Here, it seems that the manufacturer's past reputation as a producer of "good new products" is a significant factor.

Some people will buy almost anything if it is cheap enough. How often one hears the expression, "I couldn't go wrong at that price," from a new purchaser regardless of the expected benefits. On the other hand, some people will buy a product only when it is priced at a level commensurate with the benefit they expect to derive from it. Home-permanent-wave kits are a good example of this. The first kits introduced were priced at 49 cents and no one was interested. They were later reintroduced at around $1.25 and sold like hot cakes.

There are perhaps other reasons I've failed to mention, such as timing, package design, or size—all of definite importance in a wide variety of instances.

I'm not sure yet why millions of people bought hula hoops, but they did, and they'll buy many more unpredictable new products in the future. It makes for a fascinating world.

26-D CONSUMER SATISFACTION: THE MEASURE OF MARKETING EFFECTIVENESS

James U. McNeal (Marketing Educator)

Top management requires an accounting of all of its organizational units. Periodically, each department of a business must present some evidence of its effectiveness. The reason is obvious: in order for a company to succeed, each of its elements must succeed. A business firm is successful to the extent it achieves its objectives, but it can only achieve its objectives if the objectives of each of its organizational units are attained.

Today, as more and more business firms become marketing-oriented, the effectiveness of the marketing unit becomes paramount to the overall effectiveness of the firm. Consequently, increasing attention is being devoted to the measurement of marketing effectiveness.

The recent appearance of the marketing audit concept is evidence of the growing concern with marketing effectiveness. In effect, the marketing audit is a "systematic, critical, and impartial review and appraisal of the total marketing operation."[1]

While difficulty has been experienced in determining the means for measuring marketing effectiveness, it is generally conceded that the proper approach to this problem is to compare actual performance with objectives. In other words, marketing management asks, "Are we achieving what we set out to achieve so that we may make our necessary contribution to the basic goals of the firm?"

It is now fairly well established that the purpose or objective of a marketing organization is the satisfaction of a body of consumers at a profit. Practically all the textbooks that purport to teach the basics of marketing agree on this point. Consider these sample statements (italics added):

McCarthy—"The marketing job . . . is one of trying to *satisfy* a particular group of customers, the target group, with a particular goods or service."[2]

Stanton—"Customers' wants must be recognized and *satisfied effectively* (by Marketing.)"[3]

Matthews et. al.—". . . marketing (is preoccupied) with the idea of *satisfying* the needs of the customer. . . ."[4]

Field et. al.—"Marketing seeks to *satisfy* demand. . . ."[5]

Buskirk—". . . the end of all marketing activities must be to *satisfy* the desires of the people."[6]

Similar statements about the marketing-consumer relationship can be found in many other basic books as well as the advanced ones, and in numerous articles and speeches. In fact, the largest volume of proceedings ever issued by the American Marketing Association was concerned solely with this topic.[7]

While most marketing authorities apparently agree that the basic objective of marketing organizations should be consumer satisfaction

SOURCE: James U. McNeal, "Consumer Satisfaction: The Measure of Marketing Effectiveness," *MSU Business Topics,* Vol. 17 (Summer, 1969), pp. 31–35. Reprinted by permission of the publisher, the Bureau of Business and Economic Research, Division of Research, Graduate School of Business Administration, Michigan State University.

[1] Abe Shuchman, "The Marketing Audit: Its Nature, Purposes, and Problems," in William Lazer and Eugene J. Kelley, eds., *Managerial Marketing: Perspectives and Viewpoints,* rev. ed. (Homewood, Illinois: Richard D. Irwin, Inc., 1962), p. 399.

[2] E. Jerome McCarthy, *Basic Marketing, A Managerial Approach,* rev. ed. (Homewood, Illinois: Richard D. Irwin, Inc., 1962), p. 24.

[3] William J. Stanton, *Fundamentals of Marketing* (New York: McGraw-Hill Book Company, 1964), p. 5.

[4] John B. Matthews, Jr. et. al., *Marketing, An Introductory Analysis* (McGraw-Hill Book Company, 1964), p. 10.

[5] George A. Field, *Marketing Management: A Behavioral Systems Approach* (Columbus, Ohio: Charles E. Merrill Books, Inc., 1966), p. 13.

[6] Richard H. Buskirk, *Principles of Marketing: The Management View* (New York: Holt, Rinehart and Winston, Inc., 1966), p. 88.

[7] Robert M. Kaplan ed., *The Marketing Concept in Action* (Chicago: The American Marketing Association, 1964).

(at a desired profit level), these same individuals tend to avoid this goal in their discussions of measuring marketing effectiveness. Instead, attention is devoted to measuring effectiveness in terms of other marketing objectives such as profit or share of the market.[8] Tucker attempted to simplify with the economic view that "Consumer satisfaction can be best measured by what the consumer is willing to pay for a product or service."[9]

What is the marketing student and practitioner to believe when we tell him in one breath that "The performance of a marketing organization can only be evaluated in terms of the organization's objectives,"[10] and in another, that a basic objective of marketing should be consumer satisfaction? Is he not likely to assume, then, that a very important measure of a marketing organization's success or effectiveness is the extent to which it satisfies a body of consumers? And is he not likely to ask, "How do I measure the consumer satisfaction provided by a marketing organization?"

The answer to this latter question is not readily apparent in the literature. Its lack is both a gap and a dead end in marketing principles.

Some authorities avoid such a question by saying that consumer satisfaction is a philosophy rather than a goal. But calling the concept a philosophy rather than a goal or objective only creates a semantic problem, because philosophies like objectives are statements that give purpose to the marketing organization.[11]

Others avoid this problem by stating that consumer satisfaction is a social rather than a

company goal.[12] This is no more or less true than saying that profit is a social goal. Each company within the society must create consumer satisfaction as well as make a profit if the whole society is to continue to function in a desirable form.

Finally, it can sensibly be argued that consumer satisfaction is the goal of the whole firm rather than just the marketing organization.[13] Such a statement is justifiable; in fact, this is the essence of the marketing concept. But marketing, more than any other function of business, is involved with producing consumer satisfaction.

Fundamentally, management of an organization involves three functions:

- Setting objectives.

- Turning objectives into action.

- Evaluating actions to see if objectives are met.

If consumer satisfaction is the basic objective of marketing management as many authorities state, and if companies are putting the concept into action as many of them claim, then the question persists: *How does one determine if this objective, consumer satisfaction, is being met?*

The Study

A study was undertaken to determine if and how major producers of consumer goods and services ascertain the extent to which they are satisfying consumers.

A list of 128 firms was selected from *Fortune's 500* (June 1967). The particular firms selected were those considered to be leaders in their respective industries. They ranged in kind from airlines and clothing manufacturers to food and office equipment producers. Additionally, an effort was made to include any companies that, in speeches and in the literature, had reported they were operating under the marketing concept that consumer satisfaction is the goal of the entire firm. These, by definition, would be directly interested in the satisfaction of their customers.

All firms were contacted by a personal letter which contained one question, along with

---

[8] See, for example, John A. Howard, *Marketing Management Analysis and Planning*, rev. ed. (Homewood, Illinois: Richard D. Irwin, Inc., 1963).

[9] W. T. Tucker, "Marketing and Society," a paper delivered to the Southern Economic Association, 1959.

[10] Matthews et. al., *Marketing Introductory Analysis*, p. 504.

[11] This view was supported by F. J. Borch, then a vice-president of General Electric, in an address to the American Management Association more than ten years ago. See, "The Marketing Philosophy as a Way of Business Life," a reprint of the speech distributed by General Electric.

[12] Howard, *Marketing Management*, p. 17.

[13] Borch, "Marketing Philosophy," p. 3.

introductory and closing comments. Specifically, the firms were asked, "How do you determine the degree to which you are satisfying your customers?"

An open-ended question was used to gain as much latitude as possible in the responses. It was recognized that such an approach might discourage replies as contrasted to the simpler check-off type of questionnaire. Quantity of replies, however, was secondary to obtaining a good profile of the measures of consumer satisfaction employed by the firms.

Of the 128 firms contacted, fifty-eight responded. Five were discarded because they replied that there was no way to measure consumer satisfaction. One reply was discarded because the respondent apparently did not understand the question.

Findings

The fifty-two useful replies were analyzed. The results are presented in Table 1.

About 66 percent of the firms interviewed sought direct measures of consumer satisfaction. These companies performed some type of attitudinal research on their customers. The frequency of the consumer interviews were generalized by the terms "periodically," "from

TABLE 1

Factors Used by a Sample of Firms to Measure Consumer Satisfaction

Measurement Factor	Number of Companies Using Factor	Percent of Companies Using Factor
Consumer research studies	34	65.38
Unsolicited consumer responses	34	65.38
Sales volume/ trends	29	55.77
Share of market	22	41.92
Opinions of middlemen and salesmen	20	38.46
Market test results	7	13.46
Profit	1	2.0

time to time," and "often." The methodology varied considerably but the intent was to determine the degree of consumer satisfaction. For example, a leading airline replied that it used in-depth questioning of its passengers as well as a consumer panel for a broader range of questioning.

In only five cases did a firm report that it solicited attitudes of competitors' customers to see why they were not satisfied with the firm's product or service. The nature of the research question may have caused this small response concerning nonusers. If the firms, in fact, are not studying the consuming habits of competitors' customers, they are overlooking some valuable information that might provide directions for market expansion.

About two-thirds of the fifty-two companies reported that they analyzed unsolicited letters from customers to get a measure of consumer satisfaction. This is significant, since consumers typically believe that such letters to companies are treated casually, if at all. It should be recognized, however, that unsolicited comments probably do not come from a representative sample of customers.

Over one-half of the firms used sales and sales trends as barometers of consumer satisfaction. As one executive stated, "If it sells, it is satisfying people." Sales seemed to be a natural measure of consumer satisfaction to many of the respondents. Yet, there may be some danger in using this factor as completely indicative. While sales do indicate that someone desired a product, they do not indicate the degree of satisfaction. And there are many other determinants of sales, environmental elements, for example, that would prevent the conclusion that sales are a direct measure of consumer satisfaction.

Share of the market was used by 44 percent of the firms as an index of consumer satisfaction. Market share, like sales volume, seemed to be an obvious indicator of consumer satisfaction to a number of the respondents. It is a questionable index, however. It is conceivable for a company to have a major share of a market while only partially satisfying it. For instance, a minor change in a product or service might increase consumer satisfaction considerably while the market share remained the same. Stone has shown, for example, that some small retailers having only a meager share of a market are able to produce high satisfaction for certain groups of consumers.[14]

Forty-two percent of the firms reported that they used opinions of middlemen and/or company salesmen to give some idea of the extent of consumer satisfaction being generated. Companies frequently seek market data from their salesmen and dealers who have direct or near-direct contact with consumers. There is a tendency, however, for salesmen to be optimistic and dealers to be pessimistic. If their opinions about consumer satisfaction are to be used, they must be adjusted to account for their dispositions.

A few firms, 14 percent, reported that they measured the satisfaction-producing qualities of a product while it was in a test market. The implication in such a response is that the measure of satisfaction that was obtained during the test market will continue during the commercialization of the product. Follow-up measures are logically necessary.

Surprisingly, only one firm in the study viewed profits as a measure of consumer satisfaction. This is somewhat contrary to what is suggested or implied by many marketing textbooks. Apparently the companies interviewed were aware that profits, like sales, are influenced by many factors. Short-run profits may be earned while only slightly satisfying consumers. Or consumer satisfaction may be high while a firm's profits are depressed because of the oligopolistic nature of many industries.

It was noted earlier that some firms that had publicly announced they were operating under the marketing concept were included in the study. Of these firms, eighteen who reported 100 percent used direct consumer research to measure consumer satisfaction. The finding was in keeping with their philosophy.

Table 2 shows the number of indicators of consumer satisfaction used by each of the fifty-two companies interviewed. Almost two-thirds of the firms used three or more indices of consumer satisfaction. This is an impressive figure considering the costs involved in obtaining some of these factors.

TABLE 2

Number of Consumer Satisfaction Indicators Used by Firms

Number of Indicators Used	Number of Firms	Percent of Firms
1	10	19.2
2	9	17.3
3	16	30.8
4	8	15.4
5	5	9.6
6	4	7.7
Total	52	100.0

Over one-third of the firms used less than three indicators. Of the 17.3 percent using two factors, most used direct consumer research; 19.2 percent of the firms using one indicator of satisfaction used either sales volume (60 percent) or share of the market (40 percent).

All the companies known to be committed to the marketing concept used three or more measures of consumer satisfaction.

Commentary

The exploratory study discussed here was an attempt to get some idea of the measures of consumer satisfaction employed by leading companies. It is gratifying to find that a major portion of the firms conducted periodic consumer research to ascertain consumer satisfaction. Such an approach will allow a company to determine the *degree* of satisfaction. By so determining, the firm knows whether satisfaction is decreasing or increasing. This is important for it will give direction to future marketing strategy.

The frequency of consumer satisfaction studies generally was not divulged. Frequent studies, perhaps once a month, are more sensitive and useful than "one-shot" studies.[15] Thus the companies that conduct consumer satisfaction studies only once or twice a year may be obtaining tenuous data.

The firms that focus on sales volume and share of the market do not enjoy as much re-

[14] Gregory P. Stone, "City Shoppers and Urban Identification: Observations on the Social Psychology of City Life," *The American Journal of Sociology* 60 (July 1954) 36–45.

[15] Russell I. Haley and Ronald Gatty, "Monitor Your Market Frequently," *Harvard Business Review* (May–June 1968): 65–69.

fined insight into market satisfaction as those companies using direct market research. These indirect, or substitute measures of satisfaction, are at best only estimates of satisfaction and lack the sensitivity of direct measures. They probably lag behind changes in consumer satisfaction. And there are too many factors other than consumer satisfaction that influence their magnitude.

It is probable that the average firm, being much smaller than those discussed in this study, relies on the indirect measures of consumer satisfaction since they are less expensive to obtain. Consequently, such firms may have very little knowledge of the extent to which they are producing consumer satisfaction.

In sum, then, most of the firms interviewed went directly to the consumer to measure the degree of satisfaction produced rather than using indirect measures. These firms most likely have an advantage over their competitors who employ indirect measures. For those firms using substitute measures of consumer satisfaction it is recommended that they initiate a continuous program of direct market analysis. Only then will they have a record of the most logical measure of marketing effectiveness.

PRODUCT ATTRIBUTES AND THE CONSUMER

27 / The Product

A. BACKGROUND AND THEORY

The first reading (Wasson) presents the question: What is "new" about a new product? This is followed by a presentation (Wasson, Sturdivant, and Mc-Conaughy) of the acceptance length cycle for a new product.

27-A WHAT IS "NEW" ABOUT A NEW PRODUCT?

Chester R. Wasson (Marketing Educator)

Consider the case of the soup-maker who, by freezing, was able to develop commercial production of soups which previously had to be fresh-prepared—an oyster stew among them. Estimating that the market potential might be approximated by the average relationship between frozen and canned foods, he tried his soups in a single test market. The oyster stew sold out so fast that he had to withdraw it from test until he could expand production facilities even for this one market.

Or take the case of the industrial manufacturer who developed a silo-like forage storer, capable of increasing livestock production profits substantially if properly used. Yet when put into distribution through experienced dealers in heavy farm equipment, it lay dormant for more than four years. In fact, no appreciable market headway was made until it was taken out of the hands of what had seemed to be a logical channel for any kind of farm equipment.

Then, consider the business executive with soap-and-cosmetic experience who acquired rights to a promising soil improver. Trade checks indicated that consumers liked it very much, and an impartial laboratory test indicated technical properties of substance. But into a few test garden stores with no more

SOURCE: Chester R. Wasson, "What Is 'New' About a New Product?" *Journal of Marketing*, Vol. 25 (July, 1960), pp. 52–56.

than nominal advertising, sales seemed satisfactory. Nevertheless, jobbers would not take it on, and when direct sales to a wider group of dealers was tried, none of the outlets developed any major volume. Even though both amateurs and professionals who have tried it like it, and come back for more, and in spite of the fact that the economics of its use is reasonable and that theoretical demand seems attractive, the executive is about to write it off after four years of trying.

The Difference Lies in What is New

All three cases are simple examples of a too prevalent failure to analyze the "what's new?" in the new product . . . to make sure that marketing strategy, channels of distribution, and available resources are compatible with the elements of novelty in the new product. The ease or difficulty of introduction and the characteristics of the successful marketing strategy depend basically on the nature of the "new" in the new product—the new as the customer views the bundle of services he perceives in the newborn.

Take the oyster stew—what was really new, the stew itself? In "R" months, oyster stew has been traditional in homes and restaurants from Boston and San Francisco to What Cheer, Iowa . . . from the Waldorf-Astoria to Harry's Diner. Assuming adequate quality in the commercial product, oyster stew was an old and welcome dinner-table friend. Was the idea of commercial preparation new? For oyster stew, yes, of course, but not for soup. Just look at the facings in the gondolas of any supermarket, or at the empty cans in the trash of any restaurant.

Of course, the idea of a frozen soup was new, but not the concept of frozen prepared foods. Food-store freezer cases had indeed established the association of fresh-quality taste with freeze-processing. But to the consumer, the only "new" aspect about frozen oyster stew was the greater availability and convenience implied in "frozen." With this particular item, the probability of great development might have been anticipated and prepared for in advance.

The silo and the soil improver, by contrast, looked deceptively similar to known items. But actually both embodied, for the consumer, radically new ideas; and both required extreme changes in user habits and user ways of looking at familiar tasks.

The forage storer looked like the familiar silo from the outside, but really embodied a new principle of preservation whose major benefits would be realized only when livestock were taken off pasture and barn-fed harvested forage the year around. Adoption of the device meant, in effect, adoption of a radically new pattern of work organization, and even of farm buildings in some cases.

No matter how great the promised benefits, such a major turnabout of habits requires a great deal of personal selling to get even the more venturesome to try it. Traditional farm-equipment channels are not prepared to carry out the prolonged and intensive type of pioneering personal sales effort and demonstration required. A reasonable degree of success began to accrue only after the manufacturer realized these facts and made the necessary changes in his selling plan.

Likewise, the soil improver resembled other growth stimulants in that it was sold in large bags and had a granular appearance. But the method of use was entirely different from, and more difficult than, the methods of surface application common to most growth stimulants in garden use. It had to be dug in, to be physically intermixed with the soil. In addition, the benefit was an unfamiliar one, and perhaps not easily believable—simple soil aeration. True, in cultivation, all gardeners practice aeration; but they think of weed killing, not aeration, when they hoe their gardens.

With such a product, success can reasonably be expected only after a strong educational campaign based on intense advertising, wide publicity, and personal contacts with consumer groups such as garden clubs and women's clubs. The resources needed were far in excess of those available in "bootstrap" operation.

THE TONI EXAMPLE. Determination of the novel aspects of a new product is no simple mechanical process. What is new depends on what the prospective consumer perceives, or can be brought to perceive, in the new product.

Determining such potential aspects requires a high order of imagination, and spectacular successes such as the Toni Home Permanent are due in no small part to the introducer's skill in pinpointing the nature of the novel aspects of the product, and devising the kind of marketing strategy needed to fit the various types of "new" elements in his product.

When the Harrises first introduced Toni, they clearly perceived that their key problem was to gain credibility for the idea of a safe and satisfactory "permanent wave" done in the home. Home curling of hair was an old custom, but the home-produced curl had always been very temporary. Permanent waves had been available, and proven, for nearly thirty years, but only at the hand of a skilled hairdresser, and in a specially equipped beauty parlor. With the perfection of the cold-wave lotion, a true home permanent became possible, using a technique not very different from those already in use for temporary home curling. The principal benefit was one for which the times of the middle and late 1940's were ripe —a labor saving in cost as compared with the professional job.

The problem was to gain credibility for the safety and the effectiveness of the product claiming the benefit (Toni)—a problem requiring intense selling effort. The Harris strategy consisted of persuading the girl behind every cosmetic counter in town to use a kit herself before it went on sale; making sure that every cosmetic counter had a stock before the day of introduction; working one town at a time, putting the maximum advertising effort behind the introduction; plowing back all income into further advertising until market saturation was accomplished; and then using funds from established markets to open new ones.

If, on hindsight, this solution seems to have been the obvious, it should be noted that Toni was not the first cold-wave home permanent—merely the first successful one. The forgotten competitor, who was really first, never appreciated the intensity of consumer education that would be needed, and had so little success that his product is remembered by few.

Ways a Product Can be "New"

In how many ways can a product be new? Of course, each case should be analyzed on its own. Nevertheless, there are at least thirteen possibilities which should be considered:

A. Six novel attributes are positive, in the sense that they ease the job of introduction:
   1. New cost—or, better yet, price—if lower.
   2. New convenience in use—if greater.
   3. New performance—if better, more dependable and in the range of experience of the prospect—if believable.
   4. New availability, in place, or time, or both (including anti-seasonability).
   5. Conspicuous—consumption (status symbol) possibilities.
   6. Easy credibility of benefits.
B. At least four characteristics make the job more difficult, slow up market development, and usually make it costlier:
   7. New methods of use (unless obviously simpler).
   8. Unfamiliar patterns of use (any necessity for learning new habits in connection with performance of a task associated with the new product).
   9. Unfamiliar benefit (in terms of the prospect's understanding).
   10. Costliness, fancied or real, of a possible error in use.
C. Three others are ambivalent in their effect—that is, the effect on market development probably depends not only on their exact nature, but also on the cultural climate at the moment. However, extreme unfamiliarity would probably be negative in effect:
   11. New appearance, or other sensed difference (style or texture, for example).
   12. Different accompanying or implied services.
   13. New market (including different channels of sale).

The oyster stew had four of the six positive characteristics (only lower cost and conspicuous consumption omitted), and no negative ones. The silo and the soil improver had all of the negative attributes listed, and only performance among the positive. Toni had cost and performance in its favor, and marketing strategy involved an overwhelming attack on the negative aspects (fear of error and credibility of results).

The ambivalence of style should be obvious to those who have followed automobile history. The turtle-shaped DeSoto of the 1930s was one of the most spectacular design failures of history. The design was "too radical" for the motorists of that era. Twenty years later, the very similar appearance of the Volkswagen "beetle" proved no deterrent to the initiation of a radical reorientation of the American automobile market. And while the Volkswagen brought into that market items of dependable performance, greater conveniences in use, and a lower cost than had been available for some time, one element in its success was the recognition of the necessity for continuing the availability of an established implied service in the sale of the car—ready availability of parts and service. Volkswagen entered no area until it had made certain of a high-grade service network in that area.

A FOURTEENTH CHARACTERISTIC. Omission of a possible fourteenth characteristic—new construction or composition—is purposeful. This characteristic is neutral—that is, it has no consumer meaning except to the extent that it is identified with, or can be associated with, one or more of the consumer-oriented characteristics listed above.

All that is new in any product is the package of consumer-perceivable services embodied in it. The innovator leads himself astray who analyzes the novel in his newborn in terms of physical and engineering attributes.

27-B ACCEPTANCE CYCLE LENGTH

Chester R. Wasson (Marketing Educator), Frederick D. Sturdivant (Marketing Educator), and David H. McConaughy (Marketing Educator)

Nearly all products seem to go through some kind of cycle of accelerating and declining acceptance. This so-called product life cycle is usually portrayed as composed of five distinct phases as shown in Figure 1: an initial phase of relatively *slow market development,* succeeded by a rapidly accelerating *growth* period, then a period of declining growth rate —*competitive maturity*—followed by the relatively stagnant sales of *saturation,* and last, a period of *decline.* However, observation seems to indicate that product cycles vary widely, not only in total length, but in the speed of their acceptance. A great many seem to be at the extremes in the buildup of acceptance. Their divergent acceptance-acceleration patterns might be likened to the acceleration patterns of two automobiles: the high-acceleration drag racer constructed to build up fast to top speed, and the low-acceleration car which may reach just as great a terminal speed but starts out sluggishly.

High-acceleration products zoom into public

Source: Chester R. Wasson, Frederick D. Sturdivant, and David H. McConaughy, *Competition and Human Behavior.* Copyright © 1968 by Meredith Corporation. Reprinted by permission of Appleton-Century-Crofts, pp. 79–81.

favor so fast that the major introductory-period problems are those of keeping all willing dealers supplied and staying ahead of the fast-developing competition which quick profits attract. *Low-acceleration products* gain their initial acceptance slowly, and must undergo an extended period of sluggish market development during which public perception of the value of the product is slow. During this period, attracting strong dealers can be a problem. Because deficits, rather than profits, are likely to be the seller's reward during this development period, competition begins to crowd in only with the takeoff into the growth period of more rapidly accelerating sales.

The differing marketing patterns of high- and low-acceleration products are well illustrated by the contrasting histories of acceptance of black-and-white television and of color television. Acceptance of black-and-white television was strong from the outset, even in advance of much program availability. So was competition for the introducers. Misled by this mushroom sales history, the first year after the approval of color-television standards saw every TV maker enthusiastically planning a market entry. When a similar public enthusiasm did not materialize, all but RCA withdrew quickly. Being the proponent of the approved stand-

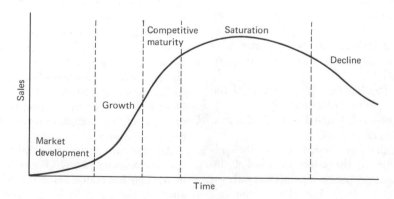

Figure 1. The standard conception of product acceptance and sales during the course of a product life cycle.

ards, RCA had to bear deficits for the ten years required to reach a perceptible growth phase. Then competition reappeared immediately.

Similar contrasting acceptance patterns can be seen on reexamination of the known sales history of two post-World War II convenience foods: frozen orange concentrate and instant coffee. First available at retail in 1947, orange concentrate sold well from its first promotion. Roughly 30 percent of peak per capita consumption had been reached by 1950, the first year for which sales estimates are given.[1] Even this climb might well have been steeper had adequate orange supply and processing and shipping facilities been available. During this shortage period, the obvious profits precipitated such a competitive scramble for a piece of this market that the resulting overexpansion in plantings and facilities forced prices to unprofitable levels by the time maturity arrived in 1952. As a result, little profit was available for any brand until a disastrous

[1] Robert D. Buzzell, "Competitive Behavior and Product Life Cycles," *New Ideas for Successful Marketing*, Proceedings of the 1966 World Congress, American Marketing Association, Chicago, Ill., 1966, pp. 46–47.

freeze a dozen years later wiped out enough groves to permit prices to rise, temporarily, to a comfortable level.

Instant coffee acceptance was quite a different story. Soluble coffee products were first introduced at the turn of the century, but achieved no mass distribution and sales until the development of an improved and cheaper product after the war. At the time of the first postwar promotion (1946), sales had reached nearly 10 percent of the eventual per capita level. Another five years was to pass before the annual growth rate started to accelerate. The climb to full market maturity and market saturation required another six years, to 1957— three times as long as the orange concentrate growth period.

Other contrasts can easily be found. Campbell's initial frozen soups, and the oyster stew especially, did not go through an extended market development phase, but a later addition to the line, fruit soup, did not sell, although most of those who tried it reported that they liked it. The important point is not their mere occurrence, but that the two divergent patterns pose quite different marketing problems, and that it is necessary to foresee the specific pattern likely to develop.

B. RESEARCH AND APPLICATIONS

This section begins with a report (Robertson) on the new-product diffusion process. It is followed by a report on research (Pessemier, Burger, and Tigert) that was undertaken in order to determine the characteristics that distinguish buyers of new products from nonbuyers.

27-C THE NEW PRODUCT DIFFUSION PROCESS

Thomas S. Robertson (Marketing Educator)

The concern of this paper is with consumer acceptance of product innovations (new products). A major difficulty is in defining what is a new product and at least four definitional criteria have frequently been used: (1) newness from existing products, (2) newness in time, (3) newness in terms of sales penetra-

SOURCE: Thomas S. Robertson, "The New Product Diffusion Process," in Bernard A. Morin, Editor, *Marketing in a Changing World* (Chicago: American Marketing Association, 1969), pp. 80–86.

tion level, and (4) consumer newness to the product.

1. *Newness from existing products.* Many authors argue that a "new product" must be *very different* from established products, although there is little attempt to make such a definition operational. The Federal Trade Commission has rendered an advisory opinion that a product may properly be called "new" "only when [it] is either entirely new or has been changed in a functionally significant and

substantial respect. A product may not be called 'new' when only the package has been altered or some other change made which is functionally insignificant or insubstantial."[1]

E. B. Weiss claims that over 80% of new products are not, in fact, "new" but "simply modifications" of existing products.[2] He does not, however, establish guidelines for distinguishing such modifications from new products. It is possible to extend this point of view to the thesis that all new products are modifications or recombinations of existing items. Barnett, an anthropologist who has studied innovation and its effects on cultural change, states that "No innovation springs full-blown out of nothing; it must have antecedents . . . ."[3] This viewpoint, which is quite prevalent in sociological thinking, looks at innovation as the outcome of an evolutionary sequence. Even an innovation such as the computer can be considered to be a recombination of existing elements coupled with a measure of technological insight.

2. *Newness in time.* Length of time on the market is a second criterion in defining a new product. There has been a pronounced tendency for firms to promote a product as new for as long as two or three years after introduction, under the assumption that the word "new" in advertising or on the package is a positive and desirable sales appeal. The Federal Trade Commission advisory opinion arbitrarily limits the use of the word new to six months after the product enters regular distribution after test marketing.[4]

3. *Newness in terms of sales penetration level.* Another new product definitional criterion is the sales level which the product has achieved. Bell[5] and Robertson,[6] for example, have arbitrarily defined products as innovations when they have not yet secured 10% of their total potential market.

4. *Consumer newness to the product.* Yet another criterion for defining a new product is that the consumer must *perceive* it to be new. There is, however, invariably some consumer who is "new" to the product and it is not particularly useful to talk in terms of any individual consumer; the aggregate consumer is generally what the marketer has in mind. Perhaps a product could be defined as new when a majority of consumers perceive it in such a way, but this is again arbitrary.

These definitions, unfortunately, need not yield the same determinations as to what products are new. For example, using the consumer perception of newness definition, an item can be new without being substantially different in function from existing products, without being particularly new to the market, and while possessing a significant sales penetration level. There is a further difficulty in the discussion to this point, and that is that a simple dichotomy is being used—a product is either new or not new. More logically, a range of "newness" would be the case.

Newness in Terms of Consumption Effects

The critical factor in defining a new product should be its effects upon established patterns of consumption. It is convenient to think in terms of: (1) continuous innovations, (2) dynamically continuous innovations, and (3) discontinuous innovations.

1. A *continuous* innovation has the least disrupting influence on established consumption patterns. Alteration of a product is almost always involved rather than the creation of a new product. Examples include: fluoride toothpaste, menthol cigarettes, and annual new-model automobile changeovers.

2. A *dynamically continuous* innovation has more disrupting effects than a continuous innovation, although it still does not generally involve new consumption pat-

[1] Federal Trade Commission, "Permissible Period of Time During which New Product May Be Described as 'New'," *Advisory Opinion Digest,* No. 120, April 15, 1967.

[2] E. B. Weiss, "That Malarky about 80% of New Products Failing," *Advertising Age,* Vol. 36, August 2, 1965, p. 101.

[3] Homer G. Barnett, *Innovation: The Basis of Cultural Change,* New York, McGraw-Hill, 1953, p. 181.

[4] Same reference as footnote 1.

[5] William E. Bell, "Consumer Innovators: A Unique Market for Newness," in *Proceedings of the American Marketing Association,* ed. Stephen A. Greyser, Chicago, 1963, pp. 85–95.

[6] Thomas S. Robertson, "Determinants of Innovative Behavior," in *Proceedings of the American Marketing Association,* ed. Reed Moyer, Chicago, 1967, pp. 328–332.

terns. It may mean the creation of a new product or the alteration of an existing product. Examples include: electric toothbrushes, electric hair curlers, and the Mustang automobile.

3. A *discontinuous* innovation involves the establishment of new consumption patterns and the creation of previously unknown products. Examples include: television, the computer, and the automobile.

This definitional framework, while recognizing that innovations are not all of the same order of newness, does not, unfortunately, distinguish new products from non-new products. It is my opinion that this decision is always arbitrary. It may be possible to agree that new sizes, new flavors, and new packages are not new products. Does, however, the addition of sugar to corn flakes or raisins to bran constitute a new product? Is an instant oatmeal a new product or a variation of the old product? No definition of innovation satisfactorily answers these and similar questions unless we rely on consumer perception and, as suggested, accept majority consumer opinion of what is and what is not an innovation.

Most Innovation Is Continuous

Most innovation in the American economy is of a continuous nature. Most innovation, especially in the consumer sector, results as an attempt to differentiate products to increase market share. Few and far between are innovations of a discontinuous nature which significantly alter or create new consumption patterns. The image of innovations resulting from the inspiration of the occasional genius does not fit the typical occurrence and even discontinuous innovations are increasingly the result of planned team research. Most innovation today results from programmed, systematic research efforts.

SOME CASE EXAMPLES. If the first detergent on the market represented a fairly discontinuous innovation, then the succeeding proliferation of brands must represent highly continuous innovations. While one brand may be a low sudser, another possess cold-water attributes, another contain bleach, and another contain disinfectant for baby clothes, all are essentially minor variations on the basic product. All of these succeeding brands are *programmed innovations*.

The automobile industry is the leading example of programmed, continuous innovations. New products appear on schedule each year and every three years major design changes occur. This planning and programming of innovation occurs across almost all industries. When a major aircraft manufacturer was considering its next venture into the commercial market, it plotted the various offerings then available in terms of such variables as runway requirements, flying range, seating capacity, and cost of operation and found the gaps in the market. These gaps were in short-range jets and high-seating-capacity jets. The company then planned to innovate in one of these areas and did so.

The Importance of Innovation to the Firm

Innovation, according to a variety of sources, occurs due to: (1) shrinking profit margins for established products, (2) shorter lives for established products, and (3) excess capacity. Schumpeter has attributed innovation to (4) a search for profit.[7] Barnett has emphasized (5) the pressure of competition and the search for product differentiation as factors leading to innovation.[8]

These reasons for the occurrence of innovation overlap considerably. Analysis of their content also reveals their all-inclusive nature. Innovation, it would appear, is the solution to all business problems. Perhaps Schumpeter's view of innovation as a search for profit summarizes all of the other reasons; although corporate marketers generally cite growth, or forward momentum, as the most important factor encouraging new product development.

MAINTAINING MOMENTUM. New products are basic to company growth and to profitability. It is seldom possible in today's economy to maintain momentum or even stability with innovations. Mattel Toymakers, for example, grew rapidly with the acceptance of Barbie Doll, but such growth could not be continued without other new products since Barbie Doll soon reached "maturity" on the product life

---

[7] Joseph A. Schumpeter. *Business Cycles* (New York, McGraw-Hill Book Company, Inc., 1939) Vol. 1, p. 97.

[8] Same reference as footnote 3 at p. 73.

cycle. It is also difficult to maintain profit margins when a product reaches maturity since competition intensifies and product advantages may be neutralized. The typical pattern in the food industry, for example, has been for profit margins to decline while sales are still increasing so that companies must quickly look to other new products for continued profit performance.[9]

EMPIRICAL DATA. The contribution of new products to the sales growth of various industries has been researched by Booz-Allen & Hamilton, Inc. Expected growth from new products varies from 46% to as much as 100%, with an average of 75%. Innovating industries are also more likely to be high growth industries.[10]

In another study, Mansfield assessed the value of technological innovation to the growth and profitability of individual firms. His concern was with the acceptance of capital goods' innovations by firms of comparable initial size in the steel and petroleum refining industries. He concludes:

> In every interval and in both industries, the successful innovators grew more rapidly than the others, and in some cases, their average rate of growth was more than twice that of the others.[11]

Innovative Competition

The importance of successfully marketing product innovations is today being recognized as never before. This is evidenced in the marketing trade magazines and academic journals as well as in the proliferation of consulting agencies devoted to new products and the establishment of new product divisions within existing agencies.

Yet, as more firms become committed to innovation, new product advantages exist for shorter time periods and the "monopoly" power of new products is soon overcome. When

General Electric quickly followed Squibb into electric toothbrushes, for example, it added innovation to innovation by marketing a cordless version which was then a new usage concept. The new product marketplace is increasingly becoming more competitive as fairly simultaneous innovations often occur and imitation is indeed rapid. Many firms, such as Mattel Toymakers, prefer to jump from product tests to national marketing since test marketing often speeds imitation.

Risks in New Products

Commitment to new products is not without serious problems and associated risks. Research and development expenditures for 1971 should approach $22.4 billion,[12]—most of which will be spent on *unsuccessful* new product ideas. Based on responses from 51 prominent companies, Booz-Allen & Hamilton report that it takes almost 60 *ideas* to result in one commercially successful new product and that three-fourths of new product expense funds go to unsuccessful products.[13] These figures, however, must be treated as estimates only, especially since this is a sample of "prominent" companies and we can probably assume greater sophistication in the research and development process.

Buzzell and Nourse, in an extensive study of product innovation in the food industry, report that of every 1,000 new product ideas:

810 are rejected at the idea stage
135 are rejected on the basis of product tests
12 are discontinued after test marketing
43 are introduced to the market
36 remain on the market after introduction[14]

According to these figures, food companies would appear to better the across-industry average reported by Booz-Allen & Hamilton. The Buzzell and Nourse figures suggest that over two successful new food products result from every 58 ideas.

NEW PRODUCT FAILURES. The greatest risk in new products and the greatest potential

[9] Robert D. Buzzell and Robert Nourse, *Product Innovation in Food Processing: 1954–1964*, Boston, Division of Research, Harvard Business School, 1967.
[10] Booz-Allen & Hamilton, Inc., *Management of New Products*, New York, 1965.
[11] Edwin Mansfield, "Entry, Gibrat's Law, Innovation, and the Growth of Firms," *American Economic Review*, Vol. 52, December, 1962, pp. 1023–1051, at p. 1036.

[12] "Research: The Cash Pours Out for Research and Development," *Business Week*, #2020, May 18, 1968, pp. 72–74.
[13] Same reference as footnote 10.
[14] Same reference as footnote 9 at p. 105. and p. 124.

monetary loss comes at the market introduction stage. Estimates of new product failures run from 10% to 80%. This wide discrepancy in estimates is due largely to three reasons: (1) *definition* of what constitutes a new product—this is seldom stated; (2) *measurement* of what failure means—while one study may include only product withdrawals from the market, another may include all unprofitable or marginally profitable products. While one study may limit itself to measurement within one or two years of introduction, another may choose a considerably longer time span; and (3) the *sample of companies* chosen—large companies are likely to market fewer failures then small companies and companies in sophisticated consumer-oriented industries are likely to market fewer failures than companies in less sophisticated, production-oriented industries.

While it is difficult, therefore, to provide an average new product failure ratio which will uniformly apply, this failure rate can be quite high. It is probably fair to say that a majority of new products fail, although it would be more meaningful to present figures by *industry* if such figures could be obtained.

WHY DO NEW PRODUCTS FAIL? New-product failures are seldom due to bad products. Analysis of the trade literature provides countless examples of basically sound new products failing after market introduction. General Foods failed with a Birds Eye line of frozen baby foods and rejected a forerunner of Instant Breakfast, Brim, in test markets. Ford Motor Company's Edsel is perhaps the classic example of a new product failure. Campbell proved unsuccessful in marketing fruit soup as well as a Red Kettle line of dry soup mixes. Coca-Cola, despite its strong consumer franchise in cola beverages, was initially unsuccessful in marketing a diet cola.

Reasons for new product failures could be discussed at length, but the foremost problem is in *marketing*. More tightly controlled test market and market experimentation procedures are necessary as well as a greater volume of marketing research in advance of new product introductions. Sophisticated models for predicting new product sales levels should be encouraged. The primary focus here, however, will not be on these concerns. It is the thesis of this paper that the probability of new product success can be increased by understanding the factors governing *diffusion* of new products, that is, acceptance by consumers.

New Product Diffusion

Diffusion is the process by which something spreads. Anthropologists have studied the diffusion of language, religion, and ideas among tribes and societies. Sociologists, particularly rural sociologists, have studied the diffusion of new ideas and new practices within societies. Physicists have studied the diffusion of atomic particles within elements. Marketers have implicitly studied diffusion for many years as they have sought to guide and control the spread of new products, but little research or conceptual thinking has been directed toward an understanding of the diffusion process itself.

The diffusion literature, as developed across a number of disciplines, offers for consideration a fairly well-developed theoretical framework which applies to the flow of information, ideas, and products. It is the integration of this framework with the traditional marketing framework which may advance our understanding of how new products disseminate and gain consumer acceptance and which may suggest means of improving new product marketing strategies.

COMPONENTS OF THE DIFFUSION PROCESS. The diffusion process can be conceptualized as: (1) the adoption, (2) of new products and services, (3) over time, (4) by consumers, (5) within social systems, (6) as encouraged by marketing activities.

Adoption refers to the use of a new item. *New products* and services will be considered in the broadest sense from highly continuous to highly discontinuous innovations. The *time dimension* distinguishes early adopters from late adopters. The *consumer adoption unit* may be the individual consumer or a family or buying committee, or even a city of consumers. *Social systems* constitute the boundaries within which diffusion occurs. In a broad sense the market segment as a whole can be viewed as a social system, or more narrowly defined, the consumer's friendship group can be considered his social system. Within these systems, communication will occur—both marketer-initiated and non-marketer-initiated. *Marketing activities* are defined as the mix of product, price, promotion, and distribution plans and strategies.

These several aspects of the diffusion process are interdependent. For example: the attributes of the new product will affect the rate of adoption over time, the types of consumers who will adopt, the kinds of social systems within which diffusion will take place, and the marketing efforts needed to achieve diffusion. Alternatively, successful new product diffusion is critically dependent upon the communication of relevant product information and the matching of new product attributes with social system and individual consumer characteristics. Marketing activities can guide and control, to a considerable extent, the rate and extent of diffusion.

Effects of Marketing Activities

The opportunities for marketing activities to affect the diffusion process *for a given new product* can be summarized as follows:

SOCIAL SYSTEM

• Marketing decisions can select the social systems (market segments) in which diffusion is most likely to be successful.

• Promotion, pricing, and distribution strategies can be combined to reach specified social systems.

• Marketing activities can, in some cases, chart the diffusion path within a social system to achieve the fastest rate of diffusion. This may be possible by reaching critical individuals first—especially innovators and opinion leaders.

CONSUMER ADOPTERS

• Marketing decisions can establish the consumer profile most likely to adopt the new product.

• Promotion, pricing, and distribution strategies can be oriented toward this consumer profile.

• Marketing activities can vary by penetration level to specifically reach different kinds of consumers. For example: advertising strategies to reach first adopters should usually be different than strategies to reach later adopters.

PRODUCT MEANING

• Marketing activities can help define product meaning and can encourage diffusion by emphasizing the most relevant product attributes. For example: should promotion for a new dessert product emphasize taste, convenience, low cost, or low calorie content?

TIME

• Marketing activities can affect *rate* of diffusion. A low price, penetration strategy, a high level of promotional expenditures, free sampling and deal activity, and intensive distribution will generally all encourage a fast diffusion rate.

These opportunities will now be assessed briefly in turn.

SOCIAL SYSTEM. The characteristics of a social system highly influence diffusion patterns for new products. This can be demonstrated by reference to a study by Graham who researched the diffusion of five innovations—television, canasta, supermarkets, Blue Cross, and medical service insurance—across social class levels. His research revealed that no single social class was consistently innovative in adopting all five innovations. Television, for example, diffused more quickly among low social classes, while the card game canasta diffused more quickly among upper social classes.[15]

Graham argues that the critical factor in determining diffusion is the extent to which the attributes of the innovation are compatible with the attributes of the culture of the receiving social system. The "cultural equipment" required for the adoption of television according to Graham, included an average education, a minimum income, and a desire for passive spectator entertainment. This cultural pattern coincided with a lower social-class level.

Other researchers have distinguished between communities exhibiting modern versus traditional norms. The modern-oriented community is receptive to innovations while the tradition-oriented community relies on established ways of doing things. The norms in effect in a social system have a sizeable bearing on diffusion rates. This may vary by region of the country and from rural to urban areas.

Innovations may also diffuse at different rates within particular spheres of a social system. A number of studies show that an innovation diffuses more quickly among socially integrated social system members than among

[15] Saxon Graham, "Class and Conservatism in the Adoption of Innovations," *Human Relations*, Vol. 9, 1956, pp. 91–100.

socially isolated members. For some products, diffusion may be most rapid among older people.

The marketer has at his discretion the choice of social systems in which to market his product or in which to place heaviest support behind his product. This decision must be based on a matching between the attributes of the new product and social system attributes. Should segmentation be on the basis of social class, ethnic group, age, or ecology? Given the selection of the most relevant social systems, what are the most appropriate promotional, distribution, and pricing strategies to reach these social systems? Finally, is it possible to initiate strategies to reach the most likely buyers within a social system? While this is frequently possible in industrial selling, it is seldom possible in reaching ultimate consumers.

CONSUMER ADOPTERS. Ultimately, diffusion is dependent upon the individual consumer. He must decide whether adoption of the new product is the appropriate course of action for him. The adoption process refers to the mental sequence of stages through which the consumer passes in arriving at an acceptance (adoption) or rejection decision. It can be conceptualized as awareness, knowledge, liking, preference, conviction, and adoption, although other conceptualizations are also available.

Considerable research evidence indicates that communication sources are not equally effective at different stages of the adoption process. While *advertising* generally has greatest impact at the earlier stages of awareness, knowledge, and liking, the consumer seeks more objective, evaluative information at the later stages of preference and conviction and *personal influence* (word-of-mouth) often becomes the dominant communication source. This, of course, varies by product and holds most when the consumer perceives a good amount of risk in buying. The important point is that a purchase decision results from the cumulative impact of a number of communication sources and the marketer must attempt to move consumers through an entire sequence of information needs.

Not all consumers within a social system have an equal initial propensity toward buying a new product and consumers adopt at different points in time. The earliest buyers, the "innovators," have generally been found to possess different characteristics from later adopters. An initial goal before marketing a new product should be to establish the profile of the most likely consumer innovators. It may then be possible to design marketing activities in line with this profile. As the innovator level of diffusion is achieved, marketing strategies should then be re-oriented to reach later buyers.

PRODUCT MEANING. Extent of a new product's diffusion and its rate of diffusion are, of course, largely a function of the particular attributes of the product. The emphasis given particular attributes and the overall brand image created are critical marketing decision areas.

There are several attribute classification schemes to account for differential diffusion rates. Rogers proposes a set of five characteristics of innovations which he believes are generally relevant. These characteristics are: (1) relative advantage, (2) compatibility, (3) complexity, (4) divisibility, and (5) communicability.[16]

Relative advantage is the degree to which an innovation is superior to the product it supersedes or with which it will compete. While the addition of fluoride to toothpaste was considered to add extra product value, many other ingredients had previously been added to toothpaste without the consumer attaching relative advantage to the resulting "new" product. A dominant marketing management function is product differentiation to encourage the consumer to perceive greater product value.

Compatibility refers to how consistent the new product is with existing ways of doing things. The greater the need for consumers to restructure their thinking and to engage in new forms of behavior, the less quickly the item is likely to diffuse.

Complexity refers to the degree of difficulty in understanding and using the new product. In general, the more complex the item, the slower its rate of diffusion and the narrower its potential market.

Divisibility refers to the extent to which a new product may be tried on a limited scale.

[16] Everett M. Rogers, *Diffusion of Innovations,* New York, The Free Press, 1962, Chapter 5.

In-store sampling of a new food product and marketing of small sizes take account of the divisibility factor.

Communicability is the degree to which word of the new product may readily be communicated to others. Conspicuous products, such as clothes, are highest on communicability.

The important point is how these characteristics are *perceived* by consumers since this is what governs response. In summary form, it can be hypothesized that rate of diffusion is positively related to relative advantage, compatibility, divisibility, and communicability, but negatively related to complexity.

Diffusion rates of technological innovations among firms have been studied by Mansfield, who hypothesizes as follows:

1. Profitability of an innovation relative to others that are available will increase the rate of adoption.

2. The larger the investment required, assuming equally profitable innovations available, the slower the rate of adoption.

3. The type of industry will affect the rate of adoption depending on its aversion to risk, market competitiveness, and financial health.[17]

Considerable work remains to be done relating innovation attributes to diffusion rates and further relating innovation attributes to consumer characteristics. For example, to the extent that a product is high on complexity, this may suggest a slower rate of diffusion, but does this also suggest a certain kind of consumer adopter? Also, when is a product attribute important? Relative advantage may be irrelevant for fashion items and for many fad items since their adoption is largely related to the perception of *newness itself* rather than to better functional performance. Diffusion patterns for fashion and fad products show a much more accelerated growth and an equally accelerated decline phenomenon.

TIME. The business firm in general wishes to shorten the diffusion time span consistent with profit maximization objectives. At times it may be desirable to gain maximum short-run penetration, while at other times a more deliberate segmentation strategy, often on the basis of price, may be followed. A strategy of maximum diffusion need not be most profitable. It is probably a fair generalization, however, that maximum diffusion (market share) is the goal for most new products. This is especially true for continuous and dynamically continuous innovations and less true for discontinuous innovations.

In a penetration strategy, maximum diffusion is sought as quickly as possible. Price tends to be set relatively low; promotion will lean heavily toward mass advertising; and intensive distribution will be used. This strategy is most necessary if little product differentiation exists for the new product and, therefore, demand is highly elastic. This strategy is also necessary if competitors are likely to introduce similar new product offerings within a fairly short period of time, despite the continuity or discontinuity of the innovation. Rapid diffusion may discourage competition, although it could also have an encouraging effect when high sales are noted—especially if the estimated potential market is large. More importantly, however, rapid diffusion will often lead to a large and brand loyal consumer franchise which is crucial to continuing sales success given the subsequent entry of competition.

A penetration strategy has implications as to the shape of the diffusion curve and encourages high acceleration. In fact, in a number of cases for new convenience *brands,* the diffusion curve is far from S-shaped. In the presweetened cereal market and in the detergent market, for example, a new brand (because of concentrated advertising and deal activity at introduction) may attain its maximum life cycle sales within a matter of a month and then settle down to a lower "maturity" level of sales. It is critical to remember that a varying proportion (sometimes very high) of beginning sales may be for *trial* purposes and need not represent *adoption,* defined in terms of acceptance and commitment to the brand as reflected in repeat purchases. A company must quickly determine its trial-adoption ratio or it can be misled into expanding production for never-to-be-realized repeat sales.

In a sales staging strategy, the typical progression is from generally high "skim the cream" pricing to relatively lower prices, from selective distribution to intensive distribution,

[17] Edwin Mansfield, "Technical Change and the Rate of Imitation," *Econometrica,* Vol. 29, October, 1961, pp. 741–766.

and from limited promotion to expanded or mass promotion. Such a strategy is more likely to be successful for specialty and durable items and is generally dependent upon a differentiated product and one which competition cannot readily duplicate. The somewhat discontinuous innovation allows, in effect, a certain degree of monopoly power.

DuPont's "Corfam" shoe material was marketed using the sales staging strategy. It was deliberately introduced to manufacturers of quality shoe products before being made available on a mass basis. Management apparently felt that maximum long-run diffusion for the product would be gained if it was not perceived as a cheap substitute for leather but instead as a quality improvement over leather. DuPont, therefore, by its choice of manufacturers to whom the product was made available, was governing intensity of distribution and pricing and extent of manufacturer advertising.

It is interesting to note that the marketer's diffusion strategy very much influences the shape of the diffusion curve. By the same token, however, the selection of a strategy is a function of the type of product and the competitive situation. A penetration or sales staging strategy must be based on accurate assessment of future market acceptance. Wasson, for example, argues that color television marketers unsuccessfully followed a penetration strategy for their products when sales to support such a strategy were not forthcoming. They misjudged rate of market acceptance and should have been following a sales staging strategy with selective distribution, relatively high price, and limited promotion until the growth seg-

ment of the diffusion process was attained.[18] We must also take cognizance of the fact that while a dichotomy of ideal types makes for expository efficiency, a considerable range of strategies between staging and penetration is available to the firm.

Conclusion

It is essentially an arbitrary decision as to what is and what is not a new product. Most "new products" on the market today, however, involve only minor changes in consumption patterns; they are of a highly *continuous* nature. Such products are the result of programmed product differentiation.

The critical value of innovation to a firm is demonstrated in many industries where over 50% of sales growth is coming from new products. Yet, the risk of new product failures is high and it is probably fair to say that a *majority* of products which are introduced to the market fail. Furthermore, these failures are seldom due to a technically unsound product but instead are largely the result of poor marketing performance.

It is the conclusion of this paper, however, that the probability of new-product success can be increased by understanding the diffusion process. Successful new-product diffusion is dependent upon the communication of relevant product information and the matching of new product attributes with social system and individual consumer attributes. Marketing strategies can guide and control, to a considerable extent, the rate and extent of new product diffusion.

[18] Chester R. Wasson, "How Predictable Are Fashion and Other Product Life Cycles?" *Journal of Marketing*, Vol. 32, July, 1968; pp. 36–43.

27-D CAN NEW PRODUCT BUYERS BE IDENTIFIED?

Edgar A. Pessemier (Marketing Educator), Philip C. Burger (Marketing Educator), and Douglas J. Tigert (Marketing Educator)

Primarily because of the paucity of relevant data, few empirical studies have appeared on the characteristics of early, late, and non-

SOURCE: Edgar A. Pessemier, Philip C. Burger, and Douglas J. Tigert, "Can New Product Buyers Be Identified?" *Journal of Marketing Research*, Vol. 4 (November, 1967), pp. 349–354.

buyers of new products. This article discusses data collected for the "Lafayette Consumer Behavior Research Project" [9]. For the project, a great deal of information was gathered about introduction of a new heavy duty detergent. The branded detergent used was promoted as having a new fluorescent ingredient with unusual brightening power. Data were obtained from diary records and two questionnaires. One questionnaire was given before the product introduction and the other after a seven-month period during which purchase diaries were kept by 265 housewives.

The theoretical basis for this study was largely derived from the literature on adoption and diffusion. Studies by rural sociologists [11], Katz and Lazarsfeld [6], C. W. King [7], Coleman, Katz and Menzel [3] and others led to the following hypotheses about variables that would discriminate among early, late, and nonbuyers of the new laundry detergent:

1. Early buyers would be more trial-prone toward brands in the product class and be heavier users of the product class (high salience) than late or nonbuyers.

2. Early buyers would actively transmit information about their experience with the brand and class; late buyers would be information receivers.

3. Early, late, and nonbuyers could be identified on the basis of demographic characteristics, mass media exposure factor scores, activity, interest, and opinion factor scores, and several product variables.

Because of the sample size (265), subjects could not be assigned to the five classifications described by Rogers [10]: innovators, early adopters, early majority, late majority, and laggards. Only the trial stage of the adoption process was investigated. The time to trial, if any, may be influenced by the level of current satisfaction, the perceived risk of trial as modified by advertising and feedback from earlier buyers, the available stock, and the rate of usage of the product class (subjects who purchase infrequently may fall by chance into the late buyer category). Subjects may develop brand preference leading to adoption after receiving information about the product and after using the product. Non-buyers may have a poor opinion of the new brand or no opinion. A great many consumer attributes could be related to these elements, for example, the independent variables that will be examined. In addition, laboratory research indicates that experimental data on buyer preferences for existing brands, and possibly for a new brand, may materially aid in predicting brand switching and market behavior for the new brand [8].

Data and Definitions

A buyer of the new detergent was anyone who bought the product at least once in the seven-month period of diary keeping. An early buyer was one who purchased the product in the first 70 days after introduction. All remaining subjects who bought were late buyers. The 70-day period was a cutoff because the number of first-time buyers per 10-day period reached a peak in the seventh 10-day period.[1] Of the 265 subjects in the sample, 52 were in the early buyer category, 62 the late buyer category, and 151 the nonbuyer category.

Fifty-seven variables (Table 1) were used to examine differences between subjects in the three buyer categories. Each variable was either a "before" or an "after" measure. The before measures were obtained by questionnaire prior to the product introduction and the after measures were gathered from questionnaires at the end of the diary period.

Some comments may clarify the variable groupings. The activity, interest, and opinion factor scores (AIO) and the media factor scores were from two sets of questions. In each case, the response sets were obliquely rotated after principal component factor analysis [12]. The product preference variable (Variable 40) was constructed as follows. Each respondent rated 16 general product characteristics for detergents on a five-point scale, from "not important" to "extremely important." She then rated each of the top ten brands that she knew about on the same set of characteristics. These two ratings were vector multiplied giving a number for each brand defined as brand preference. Only the preference score for the new detergent was used in this analysis.

The awareness score (Variable 43) resulted from summing individual responses to four questions about the new detergent. One question asked subjects to write down all brands they knew that were not already listed. A second requested names of brands introduced in the area in the past year. A third requested

[1] A plot of time to first purchase was made on Weibull probability paper. It indicated a change in the forces influencing first purchase occurred at the 70-day point on the time axis. The result parallels the effect of catastrophic and wearout failures found in the electron tube life-testing investigations of J. H. K. Kao [5].

TABLE 1

List of Variables Cross-Tabulated Against Early, Late, Nonbuyer Classifications

Socioeconomic Variables (Before Measures)

1. Number of children 18 years and under living in the home
2. Number of rooms in residence
3. Number of different residences lived in during past 15 years
4. Rent or own residence
5. Present credit buying behavior for durables, including automobiles
6. Wife's age
7. Wife's education[a]
8. Wife's employment status
9. Husband's age
10. Number of different employers husband has had since completing formal education[a]
11. Wife's religion
12. Husband's occupation
13. Husband's education
14. Total family income
15. Socioeconomic status score
16. Status consistency score

Trial-Proneness Variables

17. Certainty about current brand versus other brands (before)[a]
18. Willingness to try known but untried brands (before)[a]
19. Perceived seriousness of product failure for detergents (before)
20. Willingness to shop for preferred brand (before)
21. Feelings about experimenting with new detergents (after)[a]
22. Likelihood of trying new detergents early (after)[a]

Activity, Interest, and Opinions Factor Scores (Before Measures)

23. Health and social conformity
24. Price conscious
25. Compulsive, orderly housekeeper
26. Fashions conscious
27. Careless or irresponsible behavior in personal, financial, and shopping affairs
28. Negative attitudes towards the value of advertising
29. Conservative middle class attitudes, sociable, mature

30. Weight watcher, dieter
31. Risk avoidance
32. Outdoor, casual, activist
33. Nonparticipating sports enthusiast[a]
34. Active information seeker
35. Do-it-yourself homemaker
36. Husband-oriented, interested in husband's activities

Product Variables (After Measures)

37. Total usage rates for all detergents for period (by total weight purchased)
38. Whether housewife received a free sample of the new detergent[a]
39. For those who received the sample, how much was used[a]
40. New product preference[a]

Informational Variables (After Measures)

41. Information transmission habits for detergents[a]
42. Information receiving habits for detergents[a]
43. Awareness score for new detergent[a]
44. Advertising slogan recognition score for new detergent[a]
45. Opinion leadership

Media Exposure Factor Scores (Before Measures)

46. Factor score, cultural, intellectual magazines (*Atlantic Monthly, New York Times,* etc.)
47. Factor score, light reading magazines (*Life, Look, Readers' Digest,* etc.)
48. Factor score, fashion magazines (*Vogue, Mademoiselle, Glamour,* etc.)
49. Factor score, homemaker magazines (*Family Circle, Woman's Day,* etc.)

Judged Importance of Information Sources on New Detergents (After Measures)

50. Importance of actual trial
51. Store display
52. Television advertising
53. Magazine advertising
54. Friends and relatives
55. Package label

Social Activities (After Measures)

56. Membership in church groups
57. Membership in informal groups

[a] Significant at .05 level when cross-classified against the early, late, nonbuyer variable.

names of brands for which samples had been given in the area in the past year and the fourth, advertising copy points for new brands recently introduced.

The accurate information score was obtained by scoring responses from a list of true-false questions on product characteristics and advertising slogans for several brands. Finally, the opinion leadership measure represented the standard question from the literature: "Would you say you are more likely, about as likely, or less likely than any of your friends to be asked your advice about laundry detergents?"

The purchase data on the new product were taken from diaries for the seven-month period. For each of ten product categories, including detergents, data about date of purchase, price, brand, total weight, deal amount, and place of purchase were collected.

Techniques of Analysis

Three kinds of statistical analysis were done. First, the 57 variables in Table 1 were cross-classified against the early, late, and nonbuyers category. Second, the variables that proved significant from the cross-classification were used in a stepwise multiple regression analysis. The regression involved prediction of number of days to first purchase for the subgroup of 114 respondents who had purchased the new detergent at least once in the seven-month period. Finally, the same set of variables was used in a discriminant analysis to try to classify subjects as triers or non-triers.

Results

CROSS-CLASSIFICATION. Fourteen variables were significantly $(p < .05)$ related to the

TABLE 2
Degree of New Brand Preference Versus Kind of Buyer of New Detergent

Preference	Early Buyer	Late Buyer	Non-buyer
High (250–400)	55%	39%	19%
High Medium (200–249)	25	31	21
Low Medium (50–199)	12	12	17
Low (0–49)	8	18	43
Total	100%	100%	100%
Base	52	62	151

TABLE 3
Feelings About Present Brand of Detergent and Kind of Buyer for New Detergent

Degree of Certainty	Early Buyer	Late Buyer	Non-buyer
Very certain	17%	31%	48%
Usually certain	67	48	37
Sometimes certain or almost never certain	16	21	15
Total	100%	100%	100%
Base	52	62	151

Question: How certain are you that the brand of heavy duty detergent you are using will work as well as or better than any other brand you know of but have not tried?

kind of buyer in the cross-classification analysis. These variables (starred in Table 1) were in four distinct categories: socioeconomic, trial-proneness, product-related, and informational. Though all were significant, only those relating to specific hypotheses are examined. The opinion leadership question, the AIO factor scores on information seeking and risk avoidance, and the media factor scores were conspicuous for their inability to distinguish the kind of buyer. Also, usage rate for the product class did not differentiate among early, late, and nonbuyers.

Table 2 shows the relationship between new product brand preference and kind of buyer. Nonbuyers had the least preference for the new brand, and the early buyers the greatest.[2] Also, 19 percent of the nonbuyers indicated a high preference for the new brand. These subjects could eventually become late buyers of the new product.

Table 3 shows that early buyers were significantly less confident about their past brand purchases than late buyers, and that late buyers were less confident than nonbuyers, indicating a predisposition by early and late buyers to try new brands.

Table 4 supports the predisposition to try the new brand. When asked about willingness to buy known, but untried brands, early and late buyers indicated a greater willingness

[2] Note that the early buyers would have a longer period for evaluating the product and to develop stronger likes or dislikes for this new brand.

TABLE 4

Willingness to Try New Brands and Kind of Buyer for New Detergent

Feelings	Early Buyer	Late Buyer	Non-buyer
Very anxious or willing to try it	40%	36%	20%
Hesitant about trying it	52	53	49
Very unwilling to try it	8	11	31
Total	100%	100%	100%
Base	52	62	151

Question: When I am shopping and see a brand of heavy duty detergent that I know of but have never used, I am . . .

than nonbuyers. This result suggests that an advertising campaign aimed at shaking confidence in current brand offerings may be an effective strategy.

Two slightly different questions about innovativeness, reported in Tables 5 and 6, were part of the follow-up questionnaire. Early buyers clearly see themselves as experimenters to a significantly greater degree than late or nonbuyers (Table 5). However, early buyers

TABLE 5

Feelings About Trying New Detergents and Kind of Buyer for New Detergent

Feelings	Early Buyer	Late Buyer	Non-buyer
Enjoy experimenting with new detergents	42%	29%	13%
Prefer to wait until others have tried it	33	29	22
Prefer to wait until product has been established for some time	17	27	45
Don't know	8	15	20
Total	100%	100%	100%
Base	52	62	151

Question: (an "after test") Check the one statement that best describes your feelings about trying new detergent products.

TABLE 6

Trying New Detergents and Kind of Buyer for New Detergent

Likely to Try New Detergents	Early Buyer	Late Buyer	Non-buyer
Earlier than most people	8%	8%	1%
About the same time as most people	54	39	25
Later than most people	27	34	46
Don't know	11	19	28
Total	100%	100%	100%
Base	52	62	151

Question: In general, are you more likely to try new laundry detergents earlier, about the same time, or later than most people?

did not perceive themselves as innovators (Table 6). It seems that early buyers view their buying time for new detergents as concurrent with others. That is, there seems to be a perceived difference between experimentation and innovation. Other consumers that the early buyers had in mind might include other innovators. Literature on adoption indicates that innovative people with high interest tend to maintain active communication with one another. In this context the hypothesis seems tenable. Finally, in Tables 5 and 6, a significantly greater percentage of nonbuyers are in the "don't know" category.

Table 7 confirms an additional finding of adoption researchers about information transmission and reception. Compared with late and nonbuyers, the early buyers exhibited a higher degree of transmission of product information. However, a greater percentage of the late buyers were information receivers.

Two demographic variables were significant in the cross-classification analysis. Late buyers, compared with early and nonbuyers, had a significantly higher education. The other significant demographic variable, the number of different employers of the husband for the past 15 years, is a partial indicator of mobility. Here 43 percent of the husbands of early buyers had four or more employers; comparable figures for late and nonbuyers were 25 and 19 percent. High mobility might create the

TABLE 7

Information Transmission and Receiving About Detergents and Kind of Buyer

Information	Early Buyer	Late Buyer	Non-buyer
Kind of buyer—transmitting[a]			
Yes	40%	32%	22%
No	52	65	69
Don't know	8	3	9
Total	100%	100%	100%
Base	52	62	151
Kind of buyer—receiving[b]			
Yes	29%	43%	27%
No	65	57	65
Don't know	6	—	8
Total	100%	100%	100%
Base	52	62	151

[a] Question: Have you recently been asked your opinion on detergents or have you volunteered any information on detergents to anyone?
[b] Question: Have you recently asked or has anyone volunteered information on detergents to you?

TABLE 8

Receiving and Using Free Sample and Kind of Buyer

Free Sample	Early Buyer	Late Buyer	Non-buyer
Receiving free sample			
Did receive a free sample	67%	77%	59%
Did not receive a free sample	33	23	41
Total	100%	100%	100%
Base	52	62	151
Using free sample			
Used all of the free sample	100%	98%	73%
Used some of the free sample	—	—	16
Used none of the free sample	—	2	11
Total	100%	100%	100%
Base	35	48	89

capability to easily adjust to new elements in one's environment or might reflect dissatisfaction with present conditions.

The effect of the free sampling campaign is shown in Table 8. Sixty-five percent of all subjects reported receiving a free sample; however, in the late buyer group, 77 percent reported receiving the sample. When only those who received the sample are used as a base for studying the relationship between usage of the sample and kind of buyer, the nonbuyers do not give the sample a fair test. (Instructions on the package told housewives that several washings were needed to fully demonstrate the cumulative effects of the brightening agent in the product. Nonbuyers may have rejected the sample before trying it or after incomplete testing.)

REGRESSION ANALYSIS. To further examine differences between triers of the new product, a stepwise multiple regression analysis was done on the early and late buyers. The dependent variable was the number of days to first purchase, and the independent variables were all variables which were significant in the cross-classification analysis as well as several additional variables from Table 1. The results are shown in Table 9.

The demographic variables dominated the analysis. Early buyers lived in smaller houses, were in higher income groups, had husbands who had worked for more employers, and were less likely to buy large items on credit. In addition, early buyers expressed willingness to try new detergents, were relatively heavier readers of movie-crime magazines, and developed a higher preference for the new product. Remember, on the basis of the cross-classifica-

TABLE 9

Significant Independent Variables	Increase in R^2
Number of rooms in the house	7.3%
Total family income	5.7
Number of husband's employers	6.6
Buying on credit	4.4
Feelings about trying known but unused detergents	3.7
Media FS; movie, crime	3.4
New product preference score	1.8
Total	32.9%

tion analysis, early buyers were in relatively lower education groups. Thus, except for the income relationship, early buyers compared with late buyers appear to be typical of the lower socioeconomic classes. No convincing explanation for the income relationship appeared.

Several of the demographic variables, significant in the regression analysis, were not significant in the cross-classification analysis. The cross-classification analysis involved three groups: early, late and nonbuyers whereas the regression analysis treated only early and late buyers. Many variables that were significant in the cross-classification analysis reflected differences between triers and non-triers rather than between early and late buyers. The latter differences are reported in the discussion of the discriminant analysis. Conversely, several demographic variables, significant in the regression analysis, were not significant in the cross-classification analysis because their power to discriminate between early and late buyers was reduced after adding the third group (nonbuyers) to the cross-classification analysis.

Although the stepwise regression analysis explained only 33 percent of the variance in number of days before first purchase, the results are highly significant and suggestive of the market segment at which advertising should be aimed. For those people who made at least one purchase of the new product, one must accept the hypothesis that there were significant differences between the early and late buyers.

MULTIPLE DISCRIMINANT ANALYSIS. Also, the data can be examined for differences between triers and non-triers of the product. A two-group discriminant analysis was done on the buyer, nonbuyer classification, using the Cooley and Lohnes [4] program and then the BIMD 07M stepwise discriminant program [1]. The BIMD program was run to examine the multicollinearity among variables in the analysis. The analysis using the Cooley and Lohnes program resulted in eight significant variables not reported here. Table 10 gives the results of the stepwise discriminant analysis resulting in four significant variables, a subset of the eight variables from the Cooley and Lohnes analysis. The stepwise discriminant analysis gave the same "hit and miss" classification as the Cooley and Lohnes program

TABLE 10

Stepwise Multiple Discriminant Analysis of Buyers Versus Nonbuyers

Discriminatory Variable	F Value Contribution
Awareness of the new product (after measure)	50.1[a]
Willingness to try unused brands (before measure)	20.9[a]
Preference for new product (after measure)	10.0[a]
Likelihood of early new brand trial (after measure)	5.0[b]

| Actual Category | Classified as | |
	Buyer	Nonbuyer
Analysis Sample		
Buyer	57	23
Nonbuyer	31	79
Validation Sample		
Buyer	24	10
Nonbuyer	12	29

[a] Significant at .01 level.
[b] Significant at .05 level.

with only four rather than the original eight variables.

The buyer and nonbuyer samples were split into an analysis and validation group, and the results are shown in Table 10. For the validation sample, 72 percent of subjects were correctly classified compared with 54 percent if all subjects had been assigned to the largest group. A 72 percent classification was also achieved for the analysis group of subjects. Early buyers were more aware of the product, had a higher preference, were more willing to try new brands, and scored higher on likelihood of trying new brands early.

Conclusions

Cross-classification, regression and discriminant analysis of differences between early, late, and nonbuyers for a new brand detergent gave significant results that tended to support several hypotheses on new-product trial. Triers and non-triers of the new detergent were significantly different for product specific and trial minded variables. But given that the consumer made at least one purchase, differences between early and late trial tended to relate to socioeconomic factors.

Several important variables differentiating between buyers and nonbuyers may be interesting but impractical because they were measured after purchase. That is, are buyers more aware of the product because they purchased it, or did they purchase it because they were more aware? Similarly, did brand preference develop after buying and using, or vice versa? For some subjects a high awareness and a strong brand preference developed, which might account for the eventual wide market acceptance of the new detergent. Future research should be aimed at measuring brand preference before purchase, maybe by laboratory experiments or test marketing.

How much these findings can be generalized to other product categories or brands in this product category was not tested. The particular brand studied was heavily promoted and also free sampled, undoubtedly contributing to the high product awareness in the community. The free-sample strategy may have added to the heavy level of trial purchases. However, the findings are generally applicable. In particular, it is likely that early and late buyers are qualitatively different and that the variables that most strongly separate these groups will be different from the ones that separate buyers from nonbuyers.

REFERENCES

1. *Biochemical Computer Programs,* Health Sciences Computing Facility, Department of Preventive Medicine and Public Health, School of Medicine, University of California, Los Angeles, September 1965, 587–98.
2. Philip C. Burger, Charles W. King, and Edgar A. Pessemier, "A Large Scale Systems View of Consumer Behavior Research," University of Texas Symposium, *Exploration in Consumer Behavior,* April 1966.
3. James Coleman, Elihu Katz, and Herbert Menzel, "The Diffusion of an Innovation Among Physicians," *Sociometry,* 20 (December 1957), 253–70.
4. William W. Cooley and Paul R. Lohnes, *Multivariate Procedures for the Behavioral Sciences,* New York: John Wiley & Sons, Inc., 1962, 116–133.
5. John H. K. Kao, "A Graphic Estimation of the Mixed Weibull Parameters in Life Testing of Electron Tubes," *Technometrics,* 1 (November 1959), 389–407.
6. Elihu Katz and Paul F. Lazarsfeld, *Personal Influence,* Glencoe, Ill.: The Free Press, 1955.
7. Charles W. King, "Adoption and Diffusion Research in Marketing: An Overview," *Science, Technology and Marketing,* fall conference proceedings, American Marketing Association, August 1966, 665–84.
8. Charles W. King and Edgar A. Pessemier, *Experimental Methods of Analyzing Demand for Branded Consumer Goods with Application to Problems in Marketing Strategy,* Pullman, Wash.: Washington State University, June 1963.
9. Richard Teach, and Douglas J. Tigert, *The Consumer Behavior Research Project,* Herman C. Krannert Graduate School of Industrial Administration, Purdue University, 1965.
10. Everett M. Rogers, *Diffusion of Innovations,* Glencoe, Ill.: The Free Press, 1962.
11. Bryce Ryan and Neal C. Gross, "The Diffusion of Hybrid Seed Corn in Two Iowa Communities," *Rural Sociology,* 8 (March 1943), 115–24.
12. Douglas J. Tigert, "Consumer Typologies and Market Behavior," Unpublished doctoral dissertion, Herman C. Krannert Graduate School of Industrial Administration, Purdue University, 1966.

28 / Imagery and Symbolism

A. BACKGROUND AND THEORY

This section is comprised of material (Reynolds) on the role of the consumer in image building.

28-A THE ROLE OF THE CONSUMER IN IMAGE BUILDING

William H. Reynolds (Marketing Educator)

Product and brand images are created by consumers. Herta Herzog has defined an image as "the sum total of impressions the consumer receives from many sources. . . ."[1] This definition (which may have been an intentional oversimplification) tends to emphasize what might be called the "message milieu" and to look upon the consumer himself as a passive recipient of impressions. An image is actually the result of a more complex process. It is the mental construct developed by the consumer on the basis of a few selected impressions among the flood of total impressions; it comes into being through a creative process in which these selected impressions are elaborated, embellished, and ordered.

The exotic word "infundibular," or funnel-shaped, describes the image-building process. A great deal of work has been done in marketing on the elements in a marketer's total communications mix which actually get through to the consumer. This is the first half of the process diagrammed.[2] Less has been

done on what the consumer does with the bits of information that reach him. Yet research in this area is vital if marketers are to control their image.

To cite one example, suppose that a manufacturer of cooking oils finds that his product has an image of heaviness and viscosity and he takes steps to correct the problem. Actual reductions in viscosity—as measured by laboratory techniques—are unlikely to be effective. Housewives apparently judge viscosity in cooking oils on the basis of color. Light-colored oils are seen as less viscous. The manufacturer could change the image of his oil more successfully by changing its color than by changing its viscosity.

Image as Reputation

Belief versus fact. The question of belief *versus* fact can obscure the actual nature of an image. Images are not isolated empirical beliefs about a product or brand but are *systems of inferences* which may have only a tenuous and indirect relationship to fact.

A particular belief about a product or brand (whether true or false) can lead to dozens of other interdependent beliefs. Given a starting point, possibly only a single fact, a consumer can create (in the same way that a paleontol-

SOURCE: William H. Reynolds, "The Role of the Consumer in Image Building," *California Management Review*, Vol. 7 (Spring, 1965), pp. 69–76. © 1965 by The Regents of the University of California.

[1] Herta Herzog, "Behavioral Science Concepts for Analyzing the Consumer," in Perry Bliss, ed., *Marketing and the Behavioral Sciences* (Boston: Allyn and Bacon, Inc., 1963), p. 82.

[2] John A. Howard, *Marketing: Executive and Buyer Behavior* (New York: Columbia University Press, 1963), pp. 28–29; 136, and John C. Maloney, "Is Advertising Believability Really Important?" *Journal of Marketing*, XXVII (Oct. 1963), 3; 5.

ogist can reputedly reconstruct a dinosaur from a single bone) an amazingly detailed image of a product, the people likely to use it, and the homes in which it might be seen, complete with evaluative attitudes and emotional overtones. The proper question to ask about a belief concerning a product is not whether it is true or false but how it is interrelated functionally with other beliefs.

The Simplest Process

THE HALO EFFECT. The halo effect is the simplest process contributing to the development of an image from a relatively small amount of data. Someone liking a product because of a particular attribute with which he happens to be familiar can—and does—form opinions on other attributes of the product regardless of whether he knows anything about them or not. A food product which is liked (for whatever reason) may—because of halo—be rated high on all of its characteristics, such as quality, nutrition, and flavor. An image produced by halo looks like a real image and may function like one.

For example, college students are attracted to General Electric and consider it a good place to work. Historically, there is some probability that this attitude stems from GE's past (and present) reputation, which has filtered through faculty to students, for an atmosphere conducive to research. Currently, however, the favorable attitude toward GE seems to "float," unconnected with any specific reputational factor. The underlying reasons for the generalized attitude are almost irrelevant. GE is considered a good place to work by accountants, marketers, management types, and researchers alike. The halo consequently may cause an accounting major to sign with GE. An image strong enough to influence career decisions must in some sense be taken as real.

If a product has an unfavorable reputation with respect to one of its attributes, a manufacturer should not leap to the conclusion that this attitude is unique and singular and unrelated to other attitudes. It may stem from halo. Strategically, it may be easier for him to change other attitudes than the one in question. A garment manufacturer whose dresses are considered unfashionable and ill-made might find it hard to convince buyers

that his workmanship is good. This quality would not be visible to potential customers nor would it be something they could assess for themselves. By changing styles and aggressively promoting the fact, he might, however, be able to overcome his reputation for poor fashion. If so, halo—as people came to like his clothes—could cause his reputation for worksmanship to improve concurrently.

Plot Value

SIMPLE INFERENCE. People feel that certain attributes "go together." A suit made of good materials is usually well-cut. Expensive stores have salesladies who may snub you. Instant coffee is used by lazy women. These inferences may be right or wrong, but all of them have some prime facie validity.

Inferences can sometimes seize on one aspect of a product to the neglect of others. A product may have attributes A, B, C, and D; if A possesses more plot value than the other attributes, or—for whatever reason—attracts the attention of more consumers, it may play a disproportionately large role in the image of the product.

The respondents in a recent study were given the opportunity to examine in detail two quite different automobiles and were then asked to rate them on a list of image-type characteristics. Questions were asked about the perceived attributes of the cars themselves—sporty, elegant, fast—the people who might drive them—banker, suburban couple, teen-ager—and where and under what circumstances the cars might be seen—shopping center, opera, beach.

The same questionnaire was then administered to another group of respondents who were not shown the cars but who were told only that one of the cars was big and black and that the other was small and white. The results were substantially similar to those obtained when people were looking at the actual cars, knew their brands, and had been given a chance to become thoroughly familiar with them. The big black car, for example, was seen in both phases of the research as elegant, suitable for a banker, and likely to be seen at the opera. The images based on color and size alone were as elaborated and as detailed as those based upon the vastly greater amount of information given the first group of respondents.

Similarly, Pierre Martineau compared the images held by women familiar with two department stores with the images of the same two stores developed by another group of women, unfamiliar with the stores, but who had been shown advertisements. Again, the images based upon the limited amount of information in the advertisements were in close correspondence with the images based upon detailed information and long familiarity.[3] A marketer may be able to build an image by doing no more than establishing that his product is of a certain class; the consumer can then go on to make further inferences and, in effect, create the image himself.

Personal Associations

ASSOCIATIONAL STRUCTURES. Associations may be idiosyncratic. For example, Caroline Spurgeon in *Shakespeare's Imagery* has shown how Shakespeare associated the words "dog," "candy," and "melting," and used them in situations in his plays involving fawning and cringing.[4] Lowe's *Road to Xanadu* details the highly personal associations underlying much of Coleridge's language in *The Ancient Mariner*.[5] All of us similarly have personal associations peculiar to ourselves. Idiosyncratic associations are frequent enough, as a matter of fact, that word association tests can be used as diagnostic tools by psychologists concerned with individual personalities.

There are nevertheless sufficient uniformities from person to person in associational structures that association can be important in image building. This is generally recognized in the research conducted on names proposed for new products. It is standard practice in this research to inquire into the words suggested by a name. Consistencies are ordinarily found.

Name research is not the only area in which word association tests can be used. The word "expensive," for example, means "high-priced" or "dear" to a few people and "ostentatious" to a few others. Overwhelmingly, however, the word is associated with "quality," "fine," "elegant," "the best." An expensive product, to most people, is a good product. (The respondents in this research were asked to give the "first word to come to mind.")

Osgood's work with the semantic differential has shown that in one way associational structures are relatively simple and in another way discouragingly complex. Responses obtained when a concept is rated against a large number of adjective scales seem to be governed by three main factors, good-bad, strong-weak, and active-passive. These three factors account for almost 50 per cent of the variance when the "meaning" of particular concepts is measured, using factor analysis techniques, almost regardless of the concept, the adjectives against which it is judged, or the people doing the judging. It is in this sense that associational structures can be said to be simple; they are complex in that many opaque factors with light loadings account for the remaining unexplained 50 per cent of the variance.[6]

Associations are usually meaningful configurations. Other things being equal, a more expensive product is likely to be a better product. It is hard to establish an association between two items by repetitive juxtaposition unless the items are structurally related to each other in some way. "Progress" can be associated with General Electric but not with a buggy-whip manufacturer.

Dissonant Elements

COGNITIVE DISSONANCE. An effort to associate "progress" with a buggy-whip manufacturer would be an instance of Festinger's "cognitive dissonance."[7] Dissonance creates tension and people have evolved strategies for handling it. One strategy is to deny or to refuse to admit the existence of one of the dissonant

[3] Pierre Martineau, *Motivation in Advertising* (New York: McGraw-Hill Book Co., 1957), p. 164.

[4] Caroline Spurgeon, *Shakespeare's Imagery* (Boston: Beacon Press, 1958), pp. 195–199. (Originally published by Cambridge University Press, 1935.)

[5] John Livingston Lowe, *Road to Xanadu* (New York: Vintage Books, 1959). (Originally published by Houghton Mifflin Co., 1927).

[6] Charles E. Osgood, George J. Suci, and Percy H. Tannenbaum, *The Measurement of Meaning* (Urbana: University of Illinois Press, 1957), pp. 36–39 *passim*.

[7] Leon Festinger, *A Theory of Cognitive Dissonance* (Stanford: Stanford University Press, 1957).

elements—to insist, for example, that the buggy-whip manufacturer is not progressive, or that he is progressive but no longer manufactures buggy-whips.

Another strategy is to search for additional information or to develop broader concepts which will resolve the dissonance. A watch for ladies might be seen as both delicate and sturdy, a dissonant combination of attributes. The manufacturer could resolve this dissonance by advertising that his watch represents a breakthrough in watch design: "incredibly light, incredibly sturdy, through space-age miniaturization!"

A dissonance offers a real opportunity for the exercise of creativity; a confused image, if handled adroitly by a marketer, can be turned into an asset. A bank, for example, might offer higher interest rates than competitors but be considered "unfriendly." The obvious and usual way to counter this would be to deny the "unfriendly" element in the dissonant image and to try to create a folksy, friendly image through advertising and promotion. Another way, possibly more effective, would be to try to bring the two dissonant elements into consonance: "We offer higher interest rates because we're strictly business. Don't come to us if you want colored checks."

Use of Codes

INFORMATION THEORY. Information theory, as developed from the original work of C. E. Shannon and Bell Laboratories, offers perhaps the most general explanation of the nature of the image-building process.[8] The transmission of information can be extraordinarily efficient if codes are used which make reference to information already available to the recipient. Western Union's numbered birthday messages are an example. Transmission of one or two digits will tell the operator at the other end of the line which birthday message to pull from his file to deliver to the addressee. Similarly, computer codes such as Fortran simply tell computers conceptually which of several stored programs to use.

The consumer also has stored programs which can be activated by appropriate codes.

[8] C. E. Shannon, *The Mathematical Theory of Communication* (Urbana: University of Illinois Press, 1949).

The word "sweet" or the quality "sweetness" will prompt an array of stored associations and inferences which will differ from those which would be prompted by other code words or qualities. The word "sweet," in effect, is a constraint, which tends to reduce the uncertainty of response by making some responses more likely than others.

Sequential constraint, as the concept is used in the highly mathematical literature on information theory, refers to the reduction of uncertainty. An example is that the next item in a sequence of letters, words, or musical sounds is often predictable. If the item is completely predictable, it adds no new information and is consequently redundant. Garner points out that this can be affected by prior familiarity; a guess at the next letter in the sequence, "Now is the time for all go—" is almost certain to be an "o" to complete the sentence "—od men to come to the aid of their party."[9]

Probabilities

It should be emphasized that the process is a matter of probabilities. Constraint is rarely absolute. Osgood comments:

To use another example, "The old man——— down the road"; it is clear that the structure of English requires some verb (flew, limps, crawls, traveled, etc.), though the tense is not specified by the context; on the other hand, the presence of "old man" and "road" clearly exerts semantic selectivity on the alternatives—*limped* or *hobbled* are certainly more probable semantically than *slept, swam*, or even *ran*.[10]

A knowledgeable consumer with some background who is given a few items of information about a product or brand is often put under a similar constraint. Certain associations, attitudes, and inferences become more likely than others. The consumer will know, for example, that a car described as "big and black" would probably be heavy,

[9] R. Garner, *Uncertainty and Structure as Psychological Concepts* (New York: John Wiley and Sons, Inc., 1962), p. 213.
[10] E. Osgood, "The Representational Model and Relevant Research Methods," in Ithiel de la Sola Pool, *Trends in Content Analysis* (Urbana: University of Illinois Press, 1959), p. 79.

expensive, conservative, comfortable, and prestigious.

Image building in fact is not usually this predictable.

- People differ in the prior information at their disposal and in their creative ability to elaborate an image.
- A product or brand is a combination of attributes, and one person might construct his image on the basis of one feature and another person on another. (The story of the blind men and the elephant comes to mind.)
- Uncertainty is hardly ever reduced to zero; almost always, alternative inferences from the same facts or the same sequence of items are conceivable. For these reasons, images are statistical in nature. Different people will have different images of the same product; the number of people with a particular image is always a percentage and not the total population.

Conclusions

Images are ordered wholes built by consumers from scraps of significant detail in much the same way that writers and artists use significant detail to illumine complex totalities. *Marketers who fail to recognize the internal structure of their images and who try to correct an image problem by a frontal head-on attack are choosing, whether they know it or not, the path of most resistance.*

Millions of dollars have been spent trying to convince consumers of something about a product which they know cannot be true because it is inconsistent with the total complex of attitudes, expectations, and beliefs associated with the product. Instead, the marketer should ask himself:

1. Are there key elements in my image—not necessarily the most conspicuous—which, if changed, might lead to dissonance and to changes in the total configuration?
2. What elements in my image are structurally interrelated and give mutual support to each other? Do some of my "bad" points make my "good" points more believable?
3. How can plot value be exploited in my product design and advertising? Can I make some elements in my image more salient than others?
4. What constraints can I build into my message mix to reduce uncertainty and make consumer response more predictable?

Product and brand images arise out of a complex interaction between marketer messages and consumer creativity. It is only by recognizing the contribution of the consumer that a marketer can obtain a measure of control over the image-building process.

B. RESEARCH AND APPLICATIONS

Following is a report of research (Sommers) that deals with product symbolism and the perception of social strata.

28-B PRODUCT SYMBOLISM AND THE PERCEPTION OF SOCIAL STRATA

Montrose S. Sommers (Marketing Educator)

The question: "Why do people buy?" is constantly being answered in innumerable ways. One approach to answering it is to focus on what people buy and their perceptions of products. It was the basic objective of my

SOURCE: Montrose S. Sommers, "Product Perception and the Perception of Social Strata," in Stephen A. Greyser, Editor, *Toward Scientific Marketing* (Chicago: American Marketing Association, 1969), pp. 266–279.

research *to design a research instrument for studying perceived product symbolism* so that this concept could be more easily applied to practical marketing problems.

DESIGN OF THE RESEARCH. The project was undertaken on an exploratory basis and designed so that products became the vehicle for expression for housewives. Product symbolism was investigated within two frames of reference, the Self (S) and the described Other (O). Basically, housewives were asked to describe themselves in terms of a set of products and then to describe a particular other housewife using the same products as descriptive symbols.

When a subject adopts the frame of reference of the Self, she is saying: "What kind of a person am I? How do I see myself? What is my image of myself?" The answers elicited are in very specialized terms, in terms of products as they embody and stand for role components.

When the housewife adopts the frame of reference of the described Other, she is role playing and acting as if she were this person. From this position she is saying: "If I were she, how would I answer the same questions; what kind of a person am I? How do I see myself? What is my image of myself?"

By having subjects describe themselves and another person, it is possible to get an indication of the different descriptive symbolic values of the products used. The Self description provides an indication of perceived product symbolism and the nature of the Self perception; that is, through the relationship of product and role, which of the feminine role components are most important and their order of importance. The description of the Other provides an indication of how a subject perceives the descriptive product symbolism of another person. This description illustrates something of the perceived nature and importance of product symbols and related roles which are attributed, possibly inaccurately, to Others.

OPERATIONAL HYPOTHESES TESTED. The operational hypotheses which were tested were designed to determine whether or not a product test of the type designed could actually differentiate between members of two different social strata; the nature of the perceptions of Other and the solidarity of perception of Self and Other that exists within strata. The statement of the major hypothesis is: *members of a high stratum (H) describe Self and Other significantly differently from members of a low stratum (L).*

The second hypothesis, that *members of H are more accurate in perceiving members of L than are members of L in perceiving those of H* is suggested by the tradition of upward mobility in American society and the idea that people in higher social strata not only have had experience in reference groups in lower strata but also are more articulate regarding prestige differences and make more divisions into groups than those in lower strata.

The third hypothesis, that *members of L demonstrate greater agreement in describing Self than members of H* is based on the idea that individuals within a stratum generally have access to similar communication channels but that members of a lower stratum have fewer alternatives in terms of roles and communication channels than those of a higher stratum. Because of the smaller numbers of alternatives available to those in the lower stratum, it is expected that there will be a greater degree of homogeneity of Self descriptions in the lower stratum than in the higher one.

Hypothesis four, that *members of H demonstrate greater agreement in describing an Other than members of L* relies on the same basic position as those that preceded. Members of a higher stratum can be expected to demonstrate greater agreement in Other description than those of a lower one for the same reasons that they are expected to be more accurate in their perceptions. The better the persons and occupations are known, the more agreement concerning them.

Members of the lower stratum can be expected to have diverse concepts of Other because of their lack of actual reference group knowledge and relationships with members of groups like those in the higher stratum. In addition, the multiplicity of reference points presented by radio, television, newspapers, magazines, and other media is also expected to result in a diversity of descriptions of Other. The fifth hypothesis, that *members of H demonstrate greater agreement in describing an Other than in describing Self* develops naturally from the previous hypotheses dealing with accuracy of perceptions and agreement on Self descriptions for a higher stratum.

The sixth hypothesis is based on the same type of logic. Because *members of a lower stratum (L) have fewer role alternatives, they demonstrate greater agreement in Self description than members of H.* Because they have not had actual reference group contact with members of a higher stratum and receive much conflicting information through the mass media, their perceptions of Other are diverse and relatively inaccurate.

Measuring Perceptions of Self and Other

The basis for measuring the perceptions of products and their use lies in Q-methodology as propounded by William Stephenson.[1] Stephenson's intent was to deal with the total personality in action, with "wholes" and "descriptions" rather than traits or characteristics. The evidence of the total personality in action would be represented in the recorded reactions a person had with reference to a large number of test items. What is important in the approach is the form in which recorded reactions appear. It is the distribution of reactions, a forced normal distribution, which allows for the use of correlation and factor analysis techniques.

The test that an individual takes, under Q-methodology, is composed of items drawn from some type of population, in this case, a population of products. The methodology does not concern itself with the populations as such but with the statistical universes which are derived from them. In the product test designed for this project, the concern is not with the representativeness of the products selected, but with the manner in which an individual when she is asked to grade products on a scale, from those which best describe her to those which least describe her, arrays these products. The procedure for evaluating each item and placing it in some kind of an array is called Q-sort. The method of evaluating such arrays and the position of items within them requires the establishment of a number of classes, each with a different score, and with each class containing an appropriate number of test items so that the array takes the shape of a quasi-normal frequency distribution. The quasi-normal frequency distribution for a sample of 50 products is shown in Table 1.

Those two items which a subject places in the class on the extreme left receive a score of 9 for each. These would be the two products

[1] William Stephenson, *The Study of Behavior* (Chicago: University of Chicago Press, 1953).

TABLE 1

Frequency Distribution and Scores for Products (N = 50)

	Best Describes				Least Describes			
Score	9	8	7	6	5	4	3	2	1
Frequency	2	3	6	9	10	9	6	3	2

in the group available which best describe Self or Other. The second class contains the next three items which best describe Self or Other and each receives a score of 7. The score for items in each subsequent class is reduced to the point where the last two items, those which least describe Self or Other, receive a score of 1. From the frequency distribution it can be seen that those classes at the extremes of the distribution can be considered to be highly discriminataing and have few items falling within them while those classes in the central positions could be less discriminating and have a greater number of items falling within them. The scores which the different items receive, under the two conditions of sorting, Self and Other, becomes the basis for analysis and comparisons.

Comparisons and analysis of arrays resulting from Q-sorting operations can be made using product moment correlation (Pearson r). The array which results from the Q-sort technique can also be scored on a rank order basis with the first item placed (that one being most descriptive) scored 1 and all the other items placed (in succeeding order to least descriptive) so numbered that the last item receives lowest ranking or 50. The technique is therefore flexible from the point of view of analysis.

In determining what kinds of items are to be used for Q-sorting operations, two basic considerations are to be heeded. Care must be taken to see that none of the items included are so apparently similar as to make distinctions between them extremely difficult. In addition, a basic type of homogeneity of class of items is important so that a subject can make decisions about how the items are related and what their relative values might be. For the Q-sorting operations of this project, the items included in the test are products which can be and are used in the fulfillment of feminine role components either in the home environment, with members of the family or as a representative of the family.

Five classes of products were selected for inclusion in the product test: (1) clothing; (2) toiletries and cosmetics; (3) food; (4) household appliances; and (5) leisure products. Each class was divided into 5 products defined as standard and 5 defined as specialty; in the case of leisure products the dichotomy was made for items which have a non-participative individual or participative group orientation in use. The complete listing of products which comprised the test is shown in Table 2.

IMPLEMENTATION OF THE INSTRUMENT. The instrument, the product test, was used to test the product perceptions of housewives who represented two social strata. Fifty subjects were selected from each of two census tracts using a sampling design termed area sample

with quota controls. One census tract (designated Low or L) was generally equivalent to a combination of the Warner classifications upper lower-lower middle. The second tract (designated High or H) was generally equivalent to the Warner classification upper-middle.

Each subject, using the product test which was presented as a deck of 50 cards with a product name on each card, sorted the cards to describe Self. The Self sorts for both strata (LS and HS) were recorded and then subjects assumed the role of a member of the opposite stratum. This was done by presenting subjects with a "cue" card which characterized a typical member of H for members of L and a typical member of L for members of H. Assuming the appropriate roles and again making the descriptions of Self and Other ("as if I were this person") resulted in Other sorts

TABLE 2

Test Items by Categories and Sub-Groups

Category	Standard Sub-Group	Specialty Sub-Group
1. Clothing	Shoes skirts dresses blouses suits	hat gloves lingerie hosiery slacks
2. Toiletries and cosmetics	toothpaste hand soap deodorant facial tissue hair shampoo	hair spray permanent waves eye shadow lipstick nail polish
3. Food	catsup flour shortening potatoes bread	frozen orange juice instant coffee frozen sea food cake mix refrigerator biscuits
4. Household appliances	refrigerator iron toaster stove washing machine	electric can opener automatic dish washer rotisserie food blender automatic clothes dryer
5. Leisure products	*Non-Participative— Individual* television books magazines records Hi-Fi set	*Participative— Group* sports equipment playing cards camping equipment boating equipment cocktail set

TABLE 3

Results of Tests of the Hypotheses

Hypothesis	Operational Statement	Measurement	Finding
H I	$r_1(LS:HS) = 1.0$ and $r_2(LO:HO) = 1.0$	$r_1 = .669$ $r_2 = .185$	Accept
H II	$r_1(LS:HO) > r_2(LO:HS)$	$r_1 = .919$ $r_2 = .601$	Accept
H III	$W(LS) > W(HS)$	$W(LS) = .481$ $W(HS) = .303$	Accept
H IV	$W(LO) < W(HO)$	$W(LO) = .181$ $W(HO) = .541$	Accept
H V	$W(HS) < W(HO)$	$W(HS) = .303$ $W(HO) = .541$	Accept
H VI	$W(LS) > W(LO)$	$W(LS) = .481$ $W(LO) = .181$	Accept

for both strata; the Low stratum descriptions of H (LO) and the High stratum descriptions of L (HO).

The implementation of the test resulted in the four basic sorts; LS, LO, HS, and HO which provided the measurements necessary for hypothesis testing. The four basic sorts were obtained by developing a mean array for Self and Other for each stratum.

TEST RESULTS. The hypotheses were tested with the results shown in Table 3. Two statistics were used in demonstrating the relationships between the sorts: (1) Pearsonian r; (2) the coefficient of concordance W. Product movement correlation was used to correlate the basic product arrays, and the coefficient of concordance was used as a measure of the level of agreement to be found in each of the basic arrays.

Being able to accept the first research hypothesis, that members of different strata have different Self and Other perceptions, was a major objective of the study. This is not because the finding is significant, *per se*, but because of the method used. The support of this operational position demonstrates the ability of the Q-sort procedure, given a selection of items to be arrayed, to yield results which distinguish between members of two social strata.

An analysis of the four basic arrays LS, HS, LO, and HO (shown in Table 4), resulted in information demonstrating which products were most and least descriptive and how members of both strata viewed each other.

1. The basic product categories of Clothing, Toiletries and Cosmetics, Food, Appliances, and Leisure Products were too broad and too mixed in order to demonstrate the descriptive properties of products in terms of their item scores. By breaking the basic categories into Standard and Specialty Sub-Groups, much more accurate and descriptive information was obtained on which types of groups of products best describe Self and Other. Virtually all the Standard Sub-Group items were found to best describe with higher descriptive scores than the Specialty Sub-Group items.

2. The product categories were also found to be not accurate enough in demonstrating which types of items were responsible for differences between pairs of basic arrays. The Standard and Specialty Group sub-group breakdown showed that the largest differences between LS and HS were accounted for by the different scores given to Specialty Appliances and Standard Clothing items. The largest differences between LS and HO were accounted for by H's inaccurate perception of how members of L would score Specialty Appliances and Standard Toiletries and Cosmetics. The largest differences between HS and LO were accounted for by L's inaccuracy in perceiving how members of H would score Specialty Appliances.

3. In the analysis of descriptive ability of sub-groups related to accuracy of description, it was found that members of L were generally

TABLE 4

Product Arrays for LS, HS, LO, and HO with Items from Most Descriptive to Least Descriptive

Scores	LS	HS	LO	HO
9 (n = 2)	washing machine	washing machine	dresses	refrigerator
	stove	dresses	automatic	stove
			clothes dryer	
8 (n = 3)	refrigerator	refrigerator	shoes	electric iron
	electric iron	books	hosiery	bread
	hand soap	shoes	automatic	washing machine
			dishwasher	
7 (n = 6)	toothpaste	skirts	television	blouses
	hair shampoo	blouses	refrigerator	television
	potatoes	lingerie	lingerie	dresses
	bread	lipstick	hats	flour
	toaster	stove	washing machine	electric toaster
	television	automatic	skirt	potatoes
		dishwasher		
6 (n = 9)	dresses	hand soap	suits	frozen orange
	blouses	toothpaste	blouses	juice
	lingerie	deodorant	deodorant	shoes
	shoes	hair shampoo	gloves	deodorant
	deodorant	toaster	electric toaster	toothpaste
	facial tissues	electric iron	lipstick	shortening
	books	clothes dryer	electric	hair shampoo
	flour	records	rotisserie	hand soap
	shortening	television	hi-fi	lipstick
			stove	skirts
5 (n = 10)	skirts	slacks	hair spray	suits
	slacks	hosiery	slacks	slacks
	hosiery	suits	toothpaste	catsup
	lipstick	gloves	hair shampoo	hosiery
	hair spray	facial tissues	electric can	permanent waves
	catsup	bread	opener	books
	magazines	potatoes	hand soap	lingerie
	cake mix	playing cards	electric iron	facial tissues
	frozen orange	hi-fi	facial tissues	cake mix
	juice	frozen orange	nail polish	magazines
	refrigerated	juice	records	
	biscuits			
4 (n = 9)	frozen seafood	hats	frozen orange	instant coffee
	suits	hair spray	juice	hair spray
	gloves	nail polish	sports equipment	playing cards
	permanent waves	catsup	playing cards	gloves
	nail polish	flour	permanent waves	frozen seafood
	camping	shortening	books	hats
	equipment	magazines	eye shadow	nail polish
	records	cake mix	cocktail set	refrigerated
	clothes dryer	sports equipment	bread	biscuits
	sports equipment		blender	records

Scores	LS	HS	LO	HO

3 (n = 6)	instant coffee
	playing cards
	electric can
	  opener
	blender
	hi-fi
	hats
		instant coffee
		camping
		  equipment
		frozen seafood
		eye shadow
		blender
		refrigerated
		  biscuits
			instant coffee
			shortening
			boating
			  equipment
			frozen seafood
			magazines
			refrigerated
			  biscuits
				sports equipment
				camping
				  equipment
				automatic
				  dishwasher
				eye shadow
				automatic
				  clothes dryer
				hi-fi

2 (n = 3)	automatic
	  dishwasher
	eye shadow
	electric
	  rotisserie
		permanent waves
		electric can
		  opener
		cocktail set
			flour
			potatoes
			cake mix
				cocktail set
				blender
				electric
				  rotisserie

1 (n = 2)	boating
	  equipment
	cocktail set
		boating
		  equipment
		electric
		  rotisserie
			catsup
			camping
			  equipment
				electric can
				  opener
				boating
				  equipment

accurate in best describing members of H but they were inaccurate in being able to select items which were least descriptive of members of H. On the other hand, members of H were generally accurate in being able to select those items which both best and least describe members of L.

4. The analysis of the scores which individual items received for the descriptions of Other (LO and HO) compared to the descriptions of Self demonstrated that members of L generally focused on the differences which actually existed between LS and HS and tended to magnify them or overestimate scores. Members of H, on the other hand, tended to minimize differences between LS and HS by tending to project their own descriptions to members of L.

29 / The Brand

A. BACKGROUND AND THEORY

First, we look at the effects of brand image on the total marketing picture (Tillman and Kirkpatrick); and we then address ourselves to the question, "What is a brand?" (Stanton).

29-A BRAND IMAGE

Rollie Tillman (Marketing Educator) *and*
C. A. Kirkpatrick (Marketing Educator)

When a seller designs advertising to promote the item he sells, his concern is with his brand's image in the market; this is a product concept. When he builds advertising to promote his company, firm, or organization, his interest is in his institution's image; this is a patronage concept.

Advertisers hope and strive for favorable, attractive images, both brand and corporate, for understandable reasons. Probably the greatest contribution of attractive images is their preselling influence. The job of selling is easier when buyers are favorably inclined toward the seller and his brand. Buyers see salesmen more often, more cordially, more confidently. Relations with media, vendors, suppliers of capital, and residents of plant cities are more satisfactory. Attractive images help attract and hold desirable employees as well as desirable customers. Finally, the seller can add products to his line more successfully.

Imagery is a matter of personality. In respect to their basic nature, the image or concept you have of Ivory soap and the image you have of your instructor have much in common. Brand image is what buyers "see"

SOURCE: Rollie Tillman and C. A. Kirkpatrick, "Brand Image," in *Promotion: Persuasive Communication in Marketing* (Homewood, Illinois: Richard D. Irwin, Inc., 1968) pp. 198–199.

and "feel" when the brand name Ivory is called to their attention. It is Ivory's mental representation, Ivory's meaning to buyers; it is Ivory's impression on buyers *and* buyers' impressions of Ivory. It is the sum of the concepts and their valences which come to mind when the word "Ivory" is perceived. When buyers think of Ivory, most reactions probably are pleasant and favorable; the reaction of some persons, however, may be unfavorable. Buyers like and dislike, they are attracted to or repelled by certain brand names, just as you feel, act, and react toward certain instructors. Similarly, the ideas and attitudes buyers associate with Procter & Gamble determine corporate image.

Brand image is the buyer's picture of how that specific brand differs from other brands. Among the determinants of brand image are corporate image, consumers of the brand, retailers who stock the brand, the product's physical features, the satisfaction the brand provides, the product's price, and the ads promoting the brand. In his efforts to achieve the brand image he wants, the seller is trying to make his brand into the *specialty* type of product mentioned in the basic marketing texts. Brand image is usually stronger than corporate image because buyers know more about brands than about the firms back of the brands.

29-B WHAT IS A BRAND?

William J. Stanton (Marketing Educator)

The word "brand" is a comprehensive term, and in one way or another it includes other, more particularized terms. A *brand* is "a name, term, symbol, or design, or a combination of them which is intended to identify the goods or services of one seller or group of sellers and to differentiate them from those of competitors."[1] A brand *name* consists of words, letters, and/or numbers which may be *vocalized*. A brand *mark* is the part of the brand which appears in the form of a symbol, design, or distinctive coloring or lettering. It is recognized by sight but is not expressed when a person pronounces the brand. Tide, Cadillac, and Monsanto are examples of brand names. Brand marks are illustrated by the colonial gentleman on Quaker Oats products and the red star of Texaco petroleum products.

Importance to the Customer

A brand can be of considerable help to the consumer or industrial user. Brands are an easy way for a purchaser to identify the product or service he desires. Furthermore, the individual units of a branded item maintain a consistency of quality that buyers can depend upon. A brand also offers some protection to the consumer: it identifies the firm behind the product. A customer may have purchased a fan belt or a few yards of woolen plaid piece goods with which he was greatly pleased. When replacement parts or additional material is needed and the customer wants to get the same product, he can be assured of doing so only if the item is branded. Branding is an insurance of merchandise comparability when the buyer uses more than one source of supply. Westinghouse light bulbs are Westinghouse light bulbs, and Whitman's chocolates are Whitman's chocolates, regardless of where purchased.

Branded products tend to improve in quality over the years. Competition forces this improvement, because brand owners are constantly seeking new ways to differentiate their products in order to secure a stronger market position. In the constant search for more profitable sales volume, product improvements have frequently been the key to success. Improvements may not be perceptible on a year-to-year basis, but a 1968 Sylvania fluorescent light bulb is noticeably better than one made in 1958.

SOURCE: William J. Stanton, "What Is a Brand?" (New York: McGraw-Hill Book Company, 1967, 2nd Ed.), pp. 217–218. Copyright 1967 by McGraw-Hill Book Company. Used by permission of McGraw-Hill Book Company.
[1] Committee on Definitions, Ralph S. Alexander, Chairman, *Marketing Definitions: A Glossary of Marketing Terms*, American Marketing Association, Chicago, 1960, p. 8.

B. RESEARCH AND APPLICATIONS

The first article in this section (Kanungo) is a report on research as to the effects in awareness of fittingness, meaningfulness, and product utility. The second selection (Kassarjian and Nakanishi) compares seven different marketing research methods for selecting a brand name.

29-C BRAND AWARENESS: EFFECTS OF FITTINGNESS, MEANINGFULNESS, AND PRODUCT UTILITY[1]

Rabindra N. Kanungo (Psychologist)

The present study examines the effects of the *fittingness* or the *appropriateness* of the brand name for the product on brand awareness. Fittingness of a brand name seems to be an important characteristic that might influence the strength of brand-product association. To the present author's knowledge, no study has been reported on the effects of fittingness variable on brand awareness. The main obstacle to the systematic investigation of the effects of this variable has been the lack of any operational definition and an appropriate measure of fittingness of brand names. Many advertisers often try to select or reject brand names on the basis of their fittingness to their product, but such selections are mostly based upon their intuition or subjective feelings due to the absence of any operational measure. The present study, therefore, tries to offer an operational definition and a measure of the fittingness characteristic of the brand name, so that systematic study of the effect of the variable on brand awareness may be possible.

It is proposed that a brand name may be considered fitting or appropriate for the product if it can readily evoke associations to the product in the minds of the Ss. Thus, according to the present author, a brand name is fitting for the product if it resembles (in form, sound, or meaning) a word that belongs to one of the most frequent associations to the product. For example, if the product lipstick evokes the word "color" as one of the most frequent associations, then the brand name "Kolory" (apparently a nonsense word, but having resemblance in form and sound to the word "color") may be considered a fitting brand name for lipsticks. However, the same nonsense word will be a nonfitting brand name for the product smoking pipe if the word "color" is only a rare association to the product smoking pipe. This implies that association norms for different products may serve as a basis for selecting fitting and nonfitting brand names. Since a fitting brand name would resemble a common associate of the product, one might assume that the initial strength of the brand-product association would be greater in the case of fitting than in the case of nonfitting brand name. Thus with single or repeated exposures brand awareness would be better in the former than in the latter case.

Method

SELECTION OF BRAND NAMES. Consideration of the fittingness, the meaningfulness, and the product-utility variable manipulated in the present study influenced the selection of brand names. First, to manipulate the product-utility variable, there was a need to choose products that differed in their utility for the consumers. Thus three different categories of products were selected, namely products used by males, by females, and by both sexes. Four commonly used products from each of these categories were chosen, making a total of 12 products.

Second, in order to choose brand names that differed in their fittingness for the products,

SOURCE: Rabindra N. Kanungo, "Brand Awareness: Effects of Fittingness, Meaningfulness, and Product Utility," *Journal of Applied Psychology,* Vol. 4 (August, 1968), pp. 290–295. Copyright 1968 by the American Psychological Association, and reproduced by permission.

[1] The study was supported partly by Grant No. X-12-179 from National Research Council of Canada and partly by Grant No. X-85-8 from Dalhousie University Research Development Fund. The author is indebted to Marcia Earhard for many helpful comments.

the following procedure was employed. Each of the 12 product names was printed on a separate sheet of paper and presented to a group of 19 male and 19 female college undergraduate students. For each product, they were asked to give as many relevant associations as they could within a 30-sec. period. These Ss were instructed not to give any existing brand names as their associative responses. All the responses given by the group were found to be meaningful words. The most frequent (occurring 50% or more) and rarest (occurring only once) responses to each product were then determined from the responses given by the group. From these response words, two fitting and two nonfitting brand names for each product were constructed. One fitting and one nonfitting brand name were highly similar to a frequent and a rare response, respectively, and the other fitting and nonfitting brand names only partially resembled in sound or form a frequent and a rare response, respectively. The reason for making half the brand names more similar to the associative responses than the other half was to ensure that the former appear more meaningful than the latter.

Third, to make sure that half of the brand names had higher meaningfulness value than the other half, another 25 undergraduate students were presented with these 48 brand names. These Ss were asked to rate each brand name on a 5-point meaningful-meaningless scale. The mean meaningfulness value (m') for each of the brand names was calculated from these ratings. The products, their frequent and rare associates, and the brand names along with their m' are presented in Table 1.

DESIGN AND MATERIALS. It will be noticed from Table 1 that for each of the 12 products, there were four brand names: high meaningful–fitting (HM–F), low meaningful–fitting (LM–F), high meaningful–nonfitting (HM–NF), and low meaningful–nonfitting (LM–NF). Using each of these brand names, four different advertisements for each product were prepared. Twelve copies of each of these 48 advertisements were printed on a 14 cm. × 22 cm. art paper. In each printed layout, a brand name following the word "use" appeared at the top, and below which a picture of the product was presented. Below the

picture a short phrase containing the product name was printed. For example, in one of the nylon advertisements, at the top of the picture would appear "USE LEGS" and at the bottom of the picture would appear "for your Nylons." Farther down the page, the name and address of the advertiser (a fictitious manufacturing concern) were given.

Finally 48 booklets were compiled. Each booklet contained one advertisement of each of the 12 products in such a manner as to include a HM–F, a LM–F, a HM–NF, and a LM–NF brand name for each of the three product categories: male-use, female-use, and used-by-both products. The sequence of the 12 advertisements in each booklet was randomized to ensure varied order of presentation to Ss.

SUBJECTS. Twenty-four adult male and 24 female undergraduate students drawn from two Canadian universities served as Ss. Their ages ranged from 18 to 30 yr. The male Ss were drawn from St. Mary's University, Halifax, and the female Ss were drawn from Mount St. Vincent University, Rockingham. These Ss had never participated in any kind of psychological experiment before.

PROCEDURE. Each S was given a separate booklet and was asked to rate each brand name, in each advertisement in the booklet, on each of two 6-point scales: meaningfulness and appropriateness. The S was given 12 answer sheets, one sheet for each advertisement in the booklet, to record his ratings. The two scales were printed on the answer sheets with the following verbal labels for the 6 points: very high, high, moderate, low, very low, and none. The S was instructed to indicate his or her rating by underlining the appropriate verbal label in a scale. The order of presentation of the two scales was counterbalanced for each S. To ensure that Ss paid proper attention to the brand names in the booklet, each S was instructed to write down the brand name he or she was rating at the top of the answer sheet in a blank provided for it. The Ss were made to believe that the manufacturer intended to launch an extensive advertising campaign with a view to introducing these new products into the markets. Hence the advertiser wanted to know the reaction in terms of the two scales of various individuals toward these advertisements. The purpose of

TABLE 1

Products, Source Words, and Brand Names with Their Meaningfulness (m') Value

Product Name	High Meaningful		Low Meaningful	
	Brand Name	m'	Brand Name	m'
1. Nylons				
F	"Legs" (Leg)	4.36	"Leget" (Leg)	1.28
NF	"Feel" (Feel)	4.12	"Supet" (Superior)	1.20
2. Girdle				
F	"Shapely" (Shape)	4.48	"Tyten" (Tight)	1.24
NF	"Stately" (Stately)	4.28	"Nyten" (Night)	1.28
3. Lipstick				
F	"Colory" (Color)	2.36	"Peenkis" (Pink & Kiss)	1.32
NF	"Shiney" (Shiny)	3.52	"Crimist" (Cream)	1.40
4. Eye shadow				
F	"Blue-Lash" (Blue & Lashes)	3.36	"Loblu" (Blue)	1.36
NF	"Dark-Silk" (Dark & Silk)	3.88	"Lolid" (Lid)	1.28
5. After-shave lotion				
F	"Cooling" (Cool)	4.12	"Smelo" (Smell)	1.40
NF	"Healing" (Heal)	4.32	"Cozic" (Cozy)	1.20
6. Smoking pipe				
F	"Manly" (Man)	4.32	"Tobax" (Tobacco)	1.36
NF	"Clean" (Clean)	4.48	"Nicot" (Nicotine)	1.56
7. Briefcase				
F	"Executive" (Executive)	4.60	"Bizinet" (Business)	1.32
NF	"Important" (Important)	4.32	"Promets" (Promotion)	1.48
8. Shirts (men's)				
F	"Tie-Match" (Tie)	2.48	"Dreso" (Dress)	1.40
NF	"Party-Fit" (Party)	2.52	"Mone" (Money)	1.36
9. Writing pads				
F	"Letters" (Letter)	4.32	"Leterit" (Letter)	1.52
NF	"Economy" (Economy)	4.44	"Thicrap" (Thick)	1.24
10. Pen				
F	"Writer" (Write)	4.36	"Incko" (Ink)	1.32
NF	"Family" (Family)	4.68	"Metto" (Met)	1.40
11. Adhesive tape				
F	"Sticky" (Sticky)	4.24	"Bandes" (Bandaid)	1.48
NF	"Sporty" (Sport)	4.20	"Landes" (Land)	1.40
12. Folders				
F	"Paper-Safe" (Paper)	2.88	"Filex" (File)	1.32
NF	"Camp-Sign" (Camp & Sign)	2.52	"Firex" (Fire)	1.40

Note. Items 1–4 are female-use products, Items 5–8 are male-use products, and Items 9–12 are products used by both sexes. The bracketed word(s) next to each brand name is the associative response word(s) from which the brand name was derived.
F = fitting; NF = nonfitting.

asking Ss to rate the brand names was twofold. First, through such ratings, Ss were given incidental exposure to the advertisements, so that later tests of brand awareness would be possible. Second, Ss' ratings would directly demonstrate if Ss perceived the meaningfulness and appropriateness characteristic of the brand names in a manner intended by the experimental manipulations.

Each S was given approximately 1–1.5 min.

to rate each brand name on the two scales. After S had finished rating all brand names from the booklet, the answer sheets and the booklet were collected. The S was then given a recall sheet on which all the 12 products were listed in alphabetical order and was asked to recall as many brand names as possible and to write them beside the name of the product with which they were associated.

Results

RATINGS OF BRAND NAMES. The first part of S's task in this experiment was to rate each brand name for its meaningfulness and appropriateness. There were 48 brand names, half of which were HM and the other half LM brand names. Likewise 24 of the 48 brand names were F and the rest NF brand names (see Table 1). The advertisement booklets were distributed in such a manner that each of the 48 brand names was rated by 12 Ss (6 male and 6 female Ss) on 6-point meaningfulness and appropriateness scales. The 6 points in each scale were assigned ordinal weights of 5 (very high) to 0 (none) for the purpose of deriving the mean meaningfulness and appropriateness value for each brand name. The S's ratings indicated that the 24 HM brand names have significantly higher meaningfulness values (mean $m' = 2.74$) than those of the 24 LM brand names (mean $m' = 1.89$, $t = 3.40$, $p < .01$). The appropriateness ratings also indicate that the F brand names were considered more appropriate (mean appropriateness value = 3.07) than the NF brand names (mean appropriateness value = 1.72, $t = 4.65$, $p < .01$). This suggests that Ss did perceive the HM and LM brand names selected by the experimenter as having high and low meaningfulness, respectively. Likewise, they also perceived F and NF brand names, respectively, as more and less appropriate for the products.

EFFECTS OF FITTINGNESS AND MEANINGFULNESS. In order to determine the effects of fittingness and meaningfulness variables on brand awareness, a $2 \times 2 \times 2$ analysis of variance (Lindquist, 1953, Type VI design) was performed on the recall of brand names. The three classifications were: high and low meaningful brand names, fitting and nonfitting brand names, and male and female Ss. The two main effects of meaningfulness and fittingness and their interaction were highly

TABLE 2
Analysis of Variance of Recall Scores

Source of Variation	df	MS	F
Between Ss	47		
S's sex (S)	1	.15	<1
Error (b)	23	2.65	
Within Ss	144		
Meaningfulness (M)	1	17.52	23.67[a]
Fittingness (F)	1	24.08	66.89[a]
M × F	1	6.07	10.84[a]
M × S	1	.96	1.30
F × S	1	.27	<1
M × F × S	1	.35	<1
Error (w)	138	.55	
Error$_1$ (w)	46	.74	
Error$_2$ (w)	46	.36	
Error$_3$ (w)	46	.56	
Total	191		

[a] $p < .01$.

significant ($Fs = 23.67$, 66.89, and 10.84, respectively). These results are presented in Table 2.

The mean recall of HM–F, LM–F, HM–NF, and LM–NF brand names by all 48 Ss presented in Table 3 suggests that brand awareness is better for fitting than for nonfitting brand names and for high meaningful than for low meaningful brand names. Furthermore, these data suggest that meaningfulness variable does not influence brand awareness when the brand names are fitting ones (the difference between HM–F and LM–F recall yields a nonsignificant $t = 1.67$). However, when the brand names are of nonfitting type, the higher the meaningfulness the better is the

TABLE 3
Mean Recall Scores for Fitting and Meaningful Brand Names

	Fitting	Non-fitting	t
High meaningful	2.81	2.46	2.33[a]
Low meaningful	2.56	1.50	7.07[b]
t	1.67	6.40[b]	

Note. Means are based on the recall of all 48 Ss.
[a] $p < .05$.
[b] $p < .01$.

brand awareness (the difference between HM–NF and LM–NF yields a $t = 6.40$, $p < .01$). This is the reason for the significant interaction between meaningfulness and fittingness. The male and female Ss did not differ with respect to their recall of brand names (see Table 2). However, within each group the HM brand names were recalled significantly better than the LM brand names. For male Ss the recall means of HM and LM brand names were 5.27 and 3.87, respectively ($t = 6.67$, $p < .01$), and for the female Ss the corresponding means were 5.16 and 4.25, respectively ($t = 4.33$, $p < .01$). Similarly for both male and female Ss taken separately F brand names were recalled better than NF brand names. For male Ss the recall means of F and NF brand names were 5.21 and 3.83, respectively ($t = 6.57$, $p < .01$), and for female Ss the corresponding means were 5.33 and 4.08, respectively ($t = 5.95$, $p < .01$).

EFFECT OF UTILITY OF THE PRODUCT. A 2×3 analysis of variance was performed on the recall scores of male and female Ss for the brand names of the three categories: male-use, female-use, and used-by-both products. Out of the two main effects, the male and female Ss, and three product categories, only the latter approached significance ($F = 2.74$, $df = 2/92$, $.10 > p > .05$). The mean recall scores of the male Ss were 3.29, 3.12, and 2.87, and the corresponding recall scores of the female Ss were 3.17, 3.25, and 3.00 for male-use, female-use, and used-by-both products, respectively. These results indicate that male and female Ss did not differ in their recall patterns. The brand names for male-use and female-use products were recalled equally well by both the groups. There was a trend in both the groups to recall fewer brand names for the used-by-both products than those for the other two categories.

Discussion

The above results clearly confirm the earlier findings that brand names having higher meaningfulness values are retained better than those having low meaningfulness value (Kanungo & Dutta, 1966). In addition, the results lend strong support to the hypothesis that a fitting brand name derived from the association norms of the product is retained better than a nonfitting brand name. The fittingness variable seems to influence brand recall not only when

brand names are low meaningful ($t = 7.07$, $p < .01$) but also when they are high meaningful ($t = 2.33$, $p < .05$). The meaningfulness variable, however, influences brand recall only when brand names are nonfitting ($t = 6.40$, $p < .01$) but not when they are fitting ($t = 1.67$, $p > .05$). Such interaction effects may interest the advertisers who want to choose between two HM or LM brand names. However, further replications are needed before the advertiser can place his confidence in such interaction effects.

In practice, many advertisers choose brand names that they consider intuitively as fitting to their products. Very often, such intuitive decisions are based upon one or a few individuals' remote associative responses to the products. As suggested in this study, a better method of choosing fitting brand names would be to use the conventional laboratory word-association techniques (Cofer, 1958) with a sample of potential consumers. Generally, the association techniques have been used for the purpose of studying language and verbal learning processes (Deese, 1959; Noble, 1952) and for clinical diagnoses (Jung, 1910; Kent & Rosanoff, 1910). The present study extends its usefulness to the selection of brand names by advertisers.

The pattern of recall for brand names of the three product-utility categories does not conform to the pattern of results reported by Kanungo and Dutta (1966). The authors reported that their male Ss recalled fewer brand names of female-use products and their female Ss recalled fewer brand names of male-use products than what was expected of them. These findings supported their hypothesis that brand awareness of high-utility products is superior to that of low-utility products. In the present study, however, both male and female Ss recall male-use and female-use products equally well. These differences in the results of the two studies are presumably due to the difference in the culture patterns of Ss. The Ss used by Kanungo and Dutta (1966) were drawn from three Indian educational institutions where males and females live in a more or less segregated fashion. The cultural standards of India impose greater restrictions on free mixing among young unmarried male and female students compared to the North American cultural standards. Thus, for example, a female student in India would have less knowledge and concern about male-use products such as cigarettes or shaving blades. Likewise a male student in India would be less exposed to and interested in female-use products such as perfume or nail polish. On the other hand, the male and female Ss used in the present study share each other's interests to a greater extent due to greater exposure to each other's interests in this culture. Thus it is not surprising that both male and female Ss in the present study may be showing equal interest in both male-use and female-use products. Hence they recall the brand names of male-use and female-use products equally well. These results therefore suggest the possible role of cultural factors in brand awareness, which need to be explored more fully in the future.

Finally, it may be recalled that a trend was noticed in both the male and female Ss to recall fewer brand names for the used-by-both products as compared to the brand names for either male- or female-use products. If it is assumed that the products in the used-by-both category, such as writing pads or adhesive tape, have less personal significance for both male and female Ss compared to the products in the other two categories, such as after shave lotion, nylons, or girdles, then the trend shown by the results are consistent with the hypothesis that brand awareness of high-utility products is better than that of low-utility products. The four products belonging to the used-by-both category may have been considered somewhat less important and therefore of lower utility than the products belonging to the other two categories. Unfortunately the products were not rated on a utility scale by the Ss. Such ratings might have substantiated the above explanation.

29-D A STUDY OF SELECTED OPINION MEASUREMENT TECHNIQUES

Harold H. Kassarjian (Psychologist) and Masao Nakanishi (Marketing Educator)

Which opinion-measurement technique is the most valid and reliable? A recurring problem of attitude and opinion researchers concerned with comparisons and preferences whether they be for product, political candidate, or an advertisement is the choice of research method.

This article compares several testing methods to determine which is the most reliable. We felt the results of any investigation would depend on the technique used and hypothesized that each method would produce completely different results.

The experiment had two phases. In the first phase the following four methods were compared for the selection of a supposed brand name for a fictitious new stereophonic console phonograph:

1. Rating or Likert type scaling. Subjects rated each of 30 names on a $-2, -1, 0, 1, 2$ scale ranging from "dislike this name a great deal" to "like this name a great deal."

2. Open choice preference. Subjects checked names they particularly like as a brand name

SOURCE: Harold H. Kassarjian and Masao Nakanishi, "A Study of Selected Opinion Measurement Techniques," *Journal of Marketing Research*, Vol. 4 (May, 1967), pp. 148–153.

from the list of 30 names. The average individual selected 5.4 names.

3. Open choice objection. Subjects checked brand names they disliked. The mean number of choices was 12.6 names.

4. Limited choice. Subjects listed the best 10 names in order of preference.

The second phase repeated the study with new subjects and a reduced number of choices, from 30 to 12 brand names.

The following methods were compared:

1. Order-of-merit. Subjects listed all 12 names in order of preference.

2. Paired comparison. Each of the 12 names was paired with every other name resulting in 66 pairs. From each pair, subjects selected the most preferred name. The name appearing first in each pair was determined by a table of random numbers.

3. Open choice preference.

4. Likert scaling.

Method

Undergraduate students in an advanced marketing class were to think of possible names for the proposed stereophonic console phonograph. After eliminating duplications and obviously unusable names, there were approximately 100 brand names. Five judges checked names possibly associated with existing products, thus eliminating brand names such as Futura, Majestic, and Sound of Music. Thirty names were left for the study.

In the first phase, the 30 names were presented to 109 undergraduate business administration students at University of California, Los Angeles with differing instructions for each method. Before each set was given to the subjects, the previous set was collected so they could not refer to previous choices. The possibility that subjects might remember previous choices will be discussed. All students were

to choose the best names by all four methods; however, the order of presenting the methods was randomized. Also, the list of 30 names was presented in four separate orders so all possible combinations and permutations were possible (576 experimental forms). No two subjects received identical sets of forms.

One month later, 40 of the original subjects were retested to obtain measures of test-retest stability.

In the second phase, the list of 30 names was reduced to 12 to carry out a paired comparison test and to see if orders of preference are affected by number of names in a list.

TABLE 1

Phase 1 Order of Preference[a]

				Method		
					Limited Choice	
Brand Name	Likert Rating	Open Choice Preference	Open Choice Objection	Equal Weight	Weighted Ranks	Single Choice
Master Sound	1	2	3	1	1	2
Music Master	2	3	4	3	4	7
Stereo-Master	3	5.5	2	2	3	7
Master-Tone	4	4	1	5	6	11
Concertsound	5	1	6	4	2	1
Audio-Master	6	7	5	6	7	11
Sound Systems	7	5.5	9	7.5	5	3.5
Truetone	8	13.5	12	7.5	9	14.5
Stereo Tone	9.5	18	8	10	15	30
Coronado	9.5	8	14	11	8	5
Stereo-Fidelity	11	13.5	7	16	11	25.5
Stereo Craft	12	11	10	9	13	25.5
Stereomatic	13	13	11	13	16	18.5
Tri Fidelity	14	12	17	22	19	7
Maestro	15	16	18	14.5	12	7
Stereo Supreme	16	25.5	14	20.5	24	18.5
Sound-o-rama	17	9	20	12	10	11
Le Premier	19	10	22.5	14.5	14	18.5
Ultra-Stereo	19	15	16	18.5	20	18.5
Regal	19	18	22.5	20.5	18	14.5
Stereolife	21	22	14	17	23	18.5
Stereo Empress	22	20.5	21	23	22	18.5
Venus	23	20.5	19	18.5	17	11
Stereo-Lux	24	27.5	24	26	26	25.5
Elegencia	25	23.5	25	24	25	25.5
Phonetica	26	25.5	26	28	29	25.5
Aristola	27	29.5	28	28	28	25.5
Luxuria	28	27.5	27	28	27	25.5
Mark X Super	29	23.5	29	25	21	11
Toneonic	30	29.5	30	30	30	25.5

[a] $N = 109$.

TABLE 2

Inter-Method Correlations, Phase I

Method	Correlation	Likert Rating	Open Choice Preference	Open Choice Objection	Limited Choice Equal Weight	Limited Choice Weighted Ranks	Limited Choice Single Choice
Open choice preference	r	.89					
	r_s	.89					
Open choice objection	r	−.95	−.76				
	r_s	−.95	−.81				
Limited choice	r	.95	.91	−.86			
Equal weight	r_s	.95	.91	−.91			
Weighted ranks	r	.92	.95	−.80	.97		
	r_s	.92	.95	−.84	.96		
Single choice	r	.58	.77	−.42	.58	.73	
	r_s	.61	.74	−.49	.63	.74	

Note. r = Pearson r based on raw scores.
r_s = Spearman r based on ranks from Table 4.

From the first experiment, each of the 30 names was assigned a mean rank computed from the results of the original four methods and plotted on graph paper. The final 12 names were chosen from their mean rank scores at approximately equidistant intervals including the highest ranking name (Master Sound) and the lowest ranking name (Toneonic) to assure a better distribution of scores. In this phase, subjects consisted of 73 previously untested UCLA undergraduate students, of whom 55 were available for a retest 30 days later.

Again, the order of presenting the methods was randomized with the list of names in four separate orders. In both phases subjects were told they were selecting a name for a quality high fidelity stereophonic console phonograph soon to be marketed. They were to help select an appropriate name to reflect the high quality and high priced characteristics of this durable item. They were not told the product was imaginary.

Results

The order of preferences obtained by the methods of Phase I are in Table 1.

The rank order for each method was computed by summing the scores of each brand name for all the subjects. For example, in the Likert rating method the name Master Sound received the highest total score for all subjects. In the open choice preference method Concertsound received the greatest number of selections from all subjects, and in the open choice objection method Master-Tone received the fewest selections.

In the last three columns of Table 1 the limited choice method was processed in three ways. The subjects were first to select the 10 best names and then to rank them by preference. The last column shows the results if only the first choice name is tabulated. When each of the 109 subjects gave only one choice, many ties resulted from the single choice method, and eight names received only one selection each. The stability of the data from this column must be interpreted with extreme caution.

The next to last column considers weighted rankings of the subjects allocating 10 points to the name ranked first, nine points for the name ranked second, and finally one point for the name ranked last.[1] In the third from the last column, every choice among the best 10 is given equal weight, one point.

Though the six methods of data collection and analysis are somewhat different, they are enough alike to reject the hypothesis of dissimilarity. Master Sound received a first place rank by three methods, a second place by two methods, and a third place rank by one. In all six methods Toneonic was ranked last.[2] The

[1] Other weighting systems may also have been used. Inspection of the data, however, indicates that startling differences would not emerge.
[2] Examination of the raw scores (not presented in

results may still confuse a manager or researcher trying to recommend a single brand name, but the tests had similar results, even with a lack of independence since all subjects used all methods.

Table 2 contains inter-method correlation coefficients computed both by using raw scores and the rank-order data in Table 1. Overall, the coefficients are quite high, ranging from .97 to a low of .42.[3] The single choice method produces the poorest intercorrelations with the other methods, undoubtedly because of the basic instability of these ranks discussed above. In general, the high correlations strongly support the qualitative similarities seen in Table 1.

A method producing reliable results over a period of time, say 30 days, is more preferable because of the stable results. To test the comparative stability of the four methods, a test-retest reliability experiment was conducted for 40 original subjects. Table 3 presents the test-retest stability or reliability coefficients based on the total scores for the 40 subjects. These correlations are not strict measures of reliability as used in psychometric literature but are an indication that the same subjects produce almost identical rank orderings of preference one month later. It measures the stability of rank orders produced by a group of subjects rather than the reliability of responses from any one subject.

Correlation coefficients are high and a comparison of test-retest results does not give one method an advantage over another.

Results from the first phase show that if the only really poor technique—the single choice method—is omitted, it makes little difference which method is chosen.

EFFECT OF CHOICE RESTRICTION. The second phase of the experiment produced similar conclusions with greater clarity since subjects were given fewer choices. The orders of preference

the tables for the sake of simplicity) does not produce interesting interpretations at this point.

[3] The data in many of the tables present both a Spearman rank-order correlation and the Pearson product-moment correlation. Although the rank-order data are only in ordinal form, when the raw scores are inspected it appears that the assumptions necessary for a product-moment correlation are met. Hence, both statistics are presented for whatever additional information it may reveal to the reader.

TABLE 3

Test-Retest Correlations, Phase I

Method	Spearman Rank Order	Pearson r (Raw Scores)
Likert rating	.94	.96
Open choice preference	.88	.90
Open choice objection	.92	.95
Limited choice		
Best 10	.89	.91
Weighted ranks	.95	.94
Single choice	.94	.96

for the four methods in this phase are in Table 4.

Table 4 shows there is almost complete agreement in the rank ordering of the 12 brand names as measured by four methods.[4] There are only three reversals: in the 10th and 11th ranks of the paired comparison method, the first and second ranks of the open choice preference method, and the third and fourth ranks of the rank order method. Inspection of the raw scores indicates that these reversals are insignificant. A shift of one or two raw-score points explains the differences. In no other cell of the table will a shift of a few raw-score points make any changes in the final rank ordering of results.

Table 5 shows that inter-method correlations are extremely high.

The results of the test-retest group stability or reliability measures are in Table 6. Again, these correlations are not strict measures of reliability but a measure of the stability of the rank orders produced by a group of subjects. In view of the other findings, the extremely high correlations (.98 and .99) were not surprising.

A comparison of the stability measures for the Phase I (Table 3) with the results of Phase II (Table 6) indicates that the number of names in a list influences the outcome very little. In both phases, whether a list contains 12 or 30 names to be ranked, the test-retest comparison produces identical results.

[4] Careful inspection of the paired comparison data indicated extremely low frequency of circular triads in the transitive relationship. The hypothesis of transitivity can clearly be accepted.

TABLE 4

Phase II Order of Preferences[a]

Brand Name	Rank Order	Paired Comparison	Likert Scaling	Open Choice Preference
Master Sound	1	1	1	2
Concertsound	2	2	2	1
Stereo-Fidelity	3	4	4	4
Audio Master	4	3	3	3
Stereo Empress	5	5	5	5
Le Premier	6	6	6	6
Truetone	7	7	7	7
Sound-o-rama	8	8	8	8
Luxuria	9	9	9	9
Venus	10	11	10	10
Mark X Super	11	10	11	11
Toneonic	12	12	12	12

[a] $N = 73$.

One further comparison between the two phases: Does having a fewer or greater number of items to select affect the outcome of the preference order? Since the names for the first phase contained all 12 names used in the second set, what differences occur in the relative position of these 12 names when results of the two phases are compared? Since two selection methods, Likert scaling and open choice preference, were used in the first and second phases these comparisons can be made.

If in Table 1 only the 12 names used in Phase II were considered and the other names ignored, the first three selections in order of preference from the Likert method are Master Sound, Concertsound, and Audio Master. These are the same first, second, and third choices from the Likert scaling method in the second phase. The two names ranked last by the Likert method, Mark X Super and Toneonic, are the same in both phases even with only 12 names used in the analysis. Some shifts occur for the middle seven names, but the shifts are not significant.

Results of the first and second phases by use of the open choice preference method are similar. Concertsound, Master Sound, and Audio Master are the first three selections in both phases, and Toneonic placed last by both methods. Again, some shifts occur in the middle group of names. The Spearman rank-order correlation coefficient between Phase I and Phase II of the Likert scaling method using the 12 names is .91. For the open choice preference method, the Spearman rank correlation between the two phases is .86.

Although some shifts occur, depending on whether there are 12 or 30 items to be ranked, the differences are relatively insignificant.

TABLE 5

Inter-Method Correlations, Phase II

Method	Correlation	Rank Order	Paired Comparison	Likert Rating
Paired comparison	r	−.99		
	r_s	−.99		
Likert rating	r	−.99	.98	
	r_s	−.99	.99	
Open choice preference	r	−.98	.99	.99
	r_s	−.99	.99	.99

Note. r = Pearson r based on raw scores.

r_s = Spearman r based on ranks from Table 4.

TABLE 6

Test-Retest Correlations, Phase II

Method	Spearman Rank Order	Pearson r (Raw Scores)
Paired comparison	.99	.98
Likert rating	.97	.96
Open choice preference	.94	.95
Rank order	.93	.95

COMPARISONS WITH INDEPENDENT GROUPS. One variable that may have increased the correlation results is the effect of subjects trying to be consistent from one method to another. Since all subjects were to select their preferences by all methods, they may have remembered earlier responses, though subjects were not to refer to previous responses. However, the effect of remembering earlier responses in paper-and-pencil experiments has not been properly investigated in the literature.

To test for the effect of memory on consistency in the results, data from the second phase of the study were further analyzed, since the effect would be greater for fewer names to remember.

Since the order of presentation of the four methods was counter-balanced, each method was responded to first by nearly one-fourth of the subjects. Comparing only the first page of the questionnaire would be identical to using four randomly assigned groups, each containing 17 to 19 subjects (total sample size for the second phase was 73 subjects), with each group using a different method thus controlling for subject consistency or memory.

Table 7 contains the inter-method correlations of these data. With completely independent groups of subjects such that the methods are now independent of each other, the correlations are somewhat lower. Unfortunately, the sample size is smaller so a comparison between the independent groups of Table 7 and the correlated data of Table 5 is not possible. However, the intermethod corre-

lations are still high, ranging from a low of .67 to a high of .93. Though the possibility of subject consistency inflating the results cannot be rejected completely, the general conclusion that the various methods produce similar results has not been weakened.

RELIABILITY. A more typical kind of reliability study was used on the 55 test-retest subjects in Phase II. A method that has a higher reliability coefficient that produces high test-retest stability for any one subject, is a more useful method than one with a lower reliability coefficient, presuming that subjects do not change their opinions much in a one-month period.

Unfortunately, the usual correlation methods do not allow for a test-retest reliability measurement of each method across subjects and brand names. Therefore, subject test-retest reliability had to be computed for each of the 12 names in Phase II. Since the data were generated in such a form that Pearson r's could not be properly used, a contingency coefficient was relied on. For the analysis, 12 $n \times k$ tables were constructed for each method. For example, the contingency table for each name in the open choice preference method, was a 2×2 design, e.g., Master Sound was or was not selected the first time, and was or was not selected in the retest. The Likert scaling consisted of a 5×5 contingency table; the ranking and paired comparison methods consisted of 12×12 tables. Each contingency table was collapsed to assure an expected frequency of at least five in each cell. Chi squares were done and converted to contingency coefficients. The results of these manipulations are in Table 8.

Since these reliability coefficients are not exceptionally high, the stability of all the methods is questionable. However, a contingency coefficient will usually produce a lower correlation statistic than the more commonly used Pearson r. Where the range of a Pearson correlation is from -1.0 to 1.0, the theoretical range of a 2×2 contingency coefficient is $-.71$ to $.71$.[5]

TABLE 7

Inter-Method Comparisons with Independent Groups

Method		Correlation	Likert Rating	Rank Order	Paired Comparison
Open choice	r		.91	.75	.90
preference	r_s		.92	.67	.91
($n = 19$)					
Likert rating	r			.73	.90
($n = 17$)	r_s			.72	.93
Rank order	r				.87
($n = 18$)	r_s				.84

Note. r = Pearson r based on raw scores.
r_s = Spearman r based on ranks.

[5] The strength of association using a contingency coefficient must not be interpreted as indicating the same degree of relationship as an ordinary coefficient of the same magnitude. The upper limit for a 3×3 table is .87, for a 4×4 table, .95. The exact upper limits for rectangular tables, such

TABLE 8

Test-Retest Reliability Contingency Coefficients

Brand Name	Rank Order	Paired Comparison	Likert Rating	Open Choice Preference
Master Sound	.60[c]	.62[c]	.41[a]	.43
Concertsound	.48[e]	.50[a]	.45[a]	.42
Stereo-Fidelity	.61[c]	.56[c]	.31[a]	.41
Audio Master	.40[b]	.51[c]	.62[c]	.44
Stereo Empress	.39[a]	.41[c]	.33[a]	.40
Le Premier	.48[c]	.44[a]	.50[a]	.45
Truetone	.40[c]	.42[a]	.35[a]	.18
Sound-o-rama	.47[a]	.57[c]	.38[a]	.39
Luxuria	.47[c]	.58[d]	.60[c]	.49
Venus	.39[c]	.39[b]	.57[c]	.21
Mark X Super	.51[c]	.56[c]	.60[c]	.53
Toneonic	.38[a]	.38[c]	.22[a]	.57

[a] Contingency table with 2 degrees of freedom.
[b] Contingency table with 3 degrees of freedom.
[c] Contingency table with 4 degrees of freedom.
[d] Contingency table with 6 degrees of freedom.
[e] Contingency table with 8 degrees of freedom.
Unlettered cells are 2×2 contingency table with one degree of freedom.

Table 8 shows that the reliability measurements for the four methods are not significantly different. Although it would be meaningless to summarize the data with mean reliabilities for each method, the mean reliabilities would be .41 for open choice preference, .45 for Likert scaling, .46 for ranking and .50 for paired comparison. The four methods show almost identical results.

Summary and Conclusions

Seven methods used in marketing research for measuring attitudes, opinions, preferences, or beliefs were compared. The hypothesis that each would produce significantly different re-

as 2×3 or 3×4 tables are unknown. Further, since in Table 8 the entries are for varied sized contingency tables, relative or comparative interpretations must be made with this in mind.

sults was rejected. All methods produced high intermethod correlations whether the groups were independent of each other or consisted of all subjects using all methods. Test-retest stability measures and reliability coefficients indicate that all methods result in about the same order of preferences. The high intermethod correlations may imply a kind of convergent validity for each technique.

The selection of a research method might best be determined by reasons other than concerns about intermethod differences, the method in fashion or acceptance by clients or colleagues. The numerous articles and discussions about a method's efficiency and about the acceptability of the research plan are illaudable when concerns about validity, accuracy, costs to the client, and psychological effects on the subject, interviewer, and researcher are more significant.

A. BACKGROUND AND THEORY

This section is comprised of an article (Dichter) that defines the characteristics of a well-designed package.

30-A THE MAN IN THE PACKAGE

Ernest Dichter (Psychologist)

Aside from the product itself, the most personal contact a manufacturer has with his customers today is the package that contains his product.

Today the package must come alive at the point of purchase. The salesman may no longer be visible behind the counter, supplying a necessary living element in the selling process. But he is present, just the same.

He has stepped inside the package.

Formerly, a manufacturer had little control over the salesmen who represented his product in retail stores. They were jolly or grumpy, inept or skillful, pleasant or not, courteous or not—depending on the weather or the season or the state of their nerves.

The salesman in the package presents no such problem. He is yours to create and control.

A poorly designed package tells the consumer that the maker of the product does not care. Like an impatient salesman at five minutes before closing time, he is saying "take it or leave it." But a well-designed package is proof that the manufacturer really cares about both the customer and the product and is willing to make an extra effort to please. He is employing a friendly, interested salesman.

Just what is a well-designed package? According to research, the consumer himself is the measure of a good package.

SOURCE: Seventeen-page booklet published and copyrighted 1957 by The Paraffined Carton Research Council.

If you ask him, every consumer has a picture of the ideal package in his head. This is not simply a picture of how the package looks: it is a dramatic visualization of how it feels as he turns it around in his hand, of how it fits into his medicine chest or pantry, and of how easy it is to get at the product inside when he really needs it.

Through his emotional needs, the consumer sets up very demanding standards of good packaging. These may be listed as follows:

CONVENIENCE. Does the package hold enough of the product to satisfy his needs without being too bulky or too heavy?

ADAPTABILITY. How well does the package fit into his freezer, cupboard, glove compartment, or dresser drawer?

SECURITY. Does he feel assured that you have given him quality? Does the package make him feel it?

STATUS OR PRESTIGE. Does he feel that by buying your package he is expressing something about himself?

DEPENDABILITY. Does the package let him feel that he can rely upon you, the manufacturer?

ESTHETIC SATISFACTION. Is he pleased and satisfied by the impact of the design, color, and shape of the package?

Actually these six criteria can be described simply as combining utility, security, and esthetic appearance. This quotation from the mother of a young perfume purchaser is an example of the practical application of these criteria:

> My daughter has a perfume now that, God bless her, she can use without getting it on the floor or all over her dressing table. She used to have (name of brand) and (name of brand). One she had to shake so hard to get the perfume out that she said it gave her a charley-horse. The other one had such a big hole that whenever she used it she couldn't control it, and it spilled all over, and the whole house smelled. This new kind, now, has just the right kind of hole. And the box is so good-looking, and the bottle is so swanky. You'd think it cost twenty dollars an ounce.

Here a young girl's "dream package" fulfills all the above criteria—with special emphasis on status. The desire for status is a consumer motivation that seems to be as vitally involved in the consumer-package relationship as in the purchase of any product from premium beers to Cadillacs. Status and other factors will be examined at length later when we consider the core of all successful packaging: *how well modern packaging meets the emotional and psychological needs of to-day's consumer,* as expressed in his daily purchasing patterns and his conception of the ideal package.

A good package does not create the personality of a product. Like a good cosmetic on a beautiful girl, the desirable package merely expresses personality in a dramatic, easily recognizable way.

On the other hand, a bad package or design contradicts, underplays, or undermines a product's personality.

These are important considerations, since the personality of a product is an important determinant of brand loyalty. And so this is the place to ask: "Just what is product personality and how is it affected by package design?"

Two Images of Product Personality

Product personality consists of two parts that we can only isolate on paper. One is the *physical image*, the other is the *personality image*.

Physically a bar of soap is round, square, or octagonal; but in its personality image it may appear boldly masculine or softly feminine, modern or old-hat, of high status or low, light and delicate or heavy and coarse.

Although we have separated the two images here, the consumer never does so. He sees a unified image of the product's personality. And, significant for the package designer, any negative features of either image will affect the total picture in the consumer's head.

For example, some men might reject a bar of soap that was ovoid-shaped, strongly scented, and packaged in a frilly box. Too effeminate, they would say. But they might accept the same soap if it were brick-shaped.

Changing a Product's Personality

People like to say they never judge a book by its cover. *But they do.*

In one study, coffee was served from different coffee makers, including the most modern dripolators and the most antique coffee urns. Most of the drinkers said that the coffee poured from the antique urns tasted better. Actually it was the same coffee. This confirmed the fact that modern consumers believe that somehow things were better in the past—more wholesome, purer, etc. But more important, it indicated that the size, style, and shape of the coffee container influenced the drinker's impression of the taste.

This ability of a package or container to modify the personality of a product was further shown in a study for a pharmaceutical company. The so-called potency rating of two different-sized pills was tested. Although the potency of the drug "packaged" in the larger pill was less than that in the smaller one, not only laymen but also many doctors were fooled. The medical men insisted that the larger pill was the more potent!

The proof of the package comes the moment the consumer walks down the aisle of the supermarket. Either the package reaches out to him in a persuasive way, or it lies dead while its nearest and best competitor is chosen for the shopper's basket.

The consumer arrives in the supermarket lost in a fog of competitive claims that have been drummed into his head by newspapers, magazines, radio, TV, and billboards. The similarity of these advertising appeals often arrests the development of a distinctive product personality; this fact is responsible for the widespread lack of brand loyalty among supermarket customers today.

It is up to the package designer, to a large

extent, to attract the consumer to the particular product on the shelf. But first he must consider what has happened to the consumer's shopping experience.

In today's supermarket, passing among palisades of parallel shelves filled with hundreds of products, the consumer sees mainly a gigantic blur of boxes and cans in which there are no outstanding elements. In this chaos a package must have prominent features of design that catch the eye, hold the attention, and initiate the dramatic interplay between package and patron that makes the package come alive in the customer's hand.

The problem is more complicated than it used to be because the strolling supermarket customer seldom sees many of the packages head-on as he did in the small grocery store. Nowadays his eyes meet the shelf at an angle and he cannot perceive a clear-cut front package panel. One edge of the box and part of one side intrude on the area of vision, breaking and weakening the impact.

In examining the packaging problems arising from this "new angle" of vision, designers and manufacturers might also take into account the phenomenon of *peripheral vision*. Here, in addition to new angles of perception there is also present the factor of diminished visibility. In peripheral vision, certain colors and designs are barely perceptible. Certain forms and shapes, effective when seen directly by the consumer, become distorted, confused, and weak in impact in the dim light and abnormal angles of peripheral vision.

These visual phenomena suggest new areas for exploration in packaging—in design, typography, color, shape—to assure successful impact from whatever angle the product is viewed by the consumer. Obviously the problem is a complicated one, both technically and psychologically, but many of our major packaging designers are already meeting the challenge of new merchandising techniques.

To be successful a package must accomplish the following things when it is on display:

a. It must achieve a "reaching out" quality.

b. It must provoke uninterrupted inspection by the consumer.

c. It must "disappear" and permit the consumer to rehearse the purchase and use of the product.

A Packaging Paradox

It is clear that a package must not emphasize its own personality to the disadvantage of the product inside. In fact, the effective package must virtually "disappear" at some point in the purchase-and-use process. That is, it must disappear in the psychological sense of fading into the background while the product itself comes forward to become the "figure" that is seen, related to, and remembered by the consumer.

Sometimes, but not always, this means that an effective package should be made of transparent materials. Often the reverse is true. When we buy sausages at a meat department we want the package to fade into the finished product—the hot, crisp, aromatic meat—and not into the cold and greasy food we see through the plastic envelope.

But an opaque Duncan Hines or Betty Crocker cake mix package, with the illustration of the finished cake rich with icing, dominates the package so that within a few moments the design, the colors, the type styles and the shape of the box disappear. What the consumer sees is the luscious cake itself.

Sometimes the package refuses to disappear, and the fault can lie with the personality of the product itself. In the case of a nationally advertised food product, the package was striking, gay, bright, alive with color. But despite the achievement of the designers there was a contradiction between package and product personality.

The package radiated light-hearted gayety and frivolity, a mood that was in stark contrast to the function performed by the product. And so it failed to ring a bell in the mind of the housewife. Or still worse, it generated disbelief and even suspicion by its sharp contrast to the product's personality.

More Traits of a Good Package

PERPETUAL YOUTH. Like people, packages grow old and tired. But unlike people, they can be renewed. A tired package communicates the personality of a tired product. Today's consumer demands that his favorite products be full of freshness and youth: this calls for a constant renewal of design. Manufacturers of such products as cigarettes and breakfast foods are continually bringing out new package designs to replace those that are old and listless.

EVER-RENEWING INVOLVEMENT OF CONSUMER WITH PRODUCT. A sale does not end with the purchase of a product. Advertising and promotion continually strive to renew the relationship between consumer and product so as to create an uninterrupted flow of sales. The package on the shelf must perform a similar function—becoming more than a mere receptacle. It must resell itself to the consumer every time he sees it.

THE PLEASURE OF HANDLING. In some products a good package induces exploration with the hands, for example the Marlboro flip-top package.

CREATIVE CONSIDERATENESS. When a car manufacturer designs his windshield to give a better view from the driver's seat, he is exhibiting a concern for the consumer's needs which psychologists call creative considerateness. Consumers expect this attitude to apply to makers and designers of packages, too. Successful examples include the neat carry-home cartons of beer cans or soft drink bottles, and the development of new spouts on milk cartons which eliminate drips and spills. The presence of creative considerateness is an assurance that over-all impact of a package will be greater.

In a packaging test using the techniques of ordinary opinion research, a large number of consumers were asked to indicate their preferences among three different package designs.

The result: 62 per cent chose the most ornate design, 25 per cent the less extravagant one, and 12 per cent the simplest design. The consumer had spoken and it seemed like a green light for ornate design.

But wait. In the real-life supermarket situation, away from the questioner who had asked them a direct question about their preferences, 72 per cent bought the package *with the simplest design.*

The Motivational Answer

Only in a store or supermarket situation can a real test of buyer attitudes be made. Here the consumer is not expected to answer questions: he merely shops in his usual way. By setting up an experimental supermarket, researchers can make valid studies of consumer habits.

In a motivational research laboratory supermarket the consumer is not aware of which package is being tested. He is simply invited by the interviewer to play the "shopping game" and to enter the model store as if he were on a normal shopping trip.

He makes his purchase from among various brands of the same food product, and he has the opportunity to select his favorite brand in the current or the proposed new package—both of which appear in equally favorable positions on the shelves. If he fails to pick either package of the brand being tested, he is invited to "go back and make another purchase" until he has finally chosen one of the packages being tested.

After he has selected one of the packages being tested, he is given an interview by a psychologist who asks him about both packages—the chosen one and the rejected one. There are six steps in these interviews:

FREE ASSOCIATION. The consumer is asked to tell everything that comes to his mind as he looks at the packages. On liquid bleach, for example: "It reminds me of an ammonia bottle. I can smell the strong fumes just by looking at it." (Recommendation of the research team: change the shape of the bottle.)

STORY. "Look at this package and make up a story about it," says the psychologist. Such a third-person story permits the consumer to express his true feelings without fear of offending anyone.

COLOR. To study colors, the psychologist asks: "How do the colors make you feel?"

PERSON. To study the package's personality, the consumer is asked: "When you look at this box, what kind of person are you reminded of?" In one study of deodorants, it was found that the package impressed buyers as feminine, yet the product itself was seen as masculine. This kind of contradiction often hurts sales.

SLOGAN. The entire range of associations with the slogan are probed, and its emotional impact is estimated.

CHOICE IMPUTATIONS. The consumer is asked to tell how he thinks other consumers will react to the product. Women, for example, are asked which box they think would most likely be chosen by a boy, man, or girl.

Validation of Laboratory Tests

Finally, packages are tested in actual supermarkets. A special check-out counter is set up by trained interviewers and a board is marked to indicate the reasons for specific purchases. The consumer arranges his purchases on the board according to categories: "reminded by brand," "planned by kind," "substitute," etc.

Depth interviews (that is, extensive and probing interviews) are then conducted in the store by the interviewers.

More valuable information can be obtained from a panel of consumers. Families representing different age, income, education, national, and religious groups are asked to cooperate when a problem requires responses from specific individuals among the consuming population.

B. RESEARCH AND APPLICATIONS

This section begins with a report (Blum and Appel) that compares consumer reaction with management reaction in new package development. The second article (Friedman) explores consumer confusion in the selection of supermarket products.

30-B CONSUMER VERSUS MANAGEMENT REACTION IN NEW PACKAGE DEVELOPMENT

Milton L. Blum (Psychologist) and Valentine Appel (Psychologist)

The last decade has been one of radical change in packaging as it has in many other areas of commercial life. A real part of this packaging revolution has been the contribution which consumer research has made. In fact, the introduction of a new package without the benefit of consumer research evolution is becoming the exception rather than the rule. The study to be reported points up the importance of consumer research in such package development programs.

The writers' firm was engaged to conduct a preliminary packaging study for one of its clients. The client's objective was to develop a package for a new product line. The product was intended for use by men but to be bought by women as a gift.

The purpose of the study was to screen, from a group of 18 design renderings submitted, the designs which showed the most promise, and to indicate possible areas of design modification which might further improve the acceptance of the more promising of the design concepts. The principal intention was ultimately to evaluate the more promising designs further based upon three dimensional prototypes and larger samples of respondents.

Earlier research had detailed certain specifications which the ideal package should meet. Among these was the decision that the package should appear both as masculine and relatively expensive. Moreover, women should prefer it as a gift for their husbands, and men should prefer to receive it as a gift for themselves.

The study was unusual in that not only consumers were interviewed. The client's management, and also the design firm which created the packages, agreed to evaluate the designs from what they considered to be the female consumer's point of view. There was, therefore, the opportunity to compare the judgments of designers, management, and consumers.

Method

The study employed four independent groups of raters: female consumers ($N = 80$), male consumers ($N = 39$), advertising and marketing executives of the client company ($N = 8$), and the industrial designers who created the packages ($N = 7$). Each of the

SOURCE: Milton L. Blum and Valentine Appel, "Consumer Versus Management Reaction in New Package Development," *Journal of Applied Psychology*, 45 (August, 1961), pp. 222–224. Copyright 1961 by the American Psychological Association and reproduced by permission.

members of these groups individually rated a total of 18 different package design renderings using Stephenson's (1953) Q sort technique. The 18 designs were rated in terms of the extent to which each design was perceived as: masculine or feminine, expensive or inexpensive, and appropriate or inappropriate as a male gift. The Q sort was performed by asking the respondent to arrange the renderings into seven scaled categories, each category being assigned a score ranging from one to seven. For each respondent, this resulted in a forced frequency distribution of scores for the 18 designs. This frequency distribution was perfectly symmetrical, approached normality in shape, and had a modal rating of four which was assigned to six of the 18 designs. The forced frequency distribution and the scores assigned to each category were as follows:

Frequency	1	2	3	6	3	2	1
Score	1	2	3	4	5	6	7

The advertising and marketing executives of the client company, and the members of the design firm Q sorted the same 18 designs only on the basis of the extent to which they believed that women would be willing to give each of the packages to their husbands as a gift. This made for a total of eight variables to be analyzed; three each for the male and female consumers, and one each for management and the designers. Because of the amount of time involved in rating the designs for each variable, it was not considered desirable to request the management and design groups to rate the designs on more than one variable only. The ostensible purpose of asking management and the designers to complete the ratings was primarily as a device to explain to them the method employed.

Results

Each design was assigned an overall rating for each variable which was the mean score for the group evaluating the designs, and the mean scores were converted into ranks for each variable. To measure the extent of agreement and disagreement among the four groups of raters, the Spearman rank-difference correlations among the eight variables were calculated.

The correlations for the gift ratings between the men and women and between management and the designers were as follows: .58 between the men and women, and .55 between management and the designers. From this it can be seen that there was fair agreement between management and the designers as to which packages they believed women would be more likely to prefer as gifts for their husbands. There was also fair agreement between the men and women as to which designs they would like to give and receive. Both the male and female consumers, however, were in substantial disagreement with the other two groups on this point. The correlations between the consumers vs. the management and designer groups were as follows: −.48 between the designers and the women, −.14 between the designers and the men, −.21 between management and the women, and −.42 between management and the men. The reasons underlying this disagreement can be understood in terms of the matrix of intercorrelations among all eight variables as shown in Table 1.

TABLE 1

Rank Difference Intercorrelations Among the Eight Variables, (N = 18 designs)

Variable	1	2	3	4	5	6	7	8
1. Masculinity-men								
2. Masculinity-women	.70							
3. Gift-designers	.44	.65						
4. Gift-management	.14	.67	.55					
5. Gift-men	.23	−.08	−.14	−.42				
6. Gift-women	−.23	−.21	−.48	.21	.58			
7. Expensiveness-men	−.47	−.61	−.29	−.44	.47	.47		
8. Expensiveness-women	−.55	−.73	−.49	−.47	.41	.53	.92	

Note. With 16 degrees of freedom a correlation of .47 is significant at the .05 level. A correlation of .59 is significant at the .01 level.

Examination of this correlation matrix reveals two clearly defined clusters. The first cluster is composed of the gift ratings of management and of the designers, and of the masculinity ratings of the male and female consumers. The second cluster is composed of the gift and the expensiveness ratings of the consumers. The two clusters correlate negatively with each other. The one exception is the low positive correlation (.23) between the gift and masculinity ratings of the male consumers.

The reason for this disagreement, between the consumers on the one hand and management and the designers on the other, stems from the fact that these two groups were apparently using conflicting criteria in evaluating the designs. Management and the designers were evaluating the designs in terms of what the consumer perceived to be masculinity. Those designs which were perceived as being more masculine tended to be the same ones which the designer and management groups thought the consumers would prefer. The ratings of the consumers, on the other hand, tended to vary as a function of what they considered to be the expensive appearance of the design.

In this particular case expensiveness and masculinity appear to be relatively incompatible criteria, the correlation between them being −.73 among the women, and −.47 among the men. Since the two groups of raters tended to use one of these criteria to the relative exclusion of the other, the gift ratings of the consumers tended to correlate negatively with the ratings of the client's management and of the designers who created the designs. This is not to say that masculinity was completely unimportant among the consumer samples. It is to say that of the two variables, masculinity and expensiveness, expensiveness was the more important. Actually, among the sample of males, masculinity assumes considerable importance when the effects of perceived expensiveness are partialed out or eliminated. The partial correlations between the gift ratings and the masculinity ratings, when expensiveness is partialed out, is: .58 for the men, and −.13 for the women. The inference to be drawn here is that masculinity does contribute to preference on the part of the men when the effects of perceived expensiveness are eliminated. In the case of the women, masculinity appears to play no role at all in contributing to preference.

Discussion

The marketing implications of these findings are clear. Had the packaging decision been made on the basis of the recommendation of the design firm and on the pooled judgment of the client's marketing management, the net effect would have been to select designs which would have had the least appeal so far as the consumers sampled were concerned.

The result of the research was to outline specifications for the design group which would enable them to modify certain of the designs in ways which would cause them to be perceived by the consumer as masculine as well as expensive.

These findings point up the contribution which consumer research can make to the company involved in new packaging plans. Without the kind of information which consumer research can provide, management decisions concerning new package development remain much more of a gamble than most manufacturers can afford.

REFERENCE

Stephenson, W. *The study of behavior*. Chicago: University of Chicago Press, 1953.

30-C CONSUMER CONFUSION IN THE SELECTION OF SUPERMARKET PRODUCTS

Monroe Peter Friedman (Psychologist)

The current study attempts to objectively define the issues in the truth-in-packaging controversy by treating consumer confusion as a psychological variable capable of measurement.

Method

SUBJECTS. Thirty-three young married women who were students or the wives of students at Eastern Michigan University served as subjects (*Ss*). All *Ss* had attended college for at least 1 year and in addition had been married for 1 or more years. The *Ss* were tested in a local supermarket with which they were familiar through previous shopping; indeed most *Ss* were regular customers of the store. Recruitment of *Ss* took the form of personal requests of *Ss* through visits to their homes (mostly apartments in the married student complex of Eastern Michigan University). The *Ss* were paid for their time.

PROCEDURE. The *Ss* were instructed to select the most economical (largest quantity for the price) package for each of 20 products on sale at the selected supermarket. A time limit was enforced for each product decision, a limit based on the variety of packages on display for the product. More specifically, 10 seconds were allowed for each of the package types in the product category, unless either (*a*) there were less than six package types to a product class, in which case a 1-minute time limit was used, or (*b*) there were more than 24 package types to a product class, in which case a 4-minute time limit was employed.

In addition to stating which package she believed to be the most economical for each of the 20 products, each *S* reported to the experimenter (*E*) accompanying her the information which she used in making her decision.

Each of the 20 products employed in the study had the following characteristics:

SOURCE: Monroe Peter Friedman, "Consumer Confusion In The Selection Of Supermarket Products," *Journal of Applied Psychology*, Vol. 50 (December, 1966), pp. 529–534. Copyright 1966 by the American Psychological Association, and reproduced by permission.

1. Two or more different-sized packages of the product were on sale at the supermarket.

2. Two or more different brands of the product were on sale at the supermarket.

3. The two or more brands for each product appeared to be comparable with regard to the nature of their contents. Thus dry cereals were not selected as a product since corn flakes and raisin bran do not appear to be comparable; on the other hand, the different brands and varieties of family flour were considered comparable.

4. The products appeared to be widely used by American families.

5. The products were significant contributors to total supermarket sales. Thus table salt, which qualifies on the basis of the first four criteria, was not used in the study since it represents only about .1% of total supermarket sales.

Finally, a characteristic not of any one product, but of the whole group of 20, was that the set of products appeared to be a balanced representation of the packaged products available at American supermarkets.

The testing of the 33 *Ss* took place over a 2-day period. To aid in the testing a map of the supermarket was constructed with a specified route which touched upon the location of each of the 20 products. The *Ss* were then tested in groups of 5–10. Each member of a group was randomly paired with an *E* and the two were randomly assigned to one of the 20 product locations as their starting point in the test sequence. After *S* had responded to *E's* questions at the first location, the two proceeded along the route to the next product location, and continued in this manner until *S* had been tested at all 20 product locations. This experimental design not only permitted the testing of many *Ss* simultaneously but also allowed the effects of a variety of product sequences (20 in all) to be reflected in the results of the study.

Of the 33 *Ss*, 13 were retested 2 days after their original testing, thus permitting the determination of test-retest reliability coefficients for the experimental measures employed in the study. Concurrent validity coefficients for the measures were ascertained from correlations with Ss' pretest ratings of the 20 products. The pretest consisted of a brief story about a housewife who is undecided about which of two packages of a particular product to purchase. The two packages are equally appealing to her on a number of grounds, such as appearance and quality of contents. She finally decides to purchase the package which gives her more of the product for the price. It was pointed out to Ss that the housewife's task of determining which of the two packages is more economical would vary in difficulty for the 20 products. The Ss were instructed to rank the 20 products, using an alternation ranking procedure, with respect to the estimated difficulty the housewife would have in determining the more economical of two packages containing the product.

At the time the pretest was administered Ss were asked to indicate which of the 20 products were not usually found in their household.

MEASURES. Three behaviorally based quantitative measures of confusion in unit-price information are used in the analysis of the data. The first, Confusion Measure 1, simply indicates the number of Ss who made incorrect choices for each of the 20 products. Confusion Measure 2 calculates for each product the mean percentage increase in unit price for Ss' selected packages compared with the most economical package. Confusion Measure 3, which employs data from a supermarket trade-magazine study dealing with the total sales for each of the 20 products, provides an estimate of the increase in price which an economy-minded household unit with a specified budget would pay over a constant time-period, say a year, if its purchases reflected the values found for Confusion Measure 2. Thus Confusion Measure 3 is a weighted version of Confusion Measure 2.

The rationale behind Confusion Measure 1 is reasonably clear. It is desirable to know whether Ss are able to select the most economical package for each of the 20 common products; indeed, the number of Ss who fail in this task should be an indication of the degree of confusion associated with consumer attempts to purchase supermarket products on the basis of economy. The second measure of confusion simply reflects the magnitude of the selection errors expressed for each product as a percentage of the unit price of the most economical package. It is assumed that the larger the value found for a particular product, the greater the error which an economy-minded consumer would be expected to make when purchasing the product.

The last measure to be considered, Confusion Measure 3, represents an interaction of the estimated consumer expenditures for a supermarket product and the percentage error given by Confusion Measure 2. This third measure of confusion provides for each product a dollar-and-cents estimate of the additional expenses which an economy-minded shopper would bear due to errors in package selection. To give substance to this measure it is necessary that the actual records of consumer expenditures or estimates of such expenditures be available for processing. A search by the writer for a detailed product-by-product breakdown of the supermarket expenditures for some statistically average, or otherwise well-specified household unit, proved to be unsuccessful. Indirectly relevant data were found, however, in the *Progressive Grocer Colonial Study,*[1] which reports the percentage contribution to total sales made by each of several hundred products for six supermarkets in the southeastern United States. The six markets were members of a larger chain called the Colonial Stores. It seems clear that the results of the Colonial Study do not reflect American supermarkets or consumers as a whole. The study was conducted over an 8-week winter period within a single chain of supermarkets in one region of the country. Thus there are seasonal, regional, and probably socioeconomic reasons for suspecting differences. However, in the absence of any suitable national data dealing with either supermarket sales or consumer expenditures on an individual product basis, the results of the Colonial Study are employed in the analysis of Ss' responses of the present study. The reader is cautioned that the Colonial Study results serve only as an estimate, with strongly suspected biases, of the corresponding national data.

The percentage contributions to the total supermarket sales for the 20 products of the

---

[1] *Progressive Grocer Colonial Study.* New York: Progressive Grocer Publications (420 Lexington Avenue), 1963.

present study are perhaps made more meaningful when applied to a consumer's annual budget of say, $1,000 for supermarket expenditures. Thus the Colonial Study figure of 1.1% for powdered detergents assumes a value of $11.00 for this hypothetical budget. For this budget, Confusion Measure 3 is simply the portion of the individual product expenditure which can be assigned to error in package selection. The actual amount assigned would depend upon the value of Confusion Measure 2. Thus a household unit with economical shopping habits and a $1,000 annual supermarket budget might spend $11.00 for powdered detergents. Given a value of 24% for powdered detergents on Confusion Measure 2, we would find $^{24}/_{124}$ of the $11.00, or $2.13, as the amount over and above the minimal amount of $8.87 which our economy-minded household unit would pay if it always succeeded in purchasing the most economical package of powdered detergent. For this case then the value for powdered detergent on Confusion Measure 3 would be $2.13.

Values for other products were found in a manner similar to that described above. One first constructs a ratio consisting of the value of Confusion Measure 2 over an expression made up of the Confusion Measure 2 value plus 100. The next step is to multiply this ratio by the estimated consumer expenditure for the product. To find the value for a total supermarket expenditure different from the base of $1,000 employed here simply construct a ratio of the new total expenditure over the base of $1,000 and multiply the Confusion Measure 3 value by this fraction.

Results

Of the total of 660 decisions made by the 33 Ss, 47 represented products which Ss stated were not usually found in their homes. Since the proportion of errors for these 47 decisions did not differ significantly from the corresponding proportion for decisions involving more familiar products, the two classes of selections (familiar and unfamiliar) were pooled for the purposes of analysis.

The three measures of confusion in unit-price information were applied to the 20 products employed in the study and were found to have substantial validity when correlated with the experimental pretest (Spearman rank correlations of .59, .62, and .70 for Confusion Measures 1, 2, and 3, respectively). Likewise, substantial test-retest reliability coefficients were found (Spearman rank correlations of .91, .93, and .91 for the three numbered measures). As a check on the internal consistency of the results the 33 Ss were first divided into groups of 16 and 17, and separate mean confusion scores were computed for each group on each of the 20 products. Next Spearman rank correlations were computed between the mean confusion scores of the two groups, yielding values of .93, .93, and .96 for the three numbered measures.

The complete list of 20 products and their associated values on the three confusion measures are presented in Table 1. Also presented in Table 1 are the estimated consumer expenditures for the 20 products for a hypothetical consumer budget of $1,000.

Two nonparametric techniques, the Cochran Q Test and the Friedman χr^2 Test, were employed in the analysis of the confusion data.[2] Significant differences were found for the set of 20 products on Confusion Measure 1 (Cochran $Q = 283$, $p < .001$). The mean value of 14.3 yields an error rate of 43% for the 33 Ss. Significant differences were also found for the set of ranked product values on Confusion Measure 2 (Friedman $\chi r^2 = 214$, $p < .001$) and Confusion Measure 3 (Friedman $\chi r^2 = 242$, $p < .001$).

It is of interest to note that of the total estimated annual consumer expenditure of $121.20 for the 20 products the sum of $10.15 can be accounted for by errors in consumer selections. Thus, if it were possible for an economy-minded consumer with a $1,000 supermarket budget to always select the package giving her the largest quantity of a supermarket product for the money, she would pay an estimated $121.20 minus $10.15 or $111.05. It is estimated then that a more typical economy-minded shopper, who makes her selections in conformance with Ss' selections in the current study, would spend $10.15 more than the errorless figure of $111.05, or in other words, she would spend 9.14% more than the hypothetical consumer who was always able to select the most economical package.

[2] Siegel, S. *Nonparametric statistics for the behavioral sciences.* New York: McGraw-Hill, 1956.

TABLE 1
Confusion Values and Estimated Consumer Expenditures for 20 Supermarket Products

Product	Confusion[a] Measure 1 (Total Errors)	Confusion Measure 2 (Percentage Error)	Confusion[b] Measure 3 (Weighted Error in dollars)	Estimated[b] Annual Consumer Expenditures (dollars)
Canned peaches	8	2	.06	3.10
Canned peas	5	5	.20	4.10
Catsup	23	13	.28	2.40
Evaporated milk	2	0	0.0	6.60
Family flour	6	2	.13	6.70
Frozen orange juice	6	6	.36	6.40
Granulated sugar	0	0	0.0	10.70
Instant coffee	11	10	.92	10.10
Liquid bleach	32	32	.70	2.90
Liquid detergent	8	4	.24	6.20
Liquid shampoo	14	63	1.01	2.70
Mayonnaise	8	16	.46	3.30
Paper towels	30	12	.48	4.50
Peanut butter	7	2	.06	3.20
Potato chips	22	1	.05	5.30
Powdered detergent	33	24	2.13	11.00
Soft drinks (cola)	27	17	2.01	13.80
Solid shortening	0	0	0.0	5.50
Toilet tissue	22	5	.37	7.70
Toothpaste	22	16	.69	5.00
Sum			10.15	121.20
Mean	14.3	11.5	.507	6.06

[a] $N = 33$.

[b] Based on a total annual supermarket expenditure of $1,000.

Discussion

It is important to note that the plan and procedures of this study deal not at all with the day-to-day purchases of American consumers. It may be that economy plays a small role in many of these purchases. However, for the purposes of this study the question of what actual criteria are employed by consumers at large in their supermarket shopping is largely an irrelevant one. The question of concern is the following:

Is it possible for consumers to select, within a reasonable period of time and without the aid of paper and pencil or of computing devices, that package of a particular supermarket product which offers the largest quantity of the product for the money?

If large numbers of consumers cannot make correct selections when so instructed, and particularly if their errors are large, it would seem that the task is a confusing one. If in addition their errors are costly, there is real reason for concern.

Of course it does not necessarily follow that a confusing task results from improper packaging practices. However, for the present study significant differences were found for the set of 20 products on all three measures of confusion, and it seems unlikely that these differences can be attributed in any large part to factors other than the differences in package characteristics. For example, the possible influences of warm-up or fatigue effects were offset by the experimental variations in order of product presentation. Also level of illumination appeared to be fairly constant for the 20 product locations. In addition, in several instances packaging practices were identified which required calculations which could not be performed without great difficulty, if at all, in one's head. For example, the quantity of paper towels was presented in terms of number of sheets but the size of a sheet was not standard across brands. Indeed in the current study they ranged from a small of 7.5 inches × 11 inches to a large of 11 inches × 11 inches. Furthermore, the number of sheets in a roll varied from 75 to 200. And finally, some rolls were packaged singly and others two to a package.

Liquid bleach was a second product characterized by difficulties which were apparently influenced by packaging practices. In particular one brand of this product which formerly was made up with the commonly employed 5.25% concentration of sodium hypochlorite, the active ingredient in bleach, had been reduced in concentration to 3.25% a short time before the data were collected; the selling price of the product however had not been reduced nor for that matter had there been a change in the label or package in any manner other than the listing of the new concentration on the back of the bottle. Since most of the Ss were regular shoppers at the supermarket employed in the study it appears that rather than examining the bottle closely, they assumed the concentration had not been changed. With the original 5.25% concentration of sodium hypochlorite this bottle would have been the most economical selection; however, with the change in concentration this was no longer the case.

Since the results of this study were influenced in no small way by the time allotted for each package selection it might be well to explain the basis for selecting the unit of 10 seconds. Since S's task was considerably more demanding than day-to-day supermarket shopping it was felt that time should be provided above and beyond the normal shopping time. A recent study[3] found that it takes a shopper approximately 1 minute to select an item in a supermarket. This 1-minute period includes walking time in the store but not time at the

check-out counter. The Ss of the current study were given an average of 2.35 minutes at each product location; with the addition of walking time they had available about three times as much time as they would be expected to take for their supermarket shopping.

It is of interest to inquire what generalizations might be made from the present findings to other Ss and other settings. First, with regard to Ss of the study, it seems clear that they represent a combination of qualities that should make for extremely low confusion scores. As a group they are characterized by considerable education and by the financial strains usually associated with young married college couples. These two ingredients suggest not only strong interest in economy as a criterion for supermarket shopping, but also considerable success in meeting this criterion. It would seem then that other individuals in general, and less-educated individuals in particular, would not perform as well as Ss of the present study.

Although superficially it might appear that the results of this study would transfer readily to other supermarket settings there are differences between markets which should be considered. Although many markets carry the major brands for common products they differ in the extensiveness of sizes available and in the particular store brands which they carry. Also differences in shelf space and position for a product might well influence the ease with which a shopper could make comparisons. Problems arise too when one attempts to generalize the results for the 20 products employed here to other supermarket products. That sweeping generalizations are clearly inappropriate is indicated by a Colonial Study finding that about 30% of the consumer's supermarket expenditures are allocated to meat and produce, two foods which are not packaged beyond a simple brown bag or cellophane wrapper. With regard to more typically packaged supermarket products, again problems arise. The selection criteria for the 20 products employed in the present study have provided us with a clearly nonrandom sample of packaged products. A particularly strong bias was introduced by selecting products with a record of relatively high total sales, which would imply relatively high familiarity among shoppers.

[3] Fitzimmons, C., & Manning, S. L. *Purchases of nonfood items in selected retail stores.* Layfayette, Indiana: Cooperative Extension Department in Agriculture and Home Economics at Purdue University, 1962.

Conclusions

Within the confines of the particular experimental setting employed, the following conclusions appear to be in order.

1. The three measures of confusion in unit-price information have substantial validity and reliability.

2. The 20 products differ significantly on all three measures of confusion.

3. There is reason to believe that these differences reflect, at least in part, differences in packaging practices.

31 / The Price

A. BACKGROUND AND THEORY

The first reading (Harper) gives a definition of price. The second (Shapiro) deals with the psychology of pricing. The third selection (Oxenfeldt, Miller, Shuchman, and Winick) gives some insights into pricing from a behavioral-science point of view.

31-A DEFINITION OF PRICE

Donald V. Harper (Marketing Educator)

Prices determine how resources are to be used. They are also the means by which products and services that are in limited supply are rationed among buyers. The price system of the United States is a very complex network composed of the prices of all the products bought and sold in the economy as well as those of a myriad of services, including labor, professional, transportation, and public-utility services, and others ranging from dry cleaning to lawn-mower repair. The interrelationships of all these prices make up the "system" of prices. The price of any particular product or service is not an isolated thing. Each price is linked to a broad, complicated system of prices in which everything seems to depend more or less upon everything else.

If one were to ask a group of randomly selected individuals to define "price," many would reply that price is an amount of money paid by the buyer to the seller of a product or service or, in other words, that price is the money value of a product or service as agreed upon in a market transaction. This definition is, of course, valid as far as it goes. For a complete understanding of a price in any particular

SOURCE: Donald V. Harper, *Price Policy and Procedures* (New York: Harcourt, Brace & World, Inc., 1966), pp. 1–2. © 1966 by Harcourt, Brace and World, Inc., and reprinted with their permission.

transaction, much more than the amount of money involved must be known. Both the buyer and the seller should be familiar with not only the money amount, but with the amount and quality of the product or service to be exchanged, the time and place at which the exchange will take place and payment will be made, the form of money to be used, the credit terms and discounts that apply to the transaction guarantees on the product or service, delivery terms, return privileges, and other factors. In other words, both buyer and seller should be fully aware of all the factors that comprise the total "package" being exchanged for the asked-for amount of money in order that they may evaluate a given price.

The "true" price of a product or service changes whenever any of the associated elements in the package change, as well as when the money amount to be exchanged is altered. For example, if a department store discontinues return privileges on certain articles, or if a manufacturer of industrial machinery reduces the period during which interest will not be charged on credit transactions, the true price has been changed. The money price has not changed, but the package has.

This tends to complicate comparisons of prices on specific products or services over time. The difficulty lies in the frequency with which the conditions or factors change. For example, for many products changes in quality have been substantial over time, thereby rendering any price comparisons somewhat meaningless. Home appliances and automobiles fall into this classification.

Another source of difficulty in comparing prices over time is the fact that the "pub-lished," "quoted," "announced," or "list," price of a product or service may, in reality, not be the price actually paid. Various kinds of concealed price concessions may be given to some or all buyers. In such cases, the quoted price is not the "true" price.

31-B THE PSYCHOLOGY OF PRICING

Benson P. Shapiro (*Marketing Educator*)

One pricing concept which has been almost universally accepted by economists and businessmen is the negatively sloped demand curve. Such curves, stating that as price rises demand decreases, and vice versa, form the basis for the economic theory of the market mechanism and for the pricing policy of businessmen. The emphasis has characteristically been on such questions as: "How much will unit volume increase if we cut the price?" and "If we raise the price, will the additional revenue per unit more than compensate for the loss in unit volume?" This kind of thinking, originally developed for undifferentiated agricultural commodities in a nineteenth-century economy devoted to the fulfillment of basic needs, leaves little room for the insights of modern behavioral science. Of particular importance, the *psychology* of pricing has been neglected almost completely.

Some businessmen and academicians, however, *are* aware of certain psychological aspects of pricing. Many retailers, for example, consider a price of $2.99 much more attractive than one of $3.00; on the other hand, they know that consumers see little difference between $2.98 and $2.99. And Andre Gabor and C. W. J. Granger, both of the University of Nottingham in England, who are probably the most successful and extensive researchers in this area, have studied the connotations of prices for cost and quality.[1] What we do know about the subject may be meager, compared to the literature available on other aspects of marketing, but the evidence indicates that

consumers are not so simply motivated as the economists' demand curve implies.

One of the best examples of the strength of psychological pricing comes from an article by Oswald Knauth:

"In one case a retailer was able to purchase hosiery, having a normal market value of $2.00 per pair, for about 65 cents a pair, and offered it at $1.00. A mere handful of customers responded. Why? Reasons were searched; the values were unquestioned, the advertising forceful, the day fair. But the price of $1.00 suggested just that value, as this is a normal price for medium-grade hosiery. Two weeks later, the same goods were advertised at $1.14, which suggested higher value, with an enormous response."[2]

Customary Prices

Prices set by custom, tradition, assumed consumer psychology, and other nonobjective means are termed "customary prices." In the article just cited, Knauth writes:

Odd prices are greatly in vogue, on the theory that price just under a round number suggests to the customer a saving . . . Such prices were first named in order to suggest a saving and later became woven into the pattern of custom. [Page 10.]

(An executive of a large Midwestern department store chain told me that his store had found it had higher volume when it priced its merchandise at "odd ball" prices. In one case, many items of clothing had moved faster at $1.77 than at $1.69 in spite of the higher price.)

In a more recent article, Stanley C. Hollander states:

Psychological prices take three forms or,

SOURCE: Benson P. Shapiro, "The Psychology of Pricing," *Harvard Business Review*, Vol. 46 (July-August, 1968), pp. 14–25, at pp. 14, 18, and 20. © 1968 by the President and Fellows of Harvard College; all rights reserved.
[1] "On the Price Consciousness of Consumers," *Applied Statistics*, November 1961, p. 170.

[2] "Considerations in the Setting of Retail Prices," *The Journal of Marketing*, July 1949, p. 8.

more precisely, three degrees of rigidity. One is a belief that prices ending with certain numbers are proper while other endings are not. . . . A second somewhat more confining form of psychological pricing controls the entire figure instead of just the ending. This is illustrated by the prevalence of highly specific price lines in the women's dress trade, at both wholesale and retail. . . . . The third type of psychological pricing, an extreme form of price lining, eliminates all options except a single price point. The five cent candy bar was once . . . the prime example of a prevailing price point.[3]

Gabor and Granger, in *Economica*, suggest that the most common type of psychological

[3] "Customary Prices," *Business Topics*, Summer 1966, p. 47.

pricing, i.e., pricing just be number, is a circular process, acclimating the customer to exp customer responding over time stores continue that mode of p ... The authors offer several examples, such as nylon stockings sold at prices ending in eleven pence. When offered stockings at a price ending in ten pence, some customers could not accept that as a "real" price. It is interesting to note that consumer awareness of psychological prices caused some unusual aberrations in the Gabor and Granger data, making them more difficult to analyze.

The prevalence of customary prices shows that the consumer, in many cases, perceives price in a noneconomic manner. Price, thus, is a powerful piece of information for the consumer.

31-C ATTITUDES AND PRICING

*Alfred Oxenfeldt (Marketing Educator),
David Miller (Marketing Educator),
Abraham Shuchman (Marketing
Educator), and Charles Winick
(Psychologist)*

What attitudes are held by most business executives that are likely to affect their price decisions? What is the effect of these attitudes? Do they militate for or against price changes? Do they lead executives to charge more or less than they otherwise would? Since such attitudes are often unconscious, do they impair the ability of these executives to make efficient price decisions?

No systematic formal study has been made of attitudes which are shared by executives and influence their pricing decisions. Consequently, it is necessary to make inferences based on the extant literature and personal experience. Two attitudes that apparently affect many price decisions will be discussed briefly, for purposes of illustration, in order to explore whether most price decisions are substantially different than they would be if executives did not hold these attitudes.

SOURCE: Alfred Oxenfeldt, David Miller, Abraham Shuchman, and Charles Winick, *Insights Into Pricing from Operations Research and Behavioral Science* (Belmont, California: © Nadsworth Publishing Company, 1961), pp. 85–101. Reprinted by permission of the publisher.

First of all, most price-setters seem to believe that *prices should move parallel to costs*. This attitude represents almost a pricing formula. Indeed, according to studies that have been made of industrial pricing methods, the most commonly employed method of establishing price maintains a constant margin between some *base* cost and price.[1] This method is variously termed *cost-plus* or *average-cost* pricing.

Cost-plus pricing prevails despite the demonstrable fact that it rarely will yield maximum profit for the firm and is incompatible with the widely cited "law of supply and demand." This cost method of pricing ignores demand considerations altogether! It probably is employed, despite its inconsistency with economic doctrine, at least partly because of the power of the attitude that prices should be based upon cost alone.

It is easy to explain much anomalous price behavior by this attitude. For example, some businesses raise prices during recession, de-

[1] National Industrial Conference Board, "Pricing Practices of American Enterprise," *Business Record*, Sept. 1958.

spite a decline in sales of their product. Sometimes the rise in price is associated with an increase in wage rates won in a labor negotiation, or with a rise in raw-material prices, or with a rise in overhead costs per unit due to a decline in the firm's rate of capacity utilization.

Conversely, in innumerable cases businessmen have maintained prices despite a rise in replacement cost. It is still almost the rule for firms selling at retail not to mark up merchandise on their shelves, when the price of the merchandise has risen, until they themselves purchase new merchandise at the higher price. Their behavior seems to reflect the attitude that prices should move parallel to costs—rather than that they be set in order to obtain a maximum long-run profit for the enterprise.

This attitude is not held by business executives alone. Consumers share it; consequently, they seem to accept—almost cheerfully—increases in price associated with higher costs to the producer. Similarly, government officials in public pronouncements imply that businessmen are ignoring their civic responsibility if they raise prices beyond the rise in their costs, but have every right to recover all increases in price that they must pay.

As a result, it is practically impossible to explain price behavior or to predict the behavior of one's competitors and regulatory agencies unless one recognizes and attaches heavy weight to this attitude. Similarly, one cannot understand the operations of the United States economy (and most other industrial economies, where similar attitudes prevail) without taking this dominant attitude into account.

The attitude that prices should vary directly with costs has spawned many related and widespread attitudes. One holds that each item in a firm's entire line of products should "stand on its own feet" and "carry its own weight." As a result of this attitude, items that do not cover their "accounting" costs are dropped—even though they may greatly enhance the attractiveness of the entire line, contribute to covering overhead, and add to total profit. Also, this attitude militates against setting prices in a way that increases the profitability of an entire product line by ac-

cepting a very low price for one or a few selected items in the line.

Another significant and prevalent attitude, which is closely related to the attitude that prices should move parallel to costs, is what might be termed "public-utility-type thinking." This is the orientation that businessmen are entitled only to a "reasonable return on their investment"; consequently, even when they have an opportunity to command a very high price—because of a shortage, exceptional product features, or the like—they should not "take advantage of the situation" to demand a high price. Indeed, this attitude, as held by many businessmen and consumers alike, dictates that sellers should add a fairly uniform margin to all products they sell and that this margin should not be changed markedly over time. Many otherwise strange price phenomena—particularly "grey markets"—can be understood more readily if one takes account of attitudes like these, which may underlie the decisions of executives responsible for setting price.

A second major attitude prevalent among price-setters is that *management should "do something!" when sales decline.* Business executives, like most other groups, have a conception of their jobs and of themselves to which they attempt to adhere. Among the ingredients likely to be found in an executive's self-image is the attitude that he should be a man of action and deal quickly with difficulties as they arise; he should be resolute and prepared to take the consequences of his decisions. With this kind of general attitude among executives, one is likely to find price behavior that cannot be explained as a rational pursuit of self-interest or maximum profit for the firm.

There are many situations in which businessmen take price action when inaction would clearly be a wiser course. Such examples are especially plentiful during periods of declining sales. When sales fall throughout a market, due to broad economic forces that affect all rival firms more or less equally, it would rarely benefit any one firm to reduce its prices if all of its rivals would follow suit: all the firms would ordinarily sell essentially the same amount they would have sold had they retained the higher price, but would

receive less for their product; and, when demand revived, they would have difficulty in
raising prices back to their previous levels.
Nevertheless, price reductions are extremely
common under such circumstances—even in
industries where customers, who have been
offered a price reduction by a source they do
not patronize regularly, are able to obtain a
similar price reduction from their present
supplier. It is very difficult to explain this behavior without taking account of the tendency
of executives to regard inaction—especially
with regard to price—as perhaps the most
difficult course of action for them.[2]

Attitudes Among Customers

To understand the source and power of
most customer attitudes toward price, it is
necessary to understand their attitudes toward
money itself. The strongest attitudes that
customers carry to the purchase situation
probably relate to money itself. Their attitudes toward particular numerical prices, differentials in price for different brands of the
same product, changes in price, etc., are often
the major explanation for customer behavior;
these, however, seem less salient than their
attitudes toward money and ordinarily reflect
those attitudes quite directly.

ATTITUDES TOWARD MONEY. Since virtually
everyone beyond early childhood buys some
things, when one speaks of "customer attitudes" he is discussing the attitudes of almost
everyone in the society under consideration.
In the United States, and almost certainly in
all other highly industrialized economies, most
persons have extremely strong feelings about
money.

Psychoanalysts have helped us to understand the great strength of most peoples' feelings about money and of the attitudes that
reflect these feelings.[3] The salience and strength
of these feelings and attitudes partially derive
from their having been formed in very early

childhood. Certainly, the average person's
first contact with money often comes when he
learns that money is one reason for his not
being able to gratify his whims or desires. It
generally takes place at an extremely early
age—long before he is capable of understanding the realistic significance of money. In even
the most prosperous households, money considerations are cited to the very young child
as a major reason for his not wasting or de-
stroying things and as one reason for his not
having everything that takes his fancy. Thus,
at a very early age, the child comes to regard
money as something that is even bigger and
more powerful than his parents and something that has almost as much capacity as they
do to satisfy his wants.

Another reason for money's importance is
that it is frequently used as a reward for
children by adults. Especially in the minds of
young children, who do not understand the
true significance of money, its status as both
a reward and a goal gives it great emotional
impact and accentuates its power.

Money generates attitudes of great strength
for yet other reasons. In many homes, it is a
source of tension that is ill-disguised from even
young children and is often consciously communicated to older ones. This tension may
arise because the family income is limited or
the income-earner's employment is insecure;
or it may result from the divergent standards
of expenditure of the individual parents.
These circumstances combine to accentuate
the emotionalism which parents feel toward
money, and which they communicate to their
children.

Despite the rough similarity in the circumstances under which most individuals form
their earliest attitudes toward money, there is
very great divergence in the specific content of
those attitudes. For example, some individuals
are miserly and others are extravagant; some
make a fetish of careful management and accounting for expenditure, while others value
greatly the ability to be casual about expenditure. However, despite wide individual differences in fundamental attitudes toward
money, there are very few people whose attitudes toward money lack great salience. One
can distinguish some attitudes that strongly affect very large numbers of customers and are

[2] For a fairly detailed consideration of this
phenomenon in the steel industry, see Alfred R.
Oxenfeldt, *Industrial Pricing and Market Practices*
(Englewood Cliffs, N.J.: Prentice-Hall, 1957),
pp. 526–528.
[3] Otto Fenichel, *Psychoanalytic Theory of Neurosis*
(New York: Norton, 1945), pp. 281–283.

quite relevant to their reactions toward price, price differentials, and price changes. Other attitudes—such as the attitude toward money as the best index of "success" or "brains"—are no doubt extremely important in explaining human behavior, but are less directly relevant to an understanding of consumer behavior with respect to price. A few of these attitudes will be mentioned and described briefly in order to indicate their relevance to price and to demonstrate that it is not possible to explain consumer behavior fully or set prices effectively without taking cognizance of their content and their power.

ATTITUDE TOWARD TRANSACTIONS AS "BATTLES OF WITS." The author of Ecclesiastes in the Old Testament may have gone a bit too far when he exclaimed "Vanity of vanities; all is vanity," but it is obvious that almost everyone usually desires to convey a good impression of himself. Almost everyone has a homeostatic attitudinal balancing mechanism, which enables him to hold as high an opinion of himself as possible. Adults, and more especially parents, must recognize the purchase function as one of their important roles in the family; to make ill-advised purchases, or to pay substantially more than was necessary, thus represents ineptitude—and may even inflict injury on other members of the family. Even more important perhaps, it may signify personal "failure" and may damage one's self-esteem.

If challenged, most people become very "defensive" about their purchases. They are likely to resist the implication that they overpaid or misjudged the quality of their purchase. If they have clearly obtained poor value, they may seek a scapegoat. Generally they blame the seller, accusing him of misrepresenting, acting in poor faith, or something similar. They consider good purchasing (and thus obtaining good value for their money) to be "a matter of principle" and "an end in itself"; their purchase behavior cannot, therefore, be viewed solely in realistic and substantive terms. On substantive grounds, it may not appear to be sufficiently important for a customer of moderate income to walk several blocks to save 11 cents on a $1.00 purchase. However, as a symbol of "success" and as a mark of virtue, the extra effort will seem warranted to many and actually obligatory to some.

Little differences in price are likely to seem major items to most consumers, for the reasons discussed. Where product quality is demonstrably the same (as where the same model of the same brand of the same product sold at two stores is in question), a great barrier exists for most consumers if price differs even slightly. They require a justification for paying the higher price—and, for the large majority, it does not seem to suffice that they will save themselves some time or effort by paying the higher price. One finds many extreme examples of unrealistic behavior that can be explained only by highly salient attitudes toward money, combined with the attitude that a person reveals his intelligence and diligence by the way he makes purchases. Wealthy women who drive their limousines thirty miles through heavy traffic to save 79 cents (although they are likely to speak of it as 25 per cent) are not freaks by any means. They, and less extreme types, make up a sizable proportion of those who patronize discount houses and who patronize "regular sales" at all retail shops.

ATTITUDE THAT WASTE IS SHAMEFUL, IF NOT SINFUL. The United States is identified by many Europeans as a nation of waste. Thus, although Europeans have long regarded it as "wrong" to leave food on a plate when one has finished eating, in the United States only "crude" ill-mannered persons leave their plates absolutely bare. Indeed, the acceleration of waste has come to be viewed as a major American social contribution; and some marketing specialists proclaim that it is a virtual necessity for the continued prosperity of many industries, if not the entire economy. Most persons in the United States absorb some ascetic and "puritanical" attitudes that are most inhospitable to waste. To destroy property or to use much when little would suffice is regarded as categorically wrong in the attitude systems of most adults in the United States. Similarly, to spend more than one needs to spend may also be regarded as a categorical wrong and an unnecessary waste. Thus, the stigma attaching to waste, reinforcing the attitude that purchases involve a battle of wits, makes most consumers sensitive to the "fairness" of their purchase price; in particular, they are extremely sensitive to differences in price for the same brand of item in different retail shops.

Price assumes particular importance in an economy where brands, especially national ones, assure consumers that quality is uniform among different items of the same brand. Even though service and convenience should realistically figure in their calculations, many consumers tend to think and say that they are getting the same thing when they obtain the same brand and model of a given item. As a result, they tend to measure the "success" of any purchase by comparing the price they paid with what other customers pay or what other stores charge for the same item, rather then how the item compares in value *for them* with other things they might have purchased with those funds or with the value to them of holding those extra funds. In other words, consumers need assurance that they cannot buy the same item for less elsewhere —far more than they must be assured they need that item more than any other of equal cost. The consumer is not very vulnerable to being proved "wasteful" or foolish if he buys what he could very well have done without.

B. RESEARCH AND APPLICATIONS

The one article in this section (Frank, Green, and Sieber) is a report of a study of the correlation between selected household socioeconomic and purchasing characteristics and the average purchase price paid for a grocery product.

31-D HOUSEHOLD CORRELATES OF PURCHASE PRICE FOR GROCERY PRODUCTS

Ronald E. Frank (Marketing Educator), Paul E. Green (Marketing Educator), and Harry F. Sieber, Jr. (Marketing Educator)

To what extent, if any, is there a relationship between the average price paid per unit of a product purchased by a household and its socioeconomic and total consumption characteristics? Brands that are relatively inexpensive at any given point in time (as a result of a permanent policy of low prices or as a result of a short-run special offer) may tend to draw their market shares from different *segments* of the population, e.g., heavy versus light buyers, than brands that are typically higher priced.

The only published study directly bearing on this question is by Farley [2]. He attempted to use Stigler's theory of the economics of information [8] as a basis for studying the phenomenon of brand loyalty. Though his paper is not focused directly on our topic, the implications of the theory are relevant. He

SOURCE: Ronald E. Frank, Paul E. Green, and Harry F. Sieber, Jr., "Household Correlates of Purchase Price for Grocery Products," *Journal of Marketing Research*, Vol. 4 (February, 1967), pp. 54–58.

reasoned that the expected gain associated with searching (given that the brands in a product class are considered good substitutes) should be positively correlated with the amount purchased by a buyer. The primary reason for searching in this context would be to find lower prices. Thus one would expect heavy buyers to purchase at lower prices than light buyers, as Farley discovered.

His analysis was based on the purchasing habits of 199 households who were members of the Market Research Corporation of America's consumer panel in the Chicago metropolitan area in 1959. For each of 17 food products he compared the average price per unit paid by heavy buyers with the same quantity for light buyers within specific container sizes.

In addition, one might expect the level of a household's income to be positively associated with price paid per unit of a product for either one of two reasons, namely, that high income households (a) are faced with greater opportunity loss for time spent search-

TABLE 1

Adjusted Multiple R²'s by Product

	All Variables	Socio-economic and Purchasing only (i.e., Variables 1–14, 20)	Number of Households
Beverages			
Regular coffee	.48	.15	403
Instant coffee	.54	.09	139
Tea	.36	.18	180
Carbonated beverages	.34	.15	373
Beverages, powder and syrups	.29	.04[a]	127
Flour and baking products			
All purpose flour	.62	.14	225
Cake mixes	.21	.15	286
Oils, fats, dressings and sauces			
Margarine	.67	.17	376
Vegetable shortening	.54	.09	126
Salad dressings	.64	.19	393
Cooking oils	.47	.36	159
Peanut butter	.43	.10	215
Dairy products			
Canned milk	.33	.02[a]	178
Food specialties			
Dinners, frozen	.32	.02[a]	84
Prepared vegetables, frozen	.40	.08	151
Cereals			
Ready-to-eat cereals	.40	.04	411
Rice	.44	.15	204
Desserts and puddings			
Packaged desserts	.07	.06	357
Syrup	.36	.10	174
Snacks			
Potato chips	.82	.14	285
Soaps, cleansers and cleansing agents			
Packaged soaps and detergents	.19	.03	393
Scouring cleansers	.41	.00[a]	162
Liquid detergents	.35	.07	270
Misc. laundry aids, liquid	.24	.05	329
Macaroni, spaghetti and kindred products			
Dry spaghetti	.17	.01[a]	337
Packaged fruits and juices			
peaches	.65	.16	266
Pineapple	.36	.08	192
Fruit cocktail	.42	.13	186
Chilled orange juice	.13[a]	.17	97
Fruit, frozen	.17	.08[a]	83
Conc. fruit juices, frozen	.17	.04	280
Fruit juices	.25	.12	340

Table 1 (continued)

	All Variables	Socio-economic and Purchasing only (i.e., Variables 1–14, 20)	Number of Households
Packaged vegetables and vegetable juice			
Pork and beans	.47	.07	269
Canned corn	.48	.14	314
Tomato paste	.70	.07	276
Vegetables, frozen	.20	.04	314
Canned fish			
Tuna	.19	.14	265
Paper and paper specialties			
Toilet tissue	.07	.00[a]	409
Waxed paper	.05[a]	.01[a]	191
Paper napkins	.38	.22	224
Cleansing tissue	.25	.04[a]	270
Paper towels	.81	.10	188
Food wrappers	.27	.24	180
Condiments			
Catsup and chili sauce	.19	.12	292

[a] The equations generating these multiple R^2's had F-ratios that were not significant at the five percent level or above; all other F-ratios were significant at the five percent level or above.

ing, or they (b) tend to purchase higher quality brands.

Households owning cars might also be expected to purchase at lower prices as car ownership is apt to be positively correlated with the number of stores in which a household purchases. Finally, large families (at a given income and purchasing level) might also tend to buy at lower prices than smaller ones. Large families, at a given income level, might tend to have more incentive to use a given dollar of income more efficiently, either by purchasing the same quality product at lower prices, or by purchasing brands with slightly lower quality than those bought by smaller households. Farley did not report any results dealing with the socioeconomic correlates of price paid per unit.

To the extent that socioeconomic and total consumption characteristics are associated with price paid per unit, the price of a brand at any given point in time will tend to segment its market. That is, customers drawn to a given brand during a low-priced special will tend to have somewhat different characteristics than those drawn to it when it is sold at its regular price. Similarly, brands selling at different regular market prices will tend to draw somewhat different purchasers.

The study reported in this article analyzes the relationship between the average price paid per unit for a given product by a household and its:

1. socioeconomic characteristics,
2. total consumption of product,
3. store shopping habits,
4. private brand proneness,
5. percent purchased in small-sized containers.

The last three variables are included in the analysis to prevent their intercorrelation with socioeconomic and total consumption characteristics from biasing the estimates of the association of household socioeconomic and consumption characteristics with price paid per unit. Separate analyses are presented for each of 44 different food products (Table 1).

Data

The investigation is based on data from the *Chicago Tribune* consumer panel in 1961.[1] Purchase histories of 491 households in 44 grocery product categories, e.g., canned corn, regular coffee, and prepared cake mixes, are included. The sample was drawn from the population of the Chicago metropolitan area, the third largest metropolitan area in the country.

For each purchase by a household in a product category, a record was kept of the household's serial number, the date of purchase, the brand, the number of units, the package size, the price paid, the store where purchased, and the kind of deal involved, if any. (A deal is defined as any special price discount for merchandise at the point of sale, including cents–off coupons and cents-off packs of merchandise.)

The entire data base includes records of about 400,000 purchases. The 44 grocery products included in the study account for 18 percent of all food products purchased by households.[2]

Model

The results are based on a multiple regression analysis. A separate analysis is reported for each product. The dependent variable is the average price per unit paid by the i-th household for a given product. The definition of a unit varies from category to category. It is the measure of physical consumption normally used as the product's metric. For example, for coffee, it is pounds, while for toilet tissue it is hundreds of sheets.

The 22 independent variables are listed in Figure 1. Fourteen of these are household

[1] The authors wish to thank Donald Kline and Patrick Luby, of the *Chicago Tribune* for making these data available.
[2] This is based on *Chicago Tribune* Family Expenditure Week data for 1961. For one week in each four calendar quarters the *Tribune* creates a punch card record for every food item in a household's diary. This record includes many products that are not included as part of the standard weekly processing, such as fresh meats, poultry, and produce. These results are based on a pooling of the data for each of the four weeks in 1961.

socioeconomic characteristics, five provide a description of household store shopping behavior, one is a measure of total purchases for the product in question, the other two are the proportion of purchases devoted to private brands, as well as the proportion spent on small packages. The number of households varies for each product analysis. Households that had fewer than five purchases of a product during 1961 are eliminated from that product's regression analysis.

Socioeconomic Characteristics

1. Number of persons in family
2. Number of adults in family
3. Age of female head of family
4. Age of youngest child
5. Employment of housewife
6. Income
7. Occupation
8. Education of household head
9. Number of cars
10. Number of TV sets
11. Religion of household heads
12. Race of household heads
13. Size of building
14. Status of housewife

Store Shopping Habits

15. Proportion of total purchase for all products at A & P in 1961
16. " National
17. " Jewel
18. " Kroger
19. " Hillman

Total Consumption

20. Total purchased

Private Brand Proneness

21. Proportion of private brand purchases

Packing Size Proneness

22. Proportion of small package purchases

Two different summary statistics are used to report the results that appear in the following section. They are the multiple and partial correlation coefficients. The square of the multiple correlation coefficient (the coefficient of multiple determination) provides a measure of the proportion of variation in average price per unit that is associated with the full set of variables in the equation. The partial correlation coefficient measures the degree of association between price paid per unit and one particular variable, while holding the others constant. One multiple correlation coefficient and 22 partial correlation coefficients are generated from each regression run, based on all 22 of the independent variables specified in Figure 1. The correlation coefficient provides a direct answer to the question, to what extent are the 22 independent variables associated with the average price paid per unit by a household?

Seven household socioeconomic variables are eliminated because they are collinear with one or more of the 14 remaining variables. Those eliminated are: number of children in family, age of male head of family, number of full-time employees, religion of household (Catholic or non-Catholic), religion of household head (Jewish or non-Jewish), home ownership, and sex of household head. The highest degree of multicollinearity among the final set of independent variables (based on 491 households) is for total family income that has a squared multiple correlation coefficient of only .44 based on the linear association between it and the remaining 22 variables.

It was originally hoped that the problem of multicollinearity would be avoided by using factor analysis to generate a new set of variables that would summarize the information in the original set of multicollinear variables in a new set of factors that would not be collinear.[3] However, the effort was not successful for two reasons: (a) the resulting factors after rotation[4] were still highly correlated, and (b) the use of the factors in the product analysis regressions (using regular coffee[5]) did not achieve higher predictive or superior interpretative ability.

[3] For a recent successful application of factor analysis with this in mind, see [3].
[4] Rotation was based on the Kaiser Varimax Criterion; for a discussion, see Harman [6].
[5] Regular coffee was used as the basis for developing the final model because it is one of the categories with the highest rate of private branding activity, and it is a category one of us had considerable experience with [4, 5, 7].

Results

The first column of Table 1 reports the multiple R^2's (adjusted for sample size)[6] associated with the equations containing the 22 variables for the 44 product categories. Next, are the same statistics for each category based on equations that contain only household socioeconomic and total consumption characteristics (i.e., variables 1–14, 20). The last column reports the sample sizes on which the regressions for each product category are based.

The data of Table 1 indicate how much the set of 22 independent variables is associated with differences in the average price paid by households for particular products.

The impact of store shopping habits, as well as percent of purchases spent on private brands and small package sizes, on the price a household pays for a product is quite apparent when one contrasts the two R^2's for a product category. The average multiple R^2 (based on equations with all 22 variables) was .37. The standard deviation was .19; the range was .68. In contrast, the same three statistics for the equations with only the socioeconomic and total consumption variables were .10, .07 and .36, respectively.

The highest degree of association between the set of 22 variables and average price per unit paid by households was for potato chips (.82), paper towels (.81) and margarine (.67). When these variables (i.e., 15–19, 21, 22) are removed from the equations, these R^2's drop to .14, .10 and .17, respectively. In other words, when an unusually high degree of predictive ability (i.e., R^2) in price per unit does exist, it is primarily associated with differences in household store shopping habits, private brand consumption, and preference for small containers and not with either socioeconomic characteristics or total household purchases.

In addition to the low relative performance of the equations, i.e., small R^2, containing only household socioeconomic and purchasing variables, the absolute level of prediction is low. Twenty-two of the equations have R^2's

[6] For a discussion of the small sample size adjustment for R^2, see [1, pp. 300–4].

of less than .10; and only eight have R^2's greater than .15.

The coefficients of partial determination for the 22-variable equations are summarized in Table 2. The table contains the proportion of partial (sample) r^2's for a given variable over the 44 products that are greater than zero. For example, in 36 percent (or 12) of the 44 equations, the partial r^2 for number of persons in the family is greater than zero.

Fourteen of the 22 variables have a persistent tendency to go in one direction or the other. Each is significant at the five percent level or better. Eight of the 14 are positively

TABLE 2
Proportion of Coefficients of Partial Determination for Each Variable Greater Than Zero

Variables	Proportion of partial R^2's > 0
Number of persons in family	.36[a]
Number of adults in family	.57
Age of female head of family	.52
Age of youngest child	.48
Employment of housewife	.61
Income	.80[a]
Occupation	.27[a]
Education	.41
Number of cars	.11[a]
Number of TV sets	.41
Religion of household heads	.70[a]
Race of household heads	.30[a]
Size of building	.84[a]
Status of housewife	.52
Proportion of purchases in A & P	.59
Proportion of purchases in National	.93[a]
Proportion of purchases in Jewel	.73[a]
Proportion of purchases in Kroger	.68[a]
Proportion of purchases in Hillman's	.77[a]
Total purchases	.16[a]
Proportion of private brand purchases	.05[a]
Proportion of small packages	.82[a]

Note. Based on results for 44 product categories.
[a] Significant at the five percent level.

and six are negatively associated with average price per unit.

The results (Table 2) support all of the hypotheses mentioned in the introduction.

1. In 84 percent of the 44 product regressions, the partial r's for total consumption are negative. Heavy buyers of a product tend to purchase at lower prices than do light buyers.

2. High income families tend to purchase at higher prices, i.e., 80 percent of the partial r's were greater than zero.

3. Large families tend to pay less per unit for their product purchases than do smaller families.

4. Car owners tend to pay lower prices than do non-owners.

In addition, the effect of occupation is consistent with that of income. As a household's occupation status rises, so does the average price per unit that it pays for its purchases. The apparent inconsistency in the direction of the effects is because income increased as did its code number, while occupational status decreased as its code number increased.

Protestants have a tendency to pay higher prices per unit for food than do non-Protestants (in our sample most of the non-Protestant households are Catholic). This result may partially reflect differences in the socioeconomic profile of the two groups that are not completely adjusted for by the presence of the other socioeconomic variables in the equation.

Whites tend to pay higher prices per unit than do non-whites. Similarly, households living in large apartment buildings are also more likely to pay higher prices for their purchases. The mix of stores in the vicinity of many of the larger units probably tends to have higher prices than the mix near households living in smaller dwelling units. Many of Chicago's largest apartment buildings are located either downtown (along Michigan Avenue or Lake Shore Drive) or along Michigan Avenue on the near north side. These areas tend to consist of households with higher than average socioeconomic status for the city. The mix of available stores probably tends to reflect this upward bias in socioeconomic status.

The higher the proportion of purchases a household made at either Jewel, National, Kroger, or Hillman, the higher is the expected price per unit paid. This conflicts with the belief that supermarkets tend to have somewhat lower prices. However, it may be that customers who tend to purchase a relatively large amount of their purchases in any one chain tend to do less price shopping than those who spread their purchases among many stores.

The proportion of private brand purchases is negatively associated with price per unit, but the proportion spent on small packages is positively associated with price. Private brands tend to be less expensive, and small package sizes tend to be more expensive per unit.

Although these effects tend to be somewhat persistent among the product categories, they are usually quite small. The average partial r^2 for all 44 products is greater than one percent for only three of the 22 variables, namely, the proportion of purchases in National (.01), the proportion of private brand purchases (.03) and the proportion of small package purchases (.13).

Conclusions

Though the degree of correlation between average price paid per unit for a product by households and their socioeconomic and total consumptions characteristics is relatively modest, the direction of the effects for a number of characteristics is consistent among product categories. To some extent, the price at which a brand is sold at a point in time does segment its market.

The generality of the findings is limited partially by the variation in price from brand to brand in many of the grocery products studied. It would seem that for some nondurables and for many durables there should be higher multiple R^2's only because the vari-

ation in price for items is much greater than for grocery items. Some analysis (based on the 44 products) has been done on the relationship between variation in price in a product category and the prediction of average purchase price paid per unit by 22 variables. There appears to be virtually no relationship between the two. As for the products, it appears that predictive ability does not depend on underlying variation in price paid per unit.

REFERENCES

1. Mordecai Ezekiel and Karl A. Fox, *Methods of Correlation and Regression Analysis*, New York: John Wiley & Sons, Inc., 1959.
2. John U. Farley, "Brand Loyalty and the Economics of Information," *Journal of Business*, 37 (October 1964), 370–9.
3. John U. Farley, "Why Does Brand Loyalty Vary over Products?" *Journal of Marketing Research*, 1 (November 1964), 9–14.
4. Ronald E. Frank and William F. Massy, "Innovation and Brand Choice: The Folger's Invasion," *Proceedings of the American Marketing Association*, December 1963.
5. Ronald E. Frank and Donald G. Morrison, "The Determinants of Household Innovative Behavior for a Branded, Frequently Purchased Food Product," *Proceedings of the the American Marketing Association*, December 1964.
6. Harry Harmon, *Modern Factor Analysis*, Chicago: University of Chicago Press, 1960.
7. William F. Massy, *et al.*, "Purchasing Behavior and Personal Attributes," Stanford, Calif.: Stanford Graduate School of Business, Working Paper, forthcoming, 1966.
8. George J. Stigler, "The Economics of Information," *Journal of Political Economy*, 69 (June 1961), 213–25.

32 / The Buying Environment

A. BACKGROUND AND THEORY

The reading in this section (Engel, Kollat and Blackwell) explores the relations between consumer characteristics and store characteristics.

32-A RELATIONS BETWEEN CONSUMER CHARACTERISTICS AND STORE CHARACTERISTICS

James F. Engel (Marketing Educator), David T. Kollat (Marketing Educator), and Roger D. Blackwell (Marketing Educator)

Figure 1 is a conceptualization of how consumers select retail outlets. The scheme consists of four variables: (1) evaluative criteria; (2) perceived characteristics of stores; (3) comparison processes; and (4) acceptable and unacceptable stores. Store choice, then, is viewed as consisting of processes whereby the consumer compares the characteristics of stores as he perceives them, with evaluative criteria.

Although there is no published evidence on this point, it would appear consistent with other aspects of consumer behavior to hypothesize that consumers do not go through this process before each store visit. Instead, if past experiences with a store have been satisfactory, the store is revisited without reevaluation. Indeed, the majority of store visits that consumers make are probably not preceded by store-choice processes. The specific conditions that are likely to result in the absence of store-choice processes are unknown; considerable research is needed in this area.

Evaluative Criteria

Enough studies have been conducted to specify the following as evaluative criteria: (1) location; (2) depth and breadth of assort-

SOURCE: James F. Engel, David T Kollat, and Roger D. Blackwell, *Consumer Behavior*. Copyright © 1968 Holt Rinehart and Winston, Inc. Reprinted by permission of Holt, Rinehart and Winston, pp. 451–455.

ment; (3) price; (4) advertising and sales promotion; (5) store personnel; and (6) services.

1. LOCATION. The growth of suburban shopping centers and the loss in the market share of downtown retailers are indicative of the importance of location (and parking convenience) in influencing consumers' choice of a retail outlet. Studies have indicated that distance and parking convenience are the main reasons why many shoppers do not wish to shop in the downtown area.[1] A recent study has indicated that convenient location is the chief reason movers (new residents) make the first visit to a store.[2]

2. DEPTH AND BREADTH OF ASSORTMENT. Both merchandise variety and assortment have been found to influence store preferences. Laboratory experiments and surveys indicate that stores offering either a deep assortment or a wide variety of product lines are preferred

[1] See, for example, Charles E. Stonier, "Off-Street Parking To Attract Downtown Shoppers," *Journal of Retailing,* Vol. 36 (Fall 1960), pp. 145–149; and C. T. Jonasson, "Downtown versus Suburban Shopping" (Columbus, Ohio: Bureau of Business Research, Ohio State University, 1953), Special Bulletin No. X-58; and Robert H. Myers, "Sharpening Your Store Image," *Journal of Retailing,* Vol. 36 (Fall 1960), pp. 129–137.

[2] "The Movers," *Progressive Grocer,* Vol. 44 (November 1965), p. K-47.

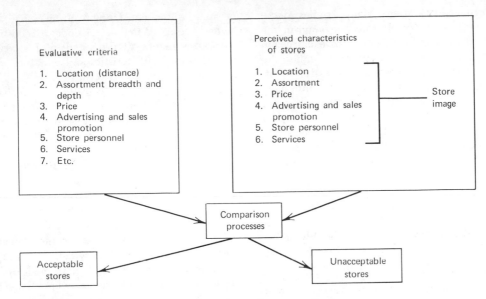

Figure 1. Store-choice processes.

over stores having medium depth or breadth of assortment.[3]

3. PRICE. The importance of price as a criterion appears to vary by product, customer, and store. For example, studies of department store[4] and supermarket[5] shoppers have found that price is often far down the list as a reason for shopping at a particular store. In the case of new car buyers, however, price is the factor most frequently cited as most important in the choice of a dealer.[6] Similarly, in some instances, price is insignificant in deciding where to buy major appliances and sport shirts.[7] One leading retailing authority has concluded that the role of price is greatly overrated.[8] Generalizations about the importance of price are not permissible at this time.

4. ADVERTISING AND SALES PROMOTION. Advertising is a quasievaluative criterion.[9] Advertisements inform consumers of sales, deals, new products, and so on. The role of sales promotion devices on store patronage is less clear. Trading stamps are of particular interest, and research in this area indicates that while many customers value and save these stamps, few attach enough significance to them to make them a determining factor in where they shop.[10]

[3] Wroe Alderson and Robert Sessions, "Basic Research on Consumer Behavior: Report on a Study of Shopping Behavior and Methods for Its Investigation," in Ronald E. Frank, Alfred A Kuehn, and William F. Massy, *Quantitative Techniques in Marketing Analysis* (Homewood, Ill.: Richard D. Irwin, Inc., 1962), pp. 129–145.

[4] Stuart U. Rich and Bernard D. Portis, "The Imageries of Department Stores," *Journal of Marketing*, Vol. 28 (April 1964), pp. 10–15.

[5] "The Movers," pp. K-35–K-58.

[6] Alderson Associates, Inc., *A Basic Study of Automobile Retailing* (Dearborn, Mich.: Ford Motor Company, 1958).

[7] George Katona and Eva Mueller, "A Study of Purchase Decisions," in Lincoln H. Clark, ed., *Consumer Behavior: The Dynamics of Consumer*

Reaction (New York: New York University Press, 1955), pp. 36–87.

[8] William R. Davidson, "The Shake-Out in Appliance Retailing," *Home Appliance Builder* (March 1965), pp. 21–29.

[9] See, for example, William Lazer and Eugene J. Kelly, "The Retailing Mix: Planning and Management," *Journal of Retailing* (Spring 1961), Vol. 37, pp. 34–41; William D. Tyler, "The Image, the Brand, and the Consumer," *Journal of Marketing*, Vol. 22 (October 1957), pp. 162–165; Pierre Martineau, *Motivation in Advertising* (New York: McGraw-Hill Book Company, Inc., 1957), Chap. 15.

[10] T. Ellsworth, D. Benjamin, and H. Radolf, "Customer Response To Trading Stamps," *Journal*

5. STORE PERSONNEL. Many studies document the importance of store personnel in the consumer's choice of a store. For example, in attempting to determine why a quality department store had been so successful in attracting Negro customers, research continually indicated that the reason was that clerks were friendlier. Similarly, neighborhood shopping centers usually rank higher than downtown stores in terms of friendliness.[11] Other studies have demonstrated that various characteristics of sales personnel, including politeness, courteousness, and product knowledge, are often used as criteria in evaluating some stores.[12]

6. SERVICES. The role of service as an evaluative criterion seems to vary considerably across both consumers and products. The following findings appear to be representative:

a. A liberal return policy is very important in determining whether consumers will shop at discount houses.[13]

b. In the purchase of new cars, expectation of good service is among the least frequently mentioned factors that buyers say caused them to select a dealer.[14]

c. Service is one of the least frequently mentioned dealer characteristics looked for by buyers of major appliances.[15] Other studies present contradictory findings.[16]

Reasons for this variation in the importance of service as a determinant of store patronage have not been empirically isolated.

Perceived Store Characteristics

What consumers perceive the price, merchandise offering, and services of a store to

be may differ considerably from what they *actually are*. Whether or not a consumer patronizes a store often depends on his *perception* of store characteristics and how they compare with evaluative criteria.

The way in which consumers perceive a store is typically referred to as a store's image. More specific definitions of store image vary from author to author. One authority, for example, defines a store's image as "the way in which the store is defined in the shopper's mind, partly by its functional qualities and partly by an aura of psychological attributes."[17] Another author defines image as "a complex of meanings and relationships serving to characterize the store for people."[18] While these definitions differ somewhat, the essential point is that the store, as perceived by the consumer, may differ from what the store "actually is" in an "objective sense."

1. DETERMINANTS OF STORE IMAGE. While there is no well-developed theory explaining how images are formed, there has been enough research to suggest several determinants. The following paragraphs describe how images are formed and how what is "perceived" may differ from "what is."

a. *Price*. The price level of a store is one determinant of image. Perceived or psychological price may differ from actual price. Consumers often form their image about a store's prices more on the basis of advertising, displays, advertising specials, and physical layout than from the actual price level of the store.

b. *Advertising*. Advertising is a major determinant of store image. The following illustrates the impact and subtle colorations and associations that advertising can produce:

One of the major mail order chains talks about expanding its market upward, attracting the middle class customer. Yet when the ads from stores of this chain were tested in three different cities where women did not know

of Retailing, Vol. 33 (Winter 1957–1958), pp. 165–169, 206; and Norman Bussel "Let's Give Trading Stamps a Weigh," *Progressive Grocer*, Vol. 44 (November 1965), pp. 154–158.

[11] Martineau, *Motivation in Advertising*, p. 181.

[12] Rich and Portis, pp. 10–15.

[13] David J. Rachman and Linda J. Kemp, "Profile of the Discount House Customer," *Journal of Retailing*, Vol. 39 (Summer 1963), pp. 1–8.

[14] Alderson Associates, Inc.

[15] Katona and Mueller, pp. 30–87.

[16] John K. Ryans, Jr., "An Analysis of Appliance Retailer Perceptions of Retail Strategy and Decision Processes," in Peter D. Bennett, ed., *Marketing and Economic Development* (Chicago: American Marketing Association, 1965), pp. 666–671.

[17] Pierre Martineau, "The Personality of the Retail Store," *Harvard Business Review*, Vol. 36 (January–February 1958), pp. 47–55, at p. 47.

[18] Leon Arons, "Does Television Viewing Influence Store Image and Shopping Frequency?" *Journal of Retailing*, Vol. 37 (Fall 1961), pp. 1–13, at p. 1.

their actual identity, in every class the stores were seen as having a lower class appeal.[19]

A leading Kansas City store's copy was tested both in Kansas City and in Atlanta. The evaluations [were] by women who had no idea of the identity of the store and who were making their judgments entirely from the physical appearance of the copy. . . . "I am not averse to bargains, but I wouldn't trust that store." "I imagine if you took something back, they would want to give you something in exchange and not give you the cash." . . . "The clerk standing there would be an immigrant, not enjoying selling. She probably could just barely speak English." . . . "I am afraid a store like this would take advantage of my ignorance on some things."[20]

c. Product and Service Mix. A store's image is affected by the products and services that consumers perceive it to offer. Other factors such as advertising and physical facilities often form the basis for perceptions of a store's product and service mix.

[19] Martineau, *Motivation in Advertising*, p. 174.
[20] Martineau, *Motivation in Advertising*, pp. 175–176.

d. Store Personnel. Sales personnel also affect a stores image. A store sometimes takes on the character of the clerks, stock boys, and those management personnel who are seen by customers. The way clerks react to customers sometimes characterizes a store as friendly, impersonal, helpful, up-to-date, or disinterested.

e. Physical Attributes. Physical attributes of a store affect consumers' perceptions of other store characteristics. The materials used on the exterior and interior, the kind of floors, the type of displays, and many other factors affect a store's image.

f. Store Clientele. The type of people shopping in a store also influences a store's image. One writer has stated this succinctly:

Their personality concept is not primarily the result of physical features of the store—it is rather the result of the group of customers who have come to shop there. Customers associate themselves with a social group, shop where that group shops, and attribute to the store characteristics of the group.[21]

[21] John H. Wingate, "Developments in the Super Market Field," *New York Retailer* (October 1958), p. 6.

B. RESEARCH AND APPLICATIONS

The discussion now turns to specific examples of retailing: a look at how consumers "really buy" meats and perishables (Tate), and a report on research done to discover some of the primary factors that bear on sales volume (Cundiff and Dommermuth).

32-B HOW CONSUMERS REALLY BUY . . . MEATS AND PERISHABLES

Russell S. Tate, Jr. (Marketing Executive)

A very unfortunate thing once happened to a well-known research man. While he was on a walking trip, he suddenly came to the edge of a stream. Being a careful researcher, he immediately consulted his maps, charts, and other data—all of which convinced him that the stream had an average depth of 2 feet. So

SOURCE: Russell S. Tate, Jr., "How Consumers Really Buy . . . Meats and Perishables," (Chicago: Super Market Institute, Inc., Copyright 1963), 5 pp.

he decided to wade across—and came mighty close to drowning because the middle was 10 feet deep. You just can't put all your faith in averages.

The same is true in the grocery business. There is no such thing as an "average" family with exactly three-and-a-fraction members. Neither is there an "average" shopper who spends a certain number of minutes in your store, selects a precise number of items, and pays an exact number of dollars and cents at the checkout counter. The "average" shopper is purely a statistical creation. You can't reach her with advertising, impress her with merchandising, or please her with courtesy.

Don't Rely on Averages

If you gear your operations to this nonexistent average shopper, you will wind up with an average store which probably won't satisfy anyone *entirely*. And then, like our unfortunate researcher, you may take an unexpected bath. Reliance on averages may be one reason why so many new stores aren't doing the weekly volume which was anticipated. In fact, there are very significant differences in the purchasing patterns of specific types of families. Some of them are obvious. Wealthy people don't buy the same way as poor people. Large families buy bigger package sizes than small families. All-purpose flour is a stronger item with rural families than metropolitan families.

If they have a choice, shoppers will favor the store which most nearly reflects their particular needs and preferences. For some of them, price may be the most important matter. Others may be interested mainly in variety. Still others may go where the meat department matches their wishes.

It follows that operators who understand the desires of the particular types of families who predominate in their trading areas—and cater to those desires—will come out ahead of the game.

The Young Homemakers

Oftentimes, the housewife's *age* is a major factor in shaping her grocery buying behavior. For example, younger housewives have a distinctly different purchasing pattern than middle-aged or older housewives. Therefore, if you are operating in a neighborhood composed mainly of young couples, you will want to be aware of these differences. They can affect your basic decisions about items to be stocked, promotions to be offered, and products to be featured in your advertising.

Young households are coming in for a lot of attention these days, and rightly so. First of all, they are a rapidly growing segment of the total population. In addition, if you can attract them at an early age—and please them—you will have a long-term customer. Finally, you

really can't afford *not* to go after the young families—or somebody else will grab them.

In view of the importance of this young group, it's surprising how many misconceptions exist about them. For example, from the standpoint of *quantities purchased,* they are not at all outstanding. On the contrary, they tend to buy significantly *less* than middle-aged families. When you stop to think of it, this is very logical—after all, younger families have fewer mouths to feed, and smaller mouths, at that. Furthermore, they haven't yet reached the age of peak income or maximum entertaining at home. It all adds up to this conclusion: Operators who open a store in a predominantly young-family neighborhood shouldn't expect to get as much volume *per household* as they would get in neighborhoods with more mature homes.

Some Cold Figures

It's pretty clear from our studies that you will get more canned fish volume, on a household-for-household basis, if your customers are between 35–44, than if they are below 35. With respect to salmon, for example, 1,000 families in the older age group will out-purchase 1,000 younger families by 50% over a six-month period. That's a lot of cases of canned fish!

Using a U. S. average based at 100 index points, families under 35 had only 82 index points for canned-salmon purchases, against 123 for the 35–44 group, 114 for the 45–54 group, and 81 for the group 55 and over.

The same base index applied to canned sardines found families under 35 rated at only 91, while the 35–44 group rated 166, the 45–54 group, 99, and the 55 and over, 94.

Now let's look at a different product—margarine. This is sometimes called "the inexpensive spread." Since young households haven't yet reached their income crest, and may be pinched for cash, margarine might be expected to have particular appeal. Well, in terms of dollars spent per household, it appears that our young families again don't measure up. In fact, they are about 10% below average, rating only 91 index points against 107 for middle-aged households and 96 for older groups.

If young families aren't heavy buyers of canned fish or margarine, how about diet items? Is this an area where they will come through strongly? On a low-calory version of a standard item, we set the purchase rate of all families at an arbitrary level of 100. All groups were well above this average, except for the under-35 homes who rated 56 index points, only a little better than half as much as the national average. Actually, since they pull down the average, their purchase rate is *less* than half the rate of any other group. The 35–44 group rated 111, the 45–54 group was highest at 132, and 55 and over rated 114.

Let's move along to coffee. Almost everybody buys some coffee—over a six-month period only 3% of the households fail to make at least one purchase. However, different families buy different amounts. Is there any pattern by age groups?

There sure is! Households under 35 represent 29% of the entire population, but buy only 19% of the regular coffee volume. Households 35–44, representing 22% of the population, bought 26% of the regular coffee, the 45–54 group, 20% of the population, bought 27%, and the 55 and over group, 29% of the population, accounted for 28% of regular coffee sales.

Could it be that the young homes are in a greater hurry, and prefer instant coffee? No, they account for even less of the instant coffee market! The under 35 households bought only 18% of instant coffee, compared to 22% for the 35–44 group, 26% for the 45–54 group, and 34% for the group 55 and over. We also get the same results with instant potatoes. Against an index of 100, the younger households rated only 79 compared to 114 for the middle-aged group and 107 for the oldest group.

I think we have seen enough statistics to make the point that young households tend to buy smaller quantities. One reason, as we suggested earlier, is that they have fewer and smaller mouths to feed. I don't want to destroy this theory, because I believe it is essentially correct, but one more measurement deserves to be mentioned. Households under 35 also buy fewer pounds of dog food, per dog-owning family, then older households. Maybe their dogs are smaller, too.

Nevertheless, a remark someone once made about women also applies to these young families—you can't live with them, but you certainly can't live without them!

Merchandising Pointers

So let's turn our attention to ways and means in which you can attract and hold the young group. From now on we will show how they differ from the older population segment in their food-preparation and eating habits. This will indicate some merchandising tactics you can use to tie in with their consumption patterns and demonstrate that your store understands their requirements.

I should point out that the measurements we have discussed until now come from MRCA's National Consumer Panel. The families in this panel report to us each week what they buy, where they bought it, how much they paid, and so on. The information about eating is taken from our National Menu Census. This is a year-long study of what happens to every food product brought into the home. It shows how all types of families combine, modify, and associate these products in preparing the family's meals. The facts we are about to present are right up to the minute. They are based on measurements made during the first six months of the current Menu Census, which will be completed on June 30 of this year.

Incidentally, although this study is primarily designed for food manufacturers, it contains a vast amount of information that can be applied to retail operations. Presumably, distributors will receive much valuable merchandising data through the courtesy of the various manufacturers who are subscribing to the Menu Census.

Let's look first at the rate-of-use for two popular types of meat: ground beef and bacon. Ground beef is relatively much more popular with the under-35 segment. During a typical two-week period, 1,000 young families will serve ground beef 3,501 times . . . while 1,000 older families will serve it only 2,888 times. Ground beef, therefore, is a better advertising and merchandising magnet when applied to young people than to older people.

When it comes to bacon, the pattern is reversed. This time, the older housewives are the more frequent users. However, both types of families serve bacon more often than they serve ground beef. In fact, bacon is the most popular single meat item of all—four out of every five families serve it at least once in a two-week period, and those who serve it do so more than five times in that span. This wide and frequent use suggests that bacon is a very good item to feature.

Incidentally, about 80% of the time bacon is eaten in its regular form—but 20% of the time it finds its way into other dishes as an ingredient or additive. And 75% of all bacon is consumed at the morning meal.

Another very popular dish is chicken, which is eaten at least once in a two-week span by almost three out of four homes. In this case, we don't find much difference by age of family. By region of the country, as you might expect, the highest percent of families serving is in the South. The lowest percent of families serving is in the West.

Interestingly, for those of you who remember the old adage "Chicken every Sunday," there is a lot of truth in the statement. It turns out that 25% of all servings of chicken take place on Sunday. From Monday through Thursday, the serving frequency is about normal. But Fridays and Saturdays just aren't chicken-serving days in the United States. In fact, Saturday is no better than Friday. As a final word on chicken, it is served fried 2½ times as often as it is served roasted.

Facts About Franks

Getting back to products where housewives under 35 act differently from housewives over 35, consider the lowly frankfurter. Here are the figures: 62% of families under 35 served frankfurters an average of 2.3 times during a 2-week period, while only 45% of families 35 and over served franks an average of once a week. Franks are clearly more popular among young families, both in percent of families serving and in serving frequency.

You may wonder whether there is a relationship between income and popularity of franks. As a matter of fact, there *is*—but possibly not in the way that many people would expect. The lowest percentage of families serving frankfurters is found in the lowest income class. Here are the figures: Of families in the under-35 age group with over $10,000 annual income, 67% served frankfurters within a 2-week period, while 70% did so in the $7,000–$10,000 income bracket; 59% for the

$4,000–$7,000 income bracket and only 58% for families with incomes under $4,000.

Frankfurters are not the poor family's dish, either below the age of 35 or above. By the way, remembering the relatively light serving of chicken on Saturdays, what's the story on franks? The answer is that they are definitely a Saturday favorite. That's when more than 22% of the total servings occur. Fridays and Sundays are both below par.

Which do you think is served more often in American homes—frankfurters of beefsteak– If you said beefsteak, you're right—and it isn't even close. The total number of servings, per 1,000 families, in a 2-week period is 1,303 for beefsteak and 1,061 for franks. Six out of ten homes serve beefsteak at least once within two weeks, and the average number of occasions is better than two.

There is not much difference by age. Families under 35 have about the same pattern as families over 35. The interesting thing is that so many families in the bottom income group serve steak. This is a higher percent than serves pork chops, or baked ham, or for that matter processed meats and cold cuts. Incidentally, steak is eaten very uniformly throughout the week. The only day slightly below par is Friday.

How About Hamburgers?

Here's another question for you. Percentagewise, are hamburger patties served more heavily in the wealthiest homes or in the poorest homes? The answer is that a higher percent of upper income homes serve hamburger patties than low income homes. The percentage of families serving hamburger patties within a 2-week period was 66% for families in the $7,000–$10,000 income range; 67% for families between $4,000–$7,000, and only 56% for families under $4,000.

We can conclude from these figures that hamburger patty is definitely not the poor man's dish in this country. In fact, they are popular across the board—and if you promote them, you will probably get considerable interest from all types of shoppers.

Staying with hamburger patties for a moment, do you think they are used more widely and frequently by small families or large families? In other words, should you think of them as something that one-and-two-member households like to place on the table, or as something that appeals particularly to a housewife with five or more mouths to feed? The answer can affect the way in which you merchandise them. Accordingly to the Menu Census, hamburger patties are served during a two-week period by about *half* of the small families . . . and by a whopping three-quarters of the large families!

Furthermore, Saturday is a relatively big day for hamburger. It ranks right up there with frankfurters. As a matter of fact, between them hamburgers and frankfurters have a stranglehold on the Saturday meat servings in this country. This might be worth keeping in mind when you plan how to conform to the eating habits of your customers: They lean heavily toward chicken on Sundays, and franks and hamburgers on Saturdays. As for the Monday through Thursday meals, that's when they eat an above average share of their pork chops, cold cuts, and ham slices.

Processed meats and cold cuts are served by a goodly number of households—more, for example, than serve baked ham. Equally important, the families who eat them do so rather frequently. These families are more apt to be young than old. The percentage of all families under 35 serving cold cuts within a 2-week period was 36%, compared to 26% for families 35 and older.

The percent of young families serving cold cuts does not vary much by income. However, when we look at family size, we do see some variations. Small families are less disposed toward these meats than average and large families—especially small families over 35.

Preferences in Fruit

It seems quite clear that the meat eating preferences of young households often differ significantly from those of more mature homes. Let's see whether the same is true for fruit. Our first example is cantaloupe. Here is a really big difference. Apparently, the taste for cantaloupe is developed in later life. Families under 35 eat cantaloupe about as often as they eat watermelon, but older families eat it more than twice as often. The message here is that cantaloupe may be a good special to pull older shoppers. Peaches are another case where older families far exceed the under-35 group

in consumption. Their rate for peaches is almost 40% higher.

As a matter of fact, we find that young families trail behind in their consumption of most fruits. The major exception is oranges. The lesson here is that fruit shouldn't be considered a highly important factor in getting the business of young housewives.

If you will agree, after the examples we have seen, that there are indeed big variations in the buying and eating behavior of different types of families, then we should consider how you can take advantage of this fact.

One conclusion, it seems to me, is that the day may be over when an operator can afford to merchandise uniformly to the mass public. Perhaps the time has come for a program of *selective* merchandising, or *bull's eye* merchandising, which recognizes that the particular people in a store's neighborhood may have unique patterns of consumption. If your merchandising program *fits* their requirements, they will have a real reason for becoming a steady customer. Conversely, if your store *doesn't* arouse any feeling of mutuality, is it any wonder that they may pass it by?

Americans don't buy like masses. But they do tend to have buying patterns which are shaped by such factors as age, income, family size, and education. Why not tie in with these patterns and make it *obvious* that they can satisfy their needs in your store?

For example, did you know that 41% of all households in the United States have only one or two members? About 23% have five or more members. Let's assume you have a store in an area composed mainly of small households, and another store in a neighborhood where large families are predominant. If, by chance, you operated both stores in the identical fashion, you would be overlooking some rather important differences in eating habits.

We mentioned earlier that hamburger patties are served by only about 50% of the small homes, compared with almost 75% of the large homes. Here's the story on frankfurters: 35% of families serving frankfurters within a 2-week period were families of 1–2 members, while 64% of families of 5 or more members served frankfurters during the same period.

Certainly, when it comes to merchandising hamburgers and frankfurters, you will do better to play them up in a neighborhood with large households than in a neighborhood with small families.

Now let's look at some comparisons by family income. I think you may be in for a bit of a surprise. Roast chicken was served by 19% of our families with incomes under $4,000 and by 18% of families over $10,000. Not much difference here between the poorest families and the wealthiest ones.

Let's take another product. Pork chops were served by 35% of our families with under $4,000 income, by 39% with incomes over $10,000. Again, this is not a significant difference. It's the same story for baked ham, served by 23% of our families under $4,000 income and by 27% of families over $10,000. The fact is, in many meat items poor families tend to have similar serving patterns as wealthy families. We can, of course, find differences if we search further. In beefsteak there is a considerable gap in favor of the upper-income group. The same is true of frankfurters. But for many meat items, it appears that the discrepancy between income classes may be smaller than might be supposed. You can't take anything for granted.

We've looked at a lot of facts and figures this morning, mainly to demonstrate that there are major differences in the way various types of families eat. We have also suggested that selective merchandising may enable you to capitalize on these differences and improve store loyalty.

Now, in conclusion, I'd like to offer just one thought for you to consider. As supermarket operators, you properly think of yourselves as grocery distributors. But in addition—and this is the big point—you are also selling a particular product. This product is your store itself —the sum total of all the items, all the fixtures and all the employees in it. The market for this product of yours is the people in your trading area.

The Store as a Product

When you think in these terms—as though your store is a package of merchandise which is offered for sale to the people in the neighborhood—you may suddenly get a much clearer view of your marketing problems and opportunities.

You have all seen many examples of grocery products which failed because they didn't match the requirements of their market. On the other hand, the fastest selling items in your stores are those which best meet the consumers' needs—in terms of price, quality, packaging, convenience, or what have you.

This concept of a store as a product may seem a little strange at first. However, it may be a springboard for fresh ideas, new insight, and more profitable over-all operations. And that, after all, is what we are looking for today.

32-C COMPARATIVE RETENTION ANALYSIS

Edward W. Cundiff (Marketing Educator) and William P. Dommermuth (Marketing Educator)

The sales volume of a retail store depends on two major determinants: (1) ability to attract shoppers, (2) ability to retain those attracted and convert them into purchasers.

Shopper Attraction

Potential customers are attracted to a store for several reasons. Perhaps the most important is the overall store image built up from personal experience, comments of other cus-

SOURCE: Edward W. Cundiff and William P. Dommermuth, "Comparative Retention Analysis," *Journal of Retailing,* Vol. 45 (Spring 1969), pp. 32–37.

tomers, and promotion. This image may be of the "in" place to shop, a convenient place to shop, or a place where the customer is most likely to find what he or she wants. Other factors that also may attract potential customers to a retail outlet are advertised promotional events, the availability of desired extra services, convenience, and special merchandise. Usually a customer is drawn to a particular store because of some combination of these attractions.

Shopper Retention

The final test of a retailer's success is his ability to sell merchandise to the potential customers who walk through his doors. Merchandising and/or salesmanship and in-store promotion are the ingredients that turn shoppers into customers. Good merchandising represents the ability to anticipate customers' desires and to have the needed merchandise available when the customer wants it. Salesmanship and in-store promotion tell customers about the availability of needed merchandise.

Despite the importance of this latter volume determinant, most retailers have no way of measuring their success in holding shoppers—turning shoppers into buyers. Small single line retailers can approximate the ratio of shoppers held by a simple head count of the number of shoppers entering the store and the number leaving without making a purchase. Thus, the man who leaves a tie store with a new tie is a shopper held, and the one who leaves without a purchase is a shopper lost. In large stores with multiple lines, however, a head count approach becomes unmanageable. The customer may have failed to find items sought in several departments, or the item actually purchased may not have been sought at all but resulted from impulse buying.

In such stores the ability of individual departments to retain customers may vary widely. This variation may rest upon differences in shopping patterns for various lines of merchandise. For example, women may shop more widely for cocktail dresses than for cookware. But this variation also reflects differences in the ability of department managers to merchandise and sell their goods. Variations in the ability of competing retailers to hold shoppers on similar merchandise, if such information were available, would provide an even better measure of the merchandising and selling efficiency of department managers. The authors have devised a method of measuring the comparative effectiveness of departments in competing retail outlets by going directly to a sample of consumers. A brief description of the method used and a presentation of comparative data from two cities follows.

The Research Technique

The survey was conducted separately in two cities, one with a population of approximately 250,000 and the other with a population slightly in excess of 100,000. In each instance, the population for the survey was defined to

TABLE 1

List of Merchandise Items Included in Survey

Item of Merchandise	Broad Category Represented
1. Costume jewelry	Costume jewelry
2. Fabric by the yard	Yard goods
3. Infant's suit or dress	Infants' wear
4. Towels or sheets	White goods
5. A boy's outer jacket	Boys' clothing
6. Girl's play clothes	Girls' play clothes and sportswear
7. Girl's dress-up dress	Girls' dress-up clothing
8. A man's dress shirt	Mens' furnishings
9. A dress for church	Women's dresses
10. A daytime blouse	Women's sportswear and casual wear
11. A ladies' coat	Women's outerwear
12. A pair of ladies' gloves	Women's accessories
13. Ladies' heels (shoes)	Women's shoes
14. A wedding gift	Gift department

include all households in the city. It was determined that adequately accurate estimates of shopping characteristics could be obtained with a sample of 400 households in the larger city and 300 households in the smaller city. In each of the cities, a random sample was drawn, using the city directory as the sampling frame.

Each respondent was contacted by telephone and asked about her shopping behavior for fourteen specific items of merchandise. The fourteen items were selected to represent most of the major merchandise categories in the typical general merchandise store. Table 1 lists these items and the broad category from which each was drawn. Care was taken to select merchandise items that would normally be purchased by a maximum number of people. Identical questions were asked concerning each item of merchandise. These questions were designed to learn the normal source of supply, all stores visited in shopping for an item, and where the purchase was finally made. Data were obtained both on recent actual purchases and on purchase preferences for items not recently purchased.

TABLE 2

Attraction of Shoppers by Selected Stores (Percentage of Market Attracted to Store)

| Merchandise Categories | City #1 | | | | | City #2 | |
| | Downtown Stores (Percent) | | Regional Center 1 (Percent) | Regional Center 2 (Percent) | | Downtown Stores (Percent) | |
	A	B	C	D	E	F	G
1. Costume Jewelry	24	1	12	6	7	12	30
2. Fabric by the Yard	16	9	10	13	7	4	29
3. Infants' Suit or Dress	17	4	10	25	13	7	20
4. Towels or Sheets	13	17	13	20	8	6	26
5. Boys' Outer Jacket	14	3	8	26	19	2	18
6. Girls' Play Clothes	15	6	9	22	13	3	28
7. Girls' Dress-up Dress	21	2	14	21	14	6	24
8. Man's Dress Shirt	14	7	12	14	12	7	23
9. A Dress for Church	20	3	14	11	11	11	28
10. A Daytime Blouse	14	6	7	10	11	10	25
11. A Lady's Coat	20	3	18	19	13	11	26
12. Ladies' Gloves	27	4	8	10	8	17	32
13. Ladies' Heels	12	—	7	4	3	7	22
14. A Wedding Gift	24	1	10	12	3	4	20

TABLE 3

Retention of Shoppers by Selected Stores
(of Shoppers Attracted Who Were Retained as Purchasers)

| Merchandise Categories | City #1 | | | | | City #2 | |
| | Downtown Stores (Percent) | | Regional Center 1 (Percent) | Regional Center 2 (Percent) | | Downtown Stores (Percent) | |
	A	B	C	D	E	F	G
1. Costume Jewelry	59	50	86	55	46	100	81
2. Fabric by the Yard	55	57	39	45	41	50	83
3. Infants' Suit or Dress	74	67	62	47	59	75	86
4. Towels or Sheets	79	86	76	81	67	72	97
5. Boys' Outer Jacket	86	33	37	63	53	50	87
6. Girls' Play Clothes	59	56	36	58	37	100	93
7. Girls' Dress-up Dress	57	33	50	60	60	40	86
8. Man's Dress Shirt	77	93	76	77	77	92	100
9. A Dress for Church	36	63	69	50	80	74	72
10. A Daytime Blouse	67	55	67	65	59	83	90
11. A Lady's Coat	29	33	47	55	14	75	84
12. Ladies' Gloves	68	67	84	87	58	83	94
13. Ladies' Heels	47	—	69	30	57	67	94
14. A Wedding Gift	84	100	76	81	67	80	97

Note. The store or stores with the highest retention in City #1 are underlined.

Findings

Retailers in the two cities met with widely varying success in respect to both shopper attraction and purchase conversion. Depending upon the type of merchandise involved, as many as 84 percent of the respondents reported failure, and as many as 100 percent reported success in satisfying their needs by shopping in given departments of given stores. Table 2 compares the ability to attract shoppers, and Table 3 compares the ability to retain shoppers in all of the major general merchandise stores in the two cities. There were five such major stores in City 1, two located in the downtown area, two in one regional type shopping center, and one in another regional shopping center. In City 2, there were two general merchandise stores of major importance.

Success in satisfying customers varied widely between lines of merchandise for each store. For example, Store A satisfied 86 percent of its customers for boys' outer jackets but only 29 percent of its customers for ladies' coats. This range of success was widest in Stores B and E, with spreads of 67 percent and 66 percent respectively. It was pointed out in the introductory part of this article that much of the variation in success in satisfying customers between departments in a single store may be explained by differences in customer shopping habits. Women might be expected to shop more widely for a coat for themselves than for an outer jacket for their sons. But variation between stores in their ability to satisfy customers for the same kind of merchandise must be explained in terms of other factors. One such factor might be the location of competition. One might expect the customer of a downtown store to be more difficult to retain because of the ease of getting to other competing stores, yet the two major downtown stores in City 1 show just as high a percentage of success in retaining their customers as do the stores in shopping centers. There does seem to be some evidence, though, that in City 2, where there are fewer alternative locations to shop, a larger proportion of consumers are retained.

It seems likely that the most important factor explaining the variations between stores is managerial ability. The departments that retain the highest percent of shoppers are doing a better job of merchandising and selling. The data in Table 2 can provide very useful control data for top management of the stores involved. For example, the women's sportswear departments in City 1 seem to be doing about equally well, since the range of customer retention varies only between 55 percent and 67 percent, a difference of 12 percent. Yet, the variation between boys' clothing departments is very wide. The manager of this department in Store B should be asked why he satisfied only 33 percent of his potential customers, while his competitor across the street managed to satisfy 86 percent. In a like manner, the costume jewelry department in Store E held only slightly more than half as many of its potential customers as did the same department in Store C. Even when the amount of variation between stores is less striking, the identification of any differences in performance provides management with a useful tool for evaluating the effectiveness of department managers.

Conclusions

The research technique described above provides a method of obtaining important control information that has not before been available to retailing management. A study of this nature would only be needed periodically as a check on managerial performance. Used in this manner it furnishes a relatively inexpensive source of information. It involves an assumption that the products listed in Table 1 provide a representative measurement of the performance of other products in the same department. However, once potentially weak departments have been identified, a second survey, including a number of products from that department, can be employed to verify the problem as well as to probe its nature and scope.

PROMOTION AND THE CONSUMER

33 / Communication

A. BACKGROUND AND THEORY

This section begins with a consideration (Hayakawa) of affective communication; and then we move to a statement by two sociologists (Broom and Selznick) that points out the effect of social status on communication.

33-A AFFECTIVE COMMUNICATION

S. I. Hayakawa (Semanticist)

First, it should be pointed out that fine-sounding speeches, long words, and the general *air* of saying something important are affective in result, regardless of what is being said. Often when we are hearing or reading impressively worded sermons, speeches, political addresses, essays, or "fine writing," we stop being critical altogether, and simply allow ourselves to feel as excited, sad, joyous, or angry as the author wishes us to feel. Like snakes under the influence of a snake charmer's flute, we are swayed by the musical phrases of the verbal hypnotist. If the author is a man to be trusted, there is no reason why we should not enjoy ourselves in this way now and then. But to listen or read in this way habitually is a debilitating habit. There is a kind of churchgoer who habitually listens in this way, however. He enjoys any sermon, no matter what the moral principles recommended, no matter how poorly organized or developed, no matter how shabby its rhetoric, so long as it is delivered in an impressive tone of voice with proper, i.e., customary, musical and physical settings. Such listeners are by no means to be found only in churches. The writer has frequently gnashed his teeth in rage when, after he has spoken before women's clubs on problems about which he wished to

SOURCE: S. I. Hayakawa, *Language in Action* (New York: Harcourt, Brace & World, Inc., 2nd ed. 1940), pp. 65–67 at p. 65.

arouse thoughtful discussion, certain ladies have remarked, "That was such a lovely address, professor. You have such a nice voice." Some people, that is, never listen to *what* is being said, since they are interested only in what might be called the gentle inward massage that the *sound* of words gives them. Just as cats and dogs like to be stroked, so do some human beings like to be verbally stroked at fairly regular intervals; it is a form of rudimentary sensual gratification. Because listeners of this kind are numerous, intellectual shortcomings are rarely a barrier to a successful career in public life, on the stage or radio, on the lecture platform, or in the ministry.

Because words are such a powerful instrument, we have in many ways a superstitious awe rather than an understanding of them—and even if we have no awe, we tend at least to have an undue respect for them. For example, when someone in the audience at a meeting asks the speaker a question, and when the speaker makes a long and plausible series of noises *without answering it, sometimes both the questioner and the speaker fail to notice that the question has not been answered; they both sit down apparently perfectly satisfied.* That is to say, the mere fact that an appropriate-sounding set of noises has been made satisfies some people that a statement has been made; thereupon they accept and sometimes memorize that set of noises, serenely confident that it answers a question or solves a problem.

33-B COMMUNICATION AND SOCIAL STATUS

Leonard Broom (Sociologist) Philip Selznick (Sociologist)

Most discussions of stratification deal with whole societies or communities, and this is the emphasis in SOCIAL STRATIFICATION. But the basic processes of stratification also occur in special-purpose associations, where they affect communication, incentive, and control. In this section we emphasize the importance of stratification for communication within large organizations.

Formal Ranks and Social Strata

The study of social stratification in organizations includes both the *formal ranking system* and the *informally patterned experiences* of the persons who occupy the positions. The formal ranking system is readily observed. It is easy to make lists of the official ranks that intervene between a five-star general and a private, between a corporation president and an unskilled worker, between the president of the American Federation of Labor and a member of a trade-union local, or between a university president and a teaching assistant.

These formal ranks tend to be associated with distinctive attitudes and interests. The diverse experiences and problems of men at different levels condition (1) how individuals in like social positions view the world and themselves, and (2) the stake they have in the organization. A man's position in the hierarchy tends to influence his general social behavior—his manners, outlook, opportunities, and power—and in this way social stratification develops.

Status is symbolized in many ways. The American office "is a veritable temple of sta-

tus."[1] The carpeted office, the memo pad, the privilege of smoking or of first-naming one's colleagues—all are cues to differential status. The way names are used is important, but the significance attached to names depends on whether one is looking up or down the hierarchy. The rank order of address by executives is definitively outlined by that student of human relations, Potter, in the case of a Lumer Farr, a company director, who liked to be called "The Guv'nor":

In the science of Christian-naming, Lumer is associated with Farr's Law of Mean Familiarity. This can be expressed by a curve, but is much clearer set down as follows:

The Guv'nor addresses:

Co-director Michael Yates as	MIKE
Assistant director Michael Yates as	MICHAEL
Sectional manager Michael Yates as	MR. YATES
Sectional assistant Michael Yates as	YATES
Apprentice Michael Yates as	MICHAEL
Night-watchman Michael Yates as	MIKE[2]

Organizations are both aided and hindered by the transformation of formal, technical rankings into social strata. On the one hand, the development of appropriate attitudes helps to sustain the system of authority. Men who have feelings of deference toward their superiors more readily accept commands. On the other hand, the development of special interests and attitudes may introduce rigidities into the organization.

SOURCE: Leonard Broom and Philip Selznick, *Sociology: A Text with Adopted Readings* (New York: Harper & Row, Publishers, 3rd ed., 1963. Copyright © 1955 Harper & Row, Publishers, Incorporated), pp. 234–235.

[1] W. H. Whyte, Jr., "Status in the American Office," *Fortune* (May, 1951).
[2] Stephen Potter, *One-upmanship* (New York: Holt, 1952), p. 44.

B. RESEARCH AND APPLICATIONS

The two readings in this section deal with some practical aspects of communication. The first article (Mendelsohn) presents the active response scale as a means of measuring the effect of communication. Then we find an analysis of various methods of measuring attitudes (Tittle and Hill).

33-C MEASURING THE PROCESS OF COMMUNICATIONS EFFECT

Harold Mendelsohn (Educator)

Let us begin with five propositions:

Proposition 1: Communications can and often do affect individuals' actions directly.

Proposition 2: Effect occurs as a broad psychological process, rather than on an either-or simple learning basis.

Proposition 3: Effect is not necessarily equally distributed among all recipients of a given communication.

Proposition 4: The dynamic through which the effect process occurs is cumulative within the individual, going from a rather rudimentary psychological brush with the communication to actually being activated by it.

Proposition 5: If effect represents a unidimensional process that operates via a cumulative dynamic, it can be measured by Guttman techniques.

Let us explore the roots and research implications of these propositions. It is evident from past communications investigations that learning is related to effect. It is also evident that emotion and activation are similarly related to effect. Taking these two considerations into account, it is possible to develop the following construct relating to the effects of communications.

In gauging whether a communication has induced action (either in terms of disposition to act or actual behavior), consideration must be given to ascertaining whether some degree of learning has taken place. However, simple learning rarely occurs in a psychological vacuum. More often than not, learning is accompanied by emotion. In fewer instances, not

only is learning accompanied by emotion, but it is also accompanied by activation.

It follows, then, that before a communication can induce action, no simple event like learning (i.e. retention of content) is sufficient to induce that action.

This leads to a hypothesis of involvement. The involvement hypothesis suggests a totality of psychological experience with a communication in terms of learning, feeling, and preparing oneself to act as a consequence of exposure. The greater the involvement that the communication produces, then the more effective it can be considered.

If the indicators of involvement can be isolated, an instrument will be available for gauging not only gross effect but the degree of effect that communications produce on different types of audiences. Such a measurement will afford an opportunity for bringing to bear new insights into the processes of effect under varying circumstances, and will ultimately lead to generalizations about the relationships between various forms of communications content and audiences on whom different types of effect are produced.

The Active Response Scale

We have been experimenting in developing such a measure for the past two years. Thus far the results of this work have been most promising on a prima-facie basis. In developing the Active Response Scale, item analysis procedures were first used to test the relationships among and between indicators, such as "recall," "liking," "believing," "accepting," and an independent criterion—disposition to act in favor of certain advertised products. After much investigation, it was determined that there was no empirical evidence in defense of

SOURCE: Harold Mendelsohn, "Measuring the Process of Communications Effect," *Public Opinion Quarterly*, Vol. 26 (Fall, 1962), pp. 411–416, at pp. 413–416.

such unitary, isolated, and variable criteria. This eliminated the possibility of an additive scale of such items.

At the same time, these preliminary investigations indicated that a number of items were "hanging together" consistently. Further study showed these items to have cumulative Guttman-like properties. At this point our thinking switched to the concept of effect as being a process—a cumulative process. By applying the H technique to the promising items, a three-item contrived scale was developed and tested.

Currently, the Active Response Scale distinguishes among three types of response to a communication: rudimentary response, emotional response, and active response. The determination of whether a recipient responds rudimentarily is based on his ability to recall something about the communication. The determination of whether a recipient responds emotionally is based on recall plus his affirmative answers to the following types of items: (1) the experience of an emotional reaction as opposed to a feeling of indifference toward the communication, (2) a feeling of greater friendliness toward the source of the communication, (3) a feeling that the communication was "getting through" to him. The determination of whether a recipient responds actively is based on recall, emotional reaction, plus responses of the following types: (1) an expression that the recipient has learned something about the idea, product, or service that will help him decide in its favor; (2) a declaration that the recipient considers the idea, product, or service worth recommending to others; (3) an expressed desire to follow up or to look into or try the idea, product, or service discussed in the communication.

Thus far, the reproducibility scores for communications tested with the Active Response technique have been well over the 90 per cent established as a minimum standard for a Guttman scale. The error ratios for these tests have fallen well below the 50 per cent limit that is considered acceptable for a Guttman scale.

Past efforts with the Active Response Scale allow for comparing the effectiveness of one communication with that of another in terms of the amount of Active Response it generates. Furthermore, by carefully probing the contributory influences of various elements in the communication on each level on the scale, it is now possible to discern without second-guessing the content factors most closely related to particular types of effect. This ability to offer relative measurement as well as to pinpoint contributory factors to effect suggests that the scale can be used simultaneously both diagnostically and metrically. It affords a simple yet powerful tool for conducting a wide variety of studies where format can be held constant and content can be altered and vice versa; where trends can not only be recorded but readily interpreted; and where predictions of likely effects can be made from audience reactions to draft versions of the finished communication.

Finally, Active Response research has indicated that the same individuals can and do react differently to different communications and that different individuals can and do react similarly to the same communications. This leads us to suspect the fruitfulness of the "persuasibility" theory of effect. At the same time, because we can actually discern the sociological and psychological characteristics of audiences who have been affected differentially by the same communication, we are now in a position to study rather systematically what the interrelationships between content appeals and audience needs, values, drives, motivations, and attitudes are under varying circumstances.

Thus far the utility of the Active Response approach has been demonstrated in its application to both diagnostic and metric problems in communications research.

For example, the Active Response Scale has been used to examine the appropriateness of humor in advertising. It was found that high Active Response is more likely to occur when the humor is at the expense of the advertiser or communicator rather than at the expense of a character with whom the audience identifies.

In another series of studies, the Active Response technique was used to determine the efficacy of simple punishment-reward appeals. The findings from these experiments suggest that both punishment and reward symbols must be in balance before effect as indicated by high Active Response can take place.

Should a "practical" or a "romantic" appeal be used to advertise a certain paper product to female consumers? When an Active Response study was addressed to this problem, it turned out that the approaches had similar strengths. That is to say, gross Active Response scores for the two different approaches were about equal. However, when the two samples were controlled for orientations and attitudes that were either practical or romantic, it became clear that each subgroup of "practicals" and "romantics" was most strongly activated by its own appropriate appeal. This particular advertiser was faced with the interesting problem of reaching two distinctive audiences with his selling messages.

In several studies of audience "post" reactions to advertisements, Active Response data helped guide decisions relating to their continuation, modification, or withdrawal. Here, not only over-all measurements were

derived of the "good" advertisements as compared with the "poor" ones, but from subgroup analyses we were able to determine precisely those elements in the communications that were responsible for differences in reactions. Thus, while the inhibiting elements in these communications were being discarded, the high Active Response stimulating elements could be rescued for future use.

Still an additional use to which the Active Response approach has been put has been in the pre-testing area. In this respect Active Response tests have predicted from reactions to "rough" and "unfinished" versions of communications how the finished versions of the same communications would be received by various strata in the target audiences.

33-D MEASURING ATTITUDES

Charles R. Tittle (Sociologist) and
Richard J. Hill (Sociologist)

The techniques evaluated were: (1) Thurstone successive-interval technique, (2) a semantic differential procedure, (3) a summated-rating (Likert) technique, and (4) a Guttman type scale. In addition, a simple self rating of attitude was examined. The efficiency of each of the five measures was assessed in terms of its correspondence with five criteria of behavior. The assessment was made under the conditions discussed above. These conditions were expected to maximize the relationship between measured attitudes and criterion behaviors.

Others have argued that if one wishes to predict a particular set of behaviors he should attempt to measure an attitude that is specific for a given individual as he relates to that class of behavior. Given this argument, maximizing the credibility of the present study required an attempt to measure a specific rather than a general attitude. One would not expect to predict an individual's personal behavior with respect to his own marriage from a measure of his attitude toward marriage as

a social institution. In the present instance, attitude toward personal participation in student political activity was taken as an appropriate measurement objective.

One hundred forty-five statements thought to reflect such an attitude were placed on a successive interval continuum by 213 student judges. The statements were formulated by the authors and several graduate students, using the literature on political participation in the larger society for suggestive outlines. These items were oriented around eight possible channels of individual political activity: (1) voting in student elections, (2) belonging to student political groups, (3) taking part in student political party activities, (4) taking part in student campaign activities, (5) keeping informed about student politics, (6) contact with student government officials, (7) interpersonal discussion of student politics, and (8) personal office holding or seeking.

The panel of judges consisted of entire classes of students, selected to give a broad representation of the student population. The statements were printed in eight-page booklets with the pages arranged randomly, and were submitted for judging with the customary instructions.[1] Following the procedures dis-

SOURCE: Charles R. Tittle and Richard J. Hill, "Attitude Measurement and Prediction of Behavior: an Evaluation of Conditions and Measurement Techniques," *Sociometry*, Vol. 30 (June, 1967), pp. 199-213, at pp. 205-210.

[1] The Seashore and Hevner method of rating items

cussed by Edwards, successive-interval scale and Q values for the statements were calculated.[2] Fifteen statements were selected so that the scale values were approximately evenly spaced on the continuum and Q values were minimal.[3] For the test sample, the median scoring technique was used.[4]

The summated rating scale was built from the same basic 145 statements. Four editors independently classified the statements as to their favorable or unfavorable content. Those statements about which all four agreed were submitted to a separate sample of 213 students. The subjects were asked to respond to each statement on a five-point scale: strongly agree, agree, undecided, disagree, strongly disagree. Responses were weighted in the standard Likert fashion from zero to four. The fifteen items that discriminated best between the top fifty and the bottom fifty subjects were selected for this scale.

A semantic differential employing nine adjectival pairs was constructed for five concepts: (1) voting in student elections, (2) discussing student political issues, (3) holding student political office, (4) helping in a student political campaign, and (5) keeping informed about student politics. The nine adjectival pairs utilized were: good-bad, valuable-worthless, clean-dirty, pleasant-unpleasant, wise-foolish, fair-unfair, complex-simple, active-passive, and deep-shallow. The first six pairs represent the evaluative or attitude dimension. They were interspersed with the remaining three to obscure the purpose of the measurement (a procedure recommended by the originators of the semantic differential).[5] Pairs were selected using the criteria suggested by

Osgood and his associates. Scores on all five concepts were summed and a mean taken as an ordinal measure of attitude toward personal participation in student political activity.

A set of items constituting a Guttman scale was derived using the same responses as those utilized for constructing the summated rating scale. A random sample of 95 questionnaires was selected from the 213 respondents. The statements were examined for scalability using the Cornell technique. Ten items, six dichotomous and four trichotomous, were found to form a scale with a coefficient of reproducibility of .928 and a minimal reproducibility of .635. All error appeared to be random.

These Guttman attitude items were retested for scalability after being administered to the test sample ($N = 301$). The items met the criteria of scalability for this sample but only when used in dichotomous form. Accordingly the four trichotomous items were collapsed into dichotomies. The final scale had a coefficient of reproducibility of .930 and a minimal marginal reproducibility of .751. Menzel's coefficient of scalability for these data was .717,[6] and Schuessler's Test I resulted in a probability of less than .001.[7]

Once the instruments were constructed they were incorporated into a questionnaire including items about the student's background, participation in student political activity, and his group affiliations on the campus. In addition, the questionnaire included an item eliciting a self-rating of attitude toward student politics on a continuum from zero to eight. This questionnaire was administered to two large sections of a course in marriage and the family, which was composed of a widely variant student population. Freshmen were

was used. See Robert H. Seashore and Kate Hevner, "A Time-Saving Device for the Construction of Attitude Scales," *Journal of Social Psychology*, 4 (August, 1933), pp. 366-372.

[2] Allen L. Edwards, *Techniques of Attitude Scale Construction*, New York: Appleton, Century, Crofts, 1957, pp. 123-138. An internal consistency test yielded an Absolute Average Deviation of .034, a value slightly higher than usually reported when the method of successive intervals is used to scale stimuli.

[3] This was not entirely possible, since only a few statements were found to have scale values near the middle of the continuum.

[4] Edwards, *op. cit.*, p. 145.

[5] Charles E. Osgood, George S. Suci, and Percy

H. Tannenbaum, *The Measurement of Meaning*, Urbana: The University of Illinois Press, 1957. The same six evaluative pairs were used by Osgood and his associates in comparing the semantic differential with other measures of attitude. See pp. 192-195.

[6] Menzel suggests the level of acceptance for scales at somewhere between .60 and .65. Cf. Herbert Menzel, "A New Coefficient for Scalogram Analysis," *Public Opinion Quarterly*, 17 (Summer, 1953), pp. 268-280.

[7] Karl F. Schuessler, "A Note on the Statistical Significance of the Scalogram," *Sociometry*, 24 (September, 1961), pp. 312-318.

TABLE 1

Interrelationship Among Criterion Measures

	Vote over Time	Guttman Index	Likert Index	Woodward-Roper Index
Vote in last election	.778	.559	.636	.632
Vote over time	—	.577	.757	.789
Guttman index of political participation	—	—	.850	.721
Likert index of political participation	—	—	—	.869

eliminated from consideration as were students who failed to provide complete data. The final set of subjects was composed of 301 upper-class students.

Development of Criterion Measures

The criterion behavior was indexed in several ways. First, the voting behavior of each subject was determined by inspecting student-voting records in an election held one week prior to the administration of the questionnaire. Second, the respondent's report of his voting behavior for the previous four elections was taken as a behavioral indicator. Third, an index of behavioral patterns was constructed by combining responses to questions about frequency of engagement in various types of student political activity. Eight activities were found to form a Guttman scale for the 301 subjects. These activities included frequency of participation in meetings of a student assembly, frequency with which the individual had written to or talked with a student representative concerning an issue, frequency of voting over the past four elections, frequency of engagement in campaign activities on behalf of a particular candidate, frequency of reading the platforms of candidates for student political office, and frequency of discussion of student political issues in talking with friends. When the items were dichotomized, the scale was characterized by a coefficient of reproducibility of .907 and a minimal marginal reproducibility of .698. Again error appeared to be random. Menzel's coefficient of scalability was .675 and Schuessler's Test I yielded a probability of less than .001.

The fourth index of student political participation was devised by summing, in Likert fashion, the categories of response concerning frequency of engagement in ten types of stu-

dent political activity. These activities included the eight previously mentioned as well as the frequency of personal office seeking and response to an item indicating whether the respondent had ever written a letter of protest to the student newspaper. A fifth measure of participation was an adaptation of the standard Woodward-Roper index of political participation involving a modified scoring of five of the activities already listed.[8]

The five criterion indexes were designed to represent alternate methods of measuring the same behavioral patterns. The degree of association between the criterion measures is reported in Table 1. In general, the magnitude of assocation is relatively high. All measures of association are in the expected direction and are significantly non-zero at a probability level less than .001. These results suggest that the various indexes measured approximately the same aspects of the students' political involvement.

The degree of interrelationship of the several attitude measures varied considerably (see Table 2). This points up the fact that various methods of measuring the same characteristic may result in the ordering of individuals quite differently. Presumably the variation is accounted for by error factors intrinsic to the measurement techniques. An assessment of the extent to which such factors affect the predictive power of the several instruments in this specific instance is presented below. Moreover, the present research design permitted certain inferences to be made about the nature of the error factors involved.

[8] See Julian L. Woodward and Elmo Roper, "Political Activity of American Citizens," *American Political Science Review*, 44 (December, 1950), pp. 872-885.

TABLE 2

Interrelationship Among Attitude Measures

	Gutt-man	Thur-stone	Sem Diff	Self-Rating
Likert	.796	.588	.619	.511
Guttman	—	.445	.523	.476
Thurstone	—	—	.432	.337
Sem Diff	—	—	—	.387

The behavioral indexes included one "objective" indicator and several "reported" indicators of activity. This raises questions with respect to the adequacy of such a design for making the assessment here proposed. Specifically, it is known that reported behavior does not always correspond to actual behavior; and that the extent of error varies with kinds of information being reported.[9] In the present instance, it was possible to compare one report of a behavior with an independent record of that behavior. The subjects were asked if they had voted in the last student election. This report was compared with the voting records. In 11 per cent of the cases, the report and the record did not coincide. In 28 of the 33 instances of non-correspondence, subjects reported that they had voted when in fact they had not. In the remaining five cases, the subject's name was not included in the voting records. In these latter instances, it was not possible to determine whether the error resulted from inadequacies of the student government's record-keeping procedures or whether the subjects had falsified their names. The degree of error observed corresponds closely to that reported in the analysis of the political behavior of other populations.[10] Thus, the self-reported data in this instance appear to provide a fairly close approximation to the actual behavior of the subjects. This conclusion is reinforced by the findings reported in Table 1 which indicate relatively high association between recorded vote and four reported indexes of related behavior.

The present research design, then, permitted

[9] Hugh J. Parry and Helen M. Crossley, "Validity of Responses to Survey Questions," *Public Opinion Quarterly,* 14 (Spring, 1950), pp. 61-80.

[10] See Charles R. Tittle and Richard J. Hill, "A Note on the Accuracy of Self-Reported Data and Prediction of Political Activity," *Public Opinion Quarterly,* forthcoming.

the assessment of the relative efficiency of scaling techniques by determining the correspondence of five measures of attitude to five measures of other behavior, including a single act and four indexes of reported configurations of behavior. All the criterion indexes were composed of, or referred to, behaviors occurring under normal social circumstances, and they represented referents for specific non-hypothetical attitude components.

Further Procedures

The attitude measures and criterion indexes used in this study were treated as ordinal data. A frequency distribution for each attitude scale was obtained, and the categories were then collapsed into six ordered classes, following the convention of equalization of marginals. The Guttman and Woodward-Roper indexes of participation also were collapsed into six categories. The seven categories of the summated index of participation were maintained to prevent a serious mal-distribution of category frequencies. The association between each scale and each index was measured by the Goodman-Kruskal gamma. Since gamma is somewhat sensitive to marginal distributions, and perhaps, the number of cells in a contingency table, care was taken to make comparisons across rows where tables with approximately equal cell numbers and marginal distributions were involved.

Results

The results reported in Table 3 indicate that only a moderate degree of correspondence between measured attitude and other behavior can be observed when (1) scaling techniques are employed to measure attitude and (2) the behavioral criterion is based upon a consideration of a series of acts occurring under normal circumstances. On the other hand, the data do show that the degree of correspondence observed is at least in part a function of the methodological conditions which maintain.

The data support the argument that greater correspondence between measured attitude and other behavior can be found when the behavioral criterion incorporates a wide range of activity with respect to the attitude object under consideration. Although the findings are not decisive, they do reveal that in five of six instances greatest association was found be-

TABLE 3

Associations[1] Between Attitude Measures and Behavioral Indexes

Behavior Index	Attitude Measure					
	15-Item Likert	10-Item Likert	Guttman	Self	Sem Diff	Thurstone
Record vote	.504	.459	.391	.285	.350	.318
Vote over time	.493	.423	.329	.365	.309	.213
Guttman index	.553	.559	.421	.410	.335	.248
Likert index	.619	.612	.535	.495	.364	.257
W-R index	.548	.535	.419	.425	.335	.238
Mean association	.543	.518	.419	.396	.339	.255

[1] Gamma.

tween the attitude measures and the Likert-type index which was derived from ten distinct kinds of behavior. The data also show that, in general, lower association was found for the voting indexes than for the Guttman and Woodward-Roper indexes based respectively on eight and five kinds of activity. Such results support the contention that the appropriate criterion measure to use in evaluating the predictive efficacy of attitude measure is one that includes sets of acts indicative of consistent or patterned behavior.

With respect to the assessment of the alternative measurement strategies, the results indicate that there is wide variation in the predictive power of the various instruments. In this instance, the Likert scale was clearly the best predictor of behavior. It was most highly associated with every one of the five behavioral indexes. The Thurstone scale showed the poorest correspondence—in only one case did it produce better prediction than any of the other measures. In fact, in four of five instances a simple self rating of attitude provided better results than the elaborate Thurstone procedure.

34 / Persuasion

A. BACKGROUND AND THEORY

The section begins with a brief look at the ethics of mass persuasion (Maloney). The second selection (Engel) points up the relevance of psychology for the understanding of economic behavior. The third reading (McGuire) is a discussion of what effect a person's awareness of an intent to persuade has on the amount of opinion change that is generated.

34-A THE ETHICS OF MASS PERSUASION

John C. Maloney (Psychologist)

All professional mind makers have been criticized at one time or another for the indiscreet use of their meager powers to manipulate the noosphere.

Science professors are criticized for instilling a narrow, mechanistic simplemindedness in their students while humanities instructors are blamed for encouraging an impractical muddle-headedness. Television and movie producers are accused of encouraging an emotional immaturity in the public mind and the press is lambasted for its vested interest in catastrophe and its supposed tendency to raise the "hostility potential" of the public.

Politicians, priests and ministers are regularly attacked by all but their own converts and advertisers are criticized for their "hidden persuasion" and inclinations to make people want things for all the wrong reasons.

Whether these criticisms are just or unjust in any given instance each group has had two consistent lines of defense. First of all, each group acknowledges a potential danger of mass persuasion by other groups but claims a

SOURCE: John C. Maloney, "Advertising Research and an Emerging Science of Mass Persuasion," *Journalism Quarterly*, Vol. 41 (Autumn, 1964), pp. 517–528, at p. 528.

singular immunity from such guilt on its own part. As a second line of defense each group points to the rugged independence of its audience membership and cites its own record of incompetence.

But the scientific study of mass persuasion puts a new face on both the criticisms and the defenses. There is surely nothing ethical or unethical about the basic process of mass persuasion itself. Any of us might agree that we would prefer to be the persuader, rather than the persuaded, but no one can deny that modern society would stop functioning effectively without some means of ordering public opinions and mass behaviors in many different spheres.

Neither is there anything sinister nor laudable in the mere fact that man is learning more about the mass persuasion processes. No advertiser, politician, minister nor any other "mind maker" can remain ethical merely by remaining incompetent.

There can be no doubt, however, that the ethics of mass persuasion take on a greater importance as sophistication in the field increases. Mass persuaders are being deprived of the generalized defense of incompetence.

In a recent address, Kingman Brewster Jr., president of Yale University, offered some advice that might well be heeded by mass persuasion scientists and practitioners alike:

Experimentation and quantification of human and social behavior will mark the intellectual revolution of your time. Do not fight it. But having welcomed it, do not expect the newly scientific study of man and society to relieve you of the moral overload of judgment.

34-B PSYCHOLOGY AND THE BUSINESS SCIENCES

James F. Engel (Marketing Educator)

The behavioral sciences have much to contribute in the way of concepts, explanations, and theories. Psychology, in particular, is highly relevant for the understanding of economic behavior. To grasp the significance of cross-fertilization at the conceptual level, however, it is necessary to examine the problems faced by the psychologist and his approach to their solution.

As might be expected, the analysis of human behavior is a complex and baffling activity. It is extremely difficult, first of all, to isolate both the causes and effects of behavior because man has an extended time perspective. His behavior is influenced by the past, the current, and the anticipated future environment. For this reason, the psychologist often has chosen to study animal behavior, because the animal lives basically in the present. Moreover, the psychological simplicity of most non-human subjects greatly simplifies the isolation and manipulation of behavioral variables. So-called "rat" psychology often is depreciated by the layman, but the contributions have been great. Animal studies can be revealing, but only if the rat is considered as an object of comparative study and not as a substitute for man.

The psychologist's task is further complicated by the fact that the mental factors determining behavior seldom can be observed directly and must, therefore, be inferred. A simple diagram may serve to clarify the nature of this problem.

Antecedents represent the complex of forces motivating behavior. The diagram indicates that mental processes stand between the antecedents of behavior and the behavior itself. One's psychological make-up might be con-

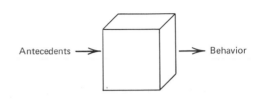

Antecedents ⟶ ⟶ Behavior

ceived as an unobservable "black box," because it is forever hidden from view.

Assume that a person is found to react vehemently when shown a Communist flag. A relationship is thus established between antecedent (the flag) and behavior (the reaction). This relationship perhaps is explained by something which took place within the "black box," but such explanations cannot be observed directly from the experiment. We might say that the subject's actions were caused by a strong anti-Communist attitude. Yet what is an attitude? An attitude represents only an inference which is made concerning whatever transpired within the black box, and the inferred explanations often are called "intervening variables." As Brown observes:

> The qualifying adjective "intervening" is used to convey the notion that postulated states, conditions, or processes intervene between behavior and its observable correlates or antecedents. Since these variables cannot be observed directly, their meanings are provided by explicit definitions and by their functional relations within the context of general theories of behavior.[1]

Important explanatory variables including such common terms as perception, drive, ego, inferiority complex, and countless others all are inferred; they have never been "proved" and never will be.[2] Unobserved intervening

SOURCE: James F. Engel, "Psychology and the Business Sciences," *The Quarterly Review of Economics and Business*, Vol. 1 (November, 1961), pp. 75–83, at pp. 75–78.

[1] Judson S. Brown, *The Motivation of Behavior* (New York: McGraw-Hill, 1961), p. 28.
[2] Intervening variables need not involve only

variables are not so common in the physical sciences, since many of the explanatory forces can be observed and measured. For instance, pressure is applied to a piece of metal and it bends. Both a cause and an effect are present, but in addition, examination may disclose that the material bent because of a rearrangement of molecules. Such verifiable explanations of cause and effect relationships will seldom be found in the behavioral sciences.

The Psychologist's Approach

Let us once again refer to the "black box" diagram.

The antecedents have now been designated as S (stimulus) and O (organic state). Behavior has been labeled R (response). While it is impossible to classify all empirical relationships, the most common analytical procedures involve (1) S-R relationships; (2) O-R relationships; and (3) R-R relationships.

1. S-R RELATIONSHIPS. The S-R relationship comprehends the manipulation of a physical or environmental factor serving to energize behavior, and the recording of subsequent responses. An inference is made from this relationship as to the explanatory factor which imparted form and direction to the response.

While S-R studies abound in the psychological literature, one especially interesting example might be cited. Asch, in a classic study, assembled groups of (usually) seven people, six of whom were briefed beforehand to behave in a certain manner. The subjects were seated and shown a number of lines one at a time on separate cards. They were then asked to indicate which of three predetermined standard lengths came the closest to representing the length of each line shown. Verbal responses were made by the knowl-

edgeable subjects before the "naïve" person responded, and in a majority of instances the group intentionally stated false replies.[3]

The naïve subject was thus exposed to a compound stimulus composed of the lines, standards of comparison, and the false responses of the group. His responses were then recorded. Evidence indicated that a majority of those placed in such a situation tended to modify their judgment to conform to group opinion, even though they were aware that this was inconsistent with their judgment. It might be concluded that the modification resulted because of a need to conform to group norms, yet it is obvious that this mental process within the black box cannot be observed or verified.

2. O-R RELATIONSHIPS. O-R relationships are very similar to S-R relationships, the only difference being the substitution of organic states for environmental stimuli. A rather obvious O-R relationship would be established if subjects were deprived of sleep for a long period and manifested the typical reactions of hallucinations and abnormal behavior. In the same sense, absence of food and the resulting behavior comprise an O-R relationship.

3. R-R RELATIONSHIPS. Dependable S-R relationships frequently present methodological hurdles because of the difficulty of isolating the behavioral effects of any given stimulus. As a result, behavior often is analyzed by patterns of responses over time in the hope of establishing predictive relationships. Explanatory variables existent within the black box then are inferred from responses without reference to behavioral antecedents.

An R-R relationship would occur if consumption of meat by a family were studied over time. Soon a fairly stable pattern of response would emerge which would hold some predictive value. Similarly, psychological test scores are occasionally found to be useful in predicting salesmen's effectiveness. The plotting of test scores against subsequent selling success or lack of success is an R-R relationship.

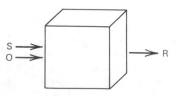

mental processes but can be accounted for by many factors such as organic states or differences in stimulus conditions.

[3] S. E. Asch, "Effects of Group Pressure Upon Modification and Distortion of Judgments," in G. E. Swanson, T. M. Newcomb, and E. L. Hartley, eds., *Readings in Social Psychology* (New York: Holt, 1952), pp. 2–11.

34-C INTENT TO PERSUADE

William J. McGuire (Psychologist)

The past several years have seen a revival of interest in what effect the subject's awareness of the source's persuasive intent has on the amount of opinion change produced by a communication. Earlier work by Hovland and his colleagues suggested that perception of intent to persuade lowered the source's credibility and thus his persuasive impact. Allyn & Festinger[1] found little difference in the persuasive impact of a speech on subjects led to suspect that their persuasibility was being measured, as compared to those led to believe that they would be asked to assess the speaker's personality after his speech. An internal analysis, however, suggested that for those subjects who felt the issue was important or had extreme initial opinion, the message had more persuasive impact in the disguised "personality" condition than in the overt "opinion" condition. Two studies by Walster & Festinger[2] showed that, when subjects listened in on a conversation from behind a one-way window, they were more persuaded by the conversation if they thought the discussants were unaware that they were being overheard (and thus couldn't be talking with the intent to persuade) than when the speakers were depicted as being aware that the subjects were listening, provided the subjects had strong initial feelings on the issue.

FOREWARNING VERSUS DISTRACTION. Festinger & Maccoby[3] suggested an alternative "distraction" interpretation for the Allyn & Festinger

results. (Seldom has so slight an effect been made to bear so heavy a burden of explanation.) According to this reinterpretation, it was not so much that the opinion orientation decreased the persuasive impact by making the source suspect, as that the personality-orientation increased the persuasive impact by distracting the subject so that the message hit with his defenses down. (From a simple learning theory interpretation one would expect distraction to have the opposite effect, interfering with comprehension of the argument and thus lowering persuasive impact.) To test their distraction notion, Festinger & Maccoby[4] presented a recorded persuasive message with a relevant or irrelevant (distraction) pictorial accompaniment. In some of their replications they found that this irrelevant film enhanced the persuasive effectiveness of the message. The difference appeared only with concerned subjects and was slight in magnitude but, in some cases, it reached the conventional levels of statistical significance.

One possible artifact in the Festinger & Maccoby study was that the distracting film was actually quite entertaining so that the subjects who were shown it during the speech may have been more persuaded because they heard it in a better humor than did the subjects who saw the dull, relevant film. Gregory Razran long ago reported that political slogans made more of an impact on subjects eating a free lunch than on subjects smelling unpleasant odors while they heard the slogans. A recent study by Janis, Kaye & Kirschner[5] showed similarly that things go better with Coke. In each of two replications they found that students showed more opinion change if they were given a snack of peanuts and Pepsi while reading a series of persuasive commu-

SOURCE: William J. McGuire, "Attitudes and Opinions," *Annual Review of Psychology*, Vol. 17 (1966), pp. 475–514, at pp. 481–482. Copyright 1966 by the American Psychological Association, and reproduced by permission.

[1] Allyn, J., and Festinger, L. "The Effectiveness of Unanticipated Persuasive Communications," *J. Abnorm. Soc. Psychol.*, 62, 35–40 (1961).
[2] Walster, E., and Festinger, L. "The Effectiveness of 'Overheard' Persuasive Communications," *J. Abnorm. Soc. Psychol.*, 65, 395–402 (1962).
[3] Festinger, L., and Maccoby, N. "On Resistance to Persuasive Communications," *J. Abnorm. Soc. Psychol.*, 68, 359–66 (1964).
[4] Same reference as footnote 3.
[5] Janis, I. L., Kaye, D., and Kirschner, P. "Facilitating Effects of 'Eating-While-Reading' on Responsiveness to Persuasive Communications," *J. Personality Soc. Psychol.*, 1, 181–86 (1965).

nications than if they were given no food while reading. There was no persuasion difference between the no-food and an unpleasant odor group. These opinion change differences cannot be attributed to gratitude to the experimenter, since he disassociated himself from the position taken in the message.

B. RESEARCH AND APPLICATIONS

In this section we consider the effects of source and message content on persuasive communication (Engel, Kollat, and Blackwell).

34-D THE PERSUASIVE COMMUNICATION: EFFECTS OF SOURCE AND MESSAGE CONTENT

James F. Engel (Marketing Educator), David T. Kollat, (Marketing Educator), and Roger D. Blackwell (Marketing Educator)

There is now an extensive literature on variations in the persuasive message and consequent attitude change. Sometimes it is naïvely assumed that these findings can be applied universally to marketing. This clearly is not true, but there are some important insights to be gained. Therefore, a wide variety of evidence is critically examined to discover the extent to which valid generalizations emerge.

Effects of the Message Source

It would seem to be plausible intuitively that a trustworthy and credible source would produce greater attitude change, all other things being equal, as opposed to one of doubtful veracity. Admittedly, the originator of the message achieves credibility by demonstrated trustworthiness and superior ability on the questions raised. Therefore, his perceived competence should enhance the persuasive power of the message.

Others, however, hypothesize quite a different effect from a favorable message source. Assume that a person who is a recognized authority on automobiles tells his neighbor that he should trade his old jalopy and switch to a different brand. The neighbor might be quite threatened by such a statement and

engage in an opposite behavior. In this case he experiences what Brehm refers to as *psychological reactance,* because he feels that his freedom of choice and viewpoint is threatened.[1] Since he perceives that a definite attempt is being made to make him change, he reacts in a contrary fashion to preserve his freedom to act and think.

As the evidence reviewed below shows, both effects have been observed, although the balance of findings favors the first hypothesis

THE EVIDENCE. A brief description of one typical study will suffice to indicate the general research approach most experimenters follow in attitude research. Hovland and Weiss exposed four groups of college students to different communications, while the only variation being in the source of the message.[2] One topic, for example, was the sale of antihistamine drugs without prescription, and source expertise was varied by attributing the communication to the *New England Journal of Biology and Medicine* in one instance and to a pictorial magazine in the other.

In general, there is a strong convergence of evidence that a credible source produces significantly greater attitude change than an

[1] J. W. Brehm, *A Theory of Psychological Reactance* (New York: Academic Press, 1966), Chap. VI.
[2] C. I. Hovland and W. Weiss, "The Influence of Source Credibility on Communication Effectiveness," *Public Opinion Quarterly,* Vol. 15 (1951), pp. 635–650.

incredible counterpart.[3] Several studies have produced contradictory findings, although there is, as yet, no convincing confirmation of Brehm's reactance hypothesis.[4]

THE DURATION OF CHANGE. By duration is meant the length of time that change persists. There are many studies indicating that the difference in change produced by credible versus incredible sources *disappears* in approximately one month's time.[5] Cohen hypothesized that the content of the message is retained while the source is forgotten.[6] With the element of credibility thus removed, the receiver evaluates the evidence as he normally would. This explanation is plausible, because most studies show that content retention seldom is affected by source credibility.[7]

IMPLICATIONS. For now it is assumed that the findings cited are valid. There is substantial basis to challenge this conclusion, but further discussion is reserved until more communication evidence is presented and evaluated.

It is interesting to speculate regarding the extent to which salesmen are perceived as being *both* expert and trustworthy, the essential requirements of credibility. It would seem that most consumers feel that the salesman has a high intent to persuade and thus would show strong reactance against what he has to say. Nevertheless, a properly trained salesman can serve as a valuable source of information, and there is no reason why credibility cannot be greatly improved in personal selling situations. Unfortunately this point is often overlooked, especially by retailers, and salesmen are not properly trained to become a credible information source.

Quite a different problem, however, is posed by an advertising manager. How can an advertisement be made credible when it is obvious that the whole intent of the message is to persuade? The recipient generally recognizes that the source is anything but impartial and unbiased. Therefore, source credibility does not appear to be a variable that can be manipulated effectively in this context, although a well-known firm clearly has an advantage in this respect. Nevertheless, an advertisement is generally perceived as a paid commercial message, and, although much valuable information and persuasive power can be imparted, this probably occurs in spite of relatively low credibility.

The fact that retention of facts remains unaffected regardless of source credibility has some interesting implications. Perhaps the salesman who was unsuccessful in closing his sale could return much later and capitalize upon the facts the prospect retains from his earlier call. This seems unlikely, however, because the appearance of the salesman once again reinstates the earlier negative feelings and minimizes his chance for success.[8] Therefore, in the typical selling situation it still

[3] See F. Haiman, "An Experimental Study of the Effects of Ethos in Public Speaking," *Speech Monographs*, Vol. 16 (1949), pp. 190–202; E. Aronson, J. Turner, and J. Carlsmith, "Communicator Credibility and Communication Discrepancy as Determinants of Opinion Change," *Journal of Abnormal and Social Psychology*, Vol. 67 (1963), pp. 31–36; E. Aronson and B. Golden, "The Effect of Relevant and Irrelevant Aspects of Communicator Credibility on Opinion Change," *Journal of Personality*, Vol. 30 (1962), pp. 135–146; H. Kelman and C. I. Hovland, "Reinstatement of the Communicator in Delayed Measurement of Opinion Change," *Journal of Abnormal and Social Psychology*, Vol. 48 (1953), pp. 327–335; and B. Bettleheim and M. Janowitz, "Reactions to Fascist Propaganda: A Pilot Study," *Public Opinion Quarterly*, Vol. 10 (1946), pp. 168–190.

[4] See B. Fine, "Conclusion Drawing, Communicator Credibility and Anxiety as Factors in Opinion Change," *Journal of Abnormal and Social Psychology*, Vol. 54 (1957), pp. 369–374; and C. I. Hovland and W. Mandell, "An Experimental Comparison of Conclusion Drawing by the Communicator and by the Audience," *Journal of Abnormal and Social Psychology*, Vol. 47 (1952), pp. 581–588.

[5] Hovland and Weiss; Kelman and Hovland; and W. Watts and W. McGuire, "Persistence of Induced Opinion Change and Retention of the Inducing Message Content," *Journal of Abnormal and Social Psychology*, Vol. 68 (1964), pp. 233–241.

[6] A Cohen, *Attitude Change and Social Influence* (New York: Basic Books, Inc., 1964), pp. 23–37.

[7] See P. Secord and C. Backman, *Social Psychology* (New York: McGraw-Hill Book Company, Inc., 1964), pp. 127–132; 187–192.

[8] Kelman and Hovland, *loc. cit.*

seems best to attempt to close the sale on the first call.

The evidence on duration of change may be of greater relevance in advertising. If advertising is often a negative source, then a cessation of advertising may be wise after initial exposure. This assumes, of course, that some content was successfully communicated. Messages might be placed in periodic "bursts," therefore, followed by periods of cessation. The facts retained hopefully will stimulate a purchase once the negative feelings are forgotten.

Regardless of the strategy used to capitalize on duration of change effects, it is extremely difficult to isolate the consumer from stimuli that remind him of the earlier message and thereby reinforce the initial negative effect. Point-of-purchase displays, for example, are reminders, but perhaps they can be designed in such a way that the basic message or campaign theme is repeated without using the symbolism of the advertisement or personal selling message presented earlier.

Finally, the evidence suggests the persuasive impact of friends or relatives who, by recommending products or brands, generally are perceived as having no "ax to grind." These *opinion leaders* thus come to be evaluated as a highly credible source under many circumstances.

Admittedly much in this area is pure speculation which is not based on research undertaken in natural field conditions using advertisements and personal selling as the variable. Nevertheless, the importance of impartiality is clearly verified. Undoubtedly the image of certain commercial spokesmen is largely attributable to this type of reputation. Arthur Godfrey, for example, is often mentioned as a credible source who would not recommend a product that does not perform as claimed. Such spokesmen who capitalize upon credibility, however, are infrequent in the mass media.

Message Content

To what extent do variations in the message content affect attitude change? It seems obvious that some approaches should be more effective than others, and the literature to be reviewed here largely supports this conclusion. The relevance of the findings for marketing,

however, is less than it might seem at first for reasons discussed later. The findings are reviewed, and the implications then are assessed.

THE EXPERIMENTAL APPROACH. The usual design of an attitude-change study uses a laboratory-type situation as opposed to natural field conditions. Generally two or more matched groups of people are asked a series of questions to determine the attitude toward a topic. Then a communication is administered to only one of the groups, and the other serves as a control. Extent of change is assessed by change in the exposed group versus the control group.

ONE SIDE VERSUS TWO SIDES. In a widely quoted study, Hovland and others studied the effects of presenting just one side of a controversial topic versus two sides.[9] The results were as follows:

1. Giving both sides produced greatest attitude change in those instances where individuals were initially opposed to the point of view presented.

2. For those convinced of the main argument, presentation of the other side was ineffective.

3. Those with higher education were most affected when both sides were presented.

While it may appear that advertisers never could capitalize upon these findings, Faison suggests that such a conclusion may be premature.[10] He presented both favorable and unfavorable product attributes in advertisements for automobiles, ranges, and floor waxes. Hovland's results were completely verified, and this suggests that a two-sided presentation may be a totally overlooked way to increase promotional effectiveness. It might be quite a task, however, to convince a manufacturer that his advertising campaign also should mention product flaws.

PRIMACY VERSUS RECENCY. There now is a

[9] C. I. Hovland, A. A. Lumsdaine, and F. D. Sheffield, *Experiments on Mass Communication*, Vol. III (Princeton, N.J.: Princeton University Press, 1948), Chap. 8.

[10] E. W. Faison, "Effectiveness of One-Sided and Two-Sided Mass Communications in Advertising," *Public Opinion Quarterly*, Vol. 25 (1961), pp. 468–469.

considerable body of evidence, much of it conflicting and contradictory, on the subject of the order in which appeals should be presented. This assumes, of course, that there are two or more main arguments either related to each other or pro and con. Some people say that the first argument presented will prove to be most effective (*primacy*),[11] while others say that the most recently presented argument will dominate (*recency*). Research investigations have focused both on the order of appeals within a single message as well as the order in a series of messages.

The most comprehensive investigations have been undertaken by Hovland and his colleagues at Yale University.[12] Here are their major findings:

1. When two sides are presented successively by different communicators, the side presented first has no particular advantage.[13]

2. If a person is asked to indicate his position publicly after hearing one side, primacy is observed in that a subsequent presentation of the other side has little effect.[14]

3. The act of stating one's opinion anonymously after hearing one side in no way interferes with the effectiveness of the other side.[15] Primacy does not operate when anonymity is present.

4. When contradictory information is presented in one communication, there is a tendency for those items mentioned first to dominate those that follow.[16] This primacy

effect is reduced, however, by interpolating other activities between the two blocks of information and by warning people against the fallibility of a first impression.

5. Presentation of information relevant to need satisfaction produces the greatest effects when it follows rather than precedes need arousal.[17]

6. Presentation of desirable information first followed by less desirable content produces more change than a reverse order.[18]

7. When favorable arguments for a point of view are to be coupled with nonsalient opposing arguments, it is best to present the material in a pro-con order.[19]

It appears that neither primacy nor recency emerges as a dominant effect. Rather, the characteristics of individual situations also interact and become integrated with the presentation itself. Therefore, it is impossible to advance a valid generalization.[20]

One factor that affects both primacy and recency is the interval between presentation of the different arguments. Miller and Campbell argue that the Hovland studies have encompassed a contiguous presentation of both arguments and an immediate measure of change, thus giving the greatest advantage to the argument presented last (recency).[21] Primacy, on the other hand, apparently becomes most pronounced as the interval be-

[11] F. J. Lund, "The Psychology of Belief: IV. The Law of Primacy in Persuasion," *Journal of Abnormal and Social Psychology*, Vol. 20 (1925), pp. 183–191.

[12] C. I. Hovland, ed., *The Order of Presentation in Persuasion* (New Haven, Conn.: Yale University Press, 1957).

[13] C. I. Hovland and W. Mandell, "Is There a 'Law of Primacy' in Persuasion?" in Hovland, *The Order of Presentation in Persuasion*, pp. 13–22.

[14] C. I. Hovland, E. H. Campbell, and T. Brock, "The Effects of 'Commitment' on Opinion Change Following Communication," in Hovland, *The Order of Presentation in Persuasion*, pp. 23–32.

[15] Hovland and Mandell, "Is There a 'Law of Primacy' in Persuasion?"

[16] A. Luchins, "Primacy-Recency in Impression Formation," in Hovland, *The Order of Presentation in Persuasion*, pp. 33–61.

[17] A. R. Cohen, "Need for Cognition and Order of Communication as Determinants of Opinion Change," in Hovland, *The Order of Presentation in Persuasion*, pp. 79–97.

[18] W. J. McGuire, "Order of Presentation as a Factor in 'Conditioning' Persuasiveness," in Hovland, *The Order of Presentation in Persuasion*, pp. 98–114.

[19] I. L. Janis and R. L. Feierabend, "Effects of Alternate Ways of Ordering Pro and Con Arguments in Persuasive Communications," in Hovland, *The Order of Presentation in Persuasion*, pp. 115–128.

[20] J. T. Klapper, *The Effects of Mass Communication* (New York: The Free Press of Glencoe, 1960).

[21] N. Miller and D. T. Campbell, "Recency and Primacy in Persuasion as a Function of the Timing of Speeches and Measurements," *Journal of Abnormal and Social Psychology*, Vol. 59 (1959), pp. 1–9.

tween presentation of the second side and measurement of attitude change increases.[22]

Three theoretical interpretations have been advanced to explain order effects: (1) set; (2) reinforcement; and (3) sensory variation.[23] None appears to be complete in itself, but each offers some important clues.

1. By set is meant a tendency to evaluate later material against or in terms of the material first received.[24] This assumes either that the person is unfamiliar with the topic or that an initial opinion has been positively reinforced by the first argument.[25] Later studies have shown that the influence of set and the primacy that results seldom occur when the material is familiar;[26] in fact, if it occurs at all, it is only after an initial presentation of new and novel material.[27]

2. The reinforcement hypothesis states that the effect of an earlier communication on the persuasiveness of later messages depends upon the extent to which the first message was rewarding.[28] Although conceptually sound, there has been no consistent support for this hypothesis.[29]

3. Finally, the sensory-variation hypothesis states that human beings seek high cortical activation and hence react more strongly to novel rather than familiar stimuli.[30] Schultz's

arguments based on this theory[31] are judged by one authority to offer the best explanation of order effects.[32] Basically, the assumption is that the second appeal provides less cortical stimulation than the first, with the result that primacy occurs. This situation prevails, however, only if the first communication is novel; if it is familiar, then the level of cortical activation is not as high. Moreover, time intervention between presentations neutralizes the cortical level induced by the first message and causes the second to be more effective through recency.

The only valid conclusion at this time is that primacy or recency depends entirely on the mediating effects of such factors as novelty, familiarity with the issue, and interpolation of activity between presentation of successive arguments. Cohen concludes that the highly confused state of findings will be clarified only when more precise theories are evoked and tested that specify these types of interactions.[33] For now, little practical use can be made of the evidence.

DRAWING A SPECIFIC CONCLUSION. When presenting a persuasive message, should a definite conclusion be drawn or should this be left to the recipient? Once again the evidence is conflicting. The most solid positive evidence is provided by Hovland and Mandell; their results showed that more than twice as many people change in the direction advocated when the conclusion was stated than when it was left to the audience to form their own conclusions.[34] Others have found similar results.[35]

In general, however, the evidence has shown a contrary tendency.[36] Some researchers claim that a conclusion stated explicitly affects only comprehension of facts and not attitude

[22] C. A. Insko, "Primacy vs. Recency in Persuasion as a Function of the Timing of Arguments and Measures," *Journal of Abnormal and Social Psychology*, Vol. 69 (1964), pp. 381–391.

[23] R. E. Lana, "Three Theoretical Interpretations of Order Effects in Persuasive Communications," *Psychological Bulletin*, Vol. 69 (1964), pp. 314–320.

[24] Lana, "Three Theoretical Interpretations. . . ."

[25] Lana, "Three Theoretical Interpretations. . . ."

[26] R. E. Lana, "Controversy of the Topic and the Order of Presentation in Persuasive Communications," *Journal of Abnormal and Social Psychology*, Vol. 62 (1961), pp. 573–577; and D. P. Schultz, "Time Awareness and Order of Presentation in Opinion Change," *Journal of Applied Psychology*, Vol. 47 (1963), pp. 280–283.

[27] W. J. McGuire, "Attitudes and Opinions," in P. R. Farnsworth, O. McNemar, and Q. McNemar, eds., *Annual Review of Psychology*, Vol. 17 (Palo Alto, Calif.: Annual Reviews, Inc., 1966), p. 488.

[28] McGuire, p. 488.

[29] McGuire, p. 488.

[30] Lana, "Three Theoretical Interpretations. . . ."

[31] Schultz.

[32] Lana, "Three Theoretical Interpretations. . . ."

[33] Cohen, *Attitude Change and Social Influence*, p. 50.

[34] Hovland and Mandell.

[35] See, for example, D. Thistlewaite, H. deHaan, and J. Kamenetsky, "The Effects of 'Directive' and 'Nondirective' Communication Procedures on Attitudes," *Journal of Abnormal and Social Psychology*, Vol. 51 (1955), pp. 107–113.

[36] See Cohen, *Attitude Change and Social influence*, p. 10.

change. Others feel that no effect will be noticed at all on uncomplicated or easily understood issues.[37] Furthermore, the greatest effects are noted when the communication is aimed at people with lower intelligence.[38]

In most circumstances, therefore, it seems best to let the audience draw their own conclusions. As Brehm has pointed out, many people seem to react negatively when a conclusion is stated and feel that an attempt is being made to influence and thereby limit their freedom of choice. When this is the reaction, then a decided "boomerang" can occur through solidification of initial opinion.

[37] D. Krech, R. Crutchfield, and E. Ballachey, *Individual in Society* (New York: McGraw-Hill Book Company, Inc., 1962), pp. 242–243.
[38] Thistlewaite, deHaan, and Kamenetsky.

35 / Advertising

A. BACKGROUND AND THEORY

The section begins with an encyclopedia definition of advertising (Britt). This leads to a statement (Stigler) about advertising and the intellectual.

35-A WHAT IS ADVERTISING?

Steuart Henderson Britt (Psychologist)

Advertising is any paid form of nonpersonal presentation and promotion of products, services, or ideas by an identifiable individual or organization.

The products advertised may be as varied as toothpaste and automobiles, and the services may range from laundries to travel agencies. The ideas advertised may involve contributing to a mental health agency, voting for a certain candidate, or going to church on Sunday. In each case the advertising points out the qualities of the product, the service, or the idea that would make it attractive to the persons the advertiser wishes to influence.

A single advertisement is usually only part of a total advertising *campaign*. Although the purpose of the campaign is to stimulate people to thought and action, this does not imply that the goal of all advertising is to make a sale. Instead, the goal of advertising is to awaken or produce predispositions to buy the advertised product or service.

This may be illustrated by the following three categories of advertising (in which, however, there is some overlapping):

1. *Immediate action.* The primary purpose of some advertising is to induce immediate action. In this category is most newspaper adver-

tising—especially for bargain-priced products, special deals, coupon offers, foods, and department-store items—as well as mail-order advertising.

2. *Awareness.* Some advertising primarily creates an awareness on the part of the listener, viewer, or reader. This category includes announcements of a new product or model, improvements in a known product, a change in price, or a change in package design.

3. *Image.* Some advertising seeks principally to create, reinforce, or change an image of a product or service (or organization) in the minds of those to whom the advertising is directed. Usually it is expected that the desired change of attitude will take place gradually over a period of time.

About three-fourths of the dollars spent for advertising messages are invested in six media —newspapers, television, direct mail, magazines, radio, and outdoor, in that order. Advertising provides the principal source of revenue for these media, which cost consumers relatively little.

Many persons object to advertising because some of it seems silly to them. They then conclude erroneously that most advertising is deceptive. Yet actual untruths are rare in most advertising. In the United States, this is especially true of products and services advertised on a nationwide basis. For example, it would be hard to find anything misleading in national advertising for insurance, shirts, soups, television sets, or pens.

SOURCE: Steuart Henderson Britt, "Advertising" (New York: *Encyclopedia Americana,* Vol. 1 (1967), pp. 195–206, at pp. 195–196. Reprinted by permission of the publishers, Grolier Incorporated, New York.

416

One difficulty is that advertising tends to have a special language of its own. Most persons do not use such phrases as "cold, crisp taste," "fast, long-lasting, safe relief," or "volcano of fashion culture." Also, in many families more time is spent watching television than any other activity, and just looking at a great number of TV commercials over a long period of time leads many people to be critical of all advertising.

Some people who want new products and buy them make advertising the scapegoat by claiming that they were duped or forced into buying something they did not need. Yet the most far-reaching advertising campaign cannot force someone to buy something he does not want.

The consumer is still king (or queen) as to what he does with his money. The consumer is free to save or to spend his money in any way he wishes.

Advertising flourishes mainly in free-market, profit-oriented countries. It is one of the most important factors in accelerating the distribution of products and in helping to raise the standard of living.

This article deals with advertising in the United States. In Canada, advertising practices are similar to those in the United States, except that in the province of Quebec advertising often is presented in both English and French.

1. The Role of Advertising in the United States

INFLUENCE OF ADVERTISING. Advertising has an important role in informing and influencing consumers. Virtually every individual in the United States is exposed to advertising. It has become one of the most important economic and social forces in society. Partly because of the influence of advertising, people have learned to want ever better products and services, to take better care of their health, and to improve their way of living.

Advertising cannot turn a poor product or service into a good one. What advertising can do—and does—is create an awareness about both old and new products and services. It stimulates wants, indicates the differences among various products (and services), and shows how various needs and wants can be satisfied. Increasingly, advertising performs one of the main functions of a salesman, by providing some advance information about products and services to consumers before they reach the place of purchase.

Advertising is one of the most important techniques of modern business enterprise. A company's decisions about advertising affect its product development, packaging, pricing, distribution, and retailing. In turn, each of these activities affects advertising. Most important of all, a company's advertising affects consumers' decisions as to what to buy or not to buy.

Advertising is especially important in product development. In a competitive market, each manufacturer attempts to improve his products and to introduce new products to gain a sales advantage. Advertising enables a business firm to tell consumers about such improvements.

MAGNITUDE OF ADVERTISING. Of some 4.4 million business firms in the United States, practically all do some advertising. Over 3,800 advertising agencies are listed in the *Standard Directory of Advertising Agencies*. They render special services to many business firms as well as to governmental agencies and nonprofit organizations.

The great majority of smaller business firms do not use an advertising agency, but almost all large firms do. The advertising agency plans, prepares, and places advertising for advertisers. However, advertising agencies account for only about 25 percent of all dollars invested in advertising in a given year.

The total dollar amount of all advertising nearly tripled in a 15-year period, rising from $5.7 billion in 1950 to $15.1 billion in 1965. See Table 1. Of this amount, national advertising—for products and services throughout the United States—accounted for about two-thirds of the total.

2. Advertising Objectives and Communication

Advertising is essentially persuasive communication. Thus, the goals set for advertising are communications tasks: to reach a defined audience, to a given extent, and during a given time period.

Consumers do not often change suddenly from uninterested individuals to convinced purchasers. In many cases they go through several steps before buying a product. In general, they

TABLE 1

Advertising Volume in the United States[a]

Advertising Medium	1955	1960	1965
Newspapers	$3,087,800	$ 3,702,800	$ 4,435,000
Radio	539,300	668,000	889,300
Magazines	729,400	940,800	1,197,700
Farm papers	33,800	34,500	33,500
Direct mail	1,298,900	1,830,200	2,271,400
Business papers	446,200	609,300	678,500
Outdoor	192,400	203,300	180,000
Television	1,025,300	1,605,000	2,497,000
Miscellaneous, including transit advertising	1,841,300	2,337,800	2,937,600
	$9,914,400	$11,931,700	$15,120,000

[a] Source: Printers' Ink.

move from unawareness of the product or service to awareness and then to knowledge, liking, preference, acceptance (or conviction), and then to purchase of the product or service.

OBJECTIVES OF ADVERTISING. The above steps in persuasive communication indicate three major objectives of advertising: (1) to produce awareness and knowledge about the product or service; (2) to create liking and preference for it; and (3) to stimulate thought and action about it.

These objectives vary with the maturity or life cycle of the product or service. As the product is introduced to the market, the major goal of advertising might be informational. Later, as the product progresses to rapid growth, emphasis might be placed on competitive appeals. Later, as the product passes into a period of maturity, advertising might be aimed at keeping the name of the product or service before consumers.

In a sense, therefore, advertising management is a process of varying the advertising objectives for each product or service in accord with the specific goals of the advertiser. It is especially important for the advertiser to set clearly defined written objectives prior to the development of advertising campaigns. Only in this way can the promotional techniques employed be directly relevant to the objectives sought. Only in this way can the effectiveness of the campaign be determined.

35-B ADVERTISING AND THE INTELLECTUAL

George J. Stigler (Economist)

The market place responds to the tastes of consumers with the goods and services that are salable, whether the tastes are elevated or depraved. It is unfair to criticize the market place for fulfilling these desires, when clearly the defects lie in the popular tastes themselves. I consider it a cowardly concession to a false extension of the idea of democracy to make

SOURCE: George J. Stigler, "The Intellectual and the Market Place," (Chicago: Graduate School of Business, University of Chicago, Sixth Printing, 1967), pp. 6–7.

sub rosa attacks on public tastes by denouncing the people who serve them. It is like blaming the waiters in restaurants for obesity.

To escape this response, the more sophisticated intellectuals have argued that people are told what to want by the market place—that advertising skillfully depraves and distorts popular desires. There is no doubt an element of truth in this response, but it is an element of trifling size. The advertising industry has no sovereign power to bend men's wills—we are not children who blindly follow the last announcer's instructions to rush to the store for soap. Moreover, advertising itself is a completely neutral instrument, and lends itself to the dissemination of highly contradictory desires. While the automobile industry tells us not to drink while driving, the bourbon industry tells us not to drive while drinking. The symphony orchestra advertises, and gets much free publicity, in its rivalry with the dance band. Our colleges use every form of advertising, and indeed the typical university catalogue would never stop Diogenes in his search for an honest man.

So I believe the intellectuals would gain in candor and in grace if they preached directly to the public instead of using advertising as a whipping boy. I believe they would gain also in virtue if they would examine their own tastes more critically: when a good comedian and a production of Hamlet are on rival channels, I wish I could be confident that less than half the professors were laughing.

B. RESEARCH AND APPLICATIONS

This section deals with some specifics. We begin with some clues (Cox) for advertising strategists. The next reading (Bucklin) reports some data on the information role of advertising. The last selection (Clement) gives an analysis of the advertising process and its influence on consumer behavior.

35-C   CLUES FOR ADVERTISING STRATEGISTS

Donald F. Cox (Marketing Educator)

The evidence which we have at our disposal seems to indicate quite clearly that people are very capable of resisting attempts to *change* their attitudes and behavior. If a persuasive communication seems incompatible with their own attitudes, they may avoid it, distort its meaning, forget it, or otherwise decide not to be influenced.

If these conclusions are valid (as they seem to be), what are the implications for advertising? Although I am unable to offer much in the way of direct evidence, I can put forth two suggestions:

• A great deal of advertising must function either to *reinforce* existing attitudes and behavior (e.g., maintenance of brand loyalty), or to *stimulate* or activate people who are already predisposed to act in the desired manner (e.g., people who enjoy reading murder mysteries are most likely to be on the lookout for, and to be influenced by, advertising of murder mysteries).

• A related implication is that advertising is not, in itself, a cause of audience effects, but rather works with and through various mediating factors such as audience predispositions and personal influence (e.g., word-of-mouth advertising).[1]

It would be a mistake to contend that predispositions are so highly developed and so rigid that attitudes and behavior patterns never change. They do. However, I would argue that *changing* a person's attitudes or behavior (as opposed to *reinforcing* present attitudes or *activating* those already predisposed) is beyond the scope of most advertising, *except* where:

1. The attitude or behavior involved is of little importance to the individual. People to whom it makes little difference which brand of toothpaste they use are more likely to be influenced to switch brands by toothpaste advertising. Even here, however, some activation of predispositions is involved; people with false teeth are less likely to use any toothpaste.

2. The mediating factors (predispositions and personal influence) are inoperative. People may be influenced directly by the adver-

SOURCE: Donald F. Cox, "Clues for Advertising Strategists: II," *Harvard Business Review*, Vol. 39 (November-December, 1961), pp. 160–182, at pp. 162–164. © 1961 by the President and Fellows of Harvard College; all rights reserved.

[1] See Joseph T. Klapper, "What We Know About the Effects of Mass Communications: The Brink of Hope," *Public Opinion Quarterly*, Volume 21, 1957–1958, pp. 453–474.

tising for a new product because they have not been able to form attitudes which would predispose them against the product.

3. The mediating factors, which normally favor reinforcement, themselves favor change. If for some reason our friends begin buying color television sets, we are more likely to be influenced by advertising for color TV sets.[2]

[2] Points (2) and (3) are taken from Klapper, op. cit.

If these contentions are realistic, it would then appear that a major function of effective advertising is to "select" people who are already predisposed to buy a product and present them with appeals (appropriate to the types of potential customers) which would hopefully trigger the desired response. *In those instances where change of important attitudes or behavior is the advertising objective, failure is more likely than success unless the advertiser can somehow work with or through the mediating factors.*

35-D   THE INFORMATIVE ROLE OF ADVERTISING

Louis P. Bucklin (Marketing Educator)

Advertising serves a purpose by providing information about the nature, availability, and location of products. Informative advertising may complement or even substitute for the central market. Advertising may limit the need for person-to-person search, or may actually supplant the negotiation process of the marketplace; for example, mail order advertising.

This article presents evidence as to whether consumers actually use advertising the way this informative role implies. Data were collected in a survey of consumer shopping patterns among a group of randomly selected female household heads residing in the communities which approximate the trading area of Oakland, California. To be included in the sample, the person sampled had to have made one shopping trip in the past month for some item (excluding foods, homes, and automobiles) costing over $5. If she had not, she was replaced from a substitute home in the same block.

The 506 women finally included in the sample were quizzed extensively about their shopping activities on this trip. They also were asked whether they had shopped for these products by checking advertisements before the trip.

Use of Advertising

Respondents reported checking advertisements for 210, or 24 percent, of the 891 products, worth five dollars or more, reported

SOURCE: Louis P. Bucklin, "The Informative Role of Advertising, *Journal of Advertising Research,* Vol. 5 (September, 1965), pp. 11–15. © by the Advertising Research Foundation, Inc., 1965.

upon. There were no replies on four products. This rate of recall, of course, does not purport to measure total exposure to advertising. What it does show is that respondents could not recall using advertising as a shopping aid more than one-quarter of the time for $5-or-better products. One might thus conclude that advertising's role as an active guide to shopping is quite restricted.

But before accepting that conclusion, let's examine the use of advertising with respect to the type of product, the last time such a product was purchased, and the item's value. Table 1 gives a breakdown of the answers on the checking of advertising by products. Rate of recall varies significantly, from 9 percent for shoes to 52 percent for furniture. These differences appear to reflect the degree of consumer familiarity with the type of product.

Where the consumer likely is most informed, such as in personal accessories, apparel, and shoes, she relies least upon advertising. Where she is not apt to know product quality, as in appliances and furniture, the effort spent checking advertising is substantially increased.

As Table 2 shows, consumers checked advertising in 18 percent of the product cases when the last purchase had been within three months. This rose to 30 percent when the most recent purchase had been 18 months ago or more, or the item had never been bought before.

Table 3 breaks down the data according to the product's value. Advertising is used much more extensively in the search for high-priced products. Advertising was checked only 14 percent of the time for products in the $5 to $9

TABLE 1

The Checking of Advertisements by Various Product Categories

	Ads Checked	No Ads Checked	Total	Base
Shoes	9%	91%	100%	(166)
Personal accessories	12	88	100	(34)
Apparel	23	77	100	(420)
Other	23	77	100	(56)
Home furnishings	26	74	100	(81)
Large Appliances	42	58	100	(31)
Small appliances	43	57	100	(21)
Toys	46	54	100	(28)
Auto accessories	50	50	100	(8)
Furniture	52	48	100	(42)
Total	24	76	100	(887)

$\chi^2 = 48.1$, $p < .001$

TABLE 2

The Checking of Advertisements by Date of Last Purchase

Date of Purchase	Ads Checked	No Ads Checked	Total	Base
Last purchased less than three months ago	18%	82%	100%	(236)
4 to 18 months	23	77	100	(311)
More than 18 months, or never	30	70	100	(274)
Total	24	76	100	(821)

$\chi^2 = 10.0$, $p < .01$

TABLE 3

The Checking of Advertisements by Product Price Level

	Ads Checked	No Ads Checked	Total	Base
$5–$9	14%	86%	100%	(370)
$10–$19	22	78	100	(198)
$20–$49	31	69	100	(176)
$50 or more	46	54	100	(123)
Total	24	76	100	(867)

$\chi^2 = 58.2$, $p < .001$

bracket. This rose to 46 percent in the $50 and over price range, a substantial and highly significant difference.

So the conclusion that advertising plays a limited role in perfecting the marketplace must be tempered in light of these results. The data lead to the hypothesis that the consumer uses advertising to the extent that she feels a need for information. If she is unfamiliar with the product, if she has not shopped for the item for some time, if it is expensive, then she will be more likely to use advertising.

Effect of Advertising

This noting of advertisements might not broaden the consumer's knowledge of the alternative product available. Instead, it might sell her on a single brand and actually reduce the scope of her information-gathering activities. To investigate this possibility, respondents

TABLE 4

The Relationship Between Checking of Ads and Brand Preference

	One Brand Pre- ferred	No Brand Pre- ferred	Total	Base
Ads checked	24%	76%	100%	(209)
No ads checked	22	78	100	(673)
Total	22	78	100	(882)

$\chi^2 = .59, p < .50$

were asked whether they had decided upon the brand before undertaking the trip in question. Answers were cross-tabulated with the checking of advertisements, and are shown in Table 4.

These data show little difference in the extent of brand preference between the two categories: 24 percent of those who checked advertisements expressed a brand preference, compared with 22 percent where advertiseing had not been checked. This difference is not significant and the notion that advertising served only to pre-sell is not substantiated.

Indeed, another computation shows that noting advertising seems to enlarge the consumer's knowledge of desirable product characteristics (Table 5).

Respondents were asked as to whether they knew all, some, few or none of the product features before they started the trip. Table 5 shows that of those who checked advertisements, 51 percent knew all the features wanted, 30 percent knew some, and only 19 percent were aware of few or none. On products for which the respondents had not checked advertisements, just 38 percent knew all features, 29 percent knew some, and 33 percent were aware of just a few. These differences

clearly suggest that advertisements aided the respondent in selecting the product characteristics that she most desired, without prejudicing her as to brand.

STORE PREFERENCES. Respondents who noted advertising also seemed much less wedded to particular stores. Respondents were asked whether they had a favorite store for purchasing each of the $5-or-more products. Cross tabulation of replies with the checking of advertisements reveals, in Table 6, a negative association: 28 percent of those who checked advertisements stated they had a preferred store for the product, as compared with 47 percent among those who did not check ads.

This relationship receives further support from evidence that respondents who checked advertising were more concerned with price. Respondents were asked for each product mentioned, what factors they considered in selecting a store. Price was mentioned as a factor for 319 of the products. Table 7 shows the cross tabulation of this question with the checking of advertisements. Price was stated as a factor for 46 percent of the products for which advertising was noted, 34 percent for those where advertising was not noted.

SHOPPING EFFORTS. Studying the extent of shopping effort by the respondents provided another view of the role of advertising. This was accomplished in two ways. First, to measure the number of shopping stops, or interstore comparisons, made for a given product, respondents were asked, with respect to the shopping trip that qualified them for the sample, to name the stores visited and the products shopped for in each. Table 8 shows the number of interstore comparisons, calculated from this information, cross-tabulated with the checking of advertisements. Where advertising was not checked, 14 percent of the products were shopped for in more than one

TABLE 5

The Relationship Between Checking Advertisements and Knowledge of Product Features Wanted

	Features Known				
	All	Some	Few or None	Total	Base
Ads checked	51%	30%	19%	100%	(207)
No ads checked	38	29	33	100	(672)
Total	41	29	30	100	(879)

$\chi^2 = 17.1, p < .001$

TABLE 6

The Relationship Between Checking Advertisements and Store Preference for the Product

	Preferred Store	No Preferred Store	Total	Base
Ads checked	28%	72%	100%	(210)
No ads checked	47	53	100	(676)
Total	42	58	100	(886)

$\chi^2 = 22.8, p < .001$

store, compared with 25 percent when advertising was checked.

Second, respondents were asked, on each product, whether they had shopped for it in a store prior to the qualifying shopping trip. A particularly strong association exists between this characteristic and the checking of advertising, as shown in Table 9. Where advertising was not checked, only 21 percent of the products had been shopped for previously; the corresponding figure where advertising had been checked was 53 percent.

Since checking of advertisements is associated with concern for price, it is fair to ask whether the relationships just cited merely reflect the price variable. To evaluate this, the two shopping activity variables were further analyzed by holding price constant within the four brackets shown on Table 3. For both interstore comparisons and extent of previous shopping, each of the four subtables revealed more extensive search activity for products for which advertising had been checked. Additive chi-squares were significant as well ($p < .001$). As a result, the relationship between

TABLE 7

The Relationship Between Checking Advertisements and Price as a Product Choice Factor

	Price Mentioned	Price Not Mentioned	Total	Base
Ads checked	46%	54%	100%	(209)
No ads checked	34	66	100	(669)
Total	36	64	100	(878)

$\chi^2 = 9.85, p < .001$

TABLE 8

The Relationship Between Checking Advertisements and the Number of Interstore Comparisons Made upon Shopping Trip

	Only One Store	More than One	Total	Base
Ads checked	75%	25%	100%	(210)
No ads checked	86	14	100	(677)
Total	84	16	100	(887)

$\chi^2 = 14.2, p < .001$

shopping assiduity and the checking of advertisements, as shown in Tables 7 and 8, is well supported.

Conclusions

The survey data build a strong case that shoppers use advertising intelligently and effectively for at least an important minority of products purchased. Advertising is used more in shopping for less familiar items, items that they have not bought recently, and high-priced items. Further, such use of advertising does not appear to lead to brand preference. On the contrary, it was associated with better product information, lower store preference, greater concern about price, and increased search.

Advertising cannot properly be termed the causative factor in all of this. Rather, advertising is part of a clearly definable, rational shopping syndrome. Advertising is simply one of several checkpoints upon which consumers

TABLE 9

The Relationship Between Checking Advertisements and Previous Shopping Trips for the Product

	Previous Shopping	No Previous Shopping	Total	Base
Ads checked	53%	47%	100%	(210)
No ads checked	21	79	100	(677)
Total	29	71	100	(887)

$\chi^2 = 78.1, p < .001$

rely to improve their purchasing abilities. In many cases where advertising was not checked, this seemed to be the result of a lack of consumer interest in investigating alternative purchases. Many such consumers perhaps felt that because of their past relationship with stores and/or brands, that making any extra effort in shopping would not be worth the time spent. Thus it may be concluded that where consumers feel a need for market information, advertising will be used as an aid to purchasing activities. In this sense, advertising may be regarded as a positive influence in the perfection of markets.

A corollary to this conclusion is ironic in the light of increasing advertising expenditures. Despite continuous exposure to advertisements, many consumers seem to have difficulty in actively checking advertisements, as indicated by their failure to do so. For the products studied in this survey, few consumers seem to be exposed to the advertising precisely when they are ready to buy. This may be because the location and whereabouts of advertisements for a wide variety of alternative products are hard to find. There is no source index with which to zero in on advertisements. Purchasing newspapers and magazines indiscriminantly is too expensive. In short, the dissemination of advertisements for more expensive products, from the standpoint of aiding the consumer when she desires this help, is very inefficiently organized. Some kind of medium is needed which the consumer can activate to produce quickly the information that she needs.

35-E AN ANALYSIS OF THE ADVERTISING PROCESS AND ITS INFLUENCE ON CONSUMER BEHAVIOR

Wendell E. Clement (Economist)

Virtually all advertising strategy and techniques for measuring its effectiveness are based on some theory of how the advertising process functions to influence behavioral patterns of consumers. Most theories view advertising as having the effect of moving consumers through several stages of a buying continuum and culminating with a purchase response. Although models describing the advertising process differ as to the number of stages in the buying continuum, they do have several stages in common. They are: (1) awareness of the advertised product, (2) attitude change, and (3) purchase response. It usually is hypothesized that these stages of the continuum are linked together in a causative chain in which advertising produces a change in consumer attitudes toward the product which in turn induces a purchase response.[1]

Although this theory of the advertising process, or slight modifications of it, is widely accepted in marketing literature, students and practitioners of marketing would have to confess virtual ignorance if pressed honestly to explain the advertising process and how it produces its results. This is evidenced by the growing body of literature expressing skepticism about the generally accepted theory of the advertising process.[2] It is an important question as to whether this model of the advertising process is valid because it has had a major influence on current advertising thought concerning advertising strategy and techniques of measuring advertising effectiveness.

The study reported on in this paper attempts to shed further light on the nature of the advertising process by empirically evaluating the system of relationships stated above. The hypothesis investigated is that the level of advertising expenditures influences consumer exposure to the advertising messages; exposure to the advertising changes consumers' attitudes; and changes in attitudes stimulate purchase responses.

SOURCE: Wendell E. Clement, "An Analysis of the Advertising Process and Its Influence on Consumer Behavior," Reed Moyer, Editor, *Changing Marketing Systems*, (Chicago: American Marketing Association, 1967), pp. 270–276, at pp. 270–275.
[1] See for example, Robert J. Lavidge and Gary A. Steiner, "A Model for Predictive Measurements of Advertising Effectiveness," *Journal of Marketing*, Vol. 25, No. 6, (Oct. 1961), pp. 59-60.

[2] One of the most persuasive arguments is given by Kristian S. Palda, "The Hypothesis of a Hierarchy of Effects: A Partial Evaluation," *Journal of Marketing Research, III*, (Feb. 1966), pp. 13-23.

The Data

Data for this analysis were made available by the American Dairy Association and the U.S. Department of Agriculture. The data were generated from a controlled experiment conducted over a two-year period to determine whether two increased levels of advertising expenditure would increase sales of fluid milk enough to justify the added cost. The experiment was conducted in six markets in which three levels of advertising expenditure were tested: (1) The present or normal level of advertising by the Association which is two cents per capita annually, (2) a medium level consisting of fifteen cents per capita annually above normal, and (3) heavy, thirty cents per capita annually above normal. The advertising expenditure pattern is based on The Extra Period Latin-Square Change-Over Design which, among other features, permits measurement of the carryover influence of the advertising expenditures.

During each of four advertising periods, about 1,500 consumers, 250 in each of the six markets, were interviewed to determine, among other things:

1. Respondent awareness of the advertising as indicated by both unaided and aided recall measurements.

2. Incidence of consumption of milk, coffee, and soft drinks.

3. Respondent scaling of forty-three statements concerning attitudes about milk.

In addition to the information obtained from the consumer surveys, data on total milk sales for each market published by the U.S. Department of Agriculture were also used.

Results of the Survey

The results observed in the study may be summarized as follows:

1. Each increased level of advertising expenditure increased the level of consumer exposure to or awareness of the advertising to a statistically significant degree. Moreover, advertising expenditures in the previous period affected level of awareness in the present period.

2. The extent of exposure, however, did not increase as a linear function of advertising expenditures. Maximizing the exposure-expenditure function indicated that, with the particular advertising mix being used, no further increase in exposure would be achieved beyond expenditures of 33.5 cents per capita suggesting that the saturation level had been reached for this particular mix.

3. Recall of the advertising themes was highest among those consumers with the most favorable attitudes but the purchase response was greatest among those with the least favorable attitudes.

4. Changes in attitudes were not as marked as changes in consumer recall. But the changes that did occur suggested that attitudes improved in the period following rather than during intensified advertising. In fact, the evidence suggests that the initial impact of the advertising was to make attitudes somewhat less favorable.

5. The pattern of sales behavior was similar to that observed for consumer exposure to the advertising, that is, sales increased with each higher level of expenditure and expenditures in the previous period had an effect on sales in the present period. Moreover, the sales response function, as in the awareness response function, is best described by a parabola.

6. Sales, when expressed as a function of consumer awareness or exposure to the advertising, were found to be linearly related. One important aspect of this function is that a one-to-one relationship did not exist between these two variables. Thus, without some knowledge of the parameter in this function, awareness studies alone cannot be used to predict purchase behavior. Another important point is that this function, being linearly related suggests that the decreasing rate of sales increase associated with each higher level of expenditure did not result from saturation of consumption, but rather from failure to achieve additional consumer exposure to the advertising.

7. Due to simplifying circumstances in the production and marketing of milk, the optimal, or most profitable level of advertising expenditure can be obtained. Increased sales represents shifting, already produced, milk from the lower price class II use to the higher price class I use. The revenue function in this diversionary program is:

(1) TR = $21X

Where TR = total revenue

    X = thousand pounds of milk per day shifted from class II to class I sales

    $21 = the difference in price per thousand pounds between class II and class I milk

The advertising cost function, as estimated from the experiment is approximately (2) TC = 78.30 − 10.7X + 1.52X.[2]

Where TC = total advertising costs per day

    X = thousand pounds of milk per day shifted from class II to class I use

The profit function may be defined as:

(3) P = TR − TC

    = 21X − (78.30 − 10.7X + 1.52X^2)

    = 78.30 + 31.7X − 1.52X^2

Where:

X = thousand pounds of sales per day

The point at which profits are a maximum is found by differentiating (3), setting the resulting function equal to zero and solving for X.

$$\frac{dp}{dx} = 31.7 - 3.04X.$$

    = 10.4 thousand pounds of sales per day

Substituting 10.4 in (2) gives optimum advertising expenditures of $131 per day per market.[3]

---

[3] It should be noted that development of the continuous curves for the advertising cost function involves considerable interpolation. Thus, other types of curves, such as a third degree curve, also could have been constructed to fit the data. If the analysis is confined to evaluating the actual points tested in the experiment, which is more technically correct, it is seen that the medium level of expenditure is optimal. For a more detailed analysis of sales, see W. E. Clement, P. L. Henderson, and C. P. Eley, *The Effect of Different Levels of Promotional Expenditures on Sales of Fluid Milk*, Economic Research Service, United States Department of Agriculture, ERS-259, Washington, D.C.: Government Printing Office, Oct. 1965.

Appraisal of Results

Perhaps the most notable finding is the fact that attitudes appeared to be changing after the sales increase rather than changing concurrently with sales. There has been considerable controversy among marketing scholars as to whether there is a logical basis for this type of behavioral pattern. Psychologists, for some years, have done considerable research on this question, although not in an advertising context. They appear convinced that change in behavior can precede change in attitudes. More recently this idea has been considered within the framework of advertising.[4]

A Theory of Attitude Behavior

The theory of cognitive dissonance, developed by Leon Festinger, appears to be most useful in explaining the results observed in this study.[5]

The major aspects of the theory with which we are concerned may be summarized as follows:

1. An important way in which dissonance may be created is by cognitive intrusion, that is, a person may be exposed to new information which is inconsistent with his present *behavior* or *beliefs*.

2. The existence of dissonance, being psychologically uncomfortable, will motivate the person to reduce the dissonance.

3. There are several ways in which dissonance might be reduced: (a) change one's action or behavior to conform to the new information; (b) change one's knowledge or change beliefs (Festinger states that either behavior or belief [attitude] may change first, but sooner or later the other will change also); (c) discredit the source of new information which created the dissonance; (d) acquire new knowledge to support one's original position; and (e) avoid the information sources that contribute to the dissonance.

---

[4] See John C. Maloney, "Is Advertising Believability Really Important?" *Journal of Marketing*, XXVII, No. 4, (Oct. 1963), pp. 1–8 and Donald F. Cox, "Clues for Advertising Strategists," *Harvard Business Review*, XXXXIV, No. 6, (Nov.-Dec. 1961), pp. 160–182.

[5] Leon Festinger, *A Theory of Cognitive Dissonance*, (Stanford, California: Stanford University Press, 1957).

The advertising messages beamed to consumers extolling the virtues of milk represented cognitive intrusion. For the group of consumers with unfavorable attitudes and little or no consumption, the advertising created dissonance because it was at variance with their belief and behavior patterns. With dissonance having been created, the affected consumers made several adjustments to reduce dissonance. The findings suggest that one method of adjustment was to discredit the advertising. This would explain the observed tendency of attitudes to initially become more unfavorable. Another method of combating dissonance may have been to ignore or forget the advertising. This is indicated by the finding that recall of the advertising themes was substantially lower among those consumers with unfavorable attitudes.

Another alternative adjustment to dissonance, as indicated by the theory, is to change either behavior or cognitions. Either may change first, but the other will also change later. It is concluded that the initial increase in sales was a change in behavior to adjust to dissonance. The subsequent improvement observed in attitude change occurred to give meaning to the already achieved behavior.

The Model Reformulated

Based on the results of this study and other evidence, it seems reasonable to conclude that the hypothesis of the advertising system investigated in this study does not apply in all situations. The model, therefore, needs to be reformulated to take into account the kinds of behavioral patterns observed here.

The reformulated advertising system is shown graphically in Figure 1. According to the reformulation, the first effect of advertising inputs is the same as before with consumers first becoming exposed to and aware of the advertising. Added to the model at this stage are "existing attitudes." It is included as an exogenous variable influencing the extent of awareness. This follows from the findings that consumers with favorable attitudes toward milk were more likely to observe the adver-

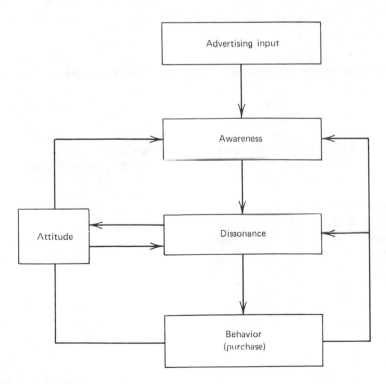

Figure 1. Model of the advertising system for a selected class of products and advertising situations.

tising than those with unfavorable attitudes, notwithstanding the fact that the former did not increase their purchases.

Another change in the model is that awareness is now shown as creating dissonance rather than directly influencing attitudes. The amount of dissonance created is a function of the advertising and of existing attitudes. The model shows that dissonance might have three separate effects: (1) there could be feedback having a depressing effect on awareness; (2) dissonance could depress existing attitudes, and (3) it could induce behavioral changes. It may be recalled that all three of these effects were observed in this study.

The effect at the behavioral level flows in two directions. If product experience yields satisfaction, attitudes become more favorable. Furthermore, there will be feedback into the system indicating that the consumer will notice the advertising more readily, experience less dissonance and become a repeat purchaser.

A second effect at the behavioral stage is that there will be a feedback on attitudes. This feedback can have a positive or negative effect depending upon the consumer's experience with the product.

Implications for Measuring Advertising Effectiveness

Clearly, the reformulated model has implications for measuring advertising effectiveness. First, it follows from the model that attitude studies, as traditionally defined and used in market research, can give quite misleading results. It is seen that three variables—exposure to the advertising, dissonance, and product experience, interact to influence the observed level of attitudes. Let us suppose that of these three variables, product experience is dominant and a firm successfully advertises and induces purchases of an inferior good. Results from traditional measurements of attitudes would suggest that advertising was ineffective

when in fact consumers' unsatisfactory experience with the product was the determining factor. Unless there is some way of untangling these complex interactions, it is not certain what the attitude survey has measured.

Awareness studies also have limitations as measures of advertising effectiveness. The revised model indicates that awareness is a function of existing attitudes in addition to advertising outlays. Thus, people who already have favorable attitudes are apt to notice the advertising to a greater extent than those with unfavorable attitudes. Moreover, the group with the greatest awareness may not be the ones who responded to the advertising. Thus, judging advertising effectiveness solely on the basis of awareness could be totally misleading. It is also to be noted that behavioral change is only one possible adjustment to awareness. Another important form of adjustment includes merely reinforcing existing attitudes with no change in behavior. We cannot tell from awareness studies alone which of these alternatives the consumer has chosen. Finally it was demonstrated that although sales were a linear function of awareness, the relationship was not one-to-one. Unless there is some knowledge of the parameter in this function, awareness studies are not very useful in predicting behavioral response.

These limitations of recall studies do not eliminate their usefulness if viewed in the proper framework. It would appear that recall studies are more of an aid to improving advertising strategy rather than a tool for measuring effectiveness. Through profile analysis they can help sharpen the program by indicating who is and who is not being reached by the advertising. They may also be used to give an indication of when a particular advertising mix has been pushed to capacity, and when attention needs to be given to manipulating some of the variables in the mix to gain additional consumer exposure.

A. BACKGROUND AND THEORY

The first selection is a careful analysis (Webster) of interpersonal communication and its connection with a salesman's effectiveness. The second article is a delineation (Taylor) of two requirements for measuring the effectiveness of promotion.

36-A INTERPERSONAL COMMUNICATION AND SALESMAN EFFECTIVENESS

Frederick E. Webster, Jr. (Marketing Educator)

The earliest, and the most persistent, answers to the question "What makes a successful salesman?" consisted of lists of the personal characteristics and traits of the salesman himself. Some of these lists generated criteria for evaluating application blanks: age, height, appearance, education, previous business experience, etc. Other lists formed the bases for, or were generated by, psychological tests: aggressiveness, dominance, extroversion, optimism, competitive spirit, etc. Despite some disenchantment with the efficacy of psychological tests, the search for the traits of successful salesmen has continued unabated, and more sophisticated and complex traits, such as "empathy" and "ego drive," have recently been suggested.[1]

Another set of answers concentrated on the salesman's actions rather than his traits. Perhaps the simplest answers were those which described the steps in the successful sales call, for example, the AIDA formula: (1) get Attention; (2) arouse Interest; (3) stimulate

SOURCE: Frederick E. Webster, Jr., "Interpersonal Communication and Salesman Effectiveness," *Journal of Marketing*, Vol. 32 (July, 1968), pp. 7–13, at pp. 7–12.
[1] David Mayer and Herbert M. Greenberg, "What Makes a Good Salesman," *Harvard Business Review*, Vol. 42 (July–August, 1964), pp. 119–125.

Desire; (4) get buying Action. This "salesmanship" approach assumed that the outcome of the sales call depends on the specific actions of the salesman.

Recognizing that the buyer played a part in determining the outcome of the call, other answers suggested that the buyer's actions were also important.

The so-called "stimulus-response theory" of selling saw the salesman as being able to elicit the desired responses if he could provide the right stimuli, and treated the prospect in essentially mechanistic terms. Like the "salesman's traits" approach, the "salesman's action" approach credited the salesman with virtually complete responsibility for the outcome of the call.

With increasing emphasis on a consumer orientation in marketing, "need satisfaction theory" provided some slightly different answers to the question "What makes a successful salesman?" These answers showed that the successful salesman was the one who could identify the prospect's needs and turn them into buying motives. Guided by this theory, the salesman learns to ask questions designed to uncover the prospect's needs, to listen carefully to the answers, and then to show how his product meets those needs. Having built the groundwork, the salesman moves in with the presentation and closes. Need satisfaction theory was really a variant of stimulus-response theory. Needs were seen as a determinant of response; to get the desired response the salesman must choose the right stimuli (selling points) which show the prospect how buying will satisfy his needs. Authors of books that define selling as "helping prospects buy" have used this explanation. While these "salesmanship" theories recognized that the prospect has a role, he was still viewed in passive terms.[2]

These three kinds of "theory" identify three important determinants of selling effectiveness: the salesman's characteristics and traits, the salesman's actions, and the prospect's needs. These elements are plausible and valid, but incomplete for explaining and predicting the outcome of the sales interview. Why is it that the same salesman, using the same actions, is not always effective with prospects with the same kinds of needs? One logical and simple explanation is that there are attributes of prospects, other than their needs, which influence the outcome of the sales call. Or, there are some complex ways in which salesman characteristics and actions combine with prospect characteristics and actions to determine outcomes.

Interaction Theory

Evans was among the first to challenge seriously the traditional "salesmanship" explanations of selling effectiveness and to suggest that the prospect played an active role in determining the progress and outcome of the sales call. He observed that:

> Very little is known about what takes place when the salesman and his prospect meet. The two parties meet in a highly structured situation, and the outcome of the meeting depends upon the resulting interaction. In this sense, the 'sale' is a social situation involving two persons. The interaction of the two persons, in turn, depends

upon the economic, social, physical, and personality characteristics of each of them. To understand the process, however, it is necessary to look at both parties to the sale as a dyad, not individually.[3]

In his study of life insurance salesmen, Evans found evidence that the probability of a sale was influenced by the extent to which there was a *matching* of the prospect's and the salesman's characteristics. This was true for such factors as age, height, income, political opinions, religious beliefs, and smoking. *Perceived* similarity for religion and politics was more important than actual similarity. Evans concluded that the successful sale was situationally determined by the interaction between prospect and salesman, and not solely by the particular characteristics of one or the other party to the interaction.[4] Other researchers have also reported evidence that successful salesmen tend to concentrate on particular kinds of prospects.[5] However, Evans' study did not consider the behavioral dynamics of the sales interaction itself.

Applying interaction theory to the study of selling recognized that selling is more than *individual* behavior. Rather, it is *social* behavior, behavior that is rewarded or punished, accepted or rejected, by another person. The essential feature of social behavior is that each of the persons in face-to-face interaction influences the behavior of the other.[6] Selling certainly fits this definition. Social behavior, or "interpersonal interaction," has also been characterized as behavior influenced by "How one person thinks and feels about another person, how he perceives him and what he expects

[2] These theories are summarized in Harold C. Cash and W. J. E. Crissy, "Ways of Looking at Selling" in William Lazer and Eugene J. Kelley (eds.), *Managerial Marketing: Perspectives and Viewpoints,* 2nd ed. (Homewood, Ill.: Richard D. Irwin, Inc., 1962), pp. 554–559.

[3] Franklin B. Evans, "Selling as a Dyadic Relationship—A New Approach," *The American Behavioral Scientist,* Vol. VI (May, 1963), pp. 76–79, at p. 76.

[4] Same reference as footnote 3, at p. 79.

[5] M. S. Gadel, "Concentration by Salesmen on Congenial Prospects," *Journal of Marketing,* Vol. 28 (April, 1964), pp. 64–66; and Lauren Edgar Crane, "The Salesman's Role in Household Decision-Making," in L. George Smith (ed.), *Reflections on Progress in Marketing* (Chicago: American Marketing Association, 1964), pp. 184–196.

[6] George Caspar Homans, *Social Behavior: Its Elementary Forms* (New York: Harcourt, Brace & World, Inc., 1961), pp. 2–3.

him to do or think, how he reacts to the actions of the other. . . ."[7]

PERCEPTION. It is a well-known fact that human beings respond to their environment in terms of their *perception* of that environment, not necessarily the objective facts of the environment. Perception is a subjective process. How a person views the environment, including other persons, is a function of his psychological structure—his goals, values, attitudes, feelings, needs, and so on. An individual's *perceptions of other people* in the environment is complicated further by the fact that he makes inferences about the intentions, attitudes, emotions, ideas, abilities, etc., which cause their behavior. Other human beings are described not only in terms of their actual behavior but in terms of the psychological attributes of their behavior. Most important of all, these attributes are looked upon as being directed toward us and having particular meaning for us. In other words, our reaction to others depends upon how we think they view their environment, including us.[8] One inference from this fact for the salesman is that just as he "sizes up" the prospect, so does the prospect "size up" the salesman. The prospect's perception of the salesman is an important determinant of the salesman's effectiveness.

ROLE EXPECTATIONS. How each person perceives or "sizes up" the other is determined by his *predispositions*: the set of opinions, attitudes, and beliefs which determines the perceiver's cognitive structure. One of the most important sources of an individual's predispositions is the role that he is in. A role is the social position occupied by an individual, including the goals of that position, and the behavioral repertoire appropriate to that position and to the attainment of those goals. Social positions (like "father," "Protestant," "Republican," "salesman," and "purchasing agent") have associated with them a set of expectations as to how persons occupying that role should behave. These expectations are "bidimensional" in that they specify both how persons

in that role should behave and how others should behave toward them.[9] Role expectations, therefore, provide important components of structure in the sales interaction in that they define the kinds of behavior that each of the actors expects both of himself and of the other person. To the extent that the prospect and the salesman have consistent role expectations (for both themselves and for each other) there will be more effective interaction and communication.

SOURCES OF ROLE EXPECTATIONS FOR THE SALESMAN. There are two particularly important sources of prospects' role expectations for salesmen. The first is the stereotype of the salesman. A "stereotype" can be defined as a "consensus of role expectations shared by a large segment of the population." It is a well-known fact that there is a stereotype of the salesman that describes him as "talkative," "easy going," "competitive," "optimistic," and "excitable." Kirchner and Dunnette found that salesmen describe themselves in these terms.[10] This stereotype is one of the reasons why the salesman is not highly regarded by a large segment of the population.[11] Perception is subjective, and it is not important whether or not the stereotype is an objectively accurate one. The prospect who does not have previous experience with a particular salesman will respond to that salesman in terms of the stereotype which he has of salesmen in general. "Inaccurate" perception of the salesman by the prospect may lead to a lack of communication. On the other hand, by the virtue of their occupation, all salesmen are regarded as having manipulative intent—they want the prospect to behave in a particular way—and communications theory indicates that the perception of manipulative intent in the communicator depends upon how much risk he perceives in the buying decision he is asked to make. Levitt's

---

[7] Fritz Heider, *The Psychology of Interpersonal Relations* (New York: John Wiley & Sons, Inc., 1958), p. 1.

[8] Ranato Tagiuri and Luigi Petrullo (eds.), *Person Perception and Interpersonal Behavior* (Stanford, California: Stanford University Press, 1958), pp. x–xi.

[9] Theodore Sarbin, "Role Theory," in Garner Lindzey (ed.), *Handbook of Social Psychology*, Vol. I (Cambridge, Mass.: Addison-Wesley, Inc., 1954), pp. 223–258.

[10] Wayne K. Kirchner and Marvin D. Dunnette, "How Salesmen and Technical Men Differ in Describing Themselves," *Personnel Journal*, Vol. 37 (April, 1959), pp. 418–419.

[11] John L. Mason, "The Low Prestige of Personal Selling," *Journal of Marketing*, Vol. 29 (October, 1965), pp. 7–10.

research mentioned above, found that the influence of the salesman's presentation was in part determined by the riskiness of the decision (that is, actual purchase vs. recommendation for further consideration) and by the self-confidence of the prospect. Cox found that women responded to a sales presentation for nylon hosiery according to their self-confidence. Women of medium self-confidence were *most* responsive. Those of low self-confidence tended to reject the salesgirl's advice because they didn't trust their ability to make a decision and because of the need to defend their egos. Those of high self-confidence rejected the advice because they didn't feel they needed it and rather preferred to trust their own judgment.[12]

Thus, the prospect's behavior in the sales interview is a function of his personal needs, his social needs, and his self-confidence, as well as the amount of risk he perceives in the buying decision. How the prospect perceives and plays his role as "buyer" determines the success of the sales call.

Another set of factors determining how the prospect plays his role in a specific sales interaction is other sources of information to which he has been exposed concerning the salesman's product. These can be grouped into two categories: impersonal, commercial sources of information such as media advertising and direct mail; and personal, noncommercial sources such as colleagues, friends, and neighbors. (The salesman can be characterized as a personal, commercial source of information.) Generally speaking, personal sources of information are known to be more effective in producing attitude change than impersonal sources.[13] On the other hand, commercial sources tend to be less effective than noncommercial sources. Therefore, salesmen tend to be more effective than advertising, but less effective than peers

(such as colleagues and friends) in developing favorable attitudes toward products.

However, the importance of alternative sources of information varies with the stage of the buyer's decision and the product life cycle. As the buyer goes through the mental stages of deciding to buy a new product (or the "adoption process"—awareness, interest, evaluation, trial, and adoption), he relies on different sources of information. Furthermore, the people who buy a new product early in its life cycle (the innovators and early adopters) tend to rely upon different sources of information than later adopters.[14]

Determinants of How the Salesman "Plays His Role"

Many of the points developed above for the prospect apply to the salesman as well. The salesman's behavior is determined by his personal needs (for example, his desire to earn a commission on the sale) and his social needs. The salesman's behavior will be influenced by his desire to meet the expectations of relevant other persons including his manager, his salesman-peers, and the prospect himself. The salesman's confidence in his own ability to "play the role" of salesman is important in determining his behavior and is determined by his knowledge, training, personality, and previous experience.

Because of the importance of the prospect's behavior in determining the success of the sales call, the salesman's ability to infer the prospect's role expectations of him is a vitally important factor. This ability has been defined as "empathy" or "empathic ability"—the ability to put oneself into the position of another person, a feeling of oneness with the other person. There is an unresolved controversy about "empathy": whether it is an inborn personality trait or can be taught and learned; and whether persons who have empathic ability are always more effective or only more effective in interactions with specific types of persons. Nonetheless, the ability to sense how the prospect expects him to behave and how the prospect is reacting to what he says is an important determinant of how successfully the salesman plays his role.

The salesman's behavior will also reflect his

[12] Donald E. Cox, "Information and Uncertainty: Their Effects on Consumer Product Evaluations," unpublished doctoral dissertation, Graduate School of Business Administration, Harvard University, 1962.

[13] Elihu Katz and Paul F. Lazarfeld, *Personal Influence* (Glencoe, Ill.: The Free Press, 1955), pp. 183–184; and Paul F. Lazarsfeld, Bernard Berelson, and Hazel Gaudet, *The People's Choice* (New York: Duell, Sloan, and Pearce, 1944), pp. 49–50.

[14] Everett M. Rogers, *Diffusion of Innovations* (New York: The Free Press, 1962).

perception of how his manager expects him to play the role of salesman. If these expectations have not been stated clearly by the manager, the salesman's behavior may not be consistent with management's expectations. Furthermore, management must be sure that its expectations about salesmen's behavior are consistent with buyer's expectations. Otherwise, the salesman is in the difficult position of having to resolve conflicting role expectations, which will lead to some frustration and anxiety, as well as reduction in his effectiveness.

The salesman's effectiveness also depends on his ability to determine the locus of responsibility for buying decisions within the buying organization. This is true for family buying decisions as well as industrial buying decisions. Where more than one person is involved in the buying decision (e.g., a purchasing agent and an engineer), the salesman may be faced with conflicting role expectations. Once again, the ability to sense and resolve conflicts in buyers' role expectations is an important determinant of his behavior.

36-B TWO REQUIREMENTS FOR MEASURING THE EFFECTIVENESS OF PROMOTION

James W. Taylor (Marketing Educator)

The idea that " 'promotion' cannot be separated out as an entity but is a composite of many other factors"[1] is an acceptable proposition to many marketing people.

However, the failure of most experiments on promotion effectiveness to produce meaningful results stems from insufficient preparation in two areas: understanding the purchasing process for the product, and appropriate use of experimental design.

Understanding the Purchasing Process

The very first step in evaluating the effectiveness of promotion, be it advertising or sales promotion, is to acquire an understanding of the whys and hows and whens that lead a customer to purchase or not purchase a product. This amounts to an outline of the route a customer travels from a point of "no need and/or desire" for the product to actual purchase of the product. Clearly the factors that influence the purchase of gasoline are different from those that influence the purchase of milk. Furthermore, the purchasing process for milk is probably different from cheese, or butter.

Any company contemplating experimental measurements of promotion effectiveness probably will already have accomplished part of the work necessary for a cohesive picture of

the purchasing process for a particular product. This work will probably consist of a number of two dimensional "photographs" of the market, such as, "21% of the customers are heavy users," or "38% of the purchasers are brand switchers." However good such data, they are insufficient until they have been fitted into a rationale that will explain how noncustomers become customers.

The dimension that most likely must be added is *time*. This amounts to viewing the purchase as the sum of a sequence of decisions, rather than a decision in itself. The customer must answer to the best of his ability a series of questions, such as: "Why should I buy it?" "Can I afford it?" "Where should I buy it?" "Do I have enough information about it?"

Sometimes these questions are resolved logically, sometimes illogically. Sometimes they are answered on a conscious level, sometimes not. The determination of which such questions go into the purchase of a product, when they are asked, and what factors influence the answers means increased understanding of the purchasing process for the product.

The difficulties in accomplishing this task may well be the "rock" on which have foundered many previous attempts at measurements of promotion effectiveness.

The first major accomplishment arising from a complete understanding of the purchasing process is the ability to establish clear objectives. Once agreement is reached that a particular group of customers must be influenced in a particular direction, objectives for a partic-

SOURCE: James W. Taylor, "Two Requirements for Measuring the Effectiveness of Promotion," *Journal of Marketing*, Vol. 29 (April, 1965), pp. 43–45.
[1] John H. Weber, "Can Results of Sales Promotion Be Predicted?" *Journal of Marketing*, Vol. 27 (January, 1963), pp. 15–19.

ular promotion can be set and appropriate measurements made.

The purchasing dynamics will show that a promotion will work only under certain conditions and at certain times. An example from gasoline retailing will illustrate this point. Under normal conditions the purchasing process for gasoline begins with "brand familiarity" for the majority of customers; that is, a particular brand will not receive purchase consideration unless it is thought to be the brand of a big, well-known company.

Consider, then, the case of a company that is well known in one area and is expanding into an area where it is not known. One of the first jobs that promotion must do is to "qualify" the brand with consumers in the new area. Thus, a measurable promotion objective is established; and the degree of success of various promotions can be determined with usual survey techniques.[2]

This is only the first step in the purchasing process. Other subsequent steps will provide measurable objectives up to and including sales and profit.

Understanding the purchasing process provides a second important benefit, namely, the ability to assess and control the other major variables influencing sales. It has been said that the results of promotion cannot be measured because "consumer response to promotion is affected by economic conditions; but the response is unknown, unmeasurable, and unpredictable."[3] This is frequently the position of the researcher who has tried to measure promotion effectiveness without *first* understanding the purchasing process. He finds that some condition in the market changed during the test; but he does not know whether it affected the test, and if so by how much.

However, if the major influences are known in advance, their effects can be controlled, or be measured and the results adjusted. The effects of inequalities in distribution, for instance, can be equalized, while competitive activity can be measured so that the final results of the test can be adjusted to compensate for measured changes, if necessary.

Suppose that economic conditions and price differential are found to be important factors for a product because they strongly influence the answers to the questions, "Should I buy?" and "Which one should I buy?" in that order. The test can then be designed to take place at points which will equalize the effects of economic conditions. The price differential at the various test points could be observed and recorded, so that the test results can be adjusted later; or the price differential might be held constant by appropriate action on the part of field marketing personnel. In either case, complete post-test data on the major factors are available.

Experimental Design

The second area where measurements of promotion effectiveness so often go astray is in the area of research techniques.

The problem is not really one of availability or adequacy of techniques. The concepts of experimental design are quite suitable for the problem at hand, and excellent reference works are available.[4]

Instead, the problem seems to be one of inadequate field application. This seems to arise in two ways: lack of knowledge of the variables to be controlled, and insufficient replications.

The first source of difficulty, lack of knowledge of the variables, will automatically become less of a problem once the purchasing process is understood. When the major variables are known, the number of test cells is fairly well fixed. If brand share has a major effect on the performance of a promotion for a product, the test may have to be conducted under a number of brand-share conditions to control this variable sufficiently.

The second source of difficulty, insufficient replications, makes analysis of test results difficult at best, and can lead to incorrect conclusions at worst. The effectiveness of a promotion can and does vary widely under field conditions. Sufficient replications will sample these variations, and allow conclusions to be drawn based on average performance.

A recent effectiveness test involving a test

[2] Lee Adler, "Sales Promotion Effectiveness *Can Be Measured*," *Journal of Marketing*, Vol. 27 (October, 1963), pp. 69–70.

[3] Weber, same reference as footnote 1, at p. 16.

[4] W. G. Cochran and G. M. Cox, *Experimental Designs* (New York: John Wiley & Sons, Inc., 2nd edition, 1957); O. L. Davies, *Design and Analysis of Industrial Experiments* (New York: Hafner Publishing Company, 1954).

cell and three controls was replicated 35 times. The final conclusion about the effectiveness of the promotion was based on average performance, and provided a useful evaluation of the profit contributed by the promotion. Individual cell results varied from a gain of 76% to a loss of 17%—far from the average effectiveness of the promotion.

Measuring Promotion Effectiveness

The effectiveness of promotions can be measured under field conditions, although inadequate preparation before the test may obscure that fact. A thorough understanding of the purchasing process for the product is mandatory *before* the test begins and rigorous adherence to experimental design *during* the test is necessary, if meaningful results are to be achieved.

Unfortunately techniques are difficult to separate from content in this area of marketing research. This tends to limit the work that can be published without divulging competitive information; and so it is difficult to move from the general to the specific in a discussion of promotion-effectiveness measurement.

However, consider one recent study in the area of promotion-effectiveness measurement, the "Super Drug X-Ray."[5] This is an interesting example of the way in which an under-

[5] The results of this study were published by the Point of Purchase Advertising Institute, Inc., in a series of four POPAI *Research Reports* entitled "The Super Drugstore Customer," "The Super Drugstore Traffic Patterns," "The Super Drugstore In-Store Displays," and "Criterion for Displays Decisions-Profit Contribution."

standing of the purchasing process is accomplished, and measurement of the sales and profit generated by various types of promotion is clearly achieved.

The study began by defining the characteristics of customers of "super" drug stores and detailing the in-store behavior of these customers. Personal interviews and recorded observations were used to collect the data used in understanding the purchasing process. Analysis of these data resulted in the modification of a number of notions about the customers of "super" drug stores and their in-store behavior.

Using this information as a base, tests of the sales performance of various types of point-of-purchase displays were designed, using experimental methods. Records of unit sales and dollar profits were kept before, during, and after the test periods. Analysis of these data clearly pointed out certain types of displays, materials, and signs as producing the most dollars of profit.

Conclusions

Three good reasons to reject the conclusion that promotion effectiveness cannot be measured are:

1. A conceptual framework can be developed to produce measurable promotion objectives.

2. The methodology to use in promotion effectiveness measurement is available.

3. When the proper conceptual framework has been developed and the proper methodology applied, promotion effectiveness *is* being measured.

B.   RESEARCH AND APPLICATIONS

The first article in this section (Evans) looks at selling as a dyadic relationship. The second selection (Kirchner and Dunnette) is a report that tells how the successful salesman sees himself.

36-C   SELLING AS A DYADIC RELATIONSHIP—A NEW APPROACH

F. B. Evans (Marketing Educator)

Very little is known about what takes place when the salesman and his prospect meet. The two parties meet in a highly structured situation, and the outcome of the meeting depends upon the resulting interaction. In this sense, the "sale" is a social situation involving two persons. The interaction of the two persons, in turn, depends upon the economic, social, physical, and personality characteristics of each of them. To understand the process, however, it is necessary to look at both parties to the sale as a dyad,[1] not individually. Specifically the hypothesis is: the sale is a product of the particular dyadic interaction of a given salesman and prospect rather than a result of the individual qualities of either alone. This approach to the selling situation is quite different from the ones typically found in business practice.

Selling Life Insurance

Life insurance selling is considered to be one of the higher types of "creative" selling. It is highly rated among sales occupations. The life insurance agent is better liked and thought to be better trained, more honest, less aggressive, and less high pressured than the automobile or real estate salesman.[2] It is also an occupation where relatively few succeed in the long run; less than a quarter of the new inexperienced agents last through the first four years.

Rarely does the life insurance purchaser seek out either the agent or the company. The agent must locate the prospect and sell him upon his need for (more) insurance. Also, few people discriminate among the major life insurance companies in the United States. The typical view is that all the large companies are equally good and that their prices and services are identical.[3] The particular life insurance agent who contacts a prospect is the critical factor in determining whether or not a sale is made. Little life insurance would be sold without the actions of the salesmen.

Dyadic Interaction in Life Insurance Selling

In spite of the recognized importance of the relationship between the life insurance agent and his prospect almost no research has been done which focuses upon them as an interacting pair.[4] A study is now being conducted to examine the interaction situation of particular salesman-prospect dyads. The sample consists of approximately 125 established and successful salesmen and some 500 of their particular prospects, half of whom purchased from the agents and half of whom did not. The analysis will focus upon the dyads, successful outcomes versus unsuccessful outcomes.

The main hypothesis of this study is that the interaction in the dyad determines the results. The more similar the parties in the dyad are, the more likely a favorable outcome, a sale. The areas being studied include the social, economic, physical, personality, and communicative characteristics of both parties. Also included are the salesman's role and the

Source: F. B. Evans, "Selling as a Dyadic Relationship," *The American Behavioral Scientist*, Vol. 65 (May, 1963), pp. 76–79.

[1] For a general discussion of dyad analysis, see M. W. Riley, *et al.*, *Sociological Studies in Scale Analysis* (New Brunswick, N.J.: Rutgers University, 1954).

[2] R. K. Bain, "The Process of Professionalization: Life Insurance Selling" (unpublished doctoral dissertation, University of Chicago, 1959, p. 342).

[3] Unpublished data, by the writer, 1959.

[4] Research on life insurance selling is commonplace but it has followed the traditional marketing methodologies. *Supra.*

TABLE 1

Comparison of Sold and Unsold Prospects' Recall and Attitudes Towards Sales Agent Who Called on Them

Interaction Indicator	Sold (Percentage)	Unsold (Percentage)
Consider salesman a friend	31	6
Consider salesman an expert	67	55
Salesman liked me as a person	78	60
Salesman enjoys his job	95	75
Salesman enjoyed talking to me	98	71
Prospect knew salesman's name	76	32
Would introduce salesman to my business friends	92	78
Would introduce salesman to my social friends	89	79
Salesman represents the best company	20	10
Denied agent's call	0	20
Company A, not represented by salesman, is best	18	17
Total dyads	(45)	(104)

prospect's view of it, sales techniques, product and company knowledge, and the influence of third parties to the selling situation.

Although this study is only about one-third completed at this time, comparisons of the sold and unsold prospects (alone) indicate the importance of their reactions to the particular salesman who called upon them. Table 1 shows that prospects who purchase insurance know more about the salesman and his company and feel more positively towards them than prospects who do not buy.

The salesmen in this study have shown a high degree of role involvement. Most feel that they are salesmen 24 hours a day, not just for working hours; they feel they work no harder than people with office jobs, and are satisfied with the way their lives have turned out. They enjoy talking to prospects and typically discuss things other than insurance with the prospects.

Half of the agents view their job as being like that of a minister; the other half think it is more like a teacher's. None believe it is like other sales jobs. They say that they hold the clients' interests higher than either a lawyer or tax accountant does. They do not feel that they are intruders upon the prospect's privacy and they claim not to be personally upset by a prospect's refusal to buy. Also they conform to rigid standards of dress which they think the role requires.

In spite of their role involvement these salesmen exhibited many conflicting attitudes.

Less than 10% of them would like to see their sons follow in their footsteps. They claimed that they enjoyed meeting new people, yet over two-thirds of them said they would quit selling if they had to make only cold canvas calls. They feel they need introductions or referrals from past clients. Three-quarters of the agents indicated no interest in the professional C.L.U. degree, nor did they believe it would in any way help their selling.

Although the agents realize that they must please their prospects, they tend to deny the importance of the interpersonal relations. They say that their prospects are the kind of people they'd like to know better as friends, the kind they'd invite to a family party or to their church's picnic. Still they claim that a prospect's age, religion, ethnic background, appearance, or whether he has children makes no difference to them. It seems quite unselective. The agents in the study are all married men with children, and the majority do not smoke.

The agents equate hard work with success. They want to tell the prospect what's best for him. They prefer to call on prospects at home, in the evening, and to talk to them in either the dining room or kitchen. A table is a handy sales tool. Some agents like to have the wife present when the sales presentation is made but most are indifferent on this point. In carrying out his role the salesman believes he knows the expectations and reactions of his prospects. In this he is only partially right.

The agent's training and his job expectations make him believe (or want to believe) that he can sell everyone. The agents tend to deny the importance of their interaction with particular kinds of prospects. However, analysis of the dyads available so far in this study points to the importance of certain similarities between the salesman and his prospect. Table 2 indicates that the successful dyads are more alike internally than the unsuccessful ones. The differences are small, but they are consistent.

The more alike the salesman and his prospect are, the greater the likelihood for a sale. This is true for physical characteristics (age, height), other objective factors (income, religion, education) and variables that may be related to personality factors (politics, smoking). It is also important to note that the perceived similarity for religion and politics is much higher and of greater importance to the sales than the true similarity.

Summary and Conclusion

Life insurance selling is commonly conceived of as depending upon the relationship

TABLE 2

Internal Pair Similarity of Sold and Unsold Dyads

Characteristic	Sold Dyads (Percentage)	Unsold Dyads (Percentage)	Total (Percentage)
Salesman same height or taller than prospect	32	68	100
Salesman shorter than prospect	28	72	100
Salesman same or better educated than prospect	35	65	100
Salesman less educated than prospect	23	77	100
Salesman and prospect less than nine years apart in age	33	67	100
Salesman and prospect more than nine years apart in age	25	75	100
Salesman earns same or more than prospect	33	67	100
Salesman earns less than prospect	20	80	100
Salesman and prospect either both smokers or both non-smokers	32	68	100
Salesman and prospect have different smoking habits	26	74	100
Salesman and prospect have same religion	32	68	100
Salesman and prospect have different religions	28	72	100
Salesman and prospect have same political party	35	65	100
Salesman and prospect have different political party	27	73	100
Prospect perceives salesman's religion the same as his own	36	64	100
Prospect perceives salesman's religion different from his own	28	72	100
Prospect perceives salesman's political party the same as his own	48	52	100
Prospect perceives salesman's political party different from his own	20	80	100
Total dyads	30 (45)	70 (104)	100 (149)

between the salesman and his prospect yet the salesman-prospect dyad has rarely been studied. The traditional marketing approach to selling has been contrasted with interaction studies in sociology and medicine. Research is now being done on the salesman-prospect dyad. Some early results of this study indicate differences in the ways sold and unsold prospects viewed the particular salesman who called upon them, how the salesman views his role, and differences in pair similarity between sold and unsold dyads. Similarity of attributes within the dyad appears to increase the likelihood of a sale.

Much more basic research into various aspects of the selling situation will be needed before any definitive and practical results may be expected.

36-D THE SUCCESSFUL SALESMAN—AS HE SEES HIMSELF

Wayne K. Kirchner (Marketing Executive) and Marvin D. Dunnette (Marketing Executive)

Personality tests, whether they be administered to salesmen, managers, or clerical help, are the most difficult kind of psychological tests to evaluate because they rely heavily upon the testee's own subjective answers. Though it may be true, under normal circumstances, that a man is the best judge of his own personality, it is a generally known and accepted fact that a job applicant is very likely to give answers on a personality test that will make him "look good."

In these circumstances it is difficult for him to be fully objective and, therefore, truthful in describing himself. He tends to put down what is most socially desirable. Aware of this limitation, psychologists are constantly searching for new approaches to personality testing that will minimize this social desirability factor and virtually force the person being tested to give as objective an answer as possible.

A relatively new approach that is now being used to achieve objective personality testing is the Adjective Checklist. In this method, the person being tested is given a checklist consisting of 36 groups of five adjectives each. His task is to pick, from each group, the adjective most descriptive of himself and the one least descriptive of himself.

The adjectives used in the checklist have been equated statistically in terms of social

desirability. (This was done by asking large numbers of people to judge the degree of favorability of a great many adjectives. From these judgments, an index of social desirability was obtained for each one.) In other words, the favorability or unfavorability of each adjective has been determined and expressed in numerical terms.

On the Adjective Checklist, those adjectives found to be most alike in social desirability are grouped together. Here, for example, is one group:

- (a) Sturdy
- (b) Handsome
- (c) Tidy
- (d) Intelligent
- (e) Cheerful

These are all, obviously, favorable adjectives; their social desirability was found to be approximately the same. It is a difficult enough task for the person being tested to pick, from such a group, the two adjectives which he considers most and least like him. It is even more difficult for him to make himself "look good" on such a test.

Eliminating Faking

Thus, the person being tested is forced to make an objective choice, thereby minimizing the social desirability factor. Consequently, the Adjective Checklist provides a more subtle approach to personality testing than the suspect method of presenting only one list of adjectives to a subject and asking him to check those which best describe himself. In addition to providing a more objective description, the

SOURCE: Wayne K. Kirchner and Marvin D. Dunnette, "The Successful Salesman—As He Sees Himself," *Personnel*, Vol. 35 (November–December, 1958), pp. 67–70. © 1958 by the American Management Association, Inc.

checklist should help, therefore, to minimize faking.

By means of the Adjective Checklist, the tendencies of various groups to make characteristic responses (i.e., to pick certain adjectives as most or least like themselves), can be observed. In the particular study under discussion here, responses to the checklist made by top-notch and less effective salesmen at the Minnesota Mining and Manufacturing Company were analyzed. The purpose was to see if the top-notch salesmen possessed a self-concept different from that possessed by the less effective salesmen. If so, the differences could be used to size up sales applicants and to predict their ultimate selling effectiveness.

As part of a large sales research project,

over 600 salesmen employed by 3M volunteered to take the series of tests being used to select sales applicants. One part of the study involved the filling out of adjective checklists. At the same time, measures of selling effectiveness were obtained for each salesman from his particular manager. In this way, the top-notch and less effective groups were identified. The two groups were then compared in terms of their answers to the various adjective combinations.

The adjectives selected most often by the top-notch and less effective salesmen as most descriptive and least descriptive of themselves are shown in Table 1, from which it will be seen that differences do exist between the way top-notch salesmen see themselves

TABLE 1
Adjectives That Differentiate Between Top-Notch and Less Effective Sales Groups

More Often Picked by Top-notch Salesmen As Most Descriptive	More Often Picked by Less Effective Salesmen As Most Descriptive	More Often Picked by Top-notch Salesmen As Least Descriptive	More Often Picked by Less Effective Salesmen As Least Descriptive
Successful	Unselfish	Scientific	Sharp-witted
Fair-minded	Leisurely	Mechanically	Directive
Uninhibited	Mechanically	inclined	Generous
Persistent	inclined	Original	Pleasure-seeking
Outspoken	Jolly	Reflective	Opportunistic
Opportunistic	Imaginative	Inventive	Clever
Spontaneous	Tough	Complicated	Emotional
Energetic	Tactful	Stolid	Thorough
Orderly	Unexcitable	Interests wide	Quick
Persuasive	Independent	Self-denying	Polished
Sociable	Loyal	Tough	Conventional
Wordy	Sentimental	Versatile	Attractive
Methodical	Unemotional	Tactful	Spunky
Thorough	Capable	Thrifty	Initiative
Unconventional	Musical	Mannerly	Trusting
Planful	Handy	Curious	Alert
Active	Contented	Sentimental	
Confident		Artistic	
Conventional		Reasonable	
Ambitious			
Stern			
Daring			
Competitive			
Excitable			

Note. The total number of top-notch salesmen was 86; the total number of less effective salesmen was 44. The less effective group is smaller because salesmen with less than two years' experience were eliminated from the sample as most were rated low in sales effectiveness. This, for the most part, actually reflected age, not ability, and would have tended to bias the sample.

and the way less effective salesmen see themselves. There are definite distinctions in the adjectives selected by the two groups.

Secondly, there seems to be an underlying logic in the adjectives chosen. For example, the adjectives selected most often by the top-notch salesmen as most descriptive of themselves tend to be adjectives that have the flavor of success about them. Top-notchers see themselves as persistent, thorough, confident, successful, opportunistic, persuasive, ambitious, and so on—all attributes usually believed to be desirable in a salesman. On the other hand, less effective salesmen tend to see themselves as a compound of qualities that, however worthy they may be, seem to have little direct bearing on successful salesmanship.

Some interesting deductions may also be made by comparing the adjectives selected by the two groups as least descriptive of themselves. Thus, the top-notchers do not see themselves as scientific, inventive, mechanically inclined, artistic, and so on. They are doers, rather than thinkers. By contrast, the less effective salesmen seem to shy away from adjectives that indicate resourcefulness, drive, or opportunism.

From these findings, we might form the hypothesis that better salesmen actually tend to see themselves as salesmen, whereas less effective salesmen do not. Logically, this makes good sense. A top-notch salesman *should* be one whose self-concept, or role in life, is focused on selling as a career and, in fact, as a total way of living.

Admittedly, the evidence for this hypothesis is not clear cut and is, at best, speculative. It does, however, tie in well with the idea sociologists have been stressing for years— that people are innately equipped to fit certain roles and that those who find their niche are the most successful.

The fact that better salesmen describe themselves differently from less effective ones and that these differences make sense may prove to be a valuable aid in sizing up new sales applicants and their chances of success in the field. Ultimately, with the checklist used in this study and others that will be derived from it, it may also become possible to provide more objective data on the personalities possessed by successful people in many other occupations.

DECISION-MAKING
BY CONSUMERS

37 / Believability

A. BACKGROUND AND THEORY

The following two selections deal with the psychology of believability. First, we consider the importance of information, discussion, and consensus in group risk-taking (Wallach and Kogan). Next, we learn about the psychology of communicator credibility (Schweitzer and Ginsburg).

37-A THE ROLES OF INFORMATION, DISCUSSION, AND CONSENSUS IN GROUP RISK TAKING

Michael A. Wallach (Psychologist) and Nathan Kogan (Psychologist)

If members of a group engage in a discussion and reach a consensus regarding the degree of risk to accept in the decisions which they make, their conclusion is to pursue a course of action more risky than that represented by the average of the prior decisions of each individual considered separately. Evidence supporting this proposition has been reported in several recent experiments, with decisions involving a wide range of content. Some of the decision contexts have been hypothetical; others have involved risks of monetary gain or loss and risks of intellectual failure; still others, risks of physical pain.

Our search for an understanding of the risky phenomenon leads to the working assumption that diffusion of responsibility is the process at issue. However, by what means does such a process operate? In all of the work conducted thus far, group discussion to a consensus has constituted the basic experimental operation for inducing the risky shift effect. When we examine group discussion to consensus more closely, we find that it pos-

SOURCE: Michael A. Wallach and Nathan Kogan, "The Roles of Information, Discussion, and Consensus in Group Risk Taking," *Journal of Experimental Social Psychology*, Vol. 1 (January, 1965), pp. 1–19, from pp. 1, 3–5, and 17.

sesses at least three distinguishable components: provision of information about others' judgments, group discussion, and achievement of consensus. Can we dissect these components and study their roles in the production of the basic phenomenon? In specifying more exactly what element within the molar condition of discussion-to-consensus leads to the risky shift effect, we should begin to understand how a mechanism of responsibility diffusion operates.

Let us consider in greater detail the three components just mentioned. In group discussion to a consensus, *information* becomes available to a person concerning the levels of individual risk taking initially favored by his peers, thereby permitting him to make judgmental comparisons with his own initial level of preferred risk. The presentation of this information concerning the risk-taking levels of others thus may serve to tell the subject that other individuals are willing to accept higher degrees of risk than he might have anticipated. As a result, the subject himself comes to favor greater risk taking. Upon this interpretation, then, the group effect, with its presumed spreading of personal responsibility, arises from the construction of a frame of reference regarding the risk-taking levels favored by others. The active causal ingredient in the situation is the comparison of one's individual decision with those made by the other group members. If this is the case, then neither group discussion nor group consensus is a necessary causal factor; rather, they constitute means for providing each member with information that permits him to compare his decisions with those made by his peers.

It is possible, on the other hand, that the necessary causal element consists of *group discussion* in itself. The fact that such verbal interaction serves as a vehicle for disseminating information may be incidental. Diffusion of responsibility may be carried only or especially by actual discussion, with the affective give-and-take which arises from face-to-face communication. Emotional involvement of the kind that discussion can create may be the precondition of a risky shift on the part of the group. Meaningful psychological contact with others may require such discussion, and diffusion of responsibility from one person to others may be possible only if contact of this kind has been established.

Consider, finally, the possible role of *consensus*. To ask a group to achieve a consensus concerning a matter of risk taking is to provide a request that may influence the type of commitment made by the group members. The requirement that a consensus be reached may engender a feeling of commitment to the group as a unit. Such an increased sense of commitment to the group might well constitute the relevant factor behind the risky shift effect, or at least a contributory factor; that is, diffusion of responsibility might be fostered or even initiated by a recentering which lifts decisional responsibility from the individual and places it squarely upon the group as a whole. A consensus requirement could well be one factor that would operate to increase an individual's degree of involvement with the decision making of other group members relative to his degree of reliance upon personal judgment.

In sum, we have analyzed the situation of group discussion to a consensus into three elements: information about the decisions of others, verbal social interaction, and achievement of consensus. Our purpose in the present research is to examine the relative efficacy of these three elements in producing the phenomenon of a group-induced risky shift. What kinds of experimental manipulations can one design toward accomplishing this end? Three conditions should provide us with the necessary data. The first of these is *discussion and consensus* (DC), the standard situation used in our previous work. Matters of risk taking are discussed by the group and a consensus is reached in each case. The second condition that we shall need to study is *consensus without discussion* (C). Here, we need to arrange a situation such that a group of individuals are required to arrive at a consensus in their decisions regarding matters of risk, but the group members cannot engage in discussion as the means of achieving consensus. Their various recommendations to one another must, nevertheless, be public rather than anonymous, so that a factor of anonymity will not distinguish the C from the DC condition. Finally, it will be necessary to investigate the effects of *discussion without consensus* (D). In the case of this condition, we must permit the processes involved in group interaction to operate, but without the requirement that a consensus be arrived at by the group members.

Conclusions

The findings of the present experiment have led us to the source of the risk-taking shifts emanating from group discussion to a consensus. Of the three elements involved in the group encounter—provision of information about the judgments of others, group discussion, and achievement of consensus—our evidence leads to the conclusion that group discussion provides the necessary and sufficient condition for generating the risky shift effect. Information about judgments given by others is not sufficient to produce the effect. The consensus factor, in turn, is neither sufficient nor necessary. In short, we have learned that the group-induced risky shift phenomenon seems to arise from the experience of discussion per se.

37-B FACTORS OF COMMUNICATOR CREDIBILITY

Don Schweitzer (Marketing Educator) and
Gerald P. Ginsburg (Marketing Educator)

The purpose of the present study was to determine the characteristics of communicators that affect recipients' judgments of the communicator's credibility. A list of characteristics was empirically derived and subjected to a factor analysis in order to assess the adequacy of the *a priori* model of communicator credibility offered by Hovland and his associates.

Method

The present study involved two phases. In the first phase subjects were asked to list the relevant characteristics of several highly credible people with whom they had had personal contact. A set of bipolar rating scales was constructed from the lists generated in Phase I. In Phase II these rating scales were used in a judgmental task and the results were factor analyzed to yield information about the number and composition of the dimensions involved in judgments of credibility. The factor analysis was done by the principal axis method with normalized varimax rotation.

PHASE I. Twenty-four students from an upper division summer school class in Educational Psychology were instructed to think of one person who fit into each of four situations specified on separate pages of an experimental booklet. The four specified situations were receiving communications from an expert, from someone whom the subject trusted, from someone who had sold him something, and from someone who had changed the subject's mind about something. The Ss were further instructed to list the characteristics of these four people that made them believe their communications. As an example, the situation concerning the trusted person read as follows:

Think of one person that you would consider worthy of your trust. That person's initials

are _____. Now consider the instances when that person has talked to you, either formally or informally. Please list the characteristics of that person which made you believe what he said.

The Ss were instructed to think of some specific acquaintance for each of the four situations so as to minimize the likelihood of their listing the characteristics contained in social stereotypes of credible persons. The four situations to which the Ss responded were selected so as to elicit characteristics related to each of the two major components of credibility (expertness and trustworthiness) plus two other situations in which credibility obviously plays a part (in addition, one of these situations—the salesman—has not received any attention in credibility studies). This procedure ensured an adequate representation of characteristics for the formation of trustworthiness and expertness factors in Phase II, if such dimensions actually are used to judge the credibility of a speaker.

After completing the lists of characteristics, the subjects were asked to answer a series of questions aimed at determining what they thought the experiment was about. In addition to a direct question about the purpose of the study the subjects were asked upon what they based their opinion, whether they had any hunches about what the experimenter expected and if so, what it was they thought he expected and what led them to believe this. These questions were included in order to determine whether the subjects had responded in terms of the instructions given them in the booklet or in terms of some other structuring of the situation which they arrived at independently of the instruction.

The lists of characteristics generated by the subjects were collated into four lists, one for each situation. The frequency with which each characteristic appeared was noted. The four lists were then combined into one list and finally were coded into general categories.[1]

SOURCE: Don Schweitzer and Gerald P. Ginsburg, "Factors of Communicator Credibility," in Carl W. Backman and Paul F. Secord, *Problems in Social Psychology: Selected Readings.* Copyright 1966 by the McGraw-Hill Book Company. Used with permission of McGraw-Hill Book Company, pp. 94–101.

[1] The coding was done independently by two persons, both very familiar with the study. There

Each of the general categories was given a label and a definition which reflected the meanings of the responses in that category. The coding process yielded twenty-four categories plus three individual responses which could not be coded into any of the categories. The categories were used to form rating scales as described below in Phase II.

PHASE II. The purpose of this phase was to investigate the factor structure of judgments of the credibility of both highly credible speakers and speakers of low credibility. This was implemented by forming bipolar rating scales based on the categories obtained in Phase I and having an independent group of subjects rate two hypothetical speakers on the scales. The judgmental responses were factor analyzed in order to assess the dimensions involved in judgments of communicator credibility.

The rating scales were derived in the following manner. From each of the twenty-four categories derived in Phase I, the most representative and most frequently mentioned characteristics were selected and paired with their opposites. From this list, two pairs from twenty-three of the twenty-four categories were selected to be included in the final set of scales.[2] Two criteria were used to select the pairs to be included in the final set of scales. First, the pair had to adequately represent the category from which it was selected; second, neither member could have a strongly negative connotation. Negatively connoted terms were avoided in an attempt to reduce the effects of any bias that the subjects might have had against characterizing others in strongly negative terms.

The forty-six pairs finally selected were ordered at random except for the restriction that the two pairs from any given category had to be separated by at least two pairs from other categories. To reduce response bias the negative member was presented first for half of the pairs. Each pair of words was used as the polar terms of a seven place rating scale. The

set of rating scales served as the measuring instrument in this phase of the study.

Data for Phase II were collected from 181 students enrolled in General Psychology. Each subject was given an experimental booklet which contained complete instructions and the introductions for two hypothetical speakers, each of which was followed by the list of rating scales. The instructions informed the Ss that they would be asked to rate two individuals on a number of scales, and gave detailed instructions on how to use the rating scale.

The topic of the would-be speeches was "The Home Disaster Shelter." The first introduction concerned a Professor Hugo Meier. The introduction stated that he had received a Ph.D. degree, served on the "President's Special Committee on Civil Preparedness," published two books and innumerable articles on the topic of civil preparedness and organized civil preparedness programs on the city, state, and national levels. In addition, hypothetical quotations lauding Dr. Meier were included. These quotations were attributed to Edward R. Murrow and *The New York Times*.

The second introduction concerned a Mr. Otto Schmidt, who was made to appear low in credibility. The description stated that he had never finished high school, accused him of shrewd business maneuvering, and said that his businesses had been investigated by the Better Business Bureau on three occasions. Included also was a hypothetical quotation from the local press that was far from complimentary to Mr. Schmidt.

Results and Discussion

The subjects in Phase I made a total of 430 responses, with a mean of eighteen responses per subject. The mean numbers of responses per subject for the four situations were 5.08, 4.67, 4.00, and 4.17 respectively. All but three of the responses were coded into the twenty-four categories mentioned earlier. The answers to the questions concerning the subject's hunches about the study indicated that the subjects had responded in terms of the instructions given to them. Thus, the purpose of the first phase was adequately met: the four situations elicited approximately equal numbers of responses, almost all of the responses were coded into a set of general descriptive cate-

---

were few inconsistencies, and these were resolved through discussion only after each other had completely finished his task.

[2] The category labeled "Appearance" was eliminated because subjects were not going to see any communicators and, therefore, could not be expected to judge them on this variable.

gories, and subjects responded in terms of the instructions.

The analysis of the rating scale data of Phase II was carried on in several stages. First, the means and variances of the responses to the forty-six rating scales were computed separately for the introduction of the highly credible speaker (Hi C Intro) and for the introduction of the speaker with low credibility (Lo C Intro). Then the rating data were factor analyzed, again separately for each of the two introductions. An examination of the means and variances is useful for interpretation of the two factor structures.

As expected, the Hi C Intro speaker was judged in generally favorable terms, while the Lo C Intro speaker was rated in generally unfavorable terms. Furthermore, the mean responses (summed over subjects) for the forty-six scales were more extreme (closer to 1 or 7) under the Hi C Intro than under the Lo C Intro. This was reflected in the much greater variance of the Hi C Intro means than of the Lo C Intro means ($t = 23.94$, $p < .001$), although the means of the two distributions of mean responses did not differ significantly ($t = .07$). In addition, there was more agreement among Ss under the Hi C Intro than under the Lo C Intro (the mean of the forty-six Hi C Intro variances was significantly smaller than that of the Lo C Intro variances, tested by t-test for correlated variances, $p < .01$). A plausible implication of these comparisons is that categories for the description of people with negative characteristics are less well defined and more poorly learned in our culture than are categories for the description of people with favorable characteristics. This would lead to lower consensus under the Lo C Intro than under the Hi C Intro.

A total of twenty-eight factors emerged in the rotated factor matrix for the Lo C Intro. This matrix accounts for 74.2 percent of the total variability of this set of responses. The first factor is a very global one that can best be interpreted as indicating a lack of trustworthiness. In addition to the components one would expect to find in terms of their model, the obtained factor contains such first order components as "intuitive," "braggard," "crude," and "unconcerned." The second factor in the matrix is also very global in nature. It clearly indicates a lack of expertise.

Factors III and IV of this matrix refer to expectations concerning the communicator's mode of presentation. The third factor indicates that the communicator was expected to lack the techniques of public speaking and to be inept in the use of English. The fourth factor reveals that this communicator was expected to be persuasive but boring and unbelievable. The fifth factor indicates that the subjects perceive this communicator as unlike themselves. Factor VI, like Factors III and IV, is concerned with mode of presentation. Here again, the speaker was expected to lack the techniques of public speaking.

The factor matrix generated by the responses to the other introduction (Hi C Intro) contains twenty-seven factors and accounts for 59.79 percent of the variance. The first factor in the matrix indicates that the subjects expected the speaker to be trustworthy. However, the inclusion of such components as "humble," "refined," and "warm" indicates that this communicator also was expected to be gracious. Factors II through IV are related to expectations concerning the mode of presentation of this communicator. Factor II indicates that the highly credible communicator was expected to be inspiring and stimulating, while Factor III reveals that he was expected to be professional, and Factor IV shows that he was expected to present the techniques of public speaking. Factors V, VI, and VII reflect expectations that the speaker will be straightforward, open minded, and adept in the use of English, respectively. The remaining factors in the matrix reveal that the communicator having high credibility was perceived as logical, sincere, professional, aware of the needs of others, problem oriented, expert, discreet, informed, a good advisor having foresight, and impartial.

A comparison can now be made between the two factor structures. First, it should be noted that more factors were generated in describing the communicator having high credibility. Second, the factors found in the Lo C Intro matrix are of a more global nature than are those found in the other matrix. It should also be noted that the substance of the factors differs between the two situations. All of these points are related to the issue raised earlier, namely, that the categories used to describe persons with negative characteristics are not as well defined in our culture as are those used to describe persons with positive characteristics. This assertion is supported by the moderate values of the means, the size of the variances, the number and global nature of the factors, and the substantive makeup of the factors related to the communicator who is low in credibility.

There is, however, another possible interpretation of these results. It may be that the characteristics used to describe communicators of low credibility are not simply the opposite of those used to describe communicators of high credibility. It should be remembered that subjects in the first phase were asked to list characteristics of communicators which made them believe what these communicators said. The terms used to define the scales in the second phase were these positive characteristics and their opposites. It may be that the crucial characteristics necessary to define communicators of low credibility were not obtained by this procedure. Regardless of which of these interpretations is correct, the fact still remains that the two factor structures differed considerably. The factors describing the highly credible communicator are much more specific than those for the communicator with low credibility. Many more factors are necessary to describe the communicator of high credibility. An "expert" factor does not emerge for the highly credible communicator. Many

factors in addition to "expertness" and "trustworthiness" are required to describe either of the communicators.

The results of this study have several important implications for the concept of communicator credibility which are not precluded by the limitations discussed above. In the first place, it seems very likely that the recipient's judgment of the credibility of a communicator is based upon more than perceptions of "trustworthiness" and "expertness." In the second place, the perceived characteristics which underlie low credibility are not necessarily the opposites of the characteristics which underlie high credibility. For example, the absence of trustworthiness and expertness cues may be condition enough for a judgment of low credibility, but the presence of those cues may not be enough for a judgment of high credibility. Thirdly, the perceived trustworthiness and perceived expertness of a communicator appear to be determined by a wide set of characteristics. Finally, the results of the present study strongly suggest that the particular cues, or perceived characteristics, which influence the recipient's judgment of credibility will vary across communication contexts and across populations of recipients. For example, cues which imply expertness of a speaker may not be influential in effecting judgments of high credibility in a college context, where expertness of the speaker is part of the everyday environment.

B. RESEARCH AND APPLICATIONS

The research selected for this section (Ehrlich, Guttman, Schonbach, and Mills) explores post decision exposure to relevant information.

37-C POSTDECISION EXPOSURE TO RELEVANT INFORMATION

Danuta Ehrlich (Psychologist), Isaiah Guttman (Psychologist), Peter Schonbach (Psychologist) and Judson Mills (Psychologist)

Under what conditions will persons voluntarily expose themselves to information? This is an important theoretical and practical question for those interested in social influence processes. It is widely accepted that the audiences of mass media are to a large extent self-selected. However, there has been little rigorous specification or systematic research concerning the variables related to seeking out or avoidance of new information. Festinger has recently proposed a theory (2) which makes some definite predictions about selective exposure to information following decisions, and it is the purpose of this study to test several of them. Before the specific predictions from the theory are stated the relevant parts of Festinger's theory will be summarized briefly.

The theory is concerned with relations among cognitive elements, that is, things which a person knows about himself or his environment. For example, knowing that one is on a picnic is a cognition about one's behavior; knowing that it is raining, a cognition about the environment. Cognitive elements may be either consonant, dissonant, or irrelevant to one another. A behavioral element is consonant with an environmental element if, considering these elements in isolation, the behavioral would follow from the environmental element; dissonant if, considering them alone, it would *not* follow. Thus knowing that it is raining is ordinarily dissonant with going on a picnic; consonant with staying home.

SOURCE: Danuta Ehrlich, Isaiah Guttman, Peter Schonbach, and Judson Mills, "Postdecision Exposure to Relevant Information," *The Journal of Abnormal and Social Psychology,* Vol. 54 (January, 1957), pp. 98–102. Copyright 1957 by the American Psychological Association, and reproduced by permission.

According to the theory, the presence of dissonance gives rise to pressure to reduce or eliminate it. The strength of these pressures is a function of the magnitude of the dissonance. The theory also states that the greater the importance or the value of the elements involved, the greater is the magnitude of the dissonance and hence the greater the pressure to reduce it.

The total magnitude of the dissonance between a behavioral element and the cluster of relevant environmental elements, assuming they are all equally important, is equal to the proportion of dissonant elements in this cluster. Therefore, one way that a person can reduce dissonance is to add new environmental elements that are consonant with his behavior. Thus the theory predicts that persons with dissonance in general seek out consonant information and avoid information that would introduce new dissonant elements.

When a person makes a decision, a corresponding behavioral element is established and his cognitions about the alternatives among which he has chosen are then consonant or dissonant with this element. All the favorable aspects of the unchosen alternatives and unfavorable aspects of the one chosen are dissonant with the choice. Consequently, the creation of dissonance is a common result of decisions. After the choice has been made, the person therefore tends, according to the theory, to expose himself to information that he perceives as likely to support the decision and to avoid information that is likely to favor the unchosen alternatives.

The purchase of a new automobile, for example, is usually a rather important decision for a person. Considerable dissonance should exist for a new car owner immediately after he has bought his car, all "good" features of the makes he considered, but did not buy, and "bad" features of the one he bought are now dissonant with his ownership of the car. He should also attempt to reduce this dissonance. In this instance of postdecision dissonance, sources of information in support of the decision are readily available. Since automobile advertising contains only material favoring the particular car advertised, reading advertisements of his own make is one way a new car owner can get information supporting his choice and thereby reduce his dissonance. On the other hand, reading advertisements of other cars may increase his dissonance.

The specific hypotheses of the study were as follows:

1. After a decision persons tend to seek out dissonance-reducing information. Thus new car owners will read advertisements of their own cars more often than those of (*a*) cars which they considered but did not buy and (*b*) other cars not involved in the choice.

2. After a decision persons tend to avoid dissonance-increasing information. Thus new car owners will read advertisements of considered cars less often than of other cars.

3. Postdecision dissonance is, in general, reduced over a period of time. Thus these selective tendencies in readership of advertising will not exist for owners of old cars.

The theory predicts other consequences of postdecision dissonance, for example, changes in desirability ratings of chosen and unchosen alternatives as investigated by Brehm (1). Our present concern is limited to the effect of decision making on exposure to information.

Method

One hundred and twenty-five male residents of Minneapolis and its suburbs, who owned one of eight popular automobile makes, were interviewed in an "advertising survey," after an appointment had been made by telephone. Sixty-five of the respondents were new car owners chosen randomly from a list of recent auto registrations, dated four to six weeks before the time of the interview. The other 60 respondents owned cars manufactured in 1952 (three years before the study was done) or before, and were selected from the Minneapolis telephone directory. (Actually about a third of the old car owners bought their cars after 1952; however, none of the purchases were made during the year in which the study was done.) The number of owners in different makes of cars was approximately equal in both groups.

During the course of the interview:

1. Each respondent was asked to recall recent automobile advertisements which had impressed him particularly and to say where and when he had seen the advertisement, whether or not his impression was favorable, and how much he had read (Recall Data).

2. Each was shown issues of popular magazines which appeared four weeks or less before the interview (after the new car owners had made their decisions) and copies of one of the two Minneapolis newspapers for seven days prior to the interview. Only those publications were included which the respondent previously indicated as having read regularly. For each issue the respondent was asked if he had seen it, and if so, he was shown each car advertisement it contained, and asked whether he had noticed the advertisement, and, if he had, whether he had "read all," "read some," or "just glanced at it" (Recognition Data).

3. Each was presented with eight large plain envelopes bearing the names of the eight popular makes. The respondent was told that his reactions to some "new automobile advertising" were desired and asked to choose two of the envelopes in order to read and comment upon the material they contained (Envelope Data).

At the conclusion of the interview the respondent was asked to name other makes which he "seriously considered" before he decided to buy his present car.

Results

As a prerequisite for the predicted selectivity in a person's exposure to information, he must have some expectation about the likelihood that a given item will reduce or increase dissonance for him. Thus the new car owners must first recognize that a particular make is being advertised, i.e., they must at least notice the advertisement. For each respondent the percentage of advertisements which he read, of those which he noticed, was therefore calculated separately for his own car, the cars he considered, other cars not involved in the choice, and also for those considered and other

TABLE 1

Mean Percentages of Advertisements Noticed and of Advertisements Read of Those Noticed[a]

Car Owners	Make Advertised			
	Own	Considered	Other	Considered Plus Other
	Percentage Noticed			
New	70 (52)	66 (50)	46 (64)	48 (64)
Old	66 (51)	52 (31)	40 (60)	41 (60)
	Percentage Read of Those Noticed			
New	67 (47)	39 (46)	34 (64)	35 (64)
Old	41 (44)	45 (20)	27 (57)	30 (57)

[a] Corresponding Ns appear in parentheses.

Note. The Ns are reduced because in some cases no advertisements of a particular kind appeared in the issues shown or none of those which appeared were noticed. They are further reduced because not all respondents named cars as "seriously considered."

cars combined. (The categories "read all" and "read some" were combined because there were too few advertisements reported as read completely to make a separate analysis feasible; results are essentially the same for these categories.) The means of these percentages for the two groups and the corresponding N's are reported in Table 1, which also contains means for the percentage of advertisements noticed of those which were shown.

It can be seen from Table 1 that new car owners read advertisements of their own make more often than advertisements of both considered and other cars. These differences do not appear among old car owners; in fact the difference between reading of own and considered car advertisements is in the opposite direction. However, it is obvious from Table 1 that new car owners do not read advertisements of considered cars less often than of other cars. Finally, it is apparent that readership of advertisements, in general, is greater among new car owners.

The significance of these differences was determined by means of the sign test. For each respondent the sign of the comparison between the percentage of advertisements read of the different categories was found and this distribution of signs was tested using the critical values given in Mosteller and Bush (3). Results of these comparisons appear in Table 2 which shows that the differences apparent from Table 1 are significant. New car owners read significantly more advertisements of their own car than of both considered and other

cars; none of the other comparisons yield significant differences. It can be seen that the Ns have been further reduced because these comparisons were not possible for all respondents.

The significance of the differences between new car and old car owners was tested by means of chi square. Results of these tests are also given in Table 2. The comparison *own vs. considered* is in the predicted direction with $p < .05$. The comparison *own vs. other* is significant at the .03 level, and the comparison *own vs. considered plus other* is significant at the .01 level; there is no significant difference for the comparison *considered vs. other*.

One other comparison in the recognition data is worth noting. New car owners were divided into two groups; those who named less than two cars as "seriously considered" and those who named two or more. The difference in reading *own vs. considered plus other* was examined separately for these two groups and was found to be greater for those who considered more than two cars. That is, new car owners who named more than one considered car read relatively more advertisements of their own car. For this group the mean difference of the percentages was 37; that of the other group was 26. The difference between the two groups was tested by a median test and the resulting (two-sided) $p = .19$ (12 of the 19 who considered two or more were above the median; only 12 of the 28 who considered less than two were above it).

TABLE 2

Sign Test Comparisons Between Percentage of Advertisements Read of Different Categories

	Car Owners	
Comparison	New	Old
% Own Minus % Considered	+21	5
	− 4	6
	$p < .01$	n.s.
Between Groups $p < .05$ ($\chi^2 = 3.90$)[a]		
% Own Minus % Other	+31	20
	− 8	16
	$p < .01$	n.s.
Between Groups $p < .03$ ($\chi^2 = 4.93$)		
% Own Minus % (Considered Plus Other)	+32	20
	− 7	17
	$p < .01$	n.s.
Between Groups $p < .01$ ($\chi^2 = 6.89$)		
% Considered Minus % Other	+19	10
	−15	7
	n.s.	n.s.
Between Groups, n.s.		

[a] Corrected for continuity.

For the Envelope Data the difference between groups is in the predicted direction but not significant. Fifty-one of 60 (85%) new car owners chose an envelope of their own car, 45 of 59 (76%) old car owners chose one of their own car. Respondents in both groups obviously chose to read and comment upon "new advertising" of their own makes far more often than would be expected by chance.

The number of impressive advertisements (Recall Data) which the respondents read is too small to make analysis of these data possible. (Of course no advertisements were included which appeared before the new car owners made their decisions or before a comparable length of time for old car owners.)

The data from the recognition of advertisements which appeared in recent publications (after the new car owners made their decisions) strongly support the prediction of Festinger's theory that, after an important decision, persons seek out consonant information. New car owners were found to read advertisements of their own car more often than those of cars they considered but did not

buy, and of other cars not involved in the choice. That this selective tendency in exposure to information is not simply a result of car ownership but is related to decision making is demonstrated by its failure to occur among old car owners. The Envelope Data also indicate that new car owners prefer to read advertisements of their own car although the difference between new and old car owners is not significant.

An alternative explanation of the results might be offered. If people do not remember accurately when they read an advertisement, and if shortly *before* buying a car, persons are more likely to read advertisements of *that* car than of others, then the advertisements of their own make may have actually been read before the decision and the obtained differences may be a result of the new car owners' inability to remember the issue in which they read them. This interpretation seems unlikely since it is plausible to suppose that, *before* their purchase, the new car owners attempted to learn as much as possible about all the different makes involved in their choice and therefore read advertisements of the makes that they considered as often as those of the make that they finally chose. Nevertheless, the possibility that it could account for the data was checked by determining whether the advertisements of the make actually chosen by the new car owners which they said they read also appeared during the month prior to their purchases. Only four of 54 such advertisements also appeared in this period. When these few instances in which the alternate explanation might apply are eliminated from the analysis the results are essentially unchanged.[1]

The prediction that new car owners would read fewer advertisements of considered cars than other cars was not substantiated. However, the data are not sufficient to reject conclusively the hypothesis that dissonance-increasing information is avoided after a decision. It is possible that some of the new car owners expected advertisements of con-

[1] There are only two small changes in the significance tests reported in Table 2 .When the four ads are eliminated the χ^2s for the comparisons between groups for *own minus considered* and for *own minus considered plus other* are reduced to 3.61 and 5.90 respectively.

sidered cars to decrease—not increase—their dissonance. They may have read the advertisements of the rejected cars not with the intention of getting further information about their advantages but for the purpose of finding fault with them, comparing them unfavorably with the chosen car. For example, an owner of a make with high horsepower who regards horsepower as an important feature of automobiles may read advertisements of considered cars of lesser horsepower to remind himself of their inferiority in this respect. We would not expect this to occur frequently but it might happen often enough to account for the failure of the prediction. The data do not provide any test of this interpretation.

The indication that new car owners who named more than one considered car tend to read relatively more advertisements of their own car than do those who named one or none is additional, suggestive evidence for Festinger's theory. Since the total magnitude of dissonance is a function of the proportion of dissonant elements, we would expect that these persons would in general have greater dissonance, for as the number of unchosen alternatives increases the proportion of dissonant elements increases. Therefore the theory predicts that they should show a greater tendency to seek out consonant information.

Summary

Readership of auto advertising by new and old car owners was investigated in order to test some predictions of Festinger's theory of dissonance concerning selective exposure to information following decisions. It was found that new car owners read advertisements of their own car more often than of cars they considered but did not buy and other cars not involved in the choice. These selective tendencies in readership were much less pronounced among old car owners. This finding supports the theoretical derivation that persons in general seek out consonant or supporting information after an important decision in an attempt to reduce dissonance resulting from it.

From the derivation that persons tend to avoid dissonance-increasing information it was predicted that new car owners would read advertisements of considered cars less often than of other cars. The data do not confirm this prediction. It was suggested that some of the new car owners may have expected the considered car advertisements to decrease—not increase—their dissonance.

REFERENCES

1. Brehm, J. W. Postdecision changes in the desirability of alternatives. *J. Abnorm. Soc. Psychol.*, 1956, **52**, 384–389.
2. Festinger, L. The relation between cognition and action. Paper read at Symposium on Cognition, Boulder, Colo., May, 1955.
3. Mosteller, F., & Bush, R. R. Selected quantitative techniques. In G. Lindzey (Ed.), *Handbook of social psychology.* Vol. I. Cambridge: Addison Wesley, 1954.

38 / Making Consumer Decisions

A. BACKGROUND AND THEORY

This section consists of an article (Festinger) that is a psychological analysis of various elements that go into making a decision.

38-A MAKING A DECISION

Leon Festinger (Psychologist)

When a person is faced with a decision between two alternatives, his behavior is largely oriented toward making an objective and impartial evaluation of the merits of the alternatives. This behavior probably takes the form of collecting information about the alternatives, evaluating this information in relation to himself, and establishing a preference order between the alternatives. Establishing a preference order does not immediately result in a decision. The person probably continues to seek new information and to re-evaluate old information until he acquires sufficient confidence that his preference order will not be upset and reversed by subsequent information. This continued information seeking and information evaluation remains, however, objective and impartial.

When the required level of confidence is reached, the person makes a decision. Undoubtedly, the closer together in attractiveness the alternatives are, the more important the decision, and the more variable the information about the alternatives, the higher is the confidence that the person will want before he makes his decision. It is probably this process of seeking and evaluating infor-

mation that consumes time when a person must make a decision.

What evidence do we have to support the above statement? The data concerning the objectivity and impartiality of the pre-decision process are rather consistent. Jecker reports data showing that before the decision is made the person spends equal amounts of time reading favorable and unfavorable information about the alternative he eventually chooses. Davidson and Kiesler and also Jecker present data which show that throughout the pre-decision period there is no noticeable divergence in the attractiveness of the two alternatives involved in the decision. In short, there is no evidence of any biasing influences before the decision is made. Of particular importance in supporting this conclusion are two experiments by Jecker in which subjects in some conditions made decisions but were uncertain of the effect their decisions would have on the outcome. In these conditions we can be quite certain that measurements were taken after the pre-decision period was completed, and yet, in these conditions, the evidence is uniform in indicating the impartiality of information seeking and the absence of any systematic, biasing re-evaluation of alternatives.

Evidence that the pre-decision activity is concerned, to a large extent, with gathering and evaluating information is more tangential. Davidson reports an experiment which

SOURCE: Leon Festinger, *Conflict, Decision, and Dissonance* (Stanford, California: Stanford University Press, 1964), pp. 152–158, at pp. 152–155. © 1964 by the Board of Trustees of the Leland Stanford Junior University.

456

shows that the more a person has thought over the relevant details before dissonance is aroused, the more rapidly does dissonance reduction proceed after the dissonance has been introduced. This experiment was done in order to help understand that the more time the person spent thinking about the alternatives in the pre-decision period, the greater was the amount of dissonance reduction in the post-decision period. Considering all the data, the most plausible interpretation of these results is that the more carefully the person thinks through and evaluates information beforehand, the more rapidly can dissonance reduction proceed once dissonance is aroused. If this interpretation is true, then there is some inferential evidence that in the pre-decision period the person does spend his time considering and evaluating information about the alternatives.

Seeking and evaluating information about the alternatives is, however, not the only thing that occurs in the pre-decision period. It certainly seems plausible to maintain that the decision maker is not a passive person, meekly accepting the decision situation as the environment poses it for him. Certainly, if the alternatives are not to his liking, he will search for other, better alternatives. If there are inevitable unpleasant consequences of making a decision, he will try to avoid making it.

There is one aspect of the pre-decision period about which we would like to speculate briefly. The pre-decision process, as we described it above, sounds like a very sane and rational process. And our data tend to support the idea that this is the way many decisions are made, at least those decisions with which a person is faced in an experimental situation. But casual observation, our own experience, and our intuition lead us to believe that occasionally, perhaps frequently, decisions are made on a rather impulsive basis. There are times when a person makes a decision, even an important one, very quickly, without considering much information about the alternatives. There are even instances when, after careful and thorough consideration of information about the alternatives, the person seems to make his decision on the basis of some minor, almost trivial, aspect. We have little understanding at present of when, and under what conditions, such impulsive decisions are made. Perhaps such behavior is a means of avoiding a situation that promises to be a difficult one. If this were the case, one would expect such impulsive decisions more frequently if the decision is important and the person thinks the alternatives would prove to be very close together in attractiveness. Perhaps such impulsive decisions are made when the information-gathering process seems almost endless. If this were the case, one would expect a greater frequency of impulsive decisions in instances where the person is faced with a large number of alternatives. Until we know more about these matters, our understanding of the pre-decision situation will remain sketchy.

Once the decision is made and the person is committed to a given course of action, the psychological situation changes decisively. There is less emphasis on objectivity and there is more partiality and bias in the way in which the person views and evaluates the alternatives. Let us be clear about the nature of the change. It is not that suddenly all objectivity disappears. Although there is a tendency to look more at consonant than at dissonant material in the post-decision period, this tendency is small and is easily overcome by other factors.

B. RESEARCH AND APPLICATIONS

The first selection (Byrnes) is a report on research that was directed to the question: Can a group of consumers actually report the probability of purchasing an item? The report (Udell) that follows deals with prepurchase behavior of buyers of small electrical appliances.

38-B CONSUMER INTENTIONS TO BUY

James C. Byrnes (Government Executive)

In 1963 the Bureau of the Census interviewed 192 suburban Detroit households about their buying intentions. The main purpose was to see whether respondents could express the likelihood of their purchasing specified durable goods during specified time periods using a probability-of-purchase scale.

Survey statisticians have been reluctant to use probability-of-purchase scales for household surveys, based in part on the belief that typical respondents do not understand the notion of probability. Also, the tendency of respondents to choose scale values at either extreme or the mid-point (clearly evident in this experiment) has led many to believe that the responses are therefore inaccurate and meaningless. However, there is no evidence whatever of what the "real" distribution looks like, and any notion that the presence of error necessarily renders a set of observations useless is patently absurd. Finally, there is the firm intuition that individuals cannot accurately predict how they will behave in the future because there are important factors which the individual does not foresee or cannot control. The economic, social, demographic, and psychological factors which affect consumer behavior during a given period may be grouped into three classes:

1. Factors which the individual has intimate knowledge about at the beginning of the period.

2. Fortuitous and unforeseen events which occur during the period, e.g., the furnace

breaks down and must be replaced, someone in the family takes ill. These affect members of the population in a nonsystematic manner.

3. Events which affect the members of the population in systematic ways, but which most consumers do not foresee, e.g., strikes which limit supply or wars.

Consumer intentions surveys seek to summarize in a useful way the first set of factors. The second and third groups will certainly affect (and bias) any forecast derived from intentions data, although the second group of factors should influence consumption as a whole in similar ways from one time period to the next and thus should not change aggregate behavior. This second group of factors will, however, contribute to the mean square error of any forecast because they affect the behavior of given individuals.

The first and third groups of factors are of major concern to the economist seeking to predict either aggregate or individual behavior. These are the traditional factors of both micro and macro analysis—employment and income, prices, psychological climate, expectations, demographic pressure, individual desires, and other events—which affect aggregate as well as individual behavior.

The successfully conducted consumer intentions survey could provide two types of information. First, it could give a current measure of the future demand for specific goods and services based on factors influencing individuals at the time of the survey, as well as perhaps a measure of the net effect of the change in such factors from one point in time to another. Second, it would give a quantitative measure of the influence of unforeseen change occurring after the forecast.

TABLE 1

Expected and Observed Prior Purchase Rates by Item for Three Periods

	6 Months			12 Months			24 Months		
	Mean scale score of expected purchase[a]	Observed prior purchase rate[b]	Difference	Mean scale score of expected purchase[a]	Observed prior purchase rate[c]	Difference	Mean scale score of expected purchase[a]	Observed prior purchase rate[d]	Difference
Kitchen range	.05	.04	+.01	.10	.06	+.04	.14	.09	+.05
Refrigerator or freezer	.04	.05	−.01	.08	.08	.00	.13	.15	−.02
Washing machine	.07	.03	+.04	.11	.06	+.05	.18	.13	+.05
Clothes dryer	.03	.01	+.02	.06	.04	+.02	.09	.07	+.02
Room air conditioner	.02	.01	+.01	.04	.04	.00	.05	.05	.00
Television set	.07	.03	+.04	.12	.09	+.03	.19	.14	+.05
Dishwasher	.02	.01	+.01	.02	.01	+.01	.03	.01	+.02
Any auto	.16	.13	+.03	.27	.30	−.03	.49	.55	−.06
New auto	.12	.10	+.02	.19	.18	+.01	.35	.35	.00
Used auto	.04	.03	+.01	.08	.12	−.04	.14	.20	−.06

[a] Survey date: November 5–6, 1963.
[b] Survey covered: November 1962–April 1963.
[c] Survey covered: November 1962–October 1963.
[d] Survey covered: November 1961–October 1963; purchases for November–December 1961 were not reported but were estimated as equal to purchases for November–December 1962.
Note: the mean scale score of expected purchases was computed by weighting all "ten" answers as 1.00 (representing certainty), the "nine" answers as .90 or 90 per cent probability, and so on.

The present experiment was designed to test the feasibility of measuring one's current subjective probability of purchase for specific items within specific periods of time and estimating rates of expected purchase for the population under study in a straightforward manner.

Method

Each respondent was first asked the month of purchase of specified items bought by household members during 1962 and 1963. Second, the respondent was given a scale with 11 points, ranging from zero to ten, and told to choose "ten" if he was certain someone in the household would purchase the item during the time interval, with the other positions trailing down to zero, the zero indicating he was certain *no* one would buy the item. Each scale position also carried a descriptive phrase, such as "About even chance, 50–50" for number five, "Almost no chance" for number one, and "Almost certain to buy" for nine. In answering, respondents were required to give the number and not just the descriptive phrase.

The respondent used the scale to indicate the chance that someone in the household would buy an auto and seven household equipment items during three periods: the next six months, the next year, and the next two years. Those who responded with a "three" or higher on the probability of purchasing an auto within two years also were asked the chance that it would be a new car. Three standard attitudinal questions included at the end of the interview also are described below.

Results

Table 1 compares for each item and time interval the rate of expected purchase and the rate of actual purchase reported for comparable periods prior to the survey. The data show a remarkably small bias that could be due to respondents' inability to accurately assess all factors. One reason for the close agreement between expected and observed (for preceding period) purchase rates may be the relative stability in income and other factors during 1962 and 1963. That the responses chosen by the 192 respondents were relevant to the questions asked seems obvious. Respondents reported, to a remarkable degree, the net sum of their desires, expectations, and financial capacity. Although the method was not tested on a cross-section of the U.S. population, the results are encouraging.

Although the respondent's assessment of his

TABLE 2

Expected and Observed Prior Purchases for 12 Months of Seven Household Equipment Items by Outlook on Economic Conditions

	Total Number of Households	Expected Purchases Per Household	Observed Prior Purchases Per Household	Difference
All Households	192	.53	.38	+.15
Jobs				
Easy to get	28	.68	.36	+.32
Hard	107	.52	.41	+.11
Other	57	.47	.33	+.14
Business				
Better	101	.63	.35	+.29
Worse	20	.65	.60	+.05
Other	71	.35	.37	−.02
Time to Buy				
Good	101	.68	.37	+.32
Bad	63	.38	.40	−.02
Other	28	.32	.39	−.07

probability of purchase may represent a biased forecast (e.g., probabilities of one or zero, representing certainty, cannot logically be taken as unbiased) the bias evident in Table 1 seems at least as small as that of any alternative cross-sectional multivariate function based on income, net worth, liquid assets, and attitudes toward spending or saving. One can state categorically that any such alternatives would prove vastly more expensive.

What is not known is the degree of bias inherent in this procedure, the degree to which the bias is due to nonsystematic random events not accurately assessed by the respondent, and the degree to which the net bias remains constant from one time period to another.

Table 2 gives the number of expected and previous purchases per household for all seven items combined, cross-classified by the responses to three attitudinal questions. The first question asked was whether jobs are easy or hard to get; the second asked whether business conditions during the next 12 months would be better or worse; and the third asked whether, "keeping in mind your present finances and your best guess about the future," now is a good or bad time to buy large durable goods.

Table 2 shows that the business conditions and the good or bad "time to buy" questions both served well in isolating those households which expected to buy more items in the coming 12 months than they reported purchasing during the previous year. Another important thing to note, though, is that while optimists sometimes reported about the same rate of expected purchases per household as did pessimists (see "business conditions"), the optimists invariably gave expected purchase rates that were greater than the previous purchase rates. Pessimists, on the other hand, almost always reported about the same rates for expected purchases as for previous purchases.

Thus responses to the probability scale reflect underlying optimism along with other factors. What is not known, though, is whether differences between rates of expected and subsequently realized purchase will be of the same character for both pessimists and optimists.

38-C PREPURCHASE BEHAVIOR OF BUYERS OF SMALL ELECTRICAL APPLIANCES

Jon G. Udell (*Marketing Educator*)

This article summarizes the results of a study of shopping behavior in the selection of small electrical appliances during December, 1964.

The primary objective was to gather data on the *types of information* and *sources of information* that consumers use in shopping for small appliances.

A second objective was to determine the extent and significance of *out-of-store shopping* and *in-store shopping* leading to the purchase. Out-of-store shopping includes all searching and information gathering which occurs outside the retail store, such as reading or listening to advertisements and discussing with other people the merits of various product and patronage alternatives. In-store shopping is the gathering of information by visiting a store or number of stores.

SOURCE: Jon G. Udell, "Prepurchase Behavior of Buyers of Small Electrical Appliances," *Journal of Marketing*, Vol. 30 (October, 1966), pp. 50–52.

The Survey

The two principal difficulties were to identify a representative sample of persons who had purchased a small electrical appliance, and to secure personal interviews with the selected respondents shortly after the date of purchase.

Because many small appliances are purchased as gifts, personal interviews could not be conducted within the purchasers' homes prior to Christmas. Rather than wait until after Christmas or use a mail questionnaire, personal interviews were conducted in retail stores immediately following the purchase of an appliance.

Interviewers were stationed in the small electrical-appliance departments of four Madison, Wisconsin, stores—including downtown, west-side, and east-side shopping center stores, that is, the major geographical areas. The areas north and south of the downtown area are comprised mainly of lakes. The stores included in the study represented the major types of retailers handling small appliances.

In the three weeks preceding Christmas, 770 shoppers were asked to be interviewed, with 705 (90%) cooperating.

Small electrical appliances up to $75 in price were included in the sample. Six products—radios, hair dryers, toasters, coffee makers, electric can openers, and irons—accounted for almost one-half the appliances bought; and 65% of the purchased appliances were priced from $7.51 to $22.51.

As for the respondents: 95% were from 19 to 65 years of age; 75% were married; 60% were males and 40% were females.

Out-of-Store Shopping

Out-of-store sources of information are *controllable* or *noncontrollable*. Controllable sources are those that manufacturers and retailers can influence or control to a substantial degree, such as advertising. Noncontrollable sources are those over which manufacturers and retailers usually have little or no control, such as discussions about products with friends and relatives.

Direct questions were used to secure data on sources of information, on the assumption that the information requested was not strongly associated with social-psychological factors that might induce biased responses. Although this could be a limitation of the study, the apparent frankness and excellent cooperation of the respondents indicated that the direct-questioning approach was appropriate.

An inability to remember may have resulted in a considerable understatement of shopping activity, especially activity related to out-of-store influences and sources of information. However, respondents clearly indicated that advertising and other out-of-store sources of information played a very important role in their shopping behavior.

The respondents were asked if they remembered getting *helpful* information from any sources of information in shopping for the appliance bought. They were also asked which of the sources (that they had mentioned) was *most useful* in providing shopping information.

Advertising in printed media was the most frequently mentioned *controllable source* in shopping for the appliances. As shown in

TABLE 1

Out-of-Store Sources of Information

Sources of Information	Percent Finding Helpful[a]	Percent Finding Most Useful[b]
Controllable:		
Newspaper advertising	25.0	9.6
Mail-order catalogs and circulars	20.7	10.2
Magazine advertising	15.0	2.4
Television advertising	14.2	3.7
Radio advertising	7.0	0.4
Noncontrollable:		
Past experience with the product brand	50.2	33.2
Discussions with friends, relatives, neighbors	33.9	18.7
Consumer rating magazines (*e.g.*, *Consumer Reports*)	9.1	3.0
Telephone calls to stores	3.5	1.0

[a] Percentages do not total 100% because many respondents mentioned more than one source of information; in addition, the less frequently mentioned sources are not shown in the table.
[b] There were 10% who could not recall obtaining helpful information from any source of information other than visiting a store.

Table 1 the most frequently mentioned advertising medium was the newspaper. Mail-order catalogs and circulars were mentioned second most frequently. A majority of the consumers indicated that some type of advertising was helpful in shopping for the purchased appliance.

The *most useful controllable sources* of information were mail-order catalogs and newspaper advertising. Respondents who had purchased at Sears selected mail-order catalogs as most useful more frequently than those purchasing elsewhere; the latter indicated that newspaper advertising was the most useful controllable source.

The most frequently mentioned and *most useful noncontrollable source* of information was past experience with product or brand. One-half found it to be helpful, and one-third said it was most useful. In addition, a substantial number of the respondents indicated that discussions with friends and relatives were helpful in shopping for their purchased appliance.

The role of out-of-store sources of information varied considerably with the demographic characteristics of the respondents. Married persons, particularly married women, mentioned newspaper advertising more frequently than single persons. Single persons, especially single women, mentioned television advertising and magazine advertising more frequently than the married respondents. In fact, television advertising was the most frequently mentioned advertising medium by single women.

Single persons mentioned discussions with friends and relatives more frequently than married persons; for example, 44% of the single men as compared with 28% of the married men mentioned discussions. Past experience with products and brands was mentioned most frequently by the single women and married men.

Families with incomes ranging from $7,500 to $10,000 mentioned newspaper advertising most frequently, and families with incomes below $3,000 mentioned this medium least frequently.

THE DECISION TO BUY. Respondents were asked *when they had tentatively decided to buy* the product which they bought, even though they might not have been sure of such things as the model, brand, and price. There were 83% who bought within one month, 50% within one week, and 22% on the same day they made their tentative purchase decision.

The men respondents indicated that they carried out their decision to purchase an appliance earlier than the women. For example, one-fourth of the male respondents purchased on the day of the decision to buy, in contrast to less than one-fifth of the women.

Respondents also were asked whether their purchase decision was made before, during, or after visiting any stores to look at the product bought. *Most of the purchases* (73%) *were planned prior to shopping in a store*— with 13% making their decision during their first store visit, and 13% after visiting a retail store (1% could not recall).

High-income purchasers were more likely to make their purchase decisions prior to visiting the retail store—85% of those with annual family incomes over $15,000 made prior decisions to buy. Also, more women (79%) than men (69%), and more married (74%) than single respondents (69%), tentatively had decided to buy prior to visiting a store.

Planning to purchase prior to visiting a store was most prevalent among consumers who purchased items priced from $27.51 to $32.51.

READINESS TO PURCHASE. The respondents who indicated that they had made a tentative decision to buy before shopping in a store were asked, "When you went to a store for the first time, did you feel that you were ready to buy on the basis of information which you already had?" *Almost two-thirds* (65%) *of the purchasers believed that they had sufficient information and were ready to buy when they made their first visit to a retail store.*

Readiness to purchase during the first store visit was more prevalent among respondents earning $15,000 or more than any other income group.

In-Store Shopping

Nearly 60% of the respondents had shopped for the small appliances only in the store where the purchase was made. There were 16% who said they had shopped in the store of purchase and one additional store, and 22% in three or more stores. The remaining 2% could not recall how many stores they had visited.

There was a direct relationship between the price of the item purchased and number of stores visited. Only 28% of the purchasers of inexpensive small appliances ($7.50 or less) shopped in two or more stores whereas 63% of the purchasers of appliances costing over $50.00 shopped in two or more stores.

There was no difference in the number of stores visited by men and women shoppers. However, more single respondents (48%) than married respondents (38%) shopped in more than one store; and those with higher levels of education tended to shop in more stores than those with less education.

The number of stores visited was negatively correlated with age. Of 173 purchasers less than 25 years of age, 52% shopped in two or more stores, whereas 37% of those over 25 years shopped in more than one store.

NUMBER OF VISITS. The majority of respondents (77%) had visited the store of purchase only once, 19% made two visits, and 4% made three or more trips. *Apparently a shopper is not likely to examine a small appliance, leave the store without buying it, and return at a later time to make the purchase.* Using the statistics of this study, there is only a 23% probability that this will occur.

The probability of occurrence is even lower if the shopper's family income is below $5,000 or above $10,000, or if the shopper is over 50 years of age. If the commodity involved is priced at less than $7.50, there is only a 3% probability that the potential purchaser will not buy during an initial visit but will return to purchase at a later date.

However, the probability of this occurring increases progressively as the value of the item increases. In fact, 57% of those buying an appliance costing over $50.00 made more than one visit to the store of purchase.

OBTAINING INFORMATION. Interviewers stated to respondents: "There are two major methods of getting information on stores, products, and prices. The first is to visit a store or stores. The second includes discussions with friends, the use of advertised information, the use of catalogs, and all additional sources other than visiting stores."

Respondents were then asked to indicate which general method was most helpful in shopping for the purchased appliance. "Visiting stores" was most helpful for 57% of the respondents, and "sources other than visiting stores" for 30%. There were 8% who stated that the two methods were equally helpful, and 5% of the respondents did not know which method of shopping was most helpful.

Implications

Both availability of shopping information and desire for convenience probably account for many of the shopping patterns revealed in this study.

In any event, it appears that the typical consumer does *not* go from store to store to gather information and to compare products and prices when shopping for small electrical appliances. He or she prefers to do much of this searching and shopping in the comfort of the home by using out-of-store sources of information, especially past experience with products and brands, discussions with friends, and printed media advertising.

This was especially true of those purchasers with higher levels of education and income. Perhaps out-of-store shopping with only one visit to the retail store is likely to become more prevalent as levels of education and income rise.

39 / Evaluating and Predicting Consumer Decisions

A. BACKGROUND AND THEORY

The only article (Kuehn and Day) selected for this section is a discussion of a number of probabilistic models than can be used to study consumer buying behavior.

39-A PROBABILISTIC MODELS OF CONSUMER BUYING BEHAVIOR

Alfred A. Kuehn (Marketing Educator) and Ralph L. Day (Marketing Educator)

The probabilistic approach to developing complex marketing models has strong parallels with the methods of nuclear physicists. In estimating shielding requirements for nuclear reactors, physicists utilize probabilistic models of the behavior of nuclear particles. Through the use of Monte Carlo techniques, they develop predictions of the levels of escaping particles with various levels of shielding. This permits the design of efficient shielding systems for proposed reactors.

In much the same way the builder of a marketing model can develop models which will reflect marketing influences and yield predictions of marketing results. The major differences are: the marketing scientist traces the purchasing behavior of individuals or households rather than nuclear particles; the relevant occurrences are exposures to merchandising influences and purchases, rather than collisions among particles; and the aggregate results are measured in the number of purchases (sales), rather than in the number of particles passing through shielding materials.

Probabilistic models of consumer behavior

SOURCE: Alfred A. Kuehn and Ralph L. Day, "Probabilistic Models of Consumer Buying Behavior," *Journal of Marketing*, Vol. 28 (October, 1964), pp. 27-31.

are still in an early stage of development relative to the progress made in nuclear physics. Emphasis so far has been on understanding the influence of marketing variables such as advertising, price changes, product variation, and special promotions rather than on forecasting sales. If a particular probabilistic model gives good predictions of market behavior, the reasons the model works are of more importance at the present stage of marketing science than the fact that it does work.

The Uncertain Consumer

The starting point in the probabilistic analysis of consumer behavior is the simple static model of the consuming unit (household or individual). The consumer is described by a set of probabilities reflecting the likelihood of his choosing any particular brand of a product class on his next purchase.

At a given time the particular brand an individual will choose is neither wholly predetermined nor a matter of pure chance. Most consumers are predisposed to prefer some brand or brands over others. These predispositions can be influenced by a great variety of factors: recent experiences, custom or habit, reference group influences, or exposures to advertising. The likelihood of purchase of particular brands will also be influenced by external factors such as the availability of favored products in stores the consumer patronizes.

Suppose there are four brands of a particular product, designated A, B, C, and D. As a result of his basic preferences, experiences, and market influences, a particular consumer might have the following probabilities of purchasing each brand: $P_A = .70$, $P_B = .20$, $P_C = .05$, and $P_D = .05$. In other words, the chances are 7 in 10 he will buy brand A, 1 in 5 he will buy B, 1 in 20 he will buy C, and 1 in 20 he will buy D.

The Dynamic Consumer

Purchase probabilities for an individual consumer can be expected to change over time. Even if no specific events directly affect the consumer's purchase probabilities, the mere passage of time will modify them as circumstances change and memories of previous experiences fade. The probability of purchasing a favored brand tends to decrease with the passage of time unless some event—such as a new purchase of the brand or an advertising message—reinforces the consumer's predisposition to buy the brand. Other events—such as purchases of competing brands or exposures to competing advertisements—tend to weaken the probability of purchase of the brand.[1]

Figure 1 illustrates how the probability of the consumer's purchase of brand A might decrease with time, in the absence of any significant events. As the probability of purchase of a favored brand declines with time, the likelihood of purchasing a competing brand increases. Pleasant associations with the favored brands and unpleasant associations with the less favored brands tend to be forgotten with time.

The Effects of Experience

The consumer's experience can be expected to have greater effect on his purchase probabilities than the mere passage of time, especially when he purchases the product often or when some or all of the brands are frequently

[1] Alfred A. Kuehn, "Consumer Brand Choice as a Learning Process," *Journal of Advertising Research*, Vol. 2 (December, 1962), pp. 10–17, at p. 14.

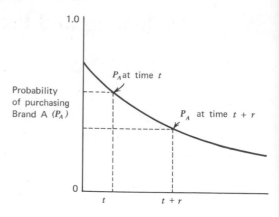

Figure 1. Decay of P_A over time (no events).

advertised. Each new purchase of the products, whether or not the most favored brand is chosen, will almost certainly modify the individual's purchase probabilities. In general, the purchase of a brand increases the probability of that brand's being chosen on the next buying occasion and decreases the purchase probabilities of other brands.

If a purchase is made under "normal" circumstances without special inducements, the expected influence of the purchase will be greater than if the purchase was made as the result of a temporary manufacturer's "deal" or retailer's "special."

Occurrences not directly related to a previous purchase, such as exposures to advertising, might also significantly alter the consumer's purchase probabilities. Figure 2 illustrates how a series of events could affect purchase probabilities and modify the time decay pattern shown in Figure 1.

The probability level which existed in time period t declined when no significant events occurred at t + 1. A repeat purchase of A in t + 2 reinforced P_A. No purchase occurred at t + 3 but an exposure to an advertisement for brand C raised P_C and lowered P_A slightly. A purchase of brand B at t + 4 caused a further reduction in P_A. Purchases of brand A in period t + 5 and t + 6 caused increases in the level of P_A. Thus Figure 2 graphically illustrates how an individual's probability of purchasing a particular brand might change with the passage of time and the occurrence of significant events.

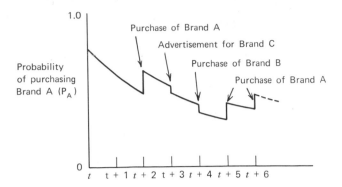

Figure 2. Changes in P_A over time with purchases and exposures to advertising.

Implications for Analysis

The rest of this article is devoted to dynamic models, but the value of the simple probability model as a static analytical concept should not be overlooked. Bothersome analytical difficulties in interpreting the results of product tests can frequently be cleared up when the housewife's behavior is viewed in probabilistic terms.[2] When a substantial number of housewives say that they prefer one of two brands in blind pair comparison tests and then say they prefer the other when the test is repeated, some researchers have concluded that housewives are inconsistent and unpredictable. Yet researchers would agree that it is unreasonable to think that housewives are absolutely infallible in making product evaluations.

In probabilistic terms, the lack of infallibility means that there is some probability on any particular trial that a housewife may choose the sample she does *not* prefer. A reversal on a repeat test merely means that she failed to choose the one she preferred on *one* of the two trials. If preferences are weak and the probability of recognizing the preferred sample is little greater than chance, then the expected number of reversals in a test panel could approach 50%. Since differences between the brands being tested are often slight, one should expect frequent reversals on repeat tests.

A Dynamic Model of Buying Behavior

A useful dynamic model of consumer brand choice behavior must provide a method of revising the individual's set of purchase probabilities to show changes induced by the passage of time, new purchase experiences, and exposures to merchandising influences. No simple structure can adequately reflect these complex changes.

Although they have gained considerable attention and are conceptually appealing, simple Markov chain models are of limited value as the basis of a brand choice model. Ronald A. Howard has classified the major problems in using Markovian analysis in three categories: irregular patterns of purchase (random interpurchase time), difficulties of aggregation, and difficulties in revising transition matrices to reflect new information.[3]

A model which has proved useful as a means of revising purchase probabilities in extensive empirical work is equivalent to a generalized form of a stochastic learning model (associative learning under conditions of reward).[4]

[2] For a more complete discussion, see Alfred A. Kuehn and Ralph L. Day, "A Probabilistic Approach to Consumer Behavior," in Reavis Cox, Wroe Alderson, and Stanley J. Shapiro, editors, *Theory in Marketing: Second Series* (Homewood, Illinois: Richard D. Irwin, Inc., 1964), pp. 380–390.

[3] Ronald A. Howard, "Stochastic Process Models of Consumer Behavior," *Journal of Advertising Research*, Vol. 3 (September, 1963), pp. 35–42.

[4] William K. Estes, "Individual Behavior in Uncertain Situations: An Interpretation in Terms of Statistical Association Theory," in R. M. Thrall, C. H. Coombs, and R. L. Davis, editors, *Decision Processes* (New York: John Wiley & Sons, Inc., 1954); and Robert R. Bush and Frederick

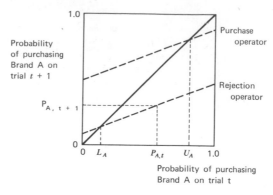

Figure 3. Revising purchase probabilities.

When the learning model is applied to the brand choice situation, the relevant "trials" are purchases of the product class. After each trial, the probability of the purchase of a particular brand on the next trial is revised in view of the choice made on that trial. If the brand in question was purchased, the probability of its purchase on the subsequent trial will normally be increased. If a brand is rejected (another brand is purchased), its probability of purchase on the next purchase occasion will normally be reduced.

The major components of the model are two functions or "operators" which determine the new probability level for a brand after each purchase. These are illustrated in Figure 3. The probability of purchasing brand A on trial t ($P_{A,t}$) is shown at the bottom scale of the diagram. The revised probability ($P_{A,t+1}$) after a purchase is made is read from the vertical scale of the diagram. The value of $P_{A,t+1}$ when another brand is purchased is read from the "rejection operator" as shown by the dotted line in Figure 3. The value of $P_{A,t+1}$ when A is purchased would be read from the "purchase operator" in a similar manner, yielding a higher value of $P_{A,t+1}$ than when another brand was purchased.

The model contains upper and lower limits on the probability of purchasing a brand on the next trial so that it can never reach either 1.0 or 0, regardless of how many continuous repeat purchases or rejections might occur.

This recognizes that a consumer never reaches the state where the purchase of a particular brand is absolutely certain on the next purchase. Conversely, the rejection of a particular brand never becomes absolutely certain. Using Bush and Mosteller's terminology, this is an incomplete learning, incomplete extinction model.[5] In Figure 3, the lower limit on P_A is designated as L_A and the upper limit is designated U_A.

The increment of change induced in the purchase probability for a brand by either a purchase or a rejection depends on the position and slope of the two operators. If the lines in Figure 3 were moved closer together, the amount of change in the purchase probability would be less than if the lines remained as shown. Similarly, changes in the slopes of the lines would change the degree of influence of the results of a particular trial.

The value of the purchase probability for trial t + 1 depends on the purchase probability for trial t, the actual outcome of trial t, and the intercepts and slopes of the lines. To incorporate the effects of the passage of time and of merchandising influences, the four parameters defining the Purchase and Rejection operators are made functions of time and merchandising influences.

Using the Model

At present, the primary use of the model is in studying patterns of consumer behavior and

Mosteller, *Stochastic Models for Learning* (New York: John Wiley & Sons, Inc., 1955).

[5] Same reference as footnote 4.

evaluating the effects of merchandising activity by studying recent purchase records of consumers. The first step in studying a particular product class is to estimate the four parameters as a function of the time elapsed between the tth and $t + 1^{st}$ purchases. The importance of differences in the frequency of purchase seems to vary considerably from product class to product class; but, in general, the influence of the most recent purchase on an individual's purchase probabilities is greater for consumers who purchase the product frequently.

In terms of the lines in Figure 3, as the time between purchases becomes small, the slopes of the lines tend to approach the diagonal and the upper limit becomes close to 1.0 and the lower limit close to 0. As the time between purchases becomes very large, the upper and lower limits come close together and the slopes of the lines approach the horizontal.

Once the effect of time between purchases is generally understood for a product class, the model can be used to study the effects of competitive marketing activity. The parameters of the model are estimated from data covering relatively short periods of time. Changes in the parameters can then be examined in relationship to the activities and policies pursued by the various brands during the period studied. Methods have been developed to estimate the parameters from consumer panel data on the basis of purchase sequences of three and four purchases. Procedures for estimating the parameters for short periods of time are necessary since merchandising conditions in the marketplace change frequently.

Evaluating Special Promotions

This model has proved useful in evaluating the effects of special promotions or "deals" (price-off packs, merchandise packs, two-for-the-price-of-one, coupons, etc.). Using consumer panel data, the buying behavior of each household was studied in chronological order along with information on the deals which it had purchased. The model provided an estimate of the probability that the household would choose any particular brand at the time each successive purchase was reported. In periods of "deal" activity when other merchandising variables were reasonably stable, differences between the estimated probabilities

and the relative purchase frequencies actually recorded could be attributed to the deal activity. Estimates of the effects of the various types of deals were developed from the aggregation of these predictions and the observed purchase records.

This permitted analysis of the degree to which sales on deals were made in lieu of regular sales, whether the sales were for current use or represented "stocking up," and the degree to which deal sales represented "new" business for the brand. Estimates of the effect on future sales of exposing additional households to a brand were also developed. Even rough measures of the "attraction effect" (getting new customers to try the product) and the "conversion effect" (keeping new customers) of different deals aid in the evaluation of the economics of "dealing" in general and of the relative value of the various kinds of deals.

Other merchandising influences probably can be studied the same way when suitable measures of the level of the particular variable are available. For example, the study of the effect of advertising may be feasible once data on exposures to advertising is available from consumer panels.

Using the brand choice model to study the effects of advertising and other marketing variables poses many problems of data specification and collection. However, the more fundamental problem facing marketing science is the development of a model which will allow the simultaneous study of all of the major marketing variables. Such a model would provide an extremely powerful tool for the study of the effects of past policies, could serve as the basis of a market simulation for "pre-testing" of proposed policies, and would provide an extremely sophisticated sales forecasting model.

In Conclusion

The probabilistic approach provides a useful conceptual framework for considering the expected purchase behavior of consumers. When the expected behavior of an individual is viewed as a set of probabilities related to the available brands, a richer and more flexible concept of "brand loyalty" is provided. When expected behavior in a product test is viewed in probabilistic terms, bothersome analytical difficulties are frequently cleared up. As useful as the simple probability model of individual consumers might be in static analysis, its use as a building block in the construction of dynamic, aggregative models of consumer brand choice behavior has been stressed in this article.

A model equivalent to a generalized form of a stochastic learning model was presented as the basis of a dynamic model of brand choice behavior. The model provides revised estimates of the purchase probability for a particular brand after each purchase occasion. The extent to which a purchase of the brand reinforces the probability of its purchase on the next purchase occasion, or the extent to which a rejection in favor of a competing brand reduces the probability, depends on the values of four parameters. These parameters

are treated as functions of time and of merchandising variables.

The parameters are estimated from sequences of purchases recorded by members of consumer panels. While the effect of time tends to vary among product classes, it is relatively stable for each product class. Once the effect of time is established for a product class, the parameters can be estimated from data covering reasonably short periods of time, and changes in purchase probabilities not attributed to the passage of time can be related to merchandising activity during the period under study.

Much remains to be done before a model can be developed which can adequately treat concomitant variation in all major marketing variables; but the probabilistic approach offers an encouraging start.

B. RESEARCH AND APPLICATIONS

The first selection (Pratt) is a report of research that was done to estimate the length of purchase-planning periods and to analyze the marketing implications involved. The concluding article (Clayclamp and Liddy) represents an analytical approach to the problem of predicting new-product performance in the marketplace.

39-B CONSUMER BUYING INTENTIONS AS AN AID IN FORMULATING MARKETING STRATEGY

Robert W. Pratt, Jr. (Marketing Executive)

When asked, "What else do you plan to consume . . . ?," Russell Baker has characterized the contemporary American housewife as responding in this manner: "Oh, you never plan. Planned consumption is almost as stifling as buying with cash. What I do is get out early in the morning with nothing very clear in mind and wander through the stores buying as impulse strikes."[1]

To those who market to American households, these words may seem an accurate de-

SOURCE: Robert W. Pratt, Jr. "Consumer Buying Intentions as an Aid in Formulating Marketing Strategy," Robert L. King, Editor, *Marketing and the New Science of Planning* (Chicago: American Marketing Association, 1968), pp. 296–302.
[1] Russell Baker, *No Cause for Panic* (J. B. Lippincott Company, 1964), pp. 195–196.

scription of observed shopping and buying behavior. Yet we know that planning does precede many consumer purchases, and a growing number of household surveys both here and abroad are asking respondents about their anticipated future behavior, including buying behavior.

The purpose of this paper is to describe one way in which intentions data can contribute to the formulation and evaluation of marketing strategy for consumer durable goods. More specifically, the paper will (1) suggest an approach to estimating the length of time required to "plan" a durables purchase and (2) discuss the marketing implications of these estimates. The applications discussed are premised on the availability of data from a reinterview or panel study.

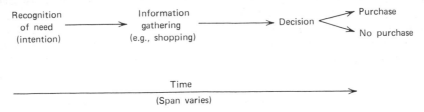

Figure 1. A paradigm of the decision process for consumer durables.

The Data

Data are from a continuous reinterview panel, maintained by the General Electric Company and described in detail in a paper presented to the American Marketing Association in December, 1967.[2] For present purposes, only a few characteristics of the research design need be reviewed.

1. Interviewing is conducted continuously throughout the year, with a new cohort entering the panel each month,

2. Each panel member is interviewed a minimum of three times at six-month intervals, and

3. Members of each cohort are selected using an area probability sample of the United States.

During the first interview, respondents are asked about their intentions to buy a large number of consumer durables, ranging from automobiles to relatively inexpensive housewares and radios.[3] When reinterviewed, they are asked a number of questions that refer directly to their earlier statements of intent.

The availability of reinterviews makes it possible to generate the following statistics:

[2] Robert W. Pratt, Jr., "Using Research to Reduce Risk Associated with Marketing New Products," in Reed Moyer (ed.), *Changing Marketing Systems* (Chicago: American Marketing Association, 1967), pp. 98–104.

[3] Respondents are confronted with a six-point scale and asked ". . . . . . which statement on this card best describes the prospects that your family will buy a (*product*) during the next six months?" The basic procedure used is patterned after that described in: F. Thomas Juster, *Consumer Buying Intentions and Purchase Probabilities—An Experiment in Survey Design*, National Bureau of Economic Research, Occasional Paper No. 99, Columbia University Press, 1966.

1. The percent of all respondents who express an intention to buy at any specified point in time.

2. On reinterviews, the percentage of intenders who actually bought.

3. Because interviews are assigned on a continuous basis, the extent to which the ratio of buyers to non-buyers among the intenders changes over time.

4. And, finally, the percentage of all those reporting a purchase on a reinterview who did not express an intention to buy on the preceding interview.

How can the types of data just described be used to estimate planning times? The answer must begin with an understanding of what is meant by a "planned" purchase. Following this, we will turn to an examination of the relationship between intentions and planning.

Planned Buying Behavior

A "planned" purchase may be thought of as one that is preceded by a decision (*i.e.*, a conscious consideration of alternatives). In this context, virtually all purchases of consumer durables are planned. A paradigm of the decision process for a consumer durable is shown in Figure 1. Although the chart is a monumental oversimplification of the actual process, it is sufficient for our purposes here.

One major characteristic of the decision process is time. However brief, planning takes time. We may consider this span of time as being bounded at its inception by the emergence of an intention, however vague, to purchase a product, and at its conclusion by a decision—either to purchase or not to purchase. Before discussing procedures for estimating this span of time, however, a few words must be said about what are usually labeled "unplanned" purchases.

If there is any validity to the assumption that virtually all consumer durables purchases are planned, then why are most analyses of buying-intentions data concerned with what are labeled "unplanned" purchases? The answer to this question can be found in an understanding of the consequences of survey design.

The length of time required to complete the planning process for a particular purchase may vary from a few minutes to a number of years. Among other things, this variation will be a function of characteristics of the product being purchased and the process by which the particular family or buying unit allocates its resources. For example, the same family will generally approach the purchase of a dishwasher in a somewhat different manner than it will approach the purchase of an electric clock; similarly, different families will approach the purchase of a dishwasher in somewhat different ways.

If the sole purpose of a consumer panel is to understand the decision process for a particular product, and if the research design calls for interviewing all respondents who are actively engaged in trying to reach a decision during the time the study is in the field, then the span of time between interviews will have to be no longer than the shortest time required by any one individual or buying unit to move from intention to decision. If the time span between interviews is longer than the shortest "decision process" then some decisions will be initiated and terminated between interviews. For many consumer durables, however, recording all decisions would require daily reinterviewing—an extremely inefficient research design for products that have a long repurchase cycle.

In the General Electric panel, one of the consequences of the six-month span between interviews is that each individual who is shown on a reinterview as having made an "unplanned" purchase, with perhaps one or two exceptions, will have completed a planning procedure identical to that experienced by respondents classified as having "fulfilled" a plan. For these so-called "unplanned purchases" the entire decision process, which with the present research design may extend to almost six months, simply took place between scheduled interviews.

Let me pause for a moment and recapitu-late. If, in fact, essentially all durables purchases are planned, and if the time between interviews is short enough, and if all survey materials and procedures are performing as intended, then, theoretically at least, a reinterview study will show no "unplanned" purchases.[4] By definition, a "perfect" study could only generate either "fulfilled" or "unfulfilled" plans. The real issue of "unplanned" purchases is procedural, not substantive. The notion of an "unplanned" or "unintended" purchase of a consumer durable is a myth!

Estimating Average Time from Intention to Purchase: A Macro Approach

As is implicit in the preceding discussion, panel data provide a basis for estimating the average (mean) length of time for buyers of a product to complete the decision process. The procedure can be demonstrated by considering an example—the case of the "Watchit," a product, that, to my knowledge, does not exist. For purposes of demonstrating the essential logic, assume first that all recorded plans to purchase a Watchit are fulfilled and that the period of time required to plan the purchase of a Watchit is always equal (but unknown). As will be shown below, for many products, relaxing these assumptions does little damage to results from the basic model being developed here. Also assume that the purchase pattern for Watchits exhibits no seasonality. The implications of this assumption cannot be so readily dismissed; they will be examined in more detail later.

Refer now to Figure 2. At any specified point in time—for example T_1—a representative sample of households will include some individuals who are in the process of planning to buy a Watchit. More specifically, given the assumptions we have made, any one sample will pick up 15.38 percent of all panel members (1) who are engaged in planning and (2) who will purchase a Watchit during the subsequent six-month period. Further, the inter-

---

[4] These assumptions do not take into account the various sources of sampling and non-sampling error. This is not meant to imply that such errors do not exist, only that their limited relevance to the basic procedure being described here does not justify detailed treatment in a paper of this length.

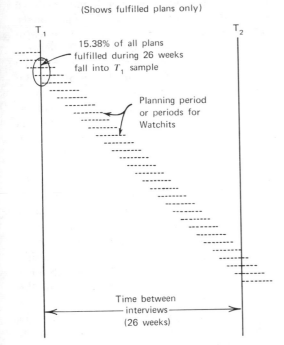

(Shows fulfilled plans only)

T_1

T_2

15.38% of all plans fulfilled during 26 weeks fall into T_1 sample

Planning period or periods for Watchits

Time between interviews (26 weeks)

Figure 2. A hypothetical example of the relationship between the prepurchase planning period for a "Watchit" and the length of time between interviews.

views will tend to be randomly distributed across the time continuum that bounds the planning process for the product. It is important to note that *regardless of how many individual planning processes are shown, 15.38 percent will be crossed by a line that represents any one point in time.*

When appropriate data are available from a panel study, a procedure for estimating the length of the purchase-planning process for a Watchit can be devised, premised on relationships that are implicit in the information shown in Figure 2. The approach is straightforward.

| Length of purchase-planning process for Watchits | = | Percentage of all buying plans that (1) will be both formulated and fulfilled during a 26-week period and (2) will be recorded at T_1 | × | Time between interviews |

$$= 15.38\% \times 26 \text{ weeks}$$
$$= 4 \text{ weeks}$$

Simple enough! But under normal survey conditions we would not have the information required to calculate the second term of this equation; that is, if we recorded 400 Watchit intenders at T_1, we would not know what percentage of all T_1-T_2 intenders they represent. Fortunately, the term can be restated as follows.

| Percentage of all buying plans that (1) will be both formulated and fulfilled during a 26-week period and (2) will be recorded at T_1 | = | Number of plans recorded at T_1 | All purchases recorded at T_2 ("planned" plus "unplanned") |

This formulation still assumes that all recorded plans are fulfilled. Clearly, interviews with members of a representative cross-sectional sample will result in the recording of plans that will *not* be fulfilled. Refering to Figure 2, the number of "unfulfilled" plans both in an absolute and in a relative sense, can only be determined for T_1 plans that are not fulfilled by T_2. Plans that both emerge and are abandoned between T_1 and T_2 will not be recorded on either interview schedule. However, *as long as the ratio of "fulfilled" plans to "unfulfilled" plans remains relatively constant through time,* the actual number of "unfulfilled" plans will in no way alter what has been said.[5] Based on our research to date, we are satisfied that this ratio does, in fact, remain reasonably constant for a large number of products. For these products, the actual estimating equation can be rewritten as follows.

---

[5] A number of the individuals who reviewed the draft of this paper questioned whether the *degree of commitment* to a purchase must not be considered in this formulation. As long as the *ratio* of "fulfilled" to "unfulfilled" plans for the particular unit of analysis (*e.g.*, generic product, product type, brand) being investigated remains constant, psychological commitment need not be explicitly taken into account. The writer has commented at some length on this problem in, Robert W. Pratt, Jr., "Understanding the Decision Process for Consumer Durable Goods: An Example of the Application of Longitudinal Analysis," in Peter D. Bennett (ed.), *Marketing and Economic Development*, American Marketing Association, 1965, especially pp. 248–254.

$$\begin{array}{l}\text{Average} \\ \text{(mean)} \\ \text{planning} \\ \text{process} \\ \text{length of} \\ \text{purchase-}\end{array} = \dfrac{\text{T}_1 \text{ plans}}{\text{Total purchases}} \times \begin{array}{l}\text{Time} \\ \text{be-} \\ \text{tween} \\ \text{inter-} \\ \text{views}\end{array}$$

Note that the first term of this equation now refers to "Average (mean)" length of the planning process. This change recognizes that planning periods for a product are not always of equal length; we are actually estimating the *mean* length.

Using data from the General Electric panel, this relationship can be used to estimate the average length of the purchase-planning process for those durables asked about on the questionnaire and that meet the general conditions specified above. The number of T_1 buying plans fulfilled by T_2 is known, as are the total number of purchases recorded at T_2 and the length of time between interviews. Results of this calculation are shown for selected appliances in Table 1.

What are the implications of assuming that the purchase pattern for a product exhibits no seasonality? With a 6-month interval between interviews, the procedure described above—if applied using data from a single cohort—will not yield an accurate estimate of the planning

TABLE 1

Estimated Length of the Purchase Planning Period for Selected Appliances[a]
(Rounded to Nearest Week)

Clothes Dryer	16 weeks
Tape Recorder	13 weeks
Refrigerator	12 weeks
Washing Machine	10 weeks
Blanket	9 weeks
Hair Dryer	8 weeks
Vacuum Cleaner	7 weeks
Television	4 weeks
Room Air Conditioner	4 weeks
Iron	4 weeks
Electric Fan	3 weeks
Electric Skillet	2 weeks
Radio	1 week

[a] Although it has been necessary to disguise absolute findings, relative differences among estimates—the crucial relationships for this paper—have been retained.

period for a product with a highly seasonal sales pattern, such as room air conditioners. But when panel interviews are assigned virtually every day (as specified in the GE design), estimates for products which deviate from the assumed sales pattern can be improved by weighting results in accordance with accumulated seasonal data. To develop a meaningful weighting scheme, it is absolutely essential that interviews be completed during the span of time within which a product reaches its seasonal sales peak. The variation in sales patterns among consumer durables argues for the kind of continuous interviewing schedule now being used by General Electric. The weighting scheme for a particular product can be further refined by reducing the time between interviews—for example, by reinterviewing monthly (rather than biannually) those members of a cohort who express an intention to buy the product.

How can the type of information shown in Table 1 be effectively used by marketing management?

Marketing Applications

First of all, purchase-planning periods provide an important input for establishing criteria needed to effectively allocate marketing dollars. In general, products having relatively short planning periods (*e.g.*, radios) require a marketing program whose characteristics approach those usually associated with frequently-purchased packaged goods—that is, relatively heavy emphasis on local advertising, wide distribution, point-of-purchase display, and so on. On the other hand, products having relatively long purchase-planning periods (*e.g.*, clothes dryer) require a different type of marketing mix—one emphasizing, for example, relatively heavy use of national media, less frequent advertising, and limited distribution. While the character of these general strategies may seem obvious, the important point here is that use of estimated planning periods introduces a *quantitative* dimension into an allocation process that traditionally has been highly subjective. It is equally important that this dimension is based on actual buying behavior.

Differences among planning periods should be reflected in differences among marketing and advertising programs. Again turning to Table 1, if the buying patterns of customers were fully taken into account, it is unlikely that the same marketing program would be considered appropriate for tape recorders and television sets. The data suggest that broad parameters of the marketing programs for tape recorders and refrigerators should be more alike than different, as should the general programs for television sets and room air conditioners. Yet both tape recorders and television sets are "consumer electronics" and, consequently, are usually grouped with other electronics for distribution and sale. Greater knowledge about the decision patterns of potential customers provides new criteria for grouping products that should increase the return from invested marketing dollars.

Two points should be noted about actual application of these data. First, the estimates shown in Table 1 do not have to be precise in order to contribute to marketing decisions. The *relative* position of a product on the list is the key item. It is important to know whether a particular product falls toward the top of the list, in the middle, or toward the bottom. But whether the estimated time is actually nine (or thirteen) weeks rather than eleven is of little practical consequence. Minor differences resulting from assumptions do not impair the application of results. Second, in application one would not group, for example, all radios. Clearly, pocket-sized radios selling for under $10.00 should not be marketed in the same way as AM/FM table radios selling for $50.00 and up. Types, models and even brands of a product can be analyzed separately. The only requirement is a sufficiently large data base.

Estimating Total Time from Intention to Purchase: A Micro Approach

A second approach to estimating purchase-planning periods is one that we think has a greater long-run payoff than the procedure just described. For clarity, and because we are still experimenting with a wide variety of procedures for implementing this general approach, I have chosen for demonstration purposes to use a hypothetical example based on a composite of our results to date.

The objective of this procedure is to estimate the time span shown in Figure 1 for *individual* purchases made by panel families. The efficacy of this approach hinges on the ability to pinpoint the two points in time that

bound the process. Fortunately, estimating the terminal point presents no unusual problems. Each respondent is asked to specify rather precisely when a purchase was made. We are convinced that results of this questioning are satisfactory. In contrast, estimating the point in time at which the planning process was initiated is substantially more difficult. We have asked respondents expressing a purchase intention as many as nineteen follow-up questions about the intended purchase—for example, when he began thinking about buying the product, whether he has talked with anyone recently about the purchase, whether he has shopped recently for the product, and whether he has been saving to make the purchase. The activities and feelings reflected in answers to these kinds of questions can be used to estimate the point in time at which meaningful deliberation began.

Fortunately, errors in estimating can be reduced because not all recorded purchases need be used for analysis. For a particular product, the analyst can select those planning periods for which he has reasonable confidence that the "beginning" of the period can be identified (assuming, of course, that an appropriate weighting scheme is used to adjust for those planning periods not used). For example, looking at Figure 2, analytical work can be limited to planning periods initiated at or close to the time of the interview. Also, as with the aggregate procedure outlined above, estimates of the total span need not be precise to be useful. Practical application is not hindered by minor inaccuracies in placing the time boundaries of the planning process.

The estimated time spans for a product can

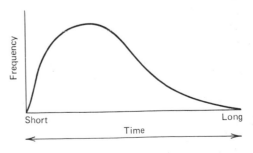

Figure 3. Frequency distribution of planning periods for the "Watchit" (hypothetical example for a "necessity").

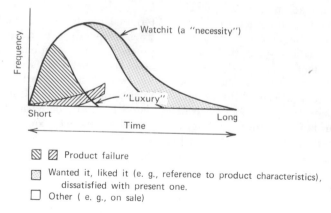

Figure 4. Planning periods and reasons for purchase (hypothetical examples).

be summarized in frequency distribution form. To demonstrate, I have classified appliances as being either "necessities" or "luxuries." A "necessity" is defined here as any appliance that has achieved a market penetration of 70 percent or higher. This category includes products that constitute the basic appliance inventory for the majority of U.S. households. Appliances falling into this category are considered by most people to be necessary to their way of life; hence, most people have them. A hypothetical frequency distribution for a "necessity"—let's continue to call it the "Watchit" —is shown in Figure 3. (For a specific product, the mean of this distribution should, of course, be identical to the estimate shown in Table 1.)

The frequency distribution for a "necessity" generally has a relatively narrow range, and is skewed right. For obvious reasons, a necessity —such as a refrigerator—often must be purchased shortly after the need to purchase is recognized; hence, many purchase-planning periods are short. On the other hand, the frequency distribution for a "luxury" usually has a relatively wide range and tends to be skewed left. "Luxury" buyers can, and often do, take their time. Why shouldn't they?

In practice, both the range and the shape of these distributions will differ widely among products.[6] After all, motivations underlying

purchases vary, as do the constraints that must be dealt with by buyers. For example, when a desire to purchase may be stimulated by an unexpected breakdown, psychological obsolescence, or other dissatisfactions with the unit, this same desire may be inhibited by financial constraints, or by a strong motivation to buy something else.

In our panel studies, respondents are asked to discuss their reasons for making a particular purchase. Because each reason can be associated with a time span, these reasons can be superimposed on the frequency distribution of planning times. Continuing with the Watchit example shown in Figure 3, the results of doing this are illustrated in Figure 4. This diagram shows, for example, that a large percentage of respondents with relatively short planning periods stated that they bought their Watchits as a result of product failure; in contrast, reasons given by those who deliberated for longer periods of time are of the type generally associated with "discretionary" buying.

Figure 4 also shows the tail of a hypothetical frequency distribution for a "luxury." As you would expect, only a small percentage of the planning periods for this product are short, and not all of the short planning periods result from product failure.

Detailed, quantified results from the type of analysis illustrated in Figure 4 can make a

[6] Also, we are convinced that the shape of these distributions will change over time as a result of both seasonal and long-term trends in buying patterns. To date, however, we have not ac-

cumulated sufficient cases to quantify these changes on a product-by-product basis.

major contribution to the formulation of marketing strategy. For example, results shown on the chart suggest that point-of-purchase and local advertising for the Watchits should emphasize product quality, durability, and after-sales service, while national advertising should emphasize appeals that are relevant to buyers who deliberate for a relatively long time. Such appeals would include outstanding product characteristics, such as color, configuration or mechanical features.

For a single product like the Watchit, this type of analysis not only tells us the percentage of buyers who deliberate for various lengths of time. It also links reasons for purchase with the various planning periods. For a line of products, an understanding of similarities and differences among the generic products, among types of a product, and even among brands can provide important quantitative underpinnings for the allocation of marketing and advertising dollars.

39-C PREDICTION OF NEW PRODUCT PERFORMANCE: AN ANALYTICAL APPROACH

Henry J. Claycamp (Marketing Educator) and Lucien E. Liddy (Marketing Executive)

Individuals with the responsibility for planning the introduction of new consumer products are painfully aware of the complexities of the problems and the magnitude of the risks involved. Despite growing sophistication in the analysis of consumer needs and wants and vast investments in product research and development, most new products introduced by firms in the consumer packaged goods industry are commercial failures.

To improve this situation both business and academic researchers have recently devoted considerable effort developing techniques to help managers plan and control new product introductions. Although the primary objective of much of this activity has been the development of more reliable methods of predicting market acceptance levels, few attempts have apparently been made to build analytical models for predicting product performance before market introduction. With one notable exception [1] nearly all of the new product models discussed in the marketing literature are, in essence, techniques for forecasting equilibrium levels of consumer trials and repeat purchases from consumer panel data obtained during the initial phase of a test market or distribution roll-out.[1]

Such techniques are valuable in identifying probable failures soon after launch. However, since marketing variables are not explicitly considered in making the forecast, they are of little value in making a priori evaluations of alternative introductory strategies or diagnosing the effects of individual elements of the marketing mix.

The purpose of this article is to present an analytical approach to the problem of predicting market responses to new consumer products which overcomes some of these limitations. In the following sections we will (a) describe the general structure of a model for predicting consumer trials and repeat purchases as a function of controllable and uncontrollable marketing variables and (b) present a detailed statistical analysis and empirical validation of the sector of the model used to predict initial trial levels.

The Model

The model presented here was designed to facilitate the planning and evaluation of alternative introductory campaigns for new consumer packaged goods. It was developed as part of a large-scale research project begun in 1965 by the advertising agency of N. W. Ayer & Son.

During the initial phase of this project, experienced marketing and advertising professionals were asked to state their operating assumptions about the way various controllable and uncontrollable variables influence consumer responses to new products. These statements and information gleaned from the marketing literature led to the specification of

SOURCE: Henry J. Claycamp and Lucien E. Liddy, "Prediction of New Product Performance," *Journal of Marketing Research*, Vol. 6 (November, 1969), pp. 414–420.
[1] For examples of these types of models, see [2, 4, 5].

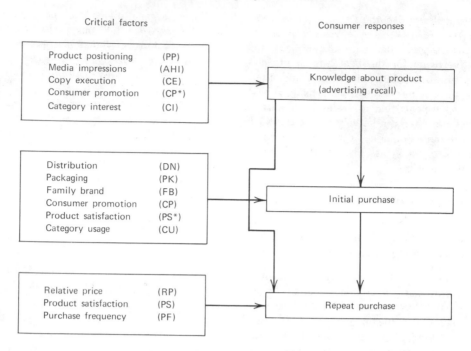

Figure 1. The Ayer new-product model.

a conceptual model involving 14 "critical factors" and three types of consumer response to a given introductory campaign (see Figure 1).

As seen from Figure 1, the initial model was specified in terms of three interconnected submodels. The first submodel implies that the new product's position as expressed in the advertising with respect to existing products in the category (PP), the number (AHI) and quality (CE) of media advertising exposures and consumer promotions containing advertising messages (CP^*), and the level of consumer interest in the product category (CI), influence consumer behavior by generating knowledge about the new product and its advertised benefits. Since consumers may become aware of the new product as a result of exposures to it in retail outlets, "correct recall of advertising claims" (AR) rather than brand or advertising awareness is used as a measure of the direct impact of these variables.

The model's second sector implies that retail distribution factors (DN), packaging characteristics (PK), a known or family brand name (FB), the amount and type of consumer promotions (CP), the extent of consumer satisfaction with the product if it has

been sampled (PS^*), the level of usage of the product category (CU), and the extent of consumer knowledge about the product, are directly associated with the level of initial purchases obtained by a new product during a given time period.

The final sector of the model implies that repeat purchase levels will depend primarily on the extent of consumer knowledge, the level of initial trials, the price of the product relative to other products in the category (RP),[2] satisfaction with prior purchases (PS), and the frequency of purchase for products in the category (PF).

The three-part structure of the model makes it possible to obtain one direct and two indirect estimates of the impact of advertising variables on consumer response to a new product campaign, i.e., the effect of PP, AHI, CE and CP^* on advertising recall, and the effect of advertising recall on initial and repeat purchases. It also takes account of the fact that

[2] Since most of the products of interest retail for less than one dollar, little risk is associated with a trial purchase. Hence, the primary impact of relative prices was assumed to be on repeat rather than purchasing behavior.

substantial numbers of initial and repeat purchases may be made by consumers who cannot recall the product's advertising messages.

Since the primary purpose of the introductory campaign is to inform consumers about the product and stimulate early trial, and most campaigns are planned in terms of 13-week cycles, a decision was made during the project's initial phase to concentrate on the first two sectors of the model shown in Figure 1.

The Data

The data used in parameter estimation and model validation were collected between mid-1965 and early 1968. During this period approximately 60 new product introductions were monitored in the Philadelphia market area. Although the sample items were classified in 32 different product categories, approximately 50 percent were food products. The remainder of the sample was made up of household supplies and personal care items. (A list of the brand names of the products used in the analysis is shown in Table 1.)

A detailed case history containing extensive information about characteristics of the introductory campaign, retail availability, and consumer responses was compiled for each product from a wide variety of data sources. For example, commercial data services and specially designed research projects were used to monitor television, radio, print and outdoor advertising, and to estimate the probable number of household exposure opportunities for each insertion.

Data on retail distribution, shelf space, in-store displays, and deals were obtained by auditing a sample of supermarkets and drug stores during the second and fourteenth week after the start of advertising for each new product.

Consumer surveys taken at the end of 13 weeks were used to estimate levels of advertising recall, initial and repeat purchases, and use of samples and coupons, product satisfaction, category usage, and category purchase frequency. Each consumer survey covered 250 housewives randomly selected from a total panel of 1200 households. Although the total panel was established on a probability basis, it is not proportionately representative of households in the total Philadelphia market since

TABLE 1

Brand Names of Products Included in Estimation and Validation Sample

Brand Name	
Apple Jacks Cereal	Scope Mouthwash
Puppets Cereal	Reef Mouthwash
Quisp & Quake	Citrisun
Maxim Coffee	Adulton
Hills Bros. Coffee	Cope
Dole Pineapple-Pink Grapefruit Drink	Measurin
Del Monte Fruit Drinks	Vanquish
Knox Flavored Gelatin Drinks	New Kotex Plus
Moo Juice	True Cigarettes
Nestle's Quik Shake	Cigarette A
Great Shakes	Cigarette B
Start Instant Breakfast Drink	Cigarette C
Shake-a-Pudding	Petal Soap
Something Diff'rent	Phase III
Bounty Pudding	Hour After Hour Deodorant
Cool Whip	Bold Laundry Detergent
Chipnics	Cold Power
Sip-n-Chips	Crew
Jus' Fried Chicken	Cinch
Lipton Dinners	Palmolive Dishwashing Liquid
Honey Suckle	Pruf Spray Starch
Kraft Noodles Romanoff	Purex Super Bleach
Spaghetti-O's	Favor Furniture Polish
Pepperidge Farm Soups	Pronto Floor Care
Great American Soups	Epic Floor Wax
Kraft Frozen Sandwich Filling	Viva Towels
Hunt's Steakhouse Catsup	Handi-Wipes
Ultra Brite Toothpaste	Gaines Variety
Fact Toothpaste	Pet'm

TABLE 2

Means and Standard Deviations of Dependent and Independent Variables for 35 New Products in Estimation Sample

Variable	Description	Mean	Standard Deviation
AR	Percent of housewives able to accurately re-call advertising claims at the end of 13 weeks	25.1	16.1
PP	Judged product positioning	35.5	15.3
AHI	Average number of media impressions/house-hold	11.5	8.5
CE	Judged quality of advertising copy execution	7.3	1.5
CP*	Coverage of consumer promotion containing advertising messages adjusted for type of promotion	36.6	57.4
CI	Index of consumer interest in the product category	37.5	5.7
IP	Percent of housewives making one or more purchases of the product during the first 13 weeks	13.9	11.9
$\widehat{AR}$	Predicted advertising recall	25.1	13.8
DN	Retail distribution, adjusted for shelf space and special displays	58.5	14.8
PK	Judged distinctiveness of package	0.556	0.132
FB	Known or family brand name	0.457	.051
CP	Coverage of consumer promotions adjusted for type and value of offer	63.9	55.1
PS*	Index of consumer satisfaction with new prod-uct samples	77.4	45.0
CU	Percent of households using products in the category	67.0	23.2

over-sampling was done in younger, higher-income areas.[3]

Quantitative values for variables such as product positioning, copy execution, and package quality were obtained by having a panel of experienced marketing and advertising executives rate each product, advertisement and package on predetermined scales. Subjective judgment was also used to develop weights for various kinds of consumer promotion, in-store displays, etc.

Starch "Ad Norm Scores" [6] were used as

a measure of category interest for each product class.

The means, and standard deviations of each of the variables used in the final model are shown in Table 2.

Parameter Estimation

METHODOLOGY. The specific model for which parameters were estimated consists of two equations with two dependent and ten independent variables.

$$(1) \quad AR = a_1 + b_{11}(PP) + b_{12}(\sqrt{AHI^*CE}) + b_{13}(CP^*) + b_{14}(CI) + e_1$$

$$(2) \quad IP = a_2 + b_{21}(\widehat{AR}) + b_{22}(DN^*PK) + b_{23}(FB) + b_{24}(CP) + b_{25}(PS^*) + b_{26}(CU) + e_2.$$

[3] To check the nature of possible biases in the sample, consumer surveys were repeated for two products on restricted random samples of housewives not included in the original panel. No significant differences between panel and non-panel statistics on advertising recall and initial purchases were found for either product.

TABLE 3

Estimation Sample Results

Variable	Regression Coefficient	Standard Error	R^2	Sy	$F(4,30)$ [a]
		Advertising Recall			
PP	.756	.122			
AHI*CE	2.122	.603			
CP*	.039	.030			
CI	.392	.302	.725	8.970	19.790
(Intercept)	−35.876				
		Initial Purchase			
					$F(6,28)$ [a]
AR	.370	.095			
DN*PK	.194	.107			
FB	9.245	2.414			
CP	.086	.024			
PS*	.022	.033			
CU	.067	.059	.709	6.933	14.100
(Intercept)	−16.011				

[a] $p[F(4,30) \geqslant 4.02] = .01$; $p[F(6,28) \geqslant 3.53] = .01$.

Equation 1 is designed to predict the level of advertising recall to be expected 13 weeks after launch from the values of four independent variables. Since CE is a quantitative index of the quality of advertising exposures measured by AHI, both are combined in a single interaction variable. The square root transformation represents an assumption of diminishing returns to media weight.

Equation 2 is designed to predict the expected level of initial purchases at the end of 13 weeks as a function of the factors assumed to be directly or indirectly related to initial trials. For example, since the values of the independent variable $\widehat{AR}$ are derived from (1), the parameter b_{21} can be interpreted as an estimate of the composite effect of the independent variables PP, AHI, CE, CP* and CI on initial purchases, as well as an estimate of the nature of the relationship between advertising recall and initial trials. This formulation of the model makes it possible to use a procedure similar to two-stage least squares[4] to estimate the effects of all the variables on initial purchases while avoiding problems of multi-

[4] Two-stage least squares would involve estimating the values of $\widehat{AR}$ from the regression of AR on all of the exogenous variables in the two equations. See [3, pp. 258–60].

collinearity and spurious correlation which occur if only one equation is specified.[5]

Stepwise least squares regression was used to estimate the parameters of the model from data on the introduction of 35 new products. Products in the estimation sample were randomly selected from a total of 58 for which data were available. The remaining 23 products were retained as a validation sample.

The parameters of Equation 1 were estimated first and used to calculate values of $\widehat{AR}$ for each of the 35 products. A second regression run was then made to obtain estimates of the coefficients in (2). The results of this analysis are shown in Table 3.

ESTIMATION SAMPLE RESULTS. Despite the use of subjective judgment to quantify several of the independent variables and the fact that many different kinds of products are included in the estimation sample, over 70 percent of

[5] A stepwise least squares regression analysis of IP on the independent variables in (1) and the last five variables in (2) was erformed at one point in the analysis. Although the R^2 in this analysis was slightly higher than that shown in Figure 3, multicollinearity among the independent variables caused the regression coefficients to fluctuate widely as variables were entered and deleted from the equation.

the variance of both dependent variables is accounted for by the independent variables listed in Table 3. The F ratios indicate that the correlations are highly significant despite the small sample size. Moreover, the signs of the regression coefficients are consistent with the hypotheses stated during the model's initial formulation, i.e., that each of the critical factors is positively related to the measures of consumer response.

The results of the regression analysis of (1) show highly significant relationships between levels of advertising recall for the 35 products in the estimation sample and the independent variables for product positioning and media advertising. Standardization of the regression coefficients indicates that these two variables are relatively far more important than CP° and CI in the relationship, e.g., the Beta weights for PP, $\sqrt{AHI^\circ CE}$, CP° and CI are .641, .411, .138, .138, respectively.

The regression statistics for $\hat{AR}$ and FB are particularly interesting. For example, the regression coefficient for AR is nearly four times as large as its standard error. Moreover, the magnitude of its β weight indicates that it is one of the most important variables in the relationship. (The β values for $\hat{AR}$, $DN^\circ PK$, FB, CB, PS°, and CU are .292, .179, .366, .374, .033, .194, respectively.) Since the values of $\hat{AR}$ are weighted sums of the independent variables in (1), this result supports the hypothesis that these variables exert an important influence on initial trial levels.

However, note that none of the independent variables in Equation 1 has a statistically significant regression coefficient at the .05 level if they are used in place of AR in (2). This result, considered without the information shown in Table 3, might lead one to conclude that initial trial levels are unrelated to product positioning and media advertising when in fact these variables are important determinants of $\hat{AR}$, and $\hat{AR}$ is one of the most important variables in the prediction of IP.

The regression coefficients for FB support the hypothesis that a known or "family" brand name on the new product has a positive net effect on trial purchases during the first 13 weeks of the campaign. The magnitude and significance levels of the coefficient are particularly surprising since FB is actually a dummy variable used as a proxy for the strength of the

brand franchise (i.e., for products with a known brand name $FB = 1.0$, for all other products $FB = 0.0$).

It is also important to note that FB is virtually uncorrelated with the other independent variables in the relationship although one might expect family branded products to obtain higher levels of advertising recall and better retail distribution. (The zero-order correlation coefficients for FB with $\hat{AR}$ and DN are $-.13$ and $.05$ respectively.)

Although the measure is crude, these results offer an important first approximation of the value of a "family brand umbrella" in the introduction of a new consumer product.

Since (1) and (2) were specified before data analysis, the results shown in Table 3 can be interpreted as a meaningful test of the model's validity. Although alternative functional forms and variable transformations were analyzed, none produced significant improvements over the initial model.

The real test of the model's validity, however, is its performance in predicting the dependent variables for a fresh set of products and its use as an operating tool. The results of these tests are discussed next.

Validation

Validation Sample Results. The regression coefficients shown in Column 2 of Table 3

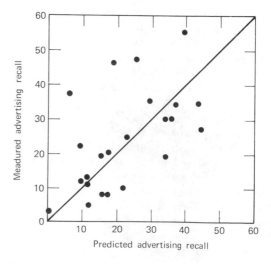

Figure 2. Measured and predicted advertising recall levels for 23 new products.

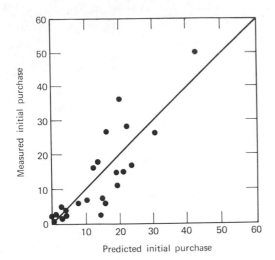

Figure 3. Measured and predicted initial purchase levels for 23 new products.

were used to predict the level of advertising recall and initial purchases for the 23 new products excluded from the regression analysis. Figures 2 and 3 show plots of the actual values of *AR* and *IP* obtained in consumer surveys and their corresponding predicted values.

It is clear from these diagrams that the model produces better predictions of initial purchases than advertising recall. For initial purchase, 13 of the predictions are within ±5 percentage points and 20 are within ±10 percentage points of the actual level. For advertising recall, however, eight are within ±5 percentage points and 15 are within ±10 percentage points of the values measured in the consumer surveys. Product moment correlations between actual and predicted values provide a more striking comparison—the simple correlation coefficient for actual and predicted initial purchase is .95, and the corresponding statistic for actual and predicted advertising recall is .56.

The correlation statistic for advertising recall is, of course, greatly influenced by large errors made for four of the products. An analysis of the introductory campaigns for these products as well as products in the estimation sample for which similar errors were made indicates that advertising recall is typically underestimated when a "catchy" jingle is used in media

advertising (e.g., one of the largest errors was found for "Spaghetti-O's").

Use of the Model. Since the model was designed to facilitate planning introductory campaigns, the most meaningful test is its usefulness in predicting, before launch, the probable outcome of a given campaign for a specific product.

The model has been used to predict initial purchase levels for seven different new products in eight widely dispersed geographic areas (Figure 4). Although the parameters were estimated from data for new product introductions in Philadelphia, seven of the eight introductions occurred outside of the Philadelphia market area.

Most of the products were owned by companies other than Ayer clients. Some of the products were actually in the market place when the predictions were made. However, only prelaunch information was used to quantify the independent variables. Each company conducted its own consumer survey using standardized data collection instruments and sampling procedures to measure the actual trial levels achieved by its product by the end of 13 weeks.

The results shown in Figure 4 are remarkably consistent with those obtained in the analysis of the 23 products in the validation sample (Figure 3) despite geographic dispersion of the markets and the fact that planned rather than measured values were used for the independent variables.

For example, in five of the eight cases the predicted value of initial purchases is within ±5 percentage points of actual trial levels obtained in the consumer surveys and only one prediction is off by as much as ten percentage points.

The largest discrepancy is for the paper product that was launched in two different market areas. Although the actual outcome is quite close in one of the markets, the measured trial level in the second market exceeds the predicted value by 13 percentage points. An ex-post analysis of this case revealed that the product achieved better than anticipated retail distribution in Market B.

Summary and Conclusions

The results of the regression analyses and the validation studies indicate that the model

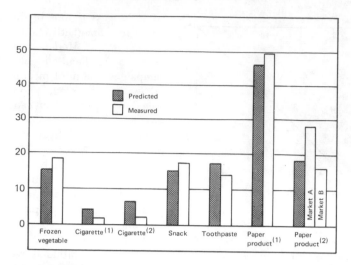

Figure 4. Measured vs. predicted initial purchase levels for seven new products in eight market areas.

produces highly accurate predictions of the level of initial purchases to be expected 13 weeks after the start of a given campaign in a particular market area. Although the 13-week trial level may not be a perfect indicator of the ultimate success or failure of the product, it is widely used to measure initial market reactions and estimate long run penetration. The initial 13-week period also accounts for much of the risk and uncertainty associated with new product introductions.

The results also show that it is possible to produce reasonably accurate estimates of advertising recall levels from data which can be obtained before market introduction. They also provide considerable evidence that "correct recall of advertising claims" is a highly relevant measure of consumer response to advertising—at least for new products.

In fact, this measure provided the key to establishing a stable relationship between advertising variables and initial purchases. By regressing measured advertising recall on data describing the content, quality, and quantity of the advertising program and consumer interest in the product category, it was possible to obtain the values of a unique interaction variable—$\widehat{AR}$—which had little correlation with the independent variables in (2) and a high degree of association with the level of initial purchases. Whereas, interaction variables are typically specified as the product of two or more independent variables, AR is the

weighted sum of the variables in (1)—regression analysis has been used to determine the weights.

Thus, the model evaluates the probable impact of a planned campaign on at least two important measures of new product performance.

REFERENCES

1. A. Charnes, *et al,* "DEMON: Decision Mapping Via Optimum GO-NO Networks—A Model for Marketing New Products," *Management Science,* 12 (July 1966).
2. Louis A. Fourt and Joseph W. Woodlock, "Early Prediction of Market Success for New Grocery Products," *Journal of Marketing,* **25** (October 1960).
3. J. Johnson, *Econometric Methods,* New York: McGraw-Hill Book Co., Inc., 1960, 258–60.
4. J. H. Parrfitt and B. J. K. Collins, "The Use of Consumer Panels for Brand Share Predictions," *Journal of Marketing Research,* **5** (May 1968), 131–45.
5. William F. Massy, "Stochastic Models for Monitoring New Product Introductions," Chapter 4 in Frank M. Bass, Charles W. King and Edgar A. Pessemier, eds., *Applications of the Sciences in Marketing Management,* New York: John Wiley & Sons, Inc., 1967.
6. Daniel Starch, Inc., *Starch 1968 Magazine Adnorms Report,* Mamaroneck, New York: Daniel Starch and Staff, 1968.

Index

DATE DUE

M